CONSONANT ORDER

ก – g^1 – 264
ข – k^4 – 272
ค – k^3 – 281
ง – ng^3 – 293
จ – ch^1 – 294
ส – s^4 – 299
ซ – s^3 – 309
ย – ny^3 – 315
ด – d^1 – 318
ต – dt^1 – 324
ฏ – t^4 – 336

ท – t^3 – 339
น – n^3 – 346
บ – b^1 – 353
ป –
ผ
ฝ
พ
ฟ
ภ
ม
ย – y^- – 386
ร – l^3 – 388

ล – l^3 – 390
ว – w^3 – 396
ห – h^4 – 3⟨⟩

9 – $--^1$ – 409
ฮ – h^3 – 411

VOWEL ORDER

×ะ	a:	แ×̌ั×	aa:/ae:	×̌ั๋	ia
×̌×	a:	แ×ั	aa/ae	×๋×	ia
×า	a	โ×ะ	o:	เ×̌ือ	eua:
×̊	i:	×̂×	o:	เ×̂ือ	eua
×̂	i	โ×	o	×̌ัว	ua:
×̊̊	eu:	เ×าะ	oh:/aw:	×̂ัว	ua:
×̂̊	eu	×̌ั×	oh:/aw:	×̂ั	ua
×̀	u:	×̊	oh/aw	×ัว×	ua
×̂	u	×̌ั×	oh/aw	ไ×	ay:/ai:
เ×ะ	e:	เ×̊	er:	ไ×	ay:/ai:
เ×̌×	e:	เ×̂	er	เ×̌า	ow:/ao:
เ×	e	เ×̌ัะ	ia:	×̀ั	a:m
แ×ะ	aa:/ae:	×̌ั×	ia	×ัย	oy:/oi:

ENGLISH-LAO, LAO-ENGLISH
DICTIONARY

English-Lao, Lao-English Dictionary

ວັຈນານຸກົມ

ອັງກິດ - ລາວະ ລາວ - ອັງກິດ

REVISED EDITION

by Russell Marcus
CHIEF EDITOR AND COMPILER

TUTTLE PUBLISHING
Tokyo • Rutland, Vermont • Singapore

Published by Tuttle Publishing, an imprint of Periplus Editions (HK) Ltd.

www.tuttlepublishing.com

Copyright © 1970
by Charles E. Tuttle Publishing Co., Inc.
All rights reserved.

LCC Card No. 77-116487
ISBN-13: 978-0-8048-0909-2

First Tuttle edition, 1970
Second (revised) edition, 1983
Printed in Singapore

Distributed by:

North America, Latin America & Europe
Tuttle Publishing
364 Innovation Drive, North Clarendon, VT 05759-9436 USA
Tel: 1 (802) 773 8930; Fax: 1 (802) 773 6993
Email: info@tuttlepublishing.com
www.tuttlepublishing.com

Japan
Tuttle Publishing
Yaekari Building, 3rd Floor
5-4-12 Osaki, Shinagawa-ku, Tokyo 141-0032
Tel: (81) 3 5437 0171; Fax: (81) 3 5437 0755
Email: sales@tuttle.co.jp
www.tuttle.co.jp

Asia Pacific
Berkeley Books Pte. Ltd.
3 Kallang Sector #04-01, Singapore 349278
Tel: (65) 6741 2178; Fax: (65) 67414 2179
Email: inquiries@periplus.com.sg
www.tuttlepublishing.com

26 25 24 23 22   25 24 23 22 21   2206MP

PUBLISHER'S FOREWORD

Prior to the compilation of this dictionary in 1966, the most comprehensive English-Lao dictionary was the LAA (Lao-American Association) Dictionary. At that time, no Lao-English dictionary was available.

Now, more than a decade has passed since the first Tuttle edition of the English-Lao, Lao-English Dictionary was published in 1970. During that time, the dictionary has become the basic communication tool between Lao people and English speakers all over the world.

It is a handy volume with many user aids such as romanized equivalents of Lao script, tone numbers indicating the tone of each syllable, vocabulary selected on the basis of frequency of use, and guidance on how to look up words both in the Lao and English alphabetized lists for those encountering either language for the first time. Having been completely revised, this language tool is all the more essential.

To the publisher's knowledge, this dictionary is still the only two-way dictionary of Lao and English in print.

ACKNOWLEDGEMENTS

As with any major project, the compilation and editing of
this dictionary required perseverance, centralized control,
and constant logistical coordination. Fortunately, the project was supported by the efforts of many people, whose time,
energy and constructive comments deserve special mention.

Ivan Izenberg and Peggy Sheppard greatly inspired and en-
couraged me to initiate the dictionary as a project in 1966.
Calvin Ellis, Dan Frederick, Sang Seunsom, Messr. Franse and
Phoui Phongsawathn advised regarding the dictionary aspects
of the Lao language. Harlan Rosacker was most instrumental in
bringing the first edition into being by devoting much of his
time to help expand and edit the vocabulary, check the romanization and prepare the manuscript for typing.

An anonymous Vietnamese man aided the project by locating
100 pages of the first edition which accidently slipped off
the back of my motorcycle and into a Vientiane rice paddy.

Others who made major contributions were the following:
- COMPILATION: Lin Thong Noinala, Niwat Sihavong, Kenechan
    Pathammavong and Harlan Rosacker.
- EDITING: Saly Chittavoravong, Lin Thong Noinala, Somsanith
    Khamvongsa and Bounmy Louangrath.
- TRANSLATION: Dao Vong Norasing, Hong Thong Norasing, Boun
    Theung Rasavongsa, Bounmy Thammavong, Sack Inthara,
    Somsanith Khamvongsa and Niwat Sihavong.
- ROMANIZATION: Niwat Sihavong, Dara Chounlamountry,
    Khamphone Sisounthone and Harlan Rosacker.
- MARKING OF TONES: Tatsuo Hoshino.
- TYPING: Phavinee Noisomsri, Khampeng Prasavath, Khamtong
    Malivong.
- REVISED MANUSCRIPT PREPARATION: Kikuko Yufu, Yukiko
    Shiratori, Rie Sago and Junko Kurimoto.

The editorial revision of this dictionary was the work of
Tatsuo Hoshino, scholar of Southeast Asian languages and
history.

Finally, the revisions in Japan was made possible by the
Japanese Overseas Cooperation Volunteers (JOCV in Nagano
Prefecture) who permitted me the use of their Lao typewriter.

Russell Marcus
May 1983

DICTIONARY FEATURES

PRACTICAL WORD SELECTION

The English-Lao section of this dictionary was compiled from the 5,000 words of the Ladder Series, the vocabulary of the English 900 Series, English for Lao Speakers, the VOA Special English Word List, books I & II of English for Today, and the 1962 LAA English-Lao Dictionary. The Lao-English Section was compiled from the vocabulary of Lao Ministry of Education primary school texts, Reader for Laotians, and a selection of words from Allen D. Kerr's excellent two-volume Lao-English Dictionary, published in 1972 by the Catholic University of America Press.

EASY-TO-USE ROMANIZATION

The system for converting Lao letters into roman letters in the English-Lao section permits Lao to be easily understood by English speakers without requiring any Lao language training. The Lao-English section does not include romanization for Lao, since the words are alphabetized by Lao letters, hence requiring that users already be familiar with the Lao alphabet. Nonetheless, as an aid to English speakers, the consonant and vowel orders with roman equivalents are summarized inside both the front and back covers of this dictionary.

TONE NUMBERS

Since Lao is a tone language, tones are crucial determinants of word meanings. The words in Lao for "near" and "far," for example, would have the same English letters, but differ in tone. In Lao, the tone of syllables is coded by the spelling (i.e., by the combination of Lao letters). Since English letters do not carry such tonal information, numbers are used to indicate the tone of romanized syllables. The numbering system, developed by Mr. Tatsuo Hoshino, as well as the Lao tone code is summarized inside both the front and back covers. Learners who are interested in speaking and reading Lao are recommended to obtain a copy of Lao for Beginners by Hoshino and Marcus (Tuttle, 1981). Besides being a useful text, this book is a complete reference source to the Lao language for beginners.

LAO ALPHABETICAL ORDER

The Lao-English section is alphabetized in accordance with
the Lao Comité Littéraire's Ruling No.77. The rules for
ordering Lao characters are summarized on page 5. The order
of Lao characters is also listed inside both the front and
back dictionary covers.

ENGLISH AIDS FOR LAO SPEAKERS

As an aid to Lao speakers learning English, English alphabet-
ical order is explained in Lao on page 4. In addition, the
following English grammatical elements are also explained in
Lao.

Item	Page	Item	Page
a	13	-ly	127
an	19	-ness	144
-er	73	-or	151
-ful	88	-'s	189
-in	109	-self	195
-ing	111	the	228
-less	122	un-	240

RULES ON ENGLISH ALPHABETICAL ORDER

(1) Letters are listed one at a time with the following priority:

- ລຽງຕົວອັງສິຕາມຣະບຽບດັ່ງຕໍ່ໄປນີ້:

a b c d e f g h i j k l m n o p q r s t u v w x y z

after	dart
bingo	dear
craft	dill
dirty	door
eager	dust

(2) Shorter words come before longer words since spaces at the end of a shorter word come before letters in a longer word.

- ລຽງຄຳສັ້ນກ່ອນຄຳທີ່ຍາວຂຶ້ງໂຕກ່ວາຽນດ້ວຍຕົວ.

a	be
an	bee
ant	been

(3) Spaces in the middle of words are ignored; hence, only the letters of words are alphabetized as in the examples below.

- ລຽງຄຳຕາມລຳດັບຕົວອັກສອນ.

humanity	public health
human rights	publicity
humans	public spirit

RULES ON LAO ALPHABETICAL ORDER

(1) The priority of single Lao letters (consonants and vowels) and tone marks is as listed below.

CONSONANTS:

ກ ຂ ຄ ງ ຈ ສ ຊ ຍ ຍ ດ ຕ ຖ ທ ນ ບ ປ ຜ ຝ
ພ ຟ ມ ຢ ຣ ລ ວ ຫ ຫງ ຫຍ ໝ ໜ ຫຼ ຫວ ອ ຮ

VOWELS:

 xະ x̆x xາ x̆ x̂ x̃ x̰ x x̂ ເxະ ເx̆x
ເx ແxະ ແx̆x ແx ໂxະ x̂x ໂx ເxາະ xɔ̆x x̂ xɔ̃x
ເx̆ ເx̂ ເx̆jະ x̆jx ເx̆j xjx ເx̂9 ເx̃9 x̂ɔະ x̆ɔx x̂ɔ
xɔx ໄx ໃx ເx̂າ xຳ

TONE MARKS:

່ ້ ໊ ໋
x x x x

(2) The letters within words are ordered according to their pronunciation, not the order in which the letters are written. Thus, ແຂວ can be found under ຂ-ແ-ວ , not ແ-ຂ-ວ.

(3) Words without tone marks are ordered before those with tone marks. The following list illustrates this rule.

ກິວ ເກາ ເກ່ມ ເກາວ ເກ່າວ ເກ້າວ ກງວ ກ່ງວ ກ້ງວ

(4) Words are ordered one syllable at a time as illustrated in the following list:

ກະ ກະທິ ກະລາ ກັມ ກັມຍາ ກາ

(5) Syllables beginning with double consonants come after syllables beginning with single consonants, as in the example below.

ຂາ ແຂວ ເຂົ້າ ຂຳ ຂວາ ແຂວງ
ຫາມ ຫຳ ເຫວກ ຫວຳ ແຫຍ

(6) Syllables which contain an unwritten letter xະ are ordered as if the letter xະ were written, as in the following list:

ສະ ສລາດ ສເວຍ ສັມ ສາ ສາສມາ ສາຍາ ເສົາ

LAO SPELLING

(Based on O.R. No.10 of Jan. 27, 1949)

<u>CONSONANTS</u>

(1) SIMPLE CONSONANTS:

Lao has 20 consonant sounds and one silent consonant. These can
be written with one of 33 consonant letters. (Note: Lao actually
has 27 distinct consonant symbols. These symbols combine, since
some letters are pairs of symbols, to make the 33 consonant
letters which are found in the dictionary.) The consonant letters are divided into three groups according to the tone on
which they are spoken as follows:

(a) 8 Akson Kang (ອັກສອນກາງ) or low tone (tone 1) consonants:

ກ ຈ ດ ຕ ບ ປ ຢ ອ
g ch d dt b bp y -

(b) 13 Akson Tam (ອັກສອນຕ່ຳ) or high tone (tone 3) consonants:

ຄ ຊ ທ ພ ຟ ຮ ງ ຍ ນ ມ ຣ ລ ວ
k s t p f h ng ny n m r l w

(c) 12 Akson Sung (ອັກສອນສູງ) or rising tone (tone 4) consonants. These cover the same basic sounds as the Akson Tam
consonants, but are spoken on a different tone level. (Note:
A 13th Akson Sung consonant exists, but is used only for
foreign words.)

ຂ ສ ຖ ຜ ຝ ຫ ຫງ ຫຍ ຫນ ໝ - ຫຼ ຫວ
k s t p f h ng ny n m l w

(2) FINAL CONSONANTS ຕົວສະກົດສຸດທ້າຍ

(a) Lao syllables always have an initial consonant and a
vowel. In addition, some syllables have a final consonant.
These final consonants fall into three categories as follows:

Nasals finals	: ng, n and m	ງ ນ ມ
Unreleased stops	: k, d and b	ກ ດ ບ
Semi-finals	: y and w	ຍ ວ

(b) The four most common of these finals have standard and variant spellings as summarized below.

Sound	Std. Spelling	Spelling Variant
-k	ກ	ຂ ຄ
-d	ດ	ຈ ສ ຊ ຕ ຖ ທ
-b	ບ	ປ ພ ຟ
-n	ນ	ຣ ລ

(c) Final consonants are written according to their pronunciation rather than according to their etymological root in Pali or Sanskrit.

ສັກຣາຊ	should be	ສັກຣາດ
ສົພ	should be	ສົບ
ສໂມສຣ	should be	ສະໂມສອນ
ອັກສຣສາຕຣ໌	should be	ອັກສອນສາດ

(d) Spelling variants of final consonants are only used within polysyllabic words as illustrated below.

ທຸຂເວທະນາ ທຸຄະຕະບຸຣຸດ ກິຈະການ ອັສະຈັນ ທັມະດາ
ຣາຊການ ອຶຕຄັດ ຣັຖະບານ ພຸທະສາສນາ
ພົລະເມືອງ ຜົລະປູກ ອັປະໂຍດ ເທພະດາ

(3) DOUBLE CONSONANTS ອັກສອນນຳ

(a) Double consonants are consonants which combine with the letters ວ , ຣ or ລ to form a single sound unit. Examples are listed below.

ຄວາຍ ຂວາ ຂວາມ ແຂວງ ຄຣູ ກຣາມ ພຣະ ພຣົມ

(b) Consonants which combine with ຫ are not double consonants, but are simply Akson Sung consonant letters. The ຫ is a silent letter. The letter ຫຣ is only used for words coming from foreign languages.

ຫງ ຫຍ ໜ ໝ ຫຣ ຫຼ ຫວ

(c) All other combinations of consonants are understood and pronounced as if the letter ×ະ came after the initial consonant. The rule concerning the writing of the letter ×ະ is to omit it in polysyllabic words.

ສງ່າ ສໄມ ສເນີ ສລາດ ຕລາດ ສຸຈຣິດ
ສາສນາ ສເນີ ຜຍາ ຂເມນ ຖນົນ ສ່ເວີຍ

(d) When two of the same consonant come together within a polysyllabic word, one of them is omitted in the written word.

ສ້ອມມະຄິດ	may be written	ສ້ອມະຄິດ
ສ້ອມມະເຄດ	may be written	ສ້ອມະເຄດ
ຄຸມມະສົມບັດ	may be written	ຄຸມະສົມບັດ
ທັມມະດາ	may be written	ທັມະດາ
ທັມມະທາມ	may be written	ທັມະທາມ
ອັມມະຄະດີ	may be written	ອັມະຄະດີ

VOWELS ສຣະ

Lao has 39 vowel symbols which can be classified into three groups: basic vowels, diphthongs and special vowels.

(1) BASIC VOWELS AND DIPHTHONGS

The nine basic vowels and three diphthongs all have short and long forms. These short and long vowels in Lao have the same basic sound; they differ only in terms of the duration over which this sound is produced.

In addition, many of these vowels have two alternative forms depending on whether the syllable they are in as a final consonant or not. The following list summarizes these different forms.

	Short	Short + final		Long	Long + final	
a:	×ະ	×̆×	a	×າ	–	
i:	×ິ	–	i	×ີ	–	
eu:	×ຶ	–	eu	×ື	–	
u:	×ຸ	–	u	×ູ	–	SIMPLE VOWELS
e:	ເ×ະ	ເ×̆×	e	ເ×	–	
aa:/ae:	ແ×ະ	ແ×̆×	aa/ae	ແ×	–	
o:	ໂ×ະ	×̂×	o	ໂ×	–	
oh:/aw:	ເ×າະ	×9×	oh/aw	×	×9×	
er:	ເ×ິ	–	er	ເ×ື	–	
ia:	ເ×ັຍະ	×̆ຽ×	ia	ເ×ັຍ	×ຽ×	DIPHTHONGS
eua:	ເ×ຶອ	–	eua	ເ×ຶອ	–	
ua:	×ົວະ	×̆ວ×	ua	×ົວ	×ວ×	

(2) SPECIAL VOWELS ສະລະພິເສດ

Although certain sounds could be written with a short vowel
together with a semi-vowel, Lao uses special vowel symbols
instead, as shown in the following list. These special vowels all
fall into the short vowel category. Rules regarding their use
are listed below.

	ay:/ai:	ow:/ao:	a:m	oy:/oi:
special vowels	ໄx	ໃx	ເx̂າ	xໍ	x9ຍ
root or alternative	xຍ	xຍ	xະ+ວ	xໍມ	x໌

    (a) After an Akson Tam or Akson Kang xໍ is used instead of x̂ມ

    (b) Although there are cases for which ໄx(ໄມ້ມະລາຍ) is inter-
changeable with ໃx(ໄມ້ມ້ວນ), in many cases the choice of symbol
determines the meaning of the word.

    (c) x9ຍ is the prefered symbol for the now little used x໌.

(3) WRITING VOWELS

    (a) Vowels written above or below a word are written over or
under the first letter of single consonants or the second letter
of combined or double consonants.

<u>single consonants</u>   <u>double consonants</u>

ປຸ່ມ ກຶມ ຣິດ ບັງ   ຫວ້າງ ພູ ຄຣຸ ພຣິນ

    (b) In polysyllabic words, the first letter xະ is omitted as
shown in the examples below.

ຕລາດ ສເມີ ສເວ້ຍ ຈປໂຍດ ປວັດ ສໄມ ປໂຍດ ອັຈມານຸກິມ

TONE MARKS ວັນນະຍຸດ

Lao has four tone marks:

(1) Common: x́ (ໄມ້ເອກ) changes the tone of all syllables to mid tone.

                  x̌ (ໄມ້ໂທ)   "   "   "   "   "   " to a falling tone

(2) Rare: x̃ (ໄມ້ຕຣີ) raises the tone of a syllable.

                  ẋ (ໄມ້ຈັຕະວາ)

TONE CODE

The combination of letters (consonants and vowels) and tone marks of a Lao syllable tells readers two things: the sound of the syllable (for example, "ban") and on what tone level to pronounce that syllable (for example, high falling). This tone code is summarized below and also inside both the front and back covers of the dictionary for quick reference.

TONE CODE

	Long or Nasal ending or Semi-vowel ending ຢ ວ	Long + stop ກ ດ ບ	Short or Short + stop ກ ດ ບ	Tone Mark ' ×̇	×̂
Kang ກ ຈ ດ ຕ ບ ປ ຢ ອ	1	6	3	2	5
Tam ຄ ງ ຍ ຊ ທ ນ ມ ຟ ນ ຣ ລ ວ ຣ	3	5	2	2	5
Sung ຂ ສ ຖ ຜ ຝ ຫ ຫງ ຫຍ ຫນ ຫມ ຫຼ ຫລ	4	6	3	2	6

Short: ×ະ ×̌× ×̌ ×̣̌ ×̣ ເ×ະ ເ×̌× ແ×ະ ແ×̌× ໂ×ະ ×̂× ເ×າະ ×ໍ9× ເ×̣̌

ເ×̌ຢະ ×̌ຽ× ເ×̣̌ອ ×̂ວ ×ວ̌× ໄ× ໃ× ເ×̂າ ×ຳ ×ອຢ

Long: ×າ ×̌ ×̣̌ ×̣ ເ× ແ× ໂ× ×̇ ×ອ× ເ×̣̌

ເ×̌ຽ ×ຽ× ເ×̣̌ອ ×̂ວ ×ວ×

<u>NUMBERS</u> ເລກ: ໑ ໒ ໓ ໔ ໕ ໖ ໗ ໘ ໙ ໐

       1 2 3 4 5 6 7 8 9 0

<u>SYMBOLS</u> ເຄື່ອງພາຍອັກສອນ: ໆ (ເກາະລະ)   ditto mark (")

                         ໆ (ເກາະລະ)   repeat the previous word

                   ໆລໆ (ຍັງມີອີກຕໍ່ໄປ)   etcetera (etc.)

<u>PUNCTUATION</u> ເຄື່ອງພາຍອັກ: (:)ສອງເມັດ   colon

                      (,)ຈຸດ   comma

                      (!)ອັສລັມ   exclamation mark

                      (-)ຂີດຂັ້ນ   hyphen

                      (...) ເມັດລະ   omission

                      (())ວົງເລັບ   parentheses

                      (.) ເມັດ   period

                      (?)ຖາມ   question mark

                      (" ")ເລັບຄູ່ອນ   quotation marks

                      (___)ຂີດພາຍ   underlining

English-Lao

ອັງກິດ - ລາວ

A

a	(see also an) def. art. ຄຳນຳໜ້າຄຳສັບທີ່ບໍ່ມີຍັງຈຸນະຂຶ້ນທ່ອນ
aback	adv. bpay: tang lang ໄປທາງຫຼັງ
abacus	b. luk kit ລູກຄິດ
abandon	n. gan bpa: tim ການປະຖິ້ມ v. bpa: tim ປະຖິ້ມ
abandonment	n. gan bpohy dtam gam ການປ່ອຍຕາມກັມ
abase	v. lot ptam long ລົດຕ່ຳລົງ
abate	v. sow: yut ເຈົ້າຢຸດ
abbey	n. bot ໂບດ
abbot	n. som pan ສົມພານ
abbreviate	v. nyoh ຫຍໍ້
abbreviation	n. gan nyoh ການຫຍໍ້
abdicate	v. sa: la: ສລະ
abdomen	n. tohng ທ້ອງ
abduct	v. bpohng ka ປ່ວງຂ້າ
abet	n. soing serm ສິ່ງເສີມ
abhor	v. saing ຊັງ
abide	v. paik a say: ພັກອາໄສ
ability	n. kwam sa mat ຄວາມສາມາດ
abject	adj. sua: hay ຊົ່ວຮ້າຍ
able	adj. sa mat ສາມາດ
abnormal	adj. piit taim ma: da ຜິດທັມມະດາ
aboard	adv. nay: ໃນ...

abode	n. ti a say: ທີ່ອາໄສ
abolish	v. nyo:k lerk ຍົກເລີກ
abominate	v. saing ຊັງ
abortion	n. gan taang luk ohk ການແທງລູກອອກ
about	adv. bpa: man pa:nam
about to	adv. geuap cha:, gaim laing cha: ເກືອບຈະ, ກໍ່ລັງຈະ
above	prep. tang terng ທາງເທິງ
above all	adv. saim kain ti su:t ສຳຄັນທີ່ສຸດ
abrade	v. fo:n ຝົນ
abrasion	n. gan fo:n ການຝົນ
abreast	adv. kiang kang ຄຽງຂ້າງ adv. ta:n ທັນ
abridge	v. nyoh ຫຍໍ້
abroad	adv. nohk bpa: tet ນອກປະເທດ
abrupt	adj. pohm bat, ta:n ti ພ້ອມບາດ, ທັນທີ
abscess	n. bpe:n nohng ເປັນໜອງ
absence	n. gan kat ການຂາດ
absent	v. kat ຂາດ
absolute	adj. yang de:t kat ຢ່າງເດັດຂາດ
absolve	v. a: ho si: ຍະໂຫສີ
absorb	v. dut ດູດ
absorbed	adj. ow: chay: say: ເອົາໃຈໃສ່
abstain	v. ngo:t we:n ງົດເອັ້ນ
abstinence	n. gan ngo:t we:n ການງົດເອັ້ນ

abstract	n. gan la:p 1ี ກ່ານລັບລີ້	accord	v. dto:k lo:ng ຕົກລົງ
	v. luap leuang ລວບເຮື່ອງ	according to	prep. dtam ຕາມ
abundance	n. kwam u: do:m so:m bun ຄວາມອຸດົມສົມບູນ	account	n. leuang low ເຮື່ອງຣາວ
			n. nay: leuang low ໃນ ເຮື່ອງຣາວ
abundant	adj. u: do:m so:m bun ອຸດົມສົມບູນ		
		accumulate	v. hi:p hom ຮີບໂຮມ
abuse	n. gan le:ng chay: ການ ເຫຼີງໃຈ	accurate	adj. ka:k naa ຄັກແນ່
	v. le:ng chay: ເຫຼີງໃຈ	accusation	n. ka:m gow la ຄຳກ່າວຫາ
academic	adj. gan hian ການຮຽນ	accuse	v. gow hay ກ່າວຫາ
academy	n. sa:m na:k seu:k sa ສຳນັກສຶກສາ	accustom	v. leuang kery ລ້ງເຄີຍ
		accustomed	adj. leung kery ລ້ງເຄີຍ
accent	n. sa:m niang ສຳນຽງ	ache	v. che:p ເຈັບ
accept	v. la:p ra:p ລັບຮັບ	achieve	v. he:t sa:m le:t ເຮັດ ສຳເຣັດ
access	n. tang kow: ທາງເຂົ້າ		
accessible	adj. kow: terng day: ເຂົາເຖີງໄດ້	acid	adj. na:m go:t ນ້ຳກົດ
		acknowledge	v. la:p hu ລັບຮູ້
accessory	n. keuang a:p bpa: gohn ເຄື່ອງອຸປະກອນ	acorn	n. gaan mak may: dto:n o:k ແກນໝາກໄມ້ຕົ້ນໂອກ
accident	n. u: bpa: dti: het ອຸປະຕິເຫດ	acquaint	v. hu cha:k ຮູ້ຈັກ
accommodate	v. hay: kwam sa: duak ໃຫ້ຄວາມສະດວກ	acquaintance	n. gan hu cha:k ma:k hu:n ການຮູ້ຈັກມັກຄຸ້ນ
accompany	v. bpay: na:m ໄປນຳ	acquire	v. day: ma ໄດ້ມາ
accomplish	v. he:t gan hay: sa:m le:t ເຮັດການໃຫ້ສຳເຣັດ	acquit	v. bpoy dtua ປ່ອຍຕົວ
		acre	n. suan piang di:n ສ່ວນພຽງດິນ
	v. he:t paan gan hay: sa:m le:t ເຮັດແຜນການໃຫ້ ສຳເຣັດ	across	prep. kam ຂ້າມ
		act	v. ta:m ta ທຳທ່າ
accomplished	adj. sa:m nan ສຳນານ		n. gan sa: daang la: kohn ການສະແດງລະคอม
accomplishment	n. po:n sa:m le:t ຜົນສຳເຣັດ	action	n. gan ga: ta:m ການກະທຳ

active	adj. wong way: ວ່ອງໄວ	admiration	n. gan so:m sery ການ
activity	n. wiak gan ວຽກການ		ຊົມເຊີຍ
actor	n. dtua la: kohn ຕົວລະຄອນ	admire	v. so:m sery ຊົມເຊີຍ
actress	n. dtua la: kohn nyi:ng	admission	n. ka pan bpa: dtu
	ຕົວລະຄອນຍິງ		ຄ່າຜ່ານປະຕູ
actual	adj. taa chi:ng ແທ້ຈິງ	admit	(confession) n. gan nyohm
acute	adj. laam ແຫຼມ		lap ການຍອມຮັບ
Adam's apple	n. koh hoy ຄໍຫອຍ		v. nyohm la:p ຍອມຮັບ
adapt	v. da:t bpaang ດັດແປງ	admittance	n. gan hay: ko:w ການໃຫ້ເຂົ້າ
add	v. so:m ສົມ	admonish	v. dteuan ເຕືອນ
	v. dteum ຕື່ມ	ado	v. gan nyu:ng nyak
addition	n. gan so:m ການສົມ		ການຫຍຸ້ງຍາກ
address	(make a speech) v. gow	adolescence	n. way: nu:m ໄວໜຸ່ມ
	kwam bpa say: ກ່າວຄຳປາໃສ	adopt	v. liang du ລ້ຽງດູ
	(speech) n. ka:m bpa say:	adoption	n. gan la:p way: bpe:n
	ຄຳປາໃສ		kohng dto:n ການລັບໄວ້ເປັນ
	(place) n. bohn yu ບ່ອນຢູ່		ຂອງຕົນ
adequate	adj. piang poh ພຽງພໍ	adore	v. bu sa ບູຊາ
aerodrome	n. dern nyo:n ເດີ່ນຍົນ	adorn	v. e ເອ
adhere	v. ti:t ga:n ຕິດກັນ	adult	n. pu nyay: ຜູ້ໃຫຍ່
adjacent	adv. gay: kiang ໃກ້ຄຽງ	adulterate	v. bpohm bpaang ປອມແປງ
adjective	n. ku:n nam ຄຸນນາມ	adultery	n. gan li:n mia leu phua
adjoin	v. dtoh ga:n ຕໍ່ກັນ		per:n ການຫຼິ້ນເມັຽຫຼືຜົວເພີ່ນ
adjourn	v. ra: nga:p way: ຣະງັບໄວ້	advance	v. luang na ລ່ວງໜ້າ
adjust	v. gaa kay: hay: moh:		n. gan luang na ການລ່ວງໜ້າ
	ແກ້ໄຂໃຫ້ເໝາະ	advantage	n. kwam day: bpiap ຄວາມໄດ້
administrate	v. bpo:k kohng ປົກຄອງ		ປຽບ
admirable	adj. bpe:n dta so:m sery	adventure	n. gan siang pay: ການສ່ຽງ
	ເປັນຕາຊົມເຊີຍ		ໄພ
admiral	n. nay po:n heua ek ນາຍພົນ	adversary	n. sa:t dtu ສັຕຣູ
	ເຮືອເອກ		

advertise	v. ໂກ ສາ: ນຳ ໂຄສນາ
advertisement	n. ການ ໂກ ສາ: ນຳ ການ ໂຄສນາ
advertiser	n. ພູ ໂກ ສາ: ນຳ ຜູ້ໂຄສນາ
advertising	n. ການ ໂກ ສາ: ນຳ ການໂຄສນາ
advice	n. ຄຳ ດຕາ:ກ ດເຕືອນ ຄຳຕັກເຕືອນ
advise	v. ດຕາ:ກ ດເຕືອນ ຕັກເຕືອນ
advisement	n. ການ ບເປີ:ກ ສາ ການ ປຶກສາ
advocate	v. ຕະ: ນາຍ ຄວາມ ທະນາຍຄວາມ n. ພູ ຕະ: ນາຍ ຄວາມ ຜູ້ ທະນາຍຄວາມ
afar	adv. ຫາງ ກາຍ: ຫາງໄກ
affable	adj. ບເປ:ນ ຕິ ຫາ:ກ ຫໍມ ເປັນທີ່ຮັກຫອມ
affair	n. ການ ງານການງານ
affect	n. ກະ: ໂຕ:ບ ກະ: ເຕືອນ ກະທົບກະ:ເທືອນ
affection	n. ຄວາມ ຫາ:ກ ຄວາມຮັກ
affirm	v. ເຢນ ຢາ:ນ ຢືນຢັນ
affirmation	n. ຄວາມ ເຢນ ຢາ:ນ ຄວາມ ຢືນຢັນ
afflict	v. ເຫ:ຕ ຫາຍ: ເດວຕ ຫໍນ ເຮັດໃຫ້ເຈັບດຮອນ
affliction	n. ຄວາມ ເດວຕ ຫໍນ ຄວາມ ເຈັບດຮອນ
afford	v. ໂພ ເຫ:ຕ ໄດ: ພໍເຮັດໄດ້

afraid	adj. ຢານ ຢ້ານ
Africa	n. ຕາ: ວິປ ອາ ຟຣີ: ກາ ທະວີບແອຟຣີກາ
after	adv. ລາ:ງ ຈາກ ຫຼັງຈາກ
afternoon	n. ຕໂຫນ ບາຍ ຕອນບ່າຍ
afterwards	(after that) adv. ພາຍ ລາ:ງ ພາຍຫຼັງ
again	adv. ອິກ ອີກ
against	prep. ຕໂຫ ສູ ຕໍ່ສູ້
age	n. ອາ: ຍຸ ອາຍຸ
aged	adj. ເຕົາ ເຖົ້າ
agency	n. ຕົວ ຕານ ໂບ ລີ: ສາ:ຕ ຕົວແທນບໍລິສັດ
agent	n. ຕົວ ຕານ ຕົວແທນ
aggregate	n. ຮວມ ຕາ:ງ ໂມ:ຕ ຮວມທັງໝົດ
aggression	n. ການ ລຸ:ກ ລານການຮຸກຮານ
aggressive	adv. ເຊີງ ລຸ:ກ ລານ ຊິງ ຮຸກຮານ
agile	adj. ໂວງ ໄວ: ວ່ອງໄວ
agitate	v. ໂກຫ ຄວາມ ຍຸ:ງ ຍາກ ກໍ່ຄວາມຍຸງຍາກ
ago	adv. ກາຍ ມາ ລາວ, ກໍຫນ ຜ່ານມາແລ້ວ, ກ່ອນ
agony	n. ຄວາມ ບປວຕ ໂລວ ຄວາມປວດ ລາວ
agree	v. ຍິ:ນ ຍໍຫມ ຍິນຍອມ
agreeable	adj. ໂພ ຍິ:ນ ຍໍຫມ ພໍ ຍິນຍອມ

agreement	(consent) n. gan dtoːk loːng ການຕົກລົງ
agriculture	n. gan bpuːk faːng ການ ປຸກຝັງ
ahead	(place) adv. tang na ທາງໜ້າ
	(time) adv. ik ອີກ
aid	v. suay leua ຊ່ວຍເຫຼືອ
	n. kwam suay leua ຄວາມ ຊ່ວຍເຫຼືອ
ail	v. heːt hay: cheːp ເຮັດໃຫ້ເຈັບ
ailment	n. gan cheːp kay: ການ ເຈັບໄຂ້
aim	n. muːng may ມຸ່ງໝາຍ v. naː ແນ
air	n. a gat ອາກາດ
air-conditioner	n. keuang bpian a gat ເຄື່ອງປ່ຽນອາກາດ
air force	n. gohng taːp a gat ກອງ ທັບອາກາດ
airlines	n. say gan biːn ສາຍ ການບິນ
airmail	n. gan soːng tang a gat ການສົ່ງທາງອາກາດ
airplane	n. heua biːn ເຮືອບິນ
airplane pilot	n. naːk biːn ນັກບິນ
airport	n. deːrːm nyoːn ເດີ່ນບິນ
airsick	n. mŏw: heua biːn ເມົາ ເຮືອບິນ
aisle	n. hohm ຮ່ອມ
akin	n. kay keu gaːn ຄ້າຍຄືກັນ
alarm	v. dteuan hay: dtoːk chay: ເຕືອນໃຫ້ຕົກໃຈ
albino	(person) n. koːn dohn ຄົນດ່ອນ
	(animal) n. saːt peuak ສັດເຜືອກ
album	n. bpeum dtiːt hup ປື້ມ ຕິດຮູບ
alcohol	n. loːw: ເຫຼົ້າ
alcoholic	adj. ki loːw: ຂີ້ເຫຼົ້າ
ale	n. loːw ເຫຼົ້າ
alert	v. dteuan hay: giam pohm ເຕືອນໃຫ້ກຽມພ້ອມ
	adj. giam pohm ກຽມພ້ອມ
alien	adj. dtaang daan ຕ່າງແດນ n. koːn dtaan daan ຄົນ ຕ່າງແດນ
alike	adj. keu gaːn ຄືກັນ adv. keu gaːn ຄືກັນ
alive	adv. mi si wiːt ມີຊີວິດ
all	adv. taːng moːt ທັງໝົດ
all over	(finished) adv. sow: laaw ໂຊ້ sow: moːt laaw ເຊົາແລ້ວ, ເຊົາ ໝົດແລວ (everywhere) n. dteːm bpay: tua tuːk bohn ເຕັມໄປທົ່ວທຸກ ບ່ອນ
allay	v. laː ngaːp ລະງັບ
allege	v. koo ang ກາວອ້າງ
allegiance	n. kwam seu dtoːng ຄວາມຊື່ຕົງ

alliance n. gan huam saːn paːn

ການຮ່ວມສັມພັນ

alligator n. kaa ແຂ້

allied adj. seuːng huam saːm pãːn

ຊຶ່ງຮ່ວມສັມພັນ

allow v. aː nuː nyat hayː

ອະນຸຍາດໃຫ້

allow for v. piː cha laː na

ພິຈາລະນາ

allowance n. bia liaːng (ເບ້ຽລ້ຽງ)

alloy n. lo haː bpaː soːm

ໂລຫະປະສົມ

all right conj. dayː laaw ໄດ້ແລ້ວ

allude v. kao pat teriːng

ກ່າວພາດເຖິງ

allure v. dut deuːng ດຸດດຶງ

ally v. huam gaːn ຮ່ວມກັນ

n. paːn taː miːt ພັນທະມິດ

almost adv. geuap ເກືອບ

alms n. kohng hayː tan ຂອງ

ໃຫ້ທານ

alone adj. diaw ດຽວ

along adv. bpay dtaːm ໄປຕາມ

aloof adj. dtang haːk ຕ່າງຕາກ

aloud adv. daːng siang ດ້ວຍສຽງ

alphabet n. dtua aːk sohn ຕົວອັກສອນ

already adv. laaw ແລ້ວ

also adv. keu gaːn ຄືກັນ

altar n. han paː ຮ້ານພະ

alter v. bpian bpaang ປ່ຽນແປງ

alternate adj. saːp bpian ສັບປ່ຽນ

alternative adj. sayː taan dayː ໃຊ້

ແທນໄດ້

n. kohng ti saːp bpian

dayː ຂອງທີ່ສັບປ່ຽນໄດ້

although conj. teriːng maan wa

ເຖິງແມ່ນວ່າ

altitude n. kwaːm suːng ຄວາມສູງ

altogether adv. huam gaːn taːng moːt

ຮວມກັນທັງໝົດ

alum n. hiːn soːm ຫີນສົ້ມ

aluminium n. aː luː miː naːm ອະລຸ

ມີນັ້ມ

always adv. leuay leuay ເລື້ອຍໆ

A.M. (ante meridiem) n. dtuhn

soːw ຕອນເຊົ້າ

AM (amplitude modulation) n.

keun taːm maː da ຄື້ນທັມະດາ

amateur n. naːk saː maːk liːn ນັກ

ສມັກຫຼິ້ນ

amaze v. heːt hayː bpaː lat

ເຮັດໃຫ້ປະຫາດ

ambassador n. ek aːk kaː rat saː

tut ເອກອັຄຣາຊຸທຸດ

ambition n. kwaːm fayː suːng ຄວາມ

ໄຝ່ສູງ

ambulance n. loːt hong moh ລົດ

ໂຮງໝໍ

amend n. gaa kay ແກ້ໄຂ

America n. aː me liː gaː ອະເມຣິກາ

American n. go:n ă: me li: ga:
คินอะเมริกา

amiable adj. bpe:n dta ha:k เป็น
ตารัก

amid prep. la wa:ng ระหว่าง

amiss adj. pi:t pat ผิดผาด

ammunition n. luk bpeun ลูกปืน

among prep. la wăng ระหว่าง

amount (quantity) n. cha:m
nŭan จำนอม

(price) n. la ka ราคา

ample n. piăng poh พัวงพ่

amplifier n. keuang ga: chay siang
เคื่องกะจายสว

amplify v. ka: nyay hay: nyay:
ยยายให้ใหย่

amuse v. pert pern เผิดเผิม

amusement n. kwam pert pern ความ
เผิดเผิม

amusement park n. suăn yohn chay: สอม
ย่อมใจ

an singular particle before
vowels ka:m na:m nă kohng sa:p
ti mi sa: la: ohk gohn
คำนำหผาอง วสียที่มีสระออกก่อม

analysis n. gan wi: koh:
ภามอิเคาะ

analyze v. wi: koh: อิเคาะ

ancestor n. ba:n pa: bu: lu:t
บ้มพะบุรถ

anchor vt. toht să: moh ท9ดสะผ

ancient adj. bo hän gow: gaa
โยรามเก้าเท่

and conj. laa: และ

anecdote n. ni: tan gohm มิทาม
ท่อม

anemic adj. leuat noy เลือดน้อย

anew adj. ik teua neu:ng อิก
เท่อ้ง

angel n. năng tê wă: da
มาๆเทอะดา

anger n. kwam chay: hay คอาม
ใจร้าย

angle n. chaa แจ

angling n. dteu:k be:t ตึกเบ็ด

angry adj. chay: hay ใจร้าย

anguish n. kwam bpauat low คอาม
ปอดธาว

angular adj. mi chaa มีเเจ

animal n. să:t สัด

animal trainer n. kwan să:t คอามสัด

ankle n. koh dtin 2ดิม

anklet n. bpohk ka ปงกขา

annals n. po:ng sa wa: dan
ผ้วสาอะดาม

annex n. dtoh dteu:m kow: ga:n
ตต่มเข้าทับ

annihilate v. guat lang ta:m lay
ภอดล้าๆทำลาย

anniversary n. wă:n ko:p hohp bpi
อัมคืยธอบปี

announce	v. bpa: gat ປະກາດ	anvil	n. taːng ທັ່ງ
announcement	n. gan bpa: gat ການປະກາດ	anxiety	n. kwam gaː woːn gaː way ຄວາມ ກະວົນກະວາຍ
announcer	n. pu bpa: gat ຜູ້ປະກາດ		
annoy	v. loːp guan ຮົບກວນ	anxious	adj. gaː woːn gaː way ກະວົນ ກະວາຍ
annoyance	n. gan loːp guan ການ ຮົບກວນ		
		any	adj. chaːk ຈັກ
annual	adj. bpa: chaːm bpi ປະ ຈໍາປີ	anybody	pu day: pu neuːng ຜູ້ໃດ ຜູ້ໜຶ່ງ
annually	adv. tuːk tuːk bpi ທຸກໆ ປີ	anymore	adj. ik leuy ອີກເລີຍ
		anyone	n. pay: pu neuːng ໃຜຜູ້ໜຶ່ງ
annul	vt. nyoːk lerk ຍົກເລີກ	anyplace	n. bohn day: day: goh day: ບ່ອນໃດກໍໄດ້
anoint	vt. tǎ naːm maːn ທານ້ຳມັນ		
another	adj. euːn ອື່ນ	anything	n. aːn day: goh day: ອັນໃດກໍໄດ້
answer	n. kaːm dtohp ຕອບ		
ant	n. moːt ມົດ	anyway	adv. chaːng day: goh dtam ຈັ່ງໃດກໍຕາມ
antagonist	n. saːt dtu ຜູ້ສັດຕຣູ		
Antarctica	n. tha wiːp aːn dtaːk dti: ga ທະວີບ ອັນຕັກຕິກາ	anywhere	adv. bohn day: goh day: ບ່ອນໃດກໍໄດ້
		apart	adj. kong dtang hak ຂອງຕ່າງຫາກ
antelope	n. dto nyeuːang ໂຕເຢືອງ		adv. dtang hak ຕ່າງຫາກ
antenna	n. say a gat ສາຍອາກາດ	apartment	n. heuːang sow: bpeːn hohng ເຮືອນເຊົ່າເປັນຫ້ອງ
anthem	n. peng saːt ເພງຊາດ		
anticipate	v. gaː dtuang ກະຕວງ	ape	n. liːng ton ລິງໂຕນ
anticipation	n. gan kat may ການຄາດ ໝາຍ	apologize	v. koh tot ຂໍໂທດ
		apology	n. kaːm koh tot ຄໍຂໍໂທດ
antidote	n. ya tohn piːt ຢາ ຖອນພິດ	appall	v. heːt hay: dtoːk chay: ເຮັດໃຫ້ຕົກໃຈ
antiseptic	adj. gaːn paː nyat ກັນ ພຍາດ	apparatus	n. keuːang bpaː gohn ເຄື່ອງ ອຸປກອນ
antler	n. kow: gwang ເຂົາກວາງ		
anus	n. taː wan naːk ທວານໜັກ	apparel	n. keuːang nuːng ເຄື່ອງນຸ່ງ

apparent	adj. bpa go:t keu ปາກົດຄື
appeal	v. hoǒng koh ຮ້ອງຂໍ
appear	(come into view) v. bpa go:t ປາກົດ
	(look) v. mi la:k sa: na: ມີລັກສມະ
appearance	(coming into view) n. gan bpa go:t ການປາກົດ
	(looks) n. la:k sa: na: ລັກສມະ
appease	v. he:t hay: sa: ngo:p lo:ng ເຮັດໃຫ້ສ່ວຍລົງ
append	v. dteu:m ຕື່ມ
appendix	n. say: dti:m ໃສ່ຕື່ງ
appetite	n. kwam saap mua ຄວາມ ແຊບນົວ
applaud	v. dto:p meu ຕົບມື
applause	n. gan dto:p meu ການຕົບມື
apple	n. mak bpohm ໝາກປ່ອມ
apple pie	n. ka: no:m mak bpohm ຂມົມໝາກປ່ອມ
appliance	n. keuang say: soy (ຄື່ອງ ໃຊ້ສອຍ
applicant	n. pu sa: ma:k ຜູ້ສມັກ
application	(paper) n. bay: sa: ma:k ໃບສມັກ
	(use) n. wi: ti say: ວິທີໃຊ້
apply	(for work) v. sa: ma:k ສມັກ
	(put on) v. ow: say: ເອົາ ໃສ່
	(concerning) v. giaw na:m ກ່ຽວນຳ
	(use) na:m ma say: ນຳ ມາໃຊ້
apply one's self	adv. dtaing chay: say: ຕັ້ງໃຈໃສ່
appoint	v. dtaang dta:ng ແຕ່ງຕັ້ງ
appointment	n. gan na:t ການນັດ
appraise	v. dti ra ka ຕີຣາຄາ
appreciate	v. hu ku:n ka ຮູ້ຄຸນຄ່າ
apprehension	n. gan hu tow: kow: chay: ການຮູ້ເທົ່າເຂົ້າໃຈ
apprentice	n. pu feu:k app ngan ຜູ້ຝຶກແຮບງານ
approach	v. kow: bpy: gay: ເຂົ້າ ໄປໄກ້
approbation	n. gan he:n di na:m ການ ເຫັນດີນຳ
appropriate	adj. moh: so:m ເພາະສົມ
	v. nyeu:t ow: ຍຶດເອົາ
approval	n. gan he:n di na:m ການ ເຫັນດີນຳ
approve	v. he:n di na:m ເຫັນດີນຳ
approximate	v. dtuang ຕວງ
April	n. deuan me sa ເດືອນເມສາ
apron	n. pa ga:n bpeuan ຜ້າກັນ ເປື່ອມ
apt	adj. moh: so:m ເພາະສົມ
aptitude	n. kwam sa: lat ຄວາມ ສລາດ

aquarium n. boh:n ka:ng sa:t na:m
ບ່ອນລ້ຽງສັດນ້ຳ

aquatic adj. ti gert ga:p na:m
ທີ່ເກີດທັບນ້ຳ

aquatics n. gi: la li:n na:m
ກິລາຫຼິ້ນນ້ຳ

arabic n. pa sa a la:p ພາສາ
ອາຫຼັບ

arbiter n. pu dta:t si:n ຜູ້ຕັດ
ສິນ

arbitrate v. dta:t si:n ຕັດສິນ

arbor v. suan may: ສວນໄມ້

arc n. kong ໂຄ້ງ

arch n. bpa: dtu go:ng ປະຕູກົ່ງ

architect n. sa: ta bpa: ni:k
ສຖາປະນິກ

architecture n. sa: ta bpa:t nya: ga:m
ສຖາປັດຍະກັມ

archives (documents) n. ek ga:
san sa:m ka:n ເອກະສານ
ສຳຄັນ
n. hohng sa: mu:t ti mi
bpeu:m gow: giaw ga:p
po:ng sa wa: dan kohng
sat laa: bpeu:m tu:k yang
giaw ga:p pa sa kohng
sat ທ່ອງສມຸດທີ່ມີເກັ່າທ່າງໂຖບ
ຜິ່ວສາລະຄາມຂອງຊາດແລະປັ້ມທຸກຢ່າງກ່ຽວ
ກັບພາສາຂອງຊາດ

archway n. tang mi bpa: dtu
kong ທາງມີປະຕູໂຄ້ງ

Arctic n. ak dti:k ອາກຕິກ

Arctic Ocean n. ma: ha sa: mu:t ak
dti: ga: ມະຫາສມຸດ ອາກຕິກາ

area n. peun ti ພື້ນທີ່

Argentina n. bpa: tet ak sa:ng dtin
ປະເທດອາກຊັງຕິນ

argue v. dto tiang ໂຕ້ຖຽງ

argument n. gan dto tiang ການ
ໂຕ້ຖຽງ

arid adj. haang laang ແຫ້ງແລ້ງ

arise v. lu:k keu:n ລຸກຂຶ້ນ

aristocracy n. puak ku:n nang
ພວກຂຸນນາງ

aristocrat n. ku:n nang ຂຸນນາງ

arithmetic n. lek ເລກ

ark n. ga:m bpa:n nyay:
ກຳປັ່ນໃຫຍ່

arm n. kaan ແຂນ

armada n. ka: buan heua lo:p
ຂວງເຮືອຣົບ

armament n. keuang a wu:t ເຄື່ອງ
ອາວຸດ

armband n. bpohk kaan ປອກແຂນ

armchair n. dta:ng i terng ຕັ່ງອີ
ເທີ່ງ

armful adj. dte:m kaan ເຕັມແຂນ

armistice n. gan sa: ngo:p ser:k
ການສງບເສີກ

armlet n. keuang bpa: da:p kaan

dtohn1 terng3 ເຄື່ອງປະດັບແຂນຕອນເທິງ

armor n. keuang2 nu:ng2 le:k6 ເຄື່ອງນຸ່ງເຫຼັກ

armory n. ka:ng3 a1 wu:t2 ຄັງອາວຸດ

armpit n. ki6 haa5 ຂີ້ແຮ້

arms n. keuang2 a1 wu:t2 ເຄື່ອງອາວຸດ

army n. gohng1 ta:p2 ກອງທັບ

around adj. ohm5 hohp5 ອ້ອມຮອບ

arouse v. he:t2 hay:6 dteu:n2 dten5 ເຮັດໃຫ້ຕື່ນເຕັ້ນ

arraign v. okk6 may4 goh:3 ern5 dtua1 ອອກໝາຍເກາະເອີ້ນຕົວ

arrange v. cha:t3 chaang1 ຈັດແຈງ

array v. cha:t3 yay1 hay:6 bpe:n1 la:2 biap6 ຈັດຢາຍໃຫ້ເປັນລະບຽບ

arrest v. cha:p3 gu:m1 ຈັບກຸມ

arrival n. gan1 ma3 te:rng4 ການມາເຖິງ

arrive n. ma3 hoht5 ມາຮອດ

arrogance n. kwam3 ki6 o:ng2 chong1 hohng4 ຄວາມຂີ້ອ່ງຈອງຫອງ

arrogant adj. ki6 o:ng2 chong1 hohng4 ຂີ້ອ່ງຈອງຫອງ

arrow n. luk5 na6 ລູກພ້າ

art (general) n. si:n3 la:2 bpa:3 ສິລປະ

(pictures) n. hup5 taam5 ຮູບແຕ້ມ

artery n. se:n6 leuat5 ເສັ້ນເລືອດ

article n. bo:t3 kwam3 ບົດຄວາມ

artificial adj. tiam3 ທຽມ

artillery n. kohng1 ta:2 han4 bpeun1 nyay:2 ກອງທະຫານປືນໃຫຍ່

artist n. na:k2 si:n4 la:2 bpi:n1 ນັກສິລປິນ

artistic adj. mi3 si:n4 la:2 bpi:n1 ມີສິລປິນ

artistry n. fi meu3 sang2 nay:3 tang3 si:n4 la:2 bpi:n1 ຝີມືຊ່າງໃນທາງສິລປະ

arts n. si:n4 la:2 bpa:3 ສິລປະ

as conj. meua2, meuan4 ເມື່ອ, ເໝືອນ

as... as toh2 ga:n1 ga:p.... ທໍ່ກັນ ກັບ.....

as soon as possible adv. way:3 ti2 su:t3 ti2 cha:3 way:3 day:5 ໄວທີ່ສຸດທີ່ຈະໄວໄດ້

ascend v. keun6 ຂຶ້ນ

ascent v. gan1 keun6 ການຂຶ້ນ

ascribe vt. ang5 i:ng1 ອ້າງອີງ

ash n. li6 tow:2 ຂີ້ເທົ່າ

ashamed adj. ay1 ອາຍ

ashtray n. a:n1 kla2 gohk6 nya1 ອັນເຂັ່ງກອກຢາ

Asia n. ta:2 wi:p2 a1 sia3 ທະວີບອາເຊັຽ

Asian adj. haang2 ta:2 wi:p2 a1 sia3 ແຫ່ງທະວີບ ອາເຊັຽ

n. ko:n3 a1 sia3 ຄົນ ອາເຊັຽ

ask	v. tam ຖາມ
asleep	adj. la:p ລັບ
asparagus	n. noh may: fla:ng ຜັກໄມ້ຝຣັ່ງ
aspect	n. la:k sa: na: ລັກສນະ
aspire	v. fay: sung lohng ໃຝ່ bering ສູງເບື້ອງ
aspirin	n. ya gaa che:p hua ຢາແກ້ເຈັບຫົວ
ass	n. ma loh ມ້າລໍ
assail	v. ta:m hay ທຳຮ້າຍ
assassin	n. pu hay ka ko:n ຜູ້ຮ້າຍຂ້າຄົນ
assassinate	v. ka ko:n ຂ້າຄົນ
assault	v. bu:k ta:m hay ບຸກທຳຮ້າຍ
assay	v. pa: nya nyam ພຍາຍາມ n. kwam pa: nya nyam ຄວາມພຍາຍາມ
assemble	v. tohn hom ga:n ທ້ອນ ໂຮມກັນ
assembly	(meeting) n. gan bpa: su:m ການປະຊຸມ (legislature) n. sa: pa ສະພາ
assert	v. yeun ya:n ຢືນຢັນ
assertion	n. gan yeun ya:n wa teuk dtohng ການຢືນຢັນ ວ່າຖືກຕ້ອງ
assets	n. so:m ba:t mi ka: ສົມ ບັດມີຄ່າ
assiduity	n. kwam ma:n pian ຄວາມ ໝັ່ນພຽນ
assign	n. dtaang dta:ng ແຕ່ງຕັ້ງ
assignment	n. wiak gan ti dtaang hay: ວຽກການທີ່ແຕ່ງໃຫ້
assist	v. suay leua ຊ່ວຍເຫຼືອ
assistance	n. kwam suay leua ຄວາມ ຊ່ວຍເຫຼືອ
assistant	n. pu suay ຜູ້ຊ່ວຍ
associate	n. pu huam na:m ຜູ້ຮ່ວມງານ v. ko:p ka ຄົບຄ້າ
association	n. sa: ma ko:m ສະມາຄົມ
assortment	v. gan cha:t bpe:n puak ການຈັດເປັນພວກ
assume	v. dtuang ຕວງ
assumption	n. gan dtuang ການຕວງ
assure	v. he:t hay: ma:n chay: ເຮັດໃຫ້ໝັ້ນໃຈ
astern	adv. tang tay heua ທາງທ້າຍເຮືອ
asthma	n. lok heut ໂຣກຫືດ
asthmatic	adj. bpe:n heut ເປັນຫືດ
astonish	v. he:t hay: bpa: lat chay: ເຮັດໃຫ້ປະຫຼາດໃຈ
astonishing	adj. bpa: lat ປະຫຼາດ
astonishment	n. kwam bpa: lat ຄວາມ ປະຫຼາດ
astound	v. he:t hay: ser ເຮັດໃຫ້ ເຊີ່
astrology	n. ho la: sat ໂຫຣະສາດ

astronaut	n. na:k a wa: gat มัก ๆอวะภาค
astronomy	n. da la sat การาสาด
at	prep. yu อยู่
at all	boh ... cha:k noy บ่ ... จักพอย
at last	nay ba:n su:t tay: ในบั้นสุดท้าย
at least	yang noy ti su:t ย่าๆ น้อยที่สุด
at once	nay: ta:n ti ta:n day: ในทันทีทันใด
athlete	n. na:k gi: la มักกีฬา
athletic	adj. gi: la กีฬา
Atlantic Ocean	n. ma: ha sa: mu:t a:t la:ng dti:k มะหาสมุดอัด ลังติก
atmosphere	n. ba:n nya gat บันยากาด
atmospheric	adj. giaw ga:p a gat ทัๆอัยยๆภาค
atom	n. a dto:m ๆตัม
atomic	adj. giaw ga:p a dto:m ทัๆอัยยๆตัม
atone	v. dtoup taan ตอบแทน
atonement	n.gan dtohp taan การตอบแทน
attach	n. dti:t na:m ติดมำ
attache	n. chow: na ti sa: tah tut เจ้าพำทิสถานทูต
attachment	n. gan dti:t na:m การ ติดมำ
attack	v. chom dti โจมตี (raid) n. gan chom dti การโจมตี
attain	v. ter:ng เถิๆ
attainment	n. gan ter:ng การเถิๆ
attempt	v. pa: nya nyam พยายาม
attend	v. bpay: huam ไปธอม
attendant	n. ko:n say: คิมใฃ้
attention	n. kwam dta:ng chay: ความตัๆใจ
attentive	adj. dta:ng chay: ra: ma:t ra: wa:ng ตัๆใจ, ระมัดระอัๆ
attest	v. pi: sut ผิสูด
attestation	n. gan ya:ng yeun การ ยิๆยืม
attic	n. kuan ค้อม
attire	v. dto:p dtaang ติบแตๆ n. gan dto:p dtaang การ ติบแตๆ
attitude	n. gi: li: nya กิริยา
attorney	n. ay: nya: gan ไอยะการ
attract	v. nyua: chay: ยิๆะใจ
attraction	n. gan nyua: luang chay: การยิๆะลอๆใจ
attractive	n. bpen dta ber:ng เป็นตาเยิๆ
attribute	n. ku:n so:m ba:t คุมสิม ฃัด

auction	n. gan kay bpa: mun ການ ຂາຍປະມູນ
audible	adj. pōh day: nyi:n day: ຜັໄດ້ຍິນໄດ້
audience	n. pu ma fa:ng ຜູ້ມາຟັງ
audit	v. guat ກວດ
audition	n gan ka:t leuak la:ng fa:ng ການຄັດເລືອກຫ້ງຟັງ v. ka:t leuak ຄັດເລືອກ
auditor	(listener) n. pu fa:ng ຜູ້ຟັງ (checker) n. pu guat ຜູ້ ກວດ
auditorium	n. hohng bpa: su:m ຫ້ວງປະຊຸມ
auger	n. sa: wa:n ສ່ວານ
August	n. deuang si:ng ha ເດືອນ ສິງຫາ
aunt	n. bpa ປ້າ (older sister of parent) n. bpa ປ້າ (younger sister of father) n. a ອາ (younger sister of mother) n. na ນ້າ
aurora	n. saang pa: a ti:t nyam dta: wa:n keun ແສງພະອາທິດ ຍາມຕະວັນຂຶ້ນ
austere	adj. ke:ng keu:m ເຄັ່ງຂຶມ
Australia	n. ot sa: dtaa li ໂອ ຕຣາລີ

authentic	adj. kohng taa la: ວງ daing derm ແທ້ແລະດັ່ງເດີມ
authenticate	v. sa: daang wa kohng taa ສແດງວ່າຂວງແທ້
authentication	n. gan sa: daany wa kohng taa ການສແດງວ່າ ຂວງແທ້
author	n. pu dtaang ຜູ້ແຕງ
authority	n. a:m nat ອຳນາດ
authorization	(power) n. gan hay: a:m nat ການໃຫ້ອຳນາດ (permission) n. gan a: nu: nyat ການອະນຸຍາດ
authorize	(power) v. hay a:m nat ໃຫ້ອຳນາດ (permit) v. a: nu: nyat ອະນຸຍາດ
autograph	n. lay se:n seu ລາຍເຊັນຊື່ v. se:n ເຊັນ
automatic	adj. bpe:n eng ເປັນເອງ
automobile	n. lo:t nyo:n ຣົຖຍົນ
autotruck	n. lo:t ba:n tu:k ຣົຖ ບັນທຸກ
autumn	n. la: du bpay: may: lo:n ຣະຄູໃບໄມ້ລົນ
auxiliary	n. pu suay ຜູ້ຊ່ວຍ adj. bpe:n keuang suay ເປັນເຄື່ອງຊ່ວຍ

avail	v. teū ow: ຖືເອົາ
available	adj. poh dày: ພໍໄດ້
avalanche	n. hiːn leu hiːm maː tì ເປ paː ໄ ໄ loːng mà dtaa terng pù ທິມຫິມະທີ່ໄຫຼພັງ ລົງມາແຕ່ເທິງພູ
avarice	n. kwam kì ti ຄວາມຂີ້ຖີ
avaricious	adj. ki tì ຂີ້ຖີ
avenge	vt. gàa kaan ແກ້ແຄ້ນ
avenger	n. pù gàa kaǎn ຜູ້ແກ້ແຄ້ນ
avenue	n. taː noːn nyaː ຖນົນ ໃຫຍ່
average	(number) n. suan saː lia ສ່ວນສະເລ່ຍ (typical) adj. poh bpan gang ພໍປານກາງ
averse	adj. ki diat ຂຍົດ
aversion	n. kwam ki diat ຄວາມຂຍົດ
avert	v. loːp lik ຫຼີບຫຼີກ
aviation	n. gan biːn ການບິນ
aviator	n. naːk biːn ນັກບິນ
avocation	n. gan ngan ການງານ
avoid	v. lik weːn ຫຼີກເວັ້ນ
await	vt. koy ta ຄອຍຖ້າ
awake	adj. hu meua keuːn ຮູ້ເມື່ອຂື້ນ
awaken	(yourself) v. dteuːn keuːn ຕື່ນຂື້ນ (someone else) v. bpuːk

awakening	n. gan bpuːk hay dteuːn ການປຸກໃຫ້ຕື່ນ
award	n. lang waːn ລາງວັນ
aware	adj. hu seuːk dtua ຮູ້ສຶກຕົວ
away	adv. gay: ohk bpay: ໄກອອກໄປ
awe	n. kwam yan ຄວາມຢ້ານ v. yan ຢ້ານ
awesome	adj. bpeːn dta yan ເປັນຕາຢ້ານ
awful	adj. pot leua ໂພດເຫຼືອ
awfully	adv. pot lay ໂພດຫຼາຍ
awhile	adv. buːt neuːng ບຶດໜຶ່ງ
awkward	adj. bpeːn kern kern ເປັນເຂີນໆ
awkwardness	n. kwam kern ຄວາມເຂີນ
axe	n. kwan ຂວານ
axis	n. chuːt pow: ຈຸດເຜົ້າ
axle	n. gan leu pow: ແກນ ຫຼືເຜົ້າ

B

baby	n. luk ohn ລູກອ່ອນ
baby carriage	n. loːt u luk ohn ຣົດ ອູ່ລູກອ່ອນ
bachelor	n. say sot ຊາຍໂສດ
back	n. laːng ຫຼັງ
back up	n. toy laːng ຖອຍຫຼັງ

backache	n. chep lang (จับຫຼัง
backbone	n. ga: duk sa:n lang ກະດູກສັນຫຼัง
backer	n. pu sa: na:p sa: nun ຜູ້ສมับสมุน
background	(scene) n. lang sak ຫຼັງສາກ
	(person) n. beuang lang ເບื้อງຫຼัງ
backward	adv. bpay: tang lang ໄປທາງຫຼัງ
bacon	n. mu ke:m sam sa:n ໝู เค็มສามชั้น
bacteria	n. seua lok เຊ้อโรก
bad	adj. sua ຊ้ว
badge	n. keuang my เคื่องໝາย
badminton	n. gi la dti bpik gay: ກีລาตีปิกไກ่
baffle	v. he:t hay: ngong เຮັดให้งง
bag	n. tong, tay: ຖิง, ไถ่
baggage	n. tong der:n tang ຖิงเดินทาง
bail	n. ngér:n bpa: gan เງินปะกัน
bait	v. ow: yeua lok เอาเหยื่อล่
bake	v. o:p ອีบ
baker	n. sang o:p ຊ่างອีบ
bakery	n. hong ka: no:m ໂຮງຂนม
balance	n. si:ng ຊ່ง
balcony	n. la: biang ລະບຽງ
bald	adj. lan ລ້ານ
bale	(of hay) n. ma:t feuang มัดเฟืອງ
	(water) v. dta:k na:m ตักน้ำ
balk	n. u: pa: sa:k อุปะสัก
ball	(round) n. mak ban ໝາກบาน
	(dancing) n. gan dte:n laim ການเต้นลำ
ballad	(literature) n. bpeu:m leuang ปึ้มเຣื่อງ
	(song) n. peng low sa: may: เพງລ่าວสไม (เພ้ງລາວสไม
ball bearing	n. luk beu:n loh ลูกปืนโล่
balloon	(children's toy) n. bpu:m bpow: ปุมเป้า
	(to ride in) n. heua hoh เຮือเຫາะ
ballot	n. ba:t ka: naan บัตคะ แนน
balm	n. kohng la: nga:p bpuat ຂອงລະງับปวด
bamboo	n. may: pay: ไม้ไผ่
ban	v. sa:ng ham ສั่งຫ้าม
banana	n. mak guy ໝາກກ้วย
band	(music) n. ka: na: do:n dti คมะดินตรี
	(maker) v. say ha:t สายธัด

bandage	n. pa hoh bat ຜ້າພັນບາດ
bandaid	n. pa dti:t bat ຜ້າຕິດ ບາດ
bandit	n. chon ໂຈນ
bang	n. siang da:ng bpa:ng ສຽງດັງບັ້ງ adj. siang da:ng bpa:ng ສຽງດັງບັ້ງ
banish	v. lay: ohk ໄລ່ອອກ
bank	n. ta: na ka:n ທະນະຄານ
bank note	n. nger:n chia ເງິນເຈັ້ຍ
bankrupt	n. lo:m la: lay ລົ້ມລະລາຍ
banner	n. bpay ປ້າຍ
banquet	n. ngan gi:n liang nyay: ການກິນລ້ຽງໃຫຍ່
bar	n. han keuang deum ຮ້ານ ເຄື່ອງດື່ມ
barbarian	n. ko:n bpa teuan ຄົນ ປ່າເຖື່ອນ
barber	n. san dta:t pom ຊ່າງ ຕັດຜົມ
barber shop	n. han dta:t pom ຮ້ານຕັດຜົມ
bare	adj. bpeuy ເປືອຍ
barefoot	adj. dtin bpo:w ຕີນເປົ່າ
barely	adv. geuap cha: boh ເກືອບ ຈະບໍ່
bargain	v. dtoh la ka ຕໍຣາຄາ
barge	n. heua ba:n tu:k hohng ເຮືອບັນທຸກຮອງ
bark	n. bpeuak may: ເປືອກໄມ້
barley	n. dto:n kow keu dto:n sa li ຕົ້ນເຂົ້າຄືຕົ້ນສາລີ
barn	n. kohk sa:t ຄອກສັດ
baron	n. nyo:t ku:n nang ຍົດ ຂຸນນາງ
barracks	n. heuan ta: han ເຮືອນທະ ຫານ
barrel	n. ta:ng ຖັງ
barren	adj. haang laang ແຫ້ງແລ້ງ
barrette	n. gi:p nip po:m ກີບນີບຜົມ
barricade	v.sand keuang ga:n ta: no:n ສ້າງເຄື່ອງກັນຖະໜົນ n. keuang ga:n ta: no:n ເຄື່ອງກັນຖະໜົນ
barrier	n. ket ga:n ເຂດກັ້ນ
barroom	n. hohng keuang deu:m ຫ້ອງເຄື່ອງດື່ມ
barter	v. laak bpian si:n ka ແລກປ່ຽນສິນຄ້າ
base	n. sa:n lu:m ຊັ້ນລຸ່ມ adj. dta:m ຕ່ຳ
baseball	n. gi: la a: me li: ga:n ກິລາຈະເມຣິກັນ
basement	n. hohng dtay: di:n ຫ້ອງໃຕ້ດິນ
bashful	adj. ki ay ຂີ້ອາຍ
basin	n. ang na:m ອ່າງນ້ຳ
basis	n. la:k laang ຫຼັກແລ້ງ
basket	v. o:w say: ga: dta ເອົາ ໃສ່ກະຕ່າ

basketball	n. gi: la li:n ban say: buaŋ ກິລາຕີ້ນການໄສ່ບ່ວງ
bat	v. dti duay kohn ຕີດ້ວຍ ຄອນ
	n. dto chia ໂຕເຈັງ
bath	n. gan ap na:m ການອາບນ້ຳ
bathe	v. ap na:m ອາບນ້ຳ
bathing suit	n. suit ap na:m ຊຸດອາບນ້ຳ
bathrobe	n. seua dtu:m ap na:m ເສື້ອ ຄຸມອາບນ້ຳ
bathroom	n. hohng ap na:m ຫ້ອງ ອາບນ້ຳ
bathtub	n. a:ng ap na:m ອ່າງອາບນ້ຳ
baton	n. kohn na:m ka: na: ຄອນ ນຳຄະນະ
batter	(cooking) n. keuang dti ເຄື່ອງຕີ
	(person) n. pu dti ຜູ້ຕີ
battery	(radio, etc...) n. tan fay: ຖ່ານໄຟ
	(car) n. moh fay: ໝໍ້ໄຟ
battle	n. gan lo:p ການລົບ
bay	n. ow ອ່າວ
be	v. maan, bpe:n ແມ່ນ, ເປັນ
	(location) v. yu ຢູ່
beach	n. hat say ຫາດຊາຍ
bead	n. gaaw mu:k ແກ້ວມຸກ
beak	(bird, chicken) n. so:p ສົບ
beam	(wood) n. keu ຂື່
	(light) n. saang ແສງ
bean	n. mak tua ໝາກຖົ່ວ
bear	n. mi ໝີ
beard	n. nuat dtay: kang ໜວດ ໄຕ້ຄາງ
bearings	n. waan hohng ແຫວນຮ່ອງ
beast	v. sa:t bpa: ສັດປ່າ
beat	v. dti, fat ຕີ, ຟາດ
beaten	adj. teuk dti ຖືກຕີ
beautiful	adj. ngam ງາມ
beautifully	adv. yang ngo:t ngam ຢ່າງງົດງາມ
beautify	vt. he:t hay: ngam ເຮັດໃຫ້ງາມ
beauty	n. kwam ngam ຄວາມງາມ
beauty parlor	n. hohng serm suay ຫ້ອງ ເສີມສວຍ
beaver	n. nu na ໜູນາ
become	v. gan bpe:n ກາຍເປັນ
bed	n. dtiang nohn ຕຽງນອນ
bedding	n. keuang bohn non ເຄື່ອງບ່ອນນອນ
bedroom	n. hohng nohn ຫ້ອງນອນ
bedstead	n. hang dtiang nohn ຮ່າງ ຕຽງນອນ
bedtime	n. we la nohn ເວລານອນ
bee	n. maa: perng ແມ່ເຜິ້ງ
beehive	n. haing perng ຮັງເຜິ້ງ
beef	n. si:n ngua ຊີ້ນງົວ
beer	n. low: bia ເຫຼົ້າເບັຽ

beet	n. pa:k gat wan ຜັກກາດຫວານ
beetle	v. maang ka:p duang ແມງຄັບດວງ
befall	v. gerd leuang ເກີດເຮື່ອງ
before	adv. gohn ກ່ອນ
beg	v. koh hohng ຂໍຮ້ອງ
beggar	n. ko:n koh tan ຄົນຂໍທານ
begin	n. dta:ng dto:n ຕັ້ງຕົ້ນ
beginning	n. gan dta:ng dto:n ການ ຕັ້ງຕົ້ນ
behalf	n. na:y: na:m ໃນນາມ
behave	v. bpa: peu:t ປະພຶດ
behind	adv. tang la:ng ທາງຫຼັງ
behold	v. he:n ເຫັນ
being	n. dtua ko:n ຕົວຄົນ
belief	n. kwam seua teu ຄວາມ ເຊື່ອຖື
believe	v. seua teu ເຊື່ອຖື
bell	n. la: ka:ng ລະຄັງ
bellow	v. ho hohng ໂຮຮ້ອງ
belly	n. tohng ທ້ອງ
belly dancer	n. na:k dte:n sa: daang ນັກເຕັ້ນສະແດງ
belong to	v. bpe:n kohng ເປັນຂອງ
belongings	n. kohng ga:m ma: si:t ຂອງກັມມະສິດ
beloved	adj. su:t ti ha:k ສຸດທີ່ຮັກ
below	adv. beuang lu:m ເບື້ອງລຸ່ມ
belt	n. say aaw ສາຍແອວ

bench	n. bpaan ma ແປ້ນມ້າ
bend	v. ko:t ຄົດ
beneath	adv. tang gohng, lu:m ທາງກ້ອງ, ລຸ່ມ
benefit	v. bpa: nyot ປະໂຍດ
benevolent	adj. ku:n kwam di ຄຸນ ຄວາມດີ
berry	n. mak fay: ຫມາກໄຟ
berth	n. dtu nohn ຕຽງນອນ
beseech	v. ohn wohn ອ້ອນວອນ
beside	prep. yu kang ຢູ່ຂ້າງ
beside the point	adv. nohk leuang ນອກເຮື່ອງ
besiege	v. lohm wa:y: ລ້ອມໄວ້
best	adj. di ti su:t ດີ ທີ່ສຸດ
bestow	v. mohp hay: ມອບໃຫ້
bet	n. gan pa: na:n ການພນັນ n. pa: na:n ພນັນ
betel	n. mak kiaw ຫມາກຄ້ຽວ
betray	v. ha:k la:ng ຫັກຫຼັງ
better	v. he:t di keun ເຮັດດີຂຶ້ນ
between	prep. la: wang ລະຫວ່າງ
beverage	n. keuang deum ເຄື່ອງດຶ່ມ
beware	v. la: wa:ng dtua ລະວັງ ຕົວ
bewilder	v. he:t hay: ngo:ng ເຮັດ nga:n ໃຫ້ງົງງວ້ນ
beyond	prep. ta:t bpay: ຖັດໄປ
bias	v. iang bpay: ຽງໄປ

bible	n. ka:m pi̤ คำพี	blade	(razor) n. mi taa มิดแถ
bicycle	n. lo:t ti̤p รົຖຖີບ		(grass) n. bay: nya ไบหย้า
bid	v. sa:ng ສັ່ງ	blame	v. dti: dtian ຕິຕຽນ
bide	v. loh ta ລໍຖ້າ	blank	adj. bpow: ເປົ່າ
big	adj. nyay: ใหย่	blanket	n. pa ho:m ผ้าท่ม
bile	n. na:m bi มร້ຍ	blast	v. la: berd ຣະເບີດ
bill	v. bpa: gat ປະກາດ	blatant	adj. ti gu:k kuan ທິກຸກກວນ
billboard	n. paan bpay ແປ້ນປ້າຍ	blaze	n. saang fay: ແສງໄຟ
billion	(1,000,000,000) n. pa:n	bleach	v. la:ng da:ng ລ້າງຖ້າງ
	lan พันล้าม		n. kohng ti say: lo:ng
billow	n. fohng na:m ຟອງນ້ຳ		da:ng ຂອງທີໃຊ້ລ້າງຖ້າງ
bind	v. yuk ma:t ผูกมัด	bleak	adj. la la ລາ ໆ
biography	n. si wa: bpa: wa:t	bleat	v. hohng keu siang gaa:
	ຊີວະປະວັດ		ຮອງຄືສຽງແກະ
birch	n. dto:n may: ຕົ້ນໄມ້	bleed	v. leuad ohg ເລືອດອອກ
bird	n. no:k ມົກ	blend	v. seuam kow: ga:n ເສື່ອມ
birth	n. gan gert ການເກີດ		ເຂົ້າກັນ
birthday	n. meu gert ມື້ເກີດ	bless	v. hay: pohn ใຫ້ພອນ
biscuit	n. ka: no:m bpa:ng ຂັ້ນມປັ້ງ	blessing	n. pohn kwam su:k ພອນ
bishop	n. chow: ka: na: kwaang		คอามสุก
	ເຈົ້າคມะແຂວງ	blight	v. ki hay: ຂີຮ້າຍ
bite	v. ga:t ກັດ	blind	v. he:t hay: dta boht ເຮັດ
bitter	adj. ko:m ຂົມ		ใຫ້ຕາບອດ
bitterly	adv. yang ko:m keu:n		adj. dta boht ຕາບອດ
	ย่าງຂົມຂึ້ນ	blindfold	v. a:t dta ຳດຕາ
black	adj. da:m ດຳ	blink	v. pa:p dta ພັບຕາ
blackboard	n. ga: dan da:m ກະດານ	bliss	n. kwam su:k คอามสุก
	ดำ	blister	v. po:ng pohng
blacksmith	n. sang le:k ຊ່າງເຫຼກ		
bladder	n. po:k ngiaw ພັກຍວ		ໂພງ, ພອງ

block	(street) n. ban dtam ho:n tang	บ้านตามถนนทาง
	(square) n. gohn si chaa	ก้อนสี่แจ
blonde	n. pu nyi:ng pom tohng	ผู้ยิงผมเทอง
blood	n. leuat	เลือด
blood relative	n. seua say	เชื้อสาย
bloom	n. ban	บาน
blossom	v. ohk dohk	ออกดอก
	n. ohk dohk ban	ออกดอกบาน
blot	n. hoy bpeuan	รอยเปื้อน
blouse	n. seua pu nyi:ng	เสื้อผู้ยิง
blow	v. bpow	เป่า
	n. gan bpow:	การเป่า
blow out	(extinguish) v. moht	มอด
	(burst) v. la: bert	ระเบิด
blow up	(explode) v. la: bert	ระเบิด
	(inflate) vt. bpow: lo:m say:	เป่าลมใส่
	(get mad) adv. chay: hay lay	ใจร้ายฑาย
blue	(color) adj. si fa	สีฟ้า
	(mood) adj. sow:	เศร้า
blues	n. peng sow:	เพงเศร้า
bluff	(cliff) n. dta: li:ng sain	ตะลิงชัน
	(liar) n. ko:n lohk luang	คนหลอกลวง
blunder	n. kwam pi:t pat	ความผิดพาด
blunt	adj. bpu:	ปู้
blur	n. kwam mua	ความมัว
blush	v. he:t hay: daang	เร็ดให้แดง
boar	n. mu bpa	หมูป่า
board	(wood) n. paan ga: dan	แผ่นกะดาน
	(committee) n. ka: na: ga:m ma: gan	คนะกัมมะกาม
boast	v. wow: uat	เอ้าอวด
boat	n. heua	เฮือ
boating	n. laan heua	แล่นเฮือ
bob	v. bpo lo keu:n laa: li:p lo:ng	โปโลขึ้นและลีบลิง
bobby pin	n. ki:p nyi:p po:m	กิบยิบผม
body	n. hang gay	ร่างกาย
	n. dto:n dtua	ตินติว
bog	n. beu:ng dto:m	บึงติม
boiler	n. keuang dto:m	เคื่องติม
bold	adj. ga han	กำหาม
bolt	(door) n. lay: bpa: dtu	ไลปะตู
	(lightning) n. saang fa laap	แสงฟ้าแลบ

(screw) n. gow⁵ giaw¹ ກ່າວ ກຽວ

(food) v. sa:³ dtaak⁶ kow:⁶ keun⁶ ສະແຕກເຂົາກິນ

(door) v. say:² lay:³ ໄສ່ໄລ

bomb n. luk⁵ la:² bert⁶ ລູກລະເບີດ
v. ti:m⁶ la:⁵ bert⁶ say:⁵ ຕິ້ມລະເບີດໃສ່

bomber n. heua³ bi:n⁶ tim⁶ luk⁶ dtaak⁶ ເຮືອບິນຕິ້ມລູກແຕກ

bond (union) n. keuang⁵ puk² ma:t⁶ ເຄື່ອງຜູກມັດ

(money) n. bai⁶t ti:² say:⁵ dtang¹ nge:rn³ ຍັດຫຶ້ໃຈຕ່າງເງິນ

bone n. ga:³ duk⁶ ກະດູກ

bonus n. ngern³ perm⁶ ເງິນເພີ້ມ

book n. bpeum⁵ ປຶ້ມ

bookcase n. dtu⁵ na:ng⁴ seu⁴ ຕູ້ໜັງສື

bookseller n. ko:n⁴ kay⁴ na:ng⁴ seu⁴ ຄົນຂາຍໜັງສື

bookstand n. bohn⁴ kay⁴ na:ng⁴ seu⁴ leu⁴ bpeum⁴ ບ່ອນຂາຍໜັງສືຫຼືປຶ້ມ

bookstore n. han⁵ kay² na:ng⁴ seu⁴ leu⁴ bpeum⁵ ຮ້ານຂາຍໜັງສືຫຼືປຶ້ມ

b(n. siang⁴ da:ng⁵ gohng⁵ ສຽງດັງກ້ອງ

boot n. gerp⁶ hu:m⁶ kaang² ເກີບຫຸ້ມແຄ່ງ ຖຸ້ມແຄ່ງ

border n. se:n⁶ ket⁶ ເສັ້ນເຂດ

bore (drill) n. choh:³ hu³ ເຈາະຮຸ

(tire) v. he:t⁶ hay:⁶ beua² ເຮັດໃຫ້ເບື່ອ

boring adj. pa³ hay:⁶ beua² nay² ພາໃຫ້ເບື່ອໜ່າຍ

born v. day: gert⁵ ໄດ້ເກີດ

borough n. meuang³ ເມືອງ

borrow n. nyeum² ຍືມ

bosom (chest) n. erik⁵ ເອິກ

(close) adj. gay⁵ si:t³ ໄກ້ສິດ

boss n. nay³ ນາຍ

both adj. ta:ng³ sohng⁴ ທັງສອງ

bother n. guan¹ chay:¹, lo:p¹ guan¹ ກວນໃຈ, ລົບກວນ

bothersome adj. goh² kwam³ la:m³ kan³ ກໍຄວາມລຳຄານ

bottle n. gaaw⁵ ແກ້ວ

bottom n. peun⁴, go:n⁵ ພື້ນ, ກົ້ນ

bough n. nga² may⁵: ງ່າໄມ້

boulder n. ngon⁴ hi:n⁴ ກ້ອນຫີນ ກ້ອນຫີນ

boulevard n. ta:³ non:³ luang³ ຖະໜົນຫຼວງ

bounce n. bat⁶ dte:n⁶ ບາດເຕັ້ນ
v. dte:n⁶ keu:n⁶ ເຕັ້ນຂຶ້ນ

bound adj. luap⁵ ຣວບ

bound to adv. ko:ng⁶ cha:² ຄົງຈະ

boundary n. ket⁴ daan⁶ ເຂດແດນ

bouquet n. soh² dohk⁶ may⁴: ຊໍດອກໄມ້

bounty	n. kwam ga: lu: nă peūa paa ຄວາມກະຣຸນາເຜຶອເຜ
bourgeois	n. ko:n sa:n ku:n năng ຄົນຊັ້ນຂຸນນາງ
bout	n. su:k dti ຊຸກຕີ
bow	(boat) n. hua heūa ຫົວເຮືອ
	(arrow) n. na ໜ້າ
bowels	n. say: ໄສ້
box	n. ga:p, aap ກັບ, ແອບ
	v. dti muay ຕີມວຍ
	(put in box) v. ow: say: ga:p ເອົາໃສ່ກັບ
boxing	n. gan dti muay ການຕີມວຍ
boy	n. de:k noy pu say ເດັກນ້ອຍຜູ້ ຊາຍ
boyfriend	n. say su ຊາຍຊູ້
boyscout	n. luk seŭa ລູກເສືອ
brace	n. say hait ສາຍຮັດ
bracelet	n. say soy kaan ສາຍສ້ອຍແຂນ
bracket	n. wo:ngle:p nyay: ວົງເລັບໃຫຍ່
brag	n. kwam uat ăng ຄວາມອວດ ອ້າງ
braid	v. ta:k san ຖັກສານ
	n. po:m bpia ຜົມເປັຽ
brake	n. keuang ham loh ເຄື່ອງ ຫ້າມລໍ້
	v. ham loh ຫ້າມລໍ້
branch	n. sa ka ສາຂາ
brand	v. ga keuang may ກາເຄື່ອງໝາຍ
brandy	n. low: waang ga:n ເຫຼົາແວງກັ່ນ
brass	n. tohng leuang ທອງເຫຼືອງ
brave	adj. ga han ກ້າຫານ
brawl	v. ha leuang pi:t ga:n ຫາເລື່ອງຜິດກັນ
bray	v. hohng keu ma loh ຮ້ອງຄືມ້າລໍ
brazen	adj. na dan ໜ້າດ້ານ
Brazil	n. bpa: tet bra sin ປະເທດ ບເຣຊິນ
breach	n. kwam dtaak nyaak chak ga:n ຄວາມແຕກແຍກຈາກກັນ
bread	n. kow: chi ເຂົ້າຈີ່
breadth	n. kwam gwang ຄວາມກວ້າງ
break	v. dtaak, ha:k ແຕກຫັກ
breakdown	(cry) hong hay: mo:t să: dti ຮ້ອງໃຫ້ມົດສະຕິ
	(destroy) ta:m lay ທຳລາຍ
	(fail to perform) pe, dtay ເປ, ຕາຍ
break in	(train) o:p lo:m ອົບລົມ
	(interrupt) ka:t kuang ຂັດຂວາງ
break off	nyu:t day ta:n ti ຢຸດ ໂດຍທັນທີ
breakfast	v. bpa:n kaw: sow: ປົນເຂົາເຈົ້າ

breakout	n. chaak yay แจกยาย
breast	n. erk, no:m เช้ก, มืม
breathe	v. haˇi:n chay: หับใจ
breathtaking	adj. piˆ: leu:k piˇ: laˆ:m ผลักผลั่
breed	n. seua เชื้อ
breeze	n. lo:m ohn ohn ลົมອอน
brew	n. gan bˇpa: so:m, gan he:t low bia ການປະສົມ ການເຮັດເຫຼົ້າເບຍ
briar	n. dto:n ku: lap nam ต้มกุลายพาม
bribe	n. si:n bo:n สินบน
brick	n. di:n chi: ดินจี่
bride	n. chow: sow เจ้าสาว
bridge	n. kua ຂົວ
	v. dti:t dtoh ติดต
bridle	v. say: nyay: maˇ ใส่ไทยมา
brief	adj. nyoh nyoh ย่อ ๆ
briefcase	n. ga: bpow: teu กะเป๋าถี
brier	n. dto:n gu: lap nam dtˆi:n กุลายพาม
bright	(light) adj. saang sa: wa:ng แสงส่าง
	(person) adj. sa: lat สลาด
	(color) adj. bat dta บาดตา
brilliant	(bright) adj. leuam เหຼื້อม
(person) adj. sa: liaw sa: lat สล้องสลาด
brim	v. kohp, him ຂອบ, ริม
bring	v. ow: ma เອົามา
bring about	he:t hay: gert keu:n เรັด ให้เກີດຂึ້ນ
bring down	he:t hay: lu:t lo:ng เรັดໃຫ້ລຸດລົງ
bring on	he:t hay: gert keu:n เรັดໃຫ້ເກີດຂึ້ນ
bring up	(raise) liang ลຽง
	(introduce a subject) ow: keu:n ma wow: เອົາ ຂึ้นมาเอົา
brink	n. kohp ຂອบ
brisk	adj. haang, wohng way: แรง, ວ່ອງໄວ
bristle	n. ko:n kaang ຂົນແຂງ
brittle	adj. dtaak ngay แตกง่าย
broad	adj. gwˆang ກ້ວາງ
broadcast	n. gan ga: chay siang ການກະจายสຽง v. ohk wi:t ta: nyu: ອອກວิทะยຸ
broad jump	n. gan dte:n gay: ການເต็มไก
broil	v. bping ปິ้ง
broker	n. nay na นายหน้า
bronchial tubes	n. loht lo:m ຫຼອดลົม

bronze	n. tohng saĭm riːt ທອງສຳຣິດ
brood	n. fung ຜູ້ງ
brook	n. huy, hong ຫ້ວຍ, ຮ່ອງ
broom	n. foy ຟອຍ
brother	(older) n. aý ອ້າຍ
	(younger) n. nohng saý ນ້ອງຊາຍ
brother-in-law	(husband of older sister) n. aý kery ອ້າຍເຂີຍ
	(husband of younger sister) n. nohng kery ນ້ອງເຂີຍ
brow	n. kiw ຄິ້ວ
bruise	n. noẃː nuːm, hoʰy saĭm ເມົານມ, ຮອຍຊ້ຳ
brush	v. paːt ປັດ
brute	n. koːn hot hay ta luːn ຄົນໂຫດຮ້າຍທາຣຸນ
bubble	n. fohng, foʰt ຟອງ, ຟົດ
buck	(deer) n. gwang ກວາງ ຜູ້
	(dollar) n. do la neuːng ໂດລາ ນຶ່ງ
	(horse) n. dit ດີດ
	(current) n. dtan ຕ້ານ
bucket	n. kuː naːm ຄຸນ້ຳ
buckle	n. hua say aaw ຫົວສາຍແອວ
bud	v. ohk noh ອອກໜໍ
Buddha	n. paː puːt taː chow ພະພຸທເຈົ້າ
Buddhist	n. puː ti naːp teu sat ຜູ້ທີ່ນັບຖື sa: na puːt ສາສນາພຸກ
budget	n. ngoːp bpaː man ງົບປມານ
buffalo	(American) kwaý bpa ຄວາຍປ່າ
	(water) n. kwaý ຄວາຍ
buffet	v. soːk, dtoy ຊົກ, ຕອຍ
bug	n. maang heuat ແມງເຮືອດ v. loːp guan ລົບກວນ
bugle	n. gaa ແກ
build	v. goh sang ກໍ່ສ້າງ
build up	heːt hay: kaang haang keuːn ເຮັດໃຫ້ແຂງແຮງຂຶ້ນ
bulgy	adj. bpuːng ປຸ້ງ
bulk	n. gohng ກອງ
bull	(animal) n. ngua pa ງົວປ່າ (talk) n. leuang ki dtua: ເຣື່ອງຂີ້ຕົວະ
bulldozer	n. loːt dtlaak dter kiːt diːn ຣົຖແຣກເຕີ ຂຸດດິນ
bullet	n. luk bpeun ລຸກປືນ
bulletin	n. baý laý ngan ໃບ ລາຍງານ

bulletin board n. bpay bpa: gad ປ້າຍ
ປະກາດ

bullfight n. gi: la dti ngua pa
ກິລາຕີງົວປ່າ

bully v. koːn heng ຂົ່ມເຫງ

bulwark n. gaːm paăng meuang
ກຳແພງເມືອງ

bum n. koːn ki kan ຄົນຂີ້ຄ້ານ

bump v. dtaːm ຕຳ

bunch v. hom gaːn ໂຮມກັນ

bundle v. puk bpeːn hoh ຜູກເປັນຫໍ
ເປັນຫໍ

bungalow n. heuan paːk ເຮືອນພັກ

burden n. keuang baːn tuːk
ເຄື່ອງບັນທຸກ

bureau (government) n. hohng gan
ຫ້ອງການ

(clothes) dtu dtaːm ຕູ້ຕັ່ງ

burglar n. koːn ki laːk ຄົນຂີ້ລັກ

burial n. gan faːng ການຝັງ

Burma adj. pa: ma ພະມ້າ

burn (to set fire) v. pow:
ເຜົາ

(on fire) may: ໄໝ້

(wound) n. bat fay may:
ບາດໄຟໄໝ້

burr n. nya chow: ຫຍ້າເຈົ້າຊູ້

burrow n. bpoːng, poːng ໂປ່ງ, ໂພງ

burst n. gan la: bert oňk
ການລະເບີດອອກ

bury v. faːng diːn ຝັງດິນຝັງ

bus n. loːt bpa: chaːm tăng
ຣົຖປະຈຳທາງ

bush n. fuːm may: ພຸ່ມໄມ້

bushel n. taːng pohng ຖັງຜອງ

business n. gan ngan ການງານ

businessman n. naːk tuː ra: giːt
ນັກທຸຣະກິດ

bust (statue) n. huːp bpaːn
keːng dtua ຮູບປັ້ນເຄິ່ງຕົວ

(woman) n. na erik
ພ້າເອິກ

bustle n. găn wohng way:
ການອ່ອງໄວ

busy adj. ka wiaːk khaọngyuk

but prep. dtaːa wa ແຕ່ວ່າ

butcher n. koːn ka saːt ຄົນຂ້າສັດ

butt (person) n. goːn ກົ້ນ

(cigarette) n. giːt gohk
ya ກີ້ຫວາຢາ

butt in kaːt kuang ຂັດຂວາງ

butter n. naːm maːn ber ນ້ຳມັນເບີ

butterfly n. maang ga: beŭa ແມງກະ
ເບື້ອ

button n. ga: duːm ກະດຸມ
v. say: ga: duːm ໃສ່ກະດຸມ

buttonhole n. hu ga: duːm ຮູກະດຸມ

buy v. seu ຊື້

buyer n. pu seu ຜູ້ຊື້

buzz	(call) v. siang heum heum ສຽງຮຳ ໆ
	(airplane) v. saaw ແສວ
by	(near) adv. gay: gay: ໄກ້ ມ່າ
	moh moh ມໍ່ ໆ
	(means) adv. doy, duay ໂດຍ, ດ້ວຍ
	(past) adv. luang lery bpay: ລ່ວງເລີຍໄປ
by all means	yang naa nohn ຢ່າງແມ່ນອນ
by and large	doy suan luam ໂດຍສ່ວນຮວມ
by the way	er ni na: ເຊີນມາ
by way of	doy tang ໂດຍທາງ
bye-bye	(interj.) la gohn ner ລາກ່ອນເນີ້

C

cab	n. loit doy san (dtaik si) ຣົດໂດຍສານ (ຕັກຊີ)
	n. loit laip chang ຣົດລັບ ຈ້າງ
cabinet	(government) n. ka: na: la: tai ta: moin dri ຄະນະ ຣັຖມົນຕຣີ
	(furniture) n. dtu: ຕູ້
cabbage	n. ga: laim bpi ກະຫຼ່ຳປີ
cable	(wire) n. say luat nyay: ສາຍລວດໃຫຍ່

	(telegraph) n. to la: le:k ໂທຣະເລກ
	v. soing to la: lek ສ່ງໂທຣະເລກ
cadaver	(natural death) n. soip ສົບ
	(violent death) n. sak soip ຊາກສົບ
cafeteria	n. han kay a han doy pu seu yi:p a han day: eng ຮ້ານຂາຍອາຫານໂດຍຜູ້ ຊື້ຂາຍຫານໄດ້ເອງ
cage	v. ka:ng say: dtu:m ຂັງໃສ່ຕຸ້ມ
	n.dtu:m no:k, dtuip ຕຸ້ມນົກ, ຄຸກ
cake	n. ka: noim kay: ຂນົມເຄ້
calculate	v. kaim nuan ຄຳນວນ
	v. lay: lek ໄລ່ເລກ
calendar	n. bpa: dti: ti:n bpe diithim ບປະ ຕິ ທິນປະຕິທິນ
	v. choit ta: bian ຈົດ ທະບຽນ
calf	(animal) n. luk ngua ລູກ ງົວ
	(lower leg) n. bi kaang ນແຄ່ງ
call	(name) v. ern ເຊີນ
call for	v. bpay: dtohn ow: ໄປຕ້ອນເອົາ
call off	v. leuan bpay: ເລື່ອນໄປ

call on	v. bpay: yiam yam ໄປ ຢ້ຽມຢາມ
call up	v. to la: sa:p ter:ng ໂທຣະສັບເຖິງ
calm	adj. sa: ngo:p ສງົບ
camera	n. gohng tay hup ກ້ອງ ຖ່າຍຮູບ
cameraman	n. sang tay hup ຊ່າງ ຖ່າຍຮູບ
camel	n. dto ut ໂຕອູດ
camp	(military) n. kay ຄ້າຍ
	(military) v. dta:ng kay ຕັ້ງຄ້າຍ
	(stay overnight) v. pa:k haam ພັກແຮມ
camping	n. gan pa:k haam ການພັກ ແຮມ
campus	n. boh li: wen ບໍຣິເວນ
can	(ability) v. day:, mi kwam sa mat ໄດ້, ມີຄວາມ ສາມາດ
	(permission) v. teuk a: nu: nyat ຖືກອະນຸຍາດ
	n. ga: bpohng ກະປ໋ອງ
canal	n. hohng ຮ່ອງ
canary	(bird) n. no:k sa: ni:t neu:ng ນົກຊະນິດນຶ່ງ
	(color) adj. si leuang ohn ສີເຫຼືອງອ່ອນ

cancel	v. nyo:k lerk ຍົກເລີກ
candidate	n. pu sa: ma:k ຜູ້ສະໝັກ
candle	n. tian ທຽນ
candy	n. ka: no:m o:m ຂນົມອົມ
canner	n. pa: na:k ngan ow: a han say: ga: bpohng; leu ga:p ຜູ້ກຽວການເຈົ້າອາທານໃສ່ ກະປ໋ອງທິຖິໄນ
cannery	n. hong ngan he:t a han ga: bpohng ໂຮງງານເຮັດອາ ການກະປ໋ອງ
cannon	n. bpeun nyay: ປືນໃຫຍ່
canoe	n. heua noy ເຮືອນ້ອຍ
can opener	n. le:k kay: ga: bpohng ເຫຼັກໄຂກະປ໋ອງ
canyon	n. wang hew gwang ຫ່ວາງ ເຫວກ້ວາງ
cap	n. muak gaa:p ໝວກເກປ v. say: muak gaa:p ໃສ່ໝວກເກປ
capability	n. sa mat dta: pap ສາມາດຜາບ
capillary	n. se:n leuat foy ເສັ້ນເລືອດຝ່ອຍ
capital	(city) n. na: kohn luang ນະຄອນຫຼວງ (funds) n. nger:n teu:n ເງິນທຶນ (letter) n. a:k sohn dtua nyay: ອັກສອນຕົວໃຫຍ່

	(important) adj. sa:m ka:n สำคัม
	(large) adj. nyay: ใหย่
capitalist	n. nay teu:n นายทึน
capitol	n. hoh la:t ta: ban ทีรัฐบาม
caps	(letters) n. a:k sohn dtua nyay: อักสอนตัวใหย่
capsules	n. ya sa: ni:t bpe:n lont ยาซนิดเป้นทูด
captain	(army) n. nay hoy ek มายธอยเอท
	(chief) n. hua na ทัวพ้า
	(navy) n. nay heua มายเธือ
capture	v. cha:p gu:m จับทุม
car	n. lo:t nyo:n ธิถยิ้ม
carat	(200mg) heua ka:m เมิงคำ
caravan	n. fung gwian ผุ้ทอวุม
carcass	n. sak sa:t dtay ฃาท สัดตาย
card	(game) n. pay: li:n ไผ่ทลิ้ม
	(invitation) n. ba:t sern บัดเฃิม
care	(look after) v. bering nyaang เบิ่ງแยว
	(watch closely) v. ha:k sa ธักสา

	(maintainence) n. gan ha:k sa ການรักสา
	(looking after) n. gan bering nyaang ການເບິ່ງແยว
	(worry) n. kwam ga:ng wo:n ความทัวอิม
careful	adj. la: ma:t la: wa:ng ระมัดระอัว
career	n. a sip อาฉับ
cargo	n. si:n ka ba:n tu:k ฉิมค้ามพุทา
cargo plane	n. nyo:n ba:n tu:k ยิมบ้มพุทา
carpenter	n. sang may: จ่าวไม้
carrot	n. hua pa:k gat daang ทือผักทาดแถว
carry on	he:t dtoh bpay: เธ็ดต่ไป่
carry out	he:t hay: sa:m le:t เธ็ดให้สำเธ็ด
cart	n. gwian ทอวุม
carton	n. hip chia kaang ทีบเจ้วแฃว
cartoon	n. hup dta: lo:k รูปถลัก
cascade	n. na:m dto:k dtat ม้ำ ติกตาด
cash	n. nger:n so:t เฃิมฃิด
cash a check	v. ber:k nger:n เบิกเฃิม v. dtaak se:k แตกเฃ็ก
cashier	n. pu la:p chay nger:n ผู้ลับ-จ่ายเฃิม

cast	(net) v. kuang คอ๋ง		cavern	n. hew เขอ
	(actor) v. to:t sohp		cavity	n. gon โกม
	ทิตสอบ		cease	n. cho:p lohng จับลิ๋ง
	n. na:k la: kohn นัก		cedar	n. dto:n so:n chín
	ละคอม			ตมสมจิม
castle	n. hoh bpa: sa:t ที่ปะสาด		ceiling	n. pe dan เพดาม
casual	adj. ba:ng ern บั๋งเชิม		celebrate	v. sa: lerm sa: lohng
casualty	n. pu bat che:p ผู้บาดเจ็บ			สเลิมสลอง
cat	n. maaw แมว		celebration	(party) n. gan sa:
catalog	n. bpeu:m lay seu dtua			lohng กามสลอง
	yang kohng ปั๋มลายชื่			(festival) n. bu:n sa:
	ตอย่างของ			lohng บุมสลอง
catch	v. ha:p cha:p รับจับ		celery	n. pa:k saan ler li
catch on	v. ko:w chay: เข้าใจ			ผักแชมเลิธิ
catcher	n. pu ha:p ผู้รับ		cell	n. ku:k meut คุกมิด
cathedral	n. bot โบถ		cellar	n. hohng dt̤y: di:n
catsup	n. na:m mak de:n			ทองใต้ติม
	น้ำพากเติม		cello	n. wi o loing nyay:
cattle	n. ngua kway วิ๋อคอาย			วีโอลิ๋งใหย่
cattle car	n. dtu ba:n tu:k sa:t			n. soh nyay: fa: la:ng
	ตู้บั๋มหุกสัด			ซ้ใหย่ผั้ง
cauliflower	n. dohk ga: la:m bpi		cement	n. bpun si me:n
	ดอกกะหฺ่ปี			ปูมธิเม็ม
cause	v. bpe:n dto:n het		cement mixer	n. cha:k pa: so:m si
	เป็นต้มเหด			ma:ng จักปะสิ๋มธิ๋มๅ
	n. dto:n het ตมเหด		cemetery	n. bpa sa ป่าซ้า
caution	v. dteuan way: เตือมไว้		censure	n. gan dti: so:m
cavalry	n. muat ta: han ma ผอด			กามติธิ๋ม
	ทะทามม้า			v. dti: so:m ติธ๋ม
cave	n. ta:m ถ้ำ			

census	n. gan saĭm luat pŏ:n la: meŭang ການສຳຫຼວດ พิລເມືອງ	chamber	n. hohng ຫ້ອງ
cent	n. neu:ng se:n ນຶ່ງເຊັນ	champion	n. pu sa: na: lert ผู้ຊมะເລີດ
centigrade	adj. suan hŏy ส่อมຮ້ອຍ $C°=5/9F°-32$	chance	(risk) v. siang pay: ສ່ຽງໄພ (happen) v. ba:ng gert keu:n ບັງເກີດຂຶ້ນ n. o' gat ໂອກາດ
central	adj. suan gang ສ່ວນกาง		
center	n. chay: gang ໃຈกาง n. sun gang ສູນกาง v. ow: way: bohn sun gang ເອົາໄວ້ບ່ອນສູນกาง	change	(difference) n. gan bpian bpaang ການປ່ຽນແປງ (money) n. nger:n nŏy ເງິນນ້ອຍ (differ) v. bpian bpaang ป่ฏมแปງ (money) v. laak bpian ແລກປ່ຽນ
century	n. sa:t dt̃a: w̃a:t ສັດວັກ		
cereal	n. ka: no:m he:t duăy kow: saa ye:n ຂນມເຮັດດ້ວຍ ເຂົ້າແຈ່ເຢັນ		
ceremony	n. pi: ti' ພິທີ	channel	n. hohng na:m ร้อງນ້ຳ
certain	adj. ka:k naa คัก่มแ่	chant	v. hohng peng ຮ້ອງເພງ
certainly	adv. yang ka:k naa ย่าງ คัก่มแ่	chaos	n. kwam sa:p so:n คอาม ສັບສົນ
certificate	n. bpa: gat sa: ni: nya: ba:t ປະກາສນີຍະບັດ	chap	n. pu say ผู้ຊาย v. he:t hăy: hăo ເຮັດໃຫ້ຮາວ
chafe	v. mi kwam ka:t keun ມີຄວາມຂັດຄືນ		
chain	v. lam so way: ล่ามโส่ไอ้ n. say so ສາຍໂສ້	character	n. u:p bpa: ni: say: ອຸປນິໄສ n. ko:n bpaak bpa: lat ຄົນແປກປລาด
chair	n. dta:ng i ຕັ່ງ อี่		
chairman	n. bpa: tan ປະທาม		
chalk	n. soh kow ສໍຂາວ	characteristic	n. la:k sa: na: ลักສນะ adj. haang la:k sa: na: ແຫ່ງลักສນะ
challenge	n. gan ta: tay ການທ້າທาย v. ta: tay ທ້າທาย		

charm	n. sa: ne̊ ສເນ່	check up on	guat laa: seup sŭan
	v. he̊it hay: lo:ng lay:		ທອດແລະສືບສວມ
	ເຮັດໃຫ້ຫຼົງໄຫຼ	check with	tam kwam ki:t he:n
charming	adj. nå ha:k ໜ້າຮັກ		ຕາມຄວາມຄິດເຫັນ
chart	n. baap paan ແບບແຜນ	checker	n. pu guat ber:ng
charter	n. bay: a: nu: nyat ໃບ		ຜູ້ທອດເບິ່ງ
	ອະນຸຍາດ	cheek	n. gaam ແກ້ມ
chaste	adj. boh li: su:t chay:	cheer	n. gan hohng hoh
	ບໍຣິສຸດໃຈ		ການຮ້ອງໂຮ
chat	n. gan lo:m ga:n li:n	chemistry	n. ke mi ເຄມີ
	ການລົມກັນຫຼິ້ນ	cherish	v. ta: nohm ha:k
	v. lo:m ga:n li:n ລົມກັນ		ຖນອມຮັກ
	ຫຼິ້ນ	chess	n. mak hu:k ໝາກຮຸກ
chauffeur	n. ko:n ka:p lo:t ຄົນຂັບ	chest	(body) n. er:k ເອິກ
	ຣົຖ		(furniture) n. dtu nŏy
cheap	adj. teuk ຖືກ		ຕູ້ນ້ອຍ
check	v. guat ber:ng ກວດເບິ່ງ	chew	v. nya:m ໜຽ້
	n. nger:n se:k ເງິນເຊັກ	chicken	n. ga:y ໄກ່
check in	(for work) v. så: ne̊r	chief	adj. sa:m ka:n ສຳຄັນ
	dtua kow: he:t gan		n. hua na ຫົວໜ້າ
	ສເມືອເຂົ້າເຮັດການ	child	(pl. children) n. de:k
	(register) v. lo:ng seu		nŏy ເດັກນ້ອຍ
	ລົງຊື	childhood	n. way: de:k nŏy ວັຍເດັກ
check out	ohk chak hong laam la:ng		ນ້ອຍ
	chak mo:t ga:m no:t ba:k	childish	adj. keu de:k nŏy
	ອອກຈາກໂຮງແຮມຫຼຸງຈາກນັດ		ຄືເດັກນ້ອຍ
	ກ່າມິດຖັກ	chili	n. mak pet ໝາກເຜັດ
check up	gen guat hang gay ການ	chill	n. kay: sa:n ໄຂ້ສັ່ນ
	ທອດຮ່າງກາຍ		v. bpe:n kay: sa:n
			ເປັນໄຂ້ສັ່ນ

chimney	n. tŏh kwăn fày:
	ທີ່ຄວັນໄຟ
chin	n. kāng ຄາງ
Chinese	(polite) n., adj. chin
	ຈີນ
	(slang) n., adj. chě:k
	ເຈັກ
chipmunk	n. kǎ: hŏhk lǎy ກະຮອກລາຍ
chirp	v. hŏng chǐap chǐap sŏ:ŋ
	ຈຽບ ໆ
chisel	n. sǐ:w sǐ:ŋ
	(cut) v. sǐ:w ohk
	ສິ່ວອອກ
	(cheat) v. lŏhk lŭang
	ຫຼອກລວງ
chocolate	n. kǎ: no:m sŏ gŏ lǎ
	ຂະໜົມໂຊໂກລາ
choice	n. gan leŭak ການເລືອກ
choose	v. leŭak ເລືອກ
chopsticks	n. mǎy: tŭ ໄມ້ຕູ່
chorus	n. pŭak nǎ:k hŏhng lŭk
	kŭ ພວກນັກຮ້ອງລູກຄູ່
Christian	adj. klí:t sǎ: dtian
	ຄຣິສຕຽນ
	n. fǎy sat sǎ: nǎ klí:t
	ຝ່າຍສາສະໜາຄຣິສ
Christmas	n. bu:n no aan ບຸນໂນແອນ
Christmastide	n. nyam no aan ຍາມໂນແອນ
Christmas tree	n. dto:n no aan ຕົ້ນ
	ໂນແອນ

cigar	n. gŏh yǎ nyay: sì gǎ ກອກ
	ຢາໃຫຍ່ ຊີກາ
cinder	n. tan fày: ຖ່ານໄຟ້
circle	n. wŏ:ng mŏ:n ວົງມົນ
	v. bpǐ:n ohm ປິ່ນອອມ
circular	adj. bpe:n wŏ:ng mŏ:n
	ເປັນວົງມົນ
	n. cho:d may wian ຈົດ
	ໝາຍວຽນ
circulation	n. gan mun wian ການໝຸນ
	ວຽນ
citizen	n. po:n lǎ: meuang ພົນ
	ເມືອງ
citizenship	n. sa:n sat ສັນຊາດ
civilization	(thing) n. kwam cha: lŏ̌:n
	ຄວາມຈະເລີນ
	(people) n. kwam sǐ wi:
	lǎy: ຄວາມສີວິໄລ
clang	n. siang lǎ: ka:ng
	ສຽງລະຄັງ
	v. he:t siang da:ng
	ເຮັດສຽງດັງ
clarify	v. he:t hay: chaam
	chaǎng ເຮັດໃຫ້ແຈ່ມແຈ້ງ
clarinet	n. gaa, gra li naat
	ແກ, ກຣາລີແນດ
clash	(fight) n. gan chom dti
	ga:n ການໂຈມຕີກັນ
	(fight) v. chom dti
	ga:n ໂຈມຕີກັນ

	(not fit) v. bòh kǒw: ga:n ບໍ່ເຂົ້າກັນ	cleave	v. pa ohk ຜ່າອອກ
class	(level) n. saín ຊັ້ນ	clergy	n. puak ku ba ພວກຄຸບາ
	(school) n. hohng hian ຫ້ອງຮຽນ	clerk	n. sa: miǎn ສມຽນ
		clever	adj. sa: lat ສລາດ
	v. cha:t bpe:n hohng bpe:n puak ຈັດເປັນຫ້ອງ ເປັນພວກ	client	n. luk ka ລູກຄ້າ
		cliff	n. na pa ໜ້າຜາ
classic	(best) adj. saín ek ຊັ້ນເອກ	climate	n. din fa a gat ດິນຟ້າອາກາດ
	(model) adj. bpe:n baap yang ເປັນແບບຢ່າງ	cling	v. goht ກອດ
		cloak	v. ba:ng ບັ້ງ
			n. sěua ku:m ເສື້ອຄຸມ
	n. bpeum baap yang ປຶ້ມ ແບບຢ່າງ	cloakroom	n. hohng way: keuang ຫ້ອງໄວ້ເຄື່ອງ
classical	adj. saín ek ຊັ້ນເອກ	clock	n. mong nyay: ໂມງໃຫຍ່
classified	(secret) adj. bpe:n tang la:p ເປັນທາງລັບ		(alarm clock) n. mong bpu:k ໂມງປຸກ
	(order) adj. bpe:n la: biap ເປັນລະບຽບ	close	adj. gay: ໄກ້
			v. a:k ອັດ
			v. bpi:t ປິດ
classroom	n. hohng hian ຫ້ອງຮຽນ	closet	n. dtu say: keuang ຕູ້ໃສ່ເຄື່ອງ
clause	(article) n. mat dta ມາຕຣາ	clothing	(general) n. keuang nu:ng ເຄື່ອງນຸ່ງ
	(sentence) n. bpa: nyok yoh ປະໂຍກໜັ້		(Lao style) n. seua pa ເສື້ອ ຜ້າ
claw	v. kut duay le:p ຄູດດ້ວຍ ເລັບ	clothing store	n. han kay keuang nu:ng ຮ້ານຂາຍເຄື່ອງນຸ່ງ
	n. le:p sa:t ເລັບສັດ	cloud	n. feua ເຝື່ອ
cleaner	n. hohng sa:k keuang ໂຮງຊັກເຄື່ອງ		v. nyu:ng nyak ຍຸ້ງຍາກ
		cloudy	adj. mèut ມົດ

clover	n. may: peut cha:m puak tua ໄມ້ຜັກຈຳຜອກຖ່ວ
clown	n. dtua dta: lo:k nay: la: kohn ຕົວຕລົກໃນລະຄອນ v. dta: lo:k lay lay ຕລົກຫຼາຍໆ
club	(stick) n. may: kohn ໄມ້ຄ້ອນ (place) n. sa: mo sohn ສະໂມສອນ n. sa ma ko:m ສະມາຄົມ
clue	n. hohng hoy ຮ່ອງຮອຍ
clumsy	adj. ser sa ເຊີຊາ
cluster	v. huam ga:n ຮວມກັນ n. ket pa:t ta: na kan, mu ເຂດຜັດຕນາການ, ໝູ່
clutch	(jerk) v. dto:k sa: nger ຕົກສະເງີ (grasp) v. kua cha:p ຄົວຈັບ n. kat o:t ຄາດອົດ
coach	(horse carriage) n. lo:t ma ລົດມ້າ (trainer) n. pu feu:k sohn ຜູ້ຝຶກສອນ (train car) n. dtu doy san lo:t fay: ຕູ້ໂດຍສານລົດໄຟ
coal	n. tan hi:n ຖ່ານຫີນ
coarse	adj. sa ຊາ
coast	n. fa:ng ta: le ຝັ່ງທະເລ v. laan doy boh say: haang cha:k ແລ່ນໂດຍບໍ່ໃຊ້ແຮງຈັກ
coastline	n. se:n fa:ng ta: le ເສັ້ນຝັ່ງທະເລ
coat	(overcoat) n. seua sa:n nohk ເສື້ອຊັ້ນນອກ (suit) n. seua ngay: ເສື້ອໃຫຍ່ (animal) n. ko:n ຂົນ
coax	v. ngua: hay: dtay chay: ຍົວະໃຫ້ຕາຍໃຈ
cock	n. gay: pu ໄກ່ຜູ້ v. keun gay: bpeun ຂຶ້ນໄກປືນ
cocoa	n. so go la na:m ໂຊໂກລານ້ຳ
coconut	n. mak pow ໝາກພ້າວ
code	(law) n. go:t la: biap ກົດລະບຽບ (secret language) n. la: ha:t ລະຫັດ
coffee	n. ga fe ກາເຟ
coffee table	n. dto: ga fe ໂຕະກາເຟ
coffin	n. long ko:n dtay ໂລງຄົນຕາຍ
coil	n. goh ກໍ້ v. goh pa:n kow: ກໍພັນເຂົ້າ
coin	n. nger:n lian ເງິນຫຼຽນ v. sang ສ້າງ

coincide	(events) v. gert keuːn pohm gaːn ເກີດຊ້ຳພ້ອມກັນ	color	n. siː ສີ
			v. sayː siː ໃສ່ສີ
	(objects) v. dteːng gaːn ເຕັ້ງກັນ	colorful	adj. mi siː lay ມີສີລາຍ
cold	n. kayː waːt ໄຂ້ຫວັດ	colored	adj. koːn daːm ຄົມດ່ຳ
	adj. now ໜາວ	colossal	adj. nyay: maː ha san ໃຫຍ່ມະຫາສານ
collar	(dog) v. bpohk koh ma ປອກຄໍໝາ	colt	(gun) n. nyi hoh bpeun ໂ ຍິ ຫໍປືນ poːk ຍັດເປັນຜັກ
	(shirt) n. koh seua ຄໍເສື້ອ		(horse) n. maː noy dtua puː ມ້ານ້ອຍຕົວຜູ້
colleague	n. muː huam ngan ຜູ້ ຮ່ວມງານ	column	(building) n. sow: heuan ເສົາເຮືອນ
collect	(money) v. geːp ເກັບ		(newspaper) n. neua leuang kohng naːng seu piːm ເນື້ອ ເລື່ອງຂອງໜັງສືພິມ
	(things) v. luap luam ລວຍລວມ		
collection	n. gan luap luam ການ ລວຍລວມ		(row) n. taaw ແຖວ
college	n. maː ha wiː taː nya layː ມະຫາວິທະຍາໄລ	comb	(hair) n. wi ຫວີ
			(rooster) n. hohn gayː ຫອນໄກ່
collision	n. gan dtaːm gaːn ການຕຳກັນ		(hair) n. wi poːm ຫວີຜົມ
colon	(punctuation) n. keuang may sohng chuːt ເຄື່ອງໝາຍ ສອງຈຸດ		(search) v. koːn ha ຄົມຫາ
		combat	n. gan chom dtiການໂຈມຕີ
	(intestines) n. sayː ໄສ້		(attach) v. chom dti ໂຈມຕີ
			(fight against) v. dtoh su ຕໍ່ສູ້
colonel	n. nay paːn eːk ນາຍພັນເອກ	combine	n. chaːk giaw kow ຈັກກ່ຽວ ເຂົ້າ
colonial	adj. haang hua meuang ແຫ່ງ ຫົວເມືອງຂື້ນ		v. bpaː soːm ປະສົມ
colony	n. hua meuang keun ຫົວເມືອງ ຂື້ນ	come	v. ma ມາ
		come about	v. gert keuːn ເກີດຊ້ຳ

come across	v. ko:n pa:p ຄົ້ມພົບ
come down with	v. bpe:n kay: duay pa: nyat ເປັນໄຂດ້ວຍພະຍາດ
come to	(recover) v. feun sa: dti: ຟື້ນສຕິ
	(total) v. luam bpe:n ລວມເປັນ
come upon	ko:n pa:p ຄົ້ມພົບ
comedy	n. la: kohn dta: lo:k ລະຄອນຕະລົກ
comet	n. dow sa: de:t ດາວສະເດັດ
comfort	n. kwam su:k sa: bay ຄວາມສຸກສບາຍ
	v. bpohp chay: ປອບໃຈ
comfortable	adj. yang su:k sa: bay ຢ່າງສຸກສບາຍ
comic	(person) n. dtua dta: lo:k ຕົວຕລົກ
comics	(books) n. bpeum hup leuang dta: lo:k ປື້ມຮູບເລື່ອງຕລົກ
comic strip	n. hup leuang yu nay: na:ng seu pi:m ຮູບເລື່ອງຢູ່ໃນໜັງສືພິມ
comma	n. keuang may chu:t (ເຄື່ອງ) ໝາຍຈຸດ
command	n. gan ba:ng ka:p ba:n sa ການບັງຄັບບັນຊາ
	v. ba:n sa gan ບັນຊາການ
commence	v. dta:ng dto:n ຕັ້ງຕົ້ນ
commencement	n. pi: ti mohp bpa: li:n nya ພິທີມອບປະລິນຍາ
commend	v. nyo:k nyohng ຍົກຍ້ອງ
comment	n. hua ki:t ຫົວຄິດ
	v. ohk kwam ki:t ອອກ ຄວາມຄິດ
commerce	adj. haang gan ka (ແຫ່ງ) ການຄ້າ
	n. gan ka kay ການຄ້າຂາຍ
commission	(rank) n. pu ba:ng ka:p gan ຜູ້ບັງຄັບການ
	(percentage) n. bper se:n ເປີເຊັນ
	(department) n. ka: na: ga:m ma ti: gan ຄມະກັມມາທິການ
	(sin) n. gan he:t sua ການ ເຮັດຊົ່ວ
commissioner	n. bpa: tan ka: na: ga:m ma ti: gan ປະທານ ຄມະກັມມາທິ ການ
commit	(someone) v. puk pa:n ຜູກ ພັນ
	(sin) v. he:t sua ເຮັດຊົ່ວ
committee	n. ka: na: ga:m ma gan ຄມະກັມມະການ
commodity	n. keuang si:n ka (ເຄື່ອງ) ສິ່ນຄ້າ
common	(ordinary) adj. ta:m ma: da sa ma:n ທັມມະດາສາມັນ
	(public) adj. sa ta la: na: ສາທາລະນະ

(together) adj. suan huam
ສ່ວນຮວມ

communicate v. dti: dtoh ຕິດຕໍ່

communication n. gan koïm na koïm
ການຄົມມາຄົມ

community n. saïng koïm ສັງຄົມ

compact n. koh dtoïk loïng gaïn
ຂັດຕລິງກັນ
adj. na naan ໜາແໜ້ນ

companion n. peuan ເພື່ອນ

company (army) n. gohng hoy ກອງ
ຮ້ອຍ

(business) n. boh liï saït
ບໍລິສັດ

(visitors) n. kaak ແຂກ

compare v. bpiap tiap ປຽບທຽບ

compass n. keïm tiït ເຂັມທິດ

compel v. baïng kaïp ບັງຄັບ

compensate n. saÿï taan ໃຊ້ແທນ

compete (skill) v. kaang gaïn
ແຂ່ງກັນ

(beauty) v. bpaï guat
ປະກວດ

competent adj. geïng
ເກັ່ງ

complain v. dtoh wa ຕໍ່ວ່າ

complete adj. koïp tuan ຄົບຖ້ວນ
v. heït hay: laaw ເຮັດ
ໃຫ້ແລ້ວ

complex adj. nyuïng ຍຸ້ງ

complexion n. piw na ຜິວໜ້າ

complicate v. heït hay: nyuïng
ເຮັດໃຫ້ຍຸ້ງ

compliment n. kwam nyoïk nyohng
ຄວາມຍົກຍ່ອງ
v. nyoïk nyohng ຍົກຍ່ອງ

compose (music) v. dtaang ແຕ່ງ
(oneself) v. laï ngaïp
chiït ລະງັບຈິດ
(made of) v. bpaï gohp
ປະກອບ

composer n. naïk dtaang ນັກແຕ່ງ

composition (mixture) n. suan bpaï gohp
ສ່ວນປະກອບ
(a work) n. leuang dtaang
ເຮື່ອງແຕ່ງ

compound (mixture) n. san bpaï gohp
ສານປະກອບ
(area) n. boh liï wen
ບໍລິເວນ
(increase) paï soïm
ຜະສົມ

comprehend v. kow: chay: ເຂົ້າໃຈ

compress v. bip kow: ບີບເຂົ້າ

compression n. kwam goït daïn, gan nyaït
ຄວາມກົດດັນ, ການນັດ

compromise n. gan soïm nyohm ການສົມ
ຍອມ
v. soïm nyohm ສົມຍອມ

computer	n. keuang kaːm nuan lek
	ເຄື່ອງຄຳນວນເລກ
comrade	(friend) n. peuan ເພື່ອນ
	(follower) saː haːy ສະຫາຍ
conceal	(hide) v. seuang ເຊື່ອງ
	(cover) v. bpiːt baːng
	ປິດບັງ
concede	v. nyohm ຍອມ
conceit	n. kwaːm uat di ຄວາມອວດດີ
conceive	(plan) v. leːrm kiːt ເລີ່ມຄິດ
	(child) v. dtaːng dtohng
	ຕັ້ງທ້ອງ
concentrate	(focus) v. chohː choːng
	ເຈາະຈົງ
	(thicken) v. heːt haːy
	kuːn ເຮັດໃຫ້ຂຸ້ນ
concept	n. naaw kwaːm kiːt
	ແນວຄວາມຄິດ
concern	(feeling) n. kwaːm puk paːn
	ຄວາມຜູກພັນ
	(business) n. boh liː saːt
	ບໍລິສັດ
	v. kohng giaw ຂ້ອງກ່ຽວ
conclude	(finish) v. saː luːp tay
	ສຸຼບທ້າຍ
	(judge) v. dtaːt siːn
	ຕັດສິນ
conclusion	n. dtohn muan tay
	ຕອນມ້ວນທ້າຍ

concrete	n. diːn si maːng ດິນຊີມັງ
	adj. saːt chaang ຢັດແຈ້ງ
condemn	v. bpaː naːm ປະນາມ
condense	(concentrate) v. heːt haːy
	kuːn ເຮັດໃຫ້ຂຸ້ນ
	(vapor) v. gay bpeːn naːm
	ກາຍເປັນນ້ຳ
condition	(terms) n. ngeuan kay
	ເງື່ອນໄຂ
	(status) n. saː pap ສະພາບ
	v. bpian dtam kwaːm maːk
	ປ່ຽນຕາມຄວາມມັກ
conduct	n. peuːt dtiː gan
	ພຶຕິກຳ
	(to lead) v. naːm nʼ
	(transmit) v. bpeːn hoːn
	tang ເປັນທິມທາງ
conductor	(bus) n. pu geːp ngeːrn
	nay loːd baːt ຜູ້ເກັບເງິນ
	ໃນລົດບັສ
	(music) n. hua na doːn dti
	ຫົວໜ້າດົນຕຣີ
cone	n. hup suay ຮູບຊວຍ
confederate	n. paːk puak ຜັກພວກ
	v. hom gaːn ໂຮມກັນ
confer	(give) v. mohp hay
	ມອບໃຫ້
	(consult) v. bpeuːk sa
	ປຶກສາ

conference	n. gohng bpa: suːm ทอງ ปະຊຸມ	conquer	v. yeuːt kohng ຍຶດຄອງ
confess	v. saː laː pạp ສາຣະພາບ	conquest	n. gan nyeuːt kohng ການ ຍຶດຄອງ
confide	v. wayː chayː ໄວ້ໃຈ	conscience	n. kwam huː seuːk ຄວາມ ຮູ້ສຶກ
confident	adj. seua chayː dtoːn eng ເຊື່ອໃຈຕົນເອງ		
confine	v. gaːk kaːng ກັກຂັງ	conscious	adj. mi saː dtiː yu ມີສະ ຕິຢູ່
confines	n. kohp ket ຂອບເຂດ	consent	n. gan dtoːk loːng kohng ການຕົກລົງຍອງ...
confirm	v. gow yeun yaːn ກ່າວຢືນຢັນ		v. dtoːk loːng ຕົກລົງ
conflict	v. gan dtoh su gaːn ການ ຕໍ່ສູ້ການ	consequence	n. poːn ຜົນ
	v. bpaː taː gaːn pะtะ ກ້ຳ	conserve	v. geːp haːk saː wayː ເກັບຮັກສາໄວ້
conform	v. daːt bpaang dtoːn eng ດັດແປງຕົນເອງ	conservative	adj. baap bo han ແບບໂບຮານ
confuse	(things) v. bpoːn gaːn ປົນກັນ		n. koːn bo han ຄົນໂບຮານ
	(ideas) v. heːt hayː ngoːng ເຮັດໃຫ້ງົງ	consider	(think over) v. piː chaː laː naː ພິຈາรະນາ
Congo	n. bpaː tet kohng goː ປະເທດ ຄອງໂກ		(judge) v. heːn wa ເຫັນວ່າ
congratulate	v. saː daang kwam nyiːn di ສແດງຄວາມຍິນດີ	considerable	adj. yang luang layː ຢ່າງ ຫຼວງຫຼາຍ
congregation	n. fuːng koːn faːng taːm maː tet saː na ຝຸງຄົນຟັງທັມ ເທດສມາ	considerate	adj. mi kwam geng chayː ມີ ຄວາມເກງໃຈ
congress	n. gan bpaː suːm saː paː ການ ປະຊຸມสะพา	consist of	v. bpaː gohp duay ປະກອບດ້ວ
connect	v. dtiːt dtoh ຕິດຕໍ່	console	v. bpohp chayː ປອບໃຈ
connection	n. gan dtoh neuang gaːn ການ ຕໍ່ເນື່ອງกัน	conspicuous	(things) adj. tiː uat ang ທີ່ອວດອ້າງ
			(actions) adj. saːt chen ຈັດເຈນ
		conspire	v. kiːt gaː boːt ຄິດກະບົດ

constant	n. ko:ng ti³ ki:ng² ຄົງທີ່
constitute	v. bpa: gohp³ ປະກອບ
constitution	(nation) n. la:t³ ta² ta:m³ ma:² nun³ ຣັຖທັມມະນູນ
	(health) n. su:³ ka:³ pap⁵ ສຸຂະພາບ
construct	v. sang ສ້າງ⁶
consul	n. go:ng su:n³ ກົງສຸນ
consult	v. bpeu:k³ sa⁴ ha⁴ leu³ ປຶກສາຫາລື
consume	v. boh li:¹ pok² ປຣິໂພກ
contact	n. dti:t³ dtoh ຕິດຕໍ່
	v. pu⁶ dti:t³ dtoh² ຜູ້ ຕິດຕໍ່
contagious	adj. dti:t³ dtoh² tua² tua² bpay: ຕິດຕໍ່ທົ່ວໄປ
contain	v. ba:n chu:³ ບັນຈຸ
	v. mi³ ມີ
container	n. hip⁶ ຫີບ
contemplate	v. dteu:k³ dtohng berng ຕຶກຕອງເບິ່ງ
contemporary	adj. huam² sa:³ may:³ ຮ່ວມສໄມ
contempt	n. kwam³ du¹ tuk⁶ ຄວາມດູຖູກ
contend	(words) v. tiang ga:n⁴ ຖຽງກັນ
	(deeds) v. dtoh su² ຕໍ່ສູ້
content	v. he:t⁶ hay: poh chay: ເຮັດໃຫ້ພໍໃຈ
	adj. poh³ chay: ພໍໃຈ
	n. kohng ba:n³ chu:³ yu⁴ nay:³ ຂອງບັນຈຸ່ໃນ
contest	(argument) n. gan³ dto¹ tiang⁵ ການໂຕ້ຖຽງ
	(rivalry) n. gan¹ bpa:³ guat⁶ ການປະກວດ
continent	n. tai² wip⁵ ທະວີບ
continually	adv. leuay⁵ leuay⁵ ເລື້ອຍໆ
continue	v. he:t³ dtoh² bpay: ເຮັດຕໍ່ໄປ
contract	n. sa:n⁴ nya³ ສັນຍາ
	(shrink) v. ho:t³ kow:⁶ ຫົດເຂົ້າ
	(acquire) v. ow:¹ kow:⁶ ma³ way⁵ ເອົາເຂົ້າມາໄວ້
contrary	adj., adv. go:ng gua:n³ kam³ ກົງກັນຂ້າມ
contrast	n. kwam³ dtaa⁶ dtang² ຄວາມແຕກຕ່າງ
	v. bpiap⁶ tiap⁵ ປຽບທຽບ
contribute	v. u:t² nun⁴ ຊຸໜູນ
contrive	v. paan⁴ gan¹ ແຜນການ
control	n. gan⁵ kuap⁵ ku:m⁶ ການຄວບຄຸມ
controversy	n. gan¹ dto¹ tiang⁴ ການໂຕ້ຖຽງ
convalescent	adj. fu:n⁵ chak⁶ kay:⁶ ຟື້ນຈາກໄຂ້
convenient	adj. sa:⁴ duak⁶ ສດວກ
convent	n. wa:t³ maa² kow⁴ ວັດແມ່ຂາວ

convention	n. saːn nya ສັມຍາ
	(custom) n. baap paan
	ແບບແຜນ
	(meeting) n. gan bpaː suːm
	ການປະຊຸມ
conversation	n. gan soːn taː naː ການສົນ
	ທະນາ
converse	v. soːn taː naː ສົນທະນາ
	n. kwam goːng gaːn kam
	ຄວາມກ່ຽວກັນຂ້ານ
convert	(exchange) v. laak bpian
	ແລກປ່ຽນ
	(change) v. bpian ປ່ຽນ
convertible	adj. bpian bpaang dayː
	ປ່ຽນແປງໄດ້
	n. loːt laːng ka bper
	ຣິດຫຼັງຄາເປີດ
convey	(things) v. koːn ຂົນ
	(ideas) v. toh hayː
	ທອດໃຫ້
convict	v. dtaːt siːn loːng tot
	ຕັດສິນລົງໂທດ
	n. koːn tot ຄົນໂທດ
convince	v. heːt hayː naa chayː
	ເຮັດໃຫ້ແນ່ໃຈ
cook	(male) n. poh kua ຜົ່ຄົວ
	(female) n. maa kua ແມ່ຄົວ
	v. heːt giːn ເຮັດກິນ
cookie	n. kaː noːm ຂນົມ

cool	(temperature) v. heːt hayː
	yeːn ເຮັດໃຫ້ເຢັນ
	adj. yeːn ເຢັນ
	(calm) adj. chayː yeːn
	ໃຈເຢັນ
coolie	n. guː liː ກຸລີ
cooperate	v. huam meu ຮ່ວມມື
cooperation	n. gan huam meu ການຮ່ວມມື
copper	n. tohng daang ທອງແດງ
copy	n. saːm now ສຳເນົາ
	v. gay ກ່າຍ
coral	n. hiːn bpaːga laːng
	ຫີນປະກາລັງ
cord	(rope) n. seuak ເຊືອກ
	(wire) n. say fayː ສາຍໄຟ
cordial	adj. yang haːk kayː ຢ່າງຮັກໃຄ່
	n. ya sayː bpua lok giaw
	gaːp hua chayː ຢາໃຊ້ບຳບັດໂຣກ
	ກ່ຽວກັບຫົວໃຈ
cork	(bottle) n. dohn gaaw ຄອນ
	ແກ້ວ
	(float) n. toy ທອຍ
	v. aːt dohn gaaw
	ຈັດຄອນແກ້ວ
corn	n. kowː saː li ເຂົາສາລີ
corn crib	n. lowː kowː saː hi law
	ເຂົາສາລີ
corner	n. chaa ແຈ
corporation	n. saː haː gan ສະທະການ
corps	n. nuaːy ພວຍ

corpse	n. sak so:p ຊາກສັບ
correct	v. guat gaa ກວດ, ແກ້
	adj. teuk ຖືກ
correspond	(equal) v. dto:ng ga:n ຕົງກັນ
	(write letter) v. dti:t
	dtoh ຕິດຕໍ
corridor	(path) n. hohm nay: heuan
	ຮອມໃນເຮືອນ
corrupt	adj. pi:t pet ຜິດເພດ
cosmopolitan	adj. haang na na sat
	ແຫງນານາຊາດ
cost	n. la ka ຮາຄາ
	v. bpe:n nger:n ເປັນເງິນ
costly	adj. paang lay ແພງຫລາຍ
costs	n. lay chay ລາຍຈາຍ
costume	n. keuang taang dtua
	ເຄືອງແຕງຕົວ
cot	n. dtia:ng de:k nohy
	ຕຽງເດັກນອຍ
cottage	n. ga: tohm ກະທ່ອມ
cotton	n. fay ຝາຍ
couch	n. boh: hohng na:ng
	ເບາະຮອງນັງ
cough	v. ay: ໄອ
could	v. sa mat ສາມາດ
council	n. sa: pa ສະພາ
counsel	(advice) n. ka:m naa: na:m
	ຄຳແນະນຳ
	(lawyer) n. ta: nay kwam
	ທະນາຍຄວາມ

count	(nobleman) n. nam nyo:t
	ມານະຍົດ
	(numbers) na:p ມັບ
count on	wa:ng per:ng kwam suay
	leua ຫວັງເພິງຄວາມຊວຍເຫຼືອ
countenance	n. si na ສີໜ້າ
counter	n. dto: kay keuang ໂຕະຂາຍ
	ເຄືອງ
	v. ka:t kan ຂັດຄ້ານ
counterfeit	v. bpohm baang ປອມແປງ
country	n. bpa: tet ປະເທດ
country club	n. sa: mo sohn ສະໂມສອນ
countryside	n. ban nohk ບ້ານນອກ
county	n. kwaang ແຂວງ
couple	adj. ku ຄູ່
	n. ku bow sow ຄູ່ບ່າວສາວ
	v. dtoh ga:n ຕໍ່ກັນ
courage	n. kwam ga han ຄວາມ
	ກ້າຫານ
course	(road) n. se:n tang ເສັ້ນ
	ທາງ
	(school)n. wi: sa ວິຊາ
of course	interj. taa laaw
	ແທ້ແລວ
court	(yard) n. der:n ເດີນ
	(law) n. san ສານ
	(king) n. lat sa: sa:m
	na:k ຮາຊສຳນັກ
	v. bpay: li:n sow ໄປ
	ຫຼິ້ນສາວ

courtroom	n. hohng pi: pak sa ຫ້ອງ ພິພາກສາ
courtesy	n. a:t ta: nya say: ອັທຍາໄສ
cousin	n. luk ay luk nohng ລູກອ້າຍ ລູກນ້ອງ
cover	n. fa bpi:t ຝາປິດ v. bpo:t bpi:t ປົກປິດ
cow	n. ngua maa ວົວແມ່
coward	n. ko:n ki yan ຄົນຂີ້ຢ້ານ
cowardly	adj. yang ki yan ຢ່າງຂີ້ຢ້ານ
cowboy	n. ko:n liang ngua ຄົນ ລ້ຽງວົວ
cousin	(female) n. luk sow kohng lu:ng kohng bpa ລູກສາວຂອງລຸງ ຂອງປ້າ
crab	(animal) n. ga: bpu ກະປູ (person) ko:n ow: chay: ຄົນ nyak ເອົາໃຈຍາກ
crack	n. hoy dtaak ຮອຍແຕກ v. dtaak haäng ແຕກແຫງ
cracker	(firecracker) n. mak ga: pok ໝາກກະໂພກ (cookie) n. ka: no:m ke:m ຂນົມເຄັມ
cradle	n. u ອູ່
craft	(profession) n. si mëu ສີມື (cunning) n. kwam lia:m ku ຄວາມຫຼ່ຽມຄູ
crane	(bird) n. no:k ga: sa ນົກກະສາ (machine) n. keuang nyo:k ເຄື່ອງຍົກ
cranium	n. ga: lok hua ກະໂລກຫົວ
crank	(person) n. ko:n ba boh ຄົນບ້າບໍ n. le:k mun ເຫຼັກໝຸນ v. mun ໝຸນ
crash	v. dto:k ຕົກ n. u: ba:t dti: het ອຸບັດຕິເຫດ
crave	v. ngaan ແງ້ນ
crawl	v. kan ຄານ
crazy	adj. ba ບ້າ
creak	n. siang la:n ສຽງລັ່ນ
cream	(milk) n. ga: ti: ກະທິ (beauty) n. bpaang na:m ta na ແປ້ງນ້ຳທາໜ້າ
create	v. sang keun ສ້າງຂຶ້ນ
creature	(product) n. si:ng ti: sang sa:n keu:n ສິ່ງທີ່ສ້າງ- ຂຶ້ນ (animal) n. sa:t ສັດ
credentials	n. ba:t bpa: cha:m dtua ບັດປະຈຳຕົວ
credit	(money) n. nger:n hay: yeum ເງິນໃຫ້ຢືມ (worthiness) n. seu siang ຊື່ສຽງ

creed	n. laːt tiː ລັກຕິ	crooked	(dishonest) adj. gong ໂກງ
creek	n. huay naːm ຫ້ວຍນ້ຳ		(things) adj. ngoh, goːng
creep	v. leua ເລື່ອ		ງໍ, ກົງ
crest	n. nyoht, hohn gayː	crop	(chicken) n. niang gayː
	ຍອດ, ຫອນ ໄກ		ພຸງໄກ່
crew	n. koːn ngan bpa chaːm heua		(plants) n. poːn bpuk ຜົນປູກ
	ຄົນງານປະຈຳເຮືອ		v. geːp giaw ເກັບກ່ຽວ
crime	n. at saː nya gaːm	croquet	n. giː la gloː geː ກິລາໂກຣເຕ້
	ອາສຍາກຳ	cross	("x") n. may dtin ga
criminal	adj. tang at saː nya gaːm		ພາມຕິນກາ
	ທາງອາສຍາກຳ		(Christian) n. may gang
crimson	adj. si daang gaa ສີແດງແກ່		ken ພາຍກາງເຂນ
cripple	adj. piː gan ພິການ		(go across) v. kam ຂ້າມ
crisis	n. pa waː suːk sern		(cross oneself) v. owː meu
	ພາວະສຸກເສີນ		heːt keung may gang ken
crisp	(brittle) adj. gohp ກອບ		ເອົາມືເຮັດເຄື່ອງພາຍທາງເຂນ
	(clear) adj. chaang ແຈ້ງ		(breed) v. bpaː soːm ປະສົມ
critic	n. pu hayː gan dti soːm		adj. chayː hayː ໃຈຮ້າຍ
	ຜູ້ໃຫການຕິຊົມ	cross out	v. kit ohk ຂີດອອກ
critical	(judicious) adj. piː kohː	crossing	(road) n. bohn kam ບ່ອນຂ້າມ
	ພິເຄາະ		(railroad) n. tang dtaːt
	(finding fault) adj. sohk		kam tang loːt fayː ທາງ
	chaːp piːt ຊອກຈັບຍົດ		ຕັດຂ້າມທາງຣົດໄຟ
	(serious) adj. sa haːt	crouch	v. mohp loːng ພອບລົງ
	ສາຫັດ	crow	n. ga ກາ
critique	n. kaːm wiː chan ຄາວິຈານ		v. kaːn ຂັນ
croak	v. heːt siang hohng keu goːp	crowd	n. fung soːn ຝູງຊົນ
	leu ga ເຮັດສຽງຮອງຄ້າຍກົບ	crown	(king) n. moːng suːt ມົງກຸດ
crocodile	n. kaa ແຂ້		(top) n. nyoht ຍອດ

crude	(person) adj. nyap sa		(promote) v. so:ng serm
	ทยาบຊ้า		ສ້ງເສິມ
	(oil) adj. di:p ดิบ	cultural	adj. haang wa:t ta: na:
cruel	adj. hot hay โຫດຮ້າย		ta:m แຫ່ງວັ້ງໝະຫ້າມ
cruise	v. laan heua แล่มເຮືอ	culture	(arts) n. wa:t ta: na:
crumb	n. set ka: no:m เສົ້ດอມ້ມ		ta:m วັທນະຫ້າม
crusade	n. so:ng kam sat sa: na		(agriculture) n. gan bpuk
	ສິ້ງคามสาสมา		fa:ng ภามปฏຝ้ว
	v. gert so:ng kam sat sa:	cunning	adj. mi le laim มີເລ່ຫ຺ຼ່ງມ
	na เทิดสิ้วคามสาสมา	cupboard	n. dtu a hah ตู้ຂ້າທาม
crush	(destroy) v. ta:m lay	curb	n. kohp ຂอบ
	ທำລາย		v. o:t chay: ວิດใจ
	(smash) v. bip บิบ	cure	n. gan ha:k sa ภามรักสา
crutch	n. may: tow: kaan sa:m la:p		(illness) v. bpin bpua ปิ่ม
	ko:n ka ha:k ไม้เຫ້າແຂມສ້າຫ້ບ		ปิอ
	คิมຂาຫ້ก		(meat, tobacco) v. ha:k sa,
crust	n. bpeuak เປືอก		ta: nohm รักสา, ຈะมອม
cry	(sob) v. hohng hay: ຮ້องใຫ້	curious	(inquisitive) adj. yak hu
	(shout) v. hohng ຮ้อງ		yak he:n ຢາກຮ້ຢາກເຫ຺ນ
crystal	(mineral) n. gaaw chia la:		(odd) adj. bpaak bpa: lat
	nay: ເໜ່อເຈ້ຽຣະไม		แปกปลาด
	(glass) n. gaaw say: แกวใส	curl	v. he:t hay: gut เຮ້ດใຫ้ກຸດ
	adj. say: ใส		n. po:m gut ผ็มภุด
cub	n. luk sa:t ลูกสัด	curly	adj. gut ກຸດ
cube	n. hup si liam mo:n to:n	currency	n. ngern เຖີม
	ຮູບສິ່ຼງ຺ຼມມ຺ນທ຺ນ	current	n. say สาย
cuff	n. bpak kaan seua ปากแຂม		(water) n. say na:m
	ເສ້อ		สายม້ำ
cultivate	(grow) v. bpuk fa:ng ปຝຝ้ว		(electricity) n. ga: saa
			กะแส

	adj. bpa: chu: bo:n
	ปะจุบัน
curry	n. gaì lì ภารี
	n. tu duay bpaang ตุ๋
	ถ้วยแปๆ
curse	v. daa ด่า
curtain	n. pa gaìng ผ้ากั้ง
curve	n. kong โค้ง
	v. kong bpay: โค้งไป
cushion	v. say: bo:n ใส่เบาะ
	n. bo:p เบาะ
custom	n. bpa: pa nì ประเพนี
customs	n. pa si si:n ka kow: laa: ohk
	ภาสีสินค้าเข้าและออก
customer	n. luk ka ลูกค้า
cut	n. bat บาด
	adj. bpe:n bat เป็นบาด
	(general) v. dta:k ตัด
	(meat) v. bpat ปาด
cut down	he:t hay: lu:t lo:ng
	เร็ดให้ลูกลั้ง
cut off	dta:t ohk ตัดออก
cut out	yu:t, sǒw: ยุด, เจ๊า
cyclist	n. ko:n ki lo:t tip
	คิมขี่รถถีบ
cyclone	n. lo:m ba mu ลิมบ้าหมู
cylinder	(shape) n. ga: bohk กะบอก
	(engine) n. sup สูบ

D

dad	n. poh พ่
dagger	n. mit sohng ko:m
	มีดสองคม
daily	adj. bpa: cha:m wa:n
	ประจำวัน
	adj. lay wa:n รายวัน
	adv. tuik meu ทุกมื้
	n. na:ng seu pe:m lay wa:n
	พังสือพมพ์ลายวัน
dainty	adj. sa: ngìam สวยๆม
dairy	n. hong ngan he:t na:m no:m
	โรงๆานเร็ดน้ำนม
dam	n. fay ga:n na:m ฝ่ายกั้มน้ำ
	v. he:t fay ga:n na:m เร็ด
	ฝ่ายกั้มน้ำ
damage	n. kwam sia hay ความเสียหาย
	v. he:t hay: sia hay เร็ด
	ให้เสียหาย
damn	v. sap saang สาบแช่ง
damp	adj. su:m ชุ่ม
dance	(classical) v. fohn ฟ้อน
	n. gan fohn ภามฟ้อน
	(modern) v. dte:n la:m
	เต้มลำ
	n. gan dte:n la:m ภาม
	เต้มลำ
dancer	n. na:k fohn มักฟ้อม

	n. na:k dte:n la:m มัก เต็มลำ
danger	n. a:n dta: lay อันตะลาย
dangerous	adj. mi a:n dta: lay มี อันตะลาย
dare	v. ga กๆ
dark	(no light) adj. meut มืด
	(color) adj. gaa แก่
darkness	n. kwam meut ความมืด
darkroom	n. hohng lang hup ห้อง ล้างฐป
darling	n. nyoht ha:k, su:t ti ha:k ยอดรัก, สุดที่รัก
darn	v. chu:n pa จุนผๆ
dart	v. bpay: yang wohng way: ไป่ย่างอ้องๆไอ
dash	v. keuang way: yang wohng way: เคื่อนไหอย่างอ้องๆไอ
	n. se:n sa:n ti dtoh ka:m เส้นสั้นๆทีต่อคำ
date	(fruit) n. mak may: sa: ni:t neu:ng ผากไม้อูมิดกิ่ง
	(day) n. wa:n ti อันที
	n. gan na:t ga:p pu sow leu pu bow การนัดถัยผู้สๆอ พู่ผู้ฐๆอ
daughter	n. luk sow ลูกสๆอ
daughter-in-law	n. luk pay: ลูกใภ้
dawn	n. we la dta: wa:n cha: keu:n เอลาตาอันจะฐื้น
day	n. meu มิ
daylight	n. kuam chaang dtohn gang wa:n ความแจ้งตอนภาง้อัม
daytime	n. meu suay, meu we:n มิ สอย, มิ้เอ้ม
daze	n. kwam ngo:ing ความงิง
dazzling	adj. bpe:n si saang nyi:p nya:p เป็นสีแสงยิยับ
dead	adj. ti dtay laaw ที ตายแล้อ
deadly	adj. sa mat he:t hay: how: dtay สามาด เรัดให้เฐๆตาย
deaf	adj. hu nuak ทูผอก
deal	n. koh sa:n nya 2ส้มยๆ
	(as cards) v. so:ng dtoh bpay: ส้อต่ไป
dealer	(trader) n. poh ka พี่คๆ
	(cards) n. pu yay pay: ผู้ฐๆยไพ่
	(agent) n. pu cha:m nay ผู้จำนๆย
dear	(darling) adj. ti ha:k ที่รัก
	(expensive) adj. paang แพง
death	n. kwam dtay ความตาย
debate	v. tiang dto wa ti ถุ้งโต้อๆที
	n. gan dto wa ti การโต้อๆที
debt	n. ni ฐี้

decay	v. now̆: , bpe̒uay ເນົ່າ, ເປື່ອຍ
deceased	n. pi dtay ຜີຕາຍ adj. dtay ຕາຍ
deceit	n. kwam lo̒hk lua̒ng ຄວາມຫຼອກລວງ
deceive	v. lo̒hk lua̒ng ຫຼອກລວງ
December	n. deu̒an ta̒in wa̒ ເດືອນທັນວາ
decent	adj. lia̒:p lo̒hn ຮຽບຮ້ອຍ
decide	v. dta̒:t sin chay: ຕັດສິນໃຈ
decision	n. gan dta̒:t sin chay: ການຕັດສິນໃຈ
deck	n. peu̒n heu̒a bohn ko̒:n yeu̒n ພື້ນເຮືອບ່ອນຄົມຢືນ v. ow̆: sa̒y: ເອົາໃສ່
declare	(announce) v. bpa̒: ga̒t ປະກາດ (tell) v. hay: gan ໃຫ້ການ
decline	(descend) v. lo̒ing ລິ່ງ (refuse) v. boh nyohm la̒:p ບໍ່ຍອມຮັບ
decorate	v. e̒ ເຍ
decrease	n. gan lo̒:t noy lo̒ing ການລົດນ້ອຍລິ່ງ v. lu̒:t noy lo̒ing ລຸດ ນ້ອຍລິ່ງ
decree	n. ka̒:m sa̒ing ຄຳສັ່ງ v. ohk ka̒:m sa̒ing ອອກຄຳສັ່ງ
dedicate	v. u̒: dt̄i:t hay: ອຸທິດໃຫ້
deed	n. gan ga̒: ta̒im ການກະທຳ
deem	v. he̒in wa̒, teu̒ wa̒ ເຫັນວ່າ, ຖືວ່າ
deep	adj. ler̆:k ເລິກ
deer	n. guang ກວາງ
defeat	n. kwam pay pa̒a ຄວາມພ່າຍແພ້
defect	n. koh bo̒:k pohng ຂໍ້ບົກ ພ່ອງ
defense	n. gan bpohng ga̒:n ປ້ອງ ການປ້ອງກັນ
defer	v. pa̒:t bpay: ຜັດໄປ
defile	v. ka̒:k ka̒n sa̒t le̒u sa̒t sa̒: n̆a ຄັດຄ້ານອາດຫຼີສາສມາ
define	v. ga̒:m no:t kwam may ກຳນົດຄວາມໝາຍ
definite	adj. n̆a sa̒:t ແນ່ນັດ
defy	v. ta̒ tay ທ້າທາຍ
degree	(school) n. bpa̒: li̒:n nya ປริญยา (temperature) n. o̒ing sa̒ ອົງສາ
deity	n. te wa̒: da ເທວະດາ
delay	v. sa̒:k sa ຊັກຊ້າ
delegate	n. pu dtang n̆a ຜູ້ຕາງໜ້າ v. mohp a̒:m nat hay: ມອບ ອຳນາດໃຫ້
deliberate	v. dteuk dtohng ຕຶກຕອງ
delicate	adj. ohn, dtaak ngay ອ່ອນ ແຕກງ່າຍ

delicious	adj. såap ແຊບ	depend	v. keu:n yu gå:p ຂຶ້ນຢູ່ກັບ
delight	v. he:t hay: nyi:n di ເຮັດ ໃຫ້ຍິນດີ	desk	n. dto: ໂຕະ
		desolate	adj. haang laang ແຫ້ງແລ້ງ
deliver	v. so:ng hay: ສົ່ງໃຫ້	despair	v. mo:t wå:ng ໝົດຫວັງ
delusion	n. gan soh go:ng, kuam lo:ng pi:t ການສໍໂກງ, ຄວາມຫລົງຜິດ		n. kwam si:n wa:ng ຄວາມ ສິ້ນຫວັງ
demand	n. kaim koh hohng ຄຳຮ້ອງຂໍ້ v. koh hohng ຂໍຮ້ອງ	despatch	n. kow duan ຂ່າວດ່ວນ v. so:ng kow ສົ່ງຂ່າວ
democrat	n. na:k bpa: sa ti: bpa: dtay: ນັກປະຊາທິປະໄຕ	desperate	adj. yang su:t kwam sa mat ຢ່າງສຸດຄວາມສາມາດ
demolish	v. ta:m lay yang si:n sering ທຳລາຍຢ່າງສິ້ນເຊີງ	despise	v. saing ຊັງ
		despite	prep. ter:ng maan wa ເຖິງແມ່ນວ່າ
demon	n. pi sat hay ຜີສາດຮ້າຍ		
demonstrate	v. sa: daang bpa: gohp ສະແດງປະກອບ	dessert	n. kohn:g wan ເຂົ້າໜົມຄວາມ
den	n. ta:m ti sa:t yu ถ้ำที่ ສັດຢູ່	destine	v. bpay: dtam bu:n dtam ga:m ໄປຕາມບຸນຕາມກັມ
denial	n. gan bpa: dti: set ການ ປະຕິເສດ	destiny	n. sok wa:t sa: na ໂຊກ ວາສນາ
denouce	v. gow: tot ກ່າວໂທດ	destroy	v. dta:m lay ທຳລາຍ
dense	adj. na naan ໜາແໜ້ນ	destruction	n. gan ta:m lay ການທຳລາຍ
dentist	(common) n. moh kaaw mi ແຂ້ວ (formal) n. ta:n dta: paat ທັນຕະແພດ	detach	v. nyaak ohk ແຍກອອກ
		detail	v. low: doy la: iat ເລົ່າ ໂດຍລະອຽດ n. lay la: iat ລາຍລະອຽດ
deny	v. bpa: dti set, boh ha:p hu ປະຕິເສດ, ບໍຮັບ ຮູ້	detailed	adj. la: iat la: oh ລະອຽດ ລະອໍ
depart	v. chak bpay: ຈາກໄປ	detain	v. ga:k dtua way: ກັກຕົວໄວ້
department	n. ga: suang ກະຊວງ	detect	v. po:p poh, hu seu:k ພົບພໍ, ຮູ້ສຶກ

determine	v. dto̎:k lo̎ing cha̗y: ຕັກລົງໃຈ	diary	n. bpeu̅m ba̗in teu̎:k la̗y ປຶ້ມ wa̎:n ບັນທຶກລາຍວັນ
detest	v. la̎ing gia̗t ລ້ງກຽຕ	dictate	(school) v. bohk ha̗y: kia̎n ບອກໃຫ້ຂຽນ
develop	(change) v. bpia̗n bpaang ປ່ຽນແປງ		dtam ຕາມ
	(photograph) v. la̅ng hu̅p ລ້າງຮູບ		(command) v. pa̎: de̎:t ຜະເດັດ
	(mature) v. pa̎:t ta̎: na̅ ພັດຕະນາ		ga̅n ການ
development	(change) n. ga̅n bpa̎i̗p ການ bpui̎:ng ປ່ຽນປູງ	dictator	n. pu̎ pa̎: de̎:t ga̅n ຜູ້ຜະເດັດ ການ
	(maturity) n. ga̅n pa̎:t ta̎: na̅ ການພັດທະນາ	dictionary	(complete) n. wa̎: cha̅: na̗ nu go̎:m ອັຈມານຸກົມ
device	n. keuang a̗i̎p bpa la̗y: ເຄື່ອງ ຣ້ບປາໄຣ		(current) n. po̗it cha̎: na̗ nu go̎:m ພົຈມານຸກົມ
	(method) n. wi̎: ti̅ ວິທິ	die	v. dta̗y ຕາຍ
devil	n. bpi sa̗t ປີສາຕ	die away	(stop) so̗w: bpa̗y: ເຊົາໄປ
devise	v. ki̎:t keu̎:n ຄິດຂື້ນ		(die) dta̗y bpa̗y: ຕາຍໄປ
devote	v. u̎it ti̎: ອຸຕທີ	die down	koy̗ koy̗ so̗w: lo̗:ng ຄ່ອຍໆ ເຊົາລົງ
devoted	adj. u̎it ti̎: ອຸຕທີ	die out	koy̗ koy̗ dta̗y bpa̗y: ຄ່ອຍໆ ຕາຍໄປ
devour	v. gi̎:n cho̗:n mo̎:t sia̅ng, daak ha̅ ກິນຈົນໝົຕສ້ຽງ, ແຕກຮໆ	diet	n. ga̅n leu̎ak gi̎:n ການເລືອກ ກິນ
dew	n. na̎:m mohk ນ້ຳພອກ		v. leu̎ak gi̎:n ເລືອກກິນ
dial	(watch) n. si̅:ng ti̅ mi̅ si̗:ng lek ໜ້າ ທີ່ມີເລກ	differ	v. dta̎ak dta̎ng ແຕກຕ່າງ
	(telephone) v. mui̎:n to̅ ໝຸນ la̎: sa̗i:p ໂທຣະສັບ	difference	n. kwa̅m dta̎ak dta̎ng ຄວາມ ແຕກຕ່າງ
		different	adj. dta̎ak dta̎ng ແຕກຕ່າງ
		difficult	adj. nya̎k ຍາກ
diamond	n. pe̎:t ເພັຕ	difficulty	n. kwa̅m nya̎k ຄວາມຍາກ
			n. kwa̅m la̎:m ba̎k ຄວາມ ລຳບາກ

dig	v. kuːt ຂຸດ	diplomatic	adj. haang gan tuːt (ແທ່ງ ການທຸດ
digest	n. bpeum ti liap liang laaw ປຶ້ມທີ່ລຽບລຽງແລ້ວ	direct	adj. seu goːng ຊື່ກົງ
	v. nyoy a han ຍ່ອຍອາຫານ (thought) v. kowː chayː ເຂົ້າໃຈ		v. naa naːm tang (ແນະນຳທາງ)
dignity	n. saːk si ສັກສີ	direction	(way) n. tiːt tang ທິດທາງ
diligence	n. kwam pian ຄວາມພຽນ		(order) n. kwam saːng, gan aːm nuay gan ຄຳສັ່ງ, ການອຳນວຍການ
dim	v. heːt hayː mi saang noy loːng (ເຮັດໃຫ້ມີແສງນ້ອຍ ລົງ	dirt	(soil) n. ki diːn ຂີ້ດິນ
	adj. poh mua mua ພໍມົວໆ		(dust) n. ki fuːn ຂີ້ຝຸ່ນ
dime	n. ngeːn aiːt siːp seːn (ເງິນ ອັດສິບເຊັນ	dirty	adj. bpeuan ເປື່ອນ
dime store	n. han kay keuang nyoy ຮ້ານ ຂາຍເຄື່ອງນ້ອຍ	disagree	v. kaːt kan ຂັດຄ້ານ
		disappear	v. hay bpayː ຫາຍໄປ
dimension	(size) n. kaː nat ຂະນາດ	disappoint	v. piːt waːng ຜິດຫວັງ
	(side) n. kang ຂ້າງ	disaster	n. kwam piː niː, payː piː baːt ຄວາມພິນາດ, ໄພພິບົດ
diminish	v. heːt hayː noy loːng (ເຮັດ ໃຫ້ນ້ອຍລົງ	discern	v. heːn saːt (ເຫັນຊັດ
dine	v. giːn kowː laang ກິນເຂົ້າແລງ	discharge	v. owː ohk (ເອົາອອກ
			n. chaːm nuan ti owː ohk ຈຳນວນທີ່ເອົາອອກ
dining room	n. hohng giːn kowː ຫ້ອງກິນເຂົ້າ	discipline	n. laː biap wiː nayː ລະບຽບວິໄນ
			v. daːt niː sayː ດັດນິໄສ
dinner	n. kowː laang ເຂົ້າແລງ	disconnect	v. dtaːt ຕັດ
dip	v. chuːm ຈຸ່ມ	discord	n. gan piːt tiang ການ ຜິດຖຽງ
diploma	n. bpaː gat saː ni nya baːt ປະກາດສະນິຍບັດ	discourse	(discussion) n. gan wowː cha ການເວົ້າຈາ
diplomat	n. naːk gan tuːt ນັກການ ທຸດ		(speech) n. bpaː taː gaː ta ປະຫະກະຖາ

discover	v. ko:n po:p ຄົ້ນພົບ
discreet	adj. mi kwam la: ma:t la wang ມີຄວາມລະມັດຣະວັງ
discrete	adj. dtaak dtang ga:n ti su:t ແຕກຕ່າງກັນທີ່ສຸດ
discuss	v. 'a: pi: 'opay ຊະຜີປາຍ
disdain	n. gan du tuk ການດູຖູກ
disease	n. lok ໂຣກ
disgrace	n. kwam ai:p ay ຄວາມອັບອາຍ
disguise	v. bpohm dtua ປອມຕົວ n. keuang ti say: bpohm dtua ເຄື່ອງທີ່ໃຊ້ປອມຕົວ
disgust	v. he:t hay: na nay ເຮັດໃຫ້ນ່າໜ່າຍ n. kwam beua nay ຄວາມ ເບື່ອໜ່າຍ
dish	(plate) n. chan ຈານ (girl) n. pu sow ngam ຜູ້ສາວງາມ
disjoin	v. nyaak chak ga:n ແຍກ ຈາກກັນ
dislike	v. laing giat ລັງກຽດ
dismal	adj. sow: chay: ເສົ້າໃຈ
dismay	v. he:t hay: dto:k chay: ເຮັດໃຫ້ຕົກໃຈ n. kwam ser: ຄວາມເຊື່
dismiss	n. nyo:k lerk ka:p lay: ຍົກເລີກ, ຍົບໄລ
dispense	v. baang hay: ແບ່ງໃຫ້
disperse	v. ga: cha:t ga: chay ກະຈັດກະຈາຍ
display	v. sa daang hay: he:n ສະແດງໃຫ້ເຫັນ n. gan wang sa: daang ການອາງສະແດງ
dispose	v. ow: ti:m ເອົາຖິ້ມ
dispute	v. pi:t tiang ga:n ຜິດຖຽງກັນ n. gan pi:t tiang ga:n ການຜິດຖຽງກັນ
dissolve	v. la: lay nay: na:m ລະລາຍໃນນ້ຳ
distant	adj. hang gay: ຫ່າງໄກ
distinct	adj. chaam chaang ແຈ່ມແຈ້ງ
distinctly	adv. yang chaam chaang ຢ່າງແຈ່ມແຈ້ງ
distinguish	v. he:t hay: na:m kwam dtaak dtaang ເຮັດໃຫ້ເຫັນ ຄວາມແປກຕ່າງ
distract	v. per:t per:n chay:, lo:p guan ເຜີດເຜີນໃຈ, ລົບກວນ
distress	v. he:t hay: deuat hohn ເຮັດໃຫ້ເດືອດຮ້ອນ
distribute	v. chaak yay ແຈກຢາຍ
district	n. ku:m, boh li: wen ຄຸມ, ບໍຣິເວນ
disturb	v. lo:p guan ລົບກວນ
ditch	n. hohng na:m ຮ່ອງນ້ຳ v. ow: ti:m ເອົາຖິ້ມ

dive	n. gan daːm naːm ການ ດຳນ້ຳ
	v. daːm naːm ດຳນ້ຳ
diver	n. naːk daːm naːm ນັກດຳນ້ຳ
divert	(attention) v. bpian
	kwam soːn chayː ປ່ຽນ
	ຄວາມສົນໃຈ
	(river) v. bpian tang dern
	ປ່ຽນທາງເດີນ
divide	(things) v. baang ແບ່ງ
	(math) v. han ຫານ
divine	(holy) adj. saːk sit ສັກສິດ
	(good) adj. di leːt ດີເລີດ
diving board	n. bpaan gaː dot naːm ແປ້ນ
	ກະໂດດນ້ຳ
division	(math) n. lek han ເລກຫານ
	(military) n. gohng paːn
	taː han ກອງພັນທະຫານ
	(a part) n. suan neuːng
	ສ່ວນໜຶ່ງ
divorce	n. gan bpaː hang ການປະຮ້າງ
	v. nyaːak tang, bpaː
	ແຍກທາງ, ປະ
dizzy	adj. laːy dta, hua sia
	ລາຍຕາ, ຫົວເສັຽ
do	v. heːt ເຮັດ
do over	heːt mayː ik ເຮັດໃໝ່ອີກ
do without	heːt doy boh chaːm bpeːn
	dtohng sayː leu dtohng mi
	ເຮັດໂດຍບໍ່ຈຳເປັນຕ້ອງໃຊ້ຫຼື
	ຕ້ອງມີ

dock	n. taː heua ທ່າເຮືອ
	v. choht heua ຈອດເຮືອ
doctor	n. tan moh ທ່ານໝໍ
	v. bpiːn bpua ປິ່ນປົວ
doctrine	n. laːt tiː ລັດທິ
document	n. ek gaː san ເອກະສານ
	v. piː sut ພິສຸດ
dodge	v. loːp lik ລິ່ງຫຼີກ
dog	n. ma ໝາ
dole	n. siːng ti chaak hayː
	ສິ່ງທີ່ແຈກໃຫ້
	v. chaak yay hayː ແຈກ
	ຍ່າຍໃຫ້
doll	n. dtuːk gaː dta ຕຸກກະຕາ
	(girl) n. pu sow ngaːm ຜູ້
	ສາວງາມ
dollar	n. ngerːn do laː ເງິນໂດລາ
domain	n. ti diːn ທີ່ດິນ
dome	n. laːng kaː goːng ຫຼັງຄາ ກົ້ງ
domestic	adj. haang ban, haang pay
	nayː bpaː tet
	ແຫ່ງບ້ານ, ແຫ່ງພາຍໃນປະເທດ
	n. koːn sayː ຄົນໃຊ້
domicile	n. heuan, puː miː laːm nowː
	ເຮືອນ, ຖຸມີລຳເນົາ
dominate	v. kohp kohng ຄອບຄອງ
dominion	n. a naː chaːk ອານາຈັກ
donation	n. gan boh liː chak ການ
	ບໍຣິຈາກ
donkey	n. ma loh ມ້າລໍ

don't	(warning) adv. ya² ย่า
do not	boh² บ่
doom	n. moh³ la:³ na:² มึระนะ
door	n. bpa: dtu³ ปะตู
doorway	n. tang kow:⁶ bpa: dtu³ ທາງເຂົ້າປະຕູ
dot	n. chu:t³ ຈຸດ
double	adj. sohng tow:² ສອງເທົ່າ
double feature	n. si ne sohng leuang³ say⁴ hohp⁵ diaw gain⁵ ຊີເນສອງເຣື່ອງສາຍຮອບດງວ ກັນ
doubt	n. koh⁶ so:ng³ say:⁴ ຂໍ້ສົງໄສ v. so:ng³ say:⁴ ສົງໄສ
dough	(bread) n. bpaeng ka:³ no:m niaw⁴ ແປ້ງຂົມໜງວ (money) n. nger:n³ ເງີນ
doughnut	n. ka:³ no:m do nait² ຂົມ ໂດໜັດ
dove	n. no:k kow:³ ນົກເຂົາ
down	adv. lu:m² ລຸມ
downstairs	n. sain⁵ laing² ຊັ້ນລ່າງ n. sain⁵ lu:m² ຊັ້ນລຸມ
downtown	n. nay³ meuang³ ໃນເມືອງ
downward	adv. bpay: tang lu:m³ ໄປ ທາງລຸມ
dozen	n. lo⁴ ໂຫຼ
draft	(conscription) n. gan² gen ta:² han⁴ ການເກນທະຫານ (air) n. keun² lo:m² ຄື່ນລົມ

drag	v. lak⁵ ລາກ
drain	(ditch) n. hohng mawang⁴ ຮ່ອງເໝືອງ (pipe) v. kay: na:m ohk⁴ ໄຂນ້ຳອອກ
drama	(singing by two people) n. la:m ku⁴ ລຳຄູ່ (singing by a group) n. la:m³ leuang³ ລຳເຣື່ອງ
draw	(picture) v. dtaam⁵ ແຕ້ມ (line) v. kit⁶ se:n⁵ ຂີດເສ້ນ
drawer	n. lin³ saik⁵ ລີ້ນຊັກ
dread	n. kwam na yan⁴ ຄວາມໜ້າຢ້ານ
dream	(sleep) n. kwam fain³ ຄວາມຝັນ (ideal) kwam fay:⁴ fain⁴ ຄວາມໄຝ່ຝັນ v. fain⁴ ຝັນ
dreary	adj. sow:⁶ mohng⁴ ເສົ້າໝອງ
dress	(normal) n. ga:³ bpong ກະໂປ່ງ (formal) n. keuang⁴ dtaang dtua⁴ ເຄື່ອງແຕ່ງຕົວ (Lao skirt) n. sin⁶ ສີ້ນ v. nu:ng⁴ keuang⁴ ນຸ່ງເຄື່ອງ
dresser	n. dtu⁵ say: keuang⁴ nu:ng⁴ ຕູ້ໃສ່ເຄື່ອງນຸ່ງ
drift	v. lay: bpay:⁴ ໄຫຼໄປ
drill	v. choh:³ hu³ ເຈາະຮູ n. sa:² wan⁴ ສະວານ

drink	n. keuang deu:m ເຄື່ອງດື່ມ	dry	adj. haang ແຫ້ງ
	v. deu:m ດື່ມ		(dry by sun) v. dtak
drip	v. yat loing ຢາດລິງ		ຕາກ
drive	v. kaip loit ຂັບຣົດ		(dry by smoke) v. yang
drive-in	n. si ne ma ti ki loit		ຢ່າງ
	bering ຊີເນມາທີ່ຣົດເຂົ້າ	duchess	n. pain la: nya kohng
driver	n. koin kaip ຄົນຂັບ		kuin tow: ພັນລະຍາຂອງຂຸນທ້າວ
drizzle	v. foin dtoik koy koy	duck	n. peit ເປັດ
	ຝົນຕົກຄ່ອຍໆ		v. muit hua dtaim loing
drone	(bee) n. pering dto pu		ມຸດຫົວຄ່າລິງ
	ເຜິ້ງໂຕ່ຜູ້	due	adj. tering we la gaim
	(noise) n. siang heu:m heu:m		noit ເຖິງເວລາກຳນົດ
	ສຽງຫຶມໆ	dues	n. ka taim niam ຄ່າທຳນຽມ
droopy	adj. koit ຄົດ	duke	n. kuin tow ຂຸນທ້າວ
drop	v. yoht bpein meit ຢອດ	dull	(life) adj. na beua ໜ້າເບື່ອ
	ເປັນເມັດ		(ignorant) adj. ngo ໂງ່
	v. dtoik ຕົກ	dumb	adj. ngo ໂງ່
drop out of	la ohk chak ລາອອກຈາກ	dungeon	n. kuik meut ຄຸກມືດ
drove	n. fuing sa:t leu koin	during	prep. la: wang ຣະຫວ່າງ
	ຝູງສັດຫຼືຄົນ	dusk	n. gohn dta: wain dtoik
drown	v. cho:m naim ຈົມນ້ຳ		ກ່ອນຕະເວັນຕົກ
drowsy	adj. ngow: nohn ເຫງົານອນ	dust	v. bpa:t fuin ປັດຝຸ່ນ
drug	n. ya ຢາ		n. ki fuin ຂີ້ຝຸ່ນ
	v. wang ya haang ວາງຢາ ແຮງ	dusty	adj. bpein fuin ເປັນຝຸ່ນ
drug store	n. han kay ya ຮ້ານຂາຍຢາ	duty	(job) n. na ti gan ໜ້າ
druggist	n. koin kay ya ຄົນຂາຍຢາ		ທີ່ການ
drum	n. gohng ກອງ		(custom) n. suay sa a gohn
	v. dti gohng ຕີກອງ		ອວຍສາອາກອນ
drunkard	n. koin ki low: ຄົນຂີ້ເຫຼົ້າ	dwarf	n. koin chaa ຄົນແຈ້
			adj. dtia ເຕັ້ຍ

dwell	v. à say: yu อาไสยู่
dye	v. nyohm si ย้อมสี
dynamite	n. diin laı bert ดิม ละเบิด
dysentery	n. lok tohng bi:t โรกท้องบิด

E

each	adj. dtaa laı a:n แต่ละอัน
each other	seuing gaın laa; gaın ซึ่ง ภัมและภัม
eager	adj. mi chay: cho:t choh ปีใจจิดจ่
eagle	n. laaw แญว
ear	n. hu หู
early	adj. dtaa sow: แต่เช้า
earmuffs	n. keuang bpohng gaın hu nyam now เคื่องป้องภัมทุยาม ผาว
earwax	n. ki hu ขี้หู
earn	v. ha ma day: ทามาได้
earnest	adj. dtang chay: ติ้งใจ
earnings	n. ngerin ti ha ma day: เงินที่ทามาได้
earth	(planet) paan di:n แผ่นดิน
	(soil) n. ki di:n ขี้ดิน
earthquake	n. paan di:n way: แผ่นดิน ไทว
ease	n. kwam sa: bay ความสะบาย

easily	(work) adv. doy ngay โดย ว่าย
	(bureaucracy) adv. doy sa: duak โดยสะดวก
east	adj. tang ti:t dta we:n ทาง ohk ทิดตาเว้นออก
eastward	adv.bpay: tang ti:t dta we:n ohk ไปทางทิดตาเว้นออก
easy	adj. ngay ว่าย
eat	v. gi:n ทีม
echo	n. siang gohng สุงก้อง
economy	(national) n. set ta: gi:t เสถฤากิด
	(personal) n. gan bpa: nya:t ภามประยัด
economics	n. get tai sat เกถทะสาด
	(study) n. hian gan ka kay ธุมภามค้าขาย
ecstasy	(joy) n. kwam di chay: yang laın leua ความดีใจ ย่างล้นเฑือ
	(rapture) n. kwam di chay: co:n leum dto ความดีใจจิม ลิมโต
edge	n. kaam แคม
edify	v. so:ng sohn hay: di สั่ง keu:nสอนใฑ้ดีอื้ม
edit	v. guat ทอด
edition	n. gan pi:m ภามผิม

editor	n. ba:n nǎ tǐ: gan ບັນນາ ທິການ	elastic	adj. tǐ yɐut kɔ́w: oňk day: ທີ່ຍືດເຂົ້າອອກໄດ້
editorial	n. bo:t ba:n na tǐ: gǎn ບົດບັນນາທິການ	elbow	n. kaǎn soňk ແຂນສອກ v. nyú duay soňk ຍູ້ດວຍ ສອກ
educate	v. oɪp lo:m ອົບໂລມ	elder	adj. tòw: gua ເຖົ້າກວ່າ
education	n. gan seú:k sǎ ການສຶກຫາ	elderly	adv. tòw: ເຖົ້າ
effect	n. po:n ຜົນ	elect	v. ka:t leuak ຄັດເລືອກ
efficiency	n. la: da:p sa:n kohng kwam sǎ mat ຣະດັບຂອງຄວາມສາມາດ	elections	n. gan leuak dtǎng ການ ເລືອກຕັ້ງ
effort	n. kwam pǎ: nyǎ nyam ຄວາມພະຍາຍາມ	electric	adj. duay fay: fǎ ດ້ວຍ ໄຟຟ້າ
egg	n. kay ໄຂ່	electrician	n. sang fay: fǎ ຊ່າງ ໄຟຟ້າ
eggbeater	n. keuang dti kay ເຄື່ອງຕີໄຂ່	electricity	n. fay: fǎ ໄຟຟ້າ
Egyptian	adj. haǎng e siǐp ແຫ່ງ ເອຊິບ	electric train	n. lo:t fay: fay: fǎ ຣົດໄຟ ໄຟຟ້າ
eight	(8) adj. bpaat ແປດ (໘)	electronics	n. gan hian giow ga:p i lek tlohn ການຮຽນກ່ຽວອັກ ອີເລັກທຣອນ
eighteen	(18) adj. siǐp bpaat ສິບແປດ		
eighth	(8th) adj. ti bpaat ທີ ແປດ	elegant	adj. yang gɔ́ sǎi ngá ຢ່າງ ໂກ້ສ່າ
eighty	(80) adj. bpaat siǐp ແປດສິບ	element	n. wa:t tu: ວັດຖຸ n. tat bpa:t, chay: ທາດ, ບັດໄຈ
either	adj. aɪn day: aɪn neuɪng ອັນໃດອັນນຶ່ງ	elephant	n. sang ຊ້າງ
elaborate	adj. yang bpa nit ຢ່າງປາ ນິດ (state) v. hay: lay la: iat ໃຫ້ລາຍລະອຽດ	elevate	(height) v. nyo:k keun ຍົກຂຶ້ນ (job) v. leuan nyo:t ເລື່ອນຍົດ

elevator	n. keuang nyo:k เคื่องยัก	emotion	n. kwam hu seu:k dteun dta:n chay: ความรู้สึกตื่นตันใจ
eleven	adj. sip et สิบเอ็ด	emperor	n. cha:k ga: pa:t จักกะพัด
eliminate	v. ka:t ohk คัด99ก		
elm	n. dto:n may: aam ก ต้มไม้แอม	emphasis	n. gan nen ka:m การเน้มคำ
eloquence	n. wo han di โอทามดิ	empire	n. ma: ha a na cha:k มะทาອามาจัก
else	adj. eun อื่ม	employ	v. chang จ้าง
	(something else) adv. si:ng eun ik สิ่งอื่มอิก	employee	n. luk chang ลูกจ้าง
	(or else) adv. a:n eun ik อัมอื่มอิก	employment	n. gan say: ko:n การไอค้ม
elsewhere	adv. bohn eun บ่อมอื่ม	empty	adj. wang bpow: ต่อางเป่า
embarrass	v. he:t hay: ka:p chay: เริดใท้คุยใจ		v. he:t hay: wang bpow: เริดใท้ท่อางเป่า
embassy	n. sai tan ek a:k ka: lat sa: tut สะ ฑามเ9ท 9คราวๆทูด	enchant	v. sab saang สายแฉ้ว
		enclose	(surround) v. lohm ล้อม
embrace	v. goht ทอด		(insert) v. soht, hom ta:ng ส9ด, โธมทา้
emerge	v. pu:t keun ผุดอึ้ม		
emergency	n. het gan su:k sern เทดภามสุทเสิ่ม	encounter	v. po:p พ้บ
		end	v. cho:p จิบ
emigrant	n. ko:n o:p nyo:p ohk cha:k bpa: tet คิมอพยิบออกจากปะเทด		n. su:t tay สุทท้าย
		endeavor	v. pai nya nyam พะยายาม
emigrate	v. o:p nyo:p ohk cha:k bpa: tet ອพิบออกจากปะเทด		n. kwam pai nya nyam คอาม พะยายาม
emigration	n. gan ni ohk nohk bpa: tet ภามพี่99ทม9ทปะเทด	endow	v. boh li: chak บริจาก
		endure	v. o:t to:n อิดทิม
eminent	adj. sung de:n สูงเด้ม	enemy	n. sa:t tu สัตธู
		energy	(motor) n. pai la:ng ngan พะลังวาม

	(people) n. ga:m la:ng ກາລັງ		ຂະຫຍາຍອອກ
engage	(marriage) v. ma:n way: ໝັ້ນໄວ້		(general) v. he:t hay: nyay: ເຮັດໃຫ້ໃຫຍ
	(hire) v. sa:n nya chang ສັນຍາຈ້າງ	enlist	(army) v. bpay: sa: ma:k ta: han ໄປສມັກທະຫານ
	(reserve) v. chang way: ຈອງໄວ້		(get support) v. day: la:p gan suay leua ໄດ້ລັບການຊ່ວຍ ເຫືອ
engagement	(contract) n. ga:n sa:n nya ການສັນຍາ	enormous	adj. nyay: lay ໃຫຍ່ຫຼາຍ
	(marriage) n. ga:n ma:n ການໝັ້ນ	enough	(stop) adv. poh ພໍ
engine	n. keuang cha:k ເຄື່ອງຈັກ		(sufficient) adj. piang poh ພຽງພໍ
engineer	n. nay sang ນາຍຊ່າງ	enquire	v. ta:m ຖາມ
	(technician) n. wi:t sa: wa: gohn ວິສະວະກອນ	enroll	v. cho:t seu ຈົດຊື່
engineering	n. wi sa: wa: ga:m wi:sa: ga:m ວິສະວະ ກຳ	ensue	v. dta:m ma ຕາມມາ
		enter	v. kow: bpay: ເຂົ້າໄປ
English	n. a:ng gi:t ອັງກິດ	enterprise	n. gan ka gi:t cha: gan ການຄ້າ, ກິດຈະການ
Englishman	n. ko:n a:ng gi:t ຄົນ ອັງກິດ	entertain	v. hay: kwam ba:n ter:ing ໃຫ້ຄວາມບັນເທີງ
enjoy	(oneself) v. sa: nu:k ສະໝຸກ	entertainment	n. kwam la lering ຄວາມລ່າ ເລີງ
	(things) v. ma:k ມັກ	enthusiasm	n. kwam di o:k di chay: ຄວາມຖືກດີໃຈ
enjoyable	adj. yang sa: nu:k sa: na:n ຢ່າງສນຸກສນານ	entire	adj. ko:p tuan ຄົບຖ້ວນ
enjoyment	n. kwam pert pern ຄວາມ ເບີດເຜີນ	entirely	adv. yang mo:t giang ຢ່າງໝົດກ້ຽງ
enlarge	(picture) v. ka: nyay o:k	entitle	(authority) v. hay: si:t ໃຫ້ສິດ
			(give title) v. hay: seu ໃຫ້ຊື່

entrance	n. tang kow: ทางเข้า
	(to delight) v. he:t hay:
	poh chay: เธ็ดให้พอใจ
entreat	v. koh hohng ຂໍຮ້ອງ
entrust	v. fak way: ฝากไว้
entry	n. gan kow: ການເຂົ້າ
envelop	v. hohm lohm ຫ້ອມລ້ອມ
envelope	n. sohng naing seu ຊອງ
	ໜັງສື
environment	n. si:ng waat lohm ສິ່ງ
	ແວດລ້ອມ
envy	n. kwam i:t sa ຄວາມອິດສາ
	v. i:t sa ອິດສາ
epidermis	n. naing ohn ໜັງອ່ອນ
episode	n. dtohn kohng leuang
	ຕອນຂອງເຮື່ອງ
equal	(straight) v. sa: mer ga:n
	ga:n ສະເໝີກັນ
	(size) v. tow: ga:n
	ເທົ່າກັນ
equip	v. bpa: gohp ປະກອບ
equipment	n. keuang bpa: gohp
	ເຄື່ອງປະກອບ
-er	(changes verbs to nouns)
	si:ng ti dteum gi: li:
	nya hay: bpe:n nam ສິ່ງ
	ທີ່ຕົມກິຣິຍາໃຫ້ເປັນນາມ
era	n. sa: may: ສໄມ
erase	v. leu:p ohk ລົບອອກ
eraser	n. yang leu:p ຢາງລົບ

erect	(upright) v. dtaing keu:n
	ຕັ້ງຂຶ້ນ
	(build) v. bpu:k keu:n
	ປຸກຂຶ້ນ
err	v. lo:ng pi:t ຫຼົງຜິດ
errand	n. tu: la: ທຣະ
error	n. ka:m pi:t, gan pi:t
	ຄຳຜິດ, ການຜິດ
escape	n. gan ni bpay: ການໜີໄປ
	v. lo:p ni ລົບໜີ
escort	v. dti:t dtam ຕິດຕາມ
	n. pu dti:t dtam ຜູ້ຕິດຕາມ
especially	adv. bpe:n pi: set ເປັນ
	ພິເສດ
essay	v. to:t lohng ທົດລອງ
	n. bo:t kwam ບົດຄວາມ
essence	n. hua koh ຫົວຂໍ້
essential	adj. seu:ng cha:m bpe:n
	ຊຶ່ງຈໍເປັນ
establish	v. dtang keu:n ຕັ້ງຂຶ້ນ
establishment	(government) n.la:t ta: ban,
	boh li: sa:t ຣັຖບານ, ບໍຣິສັດ
	(building) n. a kan ອາຄານ
estate	n. sa:p so:m ba:t ຊັບສົມບັດ
esteem	n. hua ki:t, kuam sohp poh
	ຫົວຄິດ, ຄວາມຊອບພໍ
estimate	n. gan bpa: mun ການ
	ປະມຸນ
	v. kat ka: ne, dti la ka
	ຄາດຄະເນ, ຕີລາຄາ

etc.	(et cetera) dtòh dtoh bpay: ต่าไป	everywhere	(large) adv. tuìk tuìk haang ทุกๆแห่ง
eternal	adj. dtà: lohd gan ตลอดกาน		(small unit) tu:k bohn ทุกบ่อน
Europe	n. ta: wíp yu: lóp ทะวีบยุโรบ	evidence	n. laìk tàn ผู้กฏฅาม
evaporate	v. gày bpe:n ay กายเบ็นอาย	evident	adj. chaam chaang แจ่มแจ้ง
eve	n. meu gohn มื้ก่อน	evil	n. kwàm sua hày ความชั่วช้าย adj. sua hày ชั่วช้าย
even	(numbers) adj. kùu คู่	evolve	(into) v. gày bpe:n กายเบ็น
	(equal) adj. sà: mér gan สเมีกัน		(from) mà chàk มาจาก
	(sarcasm) maan wa แม่นว่า	exact	a. ka:k naa คักแม่ v. kut hit ฏูดฮิด
	(level) piang พยง	exactly	adv. ka:k naa คักแม่ adv. yang naa nohn ย่างแม่นอน
evening	n. nyàm laang ยามแลง	exaggerate	v. wow: pot, ge:n suan เอาโพด, เกินสอม
event	n. hèt gan เหดกาน	exalt	v. nyoìk nyòhng ยักย่อง
eventual(ly)	adv. nay: tì: su:t ในที่สุด	examination	(investigation) n. gan guàt ga ภามทอดทา
ever	adv. kery เคีย		(test) n. gan sohb se:ng ภามสอบเสง
every	(spoken form) adj. tu:k tu:k ทุกๆ	examine	(investigate) v. guat ga ทอดทา
	adj. sù ain สู้อิน		(test) v. guat sohp ทอดสอบ
everybody	n. moìt tu:k ko:n หมดทุกคิม	example	n. dtua yang ตัอย่าง
everyone	n. tu:k tu:k ko:n ทุกๆคิม	exceed	v. gern ga:m no:t เกินภ้มิด
everything	(objects) n. tu:k si:ng ทุกสิ่ง		
	(categories) adv. tu:k yang ทุกย่าง		

excellent	adj. di lért ດີເລີດ
except	conj. nohk chak ນອກຈາກ
exception	n. koh nyo:k we:n ຂໍຍົກ ເວັ້ນ
exceptional	adj. bpe:n pi: set ເປັ້ນພິເສດ
excess	(beyond limit) n. gern ga:m no:t ເກີນ ກາໍນົດ
	(leftover) n. kohng leua29ງ ເຫຼືອ
exchange	(place) n. bohn laak bpian ບ່ອນແລກປ່ຽນ
	(things) n. kohng laak bpian ຂອງແລກປ່ຽນ
excite	(emotional) v. he:t hay: dteun dte:n ເຮັດໃຫ້ຕື່ນເຕັ້ນ
	(sensual)v. nyua nyuan ຢ້ວຢວນ
exciting	adj. yang dteun dte:n ປ່າງຕື່ນເຕັ້ນ
exclaim	v. hohng keu:n ຮ້ອງຂຶ້ນ
exclamation mark (!)	n. keuang may kwam sa:m ka:n ເຄື່ອງໝາຍຄວາມສໍ ຄັນ
exclude	v. nyo:k we:n ຍົກເວັ້ນ
exclusive	adj. 3a: poh: ສະເພາະ
excrement	(high) n. u:t cha la: ອຸດຈະຣະ
	(middle) n. a cho:m ອາຈົມ
	(low) n. ki ຂີ້

excuse	v. 3: nu: nyat hay: ຍາດໃຫ້
	n. ka:n gaa dtua ຄາໍແກ້ຕົວ
execute	(work) v. boh li: han ບໍຣິ ຫານ
	(kill) v. bpa: han si wi:t ປະຫານຊີວິດ
executive	adj. fay boh li: han ຝ່າຍບໍຣິຫານ
	n. pu boh li: han ຜູ້ບໍຣິຫານ
exercise	(physical) n. gan feu:k gay nya: ga:m ການຝຶກກາຍ ຍະກັນ
	(written) n. bo:t feu:k ha:t ບົດຝຶກຫັດ
	v. feu:k aap ຝຶກແອບ
exert	v. say: kwam pa: nya nyam ໃຊ້ຄວາມພະຍາຍາມ
exhaust	(tire) v. he:t hay: meuay ເຮັດໃຫ້ເມື່ອຍ
	(discard) v. say: cho:n mo:t ໃຊ້ຈົນໝົດ
	n. toh bpay siang ທໍ່ປ່ອຍ ສ່ງງ
exhibit	v. sa: daang ສະແດງ
	n. gan o:k bpa: guat ການ ອອກປະກວດ
exile	n. gan ne la: tet ການເນ ຣະເທດ

	v. nĕ lăi tĕt ເນະເຫດ		(die) v. daĭp ສັບ ດັບຊີບ
exist	(to be) v. yŭ ຢູ່	explain	(teach) v. ăi tiː bay ອະທີບາຍ
	(occur) v. bpăgŏːt keu:n ປະກົດຂຶ້ນ		(rationalize) v. si chaang ຊີ້ແຈງ
exit	n. tang ohk ທາງອອກ		
	v. ohk bpay: ອອກໄປ	explanation	n. kaĭm ăː tiː bay ຄຳ ອະທີບາຍ
expand	v. kăi nyăy ohk ຂຍາຍອອກ		n. kaĭm si chaang ຄຳຊີ້ແຈງ
expect	v. kat may ຄາດໝາຍ		
expedition	(group) n.kăː năː dern tang hă koh mŭn ຄນະເດີນທາງຫາຂໍ້ມູນ	explode	v. laː bert ລະເບີດ
	(event) n. gan dern tang ko:n ha ການເດີນທາງຄມຫາ	exploit	n. het gaĭn dan ເຫດກັນ ດານ
expel	v. kăip lăy bpay: ຂັບ ໄລ່ໄປ		v. săy: bpaː nyŏt suăn dtua ໃຊ້ປະໂຍດສ່ວມຕົວ
expend	v. săy: gaĭm lăing lĕu ngerːn ໃຊ້ກຳລັງທີ່ເງີນ	explore	(unknown) v. koːn kwă ຄົນຄວ້າ
expense	(action) n. gan chăy ການຈ່າຍ		(known) v. săim lŭat ສຳ ລ້ວດສຳຣວດ
	(result) n. lăy chăy ລາຍຈ່າຍ	export	n. gan soĭng siĭn kaĭ ohk ການສົ່ງສິນຄ້າອອກ
expensive	adj. paăng ແພງ		v. soːng siĭn kaĭ ohk ສົ່ງສິນຄ້າອອກ
experience	v. bpaː sŏːp ປະສົບ n. gan bpaː sŏːp ການ ປະສົບ	expose	(people) v. bpert pĕry ເປີດເຜີຍ
experiment	n. gan toːt lohng ການທົດ ລອງ		(film) v. bpert fiĭm hup ເປີມຟີມຮູບ
expert	adj. pu siăw săn ຜູ້ຊ່ຽວຊານ	express	n. loĭt făy: duan ຣົດໄຟ ດ່ວນ
expire	(time limit) v. mŏːt gaĭm noːt ໝົດກຳນົດ		(fast) adj. duan ດ່ວນ
			(definite) adj. kaːk naa, saːt chem ຄັກແໜ່, ວັດແຈມ
		expression	(words) n.kwam wow:, sam nuan ຄວາມເວົ້າ, ສຳນວນ

	(face) n. gan săː daang
	ການສະແຫງສີໜ້າ
exquisite	adj. laː iat laː oh
	ຣະຮງກຣະອ່
extend	(thing) v. paa ohk ແຜ່ອອກ
	(time) v. dtoh ohk ຕໍ່ອອກ
extent	(area) n. saː tan ti ti
	guang ohk ສະຖານທີ່ ທີ່ກວ້າງອອກ
	(limit) kohp keːt ຂອບເຂດ
extinguish	(turn off) v. moht ມອດ
	(put out) v. daːp loːng
	ດັບລົງ
extinguisher n. keuang moht fayː ເຄື່ອງ
	ມອດໄຟ
extra	adj. perm ເພີ່ມ
extracurricular adj. laːk sut perm ຫຼັກ
	ສູດເພີ່ມ
extraordinary adj. aiːt saː chaːn ອັສຈັນ
exterior	adj. tang nohk ທາງນອກ
external	adj. yu nohk ຢູ່ນອກ
extinct	adj. moht ມອດ
extract	v. owː ohk ເອົາອອກ
	n. kohng ti ohk ຂອງທີ່ອອກ
extravagance n. kwam fum feuay ຄວາມຟຸມ
	ເຟືອຍ
extreme	(the end) adj. suːt tay
	ສຸດທ້າຍ
	(situation) n. kaːp kaːn
	ຂັບຂັນ

extremely	adv. yang suŋ suːt, dteːm
	ti ຢ່າງສູງສຸດ, ເຕັມທີ
extremist	n. pu ti maik heːt huːn
	haang ຜູ້ທີ່ມີກເຣັດຮຸນແຮງ
eye	n. dta ຕາ
eyeball	n. huay dta ໝ້ວຍຕາ
eyebrow	n. kiw ຄິ້ວ
eyelash	n. koːn dta ຂົນຕາ
eyelid	n. naːng dta ໜັງຕາ

F

fable	(legend) n. ni tan ມີທານ
	(modern) n. niː nyay
	ນິຍາຍ
fabric	n. paan paː ແຜ່ນຜ້າ
fabricate	v. sang keuːn ສ້າງຂຶ້ນ
face	v. su na ສູໜ້າ n. na ໜ້າ
facility	n. kwam saː duak
	ຄວາມສະດວກ
fact	n. kwam chiːng ຄວາມ ຈິງ
faction	n. paːk puak ພັກພວກ
factor	n. suan, dtua bpaː gohp
	ສ່ວນ, ຕົວປະກອບ
	v. baang bpeːn suan ແບ່ງ
	ເປັນສ່ວນ
factory	n. hong ngan ໂຮງງານ
faculty	(staff) n. kaː naː a chan
	ຄະນະອາຈານ
	(ability) n. kuːn naː wuːt
	tiː ຄຸນນະອຸດທິ

fade	(color) v. dtay sĭ ຕາຍສີ
	(diminish) v. hay bpay:
	ຫາຍໄປ
fahrenheit	$(F° = 9/5C° + 3\measuredangle)$ n. gan
	taak a gat ການແທກອາກາດ
fail	(exam) v. dtoːk ຕົກ
	(task) v. boh saːm leːt
	ບໍສຳເຣັດ
faint	v. bpeːn loːm ເປັນລົມ
	v. huː seuːk wiːn wian ຮູ້
	ສຶກວິນວຽນ
fair	(festival) n. dtaː laːt naːt ຕລາດນັດ
	(beauty) n. choːp ngam
	ຈົບງາມ
	(reasonable) adj. nyuː dtiː taːm ຢຸຕິທຳ
fairly	(almost) adv. geuap ເກືອບ
	(reasonable) adj. yang nyuːt dtiː taːm ຢ່າງຢຸຕິ ທຳ
fairy	(god) n. te waː da ເທວະດາ
	(queer) n. gaː teːy ກະເທີຍ
faith	(trust) n. kwam waːy: chay: ຄວາມໄວ້ໃຈ
	(believe) n. kwam seua ຄວາມເຊື່ອ
faithful	n. puak teu sat saː naː ພວກ ຕືສາສນາ
	adj. saːt seu ສັດຊື່
fall	(action) n. gan dtoːk ການ ຕົກ
	(season) n. lʉ́ː duː bay: mai loːn ຣະດູໃບໄມ້ຫຼົ້ນ
fall asleep	nohn laːp bpay: ນອນລັບໄປ
fall through	(hole) dtoːk kuːm ຕົກຂຸມ
	(fail to happen) boh daːy: gert keuːn ບໍ່ໄດ້ເກີດຂຶ້ນ
false	(wrong) adj. piːt ຜິດ
	(untrue) boh maan taː ບໍແມນແທ້
falter	v. laːng ie, waw: gaː dtuːk ga: dtaːk lŭːy gle, ເວົາກະຕຸກກະ ຕັກ
fame	n. seu siang ຊື່ສຽງ
familiar	adj. kuːn kery ຄຸ້ນເຄີຍ
family	n. kohp kua ຄອບຄົວ
famine	n. kwam oːt yak ຄວາມ ອົດຢາກ
famous	adj. mi seu siang ມີຊື່ ສຽງ
fan	v. paːt loːm ພັດລົມ
	(motor) n. bay: paːt loːm ໃບພັດລົມ (hand) n. wĭ ວີ
fancy	adj. opa: laːt ປະຫຼາດ
	(desire) n. kwam bpaː soːng ຄວາມປະສົງ
fantastic	adj. yang boh naː seua ຢ່າງ ບໍ່ຫນ້າເຊື່ອ
far	(farther, farthest) adj. gay: ໄກ

far and wide yu bonn quang kuang ผู้ยอม
ทอางขอาง

fare n. ka dern tang ค่าเดินทาง
v. ha ma day: ทามาได

farewell n. gan la chak ทามลาจาท
intrj. bpay: di ไปดี

farm n. hay na ไร่นา
v. he:t na เริ็ดนา

farmer n. sow na, poh na
ชาวนา, ผมนา

farmhouse n. tiang na ที่งนา

farming n. gan he:t hay: he:t na
ทามเริ็ดไร่เริ็ดนา

farmland n. to:ing na ที่งนา

farsighted n. say dta gay: สายตาไท

farther adv. gay: ohk bpay: ไท
99ทไป

fascinate (beauty) v. bpe:n sa: ne
เป็นสเน

(interest) v. cha:p chay:
จับใจ

fascinating adj. yang suan hay: ha:k
ย่างจวมใหรัท

fashion v. he:t bpe:n hup เริ็ด
เป็นรูบ

(style) n. baap แบบ

fast adj. way: ไว
v. o:t a han งิดงาทาม

fasten (tie to) v. puk ผูท
(tie up) v. ma:t d t i:t มัดติด

fat (buffalo) n. kay: ไข
(pig or animal) n. na:m
ma:n น้ำมัน
(person or animal) adj.
pi ปิ
(person) adj. dtuy ตุ้ย

fatal (accident) adj. koh: hay
เคาะร้าย
(bad luck) adj. sok hay
โชทร้าย

fate n. sok sa dta โชทชะตา

father (hereditary) n. พ
(honorable) n. nya poh ยาผ
(religious) n. ku:n poh
คุนผ

father-in-law n. poh tow: ผ่เถ้า

fatherly adj. he:t meuan poh เริ็ด
เหิ็อนผ

fatigue n. kwam meuay คอามเมื่อย

fatten v. he:t hay: pi keu:n เริ็ด
ใหผิ่ชิ้ม

fault n. kwam pi:t คอามผิด

favor n. kwam ga: lu: na คอาม
ทะธ มา
v. kow: kang เข้าข้าง

favorable adj. a:m nuay, moh:
อำนอย, เพาะ

favorite adj. ti ma:k lay ti su:t
ที่มัทๆายที่สุด

fawn n. luk guang ลูททอาง

v. lia: (na) kaang

(เลี้ย (ผา) แคาง

fear   v. he:t hay: yan เธ็ด ให้ย้าน

n. kwam yan ความย้าน

feast   n. gan su:m kow: การ

ชุมเຊ็า

(people) v. su:m kow:

ชุมเຊ็า

(animal) v. su:m gi:n

ชุมกิน

feat   n. gan ga: ta:m yang ke:ng

ການກະທำຢ่าງເກ็ງ

feather   (body) n. ko:n no:k ຂນນົກ

(wing) n. bpik ปีก

v. say: ko:n ใส่ขน

feature   v. he:t hay: sa:m ka:n ti

su:t เธ็ดให้สำคัมທີ่สุด

n. na dta ພາຕາ

February   n. deuan gu:m pa (ເດືອນ

ກຸມພາ

fed up   beua laa: mo ho (ເບື່ອແລະ

ໂມໂຫ

federal   adj. sa: ha: pa:n สะຫະ

ພັນ

fee   n. nge:rn ka he:t wiak

ເງິນค่าเธ็ดວຽກ

feeble   adj. ohn pia ອ່ອນເพ้ย

feed   n. a han sa:t ອາທານສັດ

(animal) v. liang ล้ຽງ

(baby) v. bpohn ປ້ອນ

feed grinders   n. keuang bo:t a han sa:t

ເครื่องบิดอาทานสัด

feel   n. gan lup ka:m การลูบคำ

(emotion) v. hu seu:k

ธู้สึก

(touch) v. lup ลูบ

feel for   he:n chay: เທ็นใจ

feel like   yak ga: ta:m ຢາກກະທำ

feeling   n. kwam hu seu:k ความ

ธู้สึก

fell   (pp. fall) v. dta:t hay: ล้ม

lo:m ຕົກໃຫลม

fellow   n. pa:k puak ພัກພວກ

fellow student   n. peuan na:k hian

ເพื่อนมัทธุม

female   adj. pet nyi:ng (ເພດຍิ่ง

n. maa nyi:ng (ແມ່ຍิ่ง

feminine   adj. pet maa (ເພດແม่

fence   v. ohm 99ม

n. hua ธอ

fend   (push away) v. nyu ohk

ຢ99ກ

(be independent) v. pe:rng

dto:n eng (ผิ่งตินเอง

fern   n. dto:n pa:k gut ต้นผัก

ກูด

ferry   v. dtang duay heua

ຕ่າງด้อยເຮือ

n. heua ba:k (ເຮือบัท

fertile	(animals) adj. soˋm buˋn ສົມບູນ		fifties	n. naˇy: bpi neuˋ:ng paˆ:n goˆw: hoy haˆ siˋ:p ha haˇ siˋ:p goˆw: ໃນ ໑໙໕໐-໕໙
	(soil) adj. uˋ: doˋm ອຸດົມ			
festival	n. buˋn ບຸນ		fiftieth	(50th) adj. tiˋ haˇ siˋ:p tiˆ ທ²າສິບ
festive	n. laˇ leˋring ລ່າເລີງ			
fetch	v. bpay: haˆ:p maˆ ໄປຮັບມາ		fifty	(50) adj. haˇ siˋ:p ຫ້າສິບ
feud	v. taˇ: loh: wiˋ: waˇt ທະ ເລາະວິວາດ		fig	n. maˋk deuˋa ໝາກເດື່ອ
	n. gaˋn taˇ: loh: wiˋ: waˇt ການທະເລາະວິວາດ		fight	n. gaˋn choˋm dtiˋ ການໂຈມຕີ
				(battle) v. dtoˋh suˋ ຕໍ່ສູ້
				(individual) v. dtiˋ ຕີ
fever	n. kay: ໄຂ້		figure	(think) v. kiˋ:t waˇ ຄິດວ່າ
few	adj. leˋ:k noy ເລັກນ້ອຍ			(math) v. heˋ:t leˋk ເຮັດ ເລກ
	n. suˋan noy ສ່ວນນ້ອຍ			(body) n. huˋp hang ຮູບຮ່າງ
few and far between ha nˇyak ຫາຍາກ				(math) n. leˋk ເລກ
fiber	n. seˋ:n ເສັ້ນ		figure on	waˋ:ng pering ຫວັງເພິ່ງ
fiction	(story) n. leuˋang an leˋ:n ເລື່ອງອ່ານຫຼິ້ນ		figure out	(solve) gaˋa kay: baˋ:n haˇ day: ແກ້ໄຂບັນຫາໄດ້
	(make-believe) n. leuˋang dtaˋang keuˋ:n ເລື່ອງແຕ່ງຂຶ້ນ			(discover) keuˋ:t ohk day: ຄິດອອກໄດ້
field	(farm) n. toˋ:ng ທົ່ງ		figure up	lay: soˋm gaˋ:n ໄລ່ສົມກັນ
	(playing) n. saˇ: naˇm ສນາມ		file	(tool) n. dtaˇ: bay: ຕະໄບ
	(way or course) n. dern ເດີນ			(to rub) v. tuˋ dtaˇ: bay: ຖູ ຕະໄບ
fiend	n. koˋ:n pi, ki (goˋhp, yaˇ ...) ຄົນຜີ, ຂ(ກອບ, ຢາ...)			(arrange) v. geˋ:p way: ເກັບ ໄວ້
fierce	adj. taˇ luˋ:n ທາລຸນ			(catalog) n. boˋhn mian ek gaˇ: saˇn ບ່ອນມ້ຽນເອກະສານ
fifteen	(15) adj. siˋ:p ha ສິບຫ້າ			
fifth	(5th) adj. tiˋ haˇ ທີຫ້າ			(row) n. taaw ແຖວ

fill	v. heˇt hayː dteːm ເຮັດໃຫ້ ເຕັມ	finger	v. kaːm beriːng ຄ້ຳເບີ້ງ
	n. nŏn diːn, diːn toːm ໂນມຕີມ, ຕີນຕົມ		n. niːw meu ນີ້ວມື
fill in	owː dteum sayː bohn wăng ເອົາຕິມໃສ່ບ່ອນຫວ່າງ	fingernail	n. leːp meu ເລັບມື
		finish	v. moˇt laaw ໝົດແລ້ວ
fill out	kian sayː hayː laaw ຂຽນ ໃສ່ໃຫ້ແລ້ວ		n. gaˇn saˇm leːt, hohp suːt tăy ການສຳເລັດ, ຮອບສຸດທ້າຍ
fill up	owː sayː hayː dteːm moˇt ເອົາໃສ່ໃຫ້ເຕັມໝົດ	fir	n. dtoːn bɔaak ຕົ້ນແປກ (ຊະນິດໜຶ່ງ)
filling station	n. bpohm năːm măːn ປ້ຳນ້ຳມັນ	fire	(shoot) v. nyiːng ຍິງ
film	v. tay naːng ຖ່າຍໜັງ		(job) v. layː ohk gaˇn ໄລ່ອອກການ n. fayː ໄຟ
	(camera) n. fiːm hŭp ຟິມຮູບ	fireboat	n. heua daˇyp periːng ເຮືອດັບເພີ້ງ
	(layer) n. piu naːng ຜິວໜັງ		
filter	n. keuang dtohng ເຄື່ອງ	fire department	n. paˇː naak daˇyp periːng ຜແມກດັບເພີ້ງ
	v. dtohng ຕອງ		
filth	n. kohng sŏ kŏk ຂອງໂສ້ໂຄກ	fire engine	n. loˇːt daˇyp periːng ຣົດ ດັບເພີ້ງ
final	adj. suˇːt tay ສຸດທ້າຍ	firefly	n. naˇːng hiˇːng hoy ແມງ ຫິ່ງຫ້ອຍ
finally	adv. poˇːn suˇːt tay ຜົມ ສຸດທ້າຍ		
finance	n. gaˇn kaiːng ການຄັງ	fireman	n. koˇn daˇyp periːng ຄົນ ດັບເພີ້ງ
	v. hayː ngerːn teuːn ໃຫ້ເງິນທຶນ	fireplace	n. ki fayː ຄີໄຟ
find	(meet) v. poːp poh ພົບຜໍ້		(stove) n. dtowː fayː ເຕົາໄຟ
	(look for) v. sohk ຊອກ	firewood	n. feun ຟືນ
find out	dăy kŭ ໄດ້ຮູ້	fireworks	n. dohk fayː ດອກໄຟ
fine	v. bpaːp mayː ປັບໄໝ	firm	adj. naan naˇ ແໜ້ນໜາ
	n. choːp di ຈົບດີ		n. boh liˇ săːt gan ka ບໍລິສັດການຄ້າ
	adj. laː iat ລະອຽດ	first	adj. ti neuːng ທີໜຶ່ງ

fish	(net) v. hǎ bpa ทาปา	flash	n. saang fay: saín แสงไฟลั่ม
	(pole) v. dteu:k bpa ติกปา		v. sohng saang sa: wang สอมแสงสว่าง
	n. bpa ปา		
fisherman	n. ko:n hǎ bpa คิมทาปา	flat	n. siang dta:m สຽງต่ำ
fishhook	n. be:t เบ็ด		adj. piang, bpaa ผ่ຽ, แป
fishing	n. gan hǎ bpa ภามทาปา	flatten	v. he:t hay: piang เຮัด ใຫ້ผຽง
fist	n. ga:m bpa:n ກำปั้ม	flatter	v. nyohng nyoh ຍ9ງຍ່
fit	(make fit) v. he:t hay: moh: so:m เຮัดใຫ້เໝาะสົມ	flavor	n. lo:t sat ລົດຊາດ
	(fit into) v. ow: say: เ9ใส		v. he:t hay: mi lo:t sat เຮັດใຫ້มีລົດຊາດ
	(try on) v. lohng ລ9ງ		
	(fit exactly) v. he:t hay: poh di เຮັດใຫ້ผົດดิ	flax	n. ato:n opoh, opan ต็ນ, ปาม
five	(5) hǎ ຫ້າ (๕)	flee	v. pay ni ຜ່າຍໜิ
flag	v. gwaang tuing แกว่งทุງ	fleece	v. dta:t ko:n gaa: ตัด2ิมเกะ
	n. tuing ทุງ		n. ko:n gaa: 2ิมเกะ
flagpole	(small) la:k tuing ຫຼักทุງ	fleet	n. gohng heua ກ9ງเຮือ
	(big) n. sow: tuing เสົาทุງ	flexible	(thing) adj. ti kong ngoh day: ทีເຄ้วๆได้
flake	n. sa: ge:t สะເກັດ		(person) adj. da:t ngay ดัดๆาย
flame	n. bpaaw fay: แปอไฟ		
flank	v. bpay: tang kang ไປ ທາງ2าງ	flicker	v. he:t wa:p waap เຮັดอับแอบ
	n. kang 2าງ		
flap	n. pa hip, opa:k ผ่าทิบ, ปัก	flier	(pilot) n. na:k bi:n มักบิม
	v. bpiw sa: ba:t ປ໌วสะบัด		(notice) n. ba:t ko sa: na ບັດโคสมา
flare	v. bpe:n bpaaw fay: เບ້มแปอ ไฟ	flight	n. gan bi:n ภามบิม

fling	n. gan lε̌ lerng ภามล่า เลิ๋ง v. nyon โยน	flourish	n. gán uǎt ภามอวด v. maːng kaːng มั่งคั่ง
flint	n. hǐːn leːk fǎyː หินเหล็ก ไฟ	flow	v. lǎyː ไหล n. bpaaw naːm แขวงน้ำ
flip	v. dti laːng ga ตีลังกา	flower	n. dòhk máyː ดอกไม้ v. baːn ขาน
flirt	n. kòːn chowː sùː คิมเจ้าชู้ v. heːt chowː sùː เรัดเจ้า ชู้	flower bed	n. nǎn dòhk máyː พาม ดอกไม้
flit	v. biːn wayː ขิมไว	flu	n. kǎyː wàtː nyàyː ไขหวัดใหย
float	n. tuːn hěːa หุ่นเรือ v. fu ฝู	fluently	adv. koːn dtòːk gan luk chǎng คิมตกภาม, ลูกจาๆ
flock	v. bpayː bpeːn mǔ ไปเป็นฝู่ n. mǔ ฝู	fluid	n. kohng laaw ๅ9ๅเฑๅ
flood	n. náːm tuǎm น้ำถ่วม v. tuǎm ถ่วม	flunk	v. sohp dtòːk สอบตก
floor	(astonish) v. heːt hǎyː dtòːk chǎyː เรัดใหตกใจ (accelerate) v. leːng lóːt n. pěːn พื้น เลั่งลิต	flunkey	n. kòːn dtòːk gan คิมตก ภาม
		flush	(toilet) v. lang wíːt ล้างวิด (scare out) v. lǎyː ohk nòːk ไล่ออกนัก
floor plan	n. paan paːng hěːan แผม ผังเรือน	flute	n. kuːy ขุย
floor show	n. flòh sǒ ฟรโช n. gán sǎː dáːng yù bǎ ภามสะแคงยู่ขๅ	flutter	n. dtòːp bpìk ติยปีก
		fly	v. biːn ขิม n. mǎːng wǎːn แมๆวัม
florist	n. kòːn kǎyː dòhk máyː คิม ขายดอกไม้	flying	n. gán biːn ภามขิม (frequency modulation) n. kwam tì kohng kěːn wíːt tàː nyǔ ความฉี่ๅๅคั่มอิทะยุ
flour	v. kowː bpaang เข้าแป้ง	foam	n. fohng ฝๆ v. heːt bpeːn fohng เรัดเป็น fohng ฝๆ

foam rubber	n. yáng fõhng naím ຢາງ ຟອງນ້ຳ
focus	v. he:t hay: chãang bohn chù:t ເຮັດໃຫ້ແຈ້ງບົນຈຸດ n. chù:t kõhng saãng ຈຸດຂອງແສງ
foe	n. sai:t dtu ສັດຕຣູ
fog	v. he:t hay: mũa ເຮັດໃຫ້ມົວ n. naím mohk ນ້ຳໝອກ
foggy	adj. dte:m bpay: dúay mõhk ເຕັມໄປດ້ວຍໝອກ
foil	n. fai:n dap ຟັນດາບ n. paan bãng bãng ແຜ່ນບາງ ໆ v. sohn go:n ຊ້ອນກົນ
foist	v. ow! nya:t hay: ເອົາຍັດໃຫ້
fold	n. hõy pai:p ຮອຍພັບ v. pãi:p ພັບ
foliage	n. bay: mãy tũa bpay ໃບໄມ້ທວໄປ
folk	n. sów ban ຊາວບ້ານ
folksong	(north Laos) n. la:m kai:p ລຳ ຂັບ (south Laos) la:m lã ລຳລ່
follow	v. dti:t dtam ຕິດຕາມ
follower	(admirer) n. pũ sa: nai:p sã: nũn ຜູ້ສມັຍສມູນ (supporter) n. pũ nũn pũ la:hng ຜູ້ໜູນຜູ້ (crony) n. boh li: wãn ບໍລິວານ
	(religious) n. sã wo:k ສາວົກ
following	n. gan dtiì:t dtam ການຕິດຕາມ adj. dai:ng dtoh bpay: ni ດັ່ງຕໍໄປນີ້
folly	n. kwam bã ຄວາມບ້າ
fond	adj. ha:k hohm, ma:k ຮັກຫອມ, ມັກ
food	n. a han ອາຫານ
fool	v. lohk ຫຼອກ n. ko:n ngo ຄົນໂງ່
April Fool's Day	n. wãn ti nue:ng a wai: li:n wãn ti tuì:k ko:n wow: yohk gai:n day: ອັນທີໜຶ່ງ ອາວລິນ, ອັນທີ່ທຸກຄົນເວົ້າ ຢອກກັນໄດ້
foolish	adj. ngo cha ໂງ່ຈາ
foot	(pl. feet) n. dtin ຕີນ v. bpe:n nger:n ເປັນເງິນ
football	(ball) n. mak ban ໝາກ ບານ (American) n. mak ban a: me li: gai:n keu hup kay: ໝາກບານອະເມຣິກັນຄື ຮຸບໄຂ່ (soccer) n. mak ban sa go:n hup mo:n ໝາກບານສາກົນຮຸບ ມົນ
foothills	n. nern dtin pu kow: ເນີນຕີນ ພູເຂົາ

footman	n. ko:n say: ຄົນໃຊ້
footprint	(anyone) n. hoy dtin ຮອຍຕີນ
	(Buddha) n. hoy pa: bat ຮອຍພະບາດ
for	(possessive) prep. peua ເພື່ອ
	prep. sam la:p ສຳຫຼັບ
	(to) prep. bpay: nyaing ໄປຍັງ
	(support) prep. sa: na:p sa: nun ສະໜັບສະໜຸນ
for good	(id.) lery ເລີຍ
forbid	v. ham ຫ້າມ
foreboding	n. sain nyan ສັນຍານ
force	v. ba:ng ka:p ບັງຄັບ
	n. ga:m lang ກຳລັງ
forcibly	adv. doy say: ga:m la:ng ໂດຍໃຊ້ກຳລັງ
ford	v. nyang kam na:m ຍ່າງຂ້າມນ້ຳ
	n. nyi hoh lo:t si me li: ga:n ຢູ່ຮົດຂະເມຣິກັນ
fore	adj. yu na ຢູ່ໜ້າ
forehead	n. na pak ໜ້າຜາກ
foreign	adj. dtang dow ຕ່າງ ຖາວ
foreigner	n. sow dtang bpa: tet ຊາວຕ່າງປະເທດ
foremost	adj. de:n ti su:t ເດັ່ນ ທີ່ສຸດ
foresee	n. he:n gohn ເຫັນກ່ອນ
	he:n luang na ເຫັນລ່ວງໜ້າ
	hu luang na ຮູ້ລ່ວງໜ້າ
forest	n. bpa may: ປ່າໄມ້
forewarn	v. dteuan luang na ເຕືອນ ລ່ວງໜ້າ
forge	n. hong dti le:k ໂຮງ ຕີເຫຼັກ
	(metal) v. dti le:k ຕີເຫຼັກ
	(journey) v. dern sa sa ເດີນຊ້າ ໆ
forget	v. leum ລືມ
forgetful	adj. ti ma:k leum ທີ່ມັກ ລືມ
	(childish) ki leum ຂີ້ລືມ
forgive	v. nyo:k tot ຍົກໂທດ
fork	v. taeng duay sohm ແທງ ດ້ວຍສ້ອມ
	(road) n. tang sam nyaak ທາງສາມແຍກ
	(utensil) n. sohm ສ້ອມ
form	v. bpa: gohp keu:n ປະກອບຂຶ້ນ
	(shape) n. hup hang ຮູບຮ່າງ
	(school) n. sa:n ຊັ້ນ
formal	(event) adj. bpe:n tang gan ເປັນທາງການ

	(action) adj. bpe'n la: biap ເປັນລະບຽບ
	n. keuang pu nyï:ng su:t nyay: ເຄື່ອງຜູ້ຍິງຊຸດໃຫຍ່
formation	n. gan bpe:n hup hang ການເປັນຮູບຮ່າງ
former	adj. a dït 9ะถิด
formidable	adj. ga geng kam ໜ້າ ເກງຂາມ
formula	n. la:k su't ຫຼັກສຸດ
formulate	v. nyeun ka:m hong ຍືນຄ່າຮ້ອງ
fort	n. kay ta: han ti mi ga:m paang ຄ່າຍທະຫານທີ່ມີກໍາແພງ
forth	adj. ohk ma 99ກມາ
forties	n. nay: bpi pain gow: hoy si si:p ha si si:p gow: ໃນປີ ໑໙໔໐-໑໙໔໙
fortify	v. he't opohm ເຮັດປ້ອມ
fortnight	n. sohng a dti:t ສອງອາ ທິດ
fortunate	adj. sok di ໂຊກດີ
fortune	n. sok wat sa: na ໂຊກວາສນາ
forty	(40) adj. si si:p ສີ່ສິບ
forward	adv. bpay: tang na ໄປທາງໜ້າ
	v. so:ng dtoh ສົ່ງຕໍ່
foundation	(organization) n. mun ni: ti: ມຸນນິທິ
	(building) n. hak tan ຮາກຖານ
fountain	n. na:m pu: ບໍ້ນໍ້
four	(4) adj. si ສີ່ (໔)
fourscore	n. bpaat si:p ແປດສິບ
fourteen	(14) adj. si:p si ສິບສີ່
freeze	(cold) v. saa hay: ye:n ແອ່ໃຫ້ເຢັນ
	(fear) v. yeun ga: dang ຢືນກະດ້າງ
freezing	adj. ye:n lay ເປັນກາຍ
freight car	n. dtu lo:t fay: ba:n tu:k si:n ka ຕູ້ຣົດໄຟບັນທຸກ ສິນຄ້າ
freighter	n. ga:m bpain ba:n tu:k si:n ka ກໍາປັ່ນບັນທຸກສິນຄ້າ
French	adj. fla:ng ຝຣັ່ງ
french horn	n. gaa wo:ng sa: ni:t neu:ng ແກວົງສັນິດໜຶ່ງ
Frenchman	n. sow fla:ng set ຊາວຝຣັ່ງເສດ
frenzy	n. kwam ba ga:ng wo:n ຄວາມບ້າກັ່ງວົ້ນ
frequency	n. kwam ti ຄວາມຖີ່
	(often) n. leuay leuay ເລື້ອຍໆ
	(number of times) n. ka:ng kow ຄັ້ງຄາວ
frequent	v. yiam yam leuay leuay ຍ່ຽມຍາມເລື້ອຍໆ

fresh	(new) adj. so:t³ ສົດ
	(rude) adj. sua:² ຊົ່ວ
freshman	n. na:k³ seu:k⁴ sa² bpi² ti² neuing² ນັກສຶກສາປີທີໜຶ່ງ
fret	kwam³ mo³ ho³ ga:ng³ wo:n³ ຄວາມໂມໂຫກັງວົນ
	v. ga:ng³ wo:n³ ກັງວົນ
Friday	n. wa:n³ su:k³ ວັນສຸກ
friend	(one) n. peuan² ເພື່ອນ
	(many) n. mu² ໝູ່
	(lover) n. su² ຊູ້
friendship	n. mi:t² dta:² pap² ມິຕພາພ
fright	n. kwam³ yan⁵ ຄວາມຢ້ານ
frighten	v. he:t² hay:⁵ yan⁵ ເຮັດໃຫ້ຢ້ານ
fringe	n. nyoy⁶ pa² ຢອຍຜ້າ
frog	n. go:p³ ກົບ
frolic	v. la² le:ing³ ລ່າເລີງ
from	prep. chak², dta:a² ຈາກ, ແຕ່
from time to time	bpe:n² bang³ nyam³ ເປັນບາງຍາມ ບາງເວລາ
front	adj. na⁶ ໜ້າ
	adv. dtoh⁶ na⁶ ຕໍໜ້າ
	n. kang⁶ na⁶ ຂ້າງໜ້າ
frontier	n. ket² da:n³ ເຂດແດນ
frost	v. hu:m⁶ duay⁵ na:m⁵ goh:n⁵ ຫຸມຄວຍນ້ຳກ້ອນ
	n. na:m⁵ mo:k³ kang⁵ ນ້ຳໝອກ ຄ້າງ
frown	v. ga:n³ he:t² na⁶ nyu:ing⁵ ການເຮັດໜ້າຍຸ້ງ
	n. he:t² na² nyu:ing⁵ ເຮັດ ໜ້າຍຸ້ງ
frugal	adj. ki⁶ ti² ຂີ້ຖີ່
fruit	n. mak⁶ may⁵ ໝາກໄມ້
fry	(small fish) n. bpa² noy⁵ ti² ha² go:h² ge:ri:t² ປານ້ອຍທີ່ຫາກໍ່ເກີດ
	v. cheun³ ຈືນ
fuel	n. na:m⁵ ma:n³ seua³ pe:rng³ ນ້ຳມັນເຊື້ອເພີງ
fugitive	n. pu⁶ ni⁴ tot⁵ ຜູ້ໜີໂທດ
-ful	(change verbs and nouns of adjectives) ka:m² ti² bpia:n² gi:² li:² nya laa:² nam² hay: bpe:n kai:m ku:n nam² ຄຳທີ່ປ່ຽນກິລິຍາແລະນາມ ໃຫ້ເປັນຄຳຄຸນນາມ
full	adj. dte:m³ ເຕັມ
fully	adv. dte:m¹ ti² ເຕັມທີ່
fumble	(grope) v. ka:m² be:ng³ ຄຳເບິ່ງ
	(drop) v. lu:t³ meu³ ລຸດມື
fume	v. chay:¹ hay hay:⁵ ໃຈ ຮ້າຍໃຫ້
	n. gi:n² ay¹ ກິ່ນອາຍ
fun	n. gan¹ sa:² nu:k³ sa:³ nan³ ການສນຸກສນານ

function	(purpose) n. na ti ໜ້າທີ່
	(math) n. kwam dtoh ຄວາມ neuang ຕໍ່ເນື່ອງ
fund	v. chay nger:n teu:n ຈ່າຍ ເງິນທຶນ
	n. nger:n teu:n ເງິນທຶນ
fundamental	(principal) n. mun tan ມູນ ฐาน
	(base) n. go:k kow: ຮາກເຄົ້າ
	adj. ti bpe:n go:k kow: ທີ່ ເປັນຮາກເຄົ້າ
funeral	n. gan bpo:ng so:p ການ ປົງສົບ
funny	adj. na hua kwa:n ໜ້າ ຫົວຂວັນ
	n. leuang dta: lo:k ເຣື່ອງຕລົກ
fur	n. ko:n sa:t ຂົນສັດ
furious	adj. chay: hay ໃຈຮ້າຍ
furnace	n. dtow: pow: ເຕົາເຜົາ
furnish	(give) v. ow: hay: ເອົາໃຫ້
	(a room) v. dto:k dtaang ຕົກແຕ່ງ
furnishings	n. gan dto:k dtaang ການຕົກແຕ່ງ
furniture	n. keuang heuan ເຄື່ອງ ເຮືອນ
furrow	v. ku:t hohng ຂຸດຮ່ອງ n. hohng tay: ຮ່ອງໄຖ

further	adj. gay: gua: ໄກກວ່າ
fury	n. kwam mo ho ຄວາມໂມໂຫ
fuse	v. choht le:k ຈອດເຫຼັກ n. toh kohng ti say: la: bert ທໍຂອງທີ່ໃຊ້ລະເບີດ
fuss	v. ow: chay: ເອົາໃຈ n. gan pi:t tiang ການ ຜິດຖຽງ
fussy	adj. mua nyu:ng nam leuang le:k le:k nohy nohy ມົວຍຸ້ງກັບເຣື່ອງເຫຼັກ ໆ ນ້ອຍ ໆ
futile	adj. ti say: boh day: ທີ່ໃຊ້ບໍ່ໄດ້
future	n. a: na ko:t ອະນາຄົຕ

G

gain	v. day: /ga:m lay ໄດ້ກຳໄລ
gale	n. lo:m pa nyu: ລົມພະຍຸ
gallant	adj. ga han ກ້າຫານ adj. su: pap ສຸພາບ
gallery	n. hohng bpa: guat hup dtaam ຫ້ອງປະກວດຮູບແຕ້ມ
gallon	n. ga: long say: na:m ma:n ກະລ່ອນໃສ່ນ້ຳມັນ
gallop	v. hohp laan ຫອບແລ່ນ
gallows	n. bohn kwaan koh na:k tot ບ່ອນແຂວນຄໍນັກໂທດ
gaiety	n. kwam berk ban, kwam seun ban ຄວາມເບີກບານ, ຄວາມຊື່ນ ບານ

gamble	v. li:n gan pa: na:n ທີ່ມ ການພະນັນ n. gan pa: na:n bpa: pet neu:ng ການພະນັນປະເພດນຶ່ງ	(vapor) n. ay ti gert chak lo ha: seua pe:rng ອາຍທີ່ເກີດຈາກໂລຫະເຊື້ອ ເຜິງ
gambler	n. na:k gan pa: na:n ນັກການພະນັນ	gash	n. bat paa nyay: ບາດແຜ ໃຫຍ່ v. bat ບາດ
gambling	n. gan li:n gan pa: na:n ການຫຼີ້ນການພະນັນ		
gangster	n. ko:n a:n ta: pan ຄົນອັນຕະພານ	gasoline pump	n. cha:k sup na:m ma:n aat sa:ng say: lo:t ຈັກສູບນ້ຳມັນ ແອັດຊັງໃສ່ລົດ
gap	n. sohng wang ຊ່ອງວ່າງ		
garage	n. u lo:t ອູ່ລົດ	gasp	n. gan ha:n chay: hohp ການຫັນໃຈຫອບ
garb	n. keuang dtaang dto ເຄື່ອງແຕ່ງໂຕ		ha:n chay: hohp ຫັນໃຈຫອບ
garbage	n. ki nyeua ຂີ້ເຫຍື່ອ	gas station	n. bpohm na:m ma:n ປ໊ອມນ້ຳ ມັນ
garden	v. he:t suan ເຮັດສວນ n. suan ສວນ		
gardener	n. ko:n he:t suan ຄົນເຮັດສວນ	gate	n. bpa: dtu ປະຕູ
		gather	v. ge:p gohng way ເກັບ ກອງໄວ້
gardening	n. gan he:t suan ການເຮັດສວນ		
		gay	adj. muan seun ມ່ວນຊື່ນ
garden shears	n. mit dta:t bay: may: ມີດຕັດໃບໄມ້	gaze	n. gan bering ການເບິ່ງ v. chohng bering ຈ້ອງເບິ່ງ
garlic	n. hua pa:k tiam ຫົວຜັກທຽມ	gear	n. gia lo:t ເກັຽລົດ
garment	n. keuang nu:ng ເຄື່ອງນຸ່ງ	gearbox	n. ga: bpu:k gia ກະປຸກເກັຽ
		geese	n. han lay dtua ຫ່ານຫຼາຍ ໂຕ
garrison	n. kay ta: han ຄ້າຍທະຫານ	gem	n. pe:t poy ເພັດພອຍ
gas	(gasoline) n. na:m ma:n aat sa:ng ນ້ຳມັນແອັດຊັງ		v. e duay pe:t poy ເອດ້ວຍເພັດພອຍ
		gender	n. pet ເພດ

general	adj. tuā tuā bpay: ທົ່ວໆໄປ	
	n. nay po:p ນາຍພົມ	
generally	adv. doy tuā bpay:	
	ໂດຍທົ່ວໄປ	
	(ordinary) adv. dtam taim	
	ma: da ຕາມທັມມະດາ	
general practitioner	n. nay moh ນາຍ ໝໍ	
generation	n. sua hu:n ຊົວຣຸ່ນ	
generous	adj. chay: guang kuang	
	ໃຈກວ້າງຂວາງ	
genius	n. ko:n sa: lat lay	
	ຄົນສລາດຫຼາຍ	
	adj. sa: lat lay ສລາດຫຼາຍ	
gentle	adj. ohn wah ອ່ອນຫວານ	
gentleman	n. su: pap bu: lu:t ສຸ	
	ພາບບຸຣຸຕ	
gentlewoman	n. su: pap sa: dtri	
	ສຸພາບສັຕຣີ	
genuine	adj. kohng taa ຂອງແທ້	
	adj. sa:t seu ສັດຊື່	
geographical	adj. dtam pu mi sat	
	ຕາມພູມິສາດ	
geography	n. pu mi sat ພູມິສາດ	
germ	n. seua lok ເຊື້ອໂຣກ	
German	n. sow nyer la: ma:n	
	ຊາວເຢັງຣະມັນ	
gesture	n. gan si chaang ta ti	
	duay meu ການຊີ້ແຈງທ່າທີ່ດ້ວຍມື	
	v. si chaang duay meu ຊີ້ແຈງ	
	ດ້ວຍມື	

get	v. ow: ເອົາ	
get along	(with) id. teuk ga:n di	
	ຖືກກັນດີ	
get away	ni bpay: way: way:	
	ຫຼີໄປໄວໆ	
get back	go:p keun ma ກັບຄືນມາ	
get busy	id. dtang chay: he:t	
	wiak ຕັ້ງໃຈເຮັດວຽກ	
get by	gay bpay: doy boh hay:	
	he:n ກາຍໄປໂດຍບໍ່ໃຫ້ເຫັນ	
get dressed	id. nuing keuang ນຸ່ງເຄື່ອງ	
get even with	gaa kaan keun ແກ້ແຄນຄືນ	
get going	dtang dto:n he:t ຕັ້ງ	
	ຕົ້ນເຮັດ	
get hold of	cha:p ow: day: ຈັບເອົາໄດ້	
get in	(arrive) v. ma hoht ມາ	
	ຮອດ	
	(enter) kow: huam ເຂົາຮ່ວມ	
	(receive) day: la:p ໄດ້ຮັບ	
get in a fight	id. dti ga:n ຕີກັນ	
get off	lo:ng lo:t ລົງຣົດ	
get on	(bus) keu:n lo:t ຂຶ້ນຣົດ	
	(clothes) ow: seua say:	
	ເອົາເສື້ອໃສ່	
get on with	he:t dtoh bpay: ເຮັດຕໍ່ໄປ	
get out	(publish) pi:m ພິມ	
	(make known) bper pery	
	ເປິດເຜີຍ	
get over	sow: bpe:n ເຊົາເປັນ	

get over a cold id. sŏw: bpeːn waːt	n. yaːk ຍາກ
ເຈົ້າເປັນຫວັດ	giddy adj. găː dǐːk găː diăn
get ready chaːt chaang ຈັດແຈງ	ກະຕິກກະຕຸມ
get rid of (pests) gaːm chaːt ກຳຈັດ	gift n. kohng kwan ຂອງຂວັນ
(throw away) ow: tiːm	gigantic adj. nyaːy: pi leuːk ໃຫຍ່
ເອົາຖິ້ມ	ພິລິກ
get sick cheːp bpuay ເຈັບປ່ວຍ	giggle n. siang hua giːk giːk
get something across aː tiː bay hay:	ສຽງຫົວກິກກິກ
chaam chăang ຊະທີບາຍ	gin n. low: naaw neung
ໃຫ້ແຈ່ມແຈ້ງ	ເຫຼົາແມວນຶ່ງ
get something over with heːt hay: laaw	v. bpaːn ʔay ປິ່ນຝ້າຍ
ເຮັດໃຫ້ແລ້ວ	ginger n. kiːng ຂີງ
get through heːt laaw ເຮັດແລ້ວ	girdle v. kaːt say aaw ຂັດ
get to bpay: hŏht ໄປຮອດ	ສາຍແອວ
get together suːm nuːm gaːn ຊຸມນຸມກັນ	n. say aaw pu nyiːng
get undressed id. găa keuang, bpiăn	ສາຍແອວຜູ້ຍິງ
keuang ແກ້ເຄື່ອງ, ປ່ຽນ	girl n. pu sŏw ຜູ້ສາວ
ເຄື່ອງ	girl friend (for girl) n. peuang nyiːng
get up (from sleep) dteun nŏhn	ເພື່ອນຍິງ
ຕື່ນນອນ	(for boy) su ຊູ້
(stand up) yeun keuːn	give (gave pp. given) v. ow:
ຢືນຂຶ້ນ	hay: ເອົາໃຫ້
get well id. sŏw: kay ເຈົ້າໄຂ້	give away (distribute) ow: hay:
geyser n. naːm puː hohn ນ້ຳຜຸຮ້ອນ	ເອົາໃຫ້
ghastly adj. bpeːn dta yăn ເປັນ	(betray) haːk laːng ຫັກຫຼັງ
ຕາຢ້ານ	give back ow: sŏːng keuːn ເອົາສົ່ງຄືນ
adj. găː nyeuang ກະ	give in nyohm paa ຍອມແພ້
ເຍື່ອງ	give off sŏːng ohk ສົ່ງອອກ
ghost n. pi ຜີ	give oneself up nyohm mohp dtua
giant adj. nyaːy: luang ໃຫຍ່ຫຼວງ	ຍອມມອບຕົວ

give out	yáy hây: ปายให้	glisten	v. wáaw wów แวววาว
give rise to	heít hây: gèrt keu:n เธัดให้เกิดขึ้น	glitter	n. sáang wáaw wów แสງ แวววาว
give up	(hope) mo:t gà:m lang chay: ฯิฑทำลังใจ	globe	n. nuáy lók ฟ้อยโลก
	(give in) nyóhm paa ยอมแพ้	gloom	n. kwam meut mo:n ความ ฮิฑฮิม
glad	adj. dì chay: ดีใจ	glorious	adj. laít sà: mi ธสัฮิ
glance	(look) v. leuap dta ber:ng เหิฐดตาเยิ่ว		adj. tì mi gìat nyo:t ฑีฮิกฮิดยด
	(hit) v. dat ดาด	glory	n. kwam sà: leu teu nàm ความอำลิฮิมาม
	n. gan leuap dta ber:ng ทามเหิฐดตาเยิ่ว		n. laít sà: mi ธสัฮิ
glare	n. sáang sà: wang haang haang แสງสอ่าງแรງ ๆ	glossary	n. bpa: mian saíp ปะมอมสัย
	v. geung dta ber:ng ฮิ่ว ตาเยิ่ว	glove	n. to:ng meu ถิวฮิ
glass	n. gáaw แท้ว	glow	v. bpe:n si daang เย้มสิแดງ
glassware	n. keuang heít duáy gáaw เคิ่ว เธัดถอยแท้ว	glue	v. dtì:t gów ติดทาว n. yang gów ยาງทาว
glassy	adj. bpe:n gáaw เย้มแท้ว	glutinous	adj. niáw ฬฮิว
glaze	n. keuáp duáy gáaw เคิ่ย ถอยแท้ว v. sáy: gáaw ใส่แท้ว	glutton	n. ko:n gi:n láy คิฑฮิมฯาย
		gnaw	v. haan แฑม
gleam	n. wáaw dta แวວตา	go	(goes p. went pp. gone) v. bpay: ไป
	n. sáang sà: wang mua mua แสງสอ่าງมอ่ ๆ	go ahead	id. dta:ng dto:n heít gohn ติวตั้มเธัดท่อม
glide	n. kwam meun ความฮิฑ v. meun ฮิฑ	go back	id. ga:p keun bpay: ทัยคิฑไป
glimpse	n. gan leuap dta ber:ng ทามเหิฐดตาเยิ่ว	go for a walk	id. bpay: nyang li:n bpay: ย่าງฮิฑ

go into	kow: bpay: ເຂົ້າໄປ		goddess	n. tě wa: dá pǔ nɣíːng ເທະດາຜູ້ຍິງ
go off	(explode) laː bert ຣະເບີດ		gold	n. kaːm ຄຳ
	(depart) ohk dern tǎng 99ກ ເດີມທາງ		goldfish	n. bpa kaːm ປາຄຳ
	(happen) gert keuːn ເກີດຂຶ້ນ		gold leaf	n. kaːm bpiːw ຄຳປິວ
go on	heːt dtoh bpay: ເຣັດຕໍ່ໄປ		goldsmith	n. sand dti kaːm ຊ່າງຕີຄຳ
go on a picnic	id. bpay: giːn kow: bpa ໄປກິນເຂົ້າປ່າ		golden	adj. bepːn si kaːm ເປັນ ສີຄຳ
go out	(fire) moht ມອດ		golf	n. giː laː gohf ກິລາ ກ໊ອຟ
	(social activities) ohk bpay: ngan saːng koːm 99ກໄປງານສັງຄົມ		golfing	n. gan dti gohf ການຕີກ໊ອຟ
go over	(examine) guat beriːng ກວດເບິງ		good	adj. di ດິ
				(better) adj. di gwa ດິກວ່າ
	(repeat) heːt keuːn ik ເຣັດຄືນອີກ			(best) adj. di ti suːt ດິ ທີ່ສຸດ
	(succeed) bpeːn poːn saːm leːt ເປັນຜົນສຳເຣັດ		good-bye	n. la gohn ລາກ້ອນ
go to sleep	id. bpay: nohn ໄປນອນ		good afternoon	saː bay di (dtohn bay) ສບາຍດີ (ຕອນບ່າຍ)
go up	keuːn sung ຂຶ້ນສູງ		good evening	saː bay di (dtohn laang) ສບາຍດີ (ຕອນແລງ)
go with	(accompany) bpay: naːm gaːn ໄປນຳກັນ		good-hearted	adj. chay: gwang kwang ໃຈກວ້າງຂວາງ
	(match) teuk gaːn ຖຶກກັນ		goodness	n. kwaːm di ຄວາມດີ
go wrong	siːng ti piːt gert keuːn ສິ່ງທີ່ຜິດເກີດຂຶ້ນ		good night	la gohn (gang keun) ລາກ້ອນ (ກາງຄືນ)
going	n. gan bpay: ການໄປ		good morning	saː bay di (dtohn sowː) ສບາຍດີ (ຕອນເຊົ້າ)
going to	v. chaː siː 9ະ, ຊິ		goods	n. siːng kohng ສິ່ງຂອງ
goal	n. chuːt ti may ຈຸດທີ່ໝາຍ		goodwill	n. mayː dtri chiːt, kiːt di ໄມຕຣີຈິດ, ຄິດດີ
goat	n. baa ແບ			
god	n. te wa: da, pa: chow: ເທະດາ, ພະເຈົ້າ		goose	n. han dtua neuːng ຫ່ານໂຕໜຶ່ງ

gorge	v. gịn lăy ກິນຫຼາຍ
	n. hohm pu nŏy ຮອມພູ
gorgeous	adj. ngăm tỉ sụ:t ງາມທີ່
	ສຸດ
gorilla	n. lịng ton nyay: ລີງໂຕນໃຫຍ່
gossip	n. gặn wǒw: kw̌a:n ການ
	ເຈົ້າວ້ຽມ
	v. wǒw: kwa:n ເຈົ້າວ້ຽມ
got	(receive) pp. dǎy: lǎi:p
	ໄດ້ຮັບ
	(arrive) pp. bpay: ter:ng
	ໄປເຖິງ
govern	v. bpo:k kohng ປົກຄອງ
government	(general) n. gặn bpo:k
	kohng ການປົກຄອງ
	(state) n. la:t ta: ban
	ຣັຖບານ
governor	n. chǒw: kwaang ເຈົ້າແຂວງ
gown	n. seua ku:m ເສື້ອຄຸມ
grab	v. cha:p ຈັບ
gradual	adj. teua la: ncy ເທື່ອລະ
	ນ້ອຍ
gradually	adv. dǒy teua la: nŏy
	ໂດຍເທື່ອລະນ້ອຍ
graduate	n. pŭ dǎy: la:p bpa: li:n
	nya: ba:t ຜູ້ໄດ້ຮັບປຣິນຍະບັດ
	v. dǎy: lǎi:p bpa: li:n
	nya ໄດ້ຮັບປຣະລິນຍາ

graduation	n. gặn hǎi:p bpa: li:n nya
	ການຮັບປະຣິນຍາ
graft	n. si:n bo:n ສືບບິນ
	v. dtoh dto:n may: ຕໍ່ຕົ້ນໄມ້
grain	n. mě:t ເມັດ
grammar	n. wặy: nya: gohn ໄວຍະກອນ
granary	n. lǒw: kow: ເລົ້າເຂົ້າ
grand	adj. nyay: ໃຫຍ່
grandchild	n. lǎn ຫຼານ
granddaughter	n. lǎn sǒw ຫຼານສາວ
grandfather	(father's father) n. bpu
	ປູ່
	(mother's father) n. poh
	tow: ພໍ່ເຖົ້າ
grandmother	(father's mother) n. nya
	ຍ່າ
	(mother's mother) n. mǎa
	tow: ແມ່ເຖົ້າ
grandparent	(father's parents) n. bpu
	nya ປູ່ຍ່າ
	(mother's parents) poh tow:
	mǎa tow: ພໍ່ເຖົ້າ ແມ່ເຖົ້າ
grandson	n. lǎn sǎy ຫຼານຊາຍ
grange	n. hay: na suǎn ໄຮ່ນາສວນ
granite	n. hin kaang ຫິນແຂງ
grant	n. oia liang ເບ້ຽລ້ຽງ
	v. ow: hǎy: ເອົາໃຫ້
grape	n. mǎk lǎa saǎng ໝາກແຣະແຊງ
grapefruit	n. mǎk giǎng nyǎy: ໝາກກ້ຽງໃຫຍ່

grasp	n. gan cháːp ການຈັບ	greatness	n. kwam bpeːn nyày: ຄວາມ
	v. chàːp ຈັບ		ເປັນໃຫຍ່
grass	n. nya ຫຍ້າ		n. kwam sǎ lěu ຄວາມຍຸ່ງລີ
grasshopper	n. dtàːk gǎː dtaan ຕັກແຕນ	greed	n. kwam lop mǎk ຄວາມໂລບ
grassy	adj. dteːm duay nya ເຕັມ		ມາກ
	ດ້ວຍຫຍ້າ	Greek	n. sǒw grìk ຊາວກຣິກ
grateful	adj. hu buːn kuːn ຮູ້ບຸນຄຸນ	green	adj. sǐ kiaw ສີຂຽວ
gratify	v. heːt hay: poh chǎy:	greet	(bow, curtsy) v. kaːm naːp
	ເຮັດໃຫ້ພໍໃຈ		ຄຳນັບ
gratitude	n. kwam hu buːn kuːn ຄວາມ		(entertain) dtohn laːp ຕ້ອນ
	ຮູ້ບຸນຄຸນ		ຮັບ
grave	(tomb) n. luːm soːp ຫຸມສົບ	greeting	n. gan kaːm naːp ການຄຳນັບ
	(serious) adj. keng kiat		(respect) n. gǎn sǎː daang
	ເຄັ່ງຄຽດ		kuam kǒw: lǒːːp
gravel	n. hin haa ຫິນແຫ່		ການສະແດງຄວາມເຄົາລົບ
gravity	(trouble) n. kuam hay haang	grey	(color) adj. sǐ ki tow:ສີຂີ້ເຖົ່າ
	ຄວາມຮ້າຍແຮງ		(unclear) adj. moːn ມົນ
	(pulling) n. kwam tuang		(grey hair) adj. poːm
	deuːng ຄວາມຖວງດຶງ		ngohk ຜົມງອກ
gravy	n. nam sin suːk ນ້ຳຊີ້ນສຸກ	grief	n. kwam sok sow: sia chay:
gray	n. sǐ tow: ສີເຖົ່າ		ຄວາມໂສກເສົ້າເສັຽໃຈ
graze	v. giːn nya ກິນຫຍ້າ	grieve	v. sok sow sia chay: ໂສກ
grease	(food) n. kay: maːn ໄຂມັນ		ເສົ້າເສັຽໃຈ
	(car) n. cha laː biː ຈາລະບີ	grill	v. bpiːng ປິ້ງ
	v. aːt cha laː biː ອັດຈາລະບີ		(smoke) v. yang ຢ່າງ
greasy	adj. bpeːn maːn, kay maːn		(bake) v. oːp ອົບ
	ເປັນມັນ (ໄຂມັນ)		(burn in fire) v. chǐ ຈີ່
great	(bid) adj. nyay: ໃຫຍ່		n. tow: fay: heːt duay leːk
	(famous) adj. nyiːng nyay:		bpeːn diw ເຕົາໄຟເຮັດດ້ວຍເຫຼັກ
	ຊື່ງໃຫຍ່		ເປັນຕິ້ວ

grim	adj. hôt hǎy ໂຫດຮ້າຍ
grin	v. nyi:ng kaāw say: ຍິ້ງແຂວ ใส
grind	(p. & pp. ground) v. mǒ ໂມ້
	(power) v. mǒ ໂມ້
	(cocoanut)v. kut ຂຸດ
grip	n. gaǐm meu ກຳມື
groan	n. gan hohng kǎng ການ ຮ້ອງຄາງ
	v. hohng kǎng ຮ້ອງຄາງ
groom	(stable) n. kǒn liǎng na ຄົນລ້ຽງມ້າ
	(wedding) n. chow: bow ເຈົ້າບ່າວ
grocer	n. poh kā kay kohng gi:n ຜ້ຄາຂາຍຂອງກິນນ້ອຍ
	nyoy
groceries	n. keuàng gi:n ຄື່ງກິນ
grocery store	n. han kay keuàng gi:n dtang dtang ຮ້ານຂາຍຂອງ ກິນ ຕ່າງໆ
groove	n. hohng ຮ້ອງ
grope	v. ngo:m ha ງົມຫາ ຈິມຕາ
gross	adj. bpa: li: mǎn ປະຣິມານ
ground	(electricity) v. say: say di:n ໃສ່ສາຍດິນ
	(airplane) v. bi:n boh day: ບິນບ່ໍໄດ້
	(earth) n. di:n ດິນ
group	n. mu muat ໝູ່ພວກ
grove	n. bpa noy ປ່າງ9ຍ
grow	(grow up) v. nyay: keu:n ໃຫຍ່ຂຶ້ນ
	(plant) v. bpuk ປູກ
growl	v. ku, cho:m ຂູ່, ຈົມ
grow up	nyay: keu:n ໃຫຍ່ຂຶ້ນ
	n. siang kǎng keu ma ສງງຄາງຄືມາ
grub	(food) n. a han 9າຫານ
	(worm) n. nohn ໜອນ
	v. ku:t ຂຸດ
grudge	n. kwàm kaǎn chay: ຄວາມແຄ້ນໃຈ
	n. kwǎm boh poh chay: ຄວາມບໍ່ພໍໃຈ
grumble	v. cho:m ຈົມ
grunt	v. he:t siang yu nay: da:ng taan ka:m wow: ເຮັດສງງຢູ່ໃນດັງ ແທນຄຳເວົ້າ
guarantee	v. ha:p bpa: ga:n ຮັບປະກັນ
	n. gan la:p bpa lohng ການຮັບຮອງ
guard	v. yu nyàm ຢູ່ຍາມ
	n. ko:n nyam ຄົນຍາມ
guess	n. gan kat ka: ne ການຄາດ ຄະເນ
	v. tuay bering ທວາຍເບິ່ງ
guest	n. kaak pu ma yam ແຂກ ຜ້ມາຢາມ

guide	v. på bpay: ผาไป	
	(person) n. ko:n nå:m tiå:w คิมนำทาง	
	(book) n. bpeum nå:m tiå:w ปั้มนำทาง	
guild	n. sa: ha: gohn สะทะภาคม v. hum duay ka หุ้มด้วยค่า	
guilt	n. kwam sa:m neu:k pi:t ความสำนึกผิด	
guilty	adj. gå: taim pi:t กะทำผิด	
guinea pig	(animal) n. nu pu:k หนูภา	
	(person) n. pu ti bpe:n keuang to:t lohng ผู้ที่เป็น เคื่องทิดลอง	
guitar	n. gi: dta, keuang do:n dti กิตา (เคื่องดิมตรี)	
gulf	(water) n. o̊w อ่าว	
	(political gap) n. kwam kat mi:t ความฃาดมิด	
gulp	v. geun leu:t กึ่มลึก n. gan geun leu:t ภามกึ่มลึก	
gum	(chewing gum) n. su wi:ng gôm ขู่วิ้งโกม	
	(teeth) n. fein kaaw เฝ้ม แฃว	
	(tree) n. yang may: ยางไม้	
gun	n. bpeun ปืน v. nyi:ng bpeun ยิงปืน	

gunpowder	n. meu bpeun พิ้ปืน	
gunsmith	n. sang he:t bpeun ฃ่าง เธ็ดปืน	
gush	v. lay: tang ohk haang ไหพุ่งออกภาแธง n. cha:m nuan ti lay: ohk haang จำนอมที่ไหออกภาแธง	
gust	n. lo:m haang bpe:n bat bat ลิมแธงเป็นบาดา	
gusty	adj. mi lo:m haang bpe:n bat bat มีลิมแธงเป็นบาดา	
gutter	n. hang li:n ธางลิม	
guy	n. pu say nu:m ผู้ฃายหนุ่ม	
guzzle	v. deu:m lay yang way: way: ดิมฑายอย่างไว ๆ	
gymnasium	n. hohng he:t gay nya: ga:m ห้องฑัดกายยะกัม	
gymnastic	adj. giaw ga:p gay nay: boh li: han ก่อฃัยภายยะ บริฑาม	

H

habit	(character) n. ni: say: มีสัย (clothing) n. keuang nu:ng เคื่องมุง	
habitant	n. lat sa: dohn ธาสดอม	
habitation	n. sa: tan ti yu สะถามที่ยู่	
haggard	adj. ta tang hiw hoy ท่าทาง ทิวโทย	

hail	n. mak he:p ผากเຫັບ
	(rain) v. mak he:p dto:k
	ผากเຫັບຕົກ
	(greet) v. hohng dtohn la:p
	ຮ້ອງຕ້ອນຮັບ
hailstone	n. mak he:p ผากเຫັບ
hailstorm	n. pa nyu: mak he:p
	พะยุผากเຫັບ
hair	(human head) n. po:m ผົມ
	(human body or animal) n.
	ko:n ຂົນ
	(pubic) n. moy ໝອຍ
haircut	n. dta:t po:m ຕັດผົม
hair dresser	n. sang dtaang po:m
	ຊ່າງແຕ່ງผົม
hair oil	n. na:m ma:n say po:m
	ນ້ำมันใສ่ผົม
hairy	(human head) adj. mi po:m
	dok มีผົมດົກ
	(animal or human body) adj.
	mi ko:n dok มีຂົນດົກ
half	n. ker:ng ເຄິ່ງ
half-breed	(human) n. luk soht ลูกຊອດ
	(animal) n. luk ker:ng
	sat ลูกເຄິ່ງຊາດ
half time	n. ker:ng we la ເຄິ່ງເວລາ
hall	(room) n. hohng gwang
	ຫ້ອງກວ້າງ
	(corridor) n. la biang
	ລະບຽງ

halt	v. yu:t ຢຸດ
ham	(meat) n. sin ka mu
	ຊີ້ນຂາໝູ
	(actor) n. ko:n sa: daang ta
	di pu nohy ຄົนສະແດງທ່າທีผู้ນ້ອຍ
ham radio	n. wi:t ta: nyu: seu san
	ek ga: so:n ວິທະຍຸສื່ສาม
	ເອกກະຊົນ
hamburger	n. kow: chi mo:n ti mi say:
	bpe:n neua ngua ເຂົ້າຈີ່ມ້ນທີ່ມີໄສ້
	ເປັນເນື້ອວົວ
hamlet	n. ban noy ບ້ານນ້ອຍ
hammer	v. dti duay kohn ຕີດ້ວຍค້อน
	n. kohn dti ค້อนตี
hamper	v. ka:t kuang ຂັດຂວາງ
	n. ga: dta nyay: กะต่าใหย่
hand	v. nyeun hay: ຢື່ນໃຫ້
	n. meu มี
hand in	ow: nyeun hay: ເອົາຢື່ນໃຫ້
handball	n. gi: la dti luk ban noy
	duay meu
	กีลาຕີລูกບ້ານນ້ອຍດ້ວຍมี
handbill	n. bay: bpi:w ໃບປิว
handcuff	n. ga:p meu ກັບมี
handfull	adj. ga:m neung ກຳນึ่ง
handicap	(general) v. he:t hyak
	ເຮັດຍາก
	(sports) v. dtoh hay: ต่ใຫ້
	n. uip bpa: sa:k ອຸປສັก
handkerchief	n. pa paa mo:n ผ้าແผ่นมิ

handle	n. dam chaːp ດ້າມຈັບ	hardware	n. keuang leːk ເຄື່ອງເຫຼັກ
	(use hands) v. chaːp dtohng ຈັບຕ້ອງ	hardware store	n. haːn kaːy keuang leːk ຮ້ານຂາຍເຄື່ອງເຫຼັກ
	(manage) v. chaːt gan ຈັດການ	hardy	adj. toːn taːn ທົນທານ
handsome	adj. ngaːm ງາມ	hare	n. gaːy dtay bpaː ກະຕ່າຍປ່າ
handwriting	n. laːy meuː ລາຍມື	harm	n. gan sia haːy ການເສັຽຫາຍ
handy	adj. saː duak di ສະດວກດີ		(objects) v. heːt haːyː ເຮັດຫາຍ sia haːy ເຮັດໃຫ້ເສັຽຫາຍ
hang	(hang on or around) v. hoːy ຫ້ອຍ		(living things) v. heːt hayː cheːp bpuat ເຮັດໃຫ້ເຈັບປວດ
	(hang down from) v. kwaan ແຂວນ		
	(clothes) v. dtak ຕາກ	harmful	(dangerous) adj. aːn dtaː laˇy ອັນຕະລາຍ
	(person) v. kwaan koh ແຂວນຄໍ		(damaging) adj. ti bpeːn gan sia haˇy ທີ່ເປັນການເສັຽຫາຍ
hang up	(suspend) hoːy wayː ຫ້ອຍໄວ້	harmony	(music) n. niang bpaː saˇn ສຽງປະສານ
	(telephone) wang to laː saːp wayː ວາງໂທລະສັບໄວ້		(peaceful) n. kwaːm paˇ suːk ຄວາມຜາສຸກ
hangar	n. uˇ heuaˇ biːn ອູ່ເຮືອບິນ	harness	n. aˇn maː ອານມ້າ v. sayˇ aːn maˇ ໃສ່ອານມ້າ
hanger	n. koh hoˇy keuang ຂໍຫ້ອຍເຄື່ອງ	harp	v. haˇm hayˇ ຮ່ຳໄຮ n. piːn ພິນ
happen	v. geːrt keuːn ເກີດຂຶ້ນ	harsh	(voice) adj. howˇ ຫ້າວ
happiness	n. kwaːm suːk ຄວາມສຸກ		(punishment) huˇn haang ຮຸນແຮງ
happy	adj. di chayˇ ດີໃຈ		(soap) gaːt ກັດ
harbor	n. taˇ heuaˇ ທ່າເຮືອ	harvest	v. geːp giaw ເກັບກ່ຽວ
hard	(firm) adv. kaˇang ແຂງ		(action) n. gan geːp giaw ການເກັບກ່ຽວ
	(difficult) adj. nyaːk ຍາກ		
hard earned	adj. dayˇ maˇ duay kwaːm nyaˇk ໄດ້ມາດ້ວຍຄວາມຍາກ		
hardly	adv. geuap boh ເກືອບບໍ່		
hardship	n. kwaːm laːm bak ຄວາມລຳບາກ		

	(result) n. pǒìn kohng gàn geìp giǎw ຜົນຂອງການເກັບກ່ຽວ
harvester	(person) n. koìn geìp giǎw ຄົນເກັບກ່ຽວ
	(machine) n. keuang chaìk geìp giǎw ເຄື່ອງຈັກເກັບກ່ຽວ
haste	n. kwam fòw faìng ຄວາມຟ້າວ ຟັ່ງ
hasten	v. hǐb heìng ຮີບເຮັ່ງ
hat	n. mǔak ໝວກ
hatch	n. bpaì dtu yu peǔn heǔa ປະຕູຍູ້ພື້ນເຮືອ
	v. faìk kaỳ: ຟັກໄຂ່
hatchet	n. kwǎn nòy ຂວານນ້ອຍ
hate	v. saìng ຊັງ
hatred	n. kwam saìng ຄວາມຊັງ
haughty	adj. teù dtua ຖືຕົວ
haul	n. gàn gǎa ການແກ່
haunt	(to stay) v. siìng yu ສິງຢູ່
	(bother) v. lohk ຫຼອກ
have	(possess) v. mi ມີ
	(health) v. bpeìn ເປັນ
have a cold	v. bpeìn waìt ເປັນຫວັດ
have an accident	mi u: baìt het ມີອຸບັດ ເຫດ
have charge of	mi na ti laìp piìt sohp ມີໜ້າທີ່ຮັບຜິດຊອບ
have on	v. nuìng ນຸ່ງ
have time	adv. mi we lá ມີເວລາ
have to	adv. dtohng ຕ້ອງ
hawk	n. laaw ແຫຼວ
	v. kay dtam tǎ: nòìn ຂາຍຕາມຖະໜົນ
hay	n. nya haang ຫຍ້າແຫ້ງ
haystack	n. gohng nya haang ກອງຫຍ້າແຫ້ງ
hazard	v. siàng ສ່ຽງ
	n. keuang giìt kwǎng ເຄື່ອງກີດຂວາງ
haze	n. naìm mohk bang bang ນ້ຳໝອກບາງໆ
hazy	adj. mohk gua ໝອກກົ້ວ
he	pron. low (pu sǎy) ລາວ(ຜູ້ຊາຍ)
head	(body) n. hǔa ຫົວ
	(leader) n. hǔa nǎ ຫົວໜ້າ
	v. ohk naìm nǎ ອອກນຳໜ້າ
headache	n. kwam cheìp hǔa ຄວາມ ເຈັບຫົວ
	n. kwam bpuat hǔa ຄວາມ ປວດຫົວ
headdress	n. keuang suam hǔa ເຄື່ອງສວມຫົວ
head line	n. hǔa leǔang ຫົວເລື່ອງ
head light	n. dta loìt ຕາລົດ
headquarters	n. gohng baìn sǎ gàn ກອງບັນຊາການ
heal	v. bpiìn bpua ປິ່ນປົວ
health	n. su: kà: pap ສຸຂພາບ

healthy	adj. sǔ: kǎ: pǎp di สุຂພາบดี
heap	v. heːt bpeːn gohng เຮັດເປັນກอງ n. gohng ກอງ
hear	v. daỳ: nyì:n ໄດ้ยิน
hearing	n. gan daỳ: nyì:n ການໄດ้ยิน
heart	(organ) n. hǔa chay: ຫົວใจ (center) n. sǔn gang สูมกาງ
heart attack	n. hǔa chay: wǎy ຫົວใจอาย
heat	v. heːt hǎy: hohn เຮັດใຫ้ຮ้อນ n. kwǎm hohn ຄວາມຮ້อນ
heathen	n. koːn nóhk sat sǎ: nǎ ຄົນนอกสาสมา
heave	(lift) v. nyoːk keùːn ยิกຂึ้ນ (throw) v. nyòn ໂยม
heaven	n. sǎ: waǐn ສ้วม
heavy	(weight) adj. naːk ໜັກ (clothes) adj. na ໜา (traffic) adj. kaːp kaːng ຄັບຄ້ງ
heavyweight	n. koːn ka: nat naːk ຄົมมาดໜັກ
hectare	(1000 square meters or 6¼ acres) n. heːt dta (tow: gaːp paːn maaːt ga: re: mon ton leu 6¼ hai)

	เຮັກຕາ(ເທົ່າກັບ ໑໐.໐໐໐ ແມັດ ກາ: ເຣມິນທິມທຼ ຫຼ ໑/໔ ໄຣ່)
hedge	n. hǔa heːt duay dton may: ຮົ້ວເຮັດດ້วยຕົ້ນໄມ้ v. loːp lik ຫຼົບຫຼີກ
heed	(command) v. laː waịng ຣະວັງ (request) v. owː chay: say: ເອົาใจใส่
heel	n. son dtin ສົ້ນຕີນ v. nyang dtam laːng ย่าງຕາมຫຼັງ
height	n. kwǎm sung ຄວາມສูງ
heighten	v. heːt hǎy: sung keùːn เຮັດใຫ้ສูງຂึ้ນ
heir	n. pu haːp moh laː: doːk ผู้ຮັບมอละดอก
helicopter	n. nyoːn heːliː gop dtaa ยิมເຮລิໂກບແຕ
hell	n. naː: loːk naːrik ນາ: ໂລກ มะรึก (oh) intrj. aːp bpi taa taa ອຍບໍ່ແທ່າ (go to) intrj. bpay: dtay haː say: goh bpay: sa: ໄປຕາຍຮ້າใຫ้ໄປສະ
hello	interj. sǎ: baːy di ສະບາຍดี
helmet	n. muak leːk ໝວກເຫຼັກ
help	n. gan suay leǔa ການຊ່วยເຫຼือ

	v. soy leūa ຊ່ອຍເຫຼືອ
	interj. suǎy daǎ ຊ່ອຍແຕ່
helpful	adj. ti bpe:n gan suay leūa ທີ່ເປັນການຊ່ວຍເຫຼືອ
helpless	adj. mo:t waing ໝົດທ້ວງ
hem	v. lohm ລ້ອມ
	n. dtin sin ຕີນສິ້ນ
hemisphere	n. kering lōk ເຄິ່ງໂລກ
hemorrhoids	n. gon pong ກົນໂພງ
hen	n. gay: maa ໄກ່ແມ່
hence	adv. dtang dtaa ni bpay: ຕັ້ງແຕ່ນີ້ໄປ
her	pron. low (pu nyi:ng) ລາວ(ຜູ້ຍິງ)
herb	n. sa mu:n pay: ສມຸນໄພ
herd	n. mu sa:t ໝູ່ສັດ
here	adv. yu ni ຢູ່ນີ້
hereabout	adv. moh moh ni ມໍ່ໆນີ້
hereafter	n. sat na ຊາດໜ້າ
	adv. dtoh chak ni bpay: ຕໍ່ຈາກນີ້ໄປ
hereby	adv. duǎy ni ດ້ວຍນີ້
hereupon	adv. duǎy het ni ດ້ວຍເຫດນີ້
herself	pron. low eng (pu nyi:ng) ລາວເອງ (ຜູ້ຍິງ)
heritage	n. moh la: do:k ມໍລະດົກ
hermit	n. pa: leu si ພະລຶສີ
hero	(fiction) n. pa: ek ພະເອກ

	(life) n. pu ga han ຜູ້ກ້າຫານ
herring	n. bpa haa li:ng ປາແຮລິງ
hers	pron. kohng low (pu nyi:ng) ຂອງລາວ (ຜູ້ຍິງ)
hesitate	v. laing le chay: ລັງເລໃຈ
hew	v. dta:t ຕັດ
hi	interj. sa: bay di ສະບາຍດີ
hibernate	v. kow: ga:p (sa:t) ເຂົ້າກັບ (ສັດ)
hidden	adj. seung ເຊື່ອງ
hide	v. li ລີ້
	n. naing sa:t ໜັງສັດ
hide and seek	n. gan li:n mak li ການຫຼິ້ນໝາກລີ້
hideous	adj. bpe:n dta ki diat ເປັນຕາຂີ້ດຽດ
hiding place	n. bohn li ບ່ອນລີ້
hi-fi	siang hay: fay: ສຽງໄຮໄຟ
high	(height) adj. sung ສູງ
	(drunk) adj. mow: ເມົາ
	(rank) adj. nyay: ໃຫຍ່
highly	adv. yang sung ຢ່າງສູງ
highway	n. tang luang ທາງຫຼວງ
hike	v. der:n tang duay dtin ເດີນທາງດ້ວຍຕີນ
hill	n. pu noy ພູນ້ອຍ
hilly	adj. bpe:n ner:n pu ເປັນເນີນພູ

him	pron. lŏw (pŭ sǎy) ລາວ (ຜູ້ຊາຍ)
himself	pron. lŏw eng (pŭ sǎy) ລາວເອງ (ຜູ້ຊາຍ)
hind	(deer) n. guang mǎa ກວາງແມ່ adj. tang laihng ທາງຫຼັງ
hinder	(road) v. git kwang ກີດຂວາງ (idea) v. kait kwǎng ຂັດຂວາງ
hinge	n. ban paih ບານພັບ
hint	n. laik sǎ: nǎ: ລັກສນະ v. bohk laik sǎ: nǎ: ບອກລັກສນະ
hip	n. sǎ: pok ສະໂພກ
hippie	n. kŏ:n sup sǎ ຄົນສຸບຊາ
hippopotamus	n. sang na:m ຊ້າງນ້ຳ
hire	n. ka chang ຄ່າຈ້າງ v. chang ຈ້າງ
his	pron. kohng lŏw (pŭ sǎy) ຂອງລາວ(ຜູ້ຊາຍ)
hiss	v. sǎ: daang tǎ yiǎp yam ສະແດງທ່າຢຽບຢາມ
historic	adj. haang bpa: wa:t sat ແຫ່ງປະວັດສາດ
history	n. bpa: wa:t sat ປະວັດສາດ n. poing sǎ wǎ: dan ພົງສາ ວະດານ
hit	(song) n. peng sǎ: mǎy: ເພງສະໄໝ
hitch	(sore) n. hǒy dti ຮອຍຕີ (beat) v. dti ຕີ (into) v. dta:m ຕຳ (time) we la ti tuk gen ໜ້າ ope:n ta: han ເວລາທີ່ຖືກເກນເປັນທະຫານ (military) ta: han ທະຫານ (problem) n. u:p bpa: sa:k ອຸປສັກ v. mait seuak ມັດເຊືອກ
hive	n. haing pering ຮັງເຜິ້ງ
hoard	v. sǎ: soih ສະສົມ
hoarse	adj. bpak haap ປາກແຫບ
hobby	n. wiak he:t we la wang ວຽກເຮັດເວລາຫວ່າງ ອຸກເຣັກເວລາຫວ່າງ
hockey	n. gi: la dti ki ກິລາຕີຄີ
hoe	n. cho:k ຈົກ
hog	n. mu ໝູ
hoist	n. so nyo:k ໂສ້ຍົກ v. deuing keu:n ດຶງຂຶ້ນ
hold	(storage) n. bohn way: keuang ບ່ອນໄວ້ເຄື່ອງ (grip) n. gan cha:p ການຈັບ v. cha:p way: ຈັບໄວ້
hold back	(check) v. ga:n way: ກັນໄວ້ (conceal) deuang way: ເຊື່ອງ ໄວ້
hold off	kait keun ຂັດຂືນ

hold out	(obstacle) ka:t kwang ຂັດຂວາງ
	(survive) mi si wi:t yu ມີຊີວິດຢູ່
hold over	(postpone) leuan bpay: ເລື່ອນ ໄປ
	(show beyond scheduled time) leuan we la sa: daang dtoh bpay: ik ເລື່ອນ ເວລາສະແດງຕໍ່ໄປອີກ
hold up	(rob) bpu:n ປຸ້ນ
	(delay) he:t hay: sa ເຮັດໃຫ້ຊ້າ
hole	(natural) n. bpohng ປ່ອງ
	(cut) n. hu ຮູ
holiday	n. meu pa:k ngan ມື້ພັກງານ
hollow	(hole) n. bpe:n hu ເປັນຮູ
	(concave) n. gon ໂກນ
	v. he:t hay: bpe:n gon ເຮັດໃຫ້ເປັນໂກມ
holy	adj. ti sa:k ga: la: bu sa ທີ່ສັກກະລະບູຊາ
holy water	n. na:m mo:n ນ້ຳມົນ
homage	n. kwam kow: lo:p ຄວາມ ເຄົາຣົບ
home	n. ban ບ້ານ
homely	adj. ko:n bo lan ຄົນໂບຮານ
homesick	adj. ki:t hoht ban ຄິດຮອດ ບ້ານ
homework	n. gan ban ການບ້ານ
honest	adj. sa:t seu ສັດຊື່
honey	(food) n. na:m pe:ng ນ້ຳເຜິ້ງ
	(person) n. ti ha:k ທີ່ຮັກ
honor	v. hay: giat ໃຫ້ກຽດ
	(distinction) n. giat dti: nyo:t ກຽດຕິຍົດ
	(judge) n. cha san ຈຳສານ
honorary	adj. gi:t dti: ma: sa:k ກິຕິມະສັກ
hood	n. pa bpo:k hua ຜ້າປົກຫົວ
hoof	n. le:p ma ເລັບມ້າ
hook	v. goh: ເກາະ
	n. koh goh: ຂໍເກາະ
hoop	n. luk wo:ng ລູກວົງ
hope	n. kwam wa:ng ຄວາມຫວັງ
	v. wa:ng ຫວັງ
hopeful	adj. ti dte:m bpay: duay kwam wa:ng ທີ່ເຕັມໄປດ້ວຍ ຄວາມຫວັງ
hopeless	adj. mo:t wa:ng ໝົດຫວັງ
horizon	n. kohp fa ຂອບຟ້າ
horizontally	adv. tang nohn ທາງນອນ
horn	n. kow: sa:t ເຂົາສັດ
horrid	adj. bpe:n dta na yan ເປັນຕາໜ້າຢ້ານ
horror	n. kwam sa: nyo:t sa: nyohn ຄວາມສະຍົກສະຍອນ

horse	n. má ม้า		v. loːp guan ลิบกอม
horseback	n. laːng má ทั่วม้า	hour	n. sua mong จ้วโมา
horse race	n. gan kaang má ภามแข่าม้า	house	n. heuan เรือม
horseshoe	n. leːk kóp dtin má [ทูักโคย ติมม้า	household	n. keuang heuan [คื่อา [เรือม
		housekeeping	n. gan haːk sa ban ภามรักสาบ้าม
horseshoe crab	n. maang dá taː lè แมาถาทะเเ	housewife	n. maa heuan แม่เรือม
hose	v. sit naːm สิ๊ดม้ำ	how	adv. bpeːn yang daːi เป็มย่าาใด
	(sock) n. toːng dtin ถิ้วติม	how do you do	intrj. saː baːy dí สะบายถิ
	(pipe) n. toh sit naːm ทสิ๊ดม้ำ	however	adv. yang daːi goh dtam ย่าาใดก็ตาม
hospital	(common) n. hong moh โรากพ	how far	gaːy bpan daːi ไภปามใด
	(formal) hong paː nya ban โราพะยาบาม	howl	v. hohn ทอม
hospitality	n. kwam eua feua คอามเจื้อเพื่อ	how long	(time) adv. doːn bpan daːi ถิมปามใด?
			(distance) adj. nyów bpan daːi ยาอปามใด?
host	n. chow páp (pu say) เจ้าพาย (ผู้ฆาย)	how many	adv. laːy bpan daːi ฑายปามใด?
hostess	(airlines) n. nang a gat มาาาาภาถ	how much	adv. towː daːi เท้าใด?
	(party) n. chow páp (pu nyiːng) เจ้าพาย (ผู้ยิา)	how often	adv. leuay leuay boh เลื้อยๆบ่?
	(bar) n. pu sow baː ผู้สาอบาร์	how old	(things) adv. gaa bpan daːi แภ่ปามใด
hostile	adj. bpeːn saːt dtu gan เป็มสัตถูภัม		(animal or plant) adv. towː bpan daːi เถ้าปามใด
hot	adj. hohn ร้อม		(person) adv. a nyuː towː daːi อายุเท้าใด
hotel	n. hong haam โราแรม		
hound	n. má laːy neua พาไล่เมื้อ		

how tall	adv. sung bpan day: ສູງ ປານໃດ?
huddle	n. gan biat gain ການບຽດກັນ
	v. biat gain ບຽດກັນ
hue	n. si kohng si ສີຂອງສີ
hug	v. goht hait ກອດຮັດ
huge	n. nyay: ໃหຍ່
hum	n. siang heu:m heu:m ສຽງຫືມໆ
human	adj. haang ma: nu:t ແຫ່ງມະນຸດ
	n. ma: nu:t ມະນຸດ
humble	adj. tohm dtua ຖ່ອມຕົວ
	v. loit giat ລົດກຽດ
humid	adj. su:m ຊຸ່ມ
humiliate	v. heit hay: sia nyo:t ເຮັດໃຫ້ເສຍຍົດ
humor	n. a lo:m ອາຮົມ
	v. tam ta di ທຳທ່າດີ
hundred	adj. hoy ຮ້ອຍ
hunger	n. kwam yak kow: ຄວາມຢາກເຂົ້າ
hungry	adj. yak kow: ຢາກເຂົ້າ
hunt	n. gan lay: neua ການໄລ່ເນື້ອ
	v. ho neua ໂຫເນື້ອ
hunter	n. nay pan ນາຍພານ
hunting	n. gan la sa:t ການ ລ່າສັດ
hurl	v. nyon haang haang ໂຍນແຮງໆ
hurrah!	interj. e e e e (hohng hay: giat) (ຮ້ອງ (ຮ້ອງໃຫ້ກຽດ)
hurricane	n. lo:m pa nyu: her li ken ລົມພະຍຸ ເຮີຣິເຄນ
hurry	v. fow ຟ້າວ
hurt	v. heit hay: che:p ເຮັດໃຫ້ ເຈັບ
	adj. che:p ເຈັບ
husband	n. pua ຜົວ
hush	v. mi:t ມິດ
hustle	v. hip heing ຮິບເຮັ່ງ
hut	n. dtup ຕູບ
hydraulic	adj. a say: haang na:m ອາໄສແຮງນ້ຳ
hydrogen	n. hay: dro che:n ໄຮໂດຣເຈນ
hygiene	n. su: ka pi: ban ສຸຂພິບານ
hymn	n. peng sat sa:na krit ເພງສາສນາຄຣິສ

I

I	(common) pron. koy ຂ້ອຍ
	(polite) ka: noy ຂ້ານ້ອຍ
	(formal) ka pa: chow: ຂ້າພະເຈົ້າ
ice	v. heit hay: bpe:n na:m gohn ເຮັດໃຫ້ເປັນນ້ຳກ້ອນ
	n. na:m gohn ນ້ຳກ້ອນ

ice cream	n. gǎ: lǎǎm ກະແຣມ
ice skating	n. gan li:n sǎ: ge:t nǎːm gohn ການຫຼິ້ນສະເກັດນ້ຳກ້ອນ
idea	n. kwam ki:t ຄວາມຄິດ
ideal	adj. ti di le:rt ທີດີເລີດ n. u: do:m ka: dti: ອຸດົມຄະຕິ
identify	v. bohk la:k sa: na: cha:m poh: ບອກລັກສນະຈໍເພາະ
idiot	n. ko:n cha ຄົນຈາ
idle	v. yu la la ຍູ້ລາໆ adj. wang ngan ວ່າງງານ
idol	n. hup bpa:n bu sa ຮູບປັ້ນບູຊາ
if	conj. ta wa ຖ້າວ່າ
ignorance	n. kwam ngo ຄວາມໂງ່
ignorant	adj. ngo ໂງ່
ignore	v. boh hua sa ບໍ່ຫົວຊາ
ill	adj. bpuay ປ່ວຍ
illegal	(law) pi:t go:t may ຜິດກົດໝາຍ (rule) pi:t la: biap ຜິດຣະບຽບ
illness	n. kwam che:p kay: ຄວາມເຈັບໄຂ້
illuminate	v. sohng saang ສ່ອງແສງ
illusion	n. gan lohk dta ການຫຼອກຕາ
illustrate	v. dtaam hup bpa: gohp ແຕ້ມຮູບປະກອບ
image	n. hup ຮູບ
imagination	n. kwam gǎ: dtuang ຄວາມກະຕວງ
imagine	v. gǎ: dtuang ກະຕວງ
imitate	v. ow: baap yang ເອົາແບບຢ່າງ
immediate	adj. gǎy: si:t ໃຫ້ຊິດ
immediately	adv. doy tain ti tain day: ໂດຍທັນທີທັນໃດ
immense	adj. guang kuang ກວ້າງຂວາງ
immigrant	n. pu o:p pa: nyo:p kow: ma ຜູ້ອົບພະຍົບເຂົາມາ
immigrate	v. o:p pa: nyo:p ni kow: ma ອົບພະຍົບໜີເຂົາມາ
immodest	adj. nyohng dto:n eng ຍອງຕົນເອງ
immortal	adj. yeun nyo:ng ko:ng yu ຢືນຍົງຄົງຢູ່ sua ga la: nan, a: ma: dta: ຊົ່ວກາລະນານ, ອະມະຕະ
impale	v.t. taang ແທງ
impartial	(small) bpe:n gang ເປັນກາງ (large) sa:t sue ສັດຊື່
impatience	n. kwam boh o:t to:n ຄວາມບໍ່ອົດທົນ
impatient	adj. chay: hohn ໃຈຮ້ອນ
imperial	adj. haang cha:k ga: pa:t ແຫ່ງຈັກກະພັດ
implement	n. keuang meu ເຄື່ອງມື v. lo:ng meu he:t hay: sǎm le:t ລົງມືເຮັດໃຫ້ສຳເລັດ, ເຮັດໃຫ້ສ່ວງເຮັດ
implore	(god) v. wing wohn ວິງວອນ (person) v. ohn wohn ອ້ອນວອນ

imply	v. mǎy kwǎm ພາຍ ຄວາມ
import	v. ow: siːn kǎ kǒw: ເອົາສິນ ຄ້າເຂົ້າ n. siːn kǎ kǒw: ສິນຄ້າເຂົ້າ
importance	n. kwǎm sǎːm kǎːn ຄວາມສຳ ຄັນ
important	adj. sǎːm kǎːn ສຳຄັນ
impose	v. baːng kǎːp ບັງຄັບ
imposition	n. gan baːng kǎːp ການບັງຄັບ
impossible	adj. bpeːn bpay: boh day: ເປັນໄປບໍ່ໄດ້
impractical	(ability) adj. boh moh soːm ບໍ່ເໝາະສົມ (waste) bpa dtiː: baː: boh day: ປະຕິບັດບໍ່ໄດ້
impress	v. heːt hay: dteun dtaːn chay: ເຮັດໃຫ້ຕື້ນຕັນໃຈ
impression	n. kwǎm neuːk kiːt nay: chay: ຄວາມນຶກຄິດໃນໃຈ
impressionistic	n. gan dtaːm hǔp duǎy kwǎm kiːt ການແຕ້ມຮູບດ້ວຍ ຄວາມຄິດ
improve	v. gǎa kay: hay: di keun ແກ້ໄຂໃຫ້ດີຂຶ້ນ
imprison	v. chaːm kuːk ຈຳຄຸກ
improvements	n. gan heːt hay: di keun ການເຮັດໃຫ້ດີຂຶ້ນ
impulse	n. kwǎm hu seuːk suǎ kǎː naː: ຄວາມຮູ້ສຶກວູ່ວຄະນະ
in	prep. yu nay: ຢູ່ໃນ

in a hurry	adv. yang fǒw faːng ຢ່າງຟ້າວຟັ່ງ
in any event	teriːng wa chaː: mi nyaːng gert keun goh dtam ເຖິງວ່າ ຈະມີຫຍັງເກີດຂຶ້ນກໍຕາມ
in back of	tang laːng kohng ທາງຫຼັງ ຂອງ
in case of	nay: goh laː: ni ໃນກໍລະນີ
in charge of	mi naː ti laːp piː:t sohp ມີໜ້າທີ່ຮັບຜິດຊອບ
in front of	tang naː kohng ທາງໜ້າຂອງ
in order	bpeːn laː: biap ເປັນລະບຽບ
in order to	peua chaː: ເພື່ອຈະ
in the middle of	tang gang kohng ທາງກາງຂອງ
in the way	dtaːn taːng ຕັນທາງ
in time	taːn mong ທັນໂມງ
in vain	doy boh mi poːn ໂດຍບໍ່ມີຜົນ
in-	(changes meaning of adjectives to their opposite) kaːm ti bpian kaːm naːm hay: bpeːn kaːm goːng gaːn kaːm ຄຳທີ່ປ່ຽນຄຳນາມໃຫ້ເປັນ ຄຳກົງກັນຂ້າມ
inaugurate	(president) v. heːt piː: ti haːp dtaːm nǎːng may: ເຮັດພິ ທີຮັບຕຳແໜ່ງໃໝ່ (building) heːt piː: ti bpert ເຮັດພິທີເປີດ

incessant	adj. bŏh hŭ chǎːk sŏwː ບໍ່ຮູ້ຈັກເຊົາ
inch	n. nĭw ນິ້ວ
incident	n. hĕt gǎn ເຫດການ
incinerate	v. chŭt hayː mǎyː mǒːt giǎng ຈຸດໃຫ້ໄໝ້ເກ້ຽງ
incline	v. iǎng loːng ອຽງໂລ້ງ
inclination	n. kwam kow: kang noy neuːng ຄວາມເຂົ້າຂາງນ້ອຍນຶ່ງ
include	v. huǎm yŭ naːm ຮ່ວມຢູ່ນຳ
income	(interest) n. dŏhk bĭa ດອກເບ້ຍ
	(salary) n. lǎy dǎyː ຣາຍໄດ້
inconvenience	(difficult) n. kwǎm nyŭng nyǎk ຄວາມຍຸງຍາກ
	(interrupt) v. loːp guǎn ຣົບກວນ
inconvenient	adj. bpeːn tĭ nyŭng nyǎk ເປັນທີ່ຍຸ້ງຍາກ
incorrect	adj. bŏh teŭk dtŏhng ບໍ່ຖືກຕ້ອງ
increase	n. gǎn pěrm kěun ການເພີ່ມຂຶ້ນ v. pěrm kěun ເພີ່ມຂຶ້ນ
incredible	adj. leŭa seŭa ເຫຼືອເຊື່ອ
indebted	adj. bpeːn nĭ buːn kuːn ເປັນໜີ້ບຸນຄຸນ
indeed	adv. mǎan tǎa lǎaw ແມ່ນແທ້ແລ້ວ

independence	n. ĕk gǎː lǎt ເອກກະຣາດ
independent	adj. bpeːn ĕk gǎː lǎt ເປັນເອກກະຣາດ
index	(book) n. sǎ lǎː bǎn ສາຣະບານ (finger) n. nĭw sĭ mĭːǔ ນິ້ວຊີ້ມື v. chaːt hayː mĭ sǎ lǎː bǎn ຈັດໃຫ້ມີສາຣະບານ
Indian	(India) adj. kaǎk iːn dĭa ແຂກອິນເດັຍ (America) n. iːn dĭa daang ອິນເດັຍແດງ
Indian Ocean	n. maː hǎ sǎi muːt iːn dĭa ມະຫາສະມຸດອິນເດັຍ
indicate	v. sĭ bŏhk ຊີ້ບອກ
indifferent	adj. bŏh soːm chayː ບໍ່ສົນໃຈ
indignant	adj. mŏ hŏ ໂມໂຫ
individual	adj. dtaa laː ແຕ່ລະ n. buːk koːn ບຸກຄົນ
Indonesian	n. iːn do ne sǐ ອິນໂດເນຊີ
indoors	adv. tǎng nǎyː heŭan ທາງໃນເຮືອນ
induce	(persuade) v. saːk suǎn ຊັກຊວນ (electricity) dŭt deuːng fayː fá ຖຸກດຶງໄຟຟ້າ (thought) loːng tǎy duay heːt poːn ລົງທ້າຍດ້ວຍເຫດ ຜົນ

indulge	v. bpoy dtua eng ປ່ອຍຕົວເອງ	inn	n. hong haam ໂຮງແຮມ
industrial	adj. haang uï t sǎ hǎ: gaim ແຫ່ງອຸດສາຫະກັມ	innkeeper	n. pǔ cha: t gan hong haam ຜູ້ຈັດການໂຮງແຮມ
industrious	adj. du: ma:n ຄຸໝັນ	innocent	(law) adj. boh li su: t ບໍລິສຸດ
industry	(person) n. kwam du: ma:n ຄວາມຄຸໝັນ		(child) adj. boh hu diang sǎ ບໍຣູ້ງງສາ
	(business) n. uï t sǎ hǎ: gaim ອຸດສາຫະກັມ	inoculation	n. gan sǎ:k ya ການສັກຢາ
inexpensive	adj. teuk ຖຶກ		(polite) n. gǎn sit ya ການສິດຢາ
infect	(disease) v. dti: t dtoh ຕິດຕໍ່	inquire	v. sohp tam ສອບຖາມ
	(sore) v. bpe: n sǔa lok ເປັນເຊື້ອໂຣກ	insane	adj. chi: t boh poh ຈິດບໍ່ພໍ
infection	n. gan dti: t bpaat bpeuan ການຕິດແປດເປື້ອນ	insanity	n. a gan chi: t boh poh ອາການຈິດບໍ່ພໍ
inferior	adj. ti dta: m gwa ທີ່ຕ່ຳກວ່າ n. ko: n sǎn dta: m ຄົນຊັນຕ່ຳ	inscription	n. gan cha leuk ການຈາຣຶກ
		insect	n. maang may: ແມງໄມ້
infinite	adj. boh sin su: t ບໍ່ສິ້ນສຸດ	insert	(into) v. soht say: ສອດໃສ່
inflammation	n. a:k sep ອັກເສບ		(between) v. dteum kow: ຕຶມເຂົ້າ
-ing	(changes verbs to nouns) ka:m ti bpian gi: nya hay: bpe: n nam ຄຳທີ່ປ່ຽນກີຣິຍາໃຫ້ເປັນ ນາມ	inside	n. tang nay: ທາງໃນ
		insipid	adj. cheut ຈຶດ
in-law	adj. pi nohng duay gan dtaang ngan ພີນ້ອງດ້ວຍການ ແຕ່ງງານ	insist	v. ba:ng ka:p, boh nyohm bpian ta ti ບໍ່ຄົຍ, ບໍຍອມປ່ຽນທ່າທີ
inlay	n. ka:m say: kaaw ຄຳໃສ່ແກວ	inspect	v. guat ga ກວດກາ
injure	v. he: t hay: che: p ເຮັດໃຫ້ເຈັບ	inspector	n. pǔ guat gan ຜູ້ກວດກາ
		inspire	v. uan chi: t ວອນຈິດ
ink	v. dut na: m meu: k ຈຸໝນ້ຳ ຫມຶກ	install	v. cha: t dtang keun ຈັດຕັ້ງຂຶ້ນ
	n. na: m meu: k ນ້ຳຫມຶກ	installment	n. nguat ງວດ
		instance	n. goh la: ni ກໍລະນີ
		instant	adj. nay: ka: na: ໃນຂະນະ

instead	(of) adv. taan tì แทนที่	intention	n. kwam dtang chày:, che:t
intestinal	adj. giaw gàip laìm sǎy:		dta: na ความตั้งใจ, เจตนา
	ทั่วอไบลำไส้	intercourse	(communication) n. gàn giàw
intestine	n. laìm sǎy: ลำไส้		paìn gaìn การทั่วอพันกัน
instinct	n. sǎin sàt dta ñan		(sex) n. gàn sek sòim การ
	สัญชาตยาม		เสกสีม
institution	n. sài tà baìn สะถาบัน	interest	v. heìt hǎy: sòin chày:
instruct	v. sohn สอน		เธ็ดให้สนใจ
instrument	(tool) n. keuang mèu เคื่องมิ		(money) n. dohk bìa
	(music) n. keuang doìn		ดอกเบี้ย
	dtri เคื่องดิมตรี		(hobbies) n. keuang lìin
insult	(formal) v. mìin bpa: màt		เคื่องหลิ้น
	มิ่นปะมาด		(attitude) n. gàn sòin
	v. da wa ด่าอา		chày: การสนใจ
insure	(quality) v. laìp lohng	interfere	(personal) v. ñung giàw
	รับธอง		ยุ้งทั่วอ
	(logs) v. bpa: gaìn ปะกัน		(political) v. sàak saàng
intellect	n. sài dtì: bpaìn ña		แธกแธง
	สะติปันยา	interference	n. gàn sàak saàng การแธก
intelligence	(I.Q.) kwam sǎ: làt		แธง
	ความสลาด	interior	(country) adj. pǎy này:
	(spy) adj. sèup สืบ		ผายใน
intelligent	adj. sǎ: làt สลาด		(building) adj. tang này:
intend	v. dtang chày: ตั้งใจ		ทางใน
intense	(feeling) adj. lǎy tì sùt	intermission	n. gàn yuìt paìk
	ทุายที่สุด		การยุดพัก
	(heat) adj. ga lay	internal	(country) adj. haàng pay
	ภาภาย		này: แท่งผายใน
intent	adj. doy dtang chày:		(body or building) adj.
	โดยตั้งใจ		tang này: ทางใน

international	adj. haáng nǎ nǎ sát
	ແຫ່ງນານາຊາດ
interpret	v. bpaa, dti kwam may
	(ແປ, ຕີຄວາມໝາຍ
interrupt	v. ka:t koh ຂັດຄໍ
interval	n. la: wang we la
	ລະຫວ່າງເວລາ
intervene	v. kow: saak ເຂົ້າແຊກ
interview	n. gan hay: sa:m pat
	ການໃຫ້ສໍາພາດ
	v. sa:m pat ສໍາພາດ
intimate	v. bohk hay: hu ບອກໃຫ້ຮູ້
	adj. kun kery ga:n ຄຸ້ນເຄີຍ
	ກັນ
into	pron. tang nay: ທາງໃນ
intoxicate	v. he:t hay: mow: ເຮັດໃຫ້
	ເມົາ
intrigue	v. ki:t go:n u: bay
	ຄິດກົນອຸບາຍ
	n. gan keun chay: ການຊິ່ງໃຈ
introduce	v. nǎa: nǎ:m hay: hu cha:k
	ແນະນໍາໃຫ້ຮູ້ຈັກ
introduction	(book) n. kǎ:m nǎa: nǎ:m
	ຄຳແນະນຳ
	(person) n. gan nǎa: nǎ:m
	hay: hu cha:k ການແນະນໍາໃຫ້
	ຮູ້ຈັກ
intrude	v. bu:k lu:k ບຸກລຸກ
invade	v. nyo:k kow: mǎ dti
	ຍົກເຂົ້າມາຕີ

invent	v. bpa: di:t keun ປະດິດຂຶ້ນ
invest	(money) v. kow: hu:n ເຂົ້າ ຮຸ້ນ
	(rank) v. leuan nyo:t
	ເລື່ອນຍົດ
investigate	v. dtay: suan ໄຕ່ສອນ
invitation	n. gan sern ການເຊີນ
invite	v. sern ເຊີນ
involve	v. giaw kohng na:m
	ກ່ຽວຂ້ອງນໍາ
iron	(metal) n. le:k ເຫຼັກ
	(clothes) n. dtow: lit
	ເຕົາຣີດ
	v. lit pa ຣີດຜ້າ
ironing board	n. dto: lit keuang ໂຕະ
	ລິດເຄື່ອງ
irons	n. so le:k say: ko:n tot
	ໂສ່ເຫຼັກໃສ່ຄົນໂທດ
irregular	(shape) adj. boh sa: ma:m
	sa: mer ບໍ່ສະໝໍ່າສເມີ
	(action) adj. pi:t la: biap
	ຜິດລະບຽບ
irrigate	v. bpeng na:m ເບ່ງນໍ້າ
irrigation	n. gan bpeng na:m ການ
	ເບ່ງນໍ້າ
irritate	(anger) v. he:t hay: chay:
	hay ເຮັດໃຫ້ໃຈຮ້າຍ
	(itch) v. he:t hay: ka:n
	ເຮັດໃຫ້ຄັນ
	(disturb) v. guan ກວນ
island	n. goh: ເກາະ

isle	n. dohn ດອນ
isolate	v. nyáak ohk ແຍກອອກ
isolated	adj. bpìaw ປ່ຽວ
isolation	n. gan yu bpìaw ການຢູ່ປ່ຽວ
issue	(subject) n. leuang ເລື່ອງ
	v. he:t ohk ma ເຣັດອອກມາ
	(stamp) su:t ສຸດ
	(magazine) sa: ba:p ສະບັບ
it	pron. ma:n ມັນ
Italian	adj. i: dta li ອີຕາລີ
itch	n. ka:n ຄັນ
itchy	adj. bpe:n ti ka:n kay ເປັນທີ່ຄັນຄາຍ
item	n. lay gan ລາຍການ
its	pron. kohng ma:n ຂອງມັນ
it's	pron. ma:n maan ມັນແມ່ນ
itself	pron. dtua kohng ma:n eng ຕົວຂອງມັນເອງ
ivory	n. nga sang ງາຊ້າງ
ivy	n. keua ay wi ເຄືອໄອວີ

J

jab	v. taang duay si:ng kohng ແທງດ້ວຍສິ່ງຂອງ
jacket	(suit) n. seua nyay: ເສື້ອໃຫຍ່
	(pullover) n. seua su:p ga:n now ເສື້ອຊຸດກັນໜາວ

jackknife	n. mit nga:p ມີດງັບ
jade	n. nyo:k ຢົກ
jail	n. ku:k ຄຸກ
jam	n. mak may: guan ພາກໄມ້ກວນ
	v. say: li:n ໃສ່ຫຼື້ນ
jamboree	n. gan bpa: su:m (luk seua) ການປະ ຊຸມ (ລູກເສືອ)
January	n. deuan mo:k ga: la ເດືອນມົກກະລາ
Japan	n. bpa: tet nyi bpu:n ປະເທດ ຢີ່ປຸ່ນ
Japanese	adj. nyi bpu:n ຢີ່ປຸ່ນ
jar	n. hay ໄຫ
javelin	n. low ຫຼາວ
jaw	n. kang ga: dtay: ຄາງກະໄຕ
jay	n. no:k kap ນົກຂາບ
jazz	n. do:n dti sa: may: ດົນ ຕຣີສໄມ
jealous	adj. i:t sa ອິດສາ
jealousy	n. kwam i:t sa ຄວາມອິດສາ
jest	v. he:t dta: lo:k ເຣັດຕໍຼກ
	n. kwam dta: lo:k ຄວາມ ຕໍຼກ
Jesuit	n. pa: cha:m puak neu:ng kohng sat sa: na ga dto li:k ພະຈຳພວກນຶ່ງ ຂອງສາສນາກະໂຕລິກ
Jesus	n. pa: nye su ພະເຢຊູ
jet plane	n. nyo:n ay po:n ຢົນ ໄອພົ້ນ

ew n. ko:n sat yi:w ຄົນຊາດຢິວ

ewel n. keuang pe:t ເຄື່ອງເພັດ

ewelry store n. han kay ka:m ຮ້ານຂາຍຄຳ

ewish adj. haang sow yi:w ແຫ່ງ ຊາວຢິວ

b n. wiak gan ວຽກການ

ockey n. ko:n ki ma suang ຄົນ ຂີ່ມ້າຊ່ວງ

in (group) v. huam na:m ຮ່ວມ ນຳ

(things) v. ow kow: ga:n ເອົາເຂົ້າກັນ

int n. bohn dtoh ບ່ອນຕໍ່

(slang) bang sa ບັງຊາ

ke n. leuang dta: lo:k ເລື່ອງຕະລົກ

v. wow: dta: lo:k ເວົ້າ ຕະລົກ

er (person) n. ko:n dta: lo:k ຄົນຕະລົກ

(card) n. pay cho ger ໃພ້ໂຈກເກີ

ly adj. sa: nu:k sa: nan ສະໜຸກສະໜານ

t v. dteun dto:k chay: ຕື່ນຕົກໃຈ

rnal (newspaper) n. na:ng seu pi:m lay wain ໜັງສືພິມລາຍ ວັນ

(diary) n. ba:n teu:k lay ບັນທຶກລາຍ

---

wa:n ບັນທຶກລາຍວັນ

journalism (modern) n. wi: sa gan na:ng seu pi:m ວິຊາການ ໜັງສືພິມ

(formal) n. wa la: san sat ວາລະສານສາດ

journalist n. na:k na:ng seu pi:m ນັກໜັງສືພິມ

journey n. gan dern tang ການເດີນທາງ

v. dern tang ເດີນທາງ

joy n. kwam muan seun ຄວາມມ່ວນຊື່ນ

joyful adj. muan seun ມ່ວນຊື່ນ

joyous adj. sa: nu:k sa: nan ສະໜຸກສະໜານ

Judaism n. sat sa: na yi:w ສາສນາ ຢິວ

judge (formal) n. ay: nya: gan san ໄອຍະການສານ

(common) n. cha san ຈ່າສານ

v. dta:t si:n ຕັດສິນ

judgment n. gan dta:t si:n ການຕັດ ສິນ

judo n. moy yu do ໂມຍຢູໂດ

jug n. ka:n to ຄັນໂຕ

juice n. na:m mak may: ນ້ຳພາກໄມ້

juicy adj. mi na:m lay (mak may:) ມີນ້ຳລາຍ (ພາກໄມ້)

July	n. deuan goh láː gãː da ເດືອນກໍລະກະດາ
jump	(feet) v. gãː dot ກະໂດດ (parachute) v. dton chóhng ໂຕນຈ້ອງ
jumping	n. gán gãː dot ການກະໂດດ
jump rope	n. seuák dteːn ເຊືອກເຕັ້ນ
junction	n. gán saːm tòːp gaːn ການສົມທົບກັນ
June	n. deuan míː tuːnā ເດືອນ ມິຖຸນາ
jungle	n. doːng, pã dteuy ດົງ, ປາເດືອ
junior	(kid) adj. deːk nóy ເດັກນ້ອຍ (interior) adj. hohng ຮອງ (school) n. naːk seuːk sã bpiː ti sam kohng maː ha wiːt taː nyaː láy: ນັກສຶກສາຍຫ້ສາມຂອງມະຫາວິທະຍາໄລ
junk	n. keuang set nyóy ເຄື່ອງ ເສດຍ່ອຍ v. tiːm bpay: ຖີ້ມໄປ
juridical	adj. haːng sãn dtaːt siːn ເຫ່ງສານຕັດສິນ
jurisdiction	n. aːm nat sãn ອຳນາດສານ
jurisprudence	n. wíː sã goːt máy ວິຊາກົດໝາຍ
jurist	n. naːk goːt máy ນັກ ກົດໝາຍ
juror	n. gaːm maː gán dtaːt sín kwaːm ກຳມະການຕັດສິນຄວາມ

jury	n. kuːn sãn ຂຸນສານ
just	adj. tiang taːm ທ່ຽງທັມ adv. teuk dtohng (poh di) ຖືກຕ້ອງ(ພໍດີ)
justice	n. kwaːm nyuː dti taːm ຄວາມຍຸຕິທັມ
justifiable	adj. sering bpeːn gán soːː kuan ເຊິ່ງເປັນການສົມຄວນ
justification	n. gán bohk het poːn wa t dtohng ການບອກເຫດຜົນວ່າຖືກ
justify	(explain) v. bohk het poːn ບອກເຫດຜົນ (make right) v. heːt hay teuk dtohng ເຮັດໃຫ້ຖືກຕ້ອງ
jute	(big) n. dtoːn bpoh ຕົ້ນປ (small) n. dtoːn bpan ຕົ້ນ ປ່ານ
juvenile	n. nyów: waː sõːn ເຍົາວະ adj. nyów: wáy: ເຍົາໄວ

K

Kampuchea	n. kaː men ເຂມນ
kangaroo	n. dto chíːng cho ໂຕຈີງໂຈ
keel	n. tohng heua ທ້ອງເຮືອ v. loːm loːng ລົ້ມລົງ
keep	v. haːk sã wáy: ຮັກສາໄວ້ (keep quiet) v. yuː miːt ຢູ່ມິດ (keep working) v. heːt

	wiak dtoh bpay: ເຮັດວຽກການ ຕໍ່ໄປ
eep abreast of	mi kwam hu tain het gan bpa: chu: bain ມີຄວາມຮູ້ທາງ ເຮັດການປະຈຸບັນ
eep on	heit dtoh bpay: ເຮັດຕໍ່ໄປ
eep out	gain way: ກັນໄວ້
eep track of	choit way: ຈົດໄວ້
eep up	(continue) heit dtoh ເຮັດຕໍ່ (support) suay leua ຊ່ວຍເຫຼືອ
eep up with	hu tain het gan ຮູ້ທັນເຫດການ
eeper	n. koin fow: haik sa ຄົນເຝົ້າຮັກສາ
eeping	n. gan fow: haik sa ການເຝົ້າຮັກສາ
nnels	n. kohk ma ຄອກໝາ
nya	n. bpa: tet kin nya ປະເທດ ຄິນຍາ
rchief	n. pa pok hua ຜ້າໂພກຫົວ
rosene	n. naim main gait ນ້ຳມັນ ກາດ
ttle	(metal) n. ga naim ການນ້ຳ (clay) n. dtow: naim diin ເຕົາໝໍ້ນ້ຳດິນ
y	(door) n. ga: chaa ກະແຈ (problem) n. sohng tang ຊ່ອງທາງ

khaki	(color) n. si ga gi ສີກາກີ (cloth) n. pa si ga gi ຜ້າສີກາກີ
kick	n. bat dte: ບາດເຕະ v. dte: ເຕະ
kick out	lay: ohk ໄລ່ອອກ
kid	(goat) n. luk baa ລູກແບ້ v. yohk ຢອກ (child) n. deik noy ເດັກນ້ອຍ
kidnap	v. laik ow: dtua koin ລັກເອົາຕົວຄົນ
kidney	n. mak kay: laing ໝາກ ໄຂ່ຫຼັງ
kill	v. ka ຂ້າ
killer	n. kat dta: gohn ຄາດຕະກອນ
kilo	n. naim naik gi: lo ນ້ຳໜັກ ກີໂລ
kin	n. pi nohng ພີ່ນ້ອງ
kind	(to poor) adj. ga lu: na ກະຣຸນນາ n. sa: niit ຊນິດ (to people) adj. choip ຈິບ
kindergarten	n. hong hian ai: nu: ban ໂຮງຮຽນອະນຸບານ
kindle	v. daing fay: ຕັ້ງໄຟ
kindly	adj. choip ຈິບ adj. yang ga: lu: na ຢ່າງກະຣຸນນາ

kindness	n. kwam met dta ຄວາມ ເມຕຕາ
	n. kwam ga: lu: nå ຄວາມກະຣຸນາ
king	n. chow si wi:t ເຈົ້າຊີວິດ
kingdom	n. lat sa: a na cha:k ຣາຊອານາຈັກ
king-size	adj. ka: nat nyay: ຂນາດ ໃຫຍ່
kip	(name of Lao currency) nger:n gip lao ເງິນກີບລາວ
kiss	v. chup ຈູບ
	n. gan chup ການຈູບ
kitchen	n. heuan kua ເຮືອນຄົວ
kite	n. wow ວ່າວ
kitten	n. luk maåw ລູກແມວ
knee	n. hua kow: ຫົວເຂົ່າ
kneecap	n. mak ba hua kow: ພາກບ້າຫົວເຂົ່າ
kneel	v. ku: kow: ຄຸເຂົ່າ
knife	n. mit ມີດ
	v. taang duay mit ແທງດ້ວຍມີດ
knit	v. ta:k ຖັກ
knob	n. ga:m ກຳ
knock	v. koh: ເຄາະ
knot	n. koh ຂໍ
know	v. hu cha:k ຮູ້ຈັກ
know by heart	hu cho:n keun chay: ຮູ້ຈົນຂຶ້ນໃຈ

know-how	kwam sa mat pi set ຄວາມສາມາດພິເສດ
knowing	(wise) adj. sa: lat ສລາດ
	(kind) adv. mi kwam kow: chay: di ມີຄວາມເຂົ້າໃຈດີ
knowledge	n. kwam hu ຄວາມຮູ້
knuckle	n. koh niw meu ຂໍ້ນິວມື
Korea	n. bpa: tet gow: li ປະເທດເກົາຫລີ
Korean	n. ko:n sow gow: li ຄົນຊາວເກົາຫລີ

L

label	(sticker) n. bpay ປ້າຍ
	(name) n. seu ຊື່
	v. dti:t bpay ຕິດປ້າຍ
labor	(job) n. wiak ngan ວຽກງານ
	(person) n. haang ngan ແຮງງານ
	v. he:t wiak ເຮັດວຽກ
laboratory	n. hohng ko:n hua wi:t ta: nya sat ຫ້ອງຄົມຄົວ ວິທຍາສາດ
laborer	n. ko:n he:t wiak ຄົນເຮັດວຽກ
lace	v. ha:t ຮັດ
	(string) n. say ha:t ສາຍຮັດ

	(cloth) n. paˊ luk maˇy:
	ผ้าลูกไม้
lack	n. kwaˇm kat kaan
	ความขาดแคน
	adj. kern kaˊ ขาดเขิน
lad	n. deˇk noˋy puˊ saˇy
	เด็กน้อยผู้ชาย
ladder	n. kaˇn dayˊ: gay บันไดก่าย
ladies' room	n. hoˇhng naˇm suˊ: pap saˊ:
	dtri ห้องน้ำสายสัตตรี
lady	(normal) n. puˊ nyiˇ:ng
	ผู้หญิง
	(formal) n. suˊ: pap saˊ:
	dtri สุภาพสัตตรี
lag	v. saˇk saˇ วักช้า
lair	n. bohn yu kohng saˋt bpa
	(taˇm gon maˊy:) บ่อนอยู่ของ
	สัตว์ป่า (ถู่ไม้)
lake	n. taˊ: le sap ทะเลสาบ
lamb	n. luk gaˋa: ลูกแกะ
lame	adj. piˊ: gan พิการ
lament	n. kwaˇm sowˇ: saˊ: loˇit
	chayˊ: ความเศร้าสลดใจ
	v. sowˇ: saˊ: loˇit chayˊ:
	เศร้าสลดใจ
lamp	(small) n. dtaˊ: giang
	ตะเกียง
	(big) n. kom fayˇ: โคมไฟ
lance	v. taang แทง
	n. hohk หอก
land	(plane) v. loˇhng choht
	ลงจอด
	(boat) v. tiap taˋ ทูยบท่า
	n. diˊ:n ดิน
landlord	n. chow kohng ti diˊ:n
	เจ้าของที่ดิน
landmark	n. laˊ:k ket daan
	หลักเขตแดน
landscape	n. pu mi pak ผู้มิภาก
	v. daˋ:t bpaang ti diˊ:n haˇy:
	bpeˇ:n suˇan แต่งแปงที่ดินให้เป็นสวน
lane	n. tang noy ทางน้อย
language	n. paˊ sa ผาสา
language lab	n. hoˇhng faˇ:ng siang
	ห้องฟังสูง
lantern	n. kom fayˇ: โคมไฟ
Laos	(country) n. bpaˊ: tet lowˇ
	ปะเทดลาว
	(Republic) saˇ taˋ laˊ: naˊ:
	laˊ:t bpaˊ: sa tiˊ: bpaˊ: dtai
	bpaˊ: soˊ:n lowˇ
	สาทาละมะลัดปะชาทิปะไตปะชาชุมลาว
lap	v. liaˊ เลีย n. dtaˊːk ตัก
lard	(butter) n. neˊ:y เนย
	(pig) n. naˇm maˇn muˋ
	น้ำมันหมู
large	adj. gwaˇng, nyaˊ: ก้วาง, ใหญ่
largely	adv. yang gwaˇng kuˇang
	อย่างกว้างขวาง
lash	v. dti duay saˇa ตีด้วยแส้

	n. gan dti saa ການຕິແສ	launder	v. saːk keuang ຊັກເຄື່ອງ
lass	n. deːk nŏy pu nyĭːng ເດັກນ້ອຍຜູ້ຍິງ	laundry	(place) n. hŏng saːk liːt ໂຮງຊັກລີດ
last	v. toːn ທົນ		(clothes) n. keuang oʷː bpay saːk ເຄື່ອງເອົາໄປຊັກ
	adj. suːt tay ສຸດທ້າຍ		
late	adj. saː jaː ຊ້າ	law	n. goːt may ກົດໝາຍ
lately	adv. meua wayː wayː niː ເມື່ອໄວໆນີ້	lawful	adj. teuk dtohng dtam goːt may ຖືກຕ້ອງຕາມກົດໝາຍ
latest	(last) adj. saː ti suːt ຊ້າທີ່ສຸດ	lawless	adj. piːt goːt may ຜິດກົດ ໝາຍ
	(newest) adj. mayː ti suːt ໃໝ່ທີ່ສຸດ	lawn	n. deːrn nya ເດີ່ນຫຍ້າ
		lawn mower	n. loh dtaːk nya ລໍຕັດຫຍ້າ
lather	(soap) n. fohng saː bu ຟອງສະບູ	lawn tennis	n. teːn niːt ເທັນນິດ
		lawyer	n. taː nay kwam ທະນາຍຄວາມ
	(sweat) n. heua lay ເຫື່ອຫຼາຍ	lay	v. bpu, bpohng wayː ປູ, ປ່ອງໄວ້
latitude	(global) n. seːn baang lok taːng kuang ເສັ້ນແບ່ງໂລກທາງຂວາງ	lay aside	(discontinue) sowː heːt ເຊົາເຮັດ
			(save for future use) oʷː wayː sayː nayː pay na ເອົາໄວ້ໃຊ້ໃນພາຍໜ້າ
	(opportunity) n. kohp keːt kohng se li pap ຂອບເຂດຂອງເສລີພາບ	lay off	layː ohk chak ngan ໄລ່ອອກຈາກງານ
latter	adj. taːt bpayː ຖັດໄປ	lay out	gaː bpaː man nayː gan sayː chay ກະປະມານໃນການໃຊ້ຈ່າຍ
laugh	v. hua ທົວ		
	n. gan hua ການທົວ	layer	n. saːn kohng diːn ຊັ້ນຂອງດິນ
laughable	adj. bpeːn dta yaːk hua ເປັນຕາຢາກທົວ	lazily	adv. yang ki kaːn ຢ່າງຂີ້ຄ້ານ
		lazy	adj. ki kaːn ຂີ້ຄ້ານ
laughter	n. siang hua ສຽງທົວ	lead	(pioneer, guide) v. naːm paː bpay ນໍາພາໄປ
launch	n. heua ເຮືອ		(clue) v. laːk tan ຫຼັກ ຖານ
	v. bpoy loːng naːm ປ່ອຍລົງນ້ຳ		

	(metal) n. ki gua ຂີ້ກວ
	(first) n. pu na:m ຜູ້ນຳ
leader	n. hua na ຫົວໜ້າ
leaf	n. bay: may: ໃບໄມ້
	v. bpert bpeum teua la: bay: ເປີດປຶ້ມເທື່ອລະໃບ
leafless	adj. boh mi bay: ບໍ່ມີໃບ
leafy	adj. mi bay: do:k ມີໃບດົກ
league	(group) n. huam ga:n ຮວມ ກັນ
	(distance) n. la: nya: sa: me may: ລະຍະສະເມໄມ
leak	n. bohn hua ບ່ອນຮົ່ວ
	v. hua ຮົ່ວ
lean	(person) adj. choy ຈ້ອຍ
	(meat) adj. bang ບາງ
	v. ing ອີງ
leap year	n. bpi ti mi sam hoy ho:k ປີທີ່ມີສາມຮ້ອຍຫົກ si:p ho:k meu ສິບຫົກມື້
learn	v. hian ຮຽນ
learn by heart	hian cho:n keun chay: ຮຽນຈົນຂຶ້ນໃຈ
lease	n. gan sow: ການເຊົ່າ
	v. hay: sow: ໃຫ້ເຊົ່າ
least	adj. noy ti su:t ນ້ອຍທີ່ສຸດ
leather	n. nang ໜັງ
leave	(go out) v. chak bpay: ຈາກໄປ

	(remain behind) v. bpa: way: ປະໄວ້
	n. we la pa:k gan do:n ເວລາພັກການຕື່ນ ໆ
leave out	bpa: ohk ປະອອກ
leaven	n. bpaang kow: mak ແປ້ງເຂົ້າໝາກ
lecture	v. bpa: ta: ga: ta, ban nyay ປະທະກະຕະ, ບັນຍາຍ n. gan bpa: ta: ga: ta ການປະທະກະຕາ
lecturer	n. pu gow bpa: ta: ga: ta ຜູ້ກ່າວປະທະກະຕາ
ledge	n. kohp pa ຂອບພາ
ledger	n. bpeum sa: mu:t ba:n si ປຶ້ມສະໝຸດບັນຊີ
left	n. tang say ທາງຊ້າຍ
left-handed	adj. haang say ແຮງຊ້າຍ
leg	n. ka ຂາ
legal	adj. teuk dtam go:t may ຖືກຕາມກົດໝາຍ
legate	n. pu dtang na ຜູ້ຕາງໜ້າ v. dtaang dtang tut ແຕ່ງຕັ້ງ ທຸດ
legation	(house) n. sa: tan tut ສະຖານທຸດ (action) n. gan dtaang dtang tut ການແຕ່ງຕັ້ງທຸດ
legend	n. ni: tan gow ນິທານເກົ່າ

legion	n. gohng ta:p ta: han ກອງທັບຕະການ	lens	n. waan ແວ່ນ
legislate	v. dtaang go:t may ແຕ່ງກົດໝາຍ	leper	n. ko:n ki tut ຄົນຂີ້ທູດ
		leprosy	n. pa: nyat ki tut ພະຍາດຂີ້ທູດ
legislation	n. go:t may ກົດໝາຍ	less	adj. noy gua ໜ້ອຍກວ່າ
legislative	adj. mi a:m nat dtaang go:t may ມີອຳນາດແຕ່ງກົດໝາຍ	-less	(changes verbs and nouns to adjective) ti bpian gi: li: nya laa: nam hay: bpe:n ka:m ku:n nam ທີ່ປ່ຽນກິລິຍາແລະນາມ ໃຫ້ເປັນຄຳຄຸນນາມ
legislator	n. pu dtaang dtang go:t may ຜູ້ແຕ່ງຕັ້ງກົດໝາຍ		
legislature	n. ka: na: dtaang dtang go:t may ຄະນະແຕ່ງຕັ້ງກົດໝາຍ	lesson	n. bo:t hian ບົດຮຽນ
		lest	conj. yan wa ຢ້ານວ່າ
legitimate	adj. teuk dtam go:t may ຖືກຕາມກົດໝາຍ	let	(allow) v. bpoy hay: ປ່ອຍໃຫ້
leisure	n. gan pa:k pohn ການພັກຜ່ອນ		(rent) v. hay: so:m ໃຫ້ເຊົ່າ
leisurely	adv. dtam sa: bay ຕາມສະບາຍ	let alone	bon lo:p guan ບໍ່ຣົບກວນ
lemon	n. mak now tet ໝາກນາວເທດ	let down	ha:k lang ຫັກຫຼັງ
lemonade	(fresh) n. na:m mak now tet ນ້ຳໝາກນາວເທດ	let go	(allow to depart) bpoy hay: bpay: ປ່ອຍໃຫ້ໄປ
	(bottle) n. na:m so:m ນ້ຳສົ້ມ		(release) bpoy, bpa: ປ່ອຍ, ປະ
lend	v. hay yeum ໃຫ້ຢືມ	let off	a: nu: nyat ຂະນຸຍາດ
lend a hand	hay: kwam suay leua ໃຫ້ຄວາມຊ່ວຍເຫຼືອ	let out	bpoy ohk ປ່ອຍອອກ
length	(distance) n. tang nyow ທາງຍາວ	let's	v. pa ga:n ...... toh: ພາກັນ....ເທາະ
	(time) n. la: nya: we la ຣະຍະເວລາ	letter	(correspondence) n. cho:t may ຈົດໝາຍ
			(alphabet) n. dto na:ng seu ໂຕໜັງສື
lengthen	v. he:t hay: nyow ohk ເຮັດໃຫ້ຍາວອອກ	lettuce	n. pa:k sa: la:t ຜັກສະລັດ

level	n. na⌣ːm tiang, laːm daːp
	ນ້ຳທຽງ, ລຳດັບ
	(surface) v. he⌣ːt hay⌣ː
	piang ເຮັດໃຫ້ພຽງ
	(with someone) v. bo⌣hk
	kwam chi⌣ːng ບອກຄວາມຈິງ
lever	n. ma⌣y leu le⌣ːk nga⌣ːt
	ໄມ້ທີ່ເຫຼັກງັດ
levy	v. ge⌣ːp suay ເກັບຊ່ວຍ
liable	adj.ha⌣ːp pi⌣ːt sohp, ti nyohm cha⌣ː opeːn
	ຮັບຜິດຊອບ, ທ່ຽມຈະເປັນ
liar	n. ko⌣ːn ki⌣ dtu⌣a: ຄົນຂີ້ຕົວະ
liberal	adj. i⌣ːt sa⌣ː la⌣ː ອິສຣະ
liberate	(free) v. bpoy hay⌣ː bpeːn i⌣ːk sa⌣ː la⌣ː ປ່ອຍໃຫ້ເປັນອິສຣະ
	(army) v. bpo⌣ːt bpoy ປົດປ່ອຍ
liberation	n. gan opoːt opohy ການປົດປ່ອຍ
liberty	(general) n. se⌣ li⌣ pap ເສຣີພາບ
	(personal) n. kwam mi⌣ i⌣ː sa⌣ː la⌣ː ຄວາມມີອິສຣະ
librarian	(professional) n. ba⌣ːn na la⌣ːk ບັນນາຮັກ
	(clerk) n. pu fow⌣ː hohng sa⌣ː muːt ຜູ້ເຝົ້າຫໍ້ງສມຸດ
library	(room) n. hohng sa⌣ː muːt ຫໍ້ງສມຸດ
	(building) n. hoh sa⌣ː muːt ທໍ່ສມຸດ
	(bookshelf) n. ha⌣ːn bpeum ຮ້ານປຶ້ມ
license	n. bay⌣ a⌣ː nu⌣ː nyat ໃບອະນຸຍາດ
	v. a⌣ː nu⌣ː nyat hay⌣ː ອະນຸຍາດໃຫ້
	(driver's license) n. bay⌣ː ka⌣ːp ki⌣ ໃບຂັບຂີ່
lick	n. bat dti ບາດຕີ
	v. lia ເລຍ
lid	(jar) n. fa la⌣ː mi hay⌣ː ຝາຣະມີທ
	(eye) n. naːng dta ໜັງຕາ
lie	n. gan dtu⌣a: ການຕົວະ
	(fool) v. dtu⌣a: ຕົວະ
	(sleep) v. nohn ນອນ
lieutenant	n. nay⌣ hoy⌣ to ນາຍຮ້ອຍໂທ
life	n. si⌣ wi⌣ːt ຊີວິດ
life belt	(water) n. ke⌣ːm ka⌣ːt su⌣ sip ເຂັມຂັດຊູຊິບ
	(parachute) n. sa⌣y ha⌣ːt chohng ສາຍຮັດຈອງ
lifeboat	n. heua suay si wi⌣ːt ເຮືອຊ່ວຍຊີວິດ
lifeless	adj. boh ne⌣ːng dting ບໍ່ເໜັງຕີງ
lift	n. cha⌣ːk nyo⌣ːk ຈັກຍົກ
	v. nyo⌣ːk keun ຍົກຂຶ້ນ

light	(not dark) adj. chǎang แจ้ง	lime	(chemical) n. bpun kǒw ปูนขาว
	(not heavy) adj. bow: เบ๋า		(fruit) n. mak nǒw ฬากนาว
	(color) adj. ohn ออน	limestone	n. hǐːn bpun หินปูน
	n. fǎy: ไฟ	limitation	n. gan ohm ket daan ภามออมเฃตแฃน
	v. dtǎy fǎy: ใต้ไฟ		n. kohp ket ฃอบเฃต
lighten	(not dark) v. heːt hǎy: chǎang เริกให้แจ้ง	limit	(amount) v. chaːm gàːt จริภัฃ
	(not heavy) v. heːt hay: bow: เริกให้เบ๋า		(territory) v. ohm ket daan ออมเฃตแฃน
	(color) v. heːt hǎy: kǒw เริกให้ขาว		n. kohp ket ฃอบเฃต
lighter	n. leːk fǎy: ็ฏุกไฟ	limp	n. gan nyang ka ke ภาม ย้างฃาเค
	adj. bow: gùa เบ๋าภว่า		v. nyang ka ke ย้างฃาเค
lighthouse	n. heuan fǎy: nyam fǎːng เริอมไฟยามฝั้ง	line	(mark) n. seːn เส้ม
lightly	adv. yang koy koy ย่าวฅอยๆ		(row) n. taaw แถว
lightning	n. sǎy fǎ maap สายฟ้าแมบ		(cloth) v. sǎy: paa hohr tang naːy: seua
lightweight	n. naːk mǔay bow: มัภมวย เบ๋า		ใส่แผรฃวๆทาๆใมเส้อ
like	conj. kǎy keu ฅ้ายฅี	linen	n. pa fǎy liː niːn ผ้าฝ้ายลิมิม
	v. maːk มัภ	linger	v. yu dtoh ยุต
likely	adj. at cha: bpeːn dǎy: ๆาฅจะเป็มใๆ	link	n. koh dtoh ฃต
			v. dtiːt dtoh gaːn ฅิฃฅิ้
likeness	n. kwǎm meuan gaːn ฅวาม เพ้อภ้าม	linotype	n. chaːk heːt dtua piːm จัภเริฃฅอผิม
limb	(tree) n. giːng may: nyay: ภิ้วไม้ใฬย่	lion	n. dtua siːng ฅอสิๆ
	(person) n. kǎan ka แฃมฃา	lip	(person) n. hǐːm soːp ริมๆ
			(jar) n. bpak hay: ปาภใฬ

liquid	adj. bpeːn naːm ເປັນນ້ຳ	
liquor	n. lowː ເຫຼົ້າ	
list	n. lay seu ລາຍຊື່	
	v. choːt seu ຈົດຊື່	
listen	v. faːng ຟັງ	
liter	n. liːt ລິດ	
literal	adj. dtam kam woːwː ຕາມຄຳເວົ້າ	
literary	adj. haang waːn naː kaː di ແຫ່ງວັນນະຄະດີ	
literate	adj. ti an ohk kian dayː ທີ່ອ່ານອອກຂຽນໄດ້	
literature	n. waːn naː kaː di ວັນນະຄະດີ	
litter	(animal) n. fung luk saːt ຝູງລູກສັດ	
	(trash) n. ki nyeua ຂີ້ເຫຍື້ອ	
little	adj. noy ນ້ອຍ	
	(a little) adj. noy neuːng ນ້ອຍໜຶ່ງ	
live	adj. miː siː wiːt yu ມີຊີວິດຢູ່	
	v. a sayː yu ອາໄສຢູ່	
liver	n. dtaːp ຕັບ	
livestock	n. saːt liang dtang dtang ສັດລ້ຽງຕ່າງໆ	
living room	n. hohng laːp ksak ຫ້ອງຮັບແຂກ	
lizard	(ground) n. ki goː ຂີ້ໂກະ	
	(geko) n. gaːp gaa ກັບແກ	
	(chinchuck) n. chi chiam ຈີ່ຈຽມ	
	(fence) n. chi bpohm ຈີ່ປອມ	
load	v. owː sayː loːt ເອົາໃສ່ລົດ	
	n. keuang baːn tuːk ເຄື່ອງບັນທຸກ	
locomotive	n. chaːk loːt fayː ຈັກຣົດໄຟ	
lock	(hair) n. muan poːm ມ້ວນຜົມ	
	(to turn the key) v. aːt gaː chaa ອັດກະແຈ	
	(to lock up something) v. kaːng wayː ຂັງໄວ້	
	(canal) n. bpaː dtu naːm ປະຕູນ້ຳ	
	(door) n. gaː chaa ກະແຈ	
local	adj. haang tohng tiːn ແຫ່ງທ້ອງຖິ່ນ	
locate	(position) v. owː dtang ເອົາຕັ້ງ yu ຕັ້ງຢູ່	
	(find) v. sohk ha ຊອກຫາ	
locust	n. maang chaːm puak dtaːk dtaan ແມງຈຳພວກຕັກແຕນ	
lodge	v. sowː hohng ເຂົ້າຫ້ອງ	
	n. hoh paːk ທີ່ພັກ	
look	v. miː laːk saː naː, berːng ມີລັກສນະ, ເບິ່ງ	
look after	berːng nyaang ເບິ່ງແຍງ	
look at	adv. berːng ເບິ່ງ	

look different from   dtang gáːn gaːp
ຕ່າງກັນທ້ວຍ

look down on   dǔ tuk   ດູຖູກ

look for   sohk ha   ຊອກຫາ

look forward to   koy ta duay kwam poh
chàːy: ຄອຍຕ້າດ້ວຍຄວາມໝັງໃຈ

look into   guat berìːng   ກວດເບິ່ງ

look like   keu gaːn   ຄືກັນ

look on   berìːng seu seu   ເບິ່ງຊື່

look out   laː waːng: ຣະວັງ

look over   berìːng leum keun   ເບິ່ງລຶມຄືນ

look up   sohk berìːng   ຊອກເບິ່ງ

look up to   kòwː loːp   ເຄົາຣົບ

loom   n. huk   ຫູກ

loop   v. woːng seuak   ວົງເຊືອກ

loose   (not tight) adj. loːm
ຫຼົມ

   (get loose) v. luːt ohk
ລຸດອອກ

loosen   (lessen) v. maːy ohk
ມາຍອອກ

   (untie) v. gaa ohk
ແກ້ອອກ

lord   (brag) v. uat nyaː:
ອວດໃຫຍ່

   (secular) n. paː: nya
ພະຍາ

   (religious) n. paː: phaː
ພະ

lose   (a thing) v. sia   ເສັຽ

   (a game) v. liːn sia   ຫຼີ້ນ
ເສັຽ

lose face   sia na   ເສັຽໜ້າ

lose one's mind   sia chiːt   ເສັຽຈິດ

lose one's temper   a loːm sia   ອາຣົມເສັຽ

loser   n. pu sia chay: ຜູ້ເສັຽໃຈ

loss   n. kwam sia hay   ຄວາມເສັຽ
ຫາຍ

lot   (part) n. suan   ສ່ວນ

   (large amount) n. luang
lay   ຫຼວງຫຼາຍ

lotion   n. naːm hohm   ນ້ຳຫອມ

lottery   n. huay   ຫວຍ

lotus   n. dohk bua   ດອກບົວ

loud   adj. daːng   ດັງ

lounge   v. paːk pohn   ພັກຜ່ອນ

   n. hohng naːng liːn
ຫ້ອງນັ່ງຫຼີ້ນ

louse   (animal) n. dto how:
ໂຕເຫົາ

   (person) n. koːn sua sa
ຄົນຊົ່ວຊ້າ

love   v. haːk   ຮັກ

   (feeling) n. kwam haːk
ຄວາມຮັກ

   (person) n. koːn haːk   ຄົນ
ຮັກ

lovely   adj. ti na haːk   ໜ້າຮັກ

low   (position) adj. dtaːm   ຕ່ຳ

   (person) adj. suaː: sa   ຊົ່ວຊ້າ

lower	v. lo:t dta:m lo:ng ລິດຕ່ຳລົງ
	adj. dta:m gua ຕ່ຳກ່ວາ
lower classman	n. na:k hian san noy ນັກຮຽນຊັ້ນນ້ອຍ
loyal	adj. chong ha:k pa:k di ຈົງຮັກພັກດີ
loyalty	n. kwam chong ha:k pa:k di ຄວາມຈົງຮັກພັກດີ
lubricate	v. dterm na:m ma:n keuang ເຕີມນ້ຳມັນເຄື່ອງ
luck	n. sok ໂຊກ
luckily	adv. yang sok di ຢ່າງໂຊກດີ
luckless	adj. boh mi sok ບໍ່ມີໂຊກ
lucky	adj. sok di ໂຊກດີ
luggage	n. hip keuang ຫີບເຄື່ອງ
lull	n. kwam ngiap sa: ngat ຄວາມງຽບສະຫງັດ
	v. gohm (nohn) ກ່ອມ(ນອນ)
lumber	n. bpaan ແປ້ນ
lumbering	n. gan dta:t may ການຕັດໄມ້
lump	(cube) n. gohn ກ້ອນ
	(pile) n. gohng ກອງ
lump sum	n. gan chay ngern ta:n ti taing mo:t ການຈ່າຍເງິນທັນທີທັງໝົດ
lunch	n. a han gang wa:n ອາຫານກາງວັນ
	v. gi:n kow: suay ກິນເຂົ້າສວຍ
lung	n. bpoht ປອດ
lure	n. nyeua loh ເຍື່ອລໍ່
lust	v. mi dta:n ha ມີຕັນຫາ
	n. dta:n ha ຕັນຫາ
luster	n. saang ແສງ
lusty	adj. dte:m bpay: duay dta:n ha ເຕັມໄປດ້ວຍຕັນຫາ
luxuriate	v. pert pern ເພີດເພີນ
luxurious	adj. yang lu la ຢ່າງຫຼູຫຼາ
luxury	n. keuang ba:m lu:ng ເຄື່ອງ kwam su:k ບຳລຸງຄວາມສຸກ
-ly	(changes some nouns and most adjectives to adverbs) ka:m ti bpian bang nam laa: ku:n nam suan lay hay: bpe:n gi: li: nya wi: set ຄຳທີ່ປ່ຽນບາງ ນາມແລະຄຸນນາມສ່ວນຫຼາຍໃຫ້ເປັນ ກິຣິຍາພິເສດ
lyric	adj. ti giaw ga:p gap ທີ່ກ່ຽວ gohn laa: peng ກັບກາບກອນແລະ ເພງ

M

macadam	n. tang bpu duay yang ທາງປູດ້ວຍຍາງ
machine	n. keuang cha:k ເຄື່ອງຈັກ v. he:t duay cha:k ເຮັດ ດ້ວຍຈັກ

machine gun	n. bpeun goːn ປືນກົນ
machinery	n. keuang chaːk (ຄື່ງ) ຈັກ
machine shop	n. hong geuːng ໂຮງກຶງ
machinist	n. naːy saːng chaːk ນາຍຊ່າງຈັກ
mad	(angry) adj. chaːy haːy ໃຈຮ້າຍ
	(crazy) adj. baː ບ້າ
madam	n. nya maa ຍາແມ່
madden	v. heːt haːy chaːy haːy ເຮັດໃຫ້ໃຈຮ້າຍ
madhouse	n. hong moh piː baː ໂຮງໝໍປ້ິບ້າ
magazine	(paper) n. waː laː saːn ວາລະສານ
	(gun) n. dtaːp luk bpeun ຕັບລູກປືນ
magic	(trick) n. goːn ກົນ
	(voodoo) n. moːn kaː taː ມົນຄາຖາ
magician	n. koːn liːn goːn ຄົນຫຼິ້ນກົນ
magistrate	n. pu piː pak saː ຜູ້ພິພາກສາ
magnet	n. maa leːk ແມ່ເຫຼັກ
magneto	n. keuang gaːm nert faːy ເຄື່ອງກຳເນີດໄຟ

magnificence	n. kwam uː doːm soːm bun laaː diː lert ຄວາມຢຸດສົມບຸນແລະດີເລີດ
magnificent	adj. nyiːng nyaːy laaː diː lert ຍິ່ງໃຫຍ່ແລະດີເລີດ
magnify	v. heːt haːy nyaːy ເຮັດໃຫ້ໃຫຍ່
maid	n. koːn saːy (pu nyiːng) ຄົນໃຊ້ (ຜູ້ຍິງ)
maiden	n. pu sow ຜູ້ສາວ
maiden name	nam saː guːn pu nyiːng dtohn bpeːn sow ນາມລະກຸນ ຜູ້ຍິງຕອນເປັນສາວ
mail	v. soːng tang bpaːy saː niː ສ່ງທາງໄປສະນີ n. bpaːy saː niː ໄປສະນີ
mailbox	n. dtu bpaːy saː niː ຕູ້ ໄປສະນີ
mail clerk	n. saː mian chaːt choːt may saː ມຽນຈັດຈິດໝາຍ
mailman	n. koːn soːng choːt may ຄົນສົ່ງຈິດໝາຍ
maim	v. heːt haːy piː gan ເຮັດໃຫ້ພິການ
main	(things) adj. suan nyaːy ສ່ວນໃຫຍ່ (ideas) adj. chaːy kwam saːm kaːn ໃຈຄວາມສຳຄັນ n. toh naːm nyaːy ທໍ່ນ້ຳໃຫຍ່ gan dtiː gay ການຕີໄກ

mainland	n. păan di:n nyáy: ແຜ່ນ ດິນໃຫຍ່
mainly	adv. suăn nyay: ສ່ວນໃຫຍ່
maintain	v. ha:k să wáy: ຮັກສາໄວ້
maintenance	n. găn ha:k să ການຮັກສາ
majestic	adj. sa: ngá pa pėrny ສງ່າຜ່າເຜີຍ
majesty	(title) n. so:m de:t ສົມເດັດ
	(thing) n. kwám sa: ngá pa pėrny ຄວາມສງ່າຜ່າເຜີຍ
major	n. năy pa:n dti ນາຍ ພັນຕຣີ
	adj. suăn nyay: ສ່ວນໃຫຍ່
majority	n. suăn lăy sŏm ສ່ວນຫຼາຍ
make	v. he:t ເຮັດ
make a living ha liáng si wi:t ຫາລ້ຽງ ຊີວິດ	
make allowance for pi cha la: nă ພິຈາຣະ ນາ	
make believe ta:m tă ທຳທ່າ	
make certain he:t hăy: naă chay: ເຮັດໃຫ້ ແມ່ໃຈ	
make faces he:t na bpe:n dta hua ເຮັດໜ້າເປັນຕາຫົວ	
make friends ha mu ຫາໝູ່	
make fun of hua kuan ຫົວຂ້ວນ	
make money ha ngėr:n di ຫາເງິນດີ	
make over bpáang he:t may: ແປງເຮັດໃໝ	
make sure he:t hăy: naă chay: ເຮັດໃຫ້ ແມ່ໃຈ
make up v. (compose) sang kėun ສ້າງຂຶ້ນ
	(invent) bpa: di:t kėun ປະດິດຂຶ້ນ
	(apply cosmetics) dtaăng nă ແຕ່ງໜ້າ
	(become friendly again) kėun di ga:n ຄືນດີກັນ
make up for he:t taăn ເຮັດແທນ
make up one's mind dta:t si:n chay: ຕັດສິນໃຈ
make use of say: ໃຊ້
maker n. pu he:t ຜູ້ເຮັດ
makeshift n. si:ng sua kow ສິ່ງຊົ່ວຄາວ
makeup (face) n. keuang sa:m ang ເຄື່ອງສ້ອງ
	(design) n. baap ແບບ
	(story) n. leuang dtaăng ow: ເຣື່ອງແຕ່ງເອົາ
malady n. pa: nyat ພະຍາດ
malaria n. pa: nyat kay: bpa ພະຍາດໄຂ້ປ່າ
Malay adj. ma le si ມະເລຊີ
Malaysian adj. ko:n ma le si ຄົນມະເລຊີ
male n. pet pu ເພດຜູ້
malice n. kwám ki:t hăy ຄວາມຄິດຮ້າຍ

malicious	adj. mī chet dǐa: nǎ hǎy ມີເຈຕນາຮ້າຍ
malignant	adj. nyáp sá ທຍາບຊ້າ
mallet	n. kohn dti may: ຄ້ອນຕີໄມ້
malnutrition	n. gàn kàt a hǎn ການຂາດ ອາຫານ
mama	n. mǎa ແມ່
man	(men) n. pu sǎy ຜູ້ຊາຍ
manage	(supervise) v. chà:t gàn ຈັດການ
	(survise ok) v. pòh yǔ day: ຜ່ຍູ່ໄດ້
management	(people) n. ka: na: boh lí hǎn ຄະມະບໍຣິຫານ
	(action) n. gàn chà:t gàn ການຈັດການ
manager	(business) n. pu chà:t gàn ຜູ້ຈັດການ
	(sports) n. ku feu:k aap ຄູຝຶກແອບ
mandate	n. kàm sàing ຄຳສັ່ງ
mane	faàng (mǎ leu sǐng) ແຜ່ງ (ມ້າຫຼືສິງ)
mango	n. mak muang ໝາກມ່ວງ
manifest	adj. sa:t chǎang ຈັດເຈ້ງ
	(visible) v. sǎ: daang hay: he:n ສະແດງໃຫ້ເຫັນ
	(airplane) v. teuk lòng seu ki nyo:n ຕຶກລົງຊື່ຂໍ້ຍມ
manifold	adj. lay dtoh ຫຼາຍຕ
mankind	n. ma: nu:t sàt ມະນຸດຊາດ
manly	adj. yáng luk pu sǎy ຢ່າງ ລູກຜູ້ຊາຍ
manner	(behavior) n. la:k sǎ: nǎ: ລັກສະນະ
	(manners) n. gi: li: nya ກິຣິຍາ
mannerly	adj. mī gi: li: nya di ມີກິຣິຍາດີ
mansion	n. heuan nyay: ເຮືອນໃຫຍ່
mantle	n. seua ku:m ເສື້ອຄຸມ
manual	n. bpeum ku měu ປຶ້ມຄູ່ມື adj. he:t duay meu ເຮັດດ້ວຍມື
manufacture	v. bpa: di:t keun yang lay ປະດິດຂຶ້ນຢ່າງຫຼາຍ
manufacturer	n. chow kohng hong ngàn, pu pa li:t (ເຈົ້າຂອງໂຮງງານ, ຜູ້ຜະລິດ
manure	n. fu:n sà:t ຝຸ່ນສັດ
manuscript	n. dto:n sa: ba:p ຕົ້ນສະບັບ
many	adj. lay (naĭp day:) ຫຼາຍ (ນັບໄດ້)
map	v. paan tĭ ແຜນທີ່ n. he:t paan tĭ ເຮັດແຜນທີ່
maple	n. dto:n me bper:n ຕົ້ນເມເບີນ
mar	v. he:t hay: sia kwam ngam ເຮັດໃຫ້ເສ້ຍຄວາມງາມ

marble	(stone) n. hǐ:n oǐn ຫິນອ່ອນ
	(game) n. gan lǐ:n mak di:t ການຫຼິ້ນພາກດິດ
march	(parade) v. dern suan sǎ: nǎm ເດີນສວນສະໜາມ
	(battle) v. dern ta:p ເດີນທັບ
March	n. deuan mi nǎ ເດືອນມີນາ
mare	n. mǎ mǎa ມ້າແມ່
margin	(paper) n. kohp na chia ຂອບໜ້າເຈຍ
	(for error) n. kohp ket kohng kwam pi:t ຂອບເຂດຂອງ ຄວາມຜິດ
marine	n. ta: han heǔa ທະຫານເຮືອ adj. haang ta: le ແຫ່ງທະເລ
mariner	(navy) n. ta: han heǔa ທະຫານເຮືອ
	(seaman) n. ko:n a say: yu̱ heǔa ຄົນເອົາໃສຢູ່ເຮືອ
marital	adj. gǐaw ga:p gan dtaang dohng ກ່ຽວກັບການແຕ່ງດອງ
mark	n. keuang mǎy ເຄື່ອງໝາຍ v. mǎy ໝາຍ
marker	(sign) n. keuang mǎy ເຄື່ອງໝາຍ
	(grade) n. pu hay: ka: naan ຜູ້ໃຫ້ຄະແນນ
	(magic marker) n. soh

	sai lǎ:p kian keuang mǎy ສົສຳໝັບຂຽນເຄື່ອງໝາຍ
marksman	n. pu nyi:ng bpeun nǎa ຜູ້ຍິງປືນແມ່ນ
market	n. dta: lat ຕະລາດ v. kǎy kohng ຂາຍຂອງ
maroon	n. sǐ na:m dtan ke:m ສີນ້ຳຕານເຂັ້ມ v. bpoy hay; yu goh: ປ່ອຍໃຫ້ຢູ່ເກາະ
marriage	n. gan dtaang dohng ການແຕ່ງດອງ
marry	(ancient) v. dtaang dohng ແຕ່ງດອງ
	(common) v. dtaang ngan ແຕ່ງງານ
marsh	n. nohng ໜອງ
marshal	n. chohm po:n ຈອມພົນ v. cha:t chaang ຈັດແຈງ
marshmallow	n. ka: no:m fohng na:m ຂນົມຟອງນ້ຳ
martyr	n. pu nyohm dtay dtang mu ຜູ້ຍອມຕາຍຕາງໝູ່ v. soim nyohm dtay dtang ສົມຍອມຕາຍຕາງ
marvel	n. kwam ai:t sa: cha:n ຄວາມອັສຈັນ v. keu:t ka:m neu:ng, ngeu:d ngoh ຄິດຄຳນຶ່ງ, ງົດ

marvellous	(strange) adj. na᷆ bpaàk bpaː la᷇t ຜ້າແປກປລາດ	master key	n. lu᷆k gaː᷇ chaa tiˊ kaýː gaː᷇ chaa tuk baàp dayː ລູກກະແຈທີ່ໄຂກະແຈທຸກແບບ
	(excellent) adj. wiː᷇ set ວິເສດ	mastery	(control) n. kwam bpeːn nyaýː ຄວາມເປັນໃຫຍ່
masculine	adj. pet saý ເພດຊາຍ		(knowledge) n. kwam hu᷇ ຄວາມຮູ້
mash	n. kwam bpoːn gaːn ຄວາມ ປິ່ນກັນ		(ability) n. kwam saː᷇ maᴛ ຄວາມສາມາດ
	v. bpoːn bpi hayː muːn ປົ່ນປີ້ໃຫ້ມຸ່ນ	mat	n. sat ສາດ
mask	v. bpiːt ປິດ		adj. muˊa ມົວ
	n. na᷆ gak ຜ້າກາກ	match	(for cigarettes) n. gaːp fayː ກັບໄຟ
mason	n. sang goh heuan ຊ່າງກໍ່ເຮືອນ		(marriage) n. gan dtaang ngan ການແຕ່ງງານ
masonry	n. gán goh duày di᷇n chi leu hiˊ ການກໍ່ດ້ວຍດິນຈຸກຫມ		(competition) n. gan kaang kaìn ການແຂ່ງຂ້ນ
mass	(church) n. pi᷇ tiˊ suat moːn ພິທີສວດມົນ		(fit) v. kòw gaːn dayː ເຂົ້າກັນໄດ້
	(things) n. gohng nyaýː ກອງໃຫຍ່	matchbox	n. gaːp fayː ກັບໄຟ
massacre	v. ka᷆ hayː dtay moːt ຂ້າໃຫ້ຕາຍມົດ	mate	(wife) n. ku᷇ dtay ຄູ່ຕາຍ
	n. gán ka᷆ hayː dtay moːt ການຂ້າໃຫ້ຕາຍມົດ		(friend) n. peuan ເພື່ອນ
			(animal) v. seːng ເຈີ້ງ
massive	adj. naː᷇k laː nyaýː, bpeːn gohn ຫນັກແລະໃຫຍ່ເປັນກ້ອນ	material	n. keuang uːp paː gohn ເຄື່ອງອຸປກອນ
mast	n. sow gaː᷇ dong heua ເສົາກະໂດງເຮືອ	math	n. kaː᷇ niː᷇t sat ຄະນິດສາດ
master	(learn) v. hian ຮຽນ	mathematical	adj. giaw gaːp wiː᷇ sa lek ກ່ຽວກັບວິຊາເລກ
	(control) v. nyaː᷇p nyang ຍົບຍັ້ງ n. naý ນາຍ	matrimony	n. gan dtaang dohng ການແຕ່ງດອງ

matter	(substance) n. wa̍t ຖ໌ ວັດຖຸ
	(work) n. leuang ເຮື່ອງ
	(what's the matter?) chow: bpe̍n nya̍ng ເຈົ້າເປັນຫຍັງ?
	(it doesn't matter) boh bpe̍n nya̍ng ບໍ່ເປັນຫຍັງ
mattress	n. seua nohn ເສື່ອນອນ
mature	(people) v. bpe̍n pu nya̍y: ເປັນຜູ້ໃຫຍ່
	(things) adj. ga̍a ແກ່
	(behavior) adj. pu nya̍y: ຜູ້ໃຫຍ່
maximum	adj. ki̍t sung su̍t ຂິດສຸງສຸດ
may	v. a̍t cha: ອາດຈະ
May	n. deuan peu̍t sa̍ pa ເດືອນພືສຜາ
may be	adv. bang ti̍ ບາງທີ
mayor	n. chow: kwaang ga̍m paang ເຈົ້າແຂວງກ່າແຜງ
me	pron. ko̍y ຂ້ອຍ
meadow	n. tu̍ng nya̍ ທົ່ງຫຍ້າ
meager	adj. suan no̍y ສ່ວນໜ້ອຍ
meal	n. ka̍p ko̍w: ຄາບເຂົ້າ
mean	n. ga̍ng ke̍ring ກາງເຄິ່ງ
	v. ma̍y kwam wa̍ ໝາຍຄວາມວ່າ
	adj. cha̍y: ka̍sp ໃຈແຄບ
meaning	n. kwam ma̍y ຄວາມໝາຍ
meanness	n. kwam cha̍y: ka̍ap ຄວາມ ໃຈແຄບ
means	(method) n. wi̍: ti̍ ວິທີ
	(money) n. nge̍rn ເງິນ
meantime	adv. na̍y: ka̍ na̍ na̍n ໃນคมะนั้น
meanwhile	adv. na̍y: we la diaw ga̍n na̍n ໃນເอລາດຽວກັນນັ້ນ
measles	n. ka̍y: ha̍:t ໄຂ້ຫັດ
measure	(value) n. bpa̍: li man ປະຣິມານ
	(tape) n. keuang wa̍:t taak ເຄື່ອງວັດແທກ
	(distance) v. taak ແທກ
	(liquid) v. pohng ຕວງ
	(reaction) n. ta ti̍ ທ່າທີ
measurement	n. ka̍ na̍t ຂນາດ
meat	n. si̍n ຊີ້ນ
mechanic	n. sang bpaang cha̍:k ຊ່າງ ແປ່ງຈັກ
mechanical	adj. duay keuang cha̍:k ດ້ວຍເຄື່ອງຈັກ
mechanics	n. wi̍: sa giaw ga̍:p gan ne̍ng dting ວິຊາກ່ຽວກັບກັຍ ການເໜັງຕີງ
mechanism	n. leuang keuang cha̍:k ເຮື່ອງເຄື່ອງຈັກ
medal	n. ga̍ ka̍:m sohp ກາຄຳຊອບ
meddle	(disturb) v. ko̍w: nyu̍:ng giaw ເຂົ້າຍຸ້ງກ່ຽວ

	(confuse) v. hẻit hẩy nyuŉg ເຮັດໃຫ້ຫຍຸ້ງ
mediate	v. kow: kuáng gang, oṕ lŏm ເຂາະລາງກາງ, ໂອຍໂລມ
mediation	n. gǎn oṕ lom ການໂອຍໂລມ
mediator	n. pu̇ hẻit na̓ ti̓ bpe:n koɩn gang ຜູ້ເຮັດຜ້າທີ່ເປັນຄົນກາງ
medical	adj. haǎng gǎn pǎat ແກ່ງການແພດ
medicine	(drug) n. yả ຢາ
	(subject) n. wi: sǎ pǎat ວິຊາແພດ
medication	n. gǎn ha:k sǎ lok duav yǎ ການຮັກສາໂຮກດ້ວຍຢາ
meditate	vt. kow: sǎ: ma̓ ti:, hi̓n dtohng ເຂົາສະມາທ, ຮິນຕອງ
medium	adj. bpan gang ປານກາງ n. moh cha:m ໝໍຈໍ້າ
meek	adj. ohn nóhm di̓ ອ່ອນນ້ອມດີ
meet	v. po:p ພົບ
meeting	(encounter) n. gǎn po:p ga̓n ການພົບກັນ
	(conference) n. gǎn bpa: su̇m ການປະຊຸມ
Mekong River	n. maǎ na:m kohng ແມ່ນ້ຳຂອງ
mellow	adj. ohn di̓, bpa:p bpu̇ng ອ່ອນດີ, ປັ່ຍປ່ງ v. gia gohm ohn wǎn ເກ່ງກ້ອມ, ອ່ອນຫວານ
melody	n. ta:m nohng peng, kwǎm pay: roh: peng ທໍານອງເພງ, ຄວາມໄພເຣາະຂອງເພງ
melon	n. mǎk dtaǎng ໝາກແຕງ
	(watermelon) n. mak mo ໝາກໂມ
melt	v. la: lay ລະລາຍ
member	(person) n. sǎ: ma si:k ສະມາຊິກ
	(body part) n. a̓: way: nya: wa: ຊະໄວຍຢະວະ
memo	(memorandum) n. ba:n teŭ:k ບັນຝຶກ
memoir	n. ba:n teŭ:k bpa: wǎ:t kohng bu:k ko:n ບັນທຶກປະວັດ ຂອງບຸກຄົນ
memorize	v. keu:n chai ຊມໃຈ
memory	n. kwǎm cha:m ຄວາມຈໍ່າ
menace	n. gǎn ku ke:n ການຂູ່ເຂ້ມ v. ku ke:n ຂູ່ເຂ້ມ
mend	v. dtap chun ຕາບຊຸນ
men's room	n. hohng su: pap bu: lu:t ຫ້ອງຢູສຜາບບຸຣຸດ
mental	(mind) adj. haǎng chi:t chay: ແກ່ງຈິດໃຈ
	(brain) adj. haǎng ma:n sǎ: mohng ແກ່ງມັນສມອງ
mention	adj. gǎn gow ter:ng ການກ່າວເຖິງ v. wow: ter:ng ເວົ້າເຖິງ

(don't mention it) adv.
kohp chay: bòh bpe:n
nya:ng ຂອບໃຈ, ບໍ່ເປັນຫຍັງ

menu n. lay gan a hah ຮາຍການ
ອາຫານ

merchandise n. si:n ka ສິນຄ້າ

merchant n. poh ka ພໍຄ້າ

mercy n. kwam bpa ni ຄວາມປານີ

mere (only) adj. tow gan ເທ່ານັ້ນ
(small) adj. noy ນ້ອຍ

meridian n. kit sung su:t kohng,
se:n fia:ng meu
ຂົດສູງສຸດຂອງໂລກ, ເສັ້ນທ່ວງ
ເມື

merit v. kuan day: ha:p ຄວນໄດ້ຮັບ
(worth) n. ku:n ka ຄຸນຄ່າ
(virtue) n. bu:n ບຸນ

merit badge n. lian ku:n kwam di ຫຼຽນ
ຄຸນຄວາມດີ

merry adj. muan seun ມ່ວນຊື່ນ

merry-go-round n. ma may: mu:n duay
keuang cha:k keu ga:p
si:ng sa sa: wa:n ມ້າໄມ້
หมุนด้วยเครื่องจักคือบชิ่งกาล้อม

mess n. kwam hohk heua ຄວາມຮົກ
ເຮື້ອ

message n. kow ຂ່າວ

metal n. lo ha: ໂລຫະ

metallurgy n. gan seu:k sa laa: gan
say: le:k ການສຶກສາແລະ
ການໃຊ້ເຫຼັກ

metaphors n. gan bpiap tiap ko:n
say: sa:t leu si:ng kohng
ການປຽບທຽບຄິນໃສ່ສັດຫຼືສິ່ງຂອງ

meteor n. dow sa: de:t ດາວຊະເດັດ

meter (distance) n. maa:t ແມັດ
(test instrument) n.
keuang wa:t taak ເຄື່ອງ
ວັດແທກ
(music) n. cha:ng wa:
ຈັງວະ
v. wa:t taak ວັດແທກ

method n. wi: ti ວິທີ

meticulous adj. la: ma:t la: wa:ng
ระมัดระวัง

metropolitan adj. haeng meuang luang
ແຫ່ງເມືອງຫຼວງ

microbe n. maa pa: nyat ເມ່ພະຍາດ
n. seua lok ເຊື້ອໂຣກ

microphone n. mi gro fon ມິໂກຣໂຟນ

microscope n. gohng sohng be:ng kohng
nohy ກ້ອງສ່ອງເບິ່ງຂອງນ້ອຍ

midday adj. dtohn tiang ຕອນທ່ຽງ

middle adj. ke:ng gang ເຄິ່ງກາງ

Middle East n. pak dta: wa:n ohk gang ພາກ
ຕະວັນອອກກາງ

midget n. ko:n dtia ຄົນເຕ້ຍ

midnight n. tiang keun ທ່ຽງຄືນ

midst n. tam gang ທ່າມກາງ

midsummer n. gang la: du hohn
ກາງລະດູຮ້ອນ

midway	n. kerīng tang คึ่งทาง	mill	n. hŏng sĭ kŏw: โรงสีเข้า
midwife	n. nāng pa: du ing kăn		v. sĭ kŏw: สีเข้า
	มางผะดุงคัน	million	(1,000,000) n. lān ลาม
midwinter	n. gāng la: du nŏw	millionaire	n. sĕt tī เสดถี
	ภางระดูหาว	minaret	n. hŏh lāam dtam bot ĭ:t
might	v. at cha: จาถจะ		sa: lăm
	n. a:m năt อำมาถ		ทำแหฺมตามโยถอิสลาม
mighty	(power) adv. yang mī a:m	mind	v. seua fāng เชื่อฟัง
	năt lǎy ย่างมีอำมาถหฺลาย		n. chi:t chay: จิถใจ
	(strength) adv. kaang hǎang	mine	v. ku:t hǎa ฃุถแร่
	lǎy แฃงแรงหฺลาย		(cavern) n. bòh hǎa ขุมแร่
migrate	v. nyáy ohk ฃ้ายออก		(dynamite) n. la: bert
mild	adj. ohn ออน		ระเบิด
mildew	v. dto:k mo:, mu ถกโผะ, มู่	miner	n. kǒn ku:t bòh hǎa
	n. mo: โมะ		คิมฃุถแร่
mile	n. mǎy: ไมล์	mineral	n. lo hǎ: tat โลทะหาถ
milestone	(road marker) n. la:k gi lo	mingle	n. gan kow: so:m to:p
	หฺลักกิโล		ภามเฃ้าสมทบ
	(marker) n. keuang mǎy		v. kow: gan: เฃ้ากัน
	เคื่องหฺมาย	miniature	adj. hu:n ทุ่น
military	adj. giaw ga:p ta: hǎn		adj. nǒy nǒy หฺน่อยๆ
	กฺ่ยวกับทะหาน	minimum	(amount) n. yǎng nǒy
	n. gohng ta:p ภองทัพ		ย่างหฺน่อย
militia	n. ta: hǎn bǎn tะหามบ้าน		(size) n. dta:m tī su:t
milk	n. na:m nǒ:m นำ้มิม		ตำ่ที่สุถ
	v. bip na:m nǒ:m ยิบนำ้มิม	mining	n. gan ku:t bòh hǎa
milkshake	n. glaam nǒ:m sǒ:t ภแรม		ภามฃุถแร่
	มิมสิถ	minister	n. la:t ta: mo:n dtri
milky	adj. keu na:m nǒ:m		รัถมิมตรี
	คิมนำ้มิม		v. ha:p say: ธับใฃ่

ministry	(place) n. ຫ້ອງ: ສຸຫນງ ກະຊວງ
	(service) n. gan laːp saːy: buaˊ laˊː baˊːt ການ ຮັບໃຊ້ບໍ່ວຣະບັດ
minor	n. puˋ nyaˊːng noˊy ຜູ້ຍງນ9ຍ
	adj. leːk noˊy ເລັກນ9ຍ
mire	n. dun kiˊ dtoːm ດຸນຂີ້ຕົມ
	v. dtoːk dtoːm ຕົກຕົມ
minute	n. naˊ tiˊ ນາທີ
	adj. noˊy ti suˋːt ນ9ຍທີ່ສຸດ
miracle	n. het gan maˊː haˊːt saˊː: chaːn ເຫດການມະຫັສຈັນ
mirror	(big) n. gaˋː choˊːk ກະຈົກ
	(small) n. waˊan ແວ່ນ
	v. nyaˊang ແຍງ
mirth	n. kwam saˊː nuˋːk saˊː nan ຄວາມສນຸກສ9ານ
misbehave	v. boh suˊː paˊp ບໍ່ສຸພາບ
mischief	n. kiˊ deu ຂີ້ດື
miserable	(evil) adj. suaˊ haˊy ຊົ່ວຮ້າຍ
	(sick) adj. tuˊːk chaˊy: ທຸກໃຈ
miserly	adj. kiˊ tiˊ ຂີ້ຖີ່
misery	n. kwam tuˊːk nyaˊk ຄວາມທຸກຍາກ
	v. cheˊːp bpuat ເຈັບປວດ
misnomer	n. seu piˊːt ຊື່ຜິດ
miss	n. naˊng sow ນາງສາວ
miss	(loose) v. siaˊ ເສັຽ
misplace	(misplace) v. kat bpay: ຂາດໄປ
	(pine) v. kiˊːt hoht ຄິດຮອດ
	(late) v. pat bpay: ຜາດ ໄປ
Mrs.	(Mistress) n. naˊng (puˋ miˊ puˋ: laˊaw) ນາງ (ຜູ້ມີຜົວແລ້ວ)
missile	(rocket) n. chaˊː luat ຈະຣວດ
	(object) n. puak hohk loˊw, naˊː luk ພວກຫອກຫ້າວລູກນາ
missing	adj. tiˊ kat bpay: ທີ່ຂາດໄປ
mission	(errand) n. kaˊː naˊː: pu taˊan ຄະນະຜູ້ແທນ
	(group) n. kaˊː naˊː: pu sohn sat saˊː naˊ ຄະນະຜູ້ສອນສາສນາ
missionary	adj. haˊang gan sohn sat saˊː naˊ ແຫ່ງການສອນສາສນາ
	n. pu sohn sat saˊː naˊ ຜູ້ສອນສາສນາ
mist	n. mohk bang ໝອກບັງ
mistake	n. kwam piˊːt ຄວາມຜິດ
	v. piˊːt ຜິດ
mistaken	adj. piˊːt ຜິດ
mister	(high) (Mr.) n. tan ທ່ານ
	(middle) n. naˊy ນາຍ
	n. tow ທ້າວ
mistress	n. mia laːp ເມັຽລັບ

mitten	n. to:ng meu boh mi niu: ถุงมือบ่มีนิ้ว
mix	v. bpo:n ga:n ปิ้นกัน
	n. keuang bpa: so:m sa:m le:t เครื่องปะสมสำเร็ด
mob	(crowd) n. fung so:n ฝูงจูม
	(gang) n. puak a:n ta: pan พอกอ้านทะพาน
	v. b;ay: su:m nu:m, lay ko:n pa ga:n ku:m ko:n เข้าฉุมมุม, ทบคันพากันฆุมคัน
mobile	adj. ti nyay ti day: ที่ย้ายที่ได้
mobilize	(soldiers) v. gen ta: han เกนทะทาน
	(move) v. ga: gen กะเกน
mock	v. nyoh: nyery เยาะเยีย
	adj. ti bpe:n kohng tiam ที่เป็นของทูม
mode	n. baap แบบ
model	v.he:t ope:n atua yang, o4: baap เร็ดเป็นถัอย่าๆ, เอาแบบ
	(example) n. baap yang แบบอ่าๆ
	(girl) n. nang baap มาๆแบบ
moderate	adj. poh so:m kuan พัสมคอม
	n. ko:n chay: di คิมใจดี
	v. ga:m ga:p กำกับ
modern	adj. sa: may: may: สไม ใผ
modest	adj. su: pap สุพาบ
modesty	n. kwam su: pap lia:p lohy ความสุพายธูบธอย สุพายธูบธอย
modify	v. bpian bpaang ป่มแปๆ
moist	adj. su:m ๆม
molar	n. kaaw go:k แอวกัท
molasses	n. na:m oy มำ99ย
mold	(form) n. bow: loh เบ้าพล
	v. bpan hup ปั้นธุบ
	(fungus) n. mo: ใพะ
mole	(beauty spot) n. ki maang wa:n ขี้แมๆวัๆ
	(animal) n. dto dtu:n โตถุ่ม
mom	n. maa แม่
moment	n. la: nya: ธะยะ
monarch	n. chow: si wi:t เจ้าชีอืด
monastery	n. wa:t อัด
monastic	adj. se:ng giaw ga:p wa:t เจ้าก็ๆอกับอัด
Monday	n. wa:n cha:n อัมจัม
monetary	adj. haang gan nger:n แต้วทามเๆ็ม
money	n. nger:n เๆ็ม
moneybags	(sacks) n. to:ng nger:n ถิวเๆ็ม
	(person) n. set ti เสถถิ
monitor	n. pu ber:ng nyaang ผู้เบ้ๆแมย

	v. be:ring nyaang ເບີ່ງແຍງ
monk	n. ku ba̅ ຄຸບາ
monkey	n. ling ລິງ
	v. he:t dta: lo:k
	ເຮັດຄລືກ
monopolist	n. pu puk kat
	ຜູ້ຜູກຂາດ
monopolize	v. puk pat
	ຜູກຂາດ
monopoly	n. gan put kat
	ການຜູກຂາດ
monotony	n. kwam sa:m sak ຄວາມ
	ຊໍ້າຊາກ
monthly	adj. bpa: cha:m deuan
	ປະຈໍາເດືອນ
monster	(animal) n. sa:t hay nyay:
	ສັດຮ້າຍໃຫຍ່
	(spirit) n. bpi sat ຜີສາດ
month	n. deuan ເດືອນ
monument	n. a: nu: sa wa: li 9ະນຸສາ
	ວະຣີ
mood	n. a lo:m ອາຣົມ
moon	n. pa: cha:n ພຣະຈັນ
moonlight	v. he:t wiak pi: set
	ເຮັດວຽກພິເສດ
	n. saeng pa: cha:n
	ແສງພະຈັນ
mop	(hair) n. po:m do:k ຜົມດົກ
	(floor) n. may: tu heuan
	ໄມ້ຖູເຮືອນ

	v. tu heuan ຖູເຮືອນ
moral	n. si:n ta:m ສິລທໍາ
	adj. haang kohng si:n ta:m
	ແຫງຂອງສິລທໍາ
moral code	n. la:k kohng su: pa si:t
	ຫຼັກຂອງສຸພາສິດ
morale	n. ga:m lang chay: ກໍາລັງໃຈ
more	adv. ik ອີກ
	(more than) adj. lay gua
	ຫຼາຍກວ່າ
moreover	adv. dteum ik nan ຕື່ມອີກນັ້ນ
morning	n. meu so̅w: ມື້ເຊົ້າ
morrow	n. meu na̅ ມື້ໜ້າ
morsel	n. dtohn a han ຕ່ອນອາຫານ
mortal	n. ko:n sing ti dtohng dtay
	ຄົນ, ສິ່ງເຕ່ງຕາຍ
	adj. sa ha:t ສາຫັດ
mortar	(gun) n. bpun lat fa
	ປືນພາດຟ້າ
	(cement) n. si ma̅ng ສີມັງ
	(bowl) n. ko:k ຄົກ
mortgage	n. gan cha:m na̅:m ການຈໍານໍາ
	v. cha:m na:m, kay fak
	ຈໍານໍາ, ຂາຍຝາກ
mosquito	n. nyu:ng ຍຸງ
mosquito bite	n. hoy nyu:ng ga:t ຮອຍ
	ຍຸງກັດ
mosquito net	n. mu̅ng ມຸ້ງ
moss	n. ki kay: hin leu kay
	dto:n may: ຂີ້ໄຄຫີນຫຼືໄຄຕົ້ນໄມ້

most	adv. lay ti su:t ฏายทีสุด
	adj. ti su:t ทีสุด
mostly	adv. suan lay สวมฏาย
moth	n. maang ga: peua gang keun แมງກະເບື່ອກາງຄືນ
mother	n. maa แม
mother-in-law	(paternal) n. maa nya แม่ยา
	(maternal) n. maa tow: แม่เถา
motherly	adv. yang maa ยาງແມ່
mother tongue	n. pa sa kohng dtua eng ພາສາຂອງຕົວເອງ
motion	n. gan keuan way: ການເຄື່ອນໄຫວ
motion picture	n. si ne ma ຊີເນມາ
motive	n. sa het สาເหດ
motor	n. keuang cha:k ເຄື່ອງຈັກ
	adj. haang keuang: cha:k ແຫ່ງເຄື່ອງຈັກ
motorcycle	n. lo:t cha:k ຣົຖຈັກ
motto	n. ka'm su: pa si:t ຄວາມສຸພາສິດ
mould	v. bpan hup ປັ້ນຮູບ
	(form) n. bow: loh ເບ້າໂລ
	(fungus) n. mo: ໂພະ
mound	n. pon ໂພນ
mount	(get up) v. keun ki ຂຶ້ນຂີ່
	(frame) v. say: kohp ໃສ່ຂອບ

	n. pu ພູ
mountain	n. pu kow: ພູເຂົາ
mountainer	n. na:k keun kow: ນັກຂຶ້ນເຂົາ
mountainous	adj. haang pu kow: ແຫ່ງພູເຂົາ
mourn	v. way: tu:k ໄວ້ທຸກ
mouse	(mice pl.) n. nu ໜູ
moustache	n. nuat so:p ໜວດສົບ
mouth	v. wow: chak bpak ເວົາຈາກປາກ
	n. bpak ປາກ
movable	(self) adj. ti ne:ng dting day: ທີ່ເໜັງຕີງໄດ້
	(things) adj. ti nyay ti day: ທີ່ຍາຍທີ່ໄດ້
move	(self) v. ne:ng dting, keuan ti ເໜັງຕີງ, ເຄື່ອນທີ່
	(things) v. nyo:k nyay ຍົກຍາຍ
movement	(motion) n. gan ne:ng dting ການເໜັງຕີງ
	(bowel) n. a' cho:m ອາຈົມ
movie	n. si ne ma ຊີເນມາ
movie camera	n. gohng tay si ne ma ກ້ອງຖ່າຍຊີເນມາ
moving	(self) n. gan ne:ng dting day: ການເໜັງຕີງໄດ້
	(things) n. gan nyo:k nyay ການຍົກຍາຍ

much	n. lay (na:p boh day:) ຫຼາຍ (ນັບບໍ່ໄດ້)	munition	n. a² wu:t nyu:t ta³ pa:n ອາວຸດຍຸດຕະພັນ
mucus	n. (nasal) ki muk ຂີ້ມູກ	murder	v. ka³ ko:n ຂ້າຄົນ
mud	n. ki dto:m ຂີ້ຕົມ		n. gan ka ko:n ການຂ້າຄົນ
muddy	adj. bpe:n ki dto:m ເປັນຂີ້ຕົມ	murmur	v. si:m ga:n ສົ່ມກັນ
muff	v. he:t pi:t ເຮັດຜິດ		n. siang si:m ga:n ສຽງສົ່ມກັນ
muffle	v. he:t hay: siang noy lo:ng ເຮັດໃຫ້ສຽງນ້ອຍລົງ	muscle	(strength) n. gohn sin ກ້ອນຊີ້ນ
muffler	(car) n. toh ge:p siang ທໍເກັບສຽງ	muscular	adj. kaang haang ແຂງແຮງ
	(clothing) n. keuang ga:n hu ເຄື່ອງກັນຫຸ	muse	v. na:ng ki:t ນັ່ງຄິດ
mug	(glass) n. nyeuak say: na:m ເຫຍືອກໃສ່ນ້ຳ		n. si:n la: bpa: wi: ta: nya ພະເຈົ້າແຫ່ງສິນລະປະວິທຍາ pa: chow:
	(face) n. na ໜ້າ	museum	n. pi: pi:t ta: pa:n ພິພິທທະພັນ
muggy	adj. su:m laa: hohn ຊຸ່ມແລະຮ້ອນ	mush	n. kow: bpak ເຂົ້າປຸກ
mule	n. ma lua ມ້າລໍ	mushroom	n. he:d ເຫັດ
multiply	(numbers) v. kun lek ຄຸນເລກ	music	n. do:n dti ດົນຕີ
		musical	adj. giaw ga:p do:n dti ກ່ຽວກັບດົນຕີ
	(reproduce) v. ta: wi kun ທະວີຄູນ	musician	n. na:k do:n dti ນັກດົນຕີ
multitude	cha:m nuan lay ຈຳນວນຫຼາຍ	mussel	(animal) n. hoy ga: po:ng ຫອຍກະປ໋ອງ
mumble	(to oneself) v. cho:m ຈົມ	must	v. dtohng ຕ້ອງ
	(to others) v. wow: boh soh: ເວົ້າບໍ່ເສາະ	mustache	n. nuat so:p ໜວດສົບ
municipal	adj. haang tet sa: ban meuang ແຫ່ງເທສບານເມືອງ	mustard	n. na:m mak pe:t leuang ນ້ຳໝາກເຜັດເຫຼືອງ
municipality	n. tet sa: ban meuang ເທສບານເມືອງ	mute	n. ko:n bpak geuk ຄົນປາກກືກ v. a:t bpak ອັດປາກ
		mutter	v. cho:m ຈົມ
		mutton	n. sin gaa: ຊີ້ນແກະ

mutual	adj. seu̅ng ga̍i̅n la̅a̅: ga̍i̅n ຊຶ່ງກັນແລະກັນ
muzzle	(animal) n. bpak sa̍a̅:t ປາກມັດ
	(gun) n. bpak ga̍a̅: bohk bpeun ປາກກະບອກປືນ
my	adj. kohng ko̍y ຂອງຂ້ອຍ
myriad	adj. neu̅:ng meu̅:n, na̅:o boh day: ມື່ນໝືນ, ນັບບໍ່ໄດ
myself	pron. ko̍y eng ຂ້ອຍເອງ
mysterious	adj. le̅r:k la̅:p ເລັກລັບ
mystery	(secret) n. kwam le̅r:k la̅:p ຄວາມເລັກລັບ
	(movie) n. leuang le̅r:k la̅:p ເຮື່ອງເລັກລັບ
mystic	n. pu seua pi ຜູເຊື່ອຜີ
mystical	adj. haang kwam seua bu:han ແຫງຄວາມເຊື່ອຖາມ
myth	n. ni: tan bu: han ນິຖານບຸຖາມ

N

nag	(horse) n. ma nohy ມ້ານ້ອຍ v. soh ສໍ
nail	n. le̅:k dta: bpu ເຫລັກຕະປູ v. dtohk dta: bpu ຕອກເຫລັກຕະປູ
nail file	n. le̅:k tu le̅:p ເຫລັກຖູເລັບ

naked	adj. bpa: bpeuay ປະເປືອຍ
name	n. seu ຊື່ v. dtang seu ຕັ້ງຊື່
	(first name) n. seu noy ຊື່ນ້ອຍ
	(last name) n. nam sa: gu̅:n ນາມສະກຸນ
namely	adv. keu wa ຄືວ່າ
nap	n. gan nohn sua ka̍: na̅: ການນອນຊົ່ວຄະນະ v. nohn suay ນອນສວຍ
napkin	n. pa se̅:t meu ຜ້າເຊັດມື
narcotic	n. ya sep dti̅:t ຢາເສບຕິດ
narrate	v. ba̍:n nyay ບັນຍາຍ
narration	n. gan ba̍:n nyay ການບັນຍາຍ
narrative	adj. moh̍: ti cha̍: low: hay: fa̅ing ເພາະທີ່ຈະເລົ່າໃຫຟັງ
narrator	n. pu ba̍:n nyay ຜູບັນຍາຍ
narrow	v. he̅:t hay: kaap ເຮັດໃຫແຄບ adj. kaap ແຄບ
narrow-minded	adj. chay: kaap ໃຈແຄບ
nasal	adj. tang da̍ing ທາງດັ້ງ
nasty	adj. nyap kay ຫຍາບຄາຍ
natal	adj. haang gan gert ແຫງການເກີດ
nation	n. bpa: tet sat ປະເທດຊາດ
national	adj. haang sat ແຫງຊາດ

nationalism	n. la:t ti: sat ni: nyo:m	nave	(church) n. cháy gǎn si:m
	ລັດທິຊາດນິຍົມ		ໃຈກາງສິມ
nationalist	n. ko:n la:t ti: sat ni:		(person) n. ko:n ngǎn kìmງາມ
	nyo:m ຄົນລັດທິຊາດນິຍົມ	navel	n. hu say beu ຣຼສາຍບື
nationality	n. sa:n sat ສັນຊາດ	navigable	adj. ti laan heua day:
nationalize	v. hay: bpe:n kohng sat		ແລ່ນເຮືອໄດ້
	ໃຫ້ເປັນຂອງຊາດ	navigate	v. laan heua ແລ່ນເຮືອ
native	adj. haeng bǎn bert	navigation	(action) n. gan laan heua
	ແຫ່ງບ້ານເກີດ		ການແລ່ນເຮືອ
	n. ko:n peun meuang		(study) n. wi: sǎ gan laan
	ຄົນພື້ນເມືອງ		heua ວິຊາການແລ່ນເຮືອ
natural	adj. dtam ta:m ma: sǎt	navigator	(ship) n. na:k laan heua
	ຕາມທັມະຊາດ		ມັກແລ່ນເຮືອ
naturalize	v. si chaang giaw ga:p	navy	n. gohng ta:p heua
	ta:m ma: sat,dta:t sat		ກອງທັບເຮືອ
	ຊິແຈງກ່ຽວກັບທັມະຊາດ, ຕັດຊາດ	navy blue	n.si ko:m ma: ta ສີນ້ມມະຫາ
naturally	(of course) adv. taa laaw	near	adj. gay: ໄກ້
	ແຕ່ແລ້ວ	nearsighted	adj. say dta sa:n ສາຍ
	(by itself) adv. yang ta:m		ຕາສັ້ນ
	ma: sat ຢ່າງທັມະຊາດ	neat	(dress) adj. hiáp hǒy
nature	n. ta:m ma: sat ທັມະຊາດ		ຮຽບຮ້ອຍ
naughty	adj. děu ດື້		(good) adj. cho: lay
nausea	n. a gan bpu:n tohng		ຈົບຫລາຍ
	ອາການປຸ້ນທ້ອງ	necessaries	n. si:ng kohng cha:m bpe:n
nauseate	vt. he:t hay: bpu:n tohng		ສິ່ງຂອງຈຳເປັນ
	ເຮັດໃຫ້ປຸ້ນທ້ອງ	necessarily	adv. yang cha:m bpe:n
nauseous	adj. bpe:n dta bpu:n		ຢ່າງຈຳເປັນ
	tohng ເປັນຕາປຸ້ນທ້ອງ	necessary	adj. cha:m bpe:n ຈຳເປັນ
naval	adj. haeng gohng ta:p	necessity	(must) n. kwam cha:m bpe:n
	heua ແຫ່ງກອງທັບເຮືອ		ຄວາມຈຳເປັນ

	(need) n. kwăm dtŏhng găn ຄວາມຕ້ອງການ
neck	n. kŏh ຄໍ
	v. hŏhm ຫອມ
necklace	n. săy sŏy kŏh ສາຍສ້ອຍຄໍ
necktie	n. gá la: wa:t ກາລະວັດ
need	n. kwăm dtŏhng găn ຄວາມ ຕ້ອງການ
	v. dtŏhng găn ຕ້ອງການ
needle	n. kĕ:m ເຂັມ
	v. wŏw say: ເວົ້າໃສ່
needless	adj. boh chă:m bpe:n ບໍ່ຈຳເປັນ
needlework	n. ngăn nyi:p săăw ງານຫຍິບແສ່ວ
needy	adj. ti dtŏhng găn, nyak chŏ:n ທີ່ຕ້ອງການ, ຍາກຈົນ
negation	n. găn bpa: dti: set ການປະຕິເສດ
negative	n. ppa: dti: set ປະຕິເສດ
neglect	v. bpŏy bpa: ປ່ອຍປະ
negligence	n. găn bpŏy bpa: ການປ່ອຍປະ
negligible	adj. boh să:m kă:n ບໍ່ສຳຄັນ
negotiate	(peace) v. che la: cha ເຈຣະຈາ
	(price) v. dtoh la ka ຕໍ່ລາຄາ
	(object) v. bpaang ແປງ

negotiation	(peace) n. găn che la: cha ການເຈຣະຈາ
	(object) n. găn dă:t bpaang ການດັດແປງ
neighbor	n. peuan băn ເພື່ອນບ້ານ
neighborhood	n. mu băn găy: kiăng ຫມູບ້ານໃກ້ຄຽງ
neither	adj. boh măan ta:ng sŏhng ບໍ່ແມ່ນທັງສອງ
neither ... nor	adj. boh măan a:n ni... boh măan a:n na:n ບໍ່ແມ່ນອັນ ນີ້ ...ບໍ່ແມ່ນອັນນັ້ນ
nephew	n. lan say ຫລານຊາຍ
nerve	(physical) n. se:n bpa: sat ເສັ້ນປະສາດ
	(courage) n. kwăm ga hăn ຄວາມກ້າຫານ
nervous	adj. kuan ohn ຂວນໂອນ
-ness	(suffix which changes adjectives to nouns) ka:m dteu:m say: ka:m kui:n na: să:p hăy: bpe:n ka:m năm คำເຕີມໃສ່คำคุนมะไล ໃຫ້ເປັນคำนาม
nest	n. ha:ng no:k ຮັງນົກ
	v. he:t ha:ng ເຮັດຮັງ
net	adj. ta:ng mo:t ທັງໝົດ
	(hang) n. mŏhng ມອງ
	(throw) n. hăa ແຫ
	(drop) n. ga: du:ng ກະດຸ້ງ

network	n. sǎ hǔy ສາຣຸຍ	nicely	(well, neatly) adv. yǎng chóp ngám ຢ່າງຈົບງາມ
neutral	adj. bpe:n gang ເປັນກາງ		(beautifully) adv. yǎng ngám ຢ່າງງາມ
neutrality	n. kwǎm bpe:n gang ຄວາມ ເປັນກາງ	nickel	(money) n. nger:n a:t ເງິນອັດ
never	(not ever) adv. boh kery ບໍ່ເຄີຍ		(metal) n. le:k ni:k gaan ເຫຼັກນິກ
	(don't) adv. yá ... cha:k teua ຢ່າ ... ຈັກເທື່ອ	nickname	n. seu li:n ຊື່ຫຼິ້ນ ແກມຣ໌
never mind	boh bpe:n nya:ng ບໍ່ເປັນ ຫຍັງ	niece	n. lan sow ຫຼານສາວ
		night	n. gang keun ກາງຄືນ
nevermore	adv. boh mi dteum ik ບໍ່ມີດຶ່ມອີກ	nightfall	n. we la ga:m la:ng cha: meu:t ເວລາກ່າລັງຈະມືດ
nevertheless	adj. tering yang day: goh dtǎm ເຖິງຢ່າງໃດກໍ່ຕາມ	nightmare	n. fǎn hay ຝັນຮ້າຍ
new	adj. may: ໃໝ່	night table	n. dto: ncy yu hua dtiang ໂຕະນ້ອຍຢູ່ຫົວຕຽງ
news	n. kow ຂ່າວ	night time	n. we la gang keun ເວລາກາງຄືນ
newscaster	n. pu an kow tang wi:t ta: nyu: ຜູ້ອ່ານຂ່າວຕາງວິທະຍຸ	night watch	n. ko:n nyam gang keun ຄົນຍາມກາງຄືນ
newsletter	n. chó:t may kow ຈົດໝາຍຂ່າວ		
newspaper	n. na:ng seu pi:m ໜັງສືພິມ	nine	(9) adj. gow: ເກົ້າ (໙)
newsreel	n. si: ne kow ຊີເນວາວ	nine fold	adj. gow: yang ເກົ້າຢ່າງ
newsstand	n. hǎn noy noy ti kay na:ng seu pi:m ຮ້ານນ້ອຍໆທີ່ຂາຍໜັງສື ພິມ	nineteen	(19) adj. si:p gow: ສິບເກົ້າ
		nineteenth	(19th) adj. ti si:p gow: ທີ່ສິບເກົ້າ
next	adj. dtoh bpay: ຕໍ່ໄປ	ninety	(90) adj. gow: si:p ເກົ້າສິບ
nib	(pen) n. bpay bpak ga ປາຍປາກ ກາ	ninth	(9th) adj. ti gow: ທີ່ເກົ້າ
	(bird) n. bpay so:p no:k ປາຍສົບນົກ	nip	n. gan sa:p ການສັບ
nibble	v. haan ແຫນ	nipple	n. hua no:m ຫົວນົມ
nice	adj. chó:p di ຈົບດີ	nitrogen	n. tat nay: dtro chen ທາດໄນໂຕຣເຈນ

no	intrj. boh ບໍ່
no matter	(regardless) ter:ng wå.... goh dtam ເຖິງວ່າ....ກໍຕາມ
	(neither here nor there) boh sa:m ka:n ບໍ່ສ່ຳຄັນ
noble	(family) n. mi sa: gu:n sung ມີສະກຸນສູງ
	(elegent) adj. sa: ngå ngåm ສ່າງາມ
nobility	(elegence) n. kwåm sa: nga ngåm ຄວາມສ່າງາມ
	(family) n. kwåm mi sa: gu:n di ຄວາມມີສະກຸນດີ
nobleman	n. ko:n mi sa: gu:n sung ຄົນມີສະກຸນສູງ
nobody	n. boh mi pay: ບໍ່ມີໃຜ
nod	n. gan ngeu:k hua ການງຶກຫົວ
	v. ngeu:k hua ງຶກຫົວ
noise	n. siang da:ng ສຽງດັງ
noiseless	adj. mi:t ມິດ
noisy	adj. siang eu:k ga: teu:k ສຽງອຶກກະທຶກ
nominate	v. dtaang dtang ແຕ່ງຕັ້ງ
none	(thing) adv. bon mi nya:ng ບໍ່ມີຫຍັງ
	(person) adv. bon mi pay: ບໍ່ມີໃຜ
nonsense	n. boh bpe:n leuang ບໍ່ເປັນ ເຣື່ອງ
noodle	(white) n. se:n fer ເສັ້ນເຝີ
	(yellow) n. se:n mi ເສັ້ນໝີ່
	(brain) n. sa: mohng ສມອງ
noon	n. we la tiang meu ເວລາທ່ຽງມື້
no one	n. boh mi pay: ບໍ່ມີໃຜ
nor	conj. goh boh maan ກໍບໍ່ແມ່ນ
normal	(natural) adj. ta:m ma: da ທັມະດາ
	(sane) adj. sa: dti: di ສະຕິດີ
	(school) adj. o:p lo:m ku ອົບລົມຄຸ
north	n. ti:t neua ທິດເໜືອ
North America	n. a: me li: ga neua ອະເມຣິກາເໜືອ
northern	adj. haang tang ti:t neua ແຫ່ງທາງທິດເໜືອ
nose	v. sa: lohk gohk ສລອກກອກ
	n. da:ng ດັງ
nosebleed	n. leuat da:ng ເລືອດດັງ
nostril	n. hu da:ng ຮູດັງ
not	(n't) adv. boh ບໍ່
not quite	adv. boh ... bpan day: ບໍ່ ... ປານໃດ
notable	adj. ti na sa:ng get ທີ່ໜ້າສັງເກດ n. ko:n mi seu siang ຄົນມີຊື່ສຽງ
notation	n. gan ba:n teu:k way: ການບັນທຶກໄວ້

note	(writing) n. bо̄ːt cho̤ːt ยิดจิด	novelty	n. ko̤hng máyː ຂອງໃໝ່
	(music) n. no̤ːt peng ມິຕເພງ	November	n. deuan peṳːt sǎ ː chi ga̤ ເຕືອນພິສພາ
	(mental) n. máy het ພາຍເຫດ	novice	(beginner) n. ko̤ːn aáp máyː ຄົນແຫຍໃໝ່
notebook	(agenda) n. bpeum cho̤ːt ba̤ːn teṳːk ປຶ້ມຈົດບັນທຶກ		(monks) n. sa̤ːm mǎː neṳ ສາມະເນນ
	(general) n. bpeum kian ປຶ້ມຂຽນ	now	adv. diaw ní ດຽວນີ້
note paper	n. chia kian cho̤ːt may ເຈ້ຍຂຽນຈົດພາຍ	now and then	adv. bpe̤ːn beng we̤ː la̤ ເປັນບາງເວລາ
noteworthy	adj. sa̤ːm ka̤ːn ສຳຄັນ	nowadays	(present time) adv. tṳːk wa̤ːn ní ທຸກວັນນີ້
nothing	n. boh mi nya̤ːng ບໍ່ມີຫຍັງ		(generation) adv. sǎː máyː ní ສໄໝ່ນີ້
notice	(demand) n. ka̤ːm dteuan ຄຳເຕືອນ	nowhere	adv. boh mi bohn dayː lery ບໍ່ມີບ່ອນໄດເລີຍ
	(note) n. bpaː ga̤ːt ປະກາດ	nudge	v. ow̤ː sohk tohng ເອົາສອກ ຖອງ
	v. sa̤ːng ge̤ːt ສັງເກດ		
noticeable	adj. tiː sa̤ːng ge̤ːt he̤ːn dayː ngáyː ທີສັງເກດເຫັນໄດ້ງ່າຍ	nuisance	n. kwa̤ːm mṳːt mi̤ːt ຄວາມມຸດມິດ
notify	v. bohk hayː hṳ ບອກໃຫ້ຮູ້	number	(total of) n. cha̤ːm nuan ຈຳນວນ
notion	n. kwa̤ːm ki̤ːt he̤ːn ຄວາມຄິດ ເຫັນ		(numeral) n. na̤ːm ber ນ້ຳເບີ
notorious	adj. se̤u da̤ːng ຊື່ດັງ		v. sayː na̤ːm ber ໃສ່ນ້ຳເບີ
noun	n. ka̤ːm nám ຄຳນາມ		adj. tiː ທີ
nourish	v. hayː a han ໃຫ້ອາຫານ	numeral	n. dtua lek ຕົວເລກ ຄືເລກ
novel	adj. máyː ໃໝ່		adj. haang cha̤ːm nuan ແຫ່ງຈຳນວນ
	n. na̤ːng se̤u leuang ພຈ໌ສີ່ເຮື່ອງ	numerous	adj. mi la̤y ມີຫຼາຍ
novelist	n. na̤ːk kian na̤ːng se̤u a̤n li̤ːn ນັກຂຽນໜັງສື່ອ່ານຫຼິ້ນ		

nun	n. nang sǐ มางสี	(curse) n. ka:m dǎ nǎy: g
nurse	n. nang pa: nyŭ ban	sǎ ban คำด่าในทางสายาม
	มางพะยาบาม v. be:ng	oatmeal	n. kow: ot sa:m le:t hup
	nyaang. liǎng เบิ่งแยง, ลัยง	เຂ้าโอ๊ดผำເຮົกรຸຍ
nursery	(people) n. hohng liǎng	obedience	n. gan seǔa fa:ng ภาม
	de:k ห้อງລ້ຽງເດັກ	ເຊື່ອฟ้ງ
	(trees) n. bohn ga leu bo:ng		v. seǔa fa:ng ເຊື່ອฟ้ງ
	dto:n may: ບ່ອນກາເพ็บ่ງถนไม	obedient	adj. fa:ng kwam ฟ้ງคอาม
	adj. s: nǔ: ban 9ะมุบาม	object	n. si:ng kohng ลิ่ງ9อງ
nut	(tree) n. mak goh ผากก๊		v. ka:t kan ຂັດค้าม
	(bolt) n. hua ðu lohng, hua	obligation	n. gan puk mat ภามผูกมัด
	ðta: ðpu ห้อยูຂ9ງ, ห้อตะปู	oblige	(obligate) v. ba:ng kǎp
	(person) n. pi ba ผี้า		ບ້ງคับ
nylon	n. pa nǎy: lohn ผ้าไม		(help) v. puk mat ผูกมัด
	ล9ม	oblique	(crooked) adj. ko:t kong
			คิดโค้ງ
			(90) adj. ne:ng เນ้ี่ງ
	O	obscure	v. he:t hǎy: meut ເຮັດ
oak	n. dto:n may: ok	ใຫ້มิด
	ต้มไม้โ9ก		adj. meut มิด
oar	n. mǎy: pǎy ไม้พาย	obscureness	(darkness) n. kwam meut
	v. pǎy heǔa พายเຮือ	คอามมิด
oarsman	n. ko:n pǎy heǔa		(thought) n. kwam boh ka:
	คิมพายเຮือ	คอามบ่คัກ
oasis	n. bpa ti mi nohng na:m	obscurity	(vision) n. kwam meut
	nǎy: ta: le sǎy ป่าที่	คอามมิด
	ผ9ງมำในทะเล9าย		(thought) n. kwam boh ka:
oat	n. kow: ot เຂ้าโอ๊ด	คอามบ่คัກ
oath	(promise) n. ka:m sǎ ban	observation	n. gan sa:ng ĝet ภามสั่ງเภ
	คำสายาม	observatory	n. hoh bpe:ng dow ห้เບิ่ງ
			ถาอ

bserve	(look) v. saĭng gét ສັງ ເກດ
	(note) v. choːt noːt ຈົດໂນ໊ດ
bserver	n. pǔ saĭng gét ຜູ້ສັງເກດ
bstacle	n. uːp bpaː saːk ອຸປສັກ
bstinate	adj. deŭ deŭing ດຶດຶງ
tain	vt. daːy laːp ໄດ້ຮັບ
bvious	adj. tĭ heĭn daːy ngaːy ທີ່ເຫັນໄດ້ງ່າຍ
ccasion	n. ó gắt ໂອກາດ
ccasional	adj. bpeːn kaːing kow ເປັນຄັ້ງຄາວ
ccasionally	adv. bpeːn kǎːing kow ເປັນຄັ້ງຄາວ
ccident	n. pak dta weːn dtoːk ພາກຕະວັນຕົກ
ean liner	n. gaːm bpaːn doːy san taː le ກຳປັ່ນໂດຍສາມທະເລ
ccupation	(be in) n. gan nyeuːt kohng ການຍຶດຄອງ
	(job) n. a síp ອາຊີບ
ccupy	v. kow kohp kohng ເຂົາຄອບຄອງ
cur	v. bpa goːt keun ປະກົດຂຶ້ນ
ean	n. maː ha saː muːt ມະຫາສະມຸດ
clock	n. sua mong ໂຊໂມງ
tober	n. deuan dtuː laː ເດືອນຕຸລາ

octopus	n. bpá meːrːk nyay ປາ ເມິກໃຫຍ່
odd	(strange) adj. bpaak bpaː lat ແປກປລາດ
	(not even) adj. kík ຄີກ
odds	n. tang saː na ທາງຊນະ
odious	adj. tĭ na kí diat ທີ່ໜາ ຊັງຂຸດ
odor	n. giːn ກິ່ນ
odorous	adj. mĭ giːn ມີກິ່ນ
odorless	adj. boh mĭ giːn ບໍ່ມີກິ່ນ
of	(possessive) prep. kohng ຂອງ
of age	mĭ a nya sow eːt bpi leu nyay gwa ມີອາຍຸ ໒໑ ປີຫຼືກວ່າ
of course	adv. yang naːa nohn, taːa laːw ຢ່າງແນ່ນອນ, ແທ້ແລ້ວ
of no account	boh saːm kaːn ບໍ່ສຳຄັນ
of one's own accord	doy saː maːk chay doːy sa mǎːk chay ໂດຍສມັກໃຈ
off	adv. ohk ອອກ
off and on	bpeːn bang weː la ເປັນບາງເວລາ
offend	v. heːt hay boh poh chay ເຮັດໃຫ້ບໍ່ພໍໃຈ
offense	n. kwam piːt ຄວາມຜິດ
offer	n. gan nyoːk hay ການຍົກໃຫ້
	v. nyoːk hay ຍົກໃຫ້
office	(building) n. hong gan ຫ້ອງການ
	(position) n. dtaːm naːng ຕຳແໜ່ງ

office building n. dteu:k hong gan	(trees) adj. gáa ແກ
ຕຶກໂຮງການ	(things) adj. gow: ເກົ່າ
officer (organization) n. chow:	olive n. dto:n o líw ຕົ້ນໂອລິ່ວ
pa: naik ngan ເຈົ້າພນັກງານ	omen (presage) n. lang ລາງ
(soldier) n. nay ta: han	on prep. tang ter:ng ທາງ,ເທິງ
ນາຍທະຫານ	on account of nyohn wa ຍ້ອນວ່າ
(police) n. nay dta:m	on foot doy gan nyang ໂດຍການຍ່າງ
luat ນາຍຕຳຣວດ	on purpose doy dtang chay: ໂດຍຕັ້ງໃຈ
official n. ka la:t sa: gan ຂ້າລັດຖະການ	on the air ohk a gat ອອກອາກາດ
adj. bpe:n tang gan	on the alert dtiam pohm ຕຽມພ້ອມ
ເປັນທາງການ	on time tain mong dta:ng lery
officially adv. bpe:n tang gan	ທັນໂມງຕັ້ງເລີຍ
ເປັນທາງການ	once adv. kang neu:ng ຄັ້ງນຶ່ງ
officiate v.i. ga:m ga:p ກຳກັບ	once and for all teua diaw laa: teua su:
often adv. leuay leuay ເລື້ອຍໆ	tay ເທື່ອດຽວແລະເທື່ອສຸດທ້າຍ
oh interj. o ໂອ	once in a while do:n do:n teua neu:ng
oh boy! interj. to ໂທ!	ດົນໆເທື່ອນຶ່ງ
oil v. say: na:m ma:n cha:k	one (1) neu:ng ນຶ່ງ (໑)
ໃສ່ນ້ຳມັນຈັກ	one way adj. bpay: day: tang diaw
n. na:m ma:n keuang	ໄປໄດ້ທາງດຽວ
ນ້ຳມັນເຄື່ອງ	onion n. hua bpa:k bua ຫົວຜັກບົວ
adj. bpe:n na:m ma:n	only adv. tow: na:n ເທົ່ານັ້ນ
ເປັນນ້ຳມັນ	onward adv. dtoh bpay: tang na
oily adj. bpe:n na:m ma:n	ຕໍ່ໄປທາງໜ້າ
ເປັນນ້ຳມັນ	omit v. bpa: ohk ປະອອກ
okay (ok) interj. dto:k lo:ng	ooze v. lay: seu:m ໄຫຼຊຶມ
ຕົກລົງ	n. tet na:m ku:n ທາດນ້ຳ
olympic games n. gi la o li:m pi:k	opaque adj. sohng boh soht ສ່ອງບໍ
ກິລາໂອລິມປິກ	?ດ
old (people) adj. tow: ເຖົ້າ	

open	(object) v. kǎy: ໄຂ	opponent	n. ku² dtoh² su⁶ ຄູ່ຕໍ່ສູ້
	(testimony) v. bpert⁶ ເປີດ	opportunity	n. o¹ gat⁶ ໂອກາດ
	(minded) adj. bpert⁶ bery⁴ ເປີດເຜີຍ	oppose	(ideas) v. ka:t⁴ kan⁵ ຄັດຄ້ານ
	(business) adj. gáng chǎang ກາງແຈ້ງ		(fight) v. dtoh² su⁶ ຕໍ່ສູ້
opening	(crack) n. bohn² nya² ບ່ອນ ຍະ	opposite	n. go:ng⁵ gǎn⁵ kam⁵ ກົງກັນ ຂ້າມ
	(job) n. ngan⁵ wǎng⁵ ງານ ຫວ່າງ	opposition	(ideas) n. gǎn⁵ ka:t⁴ kan⁵ ການຂັດຄ້ານ
opera	n. la: kohn⁵ peng³ ອະຄອນ ເພງ		(person) n. ku² dtoh² su⁶ ຄູ່ຕໍ່ສູ້
	n. moh⁴ lam³ flǎing³ ພີລາຝລັ່ງ	oppress	v. bip¹ ba:ng² ka:p² ບີບບັງຄັບ
opera glass	n. gohng⁵ sohng⁵ ກ້ອງສ່ອງ	oppression	n. gǎn⁵ go:t³ ki¹ ko:m² he:ng³ ການກົດຂີ່ຂົມເຫັງ
operate	(surgery) v. pat³ dta:t³ ຜ່າຕັດ	optimism	n. gǎn⁵ bering³ lo⁵k nǎy:³ ngaa² di¹ ການເບິ່ງໂລກໃນແງ່ດີ
	(mechanism) v. ka:p³ ຂັບ	or	conj. leu⁵ ຫຼື
	(business) v. cha:t³ ngan³ ຈັດງານ	-or	(changes verbs to nouns) ka:m² ti¹ dteum³ gi: li: nya hay: bpe:n⁵ ka:m² nam⁵ ຄຳທີ່ເຕີມ ກີຣິຍາໃຫ້ເປັນຄຳນາມ
operation	(business) n. gǎn¹ boh¹ li:² han⁴ ການບໍລິຫານ		
	(surgery) n. gǎn¹ pa³ dta:t³ ການຜ່າຕັດ	oral	adj. duay¹ bpak¹ bpow: ດ້ວຍ ປາກເປົ່າ
	(army) n. gǎn¹ ohk³ bpa:¹ dti:³ ka:n³ ການອອກປະຕິບັດ ງານ	orange	n. mak⁶ giang⁵ ໝາກກ້ຽງ adj. ei⁴ saat⁶ ສີແສດ
opinion	n. kwam³ ki:t² he:n⁴ ຄວາມຄິດເຫັນ	orangeade	n. na:m⁵ mak⁶ giang⁵ ນ້ຳໝາກ ກ້ຽງ
opium	n. ya¹ fi:n² ຢາຝິ່ນ	orate	v. gow¹ ka:m² bpa sǎy: ກ່າວ ຄຳປາໄສ

orator n. pu bpa ta: ga ta ຜູ້ປະ
ທະກາຖາ

orbit n. tang ko chohn tang a
wa: gat ທາງໂຄຈອນທາງ
ອາວະກາດ

orchard n. suan mak may ສວນຫມາກໄມ້

orchestra n. wong doin dti nyay
ວົງດົນຕຣິໃຫຍ

orchid n. donk peung ດອກເຜິ້ງ

order v. saing ສັ່ງ
n. kaim saing ຄຳສັ່ງ

orderly adv. yang bpein lai biap
ຢ່າງເປັນລະບຽບ
n. koin haip say: ຄົນຮັບໃຊ້

ordinary adj. taim ma: da ທັມມະດາ

ordination n. gan uis bpa: soim boit
ການອຸປະສົມບົດ

ore n. haa ແຮ່

organ (body) n. a way: nya: wa:
ອະໄວຍະວະ
(music) n. kaan nyay: fla:ng
bpein hip ແຄນໃຫຍ່ເປັ່ງປັບທຽບ

organic (living) adj. haang gan
mi si wi:t ແຫ່ງຄວາມມີຊີວິດ
(necessary) adj. haang
suan cha:m bpein ແຫ່ງສ່ວນ
ຈຳເປັນ

organism n. saing mi si wi:t ສິ່ງມີ
ຊີວິດ

organization (order) n. gan cha:t dta:ng
ການຈັດຕັ້ງ
(group) n. haang hu:n suan
ແຫ່ງຮຸ້ນສ່ວນ
(foundation) n. o:ng gan
ອົງການ

organize v. cha:t dta:ng
ຈັດຕັ້ງ

orient n. pak dta: wa:n ohk ພາກ
ຕະວັນອອກ
v. bohk tang ບອກທາງ

origin n. goik kow: ກົກ
ເຄົ້າ

originate (place) v. ma chak ມາຈາກ
(event) v. gert keun ເກີດ
ຂຶ້ນ
(with) v. bpa: dti:t keun
doy ປະດິດຂຶ້ນໂດຍ

ornament n. keuang e ເຄື່ອງເອ

orphan n. deik nohy ga:m pa poh maa
ເດັກນ້ອຍກຳພ້າພາແມ່

osprey n. laaw sa: ni:t neu:ng
ແຫຼວຊະນິດນຶ່ງ

ostrich n. no:k ot li:d
ນົກໂອຕລິດ

other adj. eun ອື່ນ

otherwise adv. ta boh da:ng na:n
ຖ້າບໍ່ດັ່ງນັ້ນ

otter n. dto nak ໂຕນາກ

ought to	v. kuan chă: ຄວນຈະ
ounce	n. 1/16 na:m na:k kohng pohn ນ້ຳພັກຂອງປ່ວນ
our	adj. kohng puak how: ຂອງພວກເຮົາ
ours	pron. kohng puak how: ຂອງພວກເຮົາ
ourself	pron. dtua kohng how: eng ຕົວຂອງເຮົາເອງ
out	adv. ohk ອອກ
out of	(idiom) id. kăt ຂາດ
out-of-date	lă să: măy: ລ້າສມໄ
out of one's mind	bpe:n bă ເປັນບ້າ
out of order	say: boh day:, pe ໃຊ້ບໍ່ໄດ້, ເພ
out of print	boh mi kay ບໍ່ມີຂາຍ
out of the question	bpe:n bpay: boh day: ເປັນໄປບໍ່ໄດ້
outboard motor	n. cha:k dťi:t tay heua ຈັກຕິດທ້າຍເຮືອ
outdoors	adj. nohk heuan ນອກເຮືອນ
outer	adj. tang nohk ທາງນອກ
outfit	n. keuang nu:ng ເຄື່ອງນຸ່ງ v. boh li: chak ບໍ່ລິຈາກ
outgrow	v. nyay: gua ໃຫຍ່ກວ່າ
outhouse	v. hohng na:m nohk heuan ຫ້ອງນ້ຳນອກເຮືອນ
outlet	(electrical) n. hua su:p fay: ຫົວສຸບໄຟ (agent) n. pu taan cha:m nay ຜູ້ແທນຈຳໜ່າຍ
	(alternative) n. tang lă: bay ທາງລະບາຍ
outline	v. dtaang kong hang ແຕ່ງໂຄງຮ່າງ n. kong hang ໂຄງຮ່າງ
output	(factory) n. gan pli:t si:n ka ການຜລິຕສິນຄ້າ (motor) n. haang ma ແຮງມ້າ
outrage	v. ta:m lay ທຳລາຍ n. gan ta:m lay ການທຳລາຍ
outside	n. tang nohk ທາງນອກ
outstanding	adj. de:n ເດັ່ນ
outward	adj. pay nohk ພາຍນອກ
outweigh	v.t. mi kwam sa:m ka:n gua ມີຄວາມສຳຄັນກວ່າ
oval	adj. bpe:n hup kay: ເປັນຮູບໄຂ່
oven	n. dtow: o:p ເຕົາອົບ
over	(again) adv. ik teua neu:ng ອິກເທື່ອນຶ່ງ (above) adv. tang teri:ng ທາງເທິງ (too) adv. lay gern bpay: ຫລາຍເກີນໄປ (cross) v. kam ຂ້າມ
overall	adv. să: lu:p kwam ສະລຸບຄວາມ
overalls	n. song ka nyow ໂສ້ງຂາຍາວ
overcast	adj. meut ມືດ

overcharge (battery) adv. sak fay: lay pot ສາກໄຟຫຼາຍໂພດ

(money) adv. kay paang pot ຂາຍແພງໂພດ

overcoat n. seua ku:n ga:n now ເສື້ອຄຸມກັນໜາວ

overcome v. sa: na: ba:n ha ຊະນະ ບັນຫາ

overdo (work) v. he:t lay pot ເຮັດ ຫຼາຍໂພດ

(manners) v. he:t pot ເຮັດໂພດ

overdose n. gah hay: ya ge:n ga:m no:t ການໃຫ້ຢາເກີນກຳນົດ

overdraw v. tohn nge:n ge:n cha:m nuan ຖອນເງິນເກີນຈຳນວນ

overdue adj. sa gua ga:m no:t ຊ້າກ່ອນກຳນົດ

overeat v.t. gi:n lay ge:n bpay: ກິນຫຼາຍເກີນໄປ

overestimate v.t. kat may ge:n bpay: ຄາດໝາຍເກີນໄປ

overhaul v.t. sohm saam may: ສ້ອມ ແຊມໃໝ່

overhear v. day nyi:n doy ba:ng ern ໄດ້ຍິນໂດຍບັງເອີນ

over here adv. yu ni ຢູ່ນີ້

overload n. gan ba:n tu:k na:k ge:n bpay: ການບັນທຸກໜັກ ເກີນໄປ

overlook v. be:ng kam ເບິ່ງຂ້າມ

over night (time) adv. kam keun ຂ້າມຄືນ

(sleep) adv. kang keun ຄ້າງຄືນ

overrate v. nyohng nyoh pot ຍ່ອງ ຍໍໂພດ

overseas adj. nay: dtang bpa: tet ໃນຕ່າງປະເທດ

oversleep v.i. nohn gern ga:m no:t ນອນເກີນກຳນົດ

overtake v. gay ກາຍ

overtax (strain) v.t. say: gern bpay: ໃຊ້ເກີນໄປ

(taxes) ge:p pa si paang pot ເກັບພາສີແພງໂພດ

overthrow n. gan lo:m lang ການລົ້ມ ລ້າງ

v. lo:m lang ລົ້ມລ້າງ

overweight n. na:m na:k gern ນ້ຳໜັກ ເກີນ

overwhelm (force) v. ga:m lahng ກ້ຳລັງ neua gua ເໜືອກວ່າ

(kindness) v. hay: kwam ga: lu: na gern ໃຫ້ຄວາມກະ ລຸນາເກີນ

overwrought adj. meuay sa: mohng ເມື່ອຍ ສມອງ

owe v. dti:t ni ຕິດໜີ້

owl n. no:k kow: ນົກເຄົ້າ

wn	(possess) v. bpe:n chŏw: kohng ເປັນເຈົ້າຂອງ
	(admit) v. nyŏhm la:p ຍອມຮັບ
	adj. kohng dto:n eng ຂອງຕົນເອງ
wner	n. chŏw: kohng ເຈົ້າຂອງ
x	(oxen) n. ngŭa ງົວ
xygen	n. tat o:k sĭ ye:n ທາດໂອກຊີເຢັນ
	n. a ga:t sô:t ອາກາດສົດ
yster	n. hŏy năng lo:m ຫອຍນາງລົມ

P

abulum	n. a han sa:m la:p sa: mŏhng ອາຫານສໍລັບສມອງ
ace	n. kwam wăy: ຄວາມໄວ v. laan sa:m ແລ່ນຊ້ำ
acific	adj. sa: ngô:p sa: ngĭap di ສງົບສງຽບດີ
acification	n. gan he:t hay: mi kwam sa: ngô:p sa: ngĭap di ການເຮັດໃຫ້ມີຄວາມສງົບສງຽບດີ
Pacific Ocean	n. ma: ha sa: mu:t pa si fi:k ມະຫາສະມຸດປຊີຟິກ
acify	(country) v. he:t hay: sa: ngô:p ເຮັດໃຫ້ສງົບ (baby) v. he:t hay: mi:t ເຮັດໃຫ້ມິດ

pack	(cigarettes) n. sŏhng ຊອງ
	(package) n. hoh ຫໍ v. cha:t keuang ຈັດເຄື່ອງ
package	n. hoh ຫໍ v. ow: say: hoh ເອົາໃສ່ຫໍ
packet	n. hoh nŏy ຫໍນ້ອຍ
pact	n. koh sa:n nya ຂໍ້ສັນຍາ
pad	v. nya:t bôh: ຍັດເບາະ (ink) n. bôh: na:m meu:k ເບາະນ້ຳມຶກ kohng a:n pa: ta:p dta ຂອງອັນປະທັບຕາ (paper) n. ta:p chĭa cho:t may ຕັບເຈ້ຍຈົດໝາຍ
paddle	v. păy heua ພາຍເຮືອ n. măy: păy heua ໄມ້ພາຍເຮືອ
padlock	n. ga: chaa ກະແຈ v. say: ga: chaa ໃສ່ກະແຈ
page	v. ern seu ເອີ້ນຊື່ (paper) n. na chĭa ໜ້າເຈ້ຍ (person) n. ko:n săy: ຄົນໃຊ້
pagoda	n. tat ທາດ
pail	(no handle) n. ga: ta:ng ກະຖັງ (handle) n. ku: ຄຸ
pailful	(handle) adj. dte:m ku: ເຕັມຄຸ

	(no handle) adj. dteːm $\overset{3}{\underset{2}{s}}$aː: taːːng เต็มภะถัว
pain	n. kwam cheːp bpuat ความ เจ็บปอด
	v. cheːp เจ็บ
painful	adj. tiː heːt hayː cheːp bpuat ที่เธ็กใหเจ็บปอด
painless	adj. boh cheːp บ่เจ็บ
paint	n. naːm siː maːsi น้าสี
	(object) v. taː si ทาสี
	(picture) v. dtaam แต้ม
paintbrush	(hair) n. bpaang taː si แป๋งทาสี
	(leaf) n. foy taː si ฝอยทาสี
painter	n. sang taː si sang dtaan hup ຊ่างทาสี, ຊ่างแต้มรูบ
painting	(action) n. gan taː si ภามทาสี
	(picture) n. hup taam, chiːt taːgaːm รูบแต้ม, จิตธะภัม
pair	n. bpeːn ku เป็นคู่
	v. baang bpeːn ku แบ่ง
pajamas	n. keuang nuːng nohn เคื่อງນຸ່ງນอม
pal	n. mu ku ໝູ່ຄູ່
palace	n. paː lat saː vaːng ພะราຊວัງ
palate	n. heuak เຫือก
pale	adj. na leuang ฟ้า(ເหือງ)
paling	v. ohm hua ອ້ອມຮົວ
palm	v. seua:ng wayː nayː meu เຊื่อງໄວ້ໃນມີ
	(hand) n. fa meu ຝ່າມີ
	(tree) n. dtoːn dtan, dtoːn pao ຕົ້ນຕານ, ຕົ້ນพ้าว
palmist	n. moh beriːng lay meu ໝໍເບິ່ງລາຍมิ
palpitate	v. dteːn เต้น
palsy	adj. bpeːn bpia เປ็นເປ້ຍ
pamphlet	n. bpeum bang ปึ้มบาๆ
pan	n. moh kang ໝ้อกาๆ
	v. kua ha kaːm ຄົ້ວຫາคำ
pane	n. paan kaaw แผ่นแກ้ว
panel	(slab) n. fa ຝ่า
	(group) n. kaː naː: ຄมะ
	v. sayː fa ໃສ່ຝ้า
pang	v. heːt hayː cheːp bpuat เธ็กใหเจ็บปอด
	n. kwam cheːp bpuat ຄວามเจ็บปอด
panic	n. kwam dtaak dteun ຄວามแตกตืม
	v. wuːn wayː ວຸ່ນວາຍ
pant	v. hay chayː hohp ຫາຍໃຈ...
pantry	n. hohng wayː a han ຫ້อງໄວ້ອາຫານ
pants	n. soːng ka nyaw ສ້ວຍຍາວ...
papa	n. poh ພ่
paper	v. dtiːt chia ຕິດເຈ້ຍ

n. chia ເຈ້ຍ

adj. he:t duay chia
ເຮັດດ້ວຍເຈ້ຍ

paper clip   n. le:k nip chia ເຫຼັກ
ໜີບເຈ້ຍ

parachute   n. chohng ຈອງ

v. dton chohng ໂຕນຈອງ

parade   (military) n. gan suan sa:
nam ການສວນສະໜາມ

(religious) n. gan has ka:
buan ການແຫ່ະຂບວນ

(military) v. dern suan
sa: nam ເດີນສວນສະໜາມ

(religious) v. haa ka:
buan ແຫ່ຂບວນ

paradise   n. muang sa: wan ເມືອງ
ສວັນ

paragraph   n. wa:k neung ວັກໜຶ່ງ

parallel   adj. ku ka:n bpay: ຄູ່ກັນໄປ

paralysis   n. lok bpe:n bpia
ໂລກເປັນເປ້ຍ

paralyze   v. he:t hay: bpe:n bpia
ເຮັດໃຫ້ເປັນເປ້ຍ

parcel   n. hoh ຫໍ່

parch   v. he:t hay: haang cho:n
dtaak ເຮັດໃຫ້ແຫ້ງຈົນແຕກ

pardon   n. gan nyo:k tot ການ
ຍົກໂທດ

v. nyo:k tot hay ຍົກໂທດໃຫ້

pare   v.t. bpohk bpeuak ປອກເປືອກ

parent   n. poh maa ພໍ່ແມ່

park   v. choht lo:t ຈອດລົດ

n. suan bohn yohn chay:
ສວນບ່ອນຍ່ອນໃຈ

parley   n. gan che la: cha ການ
ເຈະຈາ

parliament   n. sa: pa haang sat ສະ
ພາແຫ່ງຊາດ

parliamentary   adj. ti giaw ga:p sa: pa
ທີ່ງ່ວກັບສະພາ

parlor   n. hohng la:p kaak
ຫອງຮັບແຂກ

parody   n. leuang he:t dta: lo:k
ເຣື່ອງເຮັດຕລົກ

v. ow: baap dta: lo:k
ເອົາແບບຕລົກ

parrot   n. no:k kaaw ນົກແກ້ວ

v. wow: ha:m hay: ເວົ້າຮ່ຳໄຮ່

part   (small unit) n. suan baang
ສວນແບ່ງ

(large unit) n. pak ພາກ

v. baang, chak bpay:
ແບ່ງ, ຈາກໄປ

(play) n. bo:t bat ບົດບາດ

partial   adj. bpe:n bang suan
ເປັນບາງສ່ວນ

participant   n. pu huam ຜູ້ຮ່ວມ

participate   v. kow: huam ເຂົ້າຮ່ວມ

particle   n. suan noy noy ສວນນ້ອຍໆ

particular	adj. cha:m poh: จำเพาะ
particularize	v.t. choh: cho:ng เจาะจิง
partisan	adj. haang gan kow: kang แห่งການเຂົ້າຂ້າງ
partition	n. keuang baang suan เຄື່ອງແບ່ງສ່ວນ
	v. baang duay keuang baang ແບ່ງດ້ວຍເຄື່ອງແບ່ງ
partner	(business) n. pu hun suan ผู้ຮ່ວມສ່ວນ
	(dancing) n. ku dte:n la:m คู่ເຕັ້ນລຳ
	(general) n. ku คู່
part-time	adj. boh dte:m we la ບໍ່ເຕັມເວລາ
party	(group) n. mu ka: na: พูคมะ
	(event) n. ngan gi:n liang ງານกິນລ້ຽງ
	v. gi:n liang กินລ້ຽງ
pass	(path) n. tang kam ທາງຂ້າມ
	v. gay bpay: ກາຍໄປ
	(ticket) n. bpi a: nu: nyat pan ບ້ຽະນຸຍາດผ่าม
pass away	dtay ຕາຍ
pass out	bpe:n lo:m ເປັນລົມ
passable	(road) adj. poh bpay: day: ผ่ไປໄດ້
	(thing) adj. poh say: day: ผ่ใຊ້ໄດ້
passage	(hallway) n. tang pan ohk laa: kow: ทางผ่ามออกและเຂົ້າ
	(tunnel) n. ka pan คำผาม
passenger	n. ko:n doy san คิมโดยสาม
passion	n. kwam lo:ng lay:, kwam ga:n na:t ความໝົງໄฑ, ความทิผัถ
passport	n. na:ng seu pan daan ໜัງສືผ่ามແถม
past	adj. gay laaw, a: di:t ภายແล้วอะถิถ
paste	n. yang gow ยาวกาว
	v. ti:t gow ถิถกาว
pastime	n. wiak leu gan li:n ka we la ວຽกເลกานລ້ຽนຂ້ำເวลา
pastry	n. ka: no:m ຂนมฺ
pasturage	n. toing nya liang sa:t ທຸ່ຍຍ้าลฺງสัถ
pasture	n. toing nya ທຸ່ຍຍ้า
	v. liang nya sa:t loing ລ້ຽนย้าสัถ ลฺง ทฺ้ยฺสัถ
pat	v. to:p koy koy ถิๆค่อยๆ
patch	v. dtap ຕາຍ
	(area) n. hoy dtap ຮอຍຕາຍ
	(tire) n. yang choht ยาว จอถ
pathetic	adj. na i du dto:n น่าอิถูถิม
pathology	n. gan hian kiaw ga:p pa: nyat ການຮฺมท่ๆวๆกัภผะยาถ
patient	adj. o:t to:n ອิถทิม
	n. ko:n che:p คิมเจัย
patriot	n. pu hai:k sat ผู้ฮัๆอาถ

159

patron	n. pu kum kohng (ผู้คุมคอง)
patter	n. siang dto:p léu nyang สงุถฺฺ่ๆุผฺ้่ๆา๑
pattern	n. baap แบบ
	v. he:t naam baap เธัดฺฺๆฺ๊แบบ
pause	v. sow: beu:t neu:ng เฃ๊ๆฺฮัดฺๆๆั๑
	n. gan sow: beu:t neu:ng กฺๆฺฆเฃ๊ๆฺฮัดฺๆๆั๑
pave	(road) v. bpu tang ปฺูๆๆๆๆ
	(understanding) v. oper:t sohng tang เปฺ๊ดฺๆๆฺๆๆๆ๑
pavillion	(officials) n. hoh koy ท์ๆ๑คๆ๑
	(exhibit) n. han sa: daang si:n ka ร้ๆมสะแฺๆๆสั๑ค้๑
paw	n. dtin sa:t ทิ๊มสัด
pay	n. nger:n deuan เ๑ๆฺฉเ๑ฺๆม
	v. chay hay: จๆๆๆฺๆ
payable	adj. ti chay hay: ท์่จๆๆๆฺๆ
pay attention	adv. hay: kwaam so:n chay: ใท์ๆฺความสฺฉมใจ
pay back	adv. ow: say: keun เ๊ๆใฉ ค๊ม
pay back	v. dtohp taan ทฺๆยแทม
pay day	n. meu berk nger:n ม๊่เปิกเๆฺม
paymaster	n. py chay nger:n ผู้จๆๆเๆฺม
payment	n. gan chay nger:n hay: กๆๆมจๆๆฺเ๑ฺมใท์
pay one's respects	bpay: ylam yam peua sa: daang kwam na:p teu ใป๊ๆฺฺมๆ๑มเพฺฺ๊สะแฺๆๆความนับ ถ
pea	n. mak tua sa:n พๆๆถฺฉสม
peace	n. kwam sa: ngo:p, sa:n dti: pap ความสฺฉย, สัมถิ๊ผๆย
peaceful	adj. sai ngo:p สฺฉย
peach	n. mak kay พๆๆคๆๆย
peacock	n. no:k nyu:ng มๆๆกฺๆ
peak	(mountain) n. chohm จฺฉม
	(trees) n. nyoht ยฺฉด
	(excitment) n. ka:n su:t nyoht ฃ๊มสฺฉยฺฉด
peanut	n. mak tua di:n พๆๆถฺฉๆถิม
pear	n. mak giang tet พๆๆก๑ๆๆ เทๆ
pearl	n. kay: mu:k ไฃๆๆยๆ
peasant	n. sow ban nohk ฃๆๆยๆๆม มๆๆ
pebble	n. hi:n haa ทิมแฮ
peck	(measurement) n. maat dtla pohng keuang มๆๆฺฉๆๆผฺๆ เค๊ๆๆ
	v. sa:p สับ
peculiar	adj. bpaak bpa: lat แปๆๆปๆๆด

peddle	(sell) v. kǎy kohng dtam baň ຂາຍຂອງຕາມບ້ານ
	(bicycle) v. tip loːt ຖີບລົດ
pedestrian	n. koːn nyǎng ຄົນຍ່າງ
peel	(fruit) v. bpohk bpeuak ປອກເປືອກ
	(sunburn) v. loːk ລອກ
peg	n. koh hoy keuang ເຄື່ອງ ເຄີ່ງ
pen	(ink) n. bpak gaː ປາກກາ
	(animal) n. kohk saːt ຄອກ ສັດ
	v. kian ຂັງ
penalty	n. tot ໂທດ
pencil	n. soh daːm ສໍດໍາ
penetrate	v. soht kow: bpaː:ǔ ໂຊດເຂົ້າໄປ
penicillin	n. ya saan ຢາແສນ
peninsula	n. laam ແຫຼມ
penknife	n. mit paːp ມີດພັບ
penny	n. ngerːn aːt aː: me liː gaːn ເງີນອັດອະເມຣິກັນ (ຮ້ອຍເປ່ນມີເຫຼັກັບນຶ່ງໂດນລາ)
pension	n. bia baːm nan ເບັ້ງບໍາ ນານ
pensioner	n. pu dayː laː:p bia baːm nan ຜູ້ໄດ້ຮັບເບັ້ງບໍານານ
people	v. heːt hay: mi koːn lay ເຮັດໃຫ້ມີຄົນຫຼາຍ n. paː: sa soːn ປະຊາຊົນ
pepper	(power) n. mak piːk tǎy: ໝາກພິກໄທ
	(chili) n. mak peːt ໝາກເຜັດ
peppery	adj. peːt ເຜັດ
per	prep. toh, laː: ຕໍ, ລະ
perambulator	n. loːt sayː deːk noy bpay: liːn ລົດໃສ່ເດັກນ້ອຍໄປຫຼີ້ນ
perceive	v. saːng get heːn ສັ່ງເກດ ເຫັນ
percent	(%) n. suan hoy ສ່ວນຮ້ອຍ
perch	v. ngoy kohn ງອຍຄອນ
	(roost) n. kohn ຄອນ
	(fish) n. pa perk ປາເຜີກ
percolate	v.t. dtohng ຕອງ
percolator	n. keuang dtohng ເຄື່ອງ ຕອງ
percussion	n. gan dtaːm leu gaː: toːp gaː tǎak keuang doːn dti sa:niːt koh ການຕີຫຼືກະທົບກະເທກເຄື່ອງດົນຕິຊະນິດເຄາ
perfect	v. heːt hay: di ເຮັດໃຫ້ດີ adj. choːp lay ຈົບຫຼາຍ
perfection	n. kwam boh liː: bun ຄວາມບໍຣິບຸນ
perfectly	adj. yang boh liː: bun ຢ່າງບໍຣິບຸນ
perform	(play) v. saː: daang ສະແດງ (work) v. paː: dtiː: baːt ປະຕິບັດ
performance	(work) n. gan gaː: tǎːm ການກະທໍາ (play) n. gan saː: daang ການສະແດງ

perfume	v. he:t hay: mi ki:n hohm ເຮັດໃຫ້ມີກິນຫອມ
	n. na:m hohm ນ້ຳຫອມ
performer	n. pu sa: daang ຜູ້ສະແດງ
perhaps	adv. bang ti ບາງທີ
peril	n. a:n dta: lay ອັນຕຣາຍ
period	n. la: nya: we la ລະຍະເວລາ
	(.) n. may yu:t ຫມາຍຢຸດ
	(menstruation) n. bpe:n la: du ເປັນຣະດູ
perish	v. dtay ຕາຍ
permanency	n. kwam ta wohm ຄວາມ ຖາວອນ
permanent	adj. nyeun nyo:ng ຍືນຍົງ
permeable	adj. seu:m day: ຊຶມໄດ້
permission	n. kwam a: nu: nyat ຄວາມອະນຸຍາດ
permit	n. bay: a: nu: nyat ໃບອະນຸຍາດ
	v. a: nu: nyat ອະນຸຍາດ
perpendicular	(90°) n. se:n ta:ng sak ເສັນຕັງສາກ
perpetual	adj. dta: loht gan ຕລອດການ
perplex	v.i. he:t hay: ngo:ng ເຮັດໃຫ້ງົງ
persecute	v.t. bia:t bian ບຽດບຽນ
persevere	v.i. pian ພຽນ
persist	v. leuay leuay bpay: ເລື້ອຍໆ ໄປ
person	n. bu:k ko:n ບຸກຄົນ
personal	adj. suan dtua ສ່ວນຕົວ
personality	(character) n. la:k sa: na: opa: cha:m dtua ou:k ko:n ລັກສມະນະປະຈຳໂຕ່ບຸກຄົນ
	(star) n. ko:n mi seu siang ຄົນມີຊື່ສຽງ
perspire	v.i. heua ohk ເຫື່ອອອກ
persuade	v. sa:k suan ຊັກຊວນ
persuasion	n. gan sa:k suan ການຊັກຊວນ
pest	n. pu lo:p guan lay, ga la: lo:k ຜູ້ຮົບກວນຫຼາຍ, ກາຣະໂຣກ
pet	n. sa:t liang yu nay: ສັດ heuan ລ້ຽງຢູ່ໃນເຮືອນ
petition	v. hohng koh ຮ້ອງຂໍ
	n. ka:m hohng ຄຳຮ້ອງ
petroleum	n. na:m ma:n ga:t ນ້ຳມັນກາດ
petticoat	n. sin sohn ສິ້ນຊ້ອນ
petty	adj. le:k le:k nohy nohy ເລັກໆນ້ອຍໆ
pharmacy	n. ha:n kay ya ຮ້ານຂາຍຢາ
phase	(project) n. dtohn ຕອນ
	(moon) n. la: nya: ຣະຍະ
	v. da:t opaang ຈັດແປ່ງ
phenomenon	n. gan pa: go:t gan ການປະກົດການ
Philippine	adj. fi lip bpin ຟິລິບປິນ
phlegm	n. ki ga: ter ຂີກະເຖິ
philosophy	n. opa:t sa: nya ປຣັຊຍາ
phone	n. keuang toh la: sa:p ເຄື່ອງໂທຣະສັບ
	v. toh la: sa:p ໂທຣະສັບ

phonograph	n. keuang li:n chan siang ຄ໌ອງหຼິ້ນຈານສຽງ
photograph	n. hup tay ຮູບຖ່າຍ v. tay hup ຖ່າຍຮູບ
photography	n. wi: sa tay hup ວິຊາຖ່າຍຮູບ
phrase	n. bpa: nyok ປະໂຍກ v. he:t hay: bpe:n ka:m wow ເຮັດໃຫ້ເປັນຄຳເວົ້າ
physical	adj. haang hang gay, haang ta:m ma: sat (ແຫ່ງຮ່າງກາຍ, ແຫ່ງທັມມະຊາດ
physician	n. tan moh ທານໝໍ
physicist	n. pu sa:m nan wi: ta: nya sat ta: ma: sat ຜູ້ຊ້ານານວິທະຍາສາດທັມມະຊາດ
physics	n. wi: ta: nya sat ta: ma: sat ວິທະຍາສາດທັມມະຊະຄ
pianist	n. na:k li:n bpi: a no ນັກຫຼິ້ນປີອາໂນ
piano	n. bpi: a no ປີອາໂນ
pick	(flower) v. de:t ເດັດ (select) v. leuak ເລືອກ (axe) n. puak siam lua ພວກສຽມ, ທຶວ
pick on	ko:m ku ຂົມຄູ
pick out	leuak ow: ເລືອກເອົາ
pick up	(take up) ge:p keun ເກັບຂຶ້ນ

	(learn easily) adv. hian dya: way: ຮຽນໄດ້ໄວ
	(truck) n. lo:t ga: pa: ຣົຖກະປະ
	(thing) v. ge:p ເກັບ
	(person) n. so pe ni teuan ໂສເພນີເຖື່ອນ
pickle	n. keuang dohng ເຄື່ອງດອງ v. dohng keuang ດອງເຄື່ອງ
picnic	n. gan gi:n kow: pa nama ກິນເຂົ້າປ່າ v. gi:n kow: pa ກິນເຂົ້າປ່າ
picture	(painting) n. hup dtaan ຮູບແຕ້ມ (photograph) n. hup pap ຮູບພາບ (movie) n. si ne ma ຊີເນມາ v. wat pap nay: sa: mohng ວາດພາບໃນສມອງ
picturesque	adj. ngam keu hup ງາມຄືຮູບ
pie	n. ka: no:m pay ຂນົມພາຍ
piece	(piece together) v. ow: say: ga:n ເອົາໃສ່ກັນ (work of art) n. hup si:n la: bpa: ຮູບສິລປະ (things) n. bpiang, dtohn ປ່ຽງ, ຕອນ
pier	n. kua tiap heua ຂົວທຽບເຮືອ

pierce	v. taang ແທງ
pig	n. mu ໝູ
	adj. giːn lǎy pôt
	ກິນຫຍາຍໂພດ
pigeon	n. noːk gang gáa
	ນົກກາງເກາ
pigskin	n. naːng mu ໜັງໝູ
pile	n. gohng ກອງ
	v. heːt bpeːn gohng
	ເຮັດເປັນກອງ
pilfer	v.t. laːk leːk laːk noy
	ລັກເລັກລັກນ້ອຍ
pilgrim	n. naːk dern tǎng kohng
	sat sǎːr na ນັກເດີນທາງຂອງ
	ສາສນາ
pill	n. ya gohn ຢາກ້ອນ
pillage	n. gan bpun saː dom
	ການປຸ້ນສະດົມ
	v. bpun ປຸ້ນ
pillar	n. sow: ເສົາ
pillow	n. mohn ໝອນ
pilot	n. naːk biːn ນັກບິນ
	v. kaːp heǔa biːn
	ຂັບເຮືອບິນ
pimple	n. siːw ສິວ
pin	n. keːm gaːt ເຂັມກັດ
	v. kaːt sǎy: ຂັດໃສ່
pincers	(tool) n. kim kíp ຄີມຄີບ
	(crab) n. ngǎm gǎː bpu
	ງາມກະປູ

pinch	v. yiːk ຢິກ
pine	n. dtoːn bpaak ແປກ(ຕະນິດໜຶ່ງ)
	v. kiːt terng ຄິດເຖິງ
pineapple	n. mak naːt ໝາກນັດ
ping pong	n. bpiːng bpohng ປິ່ງປ່ອງ
pink	adj. si buá ສີບົວ
pinnacle	n. nyoht ຍອດ
pint	n. kering liːt ເຄິ່ງລິດ
	adj. noy ນ້ອຍ
pioneer	n. pu dtaːng dtoːn ຜູ້ຕັ້ງຕົ້ນ
pious	adj. chay: bun ໃຈບຸນ
pipe	(tobacco) n. gohk ກອກ
	(water) n. toh naːm ທໍ່ນ້ຳ
	v. dtoh naːm kow: ຕໍ່ນ້ຳເຂົ້າ
piracy	n. gan bpun tǎng taː le
	ການປຸ້ນທາງທະເລ
pirate	n. chohn saː laːt ໂຈນສລັດ
pistil	n. ke sohn dohk may: (dtoː
	maa) (ກສ∘ນດອກໄມ້(ໂຕແມ່)
pistol	n. bpeun poːk ປືນພົກ
piston	n. luk sup ລູກສູບ
pit	v. nyua: hay: piːt gaːn
	ຍົວະໃຫ້ຜິດກັນ
	n. lum ຫຼຸມ
pitch	(tone) n. lai daːp siang ຣະດັບສຽງ
	(tar) n. yang bpu tǎng ຢາງປູທາງ
	v. gwaang ແກວ່ງ
pitcher	(water) n. kaːn to ຄັນໂທ
	(sport) n. pu gwaang ban
	ຜູ້ແກວ່ງບານ

pitiful	adj. nǎ sǒːng sǎn ผ้าสิ้งสาม
	adj. na iː du dtoːn ผ้าຊິຕ
	ຕິມ
pitiless	adj. bpeːn nǎ sǎing เป็นຜ້າ
	ຊ້ວ
pity	n. kwǎm sǒːng sǎn ความสิ้ง
	สาม
	v. mi kwǎm sǒːng sǎn มีความ
	ສິ້ວສາມ
placard	(paper) n. bayˈ bpaː gat
	ใบปะกาด
	(wood) n. bpay bpaː gat
	ป้ายปะกาด
place	(put) v. wang sayː bohn
	ອາງໃສ່ย่อม
	n. bohn ย่อม
	(remember) v. cheu chaːm
	ຈື່ຈำ
plague	n. paˈ nyat gaˈ laː lok
	พะยาดภาระโรก
	v. ku keːn ยู่เ็น
plain	(person) adj. yǎng liap
	liap ย่างรูบๆ
	(word) adj. ngay ง่าย
	(evident) adj. chǎam
	chǎang แจ่มแจ๋ง
	n. toːng ทง
plan	n. paǎn gan แผมภาม
	v. wang paǎn ອາງแผม
plane	(tool) n. goːp maý ภิบไม้

	(airplane) n. heǔa biːn เรือบิม
	v. goːp may: ภิบไม้
planet	n. dow noːp paː koh:
	ດາວมีบพะเคาะ
plank	n. bpǎan แป้ม
plant	n. dtoːn may: ตมไม้
	v. bpuk ปูก
plantation	n. toːng hay: ทุ่งไร่
plaster	n. si maːng lat fa สิมัง
	ລາດฝ้า
	v. bok bpun โบกปูม
plastic	adj. bpeːn bpla saː dtiːk
	เป็มปะลาสติก
	n. yang bpla saː dtiːk
	ย่างปะลาสติก
plate	n. chan จาม
	v. keuap duay เคือบด้วย
plateau	n. pu piang ผูພຽງ
platform	n. sǎn จาม
play	(game) n. gan liːn ภามຫຼິ້ม
	v. liːn ຫຼິ້ม
	(theater) n. laː kohn
	ละคอม
player	(game) n. naːk liːn มัภຫຼິ້ม
	(show) n. naːk saː daang
	มัภสะแดง
playwright	n. koːn kian boːt laː kohn
	คิมຂຽมบิดธะคอม
plea	(defense) n. koh ang
	ຊ້າງ

(appeal , request) n. kwam³ koh hohng ຄວາมຂໍ້ຮ້ອງ

plead (beg) v. ohn wohn³ ອ້ອນວອນ

(court case) v. hay: gan ໃຫ້ການ

pleasant adj. ti hay⁶ kwam³ poh³ chay: ທີ່ໃຫ້ຄວາມພໍໃຈ

please (invite) v. sern³ ເຊີມ

(request) v. ga: lu: na³ ກະຊຸນາ

(satisfy) v. he:t¹ hay: ເຮັດໃຫ້ poh³ chay: ພໍໃຈ

pleasure n. kwam³ sa: nu:k³ ຄວາມສມຸກ

pledge n. ka:m³ ma:n³ sa:n nya ຄຳພິມສັນຍາ

v. sa:n nya ສັນຍາ

plenty adj. dte:m³ bpay: duay ເຕັມໄປດ້ວຍ

pliable (objects) adj. bi:t ngoh³ day: ngay ຍືດໂຄ້ງໄດ້ງ່າຍ

(persons) adj. ti sa:k suan day: ngay ທີ່ຍັກຊ້ວມໄດ້ງ່າຍ

pliers n. kim kow ຄີມເຄົາ

plight n. a gan ອາການ

plot v. bpohng hay ປ່ອງຮ້າຍ

n. paan bpohng hay ແຜນປ່ອງຮ້າຍ

plow v. tay: na³ ໄຖນາ

n. tay: ໄຖ

plowshare n. mak so:p³ tay: ຜາກສີຍໄຖ

pluck v. lok ລອກ

plug (plug in) v. siap ສຽບ

(water) n. dohn a:t³ ຖອມອັດ

(electricity) n. hua su:p ທ່ວສຸບ

(advertize) v. ko³ sa: na³ ໂຄສະນາ

plum n. mak may: plam³ ຜາກໄມ້ຜລຳ

plumage n. koi:n no:k mo:t dto ຂມມກຜຶດໂຕ

plumber n. koi:n dtoh toh na:m ຄີມຖຜນ້ຳ

plumbing n. gan dtoh toh na:m ການຖຜນ້ຳ

plume n. koi:n no:k ti say: way: e ຂມມກທີ່ໃຈໃອເຈ

plump adj. dtui:y ຕຸ້ຍ

plunder n. kohng ti la:k ma doy gan bpu:n ຂອມທີ່ລັກມາໂດຍການປຸ້ມ

n. gan la:k, bpu:n ການລັກ, ປຸ້ມ

v. la:k, bpu:n ລັກ, ປຸ້ມ

plunge (thing) v. chu:m ຈຸ່ມ

n. gan dot loing ການໂດດລິງ

(people) v. dot loing ໂດດລິງ

plural n. cha:m nuan sohng leu lay gwa ຈຳນວມສອງຫຼືຫລາຍກວ່າ

plus (math) conj. bpa: so:m ປະສິມ

	(with) conj. ga:p ກັບ
ply	(use) v. say: ໃຊ້
	(twist) v. bi:t ບິດ
	(bend) v. go:ng ກົງ
p.m.	(post meridiem) adv. la:ng tiang ຫຼັງທ່ຽງ
pneumatic	adj. bpay: duay lo:m ໄປດ້ວຍລົມ
pneumonia	n. lok bpoht buam, bpoht kay: ໂຣກປອດບວມ, ປອດໄຂ້
poach	(steal) v. luang lam ລ່ວງລ້ຳ
	(egg) v. dti kay: say: na:m hohn dto:m ຕີໄຂ່ໃສ່ນ້ຳຮ້ອນຕົມ
pocket	n. ga: bpow: ກະເປົາ
	v. ow: say: ga: bpow: ເອົາໃສ່ກະເປົາ
pocket knife	n. mit pai p say: to:ng day: ມີດພັບໃສ່ຖົງໄດ້
pod	n. fai k ຝັກ
	(leg) n. ka gohng tay hup ຂາທ້ວງຖາຍຮຸບ
	(bean) n. fai k mak tua ຝັກໝາກຖົວ
poem	n. kong gohn ໂຄງກອນ
poet	n. pu dtaang gohn ຜູ້ແຕ່ງກອນ
poetry	n. ka:m gohn ຄຳກອນ
point	(main idea) n. chu:t koh kwam ຈຸດຂໍຄວາມ
	(sharp) n.bpay laam ປາຍແຫຼມ v. si si ຊີ

point of view	adv. kwam ki:t he:n, ta:t sa: na: ຄວາມຄິດເຫັນ, ທັດສະມະ
point out	v. si hay: be:ing ຊີໃຫ້ເບິ່ງ
pointed	adj. laam ແຫຼມ
poise	n. ta tang ທ່າທາງ
poison	n. ya beua ຢາເບຶອ v. say: ya beua ໃສ່ ຢາເບຶອ
poison ivy	n. keua "ivy" (ti mi pi:t) ເຄຶອ ອາຍວີ (ທີ່ເປັນພິດ)
poisonous	adj. bpe:n pi:t ເປັນພິດ
poke	(bag) n. ga: bpow: ກະເປົາ
	(sack) n. to:ng ຖົງ
	(for attention) v. nyaa kang ແຫຍ່ຂາງ
	(for a laugh) v. ni:ng kang ພຶງຂາງ
polar	adj. haang kua (kuan) lok ແຫ່ງຂົວ(ຂວນ)ໂລກ
polar bear	n. mi kow tang kua lok ໝີຂາວທາງຂົວໂລກ
pole	(earth) n. kua lok ຂົວໂລກ
	(post) n. lai k ຫຼັກ
pole vault	v. dte:n sow ເຕັ້ນສາວ
police	n. dta:m luat ຕຳຣວດ
police department	n. go:m dta:m luat ກົມຕຳຣວດ
policeman	n. nay dta:m luat ນາຍຕຳຣວດ
police station	sa: ta ni dta:m luat ສະຖານີຕຳຣວດ

policy	n. nǎː nyŏ bay ' มะโยบาย	pop	(father) n. pŏh ພ່
polish	v. tǔ ຖູ		(found) n. siang lǎː bert ສງຽງະເບີດ
	n. nǎːm mǎːn tǔ ນ້ຳມັນຖູ		v. la bert, dtaak
polite	adj. sǔː pǎp ສພຍາ		ຣະເບີດ, ແຕກ
political	adj. haang gan meuang	popcorn	n. kow dtohk dtaak ເຂົ້າຕອກແຕກ
	(ແຫງການເມືອງ	popular	adj. mi sue siang ມີຊສງ
politician	n. naːk gan meuang ນັກ	popularize	v. heːt hay ni nyŏːm tua
	ການເມືອງ		bpay ເຮັດໃຫ້ນິຍົມທົ່ວໄປ
politics	n. gan meuang ການເມືອງ	populate	v. perm bpaː sa soːn
poll	v. tam hua kiːt ຖາມທ່ອຄິດ		(ພີ່ມປະຊາຊົນ
	n. gan saːm luat hua kiːt	population	n. poːn lǎː meuang ພົນເມືອງ
	ການສຳຮວດທ່ອຄິດ	populous	adj. mi poːn lǎː meuang
pollen	n. ge sohn dohk maːy: (lǎː		na naan ມີພົນເມືອງຫຍາແໜ້
	ohng) (ເກສອນດອກໄມ້(ລະອອງ)		adj. oːpa sa soːn lay
pond	n. sǎː naːm ສະນ້ຳ		ປະຊາຊົນຫຼາຍ
ponder	v. dteuːk dtohng beriːng	porch	n. bpaː tu nyaːy: ປະຕູໃຫຍ່
	ຄຶດຕອງເບິ່ງ	pore	n. hu koːn ຮູໂຕ
pony	n. mǎ noy ມ້ານ້ອຍ	pork	n. siːn mu ຊີ້ນໝູ
pool	v. owː mǎ kowː gáːn	pork chop	n. siːn gaː: duk kang mu
	(ເອົາມາເຂົ້າກັນ		ຊີ້ນກະດູກຂາງໝູ
	(water) n. sǎː ap naːm	port	n. tǎ heua ທ່າເຮືອ
	ສະອາງນ້ຳ		adj. tang say kohng heua
	(common fund) v. huam suay		ທາງຊ້າຍຂອງເຮືອ
	leua ຮ່ວມຊ່ວຍເຮືອ	portable	adj. ti teu bpay: daːy:
	(billiards) n. biːn liat		ທີ່ຖືໄປໄດ້
	ບີນລຽດ	portend	v. bpeːn lang (ເປັນລາງ)
oop deck	n. tǎy heua ທ້າຍເຮືອ	porter	n. gu li hap kohng
oor	(money) adj. tuːk nyak ທຸກຍາກ		ກຸລີຫາບຂອງ
	(sad) adj. ngowː ngoy:	portion	n. suan ສ່ວນ
	(ເຫງ້າເຫງອຍ		

portrait	n. hup koːn ຮູບຄົນ
portray	v. saː daang ສະແດງ
Portuguese	n. koːn po tu gis ຄົນໂປຕຸກິສ
pose	(act) v. dtaːng taː ຕັ້ງທ່າ
	n. taː tang ທ່າທາງ
	(ask) v. tam ຖາມ
position	(place) n. saː tan ti ສະຖານທີ່
	v. dtaːng ti ຕັ້ງທີ່
	(rank) n. dtaːm naang ຕຳແໜ່ງ
positive	(suggestion) adj. bpaː nyot ປະໂຍກ
	(certain) adj. kaːk naa ຄັກແມ່
	(electricity) adj. neua ເໜືອ
possess	v. kohp kohng ຄອບຄອງ
possession	n. kwam bpeːn chowː kohng ຄວາມເປັນເຈົ້າຂອງ
possible	n. aːt chaː bpeːn bpay dayː ອາດຈະເປັນໄປໄດ້
possibility	n. gan aːt chaː bpeːn bpay dayː ການອາດຈະເປັນໄປໄດ້
post	(rank) n. dtaːm naang ຕຳແໜ່ງ
	(sign) v. diːt bpaː gat ຕິດປະກາດ
postage	n. ka bpay saː ni ຄ່າໄປສະນີ
postal	adj. haang gan bpay saː ni ແຕ່ງການໄປສະນີ
postcard	n. hup baːt ຮູບບັດ
poster	n. bpay bpaː gat ko saː naː ປ້າຍປະກາດໂຄສະນາ
postman	n. koːn soːng choːt may ຄົນສົ່ງຈົດໝາຍ
postmark	n. dtla bpay saː ni ຕຣາໄປສະນີ
post office	n. hong gan bpay saː ni ໂຮງການໄປສະນີ
postpone	v. nyay bpay ຍ້າຍໄປ
pot	(cooking) n. moh ໝໍ້
	(smoking) n. saː ຢາ
	v. ga (bia dtoːn may say moh) ກາ (ເບ້ຍຕົ້ນໄມ້ໃສ່ໝໍ້)
	(toilet) n. gaː ton kaː tohm ໂຖນ ກະໂຖມ
potato	n. maːn flaːng ມັນຝລັ່ງ
potent	(powerful) adj. aːm nat lay ອຳນາດຫຼາຍ
	(person) adj. boh li buːn ບໍລິບູນ
potential	(electrical) n. haang fay ແຮງໄຟ
	(likelihood) n. aːt chaː bpeːn bpay dayː ອາດຈະເປັນໄປໄດ້
potion	(evil) n. ya beua ຢາເບື່ອ
potter	n. sang bpaːn moh ຊ່າງປັ້ນໝໍ້

pottery	n. keūang bpaːn diːn pow: เคื่องปั้นดินเผา	(useful) adj. bpeːn bpaː nyot เป็นปะโยด	
pouch	n. toːng ถิ้ว	practice	n. gan feuːk aap ການຝຶກແອນ
poultry	n. bpeːt gayː เป็ดไก่		v. feuːk aap ฝึกแอน
pounce	v. gaː dot chaːp ກະໂດດຈັບ	prairie	n. toːng nya ທົ່ງຫຍ້າ
pound	£ (money) n. ngeːn bpohn เงิมปอม	praise	n. gan nyoːk nyohng ການ ຍົກຍ້ອງ
	lb. (weight) n. naːm naːk bpohn น้ำมักปอม		v. soːm serny ຊົມເຊີຍ
	v. dti ตี	pray	v. noːp wayː ມົບໄຫວ້
pour	(rain) v. te loːng เหลิ้ว	preach	v. tet saː na เທສມາ
	(something) v. tohk ຖອກ	preacher	n. pu tet saː na ຜູ້ เທสมา
pout	v. heːt ta mo ho เรัดทำโมโท	precaution	n. kwam laː maːt laː waːng ความระมัดระวัง
poverty	n. kwam tuːk ຄวາมทุก	precede	v. ohk na ອອກໜ້າ
powder	(face) n. bpaang แป้ง	preceding	adj. ti ohk na ທ่ออกໜ້າ
	(gun) n. meu ผี้	precept	(teaching) n. kaːm saːng sohn คำสั่งสอน
	v. heːt hayː bpeːn bpaang เรัดใຫ้เป็นแป้ง		(Buddhism) n. siːn ສີນ
power	(political) n. aːm nat ອำมาด	precious	adj. bpaː sert ปะเสิด
	(military) n. gaːm laːng ກำລัງทำลิ้ว	precipice	n. ngeuam pa เริ้มผา
powerful	(strength) adj. kaang haang แขงแรง	precise	adj. kaːk na คักแม่
	(political) adj. mi aːm nat มีอำมาด	preconceive	v. neuːk wayː gohn มึกไอ้ทอม
power mower	n. chaːk dtaːt nya จักตัดทย่า	pre-concert	adj. gohn gan liːn doːn dtri ກ່ອນການຫຼິ້ນดิมตรี
power saw	n. leuay chaːk เลื่อยจัก	predecessor	n. pu ti yu gohn ผู้ที่ยูกอม
practical	(neat) adj. ti sayː dayː ทำใຊ้ได้	predict	v. tuay ທວາย
		predicate	v. gang dtoh ກาງໂຕ
		prediction	n. gan bohk luang na ການบอกล่องໜ้า

predominate	v. mĭ laỷ gŭa มีๆฆายกว่า
preface	n. kăm năm คำนำ
prefer	v. măːk laỷ gŭa มักๆฆายกว่า
pregnant	(idiom) adj. mĭ tŏhng มีท้อง
	adj. teŭ pả măn ถือพามาม
prejudice	adj. seŭa ow: wă เຈือเอົาว່າ
	n. gan seŭa ow: wă ການเຈือเอົาว່າ
preliminary	adj. beuang dtoːn เບื້ອງต้ม
premier	adj. tĭ neuːng ที่นึง
	n. nă nyoːk laːt taː moːn dtŭri มายิกรัฐมนตรี
preoccupy	v. heːt haỷ: keuːt terng เรັดใຫ້คิดเถิງ
prepare	v. chaːt chaang จัดแจง
prepay	v.t. chảy luang nă จ่าย ຄ่ายพา
prescribe	v. sĭ chaang ຊี้แจง
prescription	(action) n. bayː sĭ chaang ใบຊี้แจง
	(medicine) n. bayː saːng ya ใบສ້งยา
presence	n. gan yu ການຢູ່
present	(person) v. năaː: năːm haỷ: hŭ แมะมำใຫ້
	(gift) n. kŏhng kwaːm 29ງ ຂอม
	(now) n. weː la bpaːt chuː baːn nĭ เอลาปะจุບัม์ນີ້

	(gift) v. mŏhp haỷ: มอบใຫ້
	adj. bpaːt chuː baːn ปะจุບัม
presentation	(introduction) n. găn năaː: naːm haỷ: hu chaːk gaːn ການแมะมำใຫ້ຮู້จักกัม
	(gift) n. găn mŏh haỷ: ການ มอบใຫ້
	(performance) n. găn săː: daang ການสะแดງ
presently	adv. taːn tĭ ni ทัมตี้ນີ້
preservation	n. găn săː: ngŭan wayː ການສ-อมไอ้
preserve	v. săː ngŭan ສ-อม
preside	v. bpeːn bpaː tăn เป็มปะ ทาม
president	(group) n. bpaː tăn ปะทาม
	(nation) n. bpaː ta nă ti boh di ปะทามาทิບໍ່ดี
press	(push) v. bip ບิบ
	n. păː: naak seu kow ผแมกสื້ຂาอ
	adj. seu kow สื້ຂาอ
	(iron) v. hĭt keuang ຣีดเคื้อງ
pressing	adj. duan ด่อม
pressure	(physical) n. kwaːm koːt daːn คอามทิดถัม
	(mental) n. găn săyː săː: mohng ການໃຊ้สมอງ
	v. suːk nyu ຊຸກยู้

prestige	n. giat ກຽດ		printer	n. pu pi:m ຜູ້ພິມ
presume	v. kat ka: ne ຄາດຄະເນ		printing	n. gan pi:m ການພິມ
pretend	v. dta:ng he:t ຕັ້ງເຮັດ		prior	adj. gohn na ກ່ອນໜ້າ
pretty	(emphasis) adj. lay ຫຼາຍ		prison	n. ku:k ຄຸກ
	adj. ngam ງາມ		prisoner	n. na:k tot ນັກໂທດ
prevail	v. de:n gwa ເດັນກວ່າ		private	n. po:n ta: han ພົນທະຫານ
prevent	v. bpohng gain ປ້ອງກັນ			adj. suan tua ສ່ວນຕົວ
previous	adj. dtaa gohn ແຕ່ກ່ອນ		privilege	n. si:t pi: set ສິດພິເສດ
previously	adv. dtaa gohn ແຕ່ກ່ອນ		prize	n. lang wa:n ລາງວັນ
prey	n. nyeua ເຫຍື່ອ		probable	adj. seung na cha: ope:n day:
price	n. la ka ລາຄາ			ຊຶ່ງຈະເປັນໄດ້
	v. dta:ng la ka ຕັ້ງລາຄາ		probably	adv. na cha: ໜ້າຈະ
priceless	adj. mun ka lo:n leua, lo:n		probe	v. sohp suan ສອບສວນ
	ka ມູນຄາລົ້ນເຫຼືອ, ລົ້ນຄາ			(action) n. gan sohp suan
prick	v. taeng ow: ແທງເອົາ			ການສອບສວນ
pride	n. kwam teu dtua ຄວາມຖືຕົວ			(thing) n. keuang to:t
priest	n. ku ba ຄຸບາ			sohp ເຄື່ອງທິດສອບ
primary	adj. beuang dto:n ເບື້ອງ		problem	(personal) n. bpa:n ha
	dto:n ຕົ້ນ			ປັນຫາ
prime	adj. noht nyi:am ປົດຢ້ຽມ			(exercise) n. lek chot
primitive	adj. mi ma dtaa derm			ເລກໂຈດ
	ມີມາແຕ່ເດີມ		proboscis	n. nguang ງວງ
prince	n. chow: say ເຈົ້າຊາຍ		procedure	n. la: biap ລະບຽບ
princess	n. chow: nyi:ng ເຈົ້າຍິງ		proceed	v. da:m nern dtoh bpay:
principal	adj. sa:m ka:n ສຳຄັນ			ດຳເມີນຕໍ່ໄປ
	n. hua na muat hong hian		proceeds	n. nge:rn lay day:
	ຫົວໜ້າຫມວດໂຮງຮຽນ			ເງິນລາຍໄດ້
principle	n. la:k gan ຫຼັກການ		process	n. wi: ti gan ວິທີການ
print	n. hoy pi:m ຮອຍພິມ			v. da:m nern dtam la:
	v. pi:m ພິມ			biap ດຳເມີນຕາມລະບຽບ

procession	n. ka: buan haa ຂະບວນແຫ່
proclaim	v. bpa: gat ປະກາດ
procrastinate	v.i. tuang we la ຖ່ວງເວລາ
procure	v. ha ma ຫາມາ
produce	v. pli:t ohk ຜລິດອອກ
	n. poin ti pli:t ohk ຜົນທີ່ຜລິດອອກ
product	n. poin ti pli:t day: ຜົນທີ່ຜລິດໄດ້
production	(output) n. gan pli:t poin ການຜລິດຜົນ
	(show) n. ngan dtang dtang ງານຕ່າງໆ
profess	v. seua teu ເຊື່ອຖື
profession	n. a' sip ອາຊີບ
professional	adj. tang a' sip ທາງອາຊີບ
	n. pu siaw san ຜູ້ຊ່ວງອງານ
professor	n. sat sa: dta a chan ສາສຕຣາຈານຈານ
profit	v. day: opa: nyot ໄດ້ປະໂຍດ
	n. poin ga:m lay: ຜົນກຳໄຣ
profound	adj. ler:k seuing ເລິກຊຶ້ງ
program	v. he:t lay gan ເຮັດຣາຍການ
	n. lay gan ຣາຍການ
progress	n. gow na ກ້າວໜ້າ
	v. he:t hay: gow na ເຮັດໃຫ້ກ້າວໜ້າ
prohibit	v. ham ຫ້າມ
prohibition	n. gan ham ການຫ້າມ
project	n. kong gan ໂຄງການ
	v. ga: kong gan ຈະໂຄງການ
prolong	v. he:t hay: nyow ເຮັດໃຫ້ຍາວ
prominent	adj. den ເດັ່ນ
promise	n. ka:m sa:n nya ຄຳສັນຍາ
	v. sa:n nya ສັນຍາ
promote	v. leuan san ເລື່ອນຊັ້ນ
promoter	n. pu ko sa: na ຜູ້ໂຄສະນາ
promotion	(rank) n. gan leuan san ການເລື່ອນຊັ້ນ
	(advertisement) n. gan ko sa: na sin ka ການໂຄສະນາ ສິນຄ້າ
prompt	adj. going dtoh we la ກົງຕໍ່ເວລາ
	v. nyua: nyow: ຍົວະເຍົາ
	v. he:t hay: cheu day: (nay: hong la: kohn) ເຮັດໃຫ້ເຈື່ອໄດ້(ໃນໂຮງລະຄອນ)
pronounce	v. ohk siang ອອກສ່ຽງ
pronunciation	n. gan wow: ohk siang ການເວົ້າອອກສ່ຽງ
proof	(evidence) n. la:k tan ຫຼັກຖານ
	(liquor) n. hoy pru:f tow: ka:p low; ha sip bper se:n ຮ້ອຍປຣຸຟ(ເຫຼົ້າກັບເຫຼົ້າ ໕໐ ເປີເຊັນ
propoganda	n. gan ko sa: na ການໂຄສະນາ
proper	adj. soim kuan ສົມຄວນ
property	n. sa:p si:n ສັບສິນ
prophet	n. moh tuay ໝໍທ່ວາຍ

proportion	(size) n. kwam day: suan		(ideas) n. gan ka:t kan
	ຄວາມໄດ້ສ່ວນ		ການຄັດຄ້ານ
	(fraction) n. a:t dta suan		(action) n. gan bpa: tuang
	ອັດຕາສ່ວນ		ການປະທ້ວງ
	v. he:t hay: day: suan	proud	(self) adj. chohng hohng ຈອງຫອງ
	ເຮັດໃຫ້ໄດ້ສ່ວນ		(of something) adj. pum
proposal	n. gan sa: ner kwam he:n		chay: ພູມໃຈ
	ການສະເໜີຄວາມເຫັນ	prove	v. pi: sut ພິສຸດ
propose	(suggest) v. sa: ner ສະເໜີ	proverb	n. su: pa si:t ສຸພາສິດ
	(marriage) v. koh dtaang	provide	v. cha:t ha hay: ຈັດຫາໃຫ້
	ngan ຂໍແຕ່ງງານ	provided	conj. ta hak wa ຖ້າຫາກວ່າ
proprietor	n. pu bpe:n chow: kohng	providence	n. sok sa dta ໂຊກຊະຕາ
	ຜູ້ເປັນເຈົ້າຂອງ	province	n. kwaang ແຂວງ
prose	n. ka:m hohy gaaw ຄຳຮ້ອຍແກ້ວ	provincial	adj. haang kwaang ແຫ່ງແຂວງ
prosecute	v. fohng san	provision	(food) n. a han ອາຫານ
	ຟ້ອງສານ		(contract) n. koh ba:n nya:t
prospect	v. sohk ha ຊອກຫາ		ຂໍບັນຍັດ
	n. kwam wa:ng ຄວາມຫວັງ	provoke	v. nyua: ຢົວະ
prosper	v. hu:ng heuang ຮຸ່ງເຮືອງ	prow	n. hua heua ຫົວເຮືອ
prosperity	n. kwam cha: lern ຄວາມ	prowl	n. gan tiaw sohk ha nyeua
	ຈະເລີນ		ການທ່ຽວຊອກຫາເຫຍື່ອ
prosperous	adj. hu:ng heuang ຮຸ່ງເຮືອງ		v. tiaw sohk ha nyeua ໄກ
protectorate	n. meuang ti yu nay: kwam		ທ່ຽວຊອກຫາເຫຍື່ອ
	ku:m kohng kohng meuang	prudence	n. kwam lohp kohp ຄວາມຮອບ
	nyay: ເມືອງທີ່ຢູ່ໃນຄວາມຄຸ້ມຄອງ		ຄອບ
	ຂອງເມືອງໃຫຍ່	prudent	adj. lohp kohp ຮອບຄອບ
protest	(ideas) v. ka:t kan ຄັດຄ້ານ	prune	n. mak may: plun ໝາກໄມ້
	(action) v. bpa: tuang ປະ		ພຣຸນ
	ທ້ວງ		v. dtohn dto:n may:, li: nga
			may: ຕອນຕົນໄມ້, ລິງາໄມ້

pry	(spy) v. soht kow: berng ສອດເຂົ້າເບິ່ງ
	(open) v. ngat ohk ງັດອອກ
psalm	v. boit sut sam ບົດສຸດງາມ
psychiatrist	n. tan moh bpua pa: nyat tang chay: ທ່ານໝໍປົວພະຍາດ ທາງໃຈ
psychology	n. chiit dta: wiit ta: nya ຈິຕວິທະຍາ
PT boat	n. heua way: mi luk dtoh pi do ເຮືອໄວມີລູກຕໍ່ປີໂຄ
public	n. bpa: sa soin ປະຊາຊົນ adj. haang sa ta la: na: ແຫ່ງສາທາຣະນະ
publication	(action) n. gan piim ການ ພິມ (book) n. naing seu piim tang tang ໜັງສືພິມຕ່າງໆ
publicity	n. gan ko sa: na ການໂຄສະນາ
publish	v. piim ພິມ
publisher	n. pu piim naing seu ຜູ້ພິມໜັງສື
pudding	n. ka: noim puit diing ຂນົມພຸດດິງ
puff	n. loim pait ລົມພັດ v. poin loim ພົນລົມ
pull	v. deuing ດຶງ
pulp	(fruit) n. siin nuan mak may: ຊີ້ນນວນໝາກໄມ້

	(paper) n. yang may: ti say: heit chia ຢາງໄມ້ທຳໃຫ້ ເຣັດເຈ້ຍ
	(magazine) n. bpeum hup giaw gaip pu nyiing ປື້ມຮູບ ກ່ຽວກັບຜູ້ຍິງ
pulpit	n. we ti saim la:p tet ເວທີສຳລັບເທດ
pulse	n. siip chohn ຊີ່ພຈອນ
pump	n. keuang sup naim ເຄື່ອງສູບນ້ຳ v. sup naim ສູບນ້ຳ
pumpkin	n. mak eu: ໝາກອື້
punch	(hit) n. gan soik ການຊົກ (hit) soik ຊົກ (hole) v. choh: ເຈາະ (liquor) n. low: pa: soim naim mak now tet ເຫຼົ້າຜະສົມ ນ້ຳໝາກນາວເທດ (hole) n. leik choh: ຫູ ເຫຼັກເຈາະຮູ
punctual	adj. going dtoh we la ກົງຕໍ່ເວລາ
punctuation	n. keuang may chuit ເຄື່ອງ ໝາຍຈຸດ
puncture	v. haang, dtaak ແທງ, ແຕກ
punish	v. taim tot ທຳໂທດ
punishment	n. gan taim tot ການທຳໂທດ
pup	n. luk ma ລູກໝາ
pupil	n. luk siit ລູກສິດ

puppy	n. mǎ nɔ́y ໝານ້ອຍ
purchase	n. gan sɛ́u ການຊື້
	v. sɛ́u ຊື້
pure	adj. bòh li: su:t ບໍລິສຸດ
purify	v. he:t hay: bòh li: su:t ເຮັດໃຫ້ບໍລິສຸດ
purple	n. si muang ສີມ່ວງ
purpose	n. chu:t bpa: so:ng ຈຸດປະສົງ
purse	n. ga: bpow nger:n ກະເປົາເງິນ
pursue	v. dti:t dtam ຕິດຕາມ
pursuit	n. ngan, gan lay: nǎ:m ງານ, ການໄລ່ນໍ
pus	n. na:m nohng ນ້ຳໜອງ
push	v. su:k nyu ຊຸກຍູ້
puss	(cat) n. luk mǎaw ລູກແມວ
	(face) n. na ໜ້າ
put	v. ow: say: ເອົາໃສ່
put away	v. ge:p way: ເກັບໄວ້
put back	v. ow: kéun way: ເອົາຄືນໄວ້
put off	v. leuang bpay: ເລື່ອນໄປ
put on	v. nu:ng, say: ນຸ່ງໃສ່
put out	(extinguish) v. mòht ມອດ
	(perturbed) v. he:t hay: boh di chay: ເຮັດໃຫ້ບໍ່ດີໃຈ
putrid	adj. now: ເນົ່າ
puzzle	v. he:t hay: so:n ເຮັດໃຫ້ສົນ n. bpi:t sa: na bpa:n ha ບິດສະນາບັນຫາ ປິສມາປັນຫາ

pyramid	n. tat hup sam liam ທາດຮູບສາມຫຼ່ຽມ
python	n. ngu leuam ງູເຫຼືອມ

Q

quack	(duck) n. siang bpe:t hohng ສຽງເປັດຮ້ອງ
	(doctor) n. tan moh bpohm ທ່ານໝໍປອມ
quaint	adj. la sa: may: ລ້າສໄມ
quake	(earth) v. way: ໄຫວ
	(person) v. sa:n ສັ່ນ
qualify	(ability) v. sa mat, sa: daang a gan ສາມາດ, ສະແດງາການ
	(add) v. ne:n ka:m ເໜັ້ນຄວາມ
quality	n. ku:n na: pap ຄຸນນະພາບ
quarrel	n. gan pi:t pat ການຜິດພາດ
	v. pi:t pat ຜິດພາດ
quarrelsome	adj. ma:k pi:ttiang ga:p pu eun ມັກຜິດຖຽງກັບຜູ້ອື່ນ
quarry	n. boh haa ບໍ່ແຮ່
	v. ku:t ko:n ຂຸດຄົ້ນ
quart	n. neu:ng guat ນຶ່ງຂວດ
quarter	(¼) n. neu:ng suan si ນຶ່ງສ່ວນສີ່
	(25¢) n. sow ha se:n ຊາວຫ້າເຊັນ
quay	n. ta heua ທ່າເຮືອ

queen	n. pa: la³ si² ni³ ພະຣາຊີນີ
queer	n. ŏpa: laak¹ ປແລກ
quench	(fire) v. moht² ມອດ
	(appetite) v. la: nga:p¹ ຣະງັບ
query	n. ka:m sa:k tam⁴ ຄຳຊັກຖາມ
	v. tam⁴ ຖາມ
quest	n. gan sa: waang ha ການສແວງຫາ
question	v. tam⁴ ຖາມ
	n. ka:m³ tam⁴ ຄຳຖາມ
questionable	adj. nyaing bpe:n ba:n⁴ ha nyu² ຍັງເປັນບັນຫາຍູ່
questionnaire	n. naing⁴ seu ka:m⁴ tam² ໜັງສືຄຳຖາມ
quick	adj. wohng way: ວ່ອງໄວ
quicken	v. he:t² hay: way: ເຮັດໃຫ້ໄວ
quickly	adv. doy way: ໂດຍໄວ
quicksilver	n. ŏpa: loht², bpian chay:ngay³ ປລອດ, ປ່ຽມໃຈ່າຍ
quiet	adj. mi:t⁴ ມິດ
quill	n. pik⁶ ປີກ
quilt	n. pa fa⁶ ຜ້າຟ້າ
quinine	n. ya gi: ni:n⁵ gaa kay: ŏpa ຢາກິນິນແກ້ໄຂ້ປ່າ
quit	(job) v. ohk chak ອອກຈາກ
quite	adv. dterp⁶ ເຕີບ
	(quite a while) adv. do:n¹ dterp ດົນເຕີບ
quite a few	(mi³) lay⁵ yu² (ມີ) ຫຼາຍຍູ່
quiver	n. ba:ng⁵ luk⁴ sohn ບັ້ງລູກສອນ

	v. sa:n⁵ ສັ້ນ
quota	n. cha:m nuan⁴ ti ga:m no:t⁵ way: ຈຳນວນທີ່ກຳນິດໄວ້
quotation	n. ka:m wow: ti wow: na:m la:n⁴ ká:m ang ຄຳເວົາທີເວົາ້ນໍ້າລ້ຫຼ້ວ, ຄຳ
quotation marks	n. may wo:ng le:p¹ (" ") ໝາຍວົງເລັບ
quote	v. wow: na:m laing, ang ເວົາຫລ້ຫຼ້ວ, ອ້າງ

R

rabbit	n. ga: day ba:n ກະຕ່າຍບ້ານ
rabid	adj. bpe:n woh³ ເປັນວໍ້
rabies	n. lok¹ bpe:n woh³ ໂຣກເປັນວໍ້
raccoon	n. nge:n sa: ni:t⁴ neu:ng ເຫງັ້ນຊນິດໜື່ງ
race	(nation) n. sat⁴ ຊາດ
	v. kaang ga:n⁵ ແຂ່ງຂັນ
	(sports) n. gan kaang ka:n⁵ ການແຂ່ງຂັນ
race course	n. sa: nam kaang ka:n³ ສນາມແຂ່ງຂັນ
racer	(person) n. na:k kaang ka:n⁵ ນັກແຂ່ງຂັນ
	(car) n. lo:t kaang ka:n ຣິດແຂ່ງ
rack	n. han⁵ ຮ້ານ
	v. he:t hay: pe pa:ng ເຮັດໃຫ້ເພພັງ
racket	n. may: dti bpik gay: ໄມ້ຕີປີກໄກ່

radiant	adj. leuam ^{6} ເຫຼື້ອມ	rain	v. fo:n dto:k ຝົນຕົກ
radiate	(light) v. so:ng saang ສ່ງແສງ		n. fo:n ຝົນ
	(steam) v. so:ng ay hohn ສ່ງອາຍຮ້ອນ	rainbow	n. huing gi:n na:m ຮຸ້ງ ກິນນ້ຳ
	(sound) n. ga: chay siang ກະຈາຍສງງ	raincoat	n. seua ga:n fo:n ເສື້ອກັນຝົນ
radiator	(house) n. keuang ga chay kwam hohn ເຄື່ອງກະຈາຍຄວາມ ຮ້ອນ	rainy	adj. mi fo:n sa: mer ມີຝົນສເມີ
	(car) n. moh na:m lo:t nyo:n ໝໍ້ນ້ຳຣົດຍົນ	raise	(breed) v. liang ລ້ຽງ
radical	adj. dtaa ga:m ner: ຕແຕ່ງກ່າເນີດ		(lift) v. nyo:k keun ຍົກຂຶ້ນ
radio	wi: ta: nyu: ວິທະຍຸ	rake	v. kat ຄາດ
raffle	n. huay ຫວຍ		n. kat noy ຄາດນ້ອຍ
raft	n. paa ແພ	ram	n. gaa: tua pu ແກະຕົວຜູ້
rag	n. pa set ຜ້າເສດ		v. taing ທັງ
rage	(anger) n. kwam mo ho hay ຄວາມໂມໂຫຮ້າຍ	ranch	n. kohk bpa: su: sa:t, to:ng liang sa:tຄອກປະສຸສັດ, ທ່ງລ້ຽງສັດ
raid	n. gan chom dti ການໂຈມຕີ	rancher	n. chow: kohng to:ng liang sa:t ເຈົ້າຂອງທ່ງລ້ຽງສັດ
	(village) v. chom dti ໂຈມຕີ	rancid	adj. me:n now: ເໝັນເໜົ່າ
	(icebox) v. gi:n hay: mo:t ກິນໃຫ້ໝົດ	random	adj. doy ba:ng er:n ໂດຍບັ້ງເຊີນ
rail	(track) n. lang lo:t fay: ລາງຣົດໄຟ	rank	(row) n. taaw ແຖວ
	(hand) n. how kain day: ຮາວຂ້ນໃດ		v. lian taaw ລຽນແຖວ
			(status) n. sa:n ຊັ້ນ
railroad	n. tang lo:t fay: ທາງຣົດໄຟ	ransom	v. tay: ໄຖ່
railway	n. tang lo:t fay: ທາງຣົດໄຟ		n. ka tay: ຄ່າໄຖ່
railway station n. sa: ta ni lo:t fay: ສະຖານີຣົດໄຟ		rap	n. gan dti koy koy ການຕີຄ່ອຍໆ
			v. dti koy koy ຕີຄ່ອຍໆ

rapid	adj. wohng way: ວ່ອງໄວ
rapids	n. gaang ແກ້ງ
rapture	n. kwam nyi:n di ຄວາມຍິນດີ
rare	adj. ha nyak ຫາຍາກ
rarely	adv. ha nyak ຫາຍາກ
rascal	n. ko:n ki deu ຄົນຂີ້ຕົວະ
rash	adj. boh hohp kohp ບໍ່ຮອບຄອບ; n. bpam daang ປ່ຳແດງ
rasp	n. dta: bay: nyap, ga: dtay ຕະ ໄບຫຍາບ, ກະຕາຍ
rat	n. nu ໜູ; v. ha:k la:ng mu sa: pa haang ngan ຫັກຫຼັງພູສະພາແຮງງານ
rate	v. ga:m no:t ka ກຳນົດຄ່າ; n. a:t dta ອັດຕາ
rather	adv. berng keu wa ເບິ່ງຄືວ່າ
ratio	n. a:t dtla suan ອັດຕາສ່ວນ
ration	n. gan bpa:n suan a han ການແບ່ງສ່ວນອາຫານ; v. baang bpe:n suan ແບ່ງເປັນສ່ວນ
rational	adj. hu cha:k ki:t day:, teu het po:n ຮູ້ຈັກຄິດໄດ້, ຖືເຫດຜົນ
rattan	n. way ຫວາຍ
rattle	v. sa:n ສັນ; n. keuang li:n de:k noy ເຄື່ອງຫຼິ້ນເດັກນ້ອຍ
ravage	v. lu:k lan ລຸກລານ
rave	v. wow: keu ba ເວົ້າຄືບ້າ
raw	adj. di:p ດິບ

ray	n. saang ແສງ
rayon	n. pa le ohn ຜ້າເຣຍອນ
razor	n. mi:t taa ມີດແຖ
reach	(grab) v. yeu ຢື້; (arrive) v. terng ເຖິງ; n. la: nya: ti cha:p terng ລະຍະທີ່ຈັບເຖິງ
react	v. bpa: dti gi: li: nya ປະຕິກິຣິຍາ
reaction	n. gan ta:m dtohp ການທຳຕອບ
read	v. an ອ່ານ
reader	(person) n. pu an ຜູ້ອ່ານ; (textbook) n. bpeum hian ປຶ້ມຮຽນ
readily	adv. yang wohng way: ຢ່າງວ່ອງໄວ
ready	adj. pohm ພ້ອມ
real	adj. se:ring be:ring dtam sa: pap taa chi:ng ເງີງເບິງຕາມສະພາບແທ້ຈິງ
realistic	adj. taa ແທ້
realize	v. hu cha:k ຮູ້ຈັກ
really!	interj. i li: taa taa ອີ່ຫຼີ, ແທ້ໆ
realm	n. a na cha:k ອານາຈັກ
reap	v. ge:p giaw ເກັບກ່ຽວ
reaper	n. ko:n giaw (kow:) ຄົນກ່ຽວ(ເຂົ້າ)
reappear	v. bpa got keun ik ປະກົດຂຶ້ນອິກ
rear	adj. tang la:ng ທາງຫຼັງ; (raise) v. liang ລ້ຽງ

       (stand up) v. nyó:k kŏh ยักคื

eason   v. hǎy: hét po:n ให้เขตผิม

        n. hét po:n   เขตผิม

easonable   adj. mi hét po:n   มีเขตผิม

eassemble   (rebuild) v. hom ga:m ik

        โฮมกันอีก

       (meet again) v. bpa: su:m

        ga:n ik ปะຊุมทันอีก

bel   v. bpe:n ga: bo:t เป็มกะบิด

        n. ga: bo:t กะบิด

bellion   n. ga:n ga: bo:t การกะบิด

bound   v. gǎ: de:n keun กะเดิมคืม

        n. gan ga: de:n keun

        การกะเดิมคืม

build   v. sang keun may: ສ້າງຂຶ້ນໃໝ່

buke   v. dti: dtian ติງูม

        n. gan dti: dtian การติງูม

call   (demand) v. ow: keun เอาคืม

       (remember) v. huan ki:t

        ter:ng ทอมคิดเถิງ

ceipt   n. bay: la:p ใบรับ

ceivable   adj. la:p day: รับได้

ceive   v. la:p รับ

ceiver   n. keuang la:p เคื่อງรับ

cent   adj. meua way: way: ni

        เมื่อไวๆนี้

ception   (action) n. gan dtohn la:p

        การต้อนรับ

       (party) n. gan gi:n liang

        การกิมล้อງ

recess   (retreat) n. gán toy ການຖອຍ

       (hollow) n. hŭ ku:m ຮູຂົມ

       (break) n. gan lerk, gán

        pa:k   ການເລີກການพัກ

        v. say: kow: bpay: noy

        neu:ng ใส่เข้าไปน้อยนึ่ງ

recipe   n. wi: ti bpu:ng ວິທີປຸງ

recital   n. gan ba:n nyay leuang

        law, gán sa: daang na:k

        do:n dti dtaa pu diaw

        ການບັນຍາຍເຣື່ອງຣາວ,

        ການສແດງດົນຕິຕແຕ່ຜູ້ດຽວ

recite   v. low:, tohng cha:m เล่า, ทอງจำ

reckon   (count) v. na:p มับ

       (judge) v. gǎ: ber:ng กะเบิ่ງ

recognize   v. cheu day: จื่ได้

recollect   v. huan la: leu:k ter:ng

        ทอมละลึกเถิງ

recommend   v. naa: na:m แมะมำ

recommendation n. gan naa: na:m fak

        faing ການแมะมำฝາກฝัງ

recompense   n. lang wa:n kwam dtohp taan

        ลาງວັນ, ความตอบแทม

reconcile   v. bpohng dohng ปรองดอງ

reconstruct   v. sang may: ສ້າງໃໝ່

record   v. ba:n teu:k บัมถึก

       (list) n. ba:n si บัมຊึ

       (phonograph) n. paan siang

        แผ่มสຽງ

recorder   (tape) n. keuang a:t siang

        เคื่อງอัดสຽງ

(flute) n. kuːy ຄຸ່ຍ	reflection n. gàn sǎ: tohn gà:p ການ
(person) n. pùu bàːn teùːk ຜູ້ບັນທິກ	ສະທ້ອນກັບ
recover (get back) v. owː keun ເອົາ ຄືນ	n. gan kìt keun lǎːng
(get well) v. sowː bpuay ເຈົ້າປ່ວຍ	ການຄິດຄືນຫຼັງ
(cover again) v. bpiːt wayː mayː ປິດເອົາໃໝ່	reform v. bpiàn bpaáng, bpaː dtìː ປ່ຽນແປງ, ປະຕິຮູບ
recreation n. gàn lerk liːn ການເລີກຫຼິ້ນ	reformer n. pùu gaa kayː dtam het ga ຜູ້ແກ້ໄຂຕາມເຫດການ
recruit v. gen ເກນ	refrain (action) v. oːt ອົດ
n. pùu teùk gen ຜູ້ຖືກເກນ	(emotion) v. gaːn ກັ້ນ
rectum n. laːm sayː dtoh gaːp dak ລຳໄສ້ຕອນທ້າຍ	n. boːt gohn luk ku ບົດທ່ອນລູ
red adj. sǐ daang ສີແດງ	refresh (body) v. seun chayː ຊື່ນໃຈ
redeem v. tayː keun ໄຖ່ຄືນ	(memory) v. heːt hayː chaːm ເຮັດໃຫ້ຈື່ຈຳ
reduce v. loːt loːng ລົດລົງ	
redwood n. mayː daang ໄມ້ແດງ	refreshment (drink) n. keuang deum yeːn yeːn ເຄື່ອງດື່ມເຍັນໆ
reed n. dtoːn oh ຕົ້ນອໍ	refrigerate v.t. heːt hayː yeːn ເຮັດໃຫ້ເຍັນ
reel v. se, werin wian ເຊ, ເອີ້ນວຽນ	refrigerator n. dtu yeːn ຕູ້ເຍັນ
n. goːing muan say beːt ກິ້ງມ້ວນສາຍເບັດ	refuge n. bohn pering ບ່ອນເພິ່ງ
refer v. ang tering ອ້າງເຖິງ	refugee n. pùu oːp paː nyoːk loːp pày: ຜູ້ອົບພະຍົກລົບໄພ
reference (mention) n. gan ang tering ການອ້າງເຖິງ	refuse n. ki nyeua ຂີ້ເຫຍື້ອ
(person) n. paː nyan ພະຍານ	v. paː dtìː set ປະຕິເສດ
(book) n. bpeum koːn kua ປຶ້ມຄົ້ນຄວ້າ	regard v. naːp teu, bering ນັບຖື
reflect (light) v. saː tohn gaːp ສະທ້ອນກັບ	n. kwam naːp teu, gán owː chayː ຄວາມນັບຖື, ການເອົາໃຈໃສ່
(recall) v. kiːt keun lǎːng ຄິດຄືນຫຼັງ	regards n. kwam waːng di, gan s daang kwam ko loːp ຄວາມຫວັງດີ, ການສະແດງຄວາມ

regarding	pron. giaw gà:p ກ່ຽວກັບ
regime	n. la: bohp ຣະບອບ
regiment	n. gohng pàn ta: hàn ກອງພັນທະຫານ
	v. he:t hay: bpe:n la: biap ເຮັດໃຫ້ເປັນລະບຽບ
region	n. kwaan, ket ແຄວ້ນ, ເຂດ
register	v. loing seu ລົງຊື້
	n. bpeum loing ta: bian ປຶ້ມລົງທະບຽນ
registrar's office	n. hohng gan loing ta: bian ຫ້ອງການລົງທະບຽນ
regret	v. sia day ເສັຽດາຍ
	n. kwam sia day ຄວາມເສັຽດາຍ
regretful	adj. na sia day ໜ້າເສັຽດາຍ
regular	(average) adj. tàm ma: da ທັມະດາ
	(daily) adj. sa: màm sa: mèr ສມ່ຳສເມີ
regulate	v. cha:t la: biap ຈັດລະບຽບ
regulations	n. go:t koh baing ka:p ກົດຂໍ້ບັງຄັບ
rehearse	v. sohm (gan sa: daang) ຊ້ອມ(ການສະແດງ)
reign	v. bpo:k kohng ປົກຄອງ
	n. lat sa: gan ຣາຊການ
reimburse	v. say: keun ໃຊ້ຄືນ
rein	n. nyay: ma ໃຫຍ່ມ້າ
	v. deuing nyay: ma ດຶງໃຫຍ່ມ້າ
reject	v. bpa: dti: se:t ປະຕິເສດ
rejoice	v. nyin di ຍິນດີ
relapse	v. ga:p dto:k sa: pap derm ກັບຕົກສະພາບເດີມ
relate	(connect) v. dti:t dtoh ຕິດຕໍ່
	(politics) v. giaw pàn ກ່ຽວພັນ
relation	(connection) n. gan dti:t dtoh ການຕິດຕໍ່
	(relative) n. pi nohng ພີ່ນ້ອງ
relationship	(relative) n. kwam giaw pàn gàn ຄວາມກ່ຽວພັນກັນ
	(political confederation) n. sàm pàn ta: pap sàm pàn ta: pap ສັມພັນທະພາບ
	(connection) n. gan dti:t dtoh ການຕິດຕໍ່
relative	adj. laaw dtaa het ແລ້ວແຕ່ເຫດ
	n. pi nohng ພີ່ນ້ອງ
relax	v. pa:k pohn ພັກຜ່ອນ
relaxation	n. gan pa:k pohn ການພັກຜ່ອນ
release	v. bpoy dtua bpay: ປ່ອຍຕົວໄປ
	n. gan bpohy hay bpe:n i: sa: la: ການປ່ອຍໃຫ້ເປັນອິສຣະ

relic n. kohng ti laː leuːk 29ŋ
ທີ່ລະລຶກ

relief n. kwam hu seuːk bainː towː
ຄວາມຮູ້ສຶກບັນເທົາ

relieve (pain) v. bainː towː ບັນເທົາ

(substitute) v. paːt
bpian ຜັດປ່ຽນ

religion n. saː saː na ສາສນາ

religious adj. haang sat saː na
ແຫ່ງສາສນາ

relish n. loːt sat keuang puːng a
han ຣົດຊາໆ, ເຄື່ອງປຸງອາຫານ
v. muan seun, siːm
ມວນຊຶນ, ຊິມ

reluctant adj. boh dteːm chayː; laïng
le chayː ບໍ່ເຕັມໃຈ, ລັງເລໃຈ

rely v. wayː chayː ໄວ້ໃຈ

remain v. kang yu ຄ້າງຢູ່

remark n. koh saing get ຂໍ້ສັງເກດ
v. saing get ສັງເກດ

remarkable adj. yang bpaː lat, den
ຢ່າງປລາດ, ເດັນ

remember v. cheu ຈື່

remind v. dteuan ເຕືອນ

remit v. soːng bpayː ສົ່ງໄປ

remnant n. kohng set leːk noy dtoːk
kang yu ຂອງເສດເລັກນ້ອຍຕົກຄ້າງຢູ່

remodel v. bpian hup mayː
ປ່ຽນຮູບໃໝ່

remote adj. hang gayː ຫ່າງໄກ

remove v. owː ohk ເອົາອອກ

rend v. nyat owː ຍາດເອົາ

render (give) v. owː hayː ເອົາໃຫ້
(give back) v. keun hayː
ຄືນໃຫ້

renew (time) v. dtoh a nyuː ຕໍ່ອາ
(shape) v. heːt hayː ເຮັດໃໝ່

renounce n. saː laː ສລະ

renown n. mi seu siang ມີຊື່ສຽງ

rent v. sowː heuan ເຊົ່າເຮືອນ
n. ngerːn ka sowː heuan
ເງິນຄ່າເຊົ່າ ເຮືອນ

reopen v.t. bpert mayː ເປີດໃໝ່

reorganization n. gan chaːt chaang mayː
ການຈັດແຈງໃໝ່

reorganize v.t. chaːt chaang mayː
ຈັດແຈງໃໝ່

repair n. gan sohm saam
ການສ້ອມແປງ
v. sohm saam ສ້ອມແປງ

repast n. a han kap neuːng neuːn
ອາຫານຄາບໜຶ່ງ ໆ

repel (push away) v. nyu ohk,
kaːp layː ຢູອອກ, ຂັບໄລ່
(dislike) v. heːt hayː
laïng giat ເຮັດໃຫ້ລັງງຽດ

repent v. koh luːt bap, saː deuː
kwam piːt
ຂລຸດບາບ, ສະເດີກຄວາມຜິ

repetition n. gan saːm ik ການຊ້ຳອີກ

replace (thing) v. ow: say: taan เอาใส่แทน	(sample) n. dtua yang ຕົວຢ່າງ
(person) v. taan bohn ແທນບ່ອນ	(business) n. dtua taan ຕົວແທນ
reply n. kam dtohp คำตอบ	**reprove** v. da wa ດ່າວ່າ
v. dtohp ຕອບ	**reptile** n. sait cha:m puak leua kan ສັດຈຳພວກເລື່ອຄານ
report n. lay ngan ลายງาม	**republic** n. sa ta la: na: lait sa ທາระນะรัฐ
v. lay ngan ลายງาม	**republican** n. bpe:n sa ta la: na: lait เป็นสาทาระนะรัฐ
reporter n. naik seu kow ນັກສື່ຂ່າວ	**repulse** (dislike) v. laing giat ລັງກຽດ
repose v. nohn paik pohn ນອນ ພັກຜ່ອນ	(push) v. nyu ohk ຍູ້ອອກ
n. gan nohn paik pohn ການນອນພັກຜ່ອນ	(flight) v. dti hay: toy ຕີໃຫ້ຖອຍ
represent (general) v. taan ແທນ	**reputation** n. seu siang ຊື່ສຽງ
(political) n. taan dtua ແທນຕົວ	**reputed** adj. mi seu siang ມີຊື່ສຽງ
repress v. go:k way: ກົກໄວ້	**request** n. gan koh hohng ການຂໍຮ້ອງ
reprint v. pi:m way: ພິມໄວ້	v. hohng koh ຮ້ອງຂໍ
n. naing seu pi:m may: ພວຽສືພິມໃໝ່	**require** v. dtohng gan ຕ້ອງການ
reproach v. dti: dtian ຕິດຽມ	**rescue** v. soy si wi:t ຊ່ອຍຊີວິດ
n. gan dti: dtian ການຕິດຽມ	**rescuer** n. pu soy si wi:t ຜູ້ຊ່ອຍຊີວິດ
reproduction (copy) n. baap ແບບ	**research** n. gan koin kua ການຄົ້ນຄວ້າ
(sexual) n. gan seup pain ການສືບພັນ	v. koin kua ຄົ້ນຄວ້າ
representative (conference) n. pu dtang na ຜູ້ຕາງໜ້າ	**resemblance** n. kwam keu gain ຄວາມຄືກັน
(government) n. sai ma si:k sai pa pu taan ສະມາຊິກສະພາຜູ້ແທນ	**resemble** v. kay keu gain ຄ້າຍຄືກັน
	resent v. ka:t kaan ຂັດແຄ້ນ

reservation	n. gan chohng wáy: ການຈອງໄວ້
reserve	n. chohng wáy: ຈອງໄວ້
	adj. sa:m lŏhng ສຳຮອງ
reserves	n. keuang sa:m lŏhng ເຄື່ອງສຳຮອງ
reservoir	n. ang nâ:m ອ່າງນ້ຳ
reside	v. a sáy: yu ອາໄສຢູ່
residence	n. bohn yu ບ່ອນຢູ່
resident	n. pu yu a sáy: ຜູ້ຢູ່ອາໄສ
resign	(quit) v. koh la ohk ຂໍລາອອກ
	(surrender) v. nyohm ຍອມ
resist	v. dtoh dtan ຕໍ່ຕ້ານ
resolute	adj. naaw naa ແໜວແໜ້
resolve	v.dta:k si:n chay: ຕັກສິນໃຈ
resort	(place) n. bohn dtak a gat ບ່ອນຕາກອາກາດ
	(alternative) n. ti per:ng a say: ທີເຜິ່ງອາໄສ
	v. bpay: leuay leuay ໄປເລື້ອຍໆ cha:t bpe:n la: biap may: ຈັດເປັນລະບຽບໃໝ
resource	n. sa:p pa: nya gohn ຊັບພະຍາກອນ
respect	n. kwam kow lo:p ຄວາມເຄົາຣົບ v. kow lo:p ເຄົາຣົບ
respectable	adj. ti na nâ:p teu ທີໜານັບຖື
respective	adj. ser:ng ga:n laa: ga:n ເຊິ່ງກັນແລະກັນ
respond	v. dtohp ຕອບ
response	n. ka:m sâ: nohng ຄຳສະໜອງ
responsible	adj. mi kwam la:p pi:t sohp ມີຄວາມຮັບຜິດຊອບ
responsibility	n. gan la:p pi:t sohp ການຮັບຜິດຊອບ
rest	(nap) n. gan yu:t pa:k pohn ການຢຸດພັກຜ່ອນ
	(final part) n. suan leua ສ່ວນເຫຼືອ
	v. yu:t pa:k pohn ຢຸດພັກຜ່ອນ
restaurant	n. hân a han ຮ້ານອາຫານ
restful	adj. sâi ngo:p ສະງົບ
restore	v. bpa:p bpu:ng dây: di ປັບປຸງໄດ້ດີ
restrain	(emotion) v. nya:p nyâng ຍັບຍັ້ງ
	(action) v. ha:m ຫ້າມ
restrict	v. cha:m ga:t ຈຳກັດ
result	v. bpe:n po:n hay: ເປັນ ຜົນໃຫ້ n. po:n ຜົນ
resume	(position) v. seup dtoh ສືບຕໍ່
	(action) v. dtaing dto:n may: ຕັ້ງຕົ້ນໃໝ່ n. chay: kwam ໃຈຄວາມ
retail	v. kay nyoy ຂາຍຍ່ອຍ n. gan kay nyoy ການຂາຍຍ່ອຍ

retain	v. geip wáy: ເກັບໄວ້
retard	v. heit háy: sã bpay: ເຮັດ ໃຫ້ຊ້າໄປ
retire	v. ohk giːn bĭa baːm nãn ອອກກິນເບັ້ຍບຳນານ
retort	v. dto dtohp ໂຕ້ຕອບ n. kãːm dto dtohp ຄຳໂຕ້ຕອບ
retreat	v. la tŏy ລ່າຖອຍ n. gan la tŏy ການລ່າຖອຍ
return	v. gaip keun ກັບຄືນ n. gaːm lay: ກຳໄລ
reunion	n. gan tohn hõm gaːn ik ການທ່ອມໂຮມກັນອີກ
reveal	v. bpert peːy ເປີດເຜີຍ
revenge	v. gãa kaan ແກ້ແຄ້ນ n. gan gãa kaan ການແກ້ແຄ້ນ
revenue	n. láy day ລາຍໄດ້
revere	v. kŏw: loːp ເຄົາຣົບ
reverend	n. paː tan achan ພະ, ທ່ານອາຈານ
reverent	adj. mi kwam yaːm geng ມີຄວາມຢຳເກງ
reverse	(turn around) v. bpian kang ປ່ຽນຂ້າງ (go backwards) v. tŏy laːng ຖອຍຫຼັງ (switch) v. bpian bpay: tang goːng gaːn kam ປ່ຽນໄປ ທາງກົງກັນຂ້າມ adj. goːng gaːn kam ກົງກັນ ຂ້າມ
review	n. láy ngan giaw gaip gan guat ລາຍງານກ່ຽວກັບການກວດ (check) v. guat beriːng ກວດເບິ່ງໆ (study again) v. hian keun ຮຽນຄືນ
revile	v.t. dã ດ່າ
revise	v. tuaːn keun ທວນຄືນ
revive	v. feun sãː dtiː ຟື້ນສະຕິ
revolt	(rebel) v. bpaː dtiː waːt dtoh dtan ປະຕິວັດຕ້ານ (disgust) v. bpuːn tohng ປັ້ນທ້ອງ
revolution	n. gan bpaː dtiː waːt ການປະຕິວັດ
revolutionary	n. pu goh gan gaː bŏːt ຜູ້ກໍ່ການກະບົດ adj. sãː may: may: ສໃໝ່ໃໝ່
revolutionize	v. bpian bpaang ປ່ຽນແປງ
revolve	(circle) v. bpiːn ohm ປິ້ນອ້ອມ (depend on) v. bpeːn bpay: dtam ເປັນໄປຕາມ
revolver	n. bpeun haːn liː ປືນຫັນລີ
reward	v. hay: laːng waːn ຮາງວັນ
rheumatism	n. lok bɔuat dtam koh dtang atãng ໂรคປວດຕາມຄຕາງໆ
rhinoceros	n. dto haat ໂຕແຮດ
rhyme	n. gohn ກອນ v. bpaː diːt gohn ປະດິດກອນ
rib	v. heit dtaː loːk ເຮັດຕລົກ n. gaː duk kang ກະດູກຂ້າງ

ribbon	(general) n. pǎ baṅg baṅg laǎ ngǒw ຜ້າບາງໆແລະຍາງ
	(typewriter) n. pǎ tep saǐm laːp chaːk piːm diːt ຜ້າເທບສໍ້າ ກົບຈັກພິມດິຕ
rice	n. kowː ເຂົ້າ
rich	adj. haːng mi ຮັ່ງມີ
rickets	n. lok ga duk ohn ໂຮກກະດູກອ່ອນ
rid	(exile) v. kaːp bpayː ຂັບໄປ
	(disease) v. sǒw ເຊົາ
	(things) v. owː tiːm ເອົາຖິ້ມ
riddle	v. heːt hayː bpeːn hu lay lay, hohn ເຮັດໃຫ້ເປັນຮູຫຼາຍໆ , ຫນ n. kwam tuay ຄວາມທວາຍ
ride	n. gan ki ການຂີ່ v. ki ຂີ່
rider	n. pu ki ຜູ້ຂີ່
ridge	n. saːn pu ສັນພູ
ridicule	v. heːt dtaː loːk ເຮັດຕຳລໍ້ກ
ridiculous	adj. naː yak huǎ ຫນ້າຢາກຫົວ
rifle	n. bpeun nyow ປືນຍາວ
right	(law) n. siːt tiː ສິດທີ
	(side) adj. faːng kua meu ທາງຂວາມື
	(correct) adj. teuk dtohng ຖືກຕ້ອງ
	(turn up) v. dtaːng keun ຕັ້ງຂື້ນ

	(correct) v. heːt hayː teuk ເຮັດໃຫ້ຖືກ
right away	adv. diǎw niː ດຽວນີ້
right-handed	adj. haǎng kua ແຮງຂວາ
right here	(-there) yu ni ni naː ຢູ່ນີ້ນີ້ນາ (yu haːn haːn na) ຢູ່ຫັນຫັນນາ
right now	diǎw niː lot ດຽວນີ້ໂລດ
rigid	(hard) adj. kaǎng ແຂງ
	(tight) adj. naǎn ແຫນ້ນ
rim	n. him ຮິມ
rind	n. peuak ເປືອກ
ring	(finger) n. waǎn ແຫວນ v. diːt gaː diːng ດິດກະດິງ
	(telephone) n. to laː saːp ໂທຣະສັບ
	(halo) n. gerng deuan ເກີ້ງເດືອນ gerng dta weːn ເກີ້ງຕະເວັ້ນ
ringworm	n. ki gak ຂີ້ກາກ
rinse	v. layː kueǔng ລ້າຍເຄືອງ
riot	n. gan cha laː choːn ການ ຈາະຈົມ v. cha laː choːn ຈາະຈົມ
rip	v. chik ຈີກ n. hoy chik ຮອຍຈີກ
ripe	adj. suːk ສຸກ
ripen	v. suːk keun ສຸກຂື້ນ

ripple	n. na⁵:m feüan ນ້ຳເຝືອນ
rise	(person) v. lu⁵:k keu³n ລຸກຂຶ້ນ
	(sun) v. keu⁶n ຂຶ້ນ
risk	v. siang a²:n dt³a: ra³y ສ່ຽງອັນຕະລາຍ
	n. gah² siang³ pa²y: ການສ່ຽງໄພ
rite	n. pi²: ti³ ພິທີ
rival	n. ku² kaang² ຄູ່ແຂ່ງ
	v. kaang² kaan⁴ ແຂ່ງຂັນ
river	n. maa² na²:m ແມ່ນ້ຳ
road	n. ta³: no³:n ຖນົນ
roam	v. tohng² tiow² ທ່ອງທ່ຽວ
roar	v. paat⁶ siang⁴ ແຜດສຽງ
roast	n. neua⁵ pi³ng laaw³ ເນື້ອປິ້ງແລ້ວ
	v. pi³ng ປິ້ງ
rob	v. ka³: mo⁵y ຂະໂມຍ
robber	n. ko³:n ka³: mo⁵y ຄົນຂະໂມຍ
robe	v. nu³:ng seua² ku³:m ນຸ່ງເສື້ອຄຸມ
	n. seua⁶ ku³:m ເສື້ອຄຸມ
robin	b. no³:k la²: du¹ bay¹: may⁵: bpo²:ng ນົກລະດູໃບໄມ້ບ່ອງ
rock	n. go³hn hi³n ກ້ອນຫີນ
	(swing) v. o²n bpay¹: o²n ma³ ໂອນໄປໂອນມາ
	(dance) v. dte³:n la²:m cha¹:ng wa²: lohk⁵ ເຕັ້ນລຳຈັ້ງ ທວະຮອກ
rocket	(space ship) n. cha³: luat⁵ ຈະຫລວດ
	(Lao type) n. ba³:ng fa⁵y: ບັ້ງໄຟ
rocky	adj. bpe³:n hi⁴n ເປັນຫີນ
rod	n. may⁵: so⁶w ໄມ້ສາວ
rogue	n. ko³:n a³:n ta²: pan¹ ຄົນອັນຕະພານ
role	n. bo³:t bat³ ບົດບາດ
roll	n. muan² ມ້ວນ
	v. gi³ing ກິ້ງ
roll up	v. pa³:n kow⁵: ພັນເຂົ້າ
romance	(story) n. leuang² kwam³ ha³:k ເຮື່ອງຄວາມຮັກ
	(love) kwam³ ha³:k ຄວາມຮັກ
romantic	adj. haang² kwam³ ha³:k ແຫ່ງ ຄວາມຮັກ
	(poetic) adj. bpak⁶ wan⁴ ປາກຫວານ
roof	v. mu³:ng la³ng ka³ ມຸງຫລັງຄາ
	n. la³ng⁴ ka³ ຫລັງຄາ
room	(chamber) n. hohng⁶ ຫ້ອງ
	(space) n. bohn² ບ່ອນ
	v. yu² hohng² diaw¹ ga³:n ຍູ່ຫ້ອງດຽວກັນ
roomy	adj. mi² bohn² la³y⁴ ມີບ່ອນຫລາຍ
roost	v. cha³:p kohn³ ຈັບຄອນ
	n. kohn³ gay¹: ຄອນໄກ່
root	(origin) n. go³:k kow⁵: ຮາກເຄົ້າ

	(plant) n. hak máy: ຣາກໄມ້	row	n. tâaw ແຖວ
rope	v. puk, kwaang seúak		v. páy heŭa ພາຍເຮືອ
	ຜູກ, ແກວ່ງເຊືອກ	rowboat	n. heŭa pay ເຮືອພາຍ
	n. seúak ເຊືອກ	royal	adj. haang gà: sà:t
rose	n. dohk gu: lap ດອກກຸຫລາບ		ແຫ່ງກະສັດ
rot	(junk) n. kohng now: ຂອງເນົ່າ	rub	v. tu ຖູ
	v. now: ເນົ່າ		n. ba:n ha ບັນຫາ
	(lie) n. kwam ki tua:	rubber	n. yang ຢາງ
	ຄວາມຂີ້ຕົວະ	rubbers	n. gerp yang gà:n bpeuan
rotate	(alternate) v. bpian pian		ເກີບຢາງກັນເປື້ອນ
	ປ່ຽນຜຽນ	rubbish	(lie) n. leuang tua: ເຣື່ອງ
	(spin) v. mu:n ຫມຸນ		ຕົວະ
rotten	adj. now: ເນົ່າ		(junk) n. ki nyeua ຂີ້ເຫຍື່ອ
rouge	n. si ta bpak ສີທາປາກ	ruby	n. ta:p ti:m ທັບທິມ
rough	(thing) adj. sa ຊາ	rudder	n. mak ka: lo:k teu tay heŭa
	(idea) adj. nyap ຫຍາບ		ພາກຄະລົກຖືຫ້າຍເຮືອ
	(strong) adj. haang ແຮງ	rude	adj. nyap sa ຫຍາບຊາ
round	v. he:t hay: mo:n ເຮັດໃຫ້	ruffle	v. he:t hay: dto:k chay:
	ມົນ		ເຮັດໃຫ້ຕົກໃຈ
	adj. mo:n ມົນ	rug	n. pa bpu ຜ້າປູ
rouse	n. kohng loh chay: ຂອງລໍ່ໃຈ	ruin	v. ta:m lay ທຳລາຍ
	v. nyu: nyo:ng ຍຸຍົງ		n. kohng bu han na: gan
rout	v. sia say: ເສັຽໃຈ		ຂອງບູຮານມະການ
route	v. so:ng bpay: na:m tang	rule	(administration) n. gan
	ສົ່ງໄປນຳທາງ		bpo:k kohng ການປົກຄອງ
	n. ho:n tang ຫົນທາງ		v. bpo:k kohng ປົກຄອງ
routine	n. la biap gan ລະບຽບການ		(regulation) n. go:t ba:ng
	adj. sa:m sak ຊ້ຳຊາກ		ka:p ກົດບັງຄັບ
rove	v. tohng tiow bpay: ທ່ອງ	ruler	(measuring stick) n. may:
	ທ່ຽວໄປ		ba:n ta:t ໄມ້ບັນທັດ

	(person) n. pu bpoːk kohng ຜູ້ປົກຄອງ
rum	n. lowː kow sǎ li ເຫຼົາເຂາສາລີ
rumble	(fight) n. gan dti gaìn ການຕີກັນ
	(noise) n. siang fa hohng ສຽງຟ້າຮ້ອງ
rumor	n. kow leu ຂາວລື
	v. lowː leu kow ເລົ່າລືຂາວ
run	n. tang laàn ທາງແລ່ນ
	v. laàn ແລ່ນ
run across	poːp doy boh kat may ພົບໂດຍບໍ່ຄາດໝາຍ
run-down	(sick) bpuay loìng ປ່ວຍລົງ
	(in need of repair) adj. peː ເພ
run out	moːt ໝົດ
rung	n. luk kaìn dayː ລູກຂັ້ນໄດ
rural	adj. haàng soːn naː boːt ແຫ່ງຊົນນະບົດ
rush	n. kwam faw ຄວາມຟ້າວ
	v. faw ຟ້າວ
Russia	n. bpaː tet laːt sia ປະເທດຣັດເຊ້ຍ
Russian	adj. ti giaw gaːp laːt sia ທີ່ກ່ຽວກັບຣັດເຊ້ຍ
rust	n. ki miang ຂີ້ໝ້ຽງ
	v. kow miang ເຂົາໝ້ຽງ
rustic	adj. haàng soːn naː boːt ແຫ່ງຊົນນະບົດ

rustle	n. siang koy koy ສຽງຄອຍໆ
	(make noise) v. heːt siang daìng koy koy ເຮັດສຽງດັງຄອຍໆ
	(steal) v. laːk ngua ລັກງົວ
rusty	adj. bpeːn ki miang ເປັນຂີ້ໝ້ຽງ
rye	n. kowː ti bpuk saːm laːp ເຂົາທີ່ປຸກຊ້ຳໆ heːt lowː laa kowː chi ເຫຼົາແລະເຂົາຈີ

S

's	(possessive suffix) kohng ຂອງ
saber	n. dap ດາບ
sack	v. sayː toìng ໃສ່ຖົງ
	n. toìng ຖົງ
sacred	adj. saːk siːt ສັກສິດ
sacrifice	(personal) n. gan sia saː laː ການເສັຍສະລະ
	(religious) n. keuang gaa baː ເຄື່ອງແກບະ
	(religious) v. gaa baː ແກບະ
	(personal) v. sia saː laː ເສັຍສະລະ
sad	adj. sow sok ເສົາໂສກ
saddle	n. an ma ອານມ້າ
	v. sayː an ໃສ່ອານ

sadness	n. kwăm sŏk sow: ຄວາມໂສກເສົ້າ
safe	adj. bpoht pay: ປອດໄພ
	n. dtu seip ຕູ້ເຊັບ ຕູ້ງມເງິນ
safely	adv. doy bpoht pay: ໂດຍປອດໄພ
safety	n. kwăm bpoht pay: ຄວາມປອດໄພ
sage	adj. să lat ສລາດ
	n. pu să lat ຜູ້ສລາດ
sail	v. laan heua bay: ແລ່ນເຮືອໃບ
	n. bay: ໃບ
sailboat	n. heua bay: lŏim ເຮືອໃບລົ່ມ
sailor	(civilian) n. pu laan heua ຜູ້ແລ່ນເຮືອ
	(military) n. ta: han heua ທະຫານເຮືອ
saint	n. naik buin ນັກບຸນ
saintly	adj. chay: pohng say: ໃຈະໆໃສ
sake	n. bpa: nyot ປະໂຍດ
salad	r. nyăm să: la:t ຍຳສລັດ
salad dressing	n. naim pă: soim nyăm să: la:t ນ້ຳປະສົມຍຳສລັດ
salary	n. ngerin deuan ເງິນເດືອນ
sale	(action) n. gan kay ການຂາຍ
	(discount) n. gan kay loit la kă ການຂາຍຫຼຸດຣາຄາ
saleable	adj. kay dăy: ຂາຍໄດ້
salesgirl	n. pa: naik ngăn pu nyĭ ing kay keuang ພັກງານຜູ້ຍິງຂາຍເຄື່ອງ
saleslady	n. pa: naik ngăn kay keuang să: dti ພັກງານຂາຍເຄື່ອງສຕຣີ
salesman	n. koin kay keyang ຄົນຂາຍເຄື່ອງ
saliva	n. naim lăy ນ້ຳລາຍ
salmon	n. bpa so moing ປາໂຊໂມ້ງ
salon	(living room) n. hohng la:p kaak ຫ້ອງຮັບແຂກ
	(dressing room) n. hohng dtaang dtua ຫ້ອງແຕ່ງຕົວ
saloon	n. ba kow boy ບາຄາວບອຍ
salt	v. say: geua săy:ເກືອໃສ່ເກິ່ງ
	n. geua ເກືອ
salute	v. kăim naip ຄຳນັບ
	n. gan kăim naip ການຄຳນັບ
salvage	(collect) v. geip tohn way: ເກັບທ່ອນໄວ້
salvation	n. gan poin tot ການພົ້ນໂທດ
salve	n. ya ki pering ຢາຂີ້ເຜິ້ງ
	v. say: ya ki pering ໃສ່ ຢາຂີ້ເຜິ້ງ
same	adj. keu gain ຄືກັນ

sample	v. to:t lohng dtua yang ทดลองถือย่างๆ n. dtua yang ตัวอย่างๆ
sanction	n. gan lo:ng tot, gan nyohm hay: การลงโทษ, การยอมให้ v. la:p lohng ow: รับรอง เอา
sand	n. di:n say ดินทราย v. pa:t duay ga: dat say ผัดด้วยกะดาดทราย
sandal	n. gerp sa:ng dan เกิบ ฮู้งดาน
sandpaper	n. ga: dat say กะดาดทราย
sandpiper	n. ni:k kaam ta: le sa: ni:t neu:ng มิกแคมทะเลชุนิดนึ่ง
sandstone	n. hin say หินทราย
sandwich	n. kow: chi nya:t say: เข้าจี่ยัดไส้
sandy	(texture) adj. dte:m bpay: duay say เต็มไปด้วยทราย (color) adj. bpe:n si di:n say เป็นสีดินทราย
sane	adj. boh bpe:n ba ย์เป็นบ้า
sanitarium	(psychological) n. hong moh lok chi:t โรงฆ้โรกจิต (physical) n. hong moh dtak a 'ga:t โรงฆ้ตากอากาด
sanitary	adj. sa: at สะอาด
Santa Claus	n. pa: nya sa:ng kan พะยา สั่งกาม

sap	n. yang may: ยางไม้ v. dut ohk ถุดออก
sapsucker	n. no:k say: มิ่กไข่
sash	n. say sa: pay baap na ผ้า nyo:k say: สายสะพายแบบ มายากใส่
satan	(devil) n. pi hay ผีร้าย (person) n. ko:n sua คิมชั่ว
satellite	(natural) n. boh li: wan duang dow บ่ริวามดวงดาว (artificial) n. dow tiam ดาวทูม (country) n. bpa: tet boh li wan ปะเทดบ่ริวาม
satin	n. paa dtuan แผดวม
satisfaction	n. kwam poh chay: ความ น้ใจ
satisfy	v. he:t hay: poh chay: เริดให้น้ใจ
Saturday	n. wa:n sow: อันเสิา
Saturn	n. dow pa: sow: ดาวพะเสิา
saucepan	n. moh mi ga:n sa:m la:p cha:p หม้กๅับสๅ้ญบ้ๆลัป
saucer	(cup) v. chan hohng chohk ga fe จามรองจอกภาเฝ (flying) n. chan bi:n จามบิม
sausage	(big) n. say: ua ไส้อั่ว (small and sweet) v. say: gohk ใส้กอก

savage	adj. bpā̃² teũan² ປ່າເຖື່ອນ
	n. koːn bpā̃² ຄົນປ່າ
save	(life) v. suay² sī³ wiːt² ຊ້ອຍຊີວິດ
	(money) v. tohn⁵ ngerːn³ ທ້ອນເງິນ
savings	n. sīng² tì² tohn⁵ wayː⁵ dayː⁵ ສິ່ງທີ່ທ້ອນໄວ້ໄດ້
savings bank	n. taː¹ nā³ kan¹ ohm³ siːn⁵ ທະນາຄາມອອມສິນ
savor	v.t. poh² chayː² nayː³ loːt² sat² ຜ່ໃຈໄມຣຶດອາດ
saw	n. leuay² ເລື່ອຍ
	v. dtaːt² duay³ leuay² ຕັດດ້ວຍເລື່ອຍ
sawdust	n. kī⁴ leuay² ຂີ້ເລື່ອຍ
sawmill	n. hong⁶ leuay² ໂຮງເລື່ອຍ
saxophone	n. bpi² bpak² ngoh⁶ ປີ່ປາກໂ
say	interj. niː¹..... ນີ້
	v. wowː² ເວົ້າ
scale	(fish) n. geːt³ bpa¹ ເກັດປ່າ
	(balance) n. siːng⁵ ຊິງ
	(size) n. saːt³ suan² ສັດສ່ວມ
	v. bpiːn² ປີມ
scan	v. an² puat⁵ paːt⁵ bpayː⁵ ฯาม ຜອດຜາດໄປ
scandal	n. kow² gan¹ gaː³ taːm¹ piːt² ຂາວກามกะทำຜิด
scant	adj. leːk⁵ leːk⁵ noy⁵ noy⁵ ເລັກໆນ້ອຍໆ
scar	v. heːt² hayː⁶ bpaaw ເຣັດໃຫ້ແປ່ອ
	n. bpaaw⁵ ແປ້ອ
scarce	adj. hā¹ nyak⁴ ຫາຍາກ
scare	v. heːt² hayː⁶ nyan² ເຣັດໃຫ້ງ່າມ
scarf	n. pa² paːn⁵ koh¹ ຜ້າພັນຄ
scatter	v. wan² bpay² ທ່ອາມໄປ
scene	(theater) n. sak⁶ ຊາກ
	(view) n. tiːw² taːt⁵ ທິອທັດ
scenery	n. pap⁵ pu³ mi⁵ bpaː² tet⁵ ຜາບຜູມິປະເທຖ
scenic	adj. pap⁵ ngoːt² ngam³ ຜາບວິດງາມ
scent	v. ta³ naːm⁵ hohm⁴ ທາมกຳທอม
	n. giːn² ກິມ
schedule	n. dta¹ lang³ weː³ la³ ຕາລາງເອລາ
scheme	v. gaː³ paan⁴ gan¹ กะแผมกาม
	n. paan⁴ gan¹ แผมกาม
scholar	n. naːk² bpat² ມັກປຣາດ
school	n. hong³ hian⁵ ໂຮງຮຽມ
	(nursery) n. aː³ nu:² ban¹ ຂະມຸຍາມ
	(elementary) n. saːn⁵ dtoːn⁵ ຂຸມຕມ
	(secondary) n. maːt² ta:³ nyoːm³ seuːk³ sa² ມັທຍມສຶກສາ
	(junior high) n. maːt² ta:² nyoːm³ pak⁵ dtoːn⁵ ມັທຍມຜາກ ຕມ

(high) n. ma:t tä: nyo:m มัทยิม	scorch v. chu:t จูด
(trade) n. pa ni:t ผานิด	score (music) n. no:t peng มิดเผง
(vocational) n. a si wa: seu:k sä อาชีวะสึกสา	(game) n. ka. naan คะแนน
schoolbook n. bpeum hian ปิ้มรฮน	v. he:t ka: naan เรัดคะแนน
schoolboy n. na:k hian say มัก รฮมจาย	scorn v. gan du tuk ภามดูถูก
schoolgirl n. na:k hian nyi:ng มัก รฮมยิง	scorpion n. maang ngow: แมงเงั้ว
schoolhouse n. dteu:k hian ถึกรฮม	scour v. pa:t tü ผัดถู
schoolmate n. mu huam hong hian ผู้รอมโรงรฮน	scourge v. dti duay saa ตีด้วยแส้
	n. may: saa ไม้แส้
schoolroom n. hohng hian ห้องรฮม	scout n. luk seua ลูกเสื้อ
science n. wi:t ta: nya sat อิทยาสาด	v. ohk lat dta: wen ออกลาดตะเว้ม
scientific adj. dtam tang wi:t ta: nya sat ตามทางอิทยาสาด	scowl v. he:t na beu:ng เรัด ผ้าบึ้ง
scientist n. na:k wi:t ta: nya sat มักอิทยาสาด	scramble (egg) v. dti hay: dtaak ตีให้แถก
	(go after) v. nyat ga:n ยาดทัม
scissors n. mit dta:t มิดตัด	scrap n. kohng set leua เอองเสดเทือ
scoff n. hua kuan kwam ki:t ทัอออมคอามคืด	scrape (object) v. kit ຂິດ
scold v. da ด่า	(self) v. gow: เภา
scoop n. chohng จอง	
v. suan ow: ຊ້อมเอา	scream v. hohng siang laam ຮອງສຽງแหม
scope (area) n. lay: nya: guang ໄลยะກວ້າງ	
(gun) n. gohng sohng ກ້อง2อง	screech v. hohng siang laam ຮອງສຽງแหม

screen	(movie screen) n. choh si ne ma จิ่เมา
	(wire) n. luat dta nang ลอดถาฟ้าๆ
screw	n. dta: bpu gow ตะปูกาว
	v. bi:t giew ขิกาว
screwdriver	n. le:k kay: kuang เท็ก ไขคาว
scrip	(money) n. bpi say: taan nger:n ขี่ใจ้แทมเวีม
script	(handwriting) n. lay meu ลายมี่
	(story) n. neua leuang เมื่อเรื่อง
scrub	n. chu:m noy noy kohng... จุมฆอยฆอย229...
	v. hu:k tu ธุกถู
sculpture	n. gan kua:t lay ภามคั้อด ลาย
sculptor	n. pu kua:t lay ผู้คั้อดลาย
sea	adj. kohng ta: le 29ๆทะเล
	n. ta: le ทะเล
seacoast	n. fa:ng ta: le ฝั่ๆทะเล
seagull	n. na:k nang n:an มีภามาๆมอม
seal	(animal) n. maaw na:m เมอมน้ำ
	(stamp) n. ga bpa: ta:p ภาปะทับ
	(envelope) v. dti:t ติด
	(close) v. a:t 9ด

seam	n. duk pa nyi:p ถูกผ้าเขับ
seaplane	n. heua bi:n na:m เรือขินน้ำ
seaport	n. ta heua ta: le ท่าเรือทะเล
search	n. gan sohk ha ภามงอกหา
	(look for) v. ko:n kua คิมคัว
	(for a person) v. ko:n kua คิมตัว
searchlight	n. fay: say nyay: ไฟสายใทย
seashell	n. gap hoy ta:le ภายทอยทะเล
seashore	n. kaam ta: le แคมทะเล
seasick	n. mow: ta: le เม๊าทะเล
season	v. say: keuang hohm ใส่ เคื่อๆทอม
	n. la: du ระถู
seat	v. ha dtang hay: na:ng ทาตั๊ๆใท้มั่ๆ
	(chair) n. bohn na:ng ข่อมมั่ๆ
	(person) n. go:n ภม
seaweed	n. sa lay ta: le สาทายทะเล
second	(2nd) adj. ti sohng ที่สอๆ
	(time) n. wi: na ti อินาทิ
	(agree with) v. sa: na:p sa nun สัมยสมุม

(substitute) n. pu sai̯m loh́ng ຜູ້ສ່ວລອງ

secondhand adj. koh́ng dtoh meu ̄ ຂອງຕົ ນີ້

n. ke:m wi: na̤ ti̥ ເຂັ ມວິ ນາ ທີ

second-rate adj. sa̤i:n ti̥ soh́ng ຊັ ນທີສອງ

secret adj. la:p ລັ ບ

n. kwa̤m la:p ຄວາມລັ ບ

secretarial adj. gia̯w ga:p le̤ ka̤ nu: gan ກ່ຽວກັ ບເລຂານຸກາມ

secretary (official) n. le̤ ka̤ nu: gan ເລຂານຸກາມ

(typist) n. sa̤: mia̤n ສມຽມ

sect n. ni̥: gay sat sa̤: na̤ ນິ ກາຍສາສນາ

section v. baang ohk bpe:n sua̤n ແບ່ງອອກເປັ ນສ່ວມ

n. pa̤: naak ຜແນກ

secure adj. bpoht pay: ປອດໄພ

v. chohng ຈອງ

security (personal) n. kwa̤m ma:n ko̤ing ຄວາມໝັ້ ນຄົ ງ

(military) n. kwa̤m bpoht pay: ຄວາມປອດໄພ

sedan n. lo:t sa̤: ni:t neu:ng ຣົ ດຊນິ ດນຶ່ ງ

see v. he:n ເຫັ ນ

see off adv. bpay: so̤:ng ໄປສົ່ ງ

seed v. wan̄ me:t ຫວ່ານເມັ ດ

n. gaan̄ ແກ່ນ

seedy adj. mi̤ nay̯: lay ມີ ໃນຫຼາຍ

(worn out) adj. go̤w: cho:n kat ເກົ່ າຈົ ນຂາດ

seeing (that) conj. meua he:n wa̤ ເມື່ ອເຫັ ນວ່າ

seek v. sohk ha̤ ຊອກຫາ

seem n. kay kay ga:e wa̤,keu si̤: ຄາຍຄາຍຄ່ວ່າ, ຄື

seep v. seum (na:m, a gat) ຊຶ ມ (ນ້ ຳ, ອາກາດ)

seine n. mohng ມອງ

v. dteu:k mohng ຕຶກມອງ

seize v. cha:p ma:n ຈັ ບໝັ້ ນ

seldom adj. noy teua ti̥ su:t ນ້ອຍເທື່ ອທີ່ ສຸດ

select adj. leuak ເລືອກ

v. leuak dta:ing ເລືອກຕັ້ ງ

selection (of things) n. gan leuak ການເລືອກ

(of people) n. gan leuak dta:ing ການເລືອກຕັ້ ງ

(object) n. kohng ti̥ leuak laaw ຂອງທີ່ ເລືອກແລ້ວ

self n. dto:n eng ຕົ ນເອງ

-self (reflexive and emphatic pronoun) dtua eng ຕົ ວເອງ

selfish adj. he:n gaa dtua ເຫັ ນແກ່ຕົ ວ

sell	v. kǎy ຂາຍ	separate	v. nyaak ohk ແຍກອອກ
seller	n. pu kǎy ຜູ້ຂາຍ		adj. tî nyaak ohk lǎaw
semi-arid	n. kerng haang lǎang		ທີ່ແຍກອອກແລ້ວ
	ເຄິ່ງແຫ້ງແລ້ງ	September	n. deuán gaín nyǎ
semicolon	n. meít chuít ມົດຈຸດ		ເດືອນກັນຍາ
senate	n. sǎ: pá sung ສະພາສູງ	sequence	n. la:m dǎip dtoh neuang
senator	n. sǎ: ma si:k sǎ: pá		ລຳດັບຕໍ່ເນື່ອງ
	sung ສະມາຊິກສະພາສູງ	serene	adj. sǎ: ngo:p, sǎy ສະງົບ, ໃສ
send	v. so:ng ສົ່ງ	serf	n. koy ka ຂ້ອຍຂ້າ
senior	adj. á wu:t so ອາວຸໂສ	serfdom	n. kwam bpe:n koy ka
	n. na:k hian bpi su:t		ຄວາມເປັນຂ້ອຍຂ້າ
	tay ນັກຮຽນປີສຸດທ້າຍ	sergeant	n. nǎy si:p ek ນາຍສິບເອກ
sensation	n. kwam hu seu:k dteun dte:n	series	n. la:m dǎip, su:t ລຳດັບ, ຊຸ
	ຄວາມຮູ້ສຶກຕຶ່ນເຕັ້ນ	serious	(person) adj. ke:ng ka:t
sense	(feeling)n. kwam hu seu:k		ເຄັ່ງຄັດ
	ຄວາມຮູ້ສຶກ		(sickness) n. á gan na:k
	v. hu seu:k ຮູ້ສຶກ		ອາການໜັກ
sensibility	n. kwam hu seu:k gǎy	seriously	(sickness) adv. yang hay
	ຄວາມຮູ້ສຶກງ່າຍ		haang ຢ່າງຮ້າຍແຮງ
sensitive	adj. mi kwam hu seu:k wǎy:		(really) adv. yang chi:ng
	ມີຄວາມຮູ້ສຶກໄວ		chaing ຢ່າງຈິງຈັ່ງ
sentence	v. dta:t si:n ຕັດສິນ	sermon	n. ka:m saing sohn ຄຳສັ່ງ
	n. bpa: nyok ປະໂຍກ		ສອນ
sentiment	n. kwam hu seu:k tang	servant	n. koìn sǎy: ຄົນໃຊ້
	chay: ຄວາມຮູ້ສຶກທາງໃຈ	serve	v. la:p sǎy: ຮັບໃຊ້
sentimental	adj. mi kwam hu seu:k dtoh	service	n.gan la:p sǎy:, ooh li: gan
	kwam na:k ມີຄວາມຮູ້ສຶກຕໍ່ຄວາມ ຮັກ		ການຮັບໃຊ້, ບໍລິການ
sentinel	n. ta: han nyam ທະຫານຍາມ		v. sohm bpaan ສ້ອມແປງ
separable	adj. nyaak ohk chak ga:n	session	(study) n. pak hian
	day: ແຍກອອກຈາກກັນໄດ້		ພາກຮຽນ

	(general) n. dtohn ຕອນ	sex	(physiology) n. pêt ເພດ
set	(group of) n. suːm ຊຸມ		(condition) n. gan maː loːm ການມະຣົມ
	(radio) n. keuang ເຄື່ອງ		
	(clock) v. dtaːng ຕັ້ງ	sexy	adj. yua yuan gam maː loːm ຍົ່ວຍວນກາມມະຣົມ
	(table) v. dtaang ແຕ່ງ		
set free	bpoy hay: bpeːn iːt saː laː: ປ່ອຍໃຫ້ເປັນອິສຣະ	shabby	adj. bpeuay kat ເປື່ອຍຂາດ
set off	(journey) ohk dern tang ອອກເດີນທາງ	shackle	n. huang leːk ຫ່ວງເຫຼັກ v. say: huang leːk ໃສ່ຫ່ວງ ເຫຼັກ
	(ignite) chut hay: laː bert ຈຸດໃຫ້ຣະເບີດ	shade	v. gaːng hoːm ກາງຮົ່ມ n. hoːm ຮົ່ມ
set out	ohk dern tang bpay: ອອກເດີນທາງໄປ	shadow	v. dtiːt dtam yang leːrːk ຕິດຕາມຢ່າງເລັກລັບ n. ngow: ເງົາ
set up	dtaːng keun ຕັ້ງຂຶ້ນ	shaft	n. gan maːy ການໄມ້
settle	(live) v. dtaːng tiːn tan ຕັ້ງຖິ່ນຖານ	shake	(agitate) v. saːn ສັ່ນ (hands) v. chaːp ຈັບ
	(argument) v. heːt hay: dtoːk loːng gaːn day: ເຮັດໃຫ້ຕົກລົງກັນໄດ້	shall	v. chaː ຈະ
		shallow	adj. dteun ຕື້ນ
seventeen	(17) adj. siːp cheːt ສິບເຈັດ	shame	n. kwam laː ay ຄວາມລະອາຍ
seven	(7) adj. cheːt ເຈັດ (ກ)	shampoo	v. saː poːm ສະຜົມ n. naːm ya saː poːm ນ້ຳຢາສະຜົມ
seventy	(70) adj. cheːt siːp ເຈັດສິບ	shape	v. heːt bpeːn hup hang ເຮັດເປັນຮູບຮ່າງ n. hup hang ຮູບຮ່າງ
several	adj. laːy ຫຼາຍ		
severe	adj. kiam kaːn ຂ້ມຂ້ນ	share	v. miː suan ມີສ່ວນ n. huːn suan ຮຸ້ນສ່ວນ
sew	(clothes) v. nyiːp saaw ຫຍິບເສື້ອ		
sewer	n. toh naːm bpeuan ທໍ່ນ້ຳ ເປື້ອນ	shark	n. bpa saː laːm ປາສລາມ

sharp	v. ໐pàt ɓang ɓang, he:t hay: siang sung ບາດບາງໆ, ເຮັດໃຫ້ສຽງສູງ	sheet	n. paan ແຜນ
	(blade) adj. ko:m ຄົມ	shelf	n. sa:n, tan, han, ໍ້ຊໍ, ຖານ, ຮ້ານ
sharpen	(blade) v.t. fo:n hay: ko:m ຝົນໃຫ້ຄົມ	shell	(sea) n. ɓpeuak hoy ເປຶອກຫອຍ
	(razor) fo:n mit taa ຝົນມີດແຖ		(bullet) n. ໐peuak luk ໐peun ເປ້ອກລູກປືນ
	(wit) v. he:t hay: sa: lat ເຮັດໃຫ້ສລາດ		(bomb) v. ti:m luk dtaak ຕິ້ມລູກແຕກ
shatter	n. he:t hay: dtaak ga: chay ເຮັດໃຫ້ແຕກກະຈາຍ		(food) v. ໐pohk ໐peuak ປອກເປຶອກ
shave	n. gan taa ການແຖ	shelter	n. ɓpohn so:n ບ່ອນຊ້ອນ
	v. taa ແຖ		v. ɓpo:k ɓpi:t ປົກປິດ
shaving cream	n. sa: bu taa nuat ສະບູ ແຖໜວດ	shelve	v. ow: say: han ເອົາໃສ່ຮ້ານ
shawl	n. pa ku:m lay: ຜ້າຄຸມ ໄຫຼ່	shepherd	n. ko:n liang gaa: ຄົນລ້ຽງ ແກະ
she	(common) pron. low ລາວ	sheriff	n. pu ɓa:ng ka:p gohng meuang ຜູ້ບັງຄັບກອງເມືອງ
	(by friend) pron. kow: ເຂົ້າ	shield	v. ɓpohng ga:n ປ້ອງກັນ
	(polite) pron. per:n ເພິ່ນ		n. keuang ɓpohng ga:n ເຄື່ອງປ້ອງກັນ
shear	v. dta:t ko:n sa:t ຕັດຂົນ ສັດ	shift	n. gan ໐pian bohn leu we la ການປ່ຽນບ່ອນທີ່ເວລາ
shears	n. mit dta:t nyay: ມີດຕັດ ໃຫຍ່		v. ໐pian bohn leu we la ປ່ຽນບ່ອນທີ່ເວລາ
shed	v. lo:n ລົ້ນ	shin	n. na kaang ໜ້າແຂ້ງ
	n. hong ge:p kohng ໂຮງ ເກັບຂອງ	shine	n. leuam ເຫຼື່ອມ
sheep	n. gaa: ແກະ		(light) v. sohng saang ສ່ອງແສງ
sheer	n. yang sa:n ຍ່າງຊ້ນ		(shoes) v. pa:t ຜັດ
	adj. taa taa ແທ້ໆ		

shingle	v. diːn muːng ດິນມຸງ
ship	n. gaːm bpaːin ກາປິ່ນ
	v. soːng ສົ່ງ
shipwreck	n. heǔa dtaak ເຮືອແຕກ
shirt	n. seǔa ເສື້ອ
shiver	v. saːn now ສັ່ນໜາວ
shock	(electric) n. gaː dtuːk ກະຕຸກ
	(surprise) n. kow dteun dteːn ຂາວດຶ່ນເຕັ້ນ
	(electric) n. gaː dtuːk ກະຕຸກ
	(surprise) v. daːy laːp kow dteun dteːn ໄດ້ຮັບຂາວດຶ່ນເຕັ້ນ
shoe	v. saːy gerp ໃສ່ເກີບ
	n. gerp ເກີບ
shoelaces	n. saːy haːit gerp ສາຍຮັດເກີບ
shoemaker	n. saːng heːt gerp ຈ່າງເຮັດເກີບ
shoot	(gun) v. nyiːng ຍິງ
	(pictures) v. taːy hup ຖ່າຍຮູບ
	n. noh maːy ໜໍ່ໄມ້
shop	n. haːn kaːy kohng ຮ້ານຂາຍຂອງ
	v. tiaw seːu kohng ຫຼົງຊື້ຂອງ
shore	n. kaːm taː leː ແຄມທະເລ
short	(time) adj. boh doːn ບໍດົນ
	(distance) adj. saːin ສັ້ນ
	(height)adj. dtaːm ຕ່ຳ
shortly	adv. doːy nyoh ໂດຍໜ້ອຍ
shortstop	n. naːik giː laː bet saː oohn koːn neuːng ນັກກິລາເບສບອລຄົນໜຶ່ງ
shot	(injection) n. yaː saːk ຢາສັກ
	(liquor) n. low: chiːp ເຫຼົ້າຈິບ
	(gun) n. bat nyiːng teua neuːng ບາດຍິງເທື່ອໜຶ່ງ
should	v. kuan chaː ຄວນ
shoulder	n. baː laːy ບ່າໄລ່
	v. ow: saːy baː ເອົາໃສ່ບ່າ
shout	n. siang hohng daːng ສຽງຮ້ອງດັງ
	v. hohng haːng haːng ຮ້ອງແຮງໆ
shove	n. gan nyu ການຍູ້
	v. suːik nyu bpay: ຊຸກຍູ້ໄປ
shovel	v. suan ຊ້ອນ
	n. suan ຊ້ອນ
show	n. gan saː daang ການສະແດງ
	(explain) v. si chaang ຊີ້ແຈງ

	(view) ow: hay: ber:ng
	เจิาใຫ້เยິ້ว
show off	uat ang ອວດອ້າງ
show up	bpa: go:t dtua ປາກົດຕົວ
showcase	n. dtu sa: daang si:n ka
	ຕູ້ສະແດງສິນຄ້າ
shower	(rain) v. fo:n dto:k ຝົນຕົກ
	(bath) v. ap na:m pu:
	ອາບນ້ຳຟຸ
	(rain) n. ha fo:n ຫ່າຝົນ
	(bath) n. gan ap na:m pu:
	ການອາບນ້ຳຟຸ
shred	n. dtohn set ຕ່ອນເສດ
	v. chik bpe:n dtohn dtohn
	ຊິກເປັນຕ່ອນໆ
shrewd	adj. sa: lat, ki gong
	ສະຫລາດ, ຂີໂກງ
shriek	v. hohng siang laam
	ຮ້ອງສຽງຫລາມ
	n. siang dta:ng chaat
	ສຽງດ້ງແຈດ
shrill	adj. (siang) laam
	(ສຽງ)ຫລາມ
shrimp	(fish) n. gu:ng nohy ກຸ້ງນ້ອຍ
	(person) n. ko:n chaa ຄົນເຈ້
shrink	(material) v. ho:t ຫົດ
	(leave) v. toy ni ຖອຍໜີ
shrine	n. si:m ສິມ
shroud	v. hoh so:p duay pa ຫໍ່ສົບ
	ດ້ວຍຜ້າ

	n. pa hoh so:p ຜ້າຫໍ່ສົບ
shrub	n. fu:m may: ຟຸ່ມໄມ້
shudder	(shake) n. gan sa:n say
	ການສັ່ນສາຍ
	v. ko:n hua lu:k ຂົນຫົວລຸກ
shuffle	(walk) v. nyang teua bpay:
	ຍ່າງເຖື່ອໄປ
	(cards) v. sa:p ສັບ
shun	v. lik ohk chak
	ຫລີກອອກຈາກ
shut	v. a:t ອັດ
shut down	a:t lo:ng ອັດລົງ
shut off	bpi:t lo:ng ປິດລົງ
shut up	sow: bpak ເຊົ້າປາກ
shutter	n. bpohng iam sa:n nohk
	ປ່ອງຢ້ຽມຊັ້ນນອກ
shy	adj. ki ay ຂີອາຍ
	v. wein ohk ເວັ້ນອອກ
Siam	n. bpa: tet tay:, sa: nyam
	ປະເທດໄທ, ສຍາມ
sick	(ill) adj. bpuay ປ່ວຍ
	(dog) v. ga:t ກັດ
	(ugly) adj. so:k ga:
	ປົກ ສົກກະປົກ
sickle	n. giaw nohy ກຽວນ້ອຍ
sickly	adj. ki pa: nyat ຂີພະຍາດ
side	(agree) v. he:n duay, kow:
	kang ເຫັນດ້ວຍ, ເຂົ້າຂ້າງ
	n. kang ຂ້າງ
side with	kow: kang ga:p ເຂົ້າຂ້າງກັບ

sidetrack   v. pā wǒw: nohk leuang ຜາເອົານອກເຣື່ອງ

n. gan pā wǒw: nohk leuang ການຜາເອົານອກເຣື່ອງ

sidewalk   n. tang nyang ທາງຍ່າງ

siege   n. gan ohm lohm ການອ້ອມ ລ້ອມ

sift   v. hohm ຮ່ອນ

sigh   n. gan hain chay: nyay: ການທັນໃຈໃຫຍ່

v. hain chay: nyay: ທັນໃຈໃຫຍ່

sight   (object) n. kohng ti he:n ຂອງທີ່ເຫັນ

(vision) n. say dta ສາຍຕາ

v. naa bpeun ແນບືນ

(gun) n. sun bpeun ສູນປືນ

sightless   (blind) adj. dta boht ຕາ ບອດ

sight seeing   n. tiaw soim sa: tan ti dtang dtang ທ່ຽວຊົມສະຖານ ທີ່ຕາງໆ

adj. naim tiaw ນ່າທ່ຽວ

sign   n. keuang may ເຄື່ອງໝາຍ

v. se:n seu ເຊັນຊື່

signal   v. hay: sa:n nyan ໃຫ້ສັນຍານ

n. sa:n nyan ສັນຍານ

signature   n. lay se:n ລາຍເຊັນ

significant   adj. sa:m ka:n ສຳຄັນ

signify   v. mi kwam may ມີຄວາມ ໝາຍ

signpost   n. bpay keuang may ປ້າຍ ເຄື່ອງໝາຍ

silence   (make quiet) v. hay bpi:t opak ໃຫ້ປິດປາກ

(command) v. mi:t mit ມິດ

n. kwam mi:t nglap ຄວາມ ມິດງຽບ

silent   adj. mi:t mi ມິດມີ

silk   n. may: ໄໝ

silkworm   n. dtua mohn ຕົວໝ່ອນ

silly   n. ngo ໂງ່

silo   n. low: (kow:) ເລົ້າ (ເເຂົ້າ)

silver   n. si nger:n ສີເງິນ

adj. nyohm si nger:n ຍ້ອມສີເງິນ

v. nger:n ເງິນ

silversmith   n. sang nger:n ຊ່າງເງິນ

silverware   n. keuang meu nger:n ເຄື່ອງມືເງິນ

similar   n. kay keu ga:n ຄ້າຍຄືກັນ

similarity   n. kwam keu ga:n ຄວາມຄື ກັນ

simple   (work) adj. ngay ງ່າຍ

(person and thing) adj. ta:m ma: da ທັມມະດາ

simplicity   n. kwam boh nyu:ng ຄວາມ ບໍ່ຍຸ່ງ

simply	(easily) adj. yang ngaay ngaay ย่างง่ายๆ
	(just) adv. piang dtaa พ่ยงแต่
sin	n. bap บาป
	v. he:t bap เร็ดบาป
since	(time) adv. dtang dtaa ตั้งแต่
	(because) adv. meua เมื่อ
sincere	(intimate) adj. sa: ni:t sa: no:m สนิดสนม
	(true) adv. taa chi:ng แท้จริง
sincerely	adv. duay kwam chi:ng chay: โดยความจริงใจ
sincerely yours	(ending of a letter) duay na:m say: chay: chi:ng ด้วยน้ำใสใจจริง
sincerity	n. kwam chi:ng chay: ความจริงใจ
sinew	n. se:n e:n เส้นเอ็น
sing	v. hohng peng ร้องเพ็ง
singe	v. lo:n ลิม
singer	(modern) n. na:k hohng นักร้อง
	(traditional) n. moh la:m พ่ลำ
single	(unmarried) adj. sot โสด
	(one) adj. diaw ถ่วง
singular	adj. ek ga: po:t, ek ga: te เอกะพ็ด, เอกะเทด
sink	n. ang na:m อ่างน้ำ
	v. cho:m จิม
sip	v. si:m (na:m) จิ้ม(น้ำ)
	n. si:m bat neu:ng จิ้มบาทนึ่ง
sir	n. tan ท่าม
siren	(noise) n. siang sa:n nyan สง่วสัมยาม
	(girl) n. pu nyi:ng ti nyua: chay: ผู้ยุ่งที่ย่วใจ
sirup	n. na:m si: lo น้ำซี้โร
sister	(elder sister) n. euay เอ้อย
	(younger sister) n. nohng sow น่องสาว
sit	v. na:ng นั่ง
	(sit down) v. na:ng lo:ng นั่งลง
sit in on	kow: huam เข้าร่วม
sit out	boh kow: huam บ่เข้าร่วม
sit up	(sitting position) lu:k keun na:ng ลุกขึ้นนั่ง
	(remain awake) yu der:k ยู่เดิก
site	n. ti da:ng ที่ตัง
situation	n. sa ta na: gan สะถามะกาม
six	(6) adj. ho:k ฟ็ก (ฝ)

sixteen	(16) adj. si:p ho:k
	ສິບຫົກ
sixth	(6th) adj. ti ho:k ທີ່ຫົກ
sixty	(60) adj. ho:k si:p ຫົກສິບ
size	(size up) v. bpa: man say:
	ປະມານໃສ່
	n. ka nat ຂນາດ
skate	(shoe) n. gerp li:n na:m
	gohn ເກີບຫຼິ້ນນ້ຳກ້ອນ
	v. li:n na:m gohn
	ຫຼິ້ນນ້ຳກ້ອນ
skeleton	n. hang ga: duk ຮ່າງກະດູກ
sketch	n. hup dtaam bpe:n hang
	ຮູບແຕ້ມເປັນຮ່າງ
	v. dtaam bpe:n hang
	ແຕ້ມເປັນຮ່າງ
ski	v. laan sa: gi ແລ່ນສະກີ
	n. gan li:n sa: gi
	ການຫຼິ້ນສະກີ
skill	n. kwam sa:m han ຄວາມ
	ຊຳນານ
skin	(animals) n. na:ng ໜັງ
	(plants) n. bpeuak ເປືອກ
	(animals) v. lohk na:ng
	ລອກໜັງ
	(plants) bpohk bpeuak
	ປອກເປືອກ
skip	n. gan dte:n ການເຕັ້ນ
	(jump) v. dte:n kam ເຕັ້ນ
	ຂ້າມ

	(omit) v. kam ຂ້າມ
skirt	v. loh: dtam kaam ເລາະ
	ຕາມແຄມ
	(Lao) n. si:n ສິ້ນ
	(Western) n. ga: bpong
	ກະໂປ່ງ
skull	n. ga: lok hua ກະໂລກຫົວ
sky	n. fa ຟ້າ
skyline	n. kohp fa ຂອບຟ້າ
skyscraper	n. heuan sung tiam fa
	ເຮືອນສູງທຽມຟ້າ
slam	(close) v. ait kow: haang
	ອັດເຂົາແຮງ
	(ridicule) hua yoh: yery
	ຫົວເຍາະເຍີ້ຍ
	n. siang ait da:ng bpa:ng
	ສຽງອັດດັງປັ້ງ
slang	n. pa sa dta: lat ພາສາ
	ຕລາດ
slant	(diagonal) n. gan ngiang
	ການງ່ຽງ
	(bias) n. gan he:t hay:
	en iang ການເຮັດໃຫ້ເອນອຽງ
slap	n. gan dto:p na ການຕົບໜ້າ
	v. dto:p na
	ຕົບໜ້າ
slash	n. hoy fai:n ຮອຍຟັນ
	v. fai:n ຟັນ

slate	(stone) n. hǐːn gàː dàn ทิมกะถาม
	(board) n. gàː dàn hǐːn กะถามทิม
slaughter	v. kȁ doy boh mī gan dtoh sū ฆ่าโดยบมิการต่สู้
	n. gan kȁ doy boh mī gan dtoh sū ການฆ่าโดยบมิการต่สู้
slaughter house	n. hong kȁ sȁːt โรงฆ่า สัถ
slave	v. hèːt wiak lǎy เรัดวຽกหนฑาย
	n. kȁ tȁt ຂ້າທາດ
slay	v. kȁ ฆ່າ
sled	v. laan lȍːt teːːng hǐː maː แล่นรัถเທิງທິມะ
	n. lȍːt tī sày laan teːːng hǐː maː ຣົຖທໃຊ້ແລ່ນເທິງທີມະ
sleep	v. nohn ນອນ
	n. gan nohn ການນອນ
sleeping bags	v. toːng nohn ถุງນອນ
sleepy	(very) adj. ngȍw nohn เຫງຶານອນ
	(a little) adj. yak nohn ຢາກນອນ
sleeve	n. kaan seua แຂນເສື້ອ
sleigh	(horse) v. deːːn tàng bpay dtaam hǐː maː เถิมทาງໄປຕາມທິມะ
	n. lȍːt maː tī sày laan teːːng hǐː maː ຣົຖມ້າທໃຊ້ແລ່ນເທິງທິມะ

slender	adj. aaw bang hang nǒy แอว ບາງຮ່າງນ້ອຍ
slice	n. paan bang bang แผ່ນบาງๆ
	v. dtȁt bpeːn paan ຕັດເປັນ แผ่น
slick	adj. meun lay มื่นหฑาย
slide	v. leuan bpay เลื่อนໄป
	(action) n. gan meun ການ ມື່ນ
	(playground) n. mak dtaː lat ພากตะลาถ
slight	n. gan du tuk ການดูฑูก
	adj. bòw bang เບົ້ายาๆ
slim	adj. bang ยาๆ
sling	(throw) v. gwaang แฑว່ງ
	(tell) v. bpaːn leuang keun เປັນເรื່อງຂຶ້ນ
	n. nǎ nohng ฑมາนอງ
slip	v. meun มื่ม
	(dress) n. sȁː lǐːp pu ຊ້າ lǐːp pu nyiːng ສລับผຍอງ
	(mistake) n. gan loːng bpert kwam laːp ການລົງ ເปิถความลับ
slipper	n. gerp dtaːa ເກີບแตะ
slippery	adj. meun มื่ม
slit	n. hoy dtaak รอยแถก
	v. bpat bpeːn seːn ปาถ เປັนເສັ້ນ

slogan	n. kwam kuan คำขวัญ	small	adj. nŏy ນ້ອຍ
slope	(hill) n. kŏy ຄອຍ	smart	(intelligent) v. sa: lat
	(triangle) n. se:n nerng		สลาด
	เส้นเນิ้ງ		v. che:p ເຈັບ
	v. kong ໂຄ້ງ		(with clothes) adj. go
slot	n. bpohng nŏy nŏy ປ່ອງນ້ອຍໆ		ໂກ້
slow	v. he:t hay: sa lo:ng		(handsome) adj. chow:
	เຮັດໃຫ້ຊ້າລົງ		su ເຈ້າຊູ້
	(motion) adj. sa ຊ້າ	smash	v. ta:p hay: dtaak
	(stupid) adj. ngo ໂງ່		ທັບໃຫ້ແຕກ
slowly	adv. yang sa sa ຢ່າງຊ້າໆ	smear	n. gan bpaat bpeuan
sludge	n. hi: ma: bpo:n na:m, dto:m		ການແປດເປື້ອນ
	ຕົມມະປົນນ້ຳ, ຕົມ		(spread) v. ta hay: bpeuan
slum	v. yiam yam bân dtup ko:n		bper: ทาใຫ້ເປື້ອນເປີ
	nyak cho:n		(ruin) n. gan ta:m lay
	ย้ามยามบ้านตุปคົມยากจົม		seu siang ການທຳລາຍຊື່
	n. bân dtup ko:n nyak cho:n		ສຽງ
	ຍ້ານຕຸບຄົນยากจิม	smell	n. gi:n ກິ່ນ
sluice	(channel) n. ga: saa na:m		(neutral) v. do:m gi:n
	chak keuan		ดิมกิ่น
	ກະແສນ້ຳจากเຊື່ອນ		(bad) v. me:n ເໝັນ
slumber	n. gan nŏhn chaap	smile	n. kwam nyi:m nyam
	ການນອນແຈບ		ความยิ้มแยม
	v. nŏhn chaapນອນແຈບ		v. nyi:m ยิ้ม
slump	(price) v. la ka dto:k	smoke	v. sup ya สูบยา
	ຣາຄາຕົກ		n. kwan fay: ຄວັນໄຟ
	(posture) v. na:ng go:m	smoker	(person) n. ko:n dud ya
	dto so ນັ່ງກົ້ມໂຕໂຊ່		ຄົນถูกยา
sly	adj. ki go:ng ຂີ້ໂກງ		(room) n. hohng ti sup
			ya day: ຫ້ອງທີ່ສูบยาໄດ້

smooth	v. he:t hay: giang ເຮັດໃຫ້ກ້ຽງ adj. giang ກ້ຽງ
smother	v. he:t hay: ha:n chay: boh day: ເຮັດໃຫ້ຫັນໃຈບໍ່ໄດ້
smuggle	v. la:k lohp pa si: ລັກລອບ ພາສີ
snack	n. a han bow: ອາຫານເບົາ v. gi:n a han hohng ກິນອາ tohng ຫານຫວ່າງທ້ອງ
snail	n. hoy leuav ຫອຍເຫຼືອວ
snake	n. ngu ງູ
snap	(break) v. ha:k ohk ຫັກ ອອກ (fingers) v. did niw ດີດນິ້ວ n. ga: du:m dtaa:p ກະດຸມແຕບ
snare	v. nyak ouang ຍັກບວງ n. buang ບວງ
snarl	v. ku ka:m lam ຂູ່ຄຳ່ຮາມ n. gan pa:n ga:n kow: ການພັນກັນເຂົາ
snatch	n. nyat ow: way: way: ຍາດເອົາໄວໆ
sneak	v. yohng ni ຍ່ອງໜີ n. pu yohng bpay: ຜູ້ຍ່ອງໄປ
sneer	n. gan hua kua:n ການຫົວຂ້ວນ

	v. hua kua:n, wow: say: ຫົວຂ້ວນເອົາໃສ່
sneeze	n. gan cham ການຈາມ v. cham ຈາມ
sniff	n. gan seup ow: gi:n ການສືບເອົາກິ່ມ v. seup gi:n ສືບກິ່ມ
snivel	v. se:t ki muk ເຊັດຂີ້ມູກ
snore	v. nohn gon ນອນໂກມ n. gan nohn gon ການນອນໂກມ
snort	n. siang da:ng gok gok ສຽງວັດ se:n mu ໂກກາດເຈັ້ນມູ v. he:t siang da:ng se:n mu ເຮັດສຽງວັດເຈັ້ນມູ
snow	v. hi: ma: dto:k ຫິມະຕົກ n. hi: ma: ຫິມະ
snowfall	n. cha:m nuan hi: ma: dto:k ຈຳນວນຫິມະຕົກ
snowflake	n. me:t hi: ma: ເມັດຫິມະ
snow shoe	n. gerp bpohng ra:n hi: ma: ເກີບປ່ອງຣ້ານຫິມມະ
snowsuit	n. keuang bpohng ga:n hi: ma: ເຄື່ອງປ່ອງກັນຫິມມະ
snug	adj. chaap di ແຈບດີ
so	(therefore) adv. da:ng na:n ດັ່ງນັ້ນ (because) adv. poh: ເພາະ
so far	adv. tering diaw ni ເຖິງກຽ ນີ້

so long	interj. bpay: gohn	sock	n. to:ng tow: sa:n
	ໄປກ່ອນ		ຖົງເທົ້າສັ້ນ
so what!	id. leåw si mi nya:ng		v. so:k ຊົກ
	gert keun ແລ້ວມິຫຍັງເກີດຂຶ້ນ	sod	n. chu:m nya ຈຸ້ມຫຍ້າ
soak	v. saa na:m ແຊ່ນ້ຳ	soda	n. na:m so da ນ້ຳໂຊດາ
soap	n. sa: bu ສະບູ	sofa	n. dta:ng i nyow ຕັ່ງອີ່ຢາວ
	v. say: sa: bu ໃສ່ສະບູ	soft	adj. ohn ອ່ອນ
soar	v. bi:n chert keun ບິນ	soften	v.i. he:t hay: ohn
	ເຈີດຂຶ້ນ		ເຮັດໃຫ້ອ່ອນ
sob	v. hohng ha: sa: eu:k	softly	adv. yang ohn ohn ຢ່າງອ່ອນໆ
	sa: eu:n ຮ້ອງໃຫ້ສະອຶກສະອຶນ	soil	v. he:t hay: bpeuan
sober	v. he:t hay: sow: mow:		ເຮັດໃຫ້ເປື້ອນ
	ເຮັດໃຫ້ເຈົ້າເມົາ		n. di:n ດິນ
	(average) adj. poh bpa:	solar	adj. giaw ga:p duang
	man ພໍປະມານ		a' ti:t ກ່ຽວກັບດວງອາທິດ
	(not drunk) adj. boh mow:	soldier	n. ta: han ທະຫານ
	ບໍ່ເມົາ	sole	v. say: peun gerp
soccer	n. gi: la dte: ban		ໃສ່ພື້ນເກີບ
	ກິລາເຕະບານ		adj. a:n diow ອັນດຽວ
social	n. gan gi:n liang		n. so:n nohng gerp
	ການກິນລ້ຽງ		ສົ້ນແຮງເກີບ
	adj. haang sa:ng ko:m	solemn	adj. yang nohp nohm
	ແຫ່ງສັງຄົມ		ຢ່າງນອບນ້ອມ
society	(status) n. sa:ng ko:m	solicit	v. koh hohng ຂໍຮ້ອງ
	ສັງຄົມ	solid	(firm) adj. kaang ແຂງ
	(group) n. su:m nu:m		(hard) adj. gaan ແກ່ນ
	ສົ້ນ ຊຸມນຸມ	solution	(answer) n. koh gaa kay:
	(organization) n. sa: ma		ຂໍແກ້ໄຂ
	ko:m ສມາຄົມ		(mixture) n. gan pa: so:m na:m,
			na:m ya ການຜະສົມນ້ຳ, ນ້ຳຢາ

solve	v. gǎa bpàːn haँ แก้ปั๋มหา	soon	adv. nayː bòh saँ niँ
somber	(color) adj. mèut มิด		ไมย่จ่านี้
	(person) adj. mìːt มิด	sooner or later wayː leu saँ ไอหลั้จ๋า
some	(mass noun) adj. chàːk	soothe	v. heːt hayː saːं bay chayː
	noy६ จักหหอย		เธัดใย้สะบายใจ
	(count noun) adj. bang,	sophomore	n. naːk hian bpi ti sohng
	langँ บา), ลา)		มักธ)มย์ปีเผิเอ)
somebody	(one person) n. koːn dayː	sordid	adj. naँ pang nayँ พ๋าผา))
	koːn neuːng คิมใดคิมมิ้)		ทาย
	(important person) n.	sore	n. bàt บาด
	koːn saːm kaːn คิมสา่คัม		adj. che̖ːp เจ็บ
someday	adv. meuँ dayँ meuँ neuँng	sorrow	n. kँam sowं sòk คอาม
	บ่ำใดมิ้)		เสก่าโสก
somehow	adv. doy wiँ ti dayँ wiँ	sorry	adj. sia chayः เสั)ใจ
	ti neuँng โดยอิทิ๋ลอิทิ๋มิ้)	sort	n. saँ niःt ว้มิด
someone	(important person) n. koːn		v. chaːm naँak ohk จ๋าแบท
	saːm kaːn คิมสา่คัม		99ก
	(one person) n. puँ dayः	soul	n. wiँn nyaँn อิมยาม
	puँ neuːng ผู้ใดผู้มิ้)	sound	v. soःng siang ผิ)ส่))
something	n. aःn dayः aःn neuःng		n. siang ส่))
	อ้มใดอ้มมิ้)	soundly	(hit) adv. yangँ naःk
sometimes	adj. bang teua บา)เทึอ		ย่า)หึก
somewhat	adj. chaँng dayः chaँng		(sleep) adv. nohn chaap
	neuːng จ๋า)ใดจ๋า)มิ้)		บอมแจบ
somewhere	adj. bohn dayः bohn neuːng		(that sounds great!) intrj
	ย่อมใดอ่อมมิ้)		er keu siː di เอ์คือ์ถ๋ถ
son	n. luk sayं ลูกฑาย	soup	n. gaang แทๆ
song	n. peng เผ)	sour	v. heːt hayː soːm เธัดใย้
son-in-law	n. luk ke̖yं ลูกเฮีย		ก้ ส่บ
			adj. soःm ก้ส่บ

source	(river) n. bòh ບໍ່	span	v. gay kŭa ກ່າຍຂົວ
	(derivation) n. tì mā ທີ່ມາ	Spanish	n. kòn sà: bpen ຄົນສະເປນ
	(origin) n. ga:m nèrt ກຳເນີດ	spank	v. dti kòn ຕີກົ້ນ
		spar	v. sohm muay ຊ້ອມມວຍ
south	(region) n. pàk dtay: ພາກໃຕ້		n. sow: ga dong hěua ເສົາກະໂດງເຮືອ
	(direction) n. tì:t dtay: ທິດໃຕ້	spare	adj. sà:m lohng ສຳລອງ
South America p.n. aï me li: ga dtay: ອະເມຣິກາໃຕ້		n. gàn sà:m lohng ການສຳລອງ
Southeast Asia p.n. a sĭ a ka: ne ອາຊີອາຄະເນ	spark	n. mà:t fay: ຜັດໄຟ
southern	adj. tang dtay: ທາງໃຕ້	sparkle	v. bpe:n saang waew wow ເປັນແສງແອວອາວ
southward	adv. dtam tang tì:t dtay: ຕາມທາງທິດໃຕ້	sparrow	n. no:k chohk ນົກຈອກ
souvenir	n. kohng tì la: leu:k ຂອງທີ່ລະລຶກ	speak	v. wow:, pàak ເວົ້າ, ປາກ
sovereign	adj. a: ti bpa: dtay: ອະທິປະໄຕ	speak up	wow: dang dang ເວົ້າດັງໆ
sow	v. wàn me:t ຫວ່ານເມັດ	speak up for	tiang suay ຖຽງຊ່ວຍ
	n. mà měa ໝູແມ່	speaker	(person) n. pû wow: ຜູ້ເວົ້າ
space	(sky) n. a wa: gàt ອາວະກາດ		(radio) n. kó sò:k ໂຄສົກ
	(vacancy) n. sohng wàng ຊ່ອງວ່າງ	spear	v. taang duay hohk ແທງດ້ວຍຫອກ
spade	(shovel) n. suan ຊ້ວນ		n. hohk ຫອກ
	v. dtohn (bpa wàn) ຕອນ(ປາວານ)	special	adj. pi: set ພິເສດ
	(cards) n. dtáam bi:t ແຕ້ມບິດ	special delivery n. gàn sòng cro:t may pi: set ການສົ່ງຈົດໝາຍພິເສດ
		specialist	n. pû siaw san ຜູ້ຊ່ຽວຊານ
		species	n. cha:m puak nyoy ຈຳພວກຍ່ອຍ
		specific	adj. choh: cho:ng ເຈາະຈົງ

specify	v. he:t hay: chŏh: cho:ng lo:ng bpay: เธ็ดให้เจาะจิๆลิๆ ไป		(time) v. săy: ใส่
specimen	n. kohng tua yang 29๋ตัๆ อ่าๆ	sphere	n. hŭp mŏ:n ธูบมน
speck	n. chu:t noy noy จุดน๋อยๆ	spice	n. keuang tĕt เคื่อๆเทด
spectacular	adj. bpe:n dta be:ring เป็นตาเบิ่ๆ		v. bpu:ng lo:t sat ปูๆธิดๆาด
spectator	n. pŭ be:ring ผู้เบิ่ๆ	spider	n. mæng mŭm แมๆมุม
speculate	(guess) v. dtuang ตๆๆ	spill	v. chŏn bpay: จ่ามไป
	(gamble) adv. siang duay kwam wa:ng สๆๆด้วย ความหๆๆ	spin	(thread) v. ke:n fay เข้มผ้าย
speech	(lecture) n. ka:m pa say: ค๋ำปาใส		(around) v. bpi:n ปิ่ม
	(accent) n. ka:m wŏw: ค๋ำเว้า	spinach	n. pa:k sa: ni:t neu:ng ผักๆะมิดมึๆ
speed	v. bpay: way:ไปไว	spine	n. ga: duk sa:n lang ๆะๆูกสัมหๆๆ
	n. kwăm way: ความไว	spirit	(energy) n. na:m chay: ม๋ำใจ
speed boat	n. hĕua way: เธือไว		(soul) n. wi:n nyan ๅิมๅาม
speedometer	n. keuang bohk kwam way: เคื่อๆบอกความไว		(ghost) n. pi ผี
spell	n. wĕt mŏ:n เวถมิม	spirits	(liquor) n. lŏw: เหๆ๋ำ
	(magic) v. sĕk mŏ:n say: เสกมิมใส่		(ghosts) n. pi lay dto ผิๆๆๆโต
	(letter) v. sa: go:t tua สะๆิดติๆ	spit	n. na:m lay ม๋ำลๆย
spelling	n. gan sa: go:t ka:m ๆามสะๆิดค๋ำ		v. to:m na:m lay ถ่มม๋ำลๆย
spend	(money) v. chay จ่าย	spite	n. kwam kaan chay: ความแค้มใจ
			v. kiat kaan, chet dta: na hay kwun kaan, เจถมาธ้าย
		(in spite of) id. te:ring ma: wa เถิๆแม่ม่ว่า

splash	n. naːm sat ນ້ຳສາດ v. owː naːm sat ເອົາ ນ້ຳສາດ
splendid	adj. saː nga ngam ສ່າງງາມ
splinter	n. sian ສ້ຽນ v. heːt hayː dtaak bpeːn bpiang ເຮັດໃຫ້ແຕກເປັນບ່ຽງ
split	v. pæ ຜ່າ n. kwam dtaak nyaak ຄວາມແຕກແຍກ
split-level house	n. heuan ti bpuːk yu neːn ເຮືອນທີ່ບຸກຢູ່ເນີນ
spoil	(person) v. dtam chayː poːt ຕາມໃຈໂພດ (good) v. heːt hayː but ເຮັດໃຫ້ບຸດ n. kohng ti dayː chek gan bpun ຂອງທີ່ໄດ້ຈາກການປຸ້ນ
spoiled	(smell) adj. but ບຸດ (rotten) adj. nowː ເນົ່າ (ruin) adj. sia ເສຍ (selfish) adj. heːn gaa dtua ເຫັນແກ່ຕົວ
spoke	n. diw loːt ຕີ້ວຣົດ pp. dayː wowː ໄດ້ເວົ້າ
sponge	v. tu duay fohng naːm ຖູດ້ວຍຟອງນ້ຳ n. fohng naːm ຟອງນ້ຳ
sponsor	v. uːm su ຊຸນຊູ
	n. puːm su ຜູ້ຊຸນຊູ
spontaneous	adj. doy taːm maː sat ໂດຍທັມມະຊາດ
spoon	n. buang ບ່ວງ v. loːm sow ລິມສາວ
spoonful	n. dteːm buang ເຕັມບ່ວງ
sport	v. teu dtiːt dtua bpayː naːm ຖືຕິດຕົວໄປນ້ຳ (game) n. giː la ກິລາ (person) n. naːk giː la ນັກກິລາ
sports car	n. loːt nyoːk noy ຣົຖຍົກນ້ອຍ
sportsman	(game) n. naːk giː la ນັກກິລາ (hunt) n. naːk la saːt ນັກລ່າສັດ
spot	(stain) v. heːt bpeːn chuːt ເຮັດເປັນຈຸດ (locate) v. heːn naa saːt ເຫັນແນ່ຊັດ (stain) n. chuːt dang ຈຸດຕ່າງໆ (place) n. bohn ບ່ອນ
spout	n. gohːk naːm ກ໋ອກນ້ຳ (water) v. pung ohk ພຸ່ງອອກ (wisdom) v. pung paa ພຸ່ງ kwam saː lat ຄວາມສະຫຼາດ ສລາດ

sprain	n. bpuat ka:t ປວດຄັດ	spy	n. na:k seup ນັກສືບ
spray	n. la: ohng na:m ละ99ງນ້ຳ		v. seup leuang la:p
	v. sit ສິດ		ສືບເຣື່ອງລັບ
sprayer	n. ba:ng sit ບັ້ງສິດ	squad	n. ta: han gohng neu:ng
spread	v. ka: ngay ohk ຂຍາຍ99ກ		ทะทามทอງໜື່ງ
	(bed) n. pa bpo:k dtiang	squadron	n. gohng po:n heua bi:n
	ຜ້າປິກຕງ		ກອງພົນເຣືອບິນ
	(cattle) n. ngua kway	square	v. nyo:k ga:m laing sohng
	ວົວຄວາຍ		ຍົກກ້ລັ້ສອງ
spring	(season) n. la: du bay:		n. hup mo:n to:n
	may: bpo:ng ຣະດູໃບໄມ້ປົ່ງ		ຮູບມົນທົມ
	(metal) n. sa: bpi:ng		adj. mo:n to:n
	ສະປິງ		ມົນທົມ
	v. dte:n keun dte:n lo:ng	square meter	n. maa:t mo:n to:n
	ເຕັ້ນຂຶ້ນເຕັ້ນລົງ		ແມັດມົນທົມ
sprout	n. noh ໜໍ	squeak	n. siang da:ng yang mu
	v. ngohk ງອກ		hohng ສງງດັງຢ່າງໝູຮ້ອງ
sprinkle	(rain) v. fo:n li:n me:t		v. he:t siang yang mu
	noy noy ຝົນລິນເມັດໜອຍໆ		ເຮັດສງຢ່າງໝູ
	(hose) v. po:m duay na:m	squeeze	n. gan bip ba:ng ka:p
	ພົມດ້ວຍນ້ຳ		ການບີບບັ້ງຄັບ
	n. fo:n me:t noy noy		v. bip ບີບ
	ຝົນເມັດໜອຍໆ	squid	n. bpa i heu ປາອື່
spur	(rooster) n. geua gay: ເກືອໄກ່	squirrel	n. ga: hohk ກະຮອກ
	(cowboy) n. le:k say:	St.	(saint) abbrv. na:k
	dtin peua taang hay: ma		bun ນັກບຸນ
	bpay: way: ເຫຼັກໃສ່ຕີນເພື່ອແທງ		(street) abbrv. ta: no:n
	ໃຫມ້າໄປໄວ		ຖນົມ
	v. cha:t hay: bpay: way:	stab	(attempt) n. kwam pa: nya
	ຈັດໃຫ້ໄປໄວ		nyam ຄວາມພະຍາຍາມ

	(action) n. ta tang tǎang ທ່າທາງແທງ	stairway	n. tang kaìn dǎy: ຫາງຂັ້ນໄດ
	v. taang dúay kohng lǎam ແທງດ້ວຍຂອງແຫຼມ	stake	(post) n. laìk hǔa ຫຼັກຮົວ
stability	n. kwam tuːn tiang, kwam maìn koːng ຄວາມໝັ້ນທ່ຽງ, ຄວາມໝັ້ນຄົງ		(gamble) n. kohng derm paìn ຂອງເດີມພັນ
stable	n. kohk ma ຄອກມ້າ		(gamble) v. wǎng derm paìn ວາງເດີມພັນ
	adj. tuːn tiang ໝັ້ນທ່ຽງ		(a claim) v. wǎng kohp ket ວາງຂອບເຂດ
stack	n. gohng ກອງ	stalk	n. goːn ກ້ນ
	v. gohng gaìn keun ກອງກັນຂຶ້ນ		v. chohp kuːp ຈອບຄຸບ
stadium	n. sa nǎm giːla ສະໜາມກິລາ	stale	adj. siːa ເສັຍ
staff	(people) n. ka: na: pu heːt wiak huam gaìn ຄະນະຜູ້ເຣັດວຽກຮ່ວມກັນ	stall	v. siːa we la dúay gan heːt aìn eun ເສັຍເວລາໂດຍ ການເຣັດອັນອື່ນ
	(stick) n. ka gang ke ຂາກາງເຂ		n. hohng nǎy: kohk saːt ຫ້ອງໃນຄອກສັດ
	v. baìn chuː koːn kow: gan ບັນຈຸຄົນເຂົ້າການ	stammer	v. bpak paːm ປາກພ້ຳ
stag	(deer) n. guang pu ກວາງຜູ້		n. gan bpak paːm ການປາກ ພ້ຳ
	(bachelor) n. sǎy sot ຈາຍໂສດ	stamp	(stamp duty) n. sa: dtaam ສະແຕມ
stage	n. we tiː ເວທີ		(feet) v. teup dtin ທຶບຕີນ
	v. sa: daang ສະແດງ		(to seal) v. bpa: ta:p dtla ປະທັບຕາ
stagger	v. se ເຊ		(seal) n. dta bpa: ta:p ຕາປະທັບ
stain	v. bpeuan ເປື້ອນ	stand	v. yeun ຢືນ
	n. hoy bpeuan ຮອຍເປື້ອນ		n. bohn wǎng ບ່ອນວາງ
stair	n. kaìn dǎy: ຂັ້ນໄດ		
staircase	n. maa kaìn dǎy: ແມ່ຂັ້ນໄດ		

stand a chance	mi tui:k a gat มีทูໂອກາດ
stand aside	yeun hang hang tang ยืนຫ่าງໆທາງๆ
stand back	toy bpay: ຖອຍไป
stand by	(help) suay leua ຊ່ວຍເຫຼືອ
	(wait) v. koy ta ຄอຍຖ้າ
stand for	(tolerate) nyohm o:t to:n ຍอມອົດໂຕນ
	(signify) may tering ໝາຍເຖິງ
stand out	bpe:n chu:t den ເປັນຈຸດເດ່ນ
stand up	v. yeun keun ຍืนຂึ້ນ
stand up for	dtoh su suay ຕໍ່ສู້ຊ่ວຍ
standard	n. mat dta tan ມາຕຕະຖານ
stanza	n. wai:k neu:ng kohng gohn leu do:n dti ອັກນ້ວຍຂອງກອນມຫຼືດົນຕรี
staple	(metal) n. le:k nyi:p chia ເຫຼັກຫຍีบເຈ້
	(food) n. kohng boh li: pô:t sai:m kai:n ຂອງບริໂພຄສำຄັນ v. nyi:p chia ຫຍิบເຈ້
star	v. sai: daang bpe:n dtua ek ສະແດງເປັນຕົວເອກ
	(movie) n. da la si ne ດາຣາຊีເນ
	(sky) n. dow ດາວ
starch	n. bpaang sai:m la:p keuang nu:ng, bpaang mai:n ແປ້ງສำຫຼັບເຄื່ອງນຸ່ງ, ແປ້ງມັນ
	v. lo:ng bpaang ລົງແປ້ງ
stare	v. geung dta bering ກຶ່ງຕາເບີ່ງ
starfish	n. bpa dow ປາດາວ
stark	adj. kaang ແຂງ
start	v. dtai:ng dto:n ຕັ້ງຕົ້ນ
startle	v. heit hay: dteun ເຮັດໃຫ້ຕื່ນ
starve	v. o:t yak a han ອົດຢາກອາຫານ
state	(nation) n. lai:t ຣັດ
	(condition) n. sa: pap ສະພາບ v. chaang hay: hu ແຈງໃຫ้ຮู້
statesman	n. lai:t ta: bu ru:t ຣັດຖະບຸຣຸດ
static	adj. sa: ti yu ສະຖີຢู่
station	n. sa: ta ni ສະຖານີ v. kow: dtai:ng way: ເຂາຕั້ງไວ້
station wagon	n. lo:t nai:ng baap go:n dtai: ຣົດນั่ງແບບກ້ນຕັດ
statistics	n. sa: ti: dti: ສະຖิຕิ
statue	(clay) n. hup bpai:n ຮูບປັ້ນ
	(brass) n. hup loh ຮູບຫຼໍ່
	(stone) n. hup sian ຮูບສ້ຽນ
stature	(height) n. luang sung ລວງສูງ

	(reputation) n. sěu siang ຊື່ສຽງ
status	n. dtaːm naang ຕ່ຳແໜງ
statute	n. goːt koh baːng kaːp ກົດຂໍ້ບັງຄັບ
stay	v. yu ຢູ່
stay in	yu heuan ຢູ່ເຮືອນ
stay out	ohk bpayː liːn ອອກໄປຫຼິ້ນ
stead	n. bohn ບ່ອນ
steady	adj. naan niow ໝັ້ນໜຽວ v. heːt hayː naan niow ເຮັດໃຫ້ໝັ້ນໜຽວ
steal	v. laːk ລັກ
steam	(cook) v. neuːng ໜື້ງ n. ay naːm ອາຍນ້ຳ
steam shovel	n. chaːk dtaːk diːn ຈັກຕັກດິນ
steel	n. leːk ga ເຫຼັກກ້າ
steep	adj. saːn ຊັນ v. chuːm ຈຸ່ມ
steeple	n. hoh laːkaːng ຫໍ່ລະຄັງ
steer	n. ngua nuːm ງົວໜຸ່ມ (boat) v. kaːt tay ຂັດທ້າຍ (control) v. baːng kaːp ບັງຄັບ
stem	v. maa chak ມາຈາກ (boat) n. hua heua ຫົວເຮືອ (plant) n. gaːn ກ້ານ (origin) n. tiː maa ທີ່ມາ
stencil	(F.) n. chia saː dtaːng siːn ເຈ້ຍສະຕັງຊີນ (Lao.) n. gaː dat kayː ກະດາດໄຂ
stenographer	n. naːk sow waː lek ນັກເຊົາວ່າເລກ
stenography	n. gan choːt sǒw waː lek ການຈົດເຊົາວ່າເລກ
step	n. bat nyang ບາດຍ່າງ v. gow ກ້າວ
step by step	teua laːkaːn ເທື່ອລະຂັ້ນ
stepfather	n. poh na ພໍ່ນາ
stepmother	n. maa na ແມ່ນາ
stepsister	n. luk sow kohng poh leu maa na ລູກສາວຂອງພໍ່ຫຼືແມ່ນາ
stepson	n. luk say kohng poh leu naa na ລູກຊາຍຂອງພໍ່ຫຼືແມ່ນາ
stereo	adj. doːn dtiː tiː miː siang nyaak ດົນຕຣີທີ່ມີສຽງຢາກແຍກ
stern	adj. kaːng kaːt ເຄັ່ງຄັດ n. tay heua ທ້າຍເຮືອ
stew	(worry) v. keuːt nyak naːm ຄິດຍາກນ້ຳ (cook) v. oh ເອາະ (food) n. oh ເອາະ (problem) n. bpaːn ha ປັນຫາ
steward	n. pu laːp say nayː heua biːn ຜູ້ຮັບໃຊ້ໃນເຮືອນບິນ
stick	(glue) v. dtiːt ຕິດ (puncture) v. taang ແທງ

sticky	adj. niaw	**stitch**	v. nyi:p หยิบ
	ໜຽວ		n. hoy nyi:p ຮ້ອຍຫຍິບ
stiff	adj. kaang	**stock**	(share) n. hu:n suan
	ແຂງ		ຮຸ້ນສ່ວນ
	n. ko:n dtay ຄົນຕາຍ		(gun) v. ge:p gohng way:
stifle	v. he:t hay: eu:t a:t		ເກັບກອງໄວ້
	ເຮັດໃຫ້ອຶດອັດ	**stocking**	n. to:ng tow: nyow
stigma	(flower) n. ge sohn dohk		ຖົງເທົ້າຍາວ
	may: ເກສອນດອກໄມ້	**stole**	n. pa paa ku:m ຜ້າແພຄຸມ
	(mark) n. keuang may		pp. day: la:k ma ໄດ້ລັກ
	bpo:m doy ເຄື່ອງໝາຍປິ່ມ		ມາ
	ດ້ອຍ	**stomach**	n. tohng ທ້ອງ
still	adj. boh ne:ng boh dti:ng		v. nyo:m la:p poh: cha:m
	ບໍ່ເໜັງບໍ່ຕີງ		bpe:n ຍອມຮັບເพาะจำเป็น
	v. he:t hay: mi:t lo:ng	**stone**	n. hi:n ຫີນ
	ເຮັດໃຫ້ມິດລົງ		v. gwaang hi:n ແກວ່ງຫີນ
	adv. nya:ng ຍັງ		adj. he:t duay hi:n
stimulate	(inspire) v. deu:ng dut		ເຮັດດ້ວຍຫີນ
	chi:t chay: ດຶງດູດຈິດໃຈ	**stony**	adj. bpe:n hi:n ເປັນຫີນ
	(push) v. suay nyu	**stool**	(chair) n. dta:ng sam ka
	ຊວຍຍູ້		ຕັ່ງສາມຂາ
sting	(thorn) v. bpa:k ປັກ		(movement) v. dtua yang
	(bee) v. dtoht ຕອດ		ki ຕົວຢ່າງຂີ້
stink	v. me:n ເໝັນ	**stoop**	v. go:m lo:ng ກົ້ມລົງ
	n. gi:n me:n ກິ່ນເໝັນ	**stop**	v. yu:t ຢຸດ
stir	v. ko:n ຄົນ		n. gan yu:t ການຢຸດ
stir up	goh hay: gert keun	**store**	n. han ka ຮ້ານຄ້າ
	ກໍໃຫ້ເກີດຂຶ້ນ		v. ge:p way: ເກັບໄວ້
stirrup	n. bohn yiap we la ki ma		(supplies) n. kohng ti
	ບ່ອນຢຽບເວລາຂີ່ມ້າ		mian way: ຂອງທີ່ມ້ຽນໄວ້

	(department store) n. hân
	ka nyay: ຣ້ານຄ້າໃหย่
storm	v. kow: chom dti ເຂົ້າໂจมติ
	n. pa nyu: พายุ
stormy	adj. mi pa nyu: มีพายุ
story	(old) n. ni: tan มิทาม
	(new) n. kow ຂ່າວ
	(floor) n. sân ຊັ້ນ
stout	adj. uan nyay: ອ້ວນໃหย่
stove	n. dtow: fay: ເຕົາไฟ
straight	adj. seu ຊື່
strain	v. ke:ng ເຄ້ງ
	(pressure) n. kwam ke:ng dteu:ng ความเค้งติ๊ງ
	(a bit of) n. kwam bpo:n cheua yu ความบิมเจือຢู่
strait	n. hohng kaa kohng na:m ta: le ຮ່ອງแคະຽ ງน้ำทะเล
strange	adj. bpa: lat ปลาด
stranger	n. ko:n bpaak na คิมแปກ พา
strap	n. say ha:t สายรัด
	v. ha:t duay say ha:t รัดด้วยสายรัด
straw	(rice) n. feuang ເพື່ອງ
	(hay) n. nya haang หຍ้า แຫ້ງ
	(drink) n. loht dut ຫຼດດູດ
strawberry	n. mak mohn sa: ni:t neu:ng

	ພาກมงมอຈะมิดมัว
stray	n. sa:t ti ha boh he:n สัດທິ่ทางเติบ
	v. bpay: tua tip ไปທั่วทิບ
streak	n. say, dta สาย, ตา
	v. he:t hay: bpe:n say เรັດใต้เป็นสาย
stream	(current) n. ga: saa ทะแล
	(river) n. huay ຫ້ວຍ
	v. lay: ohk ไຫຼออก
street	n. tâ: no:n ถนิม
street car	n. lo:t lang ຣົດລาງ
strength	n. ga:m la:ng ກำลัງ
strenuous	adj. ke:ng kiat ເຄ້ງຄງก
stress	v. ne:n ເນ້ນ
	n. na:m na:k บ้ำขัก
stretch	(tense) v. yiat ຢ່ງດ
	(lengthen) v. keu:ng ohk ຊี້ออก
	(area) n. neua ti ເນื້อທี่
	(prison) n. we la yu ku:k ເวลาຢู่คุก
stretcher	n. dtiang ham ຕຽງຫาม
strict	adj. ke:ng ka:t ເຄ້ງคิด
stride	(step) n. yop guang ໂຍບກ້າງ
	(progress) n. kwam gow na ความก้าวໜ້า
	v. yop guang ໂຍບກ້າງ

strife	n. gan pi:t tiang ga:n ການຜິດຖຽງກັນ
strike	(hit) v. dtohy ຕ່ອຍ
	(hit) n. gan dtohy dti ການຕ່ອຍຕີ
	(work) n. gan na:t yu:t ngan ການນັດຢຸດງານ
	(work) v. bpa: dti: wa:t yu:t ngan ປະດີວັດຢຸດງານ
string	n. seuak ເຊືອກ
	v. ma:t duay seuak ມັດດ້ວຍເຊືອກ
strip	(long piece) n. se:n ເສັ້ນ
	(bars) n. ku:m so pe ni ຄຸ້ມໂສເພນີ
	(fruit) v. bpohk ohk ປອກອອກ
	(clothes) v. gaa seua pa ohk ແກ້ເສື້ອຜ້າອອກ
stripe	n. lay ລາຍ
	v. kit lay ຂີດລາຍ
strive	v. pa: nya nyam ພະຍາຍາມ
stroke	n. bat ບາດ
	v. he:t bpe:n bat ເຮັດເປັນບາດ
stroll	v. nyang li:n ຍ່າງຫຼິ້ນ
	n. gan nyang li:n ການຍ່າງຫຼິ້ນ
strong	(muscles) adj. kaang haang ແຂງແຮງ
	(hard) adj. kaang ແຂງ
structure	n. paan sang ແຜນສ້າງ
	v. cha:t hay: bpe:n paan sang ຈັດໃຫ້ເປັນແຜນສ້າງ
struggle	v. di:n lo:n ດີ້ນຮົນ
	n. gan di:n lo:n ການດີ້ນຮົນ
stubborn	adj. deu deu:ng ດື້ດຶງ
	(figurative) adj. hua kaang ຫົວແຂງ
stuck	adj. ka ຄາ
stuck-up	ki o:ng ຂີໂອ່ງ
student	(listener) n. luk si:t ລູກສິດ
	(devoted) n. na:k hian ນັກຮຽນ
	(university) n. na:k seu:k sa ນັກສຶກສາ
studio	(art room) n. hohng si:n la: bpa: ຫ້ອງສິລປະ
	(workroom) n. hohng bpa: dti: ba:t ngan ຫ້ອງປະຕິບັດງານ
study	n. hohng kian ຫ້ອງຮຽນ
	v. seu:k sa ສຶກສາ
study hall	n. dteu:k hian ຕຶກຮຽນ
stuff	v. nya:t say: ຍັດໃສ່
	n. si:ng kohng ສິ່ງຂອງ

tumble	v. dte: sa: du:t เตะสะดุด
tun	v. he:t hay: เຮັດໃห้เຢ໌
stunt	n. gan sa: daang go:n ການสะແດງກົນ
stupid	adj. ngo โງ່
sturdy	adj. na:m, to:n tan พํา, ທົນທານ
style	(sample) n. baap ແບບ
	(clothing) n. song ຊົງ
	(manner) n. wat ວາດ
	v. ohk baap keuang ອອກ ແບບເຄື່ອງ
subdue	v. bpap bpam ປາບປາມ
subject	(grammar) n. bpa: tan ປະທານ
	(topic) n. hua leuang ຫົວເຣື່ອງ
	(of king) n. se na a mat ເສນາອາມາດ
	v. he:t hay: day: la:p เຮັດໃห้ได้ ร຺ับเริดให้ได้รับ
sublime	adj. di lert ดีเลิด
submerge	v. cho:m จิม
submarine	n. heua da:m na:m ເຮືອດຳ ນ້ຳ
submit	(give up) v. nyohm ยอม
	(for approval) v. mohp hay: มอบให้
subordinate	(person) n. pu yu dtay: ba:ng ka:p ba:n sa ผู้ยูใต บ่งคับบันຊา
subscribe	(grammar) n. a: nu: bpa: nyok ອະนุปะโยก
	v. he:t hay: yu gohng ba:ng ka:p เริดใหยู่ทอງข้ง ค຺ับ
	(magazine) v. chong na:ng seu จอງພ຺ัวลิ
	(believe) v. he:n di เຫ້ນดิ
subscription	n. gan chohng na:ng seu pi:m ການจองພ຺ัวลิພิม
subsequent	adj. dtam ma ตามมา
subsist	v. nyaing ko:ng yu day: ຢ຺ังคือยู่ได້
substance	(thing) n. gaan san ແกนสาม พาวะมะ
	(idea) n. koh kwam 2ความ ເນື້ອความคิด
substitute	n. dtua taan ตົວແທม
	v. say: taan ga:n ใຊ໌ ແທมກัม
subtle	adj. ler:k seung เลิกຊ຺ึ
subtract	v. lo:p ohk ลิบออก
suburb	n. ku:m nohk meuang ค຺ุมนอกเมือງ
subway	n. lo:t fay: dtay: di:n ร຺ถไฟใต้ดิม
success	n. kwam sa:m le:t ความสำเร็ด
successful	adj. bpe:n po:n sa:m le:t เປ຺ັนผิมสำเร็ด

succeed	v. day: la:p po:n sa:m le:t ໄດ້ຮັບຜົນສຳເລັດ	suitcase	n. hip dern tang ຫີບເດີມທາງ
such	adj. se:n ເຊັ່ນ	sullen	adj. but beu:ng ບູດບຶ້ງ
suck	v. dut gi:n ດູດກິນ	sulphur	n. mat ມາດ
sudden	adj. ta:n ti ta:n day: ທັນທີທັນໃດ	sultan	n. chow: haang sat sa: na i:t sa: lam ເຈົ້າແຫ່ງສາສນາ ອິສລາມ
suddenly	adv. ta:n day: na:n ທັນໃດນັ້ນ	sultry	adj. hohn ho:n ຮ້ອນຮົນ
sue	v. fohng ຟ້ອງ	sum	n. cha:m nuan ຈຳນວນ v. sa: lu:p ສລຸບ
suffer	v. toin toh la: man ທົນທຸລະມານ	sum up	v. nyoh leuang ຫຍໍ້ເຣື່ອງ
sufficient	adj. bpiang poh ພຽງພໍ	summary	n. chay: kwam ໃຈຄວາມ
suffrage	(vote) n. gan lo:ng ka: naan siang ການລົງຄະແນນ ສຽງ (prayer) n. gan no:p way: ການນົບໄຫວ້	summer	n. la: du hohn ຣະດູຮ້ອນ
		summertime	n. nyam hohn ຍາມຮ້ອນ
		summit	adj. ti sung su:t ທີ່ສູງສຸດ n. nyoht kow: ຍອດເຂົ້າ
sugar	n. na:m dtan ນ້ຳຕານ	summon	v. ow: dtua ma ເອົາຕົວມາ
suggest	v. sa: ner ສເນີ	summons	n. may goh: ຫມາຍເກາະ
suggestion	n. sa: ner, gan si naaw tang hay: ການສເນີ, ການຊີແນວທາງໃຫ້	sun	n. dta wa:n ຕາເວັນ v. dtaak daat ຕາກແດດ
suicide	n. gan ka dtua dtay ການຂ້າຕົວຕາຍ	sunlight	n. saang daat ແສງແດດ
		sunny	adj. mi daat ມີແດດ
suit	(suitable) v. moh: so:m ga:n ເໝາະສົມກັນ (law) n. gan fohng hohng ການຟ້ອງຮ້ອງ (clothes) n. su:t nay: ຊຸດໃຫຍ່ (ເສື້ອຜ້າ)	sunrise	n. we la dta: we:n keun ເວລາຕະເວັນຂຶ້ນ
		sunset	n. we la dta: we:n dto:k ເວລາຕະເວັນຕົກ
		sunshine	n. daat ແດດ ແສງແດດ
		superb	adj. wi: set ວິເສດ
suitable	adj. ti moh: so:m ທີ່ເໝາະສົມ	superintendent	n. pu guat gan ຜູ້ກວດ ການ

uperior	adj. ti sung gua ທີ່ສູງກວ່າ
	n. pu sung gua ຜູ້ສູງກວ່າ
uperstition	n. gan seua sok seua lang
	ການເຊື່ອໂຊກເຊື່ອລາງ
upervise	v. bering nyaang ເບິ່ງແຍງ
upervisor	n. pu bering nyaang guat ya
	ຜູ້ເບິ່ງແຍງກວດກາ
upper	n. a han kam ອາຫານຄ່ຳ
upplement	v. dteum say: ຕື່ມໃສ່
	n. suan serm dterm dtoh
	ສ່ວນເສີມເຕີມຕໍ່
upply	n. gan chat hay: ການ
	ຈັດຫາໃຫ້
	v. chaak chay hay:, so:ng sa:
	biang ແຈກຈ່າຍໃຫ້, ສ່ວງສະບຽງ
upport	v. uit nun ອຸດໜູນ
uppose	v. so:m muit wa ສົມມຸດວ່າ
uppress	v. ko:m way:, pap ຍນໄວ, ຜາບ
upreme	adj. sung suit ສູງສຸດ
ure	adj. maa chay: ແນ່ໃຈ
	(that's for sure) intrj.
	nai:n bpe:n kwam chi:ng
	ນັ້ນເປັນຄວາມຈິງ
urely	adv. yang kaik naa ຢ່າງຄັກແນ່
urge	v. pu:ng bpay: bpe:n gu:m
	ພຸ່ງໄປເປັນກ້ອນ
	n. ga: saa pu:ng ohk, fohng
	na:m sung ກະແສຜຸ່ງອອກ, ຟອງນ້ຳສູງ
urface	n. na ໜ້າ

	v. bpo lo keun, soht keun
	ໂປໂລຮ້ນ, ຊອດຂຶ້ນ
surgeon	n. moh bpat ໝໍ່ປາດ
surgery	n. gan pa dta:t ການຜ່າຕັດ
surmise	v. dow: ເດົາ
surpass	v. he:t di gua ເຮັດດີກວ່າ
surplus	n. cha:m nuan ti lo:n
	leua ຈຳນວນທີ່ລົ້ນເຫຼືອ
surprise	n. kwam dteun dte:n
	ຄວາມຕື່ນເຕັ້ນ
	v. he:t hay: dteun
	ເຮັດໃຫ້ຕື່ນ
surrender	v. nyohm paa ຍອມແພ້
surround	v. ohm lohm ອ້ອມລ້ອມ
survey	v. sa:m luat ສຳຮວດ
	n. gan sa:m luat ການສຳຮວດ
survival	n. gan nya:ng mi si wi:t
	yu ການຍັງມີຊີວິດຢູ່
survive	v. loht si wi:t ຣອດຊີວິດ
suspect	n. pu teuk so:ng say:
	ຜູ້ຖືກສົງໄສ
	v. so:ng say: ສົງໄສ
suspend	(revoke) v. nyeu:t way:, ngo:t
	bpay: gohn ຍືດໄວ້ງົດໄປກ່ອນ
	(hang) v. kwaan way: ແຂວນໄວ້
suspension	(car) n. naap lo:t ແໜບລົດ
	(hanging) n. gan kwaan
	way: ການແຂວນໄວ້
suspicious	adj. ti bpe:n dta so:ng
	say: ທີ່ເປັນຕາສົງໄສ

sustain	v. ka:m su⁵ way³ ຄ້ຳຊູ່ໄວ້	swim	v. way⁶ na:m ທ່ອຍນ້ຳ
swallow	(gulp) n. gan¹ geun¹ ການກືນ		n. gan¹ way⁶ na:m ການທ່ອຍນ້ຳ
	(bird) n. no:k aan ມົກແອນ	swimmer	n. na:k² way⁶ na:m ນັກທ່ອຍນ້ຳ
	v. geun¹ ກືນ	swimming pool	n. sa:³ way⁶ na:m⁵ ສະທ່ອຍນ້ຳ
swamp	n. beu:ng ບຶງ	swine	(pig) n. mu⁴ ຫມູ
	(overturn) v. chu:m ຈຸມ		(person) n. ko:n³ sua ຄົນ
	(overrun) v. mi³ wiak⁵ lay⁴		ຊົວ
	pot ມີວຽກຫລາຍໂພດ	swing	n. on sa³ ໂອນຊາ
swarm	v. bpay: bpe:n fu:ng ໄປເປັນຝູງ		v. gwaang bpay: ma³ ແກວ່ງໄປມາ
	n. fu:ng¹ ຝູງ	swirl	v.i. mun¹, ha:n³ ຫມຸນ, ຫັນ
sway	v. gwaang gway⁴ ແກວ່ງໄກວ		ຫມຸນໄວ
swear	(official) v. sa⁴ ban ສາບານ	switch	(stick) n. may⁵ saa ໄມ້ແສ້
	(curse) v. cho:m da² ຈົມດ່າ		(control) n. go:ng dta:k³ fay: fa ກົງຕາກໄຟຟ້າ
sweat	n. heua ເຫື່ອ		v. bpian ປ່ຽນ
	v. heua ohk ເຫື່ອອອກ	swollen	adj. buam ບວມ
sweater	n. seua ko:n⁴ sa:t³ ta:k³ ເສື້ອກົນສັດຖັກ	swoon	v. bpe:n lo:m³ ເປັນລົມ
sweep	v. pa:t¹ ປັດ	sword	n. dap⁶ ດາບ
sweet	adj. wan¹ ຫວານ	syllable	n. pa:² nyang³ ພະຍາງ
sweeten	v.i. he:t hay: wan⁴ ເຮັດໃຫ້ຫວານ	symbol	n. sa:n⁴ nya la:k³ ສັນຍາລັກ
sweetheart	n. su⁵ 2	symbolize	v. bpe:n sa:n¹ nya⁴ la:k³² ເປັນສັນຍາລັກ
swell	adj. di, go⁵ ດີ, ໂຕ້	sympathy	n. kwam he:n³ o:k⁴ he:n³ chay:⁴ ຄວາມເຫັນອົກເຫັນໃຈ
	v. kay: keun² ໃຫຍ່ຂຶມ	symphony	n. wo:ng³ du:³ li:³ nyang³ ວົງດຸລະຍາງ
swift	adj. wohng way:² ວ່ອງໄວ	symptom	n. a¹ gan¹ kohng⁴ lok⁵ ອາການຂອງໂຣກ
	adj. luat lew³ ລວດເລວ		

T

table n. dto: ໂຕະ

tablecloth n. pa bpu dto: ຜ້າປູໂຕະ

tablespoon n. buang so:t gaang
ບ່ວງຊຸດແກງ

tablet (stone) n. gohn ກ້ອນ

(pill) n. me:t ເມັດ

(paper) n. dta:p ຕັບ

tack (thumbtack) n. dta: bpu
waa ຕະປູແວ້

(carpet tack) n. dta: bpu
noy ຕະປູນ້ອຍ

v. dtohk le:k dta: bpu
ຕອກເຫຼັກຕະປູ

tackle (jump) v. dot say: hay:
lo:m ໂດດໃສ່ໃຫ້ລົ້ມ

(finish) v. he:t hay: laaw
ເຮັດໃຫ້ແລ້ວ

tact n. pi:k way: ພິກໄຫວ

tactics n. paan gan ແຜນການ

tadpole n. luk huak ລູກຮວກ

tag (label) n. pi dti:t ga:
bpow: ປ້າຍຕິດກະເປົາ

(game) n. li:n mak li
ຫຼິ້ນພາກລິ

(label) v. dti:t bpay
ຕິດປ້າຍ

(tag along) v. dti:t dtam
ຕິດຕາມ

tail n. hang ຫາງ

v. dti:t dtam ຕິດຕາມ

tailor n. sang dta:t keuang
ຊ່າງຕັດເຄື່ອງ

v. dta:t keuang ຕັດເຄື່ອງ

tailors n. han dta:t keuang ຮ້ານ
ຕັດເຄື່ອງ

taint (soil) v. he:t hay: dang
ເຮັດໃຫ້ດ່າງ

(defile) v. he:t hay: mi
mo:n ti:n ເຮັດໃຫ້ມີມົນທິນ

take (grab) v. cha:p ຈັບ

(receive) v. ow: ເອົາ

take a bus ki lo:t me ຂີ່ລົດເມ

take a bath ap na:m ອາບນ້ຳ

take a nap nohn suay ນອນສວຍ

take a picture tay hup ຖ່າຍຮູບ

take a test sohp se:ng ສອບເສັງ

take after kay keu ຄ້າຍຄື

take apart mang ohk ມ້າງອອກ

take away one's breath he:t hay: dteun
laa: bpaak chay: ເຮັດໃຫ້ຕື່ນ
ແລະແປກໃຈ

take back (return) v. ow: bpay:
so:ng keun ເອົາໄປສົ່ງຄືນ

(retract) v. ow: keun
ເອົາຄືນ

take care of ber:ng nyaang ເບິ່ງແຍງ

take charge of la:p na ti ha:p pi:t sohp
ຮັບໜ້າທີຮັບຜິດຊອບ

take down	(lower) v. ow: lo:ng	เอาลง
	(record) v. cho:t way:	จดไว้
take for granted	teu wa boh mi bai:n ha	
	a' ถือว่าบ่มีบันหา	
take in	bpay: ber:ng ไปเบิ่ง	
take into account	pi: cha la: na	พิจารณา
take it easy	koy koy he:t ค่อยๆเร็ด	
take off	(rise from the ground)	
	keun chak dern ขึ้นจากเดิม	
	(remove) v. gaa ohk แก้ออก	
take on	(hire) v. chang จ้าง	
	(undertake) v. la:p pa la:	
	รับภาระ	
take one's time	he:t dtam sa: bay	
	เร็ดตามสะบาย	
take out	(accompany) pa bpay: li:n	
	gan keun พาไปเทียวกางคืม	
	(remove) v. ow: ohk เอาออก	
take over	la:p na ti ha:p pi:t sohp	
	รับพาทรับผิดชอบ	
take pains	he:t yang la: ma:t la: wa:ng,	
	pian เร็ดอย่างระมัดระวัง, ผงม	
take part in	kow: huam เข้าร่วม	
take place	mi keun, gert keun	
	มีขึ้น, เกิดขึ้น	
take sides with	kow: kang เข้าข้าง	
take someone out	pa bpay: พาไป
take time off	pa:k gan พักกาน
take time out	sow: he:t wiak noy	
	neuing เอาเร็ดงานพ่อยนิ่ง	
take turns	bpian pian ปง่มผูง่ม
take up	(study) v. ler:m hian เริ	
	(occupy) v. say: we la,	
	bohn ไช้เอลา, ไช้บอม	
take your time	id. he:t dtam sa: bay	
	เร็ดตามสะบาย	
tale	(episode) n. leuang low	
	เรื่องราว	
	(legend) n. ni: tan มีทาม	
talent	n. kwam sa mat คอามสามา	
talk	v. lo:m ลม	
	(lecture) n. gan ba:n nya	
	ทามบันยาย	
talk over	pi: cha la: na duay gan	
	so:n ta: na พิจารณาด้อย	
	ทามสัมทะมา	
talker	(like to talk) n. ko:n	
	wow: du: คิมเอ้าๆ	
	(flatter) n. ko:n ta:	
	laang คิมฤแลง	
tall	adj. suhg สูง	
tambourine	n. gohng mak ga: sa:	
	ทองฺมากกะแจะ	
tame	adj. keu:n คุ้ม	
	v. he:t hay: keu:n	
	เร็ดใหคุ้ม	

an

(leather) v. fohk naːng
ฟอกหนัง

(sun tan) v. ap daat
อาบแดด

n. siː daat mayː สีแดดใหม่

angle

n. gan nyuːng ການທ່ຽງ

v. heːt hayː nyuːng
ເຮັດໃຫ້ທ່ຽງ

adj. nyuːng ທ່ຽງ

ank

(army) n. loːt taːng
ລົດຖັງ

(container) n. taːng sayː
naːm ຖັງໃສ່ນ້ຳ

(tank up) v. owː sayː
taːng ເອົາໃສ່ຖັງ

anker

n. gaːm bpaːn baːn tuːk
naːm maːn ກຳປັ່ນບັນທຸກນ້ຳມັນ

anner

n. koːn fohk naːng ຄົນ
ฟอกหนัง

ap

n. gohk naːm ກ໊ອກນ້ຳ

(drain) v. owː ohk ເອົາ
ອອກ

(rap) v. dtohː koy koy
ເຕາະຄ່ອຍໆ

ape

(stick) v. dtiːt duay tap
ຕິດດ້ວຍເທບ

(record) v. baːn teuːk
siang ບັນທຶກສຽງ

(stick) n. tep dtiːt ເທບ
ຕິດ

(record) n. dtep baːn
teuːk siang ເທບບັນທຶກສຽງ

tape measure (cloth) n. pa saːm laːp
taak ຜ້າສາມລັບແທກ

(metal) n. paan leːk saːm
laːp taak ແผ່นເหล็กสามลับแทก

taper

n. tian noy ທຽນນ້ອຍ

v. laːm loːng ແหลมลง

tape recorder n. keuang baːn teuːk
siang ເຄื່ອງບັນ
ທຶກສຽງ

tar

n. yang bpu taːng ຢາງປູທາງ

tardy

adj. saːk sa ຊັກຊ້າ

target

n. bpowː may ເປ້າໝາຍ

tariff

n. aːt dta pa siː ka kowː laa
ohk ອັດຕາພາສີຂາເຂົາແລະ99ก

n. laːy gan laː ka ລາຍການ
ราคา

tart

n. kaːː noːm saiː niːt
neuːng ຂนมຊໄนิด
neuːng ຂนมชุมีนึ่ง

adj. loːt haːng, soːm ຮົດແຮງ, ສົມ

task

n. wiak naːk ວຽກໜັກ

v. heːt hayː naːk nuang
ເຮັດໃຫ້ໜັກໜ່ວງ

taste

n. loːt sat ຮົດຊາດ

v. siːm ຊີມ

tasteless

adj. boh mi loːt sat
ບໍ່ມีรົດຊາດ

taunt

n. gan nyohːnyery
ການເຢາະເຢີ້ຍ

v. nyohː nyery ເຢາະເຢີ້ຍ ,

tavern	n. hong kay lowː ໂຮງ ຂາຍເຫຼົ້າ
tax	n. pa siꞌ ພາສີ v. geːp pa siꞌ ເກັບພາສີ
taxi	n. (taxicab) n. loːt doy san ຣົດໂດຍສານ v. lerːm laan okh, doy san ເຣີມແລ່ນອອກ, ໂດຍສານ
tea	(drink) n. naːm saꞌ ນ້ຳຊາ (leaves) n. bayꞌ saꞌ ໃບຊາ
teach	v. sohn ສອນ
teacher	n. nay ku ນາຍຄູ
teakwood	n. mayː saːk ໄມ້ສັກ
team	n. kaː naiꞌ ຄມະ
teapot	n. ga naːm saꞌ ການ້ຳຊາ
tear	n. naːm dta ນ້ຳຕາ (rip) v. chik ຈີກ (move) v. keuan tiꞌ wayː wayː ເຄື່ອນທີ່ໄວໆ (tore) p. dayː chik ໄດ້ຈີກ (torn) pp. teuk chik ຖືກ ຈີກ
tear down	taːm layꞌ loːng ທຳລາຍລົງ
tear up	taːm layꞌ doy chik bpeːn dtohn noy noy ທຳລາຍໂດຍຈີກ ເປັນຕ່ອນນ້ອຍໆ
tease	(strip tease) n. laː baːm bpo ລະບຳໂປ້ (one who teases) n. pu maːk yohk ຜູ້ມັກຍອກ

	v. yohk ຍອກ
teaspoon	n. buang naːm saꞌ ບ່ວງ ນ້ຳຊາ
technical	adj. wiː saꞌ gan ວິຊາການ n. tek niːk ເຕັກນິກ
technician	n. sang pu siow saːn ຊ່າງຜູ້ຊ່ວຍຊານ
technology	n. uit saꞌ haꞌ gaːm saːt ອຸດສາຫະກັມສາດ
tedious	adj. laː iat choːn iːt ohn ລະອ່ຽດຈີມຊີດອ່ອນ
teem	v. dteːm bpayː duay ເຕັມໄປດ້ວຍ
teens	n. aꞌ nyuː laː wang siːp sam teriːng siːp gow ອາຍຸລະຫວ່າງ ໑໓ ເຖິງ ໑໙
teenagers	n. puak nuːm sow ພວກໜຸ່ມ ສາວ
teeter totter	n. bpaan liːn duːp deuang ແປ້ນຫຼິ້ນດຸບເດີ່ງ
teeth	n. kaaw ແຂ້ວ
telegram	n. to laː lek ໂທະເລກ
telegraph	n. keuang soːng to laː lek ເຄື່ອງສົ່ງໂທະເລກ v. dti say ຕີສາຍ
telephone	n. keuang to laː saːp ເຄື່ອງໂທະສັບ v. wow to laː saːp ເວົ້າໂທະສັບ

telescope	n. gohng sohng tang gay: ກ້ອງສ່ອງທາງໄກ
	v. sup kow: ga:n day: ສຸບເຂົາກັນໄດ້
television	n. to la: pap ໂທລະພາບ
tell	(inform) v. bohk ບອກ
	(relate) v. low: ເລົ່າ
tell apart	bohk kwam dtaak dang ບອກຄວາມແຕກຕ່າງ
tell time	bohk we la ບອກເວລາ
temper	(momentary mood) n. a lo:m ອາຣົມ
	(to moderate) v. he:t hay: poh di ເຮັດໃຫ້ພໍດີ
	(steel) v. he:t hay: kaang ເຮັດໃຫ້ແຂງ
temperate	adj. poh bpan gang ພໍປານກາງ
temperature	n. u:n ha: pum ອຸນຫະພູມ
tempest	n. lo:m pa nyu: ລົມພາຍຸ
temporary	adj. sua kow ຊົ່ວຄາວ
temple	n. wi: han ວິຫານ
tempt	v. loh hay: he:t sua ລໍ້ໃຫ້ເຮັດຊົ່ວ
temptation	v. si:ng loh chay: ສິ່ງລໍ້ໃຈ
ten	adj. si:p ສິບ
tenant	n. pu sow: ຜູ້ເຊົ່າ
tend	v. bper:ng nyaang, fow: ເບິ່ງແຍງ, ເຝົ້າ
	v. en iang bpay: tang ເອນຍງໄປທາງ
tendency	n. kwam en iang ຄວາມ ເອນຍ່ງ
tender	(person) adj. ohn wan ອ່ອນຫວານ
	(food) adj. poy ເປ່ອຍ
	n. pu ber:ng nyaang, ka:m sa: ner ຜູ້ເບິ່ງແຍງ, ຄົາສເນີ
tendon	n. se:n e:n ເສັ້ນເອັນ
tennis	n. te:n ni:t ເຫັນນິດ
tense	adj. ke:ng ເຄັ່ງ
	v. he:t hay: ke:ng dteu:ng ເຮັດໃຫ້ເຄັ່ງຕຶງ
	n. we la se:n a: dit, bpa chu: ba:n, a: na ko:t ເວລາເຊິ່ງອະດິດ, ປະຈຸບັນ, ອະນາຄົດ
tent	n. dtup pa ຕຸບຜ້າ
tenth	adj. ti si:p ທີສິບ
term	(school) n. pak hian ພາກຮຽນ
	(time) n. sa: may: ສະໄມ
	(word) n. ka:m sa:p ຄຳສັບ
	v. say: seu ໃສ່ຊື່
terms	(conditions) n. ngeuan kay: ເງື່ອນໄຂ
	(relations) n. kwam giaw pa:n ຄວາມກ່ຽວພັນ
terrace	(house) n. sa:n dtam kang pu ຊັ້ນຕາມຂ້າງພູ
	(patio) n. la: biang peun ລະບຽງພື້ນ

(farmland) v. he:t hay:
bpe:n sa̅:n d̆tam kang pu
ເຮັດໄຮ່ເປັນສວນຕາມ
ຂາງພູ

terrible (frightening) adj. bpe:n
d̆ta nyan ເປັນຕາຍ້ານ

(disgusting) adj. bpe:n
d̆ta nay ເປັນຕາໜ່າຍ

territory (land) n. di:n daan
ດິນແດນ

(area) n. ti:n ຖິ່ນ

terror adj. bpe:n d̆ta yan
ເປັນຕາຍ້ານ
n. kwam sa̅: tan yan gua
ຄວາມສະທ້ານຍ້ານກົວ

test (trial) n. gan to:t lohng
ການທົດລອງ

(exam) n. gan sohp se:ng
ການສອບເສງ

(try) v. to:t lohng
ທົດລອງ

(exam) v. se:ng ເສງ

testament n. pi: nay: ga:m
ພິໄນຍກັມ

testify v. sa̅: daang hay: he:n
wa̅ ສະແດງໃຫ້ເຫັນວ່າ

testimony (trial) n. kwam hay: gan
ຄວາມໃຫ້ການ

(proof) koh pi: sut
ຂໍພິສຸດ

text (contents) n. bo:t kohng
leuang ບົດຂອງເຣື່ອງ

(textbook) n. bpeum hian
ຫັ້ນຮຽນ

textile (cloth) n. pa paa ຜ້າແພ

(raw material) n. si:ng
ti say: d̆ta:m bpe:n pa
ສິ່ງໃຊ້ທຳເປັນຜ້າ

Thai n. tay: ໄທ

Thailand n. bpa: tet tay: ປະເທດໄທ

than conj. gua ກ່ວາ

thankful adj. hu seu:k kohp chay:
ຮູ້ສຶກຂອບໃຈ

thanks id. kohp chay: der
ຂອບໃຈເດີ້

thank you id. kohp chay: ຂອບໃຈ

that adj. na:n ນັ້ນ
conj. se:ng, ti ນັ້ນເຊິ່ງ, ທີ

thaw v. bpeuay bpe:n na:m
ເປື່ອຍເປັນນ້ຳ

the (definite article) adj.
ka:m na:m na kohng nam
ຄຳນຳໜ້າຂອງນາມ
ຄຳນີ້ຜ້າຂອງນາມ (ໃຊ້ທັງງ
ແລະນ້ອຍ)

theater (play) n. hong la: kohn
ໂຮງລະຄອນ

(movie) n. hong si: ne
ໂຮງຊີເນ

theft n. gan ka: moy ການຂະໂມຍ

their	adj. kohng puak ka: chow: ຂອງພວກເຈົ້າ
them	pron. puak ka: chow: ພວກຂະເຈົ້າ
theme	(music) n. ta:m nohng ທໍານອງ
	(story) n. neua ha ເນື້ອຫາ
themselves	pron. dtua kohng ka: chow: eng ຕົວຂອງຂະເຈົ້າເອງ
then	(at that time) adj. nay: we la na:n ໃນເວລານັ້ນ
	(after that) adv. laaw ແລ້ວ
theory	n. ti:t sa: di ທິສຕິ
there	adv. ha:n ຫັ້ນ
thereabout	adv. taap taap na:n ແຖບໆ ນັ້ນ
thereafter	adv. la:ng chak na:n ຫຼັງຈາກນັ້ນ
there is	(there are) id. mi ມີ
therefore	adv. poh: sa: na:n ເພາະສັ້ນ
thermometer	n. ba loht ບາໂຫຼດ
these	adj. low: ni ເຫຼົ່ານີ້
	pron. si:ng low: ni ສິ່ງເຫຼົ່ານີ້
they	pron. ka: chow: ຂະເຈົ້າ
thick	(solid) adj. na ໜາ
	(liquid) adj. ku:n ຂຸ້ນ
thicket	n. fu:m may: ພຸ່ມໄມ້
thief	n. ko:n ki la:k ຄົນຂີ້ລັກ
thigh	(people) n. gok ka ກົກຂາ
	(people or animals) n. ka dto ຂາໂຕ
thimble	n. bpohk niw meu ປອກນິ້ວມື (ສໍາຫຼັບຫຍິບເຍັບ(ຄື້ວ))
thin	adj. bang ບາງ
	(liquid) adj. say: ໄສ
	v. he:t hay: say: ເຮັດໃຫ້ໄສ
thing	(concrete) n. keuang kohng ເຄື່ອງຂອງ
	(concrete or abstract) n. si:ng ສິ່ງ
think	v. ki:t, keu:t ຄຶດ, ຄິດ
think highly of	nyo:k nyohng laa: na:p teu ຍົກຍ້ອງແລະນັບຖື
think of	keu:t ha ຄິດຫາ
think out	keu:t ohk ຄິດອອກ
think over	ki:t pi: cha la: na ຄິດພິຈາລະນາ
think up	ki:t keun ຄິດຂຶ້ນ
third	adj. ti sam ທີສາມ
thirst	(water) n. kwam yak na:m ຄວາມປາກນ້ຳ
	(general) n. kwam yak ຄວາມປາກ
thirsty	adj. yak na:m ປາກນ້ຳ
thirteen	(13) adj. si:p sam ສິບສາມ

thirteenth	(13th) adj. ti si:p sam ທີສິບສາມ
this	pron. ain ni ອັນນີ້
	adj. ni ນີ້
thistle	n. peut nam ຜີດນາມ
thorn	n. nam ຫນາມ
thorax	n. na er:k ຫນ້າເອິກ
thorough	adj. doy dta: loht ໂດຍຕລອດ
thoroughbred	adj. pain leuat diow ພັນເລືອດດຽວ
those	adj. low: na:n ເຫຼົ່ານັ້ນ
	pron. si:ng low: na:n ສິ່ງເຫຼົ່ານັ້ນ
though	adj. te:ng maan wa ເຖິງແມ່ນວ່າ
thought	n. kwam ki:t ຄວາມຄິດ
thoughtful	(full of thought) adj. hohp kohp ຮອບຄອບ
	(considerate) adj. ti he:n o:k he:n chay: pu eu:n ທີ່ເຫັນອົກເຫັນໃຈຜູ້ອື່ນ
thousand	adj. pain ພັນ
thrash	v. kian dti ຂ້ຽນຕີ
thread	(screw) n. giow ກຽວ
	(sewing) n. may: nyi:p ໄໝຫຍິບ
	v. hoy ke:m ຮ້ອຍເຂັມ
threat	n. gan ku ke:n ການຂູ່ເຂັນ
threaten	v.t. ku ke:n ຂູ່ເຂັນ
three	adj. sam ສາມ (ມ)
thresh	v. fat kow: ຟາດເຂົ້າ
threshold	n. dtin bpa: dtu ຕິນປະຕູ
thrice	(3X) adv. sam teua ສາມເທື່ອ
thrift	n. gan ma:t ta: nya:t, gan bpa: ya:t ການມັທຍັດ, ການປະຍັດ
thrifty	adj. ma:t ta: nya:t ມັທຍັດ
thrill	v. he:t hay: dteun dte:n leu sa: teuan ເຮັດໃຫ້ຕົນເຕັ້ນຫຼືສະເທືອນ n. si:ng ti he:t hay: dteun dte:n leu sa: teuan ສ່ວງທີເຮັດໃຫ້ຕົນເຕັ້ນຫຼືສະເທືອນ
thrilling	adj. dteu:n dte:n ຕື່ນເຕັ້ນ
thrive	v. cha: re:rin ຈະເຣີນ
throat	n. koh hoy ຄໍຫ້ອຍ
throb	v. sa:n ສັ່ນ
throe	n. sa:n bpe:n bat, bpe:n bat ສັ້ນເປັນບາດ, ເປັນບາດ
throne	n. ba:n la:ng ບັນລັງ
throng	(people) n. fu:ng so:n ຝູງຊົນ
	(things) n. su:m ຊຸມ v. hom ga:n bpe:n gu:m ໂຮມກັນເປັນກຸ່ມ
through	(motion) prep. pan ຜ່ານ
	(beginning to end) adj. dta: loht ຕລອດ
	(by means of) prep. doy ໂດຍ

through street id. ta: no:n ti boh mi bpay yu:t ຖນົນທີ່ບໍ່ມີປ້າຍຢຸດ

through train id. lo:t duan ຣົດດ່ວນ

throw v. kwuang ຂວ້າງ

throw away v. kwuang ti:m ຂວ້າງຖິ້ມ

throw out ko:m ku hay: ni ຂົມຂູ່ໃຫ້ໜີ

throw up hak ຮາກ

thrust v. nyu haang haang ຍູ້ແຮງໆ

(motion) n. gan suk nyu ການຊຸກຍູ້

thumb n. bpo meu ໂປ້ມື

thump n. siang tu:p ສຽງທຸບ

v. tu:p dti ທຸບຕີ

thunder n. (siang) fa hohng (ສຽງ)ຟ້າຮ້ອງ

v. fa hohng ຟ້າຮ້ອງ

thunderbolt n. fa pa ຟ້າຜ່າ

thunder clap n. siang bat fa pa ສຽງບາດຟ້າຜ່າ

thunder storm n. pa nyu: fo:n ພາຍຸຝົນ

Thursday n. wa:n pa: ha:t ວັນພະຫັດ

thus adv. poh: sa: na:n ເພາະສະນັ້ນ

tick (sound) n. siang da:ng baap mong dta:ng ສຽງດັງແບບໂມງຕັ້ງ

v. may keuang ໝາຍເຄື່ອງ

(insect) n. he:p ເຫັບ

ticket (movie, train) n. pi ປີ້

(label) n. nyi hoh ຍີ່ຫໍ້

(to label) v. dti:t nyi hoh ຕິດຍີ່ຫໍ້

tickle (action) v. he:t hay: ga: diam ເຮັດໃຫ້ກະດຽມ

(feeling) v. ga: diam ກະດຽມ

tide (high) v. na:m keun ນ້ຳຂຶ້ນ

(low) n. na:m bo:k ນ້ຳບົກ

tidings n. kow ຂ່າວ

tie (rope) v. ma:t ມັດ

(score) adj. day: ka: naan tow: ga:n ໄດ້ຄະແນນເທົ່າກັນ

(necktie) n. ga la: wa:t ກາຣະວັດ

(F.) n. ka: naan tow: ga:n ຄະແນນເທົ່າກັນ

tiger n. seua ເສືອ

tight (collar, crowd) adj. ka:p ຄັບ

(taut, packed) adj. naan ແໜ້ນ

tighten v. ha:t kow: ຮັດເຂົ້າ

tigress n. seua maa ເສືອແມ່

tile (roof-clay) n. di:n koh ດິນຂໍ

(roof-cement) n. di:n ga: beuang ດິນກະເບື້ອງ

	(F.) (floor) n. di:n ga ¹ ¹ ໂອ ດິນກາໂຣ
till	n. li:n sa:k say nger:n ⁵ ² ² ³ ລິ້ນຊັກໃສ່ເງິນ
	prep. choh:n gua ¹ ² ຈິນກວ່າ
	v. tay: ⁴ ໄຕ
tilt	v. ngiang ² ວ່ງງ
timber	n. may: heuan ⁵ ³ ໄມ້ເຮືອນ
time	(period) n. we la ³ ³ ເວລາ
	(repetition) n. teua ² ເທື່ອ
time off	we la nyu:t gan ³ ³ ³ ເວລາຫຍຸດການ
timetable	n. dta lang we la ³ ³ ³ ຕາລາງເວລາ
timid	adj. ki ay ⁶ ¹ ຂີ້ອາຍ
tin	n. di bu:k ¹ ³ ດີບຸກ
	n. ga: bpohng ³ ກະປ໋ອງ
tincture	n. ya daang ¹ ³ ຢາແດງ
tinge	(color) n. si ohn ohn ⁴ ² ² ສີອອນໆ
	(flavor) n. lo:t ohn ohn ² ² ² ຣົດອອນໆ
tingle	v. che:p nohy nohy nyohn teuk ³ ⁵ ⁵ ⁵ ⁶ dtohk ⁶ ເຈັບໜ້ອຍໆຍ້ອນຖືກຕຸກ
tinker	n. sohm bpaang doy boh mi ⁶ ⁶ ¹ ¹ ² kwam sa:m nan ³ ³ ³ ສ້ອມແປງໂດຍ ບໍ່ມີຄວາມຊຳນານ
tinkle	v. sa:n ga: di:ng ² ³ ³ ສັ່ນກະດິງ n. siang ga: di:ng ¹ ³ ³ ສງງກະດິງ
tint	v. si ohn ohn ⁴ ² ² ສີອອນໆ v. say: si ² ⁴ ໃສ່ສີ

tiny	adj. noy noy ⁵ ⁵ ໜ້ອຍໆ
tip	(point) n. so:m ² ສົ້ມ
	(money) n. nger:n lang ³ ³ ເງິນລາງ wa:n ³ ເວີນຣາງວັນ
	(to give money) v. hay: ⁶ lang wa:n ³ ³ ໃຫ້ຣາງວັນ
	(to upset) v. he:t hay: ² ⁶ lo:m ⁵ ເຣັດໃຫ້ລົມ
tiptoe	v.i. nyohng bpay: ² ¹ ຍ່ອງ ໄປ
tiptop	(excellent) n. bohn di ² ¹ lert ⁵ ບ່ອນດີເລີດ adj. di lert ¹ ⁵ ດີເລີດ
tire	(become tired) v. meuay ² ເມື່ອຍ
	(make tired) v. he:t hay ² ⁶ meuay ເຣັດໃຫ້ເມື່ອຍ
tired	(physical) adj. meuay ² ເມື່ອຍ
	(mental) v. beua ² ເບື່ອ
tissue	(cloth) n. pa bang bang ² ຜ້າບາງໆ (paper) n. chia bang ⁵ ¹ bang ¹ ເຈ້ຍບາງໆ
title	(rank) n. nyo:t ² ຍົດ (theme) n. seu hua ² ⁴ leuang ⁵ ຊື່ຫົວເຣື່ອງ
to	(until) prep. ter:ng ⁴ ເຖິງ (to someone) adv. bpay: ⁷ ha ໄປຫາ

toad	n. ka:n kak ຄັນຄາກ
toast	(bread) n. kow: chi bpi:ng ເຂົ້າຈີ່ປິ້ງ
	(drink) n. gan uay say: ການອວຍໄຊ
	(to drink) v. uay say: ອວຍໄຊ
	(to brown bread) v. bpi:ng kow: chi ປິ້ງເຂົ້າຈີ່
toaster	n. keuang bpi:ng kow: chi ເຄື່ອງປິ້ງເຂົ້າຈີ່
tobacco	n. ya se:n ຢາເສັ້ນ
today	adv. meu ni ມື້ນີ້
toe	n. niw dtin ນິ້ວຕີນ
together	adv. na:m ga:n ນຳກັນ
toil	n. wiak lay ວຽກໜາຍ v. he:t wiak lay ເຮັດວຽກໜາຍ
toilet	(polite) n. hohng na:m ຫ້ອງນ້ຳ
	(common) n. suam ສ້ວມ
toilet articles	n. keuang sa:m ang ເຄື່ອງສຳອາງ
token	(money) n. nger:n a:t say: taan nger:n ເງິນອັດໃຊ້ແທນເງິນແທ້
	(symbol) a: nu: sohn ອະນຸສອນ
tolerant	adj. pohn sa:n pohn nyow ຜ່ອນສັ້ນຜ່ອນຍາວ
toll	n. ka nay: gan say: ຄ່າໃນການໃຊ້ n. dti la: ka:ng koy ອາກອນ peua hohng ຕິຣະຄ້ຽຄ້ອຍເພື່ອ ຮອງ
tomato	n. mak de:n ໝາກເດັ່ນ
tomb	n. ka:m fa:ng so:p ຂຸມຝັງສົບ
tomorrow	n. meu eun ມື້ອື່ນ
ton	n. dton ໂຕນ
tone	n. sa:m niang ສຳນຽງ
tongue	n. li:n ລີ້ນ
tonic	n. ya ba:m lu:ng ga:m la:ng ຢາບຳລຸງກຳລັງ
tonight	n. meu laang ni ມື້ແລງນີ້
too	(also) adv. meuan ga:n ເໝືອນກັນ
	(too much) adv. pot ໂພດ
tool	n. keuang meu ເຄື່ອງມື
tooth	n. kaaw ແຂ້ວ
toothache	n. che:p kaaw ເຈັບແຂ້ວ
toothbrush	n. bpaang tu kaaw ແປງຖູແຂ້ວ
toothpaste	n. ya tu kaaw ຢາຖູແຂ້ວ
toothpick	n. may: chi:m kaaw ໄມ້ຈີ້ມແຂ້ວ
toothless	adj. boh mi kaaw ບໍ່ມີແຂ້ວ
top	n. choh:m ຈອມ
topic	n. hua leuang ຫົວເລື່ອງ

torch	n. gaː bohng กะบอง	tourist	n. naːk tohng tiow นักท่องท่ຽว
torment	n. gan toh laː man การทระมาน	tournament	n. gan kaang kan siːng saː naː การแข่งขันจิงจะมะ
	v. toh laː man ทระมาน	tow	v. gaa แก
torpedo	n. luk bpeun nyaːy: kohng rue dam: namː ลูกปืมใหย่ຂອງเริงດຳน้ำ	towards	(come) prep. ma haː มาทา
			(go) prep. bpay haː ไปทา
torrent	n. gaː saa naːm ti lay: haang กะแสน้ำที่ไหลแรง	towel	n. pa seːt dto ผ้าเจ็ดโต
tortoise	n. dtow: fa เຕ่าฟา	tower	n. hoh koy ทໍคอຍ
torture	n. gan toh laː man การทระมาน		v. sung tuam ฟูงถ่ວม
	v. toh laː man ทระมาน	town	n. meuang เมือง
toss	v. nyon bpay: โยมไป	toxic	adj. beua เบื่ອ
total	n. chaːm nuan taːng moːt จำมวมทังฟิด		adj. bpeːn piːt เป็นฟิດ
	v. huam kow: gaːn รอมเຂ้าทัม	toxin	n. piːt saːt dtang dtang ฟิดสัดต่າງๆ
	adj. tang moːt ทังฟิด	toy	n. keuang liːn deːk noy เครื่ງทิ้มເດักม้อຍ
totter	v. nyang seː ຍ່າງເຊ		v. liːn naːm ทิ้มม่ำ
touch	(action) n. gan saːm paːt การสัมผัด	trace	n. hoy รอຍ
	(skill) n. kwam saːm nan คอามฉ่ำมาม		(follow) v. naːm hoy ມ່ຽรอຍ
	v. bay ບาຍ	track	n. hoy dtin รอຍຕິມ
tough	(strong) adj. kaang haang แຂງแรง		(follow) v. naːm hoy dtin ມ່ຽรอຍຕິມ
	(meat) n. nyap ทຍาບ		(railroad) n. lang loːt fay: ลางຣิດไฟ
tour	n. gan tohng tiow การท่องท่ຽว	tract	(land) n. dtohn ຕອມ
	v. tohng tiow ท่ງท่ຽว		(essay) n. leuang เรื่ອງ
		tractor	n. loːt duːt ຣິດດຸດ
		trade	n. gan ka kay การคาຂาຍ

	(sell) v. ka kay คำຂาย
	(swap) v. bpian gain ປ່ຽນກັນ
trade-in	v. ow! kohng gow! bpay: bpian ເອົາຂອງເກົ່າໄປ bpian ປ່ຽນ
trademark	n. nyi hoh gan ka ໝາຍການຄ້າ
trading	n. gan ka kay ການຄ້າຂາຍ
trading post	n. han kay kohng nyoy ຮ້ານຂາຍຂອງຍ່ອຍ
tradition	n. hit kohng ຮີດຄອງ
traditional	adj. dtam hit kohng ຕາມຮີດຄອງ
traffic	(sell) v. ka kay คำຂาย
	(trade) n. gan ka ການ ค้า
	(cars) n. gan cha la chohn ການຈາຣະຈอน
tragedy	n. leuang sok ເລື່ອງໂສກ
trail	v. dtit dtam ຕິດຕາມ
	n. hoy ຮອຍ
train	v. feu:k aap ຝຶກແອບ
	n. lo:t fay: ລົດໄຟ
trainer	n. pu feu:k aap ຜູ້ຝຶກແອບ
trait	(general) n. u:p bpa: ni: say: ອຸປນິໄສ
	(bad) n. sa:n dan ສັນດານ
tramp	n. ko:n pa: ne chohn คิมພະເນຈอน
	v. nya:m ย่ำ

tranquil	n. kwam mi:t mi ความมิดมิ่
transaction	n. gan dti:t dtoh gain ການຕິດຕໍ່ກັນ
transcribe	v. gay ow: dtam sa: ba:p dto:n ถ่ายเอาตามสะบับถิม
transfer	(things) v. on ໂอน
	(person) v. nyay ຍ້າย
	(ticket) n. bay: bpian lo:t me ใบปฺ่ฌนลิถเม
transform	v. bpian sa: pap ปฺ่ฌนสะ พาย
transfusion	n. tay leuat ຖ່າຍເລືอด
transistor	n. wa:t tu say: taan loht wi:t ta: nyu: อัดถุใจแทม ທຼງถุอิทะยุ
transit	(survey) n. gohng sohng tang ก้วงส่วงทาง
	(crossing) n. gan dern pan ການເດີນผ่าม
translate	v. bpaa ແປ
translator	n. pu bpaa ຜູ້ແປ
transmit	v. so:ng bpay: ສ່งไป
transmitter	n. keuang so:ng wi:t ta: nyu: ເคื่องส่งอิทะยุ
transparent	adj. sohng soht ส่องຊอด
transport	n. gan ko:n so:ng ການຂົนส่ง
	v. ko:n so:ng ຂົนส่ง
trap	n. haaw ແຮວ
	v. da:k cha:p ถักจับ

trapeze	n. huy si liam dan boh	treaty	n. so:n ti: sa:n nya
	tow: ga:n ຮູບສີ່ຫຼ່ຽມດ້ານ		ສົນຕິສັນຍາ
	ບໍ່ເທົ່າກັນ	tree	n. dto:n may: ຕົ້ນໄມ້
trapeze artist	n. na:k hoy hon ນັກ		v. lay: keun dto:n may:
	ຫ້ອຍໂຕນ		ໄລຂຶ້ນຕົ້ນໄມ້
trashman	n. ko:n ge:p ki nyeua	tremble	v. sa:n sa: teuan ສັ່ນ
	ຄົນເກັບຂີ້ເຫຍື່ອ		ສະເທືອນ
travel	v. dern tang ເດີນທາງ	tremendous	adj. nyay: leua ger:n
travels	n. gan dern tang		ໃຫຍ່ເຫຼືອເກີນ
	ການເດີນທາງ	trench	n. ku:m li ser:k ຂຸມລີ້
traveller	n. ko:n dern tang		ເສີກ
	ຄົນເດີນທາງ	trend	n. kwam bpe:n bpay:
travelling	n. gan dern tang		ຄວາມເປັນໄປ
	ການເດີນທາງ	trespass	v.t. luang la:m ket daan
tray	n. pa tat ພາຖາດ		ລ່ວງລ້ຳເຂດແດນ
treachery	n. gan toh la: nyo:t	trial	n. gan sohp, ka: di san
	ການທໍຣະຍົດ		ການສອບ, ຄະດີສານ
tread	v. yiap ຢຽບ	triangle	n. huy sam liam ຮູບສາມ
	(tank) n. dtin koh: ຕີນເກາະ		ຫຼ່ຽມ
treason	n. ga: bo:t dtoh sat	tribe	n. low: pow: ເຜົ່າ, ເຜົ່າ
	ກະບົດຕໍ່ຊາດ	tributary	n. sa ka kohng maa
treasure	n. sa:p so:m ba:t ຊັບສົມບັດ		na:m ສາຂາຂອງແມ່ນ້ຳ
	v. tohn hom so:m ba:t way:	tribute	(tax) n. suay sa a' gohn
	ທ້ອນໂຮມສົມບັດໄວ້		ສ່ວຍສ່າອາກອນ
treasury	n. ka:ng nger:n ຄັງເງິນ		(respect) v. ta: wuay
treat	(doctor) v. ha:k sa		ba:ng ko:m ຖວາຍບັງຄົມ
	ຮັກສາ		(offering) n. keuang ba:n
	(gift) v. liang ລ້ຽງ		na gan ເຄື່ອງບັນນາການ
	n. si:ng ti liang ສິ່ງທີ່	trick	(magic) n. u: bay ອຸບາຍ
	ລ້ຽງ		

	(cheat) n. gan lohk luang ການຫຼອກລວງ
	v. lohk ow: ຫຼອກເອົາ
trickle	v. yoht loing bpa:p bpa:p ຢົດຫຼິ່ງບັບໆ
tricycle	n. loit sam loh ຣົດສາມລໍ້
trigger	n. gay: bpeun ໄກປືນ v. dta:ing dto:n ຕັ້ງຕົ້ນ
trifle	n. kohng noy noy ຂອງນ້ອຍໆ
trim	v. dta:t kohp ohk ຕັດຂອບ ອອກ
trip	v. goh: ka ເກາະຂາ n. gan dern tang bpay: ການເດີນທາງໄປ
triple	adj. sam tow: ສາມເທົ່າ
triumph	n. say: sa: na: ໄຊຊະນະ v. day: la:p say: sa: na: ໄດ້ຮັບໄຊຊະນະ
trivial	adj. le:k le:k noy noy ເລັກໆນ້ອຍໆ
trombone	n. gaa deu:ng kow: deu:ng ohk ແກເດິງເຂົ້າດິງອອກ
troop	n. mu ka: na: ພວກຄະນະ v. nyang ope:n mu ຍ່າງ ເປັນໝູ່
trophy	n. lang wa:n say: sa: na: ຣາງວັນໄຊຊະນະ
tropical	adj. giaw ga:p ket hohn ກ່ຽວກັບເຂດຮ້ອນ

tropics	n. ket hohn ເຂດຮ້ອນ
trot	v. laan sa:m ແລ່ນບູ່າ
trouble	n. kwam deuat hohn ຄວາມເດືອດຮ້ອນ v. lo:p guan ຣົບກວນ
trousers	n. so:ng ka nyow ສົ້ງ ຂາຍາວ
trout	n. opa na:m cheut sa: ni:t neu:ng ປານ້ຳຈືດຊະນິດໜຶ່ງ
trowel	n. meu bpa: tay ມີປະທາຍ
truce	n. gan pa:k lo:p ການຜັກລົບ
truck	n. loit ba:n teu:k ຣົດບັນທຸກ v. ko:n ຂົນ
trudge	v. nyang bpay: duay kwam meuay ຍ່າງໄປດ້ວຍຄວາມເມື່ອຍ
true	adj. taa ແທ້
trumpet	n. gaa ແກ (elephant) v. paat siang ແຜດສຽງ (ເຮິ່ມຊ້າງ)
trunk	(elephant) n. nguang sang ງວງຊ້າງ (tree) n. la:m dto:n ລຳຕົ້ນ (suitcase) n. hip nyay: ຫີບໃຫຍ່
trunks	n. so:ng ka sa:n ສົ້ງຂາສັ້ນ
trust	v. seua chay: ເຊື່ອໃຈ n. kwam way: wang chay: ຄວາມໄວ້ວາງໃຈ

trustworthy	adj. so:m kuan way: wang chay: ສົມຄວນໄວ້ວາງໃຈ
truth	n. kwam chi:ng ຄວາມຈິງ
truthfully	adv. yang chi:ng cha:ng ຢ່າງຈິງຈັງ
try	n. gan to:t lohng ການທົດລອງ
	(patience) v. lohng chay: ລອງໃຈ
	(attempt) v. pa nya nyam ພະຍາຍາມ
	(experiment) v. to:t ທົດ lohng ລອງ
	(investigate) v. dtay: suan ໄຕ່ສວນ
try on	lohng keuang nu:ng gohn cha: seu ລອງເຄື່ອງນຸ່ງກ່ອນຈະຊື້
tub	n. ang nyay: ອ່າງໃຫຍ່
tube	(radio) n. loht ຫຼອດ
	(hose) n. toh ທໍ
tuberculosis	n. lok bpoht haeng ໂຮກປອດແຫ້ງ
tuck	(put in) v. nya:t kow: ຍັດເຂົ້າ
	(fold up) v. pa:p keun ພັບຂຶ້ນ
Tuesday	n. wa:n a:ng kan ວັນອັງຄານ
tuft	(bunch) n. puang ພວງ
	(clump) n. chu:k ຈຸກ
tug	n. gan deu:ng ການດຶງ
	v. deu:ng ດຶງ
tumble	v. dti la:ng ga ຕີລັງກາ
tumult	n. siang eu:k ga: teu:k ສຽງອຶກກະທຶກ
tune	n. ta:m nohng peng ທຳນອງເພງ [ພງ]
	(radio) v. bi:t ha sa: ta ni ບິດຫາສະຖານິ
	(instrument) v. bpa:p siang ປັບສຽງ
tunnel	n. u: mong ອຸໂມງ
	v. choh: bpe:n u: mong ເຈາະເປັນອຸໂມງ
turf	n. der:n nya ເດີ່ນຫຍ້າ
turkey	n. gay: nguang ໄກ່ງວງ
turn	(direction) n. gan liaw ການລ້ຽວ
	(chance) n. pian ຜ່ຽນ
	v. liaw ລ້ຽວ
turn back	adv. ga:p ma ກັບມາ
turn down	(refuse) bpa: dti: set ປະຕິເສດ
	(reduce the volume) adv. bi:t lohng ບິດຄ່ອງ
turn in	(go to bed) adv. bpay: nohn ໄປນອນ
	(submit) adv. nyeun hay: ຍື່ນໃຫ້
turn off	v. moht ມອດ
turn on	v. bpert ເປີດ

turn out	(result) adv. mi^3 po^{4}n
	ມີຜົນ
	(appear) bpa go:t^3 keun^6
	ປະກົດຂຶ້ນ
	(manufacture) he:t^2 o^{6}k
	kay^4 ເຮັດອອກຂາຍ
turn over	kam lo:ng^6 ຂຳລົງ
turn to	v. uay^2 ha^4 ຊວຍຫາ
turnip	n. hua^4 pa:k^3 gat^6
	ຫົວຜັກກາດ
turret	n. bpohm^5 nyam ປ້ອມຍາມ
turtle	n. dtow^2 ເຕົ່າ
tusk	(elephant) n. nga^3 sang^5
	ງາຊ້າງ
	(boar) n. kaaw^6 ngaa^3 mu^4
	ແຂວແກ້ມ
tutor	n. ku^3 sohn^4 pi:^{2} set^6
	ຄູສອນພິເສດ
	v. sohn^4 pi:^{2} set^6 ສອນພິເສດ
tuxedo	n. su:t^6 pa^3 say^5 gi:n^3 liang^3
	nay:^{3} la dtli^3 sa:^{3} mo sohn^4
	ຊຸດຜູ້ຊາຍກິນລ້ຽງໃນรา
	ຕรีสะโมสอน
TV	n. to^3 la:^{2} pa^{5}p ໂທຣະພາບ
tweed	n. pa^6 ko:n^4 sa:t^6 ผ้าຂົນສัດ
tweezers	n. le:k^3 kim^5 ເຫຼັກຄີມ
twelfth	(12th) adj. ti^2 si:p^3 sohng^4
	ที่สิบสอງ
	(1/12) adj. neu:ng^2 nay:^{3}
	si:^{3}p sohng^4 ໜึ่งในสิบສอງ
twelve	(12) adj. si:^{3}p sohng^4
	ສิບສอງ
twenty	(20) adj. sow^3 ຊາວ
twice	(2x) adv. sohng^4; teua^2
	ສອງເທื่อ
twig	n. gi:ng^2 may^5; noy^5
	ກิ่งໄມ້ນ้อย
twinkle	v. bpe:n^1 saang^4 nyi:^{3}p
	ຍา:ບ ເປັมແສງຫຍິບຍับ
	n. waaw^4 dta^2 ແວວຕา
twilight	(evening) n. nyam^3 sa^4
	nya:n^3 ຍามສาຍัน
	(morning) n. nyam^3 dta:^{3}
	wa:n^3 keun^6 ຍามตะເວັนຂึ้น
twin	adj. fa^4 faat^6 ຝาແຝด
	n. luk^4 fa faat^6 ลูกฝาแฝด
twist	(turn) v. bi:t^3 ບິด
	(dance) n. dte:n^5 la:m^3
	ta: wi:t^2 ເຕ้นລำทะວิด
twitch	v. din^5 ดิ้ม
	n. gan din^5 ການดิ้ม
two	(2) adj. sohng^4 ສอງ (6)
two-seater	n. pa^3 ha:^{3} na:^{2} sohng^3 bohn^3
	na:ng^2 ผาทะมะສອງບ່ອນນั่ງ
two-storey house	n. heuan^3 sohng^4 sa:n^5
	ເຮือนສອງຊั้ม
type	(printing) n. dtua^3 pi:^{3}m
	ตัวพิม
	(sample) n. baap^6 yang^2
	ແບบย่าງ

	(kind) n. sa: ni:t ຊນິດ	ulterior	(come after) adj. ti ma
	v. dti pi:m ຕີພິມ		na:m lang ທີ່ມາພາຍຫຼັງ
typewrite	v. dti cha:k ຕີຈັກ		(motive) adj. ti fa:ng
typewriter	n. cha:k dti pi:m		nyu nay: ທີ່ຊ້ວງຢູ່ໃນ
	ຈັກຕີພິມ	ultimate	(final) adj. su:t tay
typhoid	n. kay: say:		ສຸດທ້າຍ
	ໄຂ້ໃສ່		(highest) adj. ka:n su:t
typhoon	n. lo:m pa nyu: nyay:		nyoht ຂັ້ນສຸດຍອດ
	nay: ta: le ລົມພາຍໃຫຍ່ໃນ	umbrella	n. ka:n ho:m ຄັນຮົ່ມ
	ທະເລ	umpire	(committee) ga:m ma: gan
typical	adj. dtua yang ຕົວຢ່າງ		ກັມມະການ
typify	v. he:t bpe:n dtua yang		(referee) n. pu dta:t
	ເຮັດເປັນຕົວຢ່າງ		si:n ຜູ້ຕັດສິນ
typist	n. ko:n dti cha:k ຄົນຕີ		v. dta:t si:n ຕັດສິນ
	ຈັກ	un-	(changes meaning of
tyrannize	v. bpo:k kohng yang go:t		adjectives to their
	ki ko:m heng ປົກຄອງຢ່າງກົດຂີ່ຂົ່ມ		opposite) bpian ku:n sa:p
	ເຫງ		hay: bpe:n ka:m going ga:n
tyrant	n. pu bpo:k kohng yang		kam ປ່ງນຄຸມໄຊຍໃຫ້ເປັນຄຳກົງກັນ
	say: a:m nat ຜູ້ປົກຄອງຢ່າງໃຊ້		ຂ້າມ
	ອຳນາດ	unable	adj. boh sa mat ບໍ່ສາມາດ
		unanimous	adj. po:m chay: ga:n
	# U		bpe:n ek ga: sa:n ພ້ອມໃຈ
udder	n. dtow: no:m sa:t		ກັນເປັນເອກກະສັນ
	ເຕົ້ານົມສັດ	unbelievable	adj. boh bpe:n dta seua
ugly	n. bpe:n dta ki diat		ບໍ່ເປັນຕາເຊື່ອ
	ເປັນຕາຂີ້ດຽດ	unbutton	v. gaa ga: du:m ohk
ulcer	n. fi ຝີ		ແກ້ກະດຸມອອກ
ulcerate	v. gay bpe:n fi	uncle	(maternal and younger) n.
	ກາຍເປັນຝີ		na bow ນ້າບ່າວ

(older) n. luːng³ ລຸງ	undertake (start work) v. loːng³ meu³ heːt³ ລົງມືເຮັດ
(paternal and younger) n. ow¹ ອາວ	(responsibility) laːp³ pa laː² ຮັບພາລະ
uncomfortable adj. huːn⁴ huay⁴ ขมมอาย	underwear n. seua⁶ leu⁴ soːng⁶ sohn⁵ ເສື້ອຫລືຂ້ອງຊ້ອນ
adj. boh² saː³ bay¹ ບໍ່ສະບາຍ	
under (underneath) prep. yu² luːm² ຢູ່ລຸ່ມ	underweight adj. naːm³ naːk³ boh² poh⁵ ນ້ຳໜັກບໍ່ພໍ
(less) prep. noy² gua² ໜ້ອຍກວ່າ	underworld (hell) n. na loːk⁶ naɾok² ນະໂລກນາຮົກ
underbrush n. fuːm² may⁵ ປຸ່ມໄມ້	(crime) n. saː³ ma koːm⁶ aːn¹ taː² pan³ ສະມາຄົມອິ່ມຕະ
undergo v. day³ paɲ³ kwam laːm³ bak⁶ chak... ໄດ້ผ่ามความລำบາກจาก...	ພາມ
underground (beneath) adj. dtay³ diːn⁵ ใต้ดิม	undo (untie) v. gaa⁴ ohk⁶ ແກ້ອອກ
(secret) adj. laːp⁵ lap⁴ ลับ	(destroy) v. taːm³ lay³ ທຳລາຍ
n. hohng⁶ dtay⁵ diːn⁵ ຫ້ອງໃຕ້ດິນ	undress v. gaa⁵ seua⁶ ແກ້ເສື້ອ
(rebels) n. kaː² naː² paː² dti paːk³ ຄມະปะທຶปัก	undulate (water) v. lay⁴ bpeːn¹ keun² ໄກ¢ปัมคูม
underline (draw) v. kit⁶ seːn⁶ gohng⁵ ຂີດເສັ້ນໂຄງ	(motion) v. mi³ li³ la³ ohn¹ soy⁵ ມີລິລາອອນຊ້ອຍ
(emphasize) neːn⁵ ເໜັ້ນ	unfair adj. boh² nyuːt² dti² taːm³ ບຍຶ່ຫຳ
underneath prep. gohng⁵, luːm² ກ້ອງ, ລຸ່ມ	unforeseen adj. boh² kat² luang⁵ na⁶ ບຄາຕລ່ວງໜ້า
understand v. kow⁶ chay¹ ເຂົ້າ ໃจ	unfortunate adj. sok⁵ boh² di² ໂຊກບໍດີ
understanding n. kwam³ kow⁶ chay¹ ຄວາມເຂົ້າใจ	unfurnished adj. ti² boh² mi² keuang³ heuan³ ທີ່ບໍ່ມີເຄື່ອງເຮືອນ
adj. heːn⁴ oːk³ heːn⁴ chay⁴ ເຫັນອົກເຫັນໃจ	ungrateful adj. boh² hu² buːn² kuːn⁵ ບຊຍນຄົມ
	unhappy adj. boh² mi² kwam³ suːk³ ບໍ່ຄວາມสุก

uniform	adj. bpe:n a:n diaw ga:n
	ເປັນອັນດຽວກັນກົດ
	n. keuang baap ເຄື່ອງແບບ
unify	v. tohn hom kow: ga:n
	ທ້ອມໂຮມເຂົ້າກັນ
union	(connection) n. gan hom
	ga:m ການໂຮມກັນ
	(Soviet) n. sa: ha: pap
	ສະຫະພາບ
	(organization) n. sa:
	ma ko:m ສະມາຄົມ
unique	(only one) adj. a:n diaw
	ອັນດຽວ
	(different) adj. boh mi
	a:n meuan ບໍ່ມີເໝືອນ
	(superior) adj. boh mi
	a:n bpiap ບໍ່ມີປຽບ
unite	v. huam kow: ga:n ຮ່ວມ
	ເຂົ້າກັນ
United States of America	n. sa: ha:
	lait a: me li: ga ສະຫະຣັດ
	ອະເມຣິກາ
United Kingdom	n. sa: ha: lat sa: a na
	cha:k a:ng gi:t ສະຫະຣາຊອາ
	ນາຈັກອັງກິດ
universal	adj. tua lok ທົ່ວໂລກ
universe	n. cha:k ga: wan ຈັກກະວານ
university	n. ma: ha wi:t ta: nya
	lay: ມະຫາວິທະຍາໄລ
unkind	(cruel) adj. hot hay ໂຫດຮ້າຍ
	(impolite) adj. boh su:
	pap ບໍ່ສຸພາບ
unknown	adj. ti boh mi pay: hu:
	cha:k ບໍ່ໄຜ່ຮູ້ຈັກ
unless	prep. nyo:k we:n ຍົກເວັ້ນ
	conj. nohk chak wa
	ນອກຈາກວ່າ
unload	v. ko:n lo:ng ຂົນລົງ
unlock	v. kay: ga: chaa ໄຂ
	ກະແຈ
unlucky	adj. boh mi sok ບໍ່ມີໂຊກ
unnatural	(not natural) adj. pi:t
	ta:m na: sat ຜິດທັມະຊາດ
	(not usual) adj. pi:t
	ta:m ma: da ຜິດທັມະດາ
unpleasant	adj. boh bpe:n ti poh
	chay: ບໍ່ເປັນທີ່ພໍໃຈ
unpopular	adj. ti boh mi pay: ni:
	nyo:m ທີ່ບໍ່ໄຜ່ນິຍົມ
unprecedented	adj. boh kery mi ບໍ່ເຄີຍມີ
unreal	adj. boh maan taa ບໍ່ແມ່ນ
	ແທ້
unrealistic	adv. fay: fa:n ໄຝ່ຝັນ
unusual	adv. bpaak bpa: lat ແປກ
	ປລາດ
up	prep. te:ring ເທິງ
up-to-date	tain sa: may: ທັນສມັຍ
up to someone	bpe:n na ti kohng....
	ເປັນໜ້າທີ່ຂອງ....
up to the minute	tain sa: may: ທັນສມັຍ

uphold v. sa: na:p sǎ: nǔːn ສະໜັບສະໜຸນ	**upward** adj. sǔːng keun bpay: ສູງຂຶ້ນໄປ
upon prep. meua ເມືອ	adv. bpay: tang terng ໄປທາງເຕີງ
upper adj. kaːn sung ຂັນສູງ	**urban** adj. haàng gaːm paang ແຫງກາມປາງ
upperclassman n. naːk seuːk sa ɔɔi tiː saw leu sǐ ນັກສຶກສາຊະຫຼານກຸສ	meuàng ເມືອງກຳແພງເມືອງ
upright (position) adj. yeun goːing ຢືນກົງ	**urge** (excite) v. ka: nya:n ka: nyɔh ຂະໜ່ຍຂໍໜ່ຍ
(honest) adj. seu sa:t ຊື່ສັດ	(encourage) v. hay: gaːm laːng chay: ໃຫ້ມາໃຈງໃຈ
uprising (organization) n. gan gaː: boːt ການກະບົດ	n. kwam dtohng gan kohng a loːm ຄວາມຕ້ອງການຂອງ ອາຣົມ
(action) n. gan chaː: la choːin ການຈາຣະຈິມ	**urgency** n. gnn duan ການດ່ວນ
uproot (plant) v. tohn hak ຖອນຮາກ ຮາກ	**urgent** adj. duan, gaː: taːn haːn ດ່ວນ, ກະທັນທັນ
(person) v. nyay ban ຍ້າຍ ບ້ານ	**urinal** n. tohn saːm laːp bpaːt sa: waː: ຍອນສາຫ້ຍປຜ້ວະ
upset adj. a loːm sia ຈາຣົມເສັງ	**urinate** (polite) v. bpay: suam ໄປຍ້ອມ
(person) v. heːt hay: a loːm sia ເຮັດໃຫ້ອາຣົມເສັງ	(oblique) v. taːy bow: ຖ່າຍເບົ້າ
(things) v. loːm loːing ລົ້ມລົງ	(familiar) v. nyiaw ຫ່ຍວ
(plans) loːm lew ລົ້ມເຫຼວ	**urine** (polite) n. naːm bpaːt sa: waː: ນ້ຳປຍສ້ວະ
upside down (inverted) luang bpiːn ຄວງປົ້ມ	(familiar) n. naːm nyiaw ນ້ຳຫ່ຍວ
(disarranged) boh bpeːn la: biap ບໍເປັນຣະບຽບ	**urn** n. ang ອ່າງ
upstairs adh. yu teriːng ຍໍເຕິງ	**usage** n. gan saːy: ການໃຊ້
uptown adv. tang neua meuàng ທາງເໜືອເມືອງ	

use	(function) n. bpa: nyot ปะโยก
	v. say: ใช้
use up	adv. say: cho:n mo:t ใช้จົນໝົດ
used to	adv. kery เคีย
useful	adj. bpe:n bpa: nyot เป็นปะโยก
usefulness	n. gan mi bpa: nyot ການมีปะโยก
useless	adj. boh mi bpa: nyot ບໍ່มีปะโยก
usher	v. pu si bohn na:ng hay: ผู้ຊอมมาใຫ
usual	adj. ta:m ma: da ທำมะถา
usually	(as usual) adv. dtam kery ตามเคีย
	(natural) adv. dtam ta:m ma: da ตามທำมะถา
	(regularly) adv. dtam bpo:k ga: dti: ตามปิກກะถิ
utensil	n. keuang say: soy nay: kua เคื่อງใช้ສอยໃນคົว
utter	v. wow: ohk ma เว้าອອกມา
utmost	adj. suit ga:m la:ng สุถกำลัງ
utility	n. bpa: nyot ปะโยก
utilize	v. say: hay: bpe:n bpa: nyot ใช้ใຫ้เป็ນปะโยก
uvula	n. lin gay: (kohng ko:n) ลิ้นไก่(ຂອງคົม)

unripe	adj. di:p ถิบ
untie	v. gaa ohk แກ້ອອก
until	conj. cho:n teri:ng จົນເຖิง
unto	prep. dtoh ถໍ

V

vacancy	(position) n. dta:m naang wang ถำแໜ່ງอ่าງ
vacant	(empty) adj. bpow: wang เປ່ົาໜ່าງ
	(available) adj. wang อ่าງ
vacate	v. he:t hay: bpow: เຮັດใຫ້เป่า
vacation	n. nyam pa:k ยามພัก
vaccinate	v. sa:k ya bpohng ga:n pa: nyat ສักยาป่อງກັนພะยาถ
vaccination	n. gan sa:k ya bpohng ga pa: nyat ການສักยาป่อງກັนພะ ยາถ
vaccine	n. ya sa:m la:p sa:k bpohng ga:n pa: nyat ยาสำลัບສักປ่อງກັนພะ ยາถ
vaccuum	n. kwam wang bpow: คอามอ่าງเป่ົา
vacuum cleaner	n. keuang dut ki fu:n เคื่อງถูถຂີ້ຝຸ່ນ

agabond	adj. ko:n pa: ne chohn คົນພະເนจอน
ague	adj. boh chaam chaang ບໍ່ແຈ່ມແຈ້ງ
ain	(conceited) adj. uat o:ng ອວດອ່ງ (worthless) adj. boh mi bpa: nyot ບໍ່ມີປະໂຍດ
aliant	adj. ga han ກ້າຫານ
alid	(reasonable) adj. mi het po:n ມີເหตุผົນ (legal) adj. teuk dtohng dtam go:t may ถึกต้องตามກົດ ໝาย
alise	n. ga: bpow hiw ກະເປົ໋າหิ้ວ
alley	n. mohm pu ຮ່ອມพู
alor	n. kwam ga han ຄວາມກ້າ ຫານ
aluable	(of value) adj. mi ka ມີຄ່າ (expensive) adj. mi la ka paang ມີราຄาແพງ
alue	v. dti la ka ຕีราຄา n. la ka ราຄา
alve	(engine) n. lin sup ลิ้มสุบ (pipe) n. su:p bpa:p สุบยับ
andal	n. puak bpa teuan ta:m lay kohng di ผอกป่าเຖื່ອมทำลาย ຂອງดี

vane	(weather) n. keuang sa:m la:p bering tang dern เคื่ອງ kohng lo:m สำຫรับເບ້ຶๆทางเดิม ຂອງລົม (propeller) bay: pa:t kohng keuang nyo:n tang tang ใบพัด ຂອງเคื່ອງຍົมต่างๆ
vanilla	n. wa: ni la na:m su lo:t laa: gi:n อะมิลานำ ຣูລິຕແລະກิ່ม
vanish	v. hay bpay: หายไป
vanity	n. kwam ta: no:ng dtua ຄວາມທະມົງติว
vanquish	v. bpap hay: mo:t ปาบใຫ້ພິด
vapor	v. ay (na:m) ຮาຍ(ນ້ำ)
vaporize	(to became vapor) v. gay bpe:n ay ภายເປ້ນຮาຍ (to make vapor) v. he:t hay: gert ay ເຮັດใຫ້ເกิดຮาຍ
variable	n. bpian bpaeng day: ປ່ຽมແປ່ງได
variety	(many kinds) n. si:ng dtang dtang ສ່ງต่างๆ (kind) n. sa: ni:t ຊມິด
various	(miscellaneous) adj. dtang dtang ต่างๆ (many) adj. lay ຫລາຍ
varnish	v. ta hay: leuam ทาใຫ້ ເຫ້ือม

n. naːm maːm saːm laːp taˈ
hayː leuam ນ້ຳມັນສຳຫຼັບທາໃຫ້
ເຫຼື້ອນ

vary (differ) v. dtaak dtang
ແຕກຕ່າງ

(change) v. bpian bpaang
ປ່ຽນແປງ

vase n. to sayː doh mayː
ໂຖໃສ່ດອກໄມ້

vassal (slave) n. kaˈ tat ຂ້າທາດ

vast adj. guang nyayː ກ້ວາງໃຫຍ່

vault (cellar) n. hohng dtayː
diːn ຫ້ອງໃຕ້ດິນ

(curved roof) n. peˈ danˈ
goːng ເພດານກົ້ງ

(bank) n. hohng mian
ngeˈrːn ຫ້ອງມ້ຽມເງິນ

v. dteˈn ເຕັ້ນ

veal n. sin ngua noy ຊີ້ນງົວນ້ອຍ

vegetable n. paːk ຜັກ
adj. dayː ma chak paːk
ໄດ້ມາຈາກຜັກ

vehicle n. nyoːn nyan ຍົນຍານ

veil n. pa bpoːk na ຜ້າປົກໜ້າ

(cover) v. bpoːk ປົກ

(hide) v. baːng ບັງ

vein (blood vessel) n. seˈn
leuat daːm ເສັ້ນເລືອດດຳ

(leaves) n. seˈn bayː mayː
ເສັ້ນໃບໄມ້

(mineral) n. tan tat haa
nayː diːn ຖ່ານທາດແຮ່ໃນດິນ

(mood) n. aˈ loːm ອາລົມ

velvet n. gaːm maˈ nyiˈ ກຳມະຍີ່
adj. ohn keu gaːm maˈ
nyiˈ ອ່ອນຄືກຳມະຍີ່

venerable adj. bpeːn dta naːp teu
ເປັນຕານັບຖື

venerate v. naːp teu ນັບຖື

veneration n. gan naːp teu ການນັບຖື
ການມັຍຍຕິ

vengeance n. gan gaa kaan
ການແກ້ແຄ້ນ

venom n. piˈt ພິດ

venomous (snake) adj. mi piˈt ມີພິດ

(plants) adj. beua ເບຶອ

(speech) adj. bpeːn piˈt
ເປັນພິດ

ventilate v. tay aˈ gat ຖ່າຍອາກາດ

ventilator n. paːt loːm ພັດລົມ

venture n. gan paː choːn pay
ການຜະຈົນໄພ

v. siang ສ່ຽງ

veranda n. laˈ biang ລະບຽງ

verb n. kaːm giˈ liˈ nya
ຄຳກິຣິຍາ

verdict n. kaːm dtaːt siˈn
ຄຳຕັດສິນ

verge n. kohp ຂອບ
v. gayˈ chaˈ ໃກ້ຈະ

verification	n. gan guat sohp ການກວດສອບ
verify	v. guat sohp ກວດສອບ
verse	v. bo:t gohn ບົດກອນ
version	(translation) n. bo:t bpaa ບົດແປ (viewpoint) n. kwam he:n ຄວາມເຫັນ (variation) n. gan da:t bpaang ການດັດແປງ
vertical	adj. bpe:n se:n dta:ng ເປັນເສັ້ນຕັ້ງ
very	(many) adj. lay ຫຼາຍ (indeed) adj. taa ແທ້
vessel	(dish) n. tuay sam ຖ້ວຍຈານ (blood) n. se:n leuat ເສັ້ນ ເລືອດ (ship) n. heua ເຮືອ
vest	n. seua sohn nay: ເສື້ອຊ້ອນໃນ v. mohp si:t hay: ມອບ (ສິດໃຫ້)
veteran	(from war) n. ta: han pan ser:k ທະຫານຜ່ານເສິກ (ex-soldier) n. ta: han gow: ທະຫານເກົ່າ adj. sa:m nan ຊຳນານ
veterinarian	n. sa:t dta: wa: paat ສັດຕະແພດ
veterinary	adj. giaw ga:p gan ha:k sa sa:t ກ່ຽວກັບການຮັກສາສັດ

	n. sa:t dta: wa: paat ສັດຕະແພດ
veto	(reject) v. ka:t kan ຂັດຄ້ານ (forbid) v. ham ຫ້າມ
vex	(annoy) v. lo:p guan ຣົບກວນ (puzzle) v. he:t hay: nyu:ng ເຮັດໃຫ້ຫຍຸ້ງ
via	prep. doy pan ໂດຍຜ່ານ
vibrant	(lively) adj.mi si wi:t si wa ມີຊີວິດຊີວາ (vigorous) adj. kaang ka:n ແຂງກ້ານ
vibrate	v. sa: teuan ສະເທືອນ
vibration	n. gan sa: teuan ການສະ ເທືອນ
vice	(crime) n. gan ga: ta:m pi:t ການກະທຳຜິດ (habit) n. kwam bpa: peu:t sua ຄວາມປະພຶດຊົ່ວ adj. lohng ຣອງ
vicinity	n. boh li: wen gay: kiang ບໍຣິເວນໃກ້ຄຽງ
vicious	(person) adj. ta lu:n ທາລຸນ (animal) adj. hot hiam ໂຫດຮ້າມ
victim	n. pu la:p koh: ຜູ້ຮັບເຄາະ
victor	n. pu mi say: sa: na: ຜູ້ມີໄຊຍະມະ

victory	n. say: sa: na: ໄຊຊນະ	vineyard	n. suan mak laa saang
Vietnamese	(slang) adj. gaäw ແກວ		ສວນໝາກລະແຣແຣງ
	(polite) adj. koïn wiat nắm ຄົນຫຼວດນາມ	violate	(not respect) v. la: mert ຣະເມີດ
view	(object of sight) n. bohn ti liaw heïn ບ່ອນທີ່ຫຼຽວເຫັນ		(to ruin) v. ta:m lay ທຳຮ້າຍ
	(scene) n. tiːw taːt ຫົວ ຫັດ	violence	n. kwam huïn haang ຄວາມຮຸນແຣງ
	(opinion) n. kwam heïn ຄວາມເຫັນ	violent	adj. huïn haang ຮຸນແຣງ
	v. bering ເບິ່ງ	violet	adj. si muang ສີມ່ວງ n. dohk may: si muang sa: n neuïng ດອກໄມ້ສີມ່ວງຊະນີດໜຶ່ງ
viewpoint	n. ngaa kwam ki:t ແງ່ ຄວາມຄິດ	violin	n. soh flaïng ຊໍຝຣັ່ງ n. naːk si soh flaïng ນັກຊີຊໍຝຣັ່ງ
vigil	(watch) n. gan nyam ການ der:k ຍາມເດີກ	virgin	adj. boh liː suːt ບໍລິສຸດ n. sow poːm maː cha li ສາວພົມມະຈາຣິ
	(without sleep) n. gan oːt nohn ການອົດນອນ	virtual	(real) adj. taa chiːng ເເມ່ຈິງ
	(alert) n. gan la: waïng ການຣະວັງແວງເບິ່ງ		(equivalent) adj. tow: ga:p wa ເທົ່າກັບວ່າ
vigor	(vigor) n. kwam kaäng haang ຄວາມເຂັ້ມແຣງ	virtue	n. kuïn ngam kwam di ຄຸນງາມຄວາມດີ
vile	(wicked) adj. sua sa ຊົ່ວຊ້າ	visa	n. gan dti ga a: nu: nyad ha kow: bpa: tet ການຕິການະນຸຍາດໃຫ້ເຂົາປະເທດ
	(smelly) adj. meːn lay ເໝັນຫຼາຍ		
village	n. muːban ໝູ່ບ້ານ	vise	n. bpak leːk saːm laːp kắp, maä haang
villain	n. pu hay ຜູ້ຮ້າຍ		ປາກເຫຼັກສ້ຳເຂັບຄາບ, ເເໝຮັງ
vine	n. keua (may:) ເຄືອ (ໄມ້)	visible	adj. ti sohng keïn day: ທີ່ສ່ອງເຫັນໄດ້
vinegar	n. naːm soːm ນ້ຳສົ້ມ		

vision	(opinion) n. naaw³ kwam³ keu:t² ແນວຄວາມຄິດເຫັນ
	(dream) n. kwam³ fan⁴ ຄວາມ ຝັນ
	(eyesight) n. say⁴ d̄ta ສາຍຕາ
visit	n. gan¹ yiam⁵ yam¹ ການຢ້ຽມຢາມ
	v. yam¹ ຢາມ
visitor	(guest) n. kaak⁶ ban⁵ ແຂກບ້ານ
	(tourist) n. pu⁶ ma³ yam ຜູ້ມາຢາມ
visualize	v. hay⁶ he:n⁴, keu:t² pen¹ hup⁵ keun³ nay: chay: ໃຫ້ເຫັນ, ຄິດເປັນຮູບຂຶ້ນໃນໃຈ
vital	(concerning) adj. ti² giaw² gap³ si³ wi:t² ທີ່ກ່ຽວກັບຊີວິດ
	(necessary) adj. cha:m¹ bpe:n¹ ຈຳເປັນ
vitamin	n. ya¹ wi:² d̄ta mi³n ຢາວິຕາມິນ
vivid	adj. chaam² say:⁴ ແຈ່ມໃສ
vocabulary	n. ka:m³ sa:p³ ຄຳສັບ
vocal	(spoken) adj. giaw² gap³ siang⁴ chak⁶ hu⁵ koh³ ກ່ຽວກັບ ສຽງຈາກຮູຄໍ
	(talkative) adj. bpe:n¹ ko:n³ wow⁵: du:² ເປັນຄົນເວົ້າດຸ
vocation	n. a¹ sip⁵ ອາຊີບ
voice	n. siang⁴ chak⁶ hu⁵ koh³ ສຽງຈາກ ຮູຄໍ
	v. ohk⁶ siang⁴ ອອກສຽງ
void	adj. bpow:² wang² ເປົ່າວ່າງ
	v. leu:p² lang⁵ ລົບລ້າງ
volcano	n. pu³ kow⁴: fay:³ ພູເຂົາໄຟ
volleyball	n. wohn³ le³ ban³ ໂວນເລບານ
volt	n. nuay² haang³ fay:³ fa⁵ ຫົວຍແຮງໄຟຟ້າ
voltmeter	n. keuang² taak⁵ haang³ fay:³ fa⁵ ເຄື່ອງແທກແຮງໄຟຟ້າ
volume	n. boh¹ li:² mat⁵ ປໍລິມາດ
	(magazine) n. sa:¹ bap⁵ ສະບັບ
	(books) n. hua⁴ tho³ ຫົວ ທໍ
	(amount) n. cha:m¹ nuan² ຈຳນວນ
voluntary	adj. sa:¹ ma:k³ chay:² ສັມກ ໃຈ
volunteer	n. pu⁶ a¹ sa⁴ sa:³ ma:k² ຜູ້ອາສາສມັກ
	v. sa:³ ma:k² ສມັກ
vomit	v. hak⁵ ຮາກ
	n. hak⁵ ຮາກ
vote	v. lo:ng³ ka:² naan² siang⁴ ລົງຄະແນນສຽງ
	n. gan¹ ohk⁶ siang⁴ lo:ng³ ka:² naan² ການອອກສຽງລົງຄະແນນ
voter	n. pu⁶ lo:ng³ ka:² naan² siang⁴ ຜູ້ລົງຄະແນນສຽງ
vow	v. sa⁴ ban¹ ສາບານ
	n. ka:m³ sa⁴ ban¹ ຄຳສາບານ
vowel	n. sa:³ la:² ສຣະ

voyage	n. gan dern tang ການເດີນ ທາງເດີນທາງ	waist	n. aaw ແອວ
	v. dern tang ເດີນທາງ	wait	(stop a while) v. ta ຖ້າ
vulgar	(common) adj. tua tua bpay: ທົ່ວໆໄປ		v. koy ta ຄອຍຖ້າ
			(serve) v. kohy la:p say: ຄອຍຮັບໃຊ້
	(profane) adj. nyap kay ຫຍາບຄາຍ	wait on	kohy la:p say: ຄອຍຮັບໃຊ້
vulture	n. haang ແຮ້ງ	waiter	n. pu sya la:p say: nay: han a han ຜູ້ຊາຍຮັບໃຊ້ໃນ ຮ້ານອາຫານ

W

waddle	v. nyang keu bpe:t ຍ່າງຄືເປັດ		(Eng.) n. boy ບອຍ
wade	v. lu:y na:m ລຸຍນ້ຳ		(headwaiter) n. hua na boy ຫົວໜ້າບອຍ
wag	(sway) v. gwaang gway: ແກວ່ງກວາຍ	waitress	n. pu nyi:ng la:p say: nay: han a han ຜູ້ຍິງຮັບໃຊ້ໃນຮ້ານອາຫານ
	(shake) v. ga: di:k ກະດິກ		
wage	v. da:m nern ດຳເນີນ	wake	(somebody else) v. bpu:k ປຸກ
	n. ka chang ຄ່າຈ້າງ		(yourself) v. dteun ຕື່ນ
wager	n. ka pa: na:n ga:n ຄ່າພະນັນກ້ານ		n. ngan so:p gang keun ງານສົບກາງຄືນ
	v. pa: na:n pa:n ພະນັນ	walk	(stroll) n. gan nyang li:n ການຍ່າງຫຼິ້ນ
wagon	n. lo:t si dtin say: ba:n tu:k kohng ລົດຕີນຊື່ ຕິມໃຊ້ບັນທຸກເຄື່ອງ		(footpath) n. tang tiaw ທາງທຽວ
			v. nyang ຍ່າງ
wail	(howl) v. hohng kang ຮ້ອງຄາງ	wall	(inside) n. fa ຝາ
			(outside) n. ga:m paang ກຳແພງ
	(moan) v. kang kang ຄາງຄາງ		v. heit fa ເຮັດຝາ
	(complain) v. ha:m hay: ຮ່ຳໄຮ	wallet	(money) n. ga: bpow: ngern ກະເປົາເງິນ

	(travel) n. gä: bpow: hiw กะเปาทือ
wallow	n. buak kway ขวกควาย
	(in mud) v. gi:ng geuak กิ้งเกือก
	(in water) v. fum na:m ผุ่มมน้ำ
	(in luxury) v. mo:k mu:n พัวมุน
	(degenerate) v. mi sa: pap sua hay มีสะพาบฉัวร้าย
wallpaper	n. chia hum fa เจ้ยหุมฝา
walnut	(nut) n. mak nua พากนัว
	(wood) may: mak nua ไม้พากนัว
wander	v. bpay: yang boh mi chu:t may ไปย่างยังบ่มีจุดพาย
want	(need) v. dtohng gan ต้องการ
	(desire to) v. yak ยาก
	(desire) v. yak day: ยากได้
	n. kwam dtohng gan ความต้องการ
war	v. he:t ser:k so:ng kam เຮັດเสิกสงคาม
	n. ser:k so:ng kam เสิกสงคาม

ward	n. pu yu nay: kwam bpo:k kohng ผู้ຢูในความปิกคอง
warden	(supervisor) n. pu ber:ng nyaang ผู้เบิ่งแยง
	(prison) n. pu a:m nuay gan ku:k ผู้อำนอยการคุก
wardrobe	n. seua pa เสื้อผ้า
ware	(goods) n. si:n ka ສິນค้า
	(utensil) n. keuang say: dtang dtang เคื่องใช้ต่างๆ
warehouse	n. sang mian keuang ສາງมຽมเคื่อง
warfare	n. ser:k so:ng kam เสิกสงคาม
warm	v. u:n keun ฉุ่นຂึ้ม
	(welcome) adj. o:p u:n ฉบฉุ่น
	(temperature) adj. u:n ฉุ่ม
warn	v. dta:k dteuan ตักเตือม
warp	(to bend) n. ngoh ว์
	(to curve) n. go:ng ก็ว
warrant	(court writ) n. may goh: พายเกาะ
	(deserve) v. so:m kuan day: la:p ສົมຄอมได้รับ
	(gurarantee) n. gan la:p bpa: ga:n ການธับปะมัน
warrior	n. na:k lo:p มักຮົบ
warship	n. ga:m bpa:n lo:p กำปั่มธົບ

wash	n. pa ti sa:k ຜ້າຫຸ້ນ
(clothes) v. sa:k ຊັກ	
(things) v. lang ລ້າງ	
(people) v. ap ອາບ	
wash basin	n. ang suay na ອ່າງສ່ວຍຜ້າ
washer	n. wo:ng wáan (sa:m la:p bu lohng) ວົງແຫວນ (ສຳຫຼັບບຸ ລອງ)
washing machine n. cha:k sa:k pa ຈັກຊັກຜ້າ	
Washington, D.C. n. gu/ing woh si/ing dta:n ກຸງວໍຊິງຕັນ	
wasp	n. dto dtoh ໂຕໂຕ້
waste	v. he:t hay: sia ເຮັດໃຫ້ເສັຽ
	n. kohng ti:m ຂອງຖິ້ມ
wastebasket	n. ga: dta ti:m ki nyeua ກະຕ່າຖິ້ມຂີ້ເຫຍື້ອ
watch	(watchman) n. ko:n nyam ຄົນຍາມ
	(wristwatch) n. mong say: kaan ໂມງໃສ່ແຂນ
	v. ber:ng ເບິ່ງ
watch maker	(craftsman) n. sang he:t mong ຊ່າງເຮັດໂມງ
	(repairman) n. sang bpaang mong ຊ່າງແປງໂມງ
watchman	(large area) n. ko:n nyam ຄົນຍາມ
	(specific thing) n. pu fow ຜູ້ເຝົ້າ

water	n. na:m ນ້ຳ
	v. ho:t na:m ຕົດນ້ຳ
water buffalo n. kway ຄວາຍ	
water color	(paint) n. si na:m ສີນ້ຳ
	(picture) n. hup dtaam duay si na:m ຮູບແຕ້ມດ້ວຍ ສີນ້ຳ
waterfall	n. na:m dto:k (dtat) ນ້ຳຕົກ (ຕາດ)
waterfront	n. bohn dtoh na ta na:m ບ່ອນແພຫາມນ້ຳ
watermelon	n. mak mo ໝາກໂມ
waterproof	v. he:t hay: na:m kow: boh day: ເຮັດໃຫ້ນ້ຳເຂົ້າໃຫ້ໄດ້ adj. ti ga:n na:m day: ທີ່ກັນນ້ຳໄດ້
water skiing	n. gan li:n sa: gi na:m ການຫຼິ້ນສະກີນ້ຳ
waterway	n. tang na:m ທາງນ້ຳ
watery	(wet)adj. bpiak ປຽກ
	(soft) adj. ohn keu na:m ອ່ອນຄືນ້ຳ
watt	n. nuay ga:m la:ng fay: fa ໜ່ວຍກຳລັງໄຟຟ້າ
wave	(heat wave) n. we la ti hohn ti su:t ເວລາທີ່ຮ້ອນທີ່ສຸດ
	(radio wave) n. keun wi:t ta: nyu: ຄື້ນວິທະຍຸ

	(wave of water) n. fohng³ na:m⁵ ຟອງນ້ຳ		(things) n. sa:p² so:m⁴ ba:t ຊັບສົມບັດ
	v. bok⁶ meu³ ໂບກມື	wealthy	(from possessions) adj. ha:ng³ ຣັ່ງ
	(sound wave) n. keun² ຄື້ນ		(from work or luck) adj. luay³ ລວຍ
	(light wave) n. ga:³ saa⁴ ກະແສ	weapon	n. a¹ wu:t² dtang² dtang² ອາວຸດຕ່າງໆ
waver	v. sa:n² ສັ່ນ		
	n. gan¹ bpa:³ dti:³ set⁶ ການປະຕິເສດ	wear	n. kwam³ hu:n⁶ hian⁶ ຄວາມຫຸ້ນຫຽນ
wavy	adj. bpe:n keun² ເປັນຄື້ນ		v. nu:ng³ ນຸ່ງ
wax	v. nyay: keun² (se:n deuan bpe:n dto:n) ໃຫຍ່ຂື້ນ (ເຊັ່ນ ເດືອນເປັນຕົ້ນ)	wear away	id. he:t³ hay: hu:n⁶ kow:⁶ ເຮັດໃຫ້ຫຸ້ນເຂົາ
	(candle) n. ki pering⁶ ຂີ້ເຜິ່ງ	wear off	he:t² hay: mi⁶ noy³ lo:ng³ ເຮັດໃຫ້ມີໜ້ອຍລົງ
	(ear) n. ki hu⁴ ຂີ້ຫູ	wear someone out	id. he:t³ hay: meuay² ເຮັດໃຫ້ເມື່ອຍ
way	(way of life) n. wi:² ti³ tant³ ວິທີທາງ	weary	adj. meuay², beua² nay² ເມື່ອຍ, ເບື່ອໜ່າຍ
	(road) n. ho:n⁴ tang³ ຫົນທາງ	weather	v. to:n³ day:⁵ ທົນໄດ້
	(direction) n. tang³ ທາງ		n. a¹ gat⁶ ອາກາດ
wayward	adj. deu⁵ deu:ng¹ ດື້ດຶງ	weave	(cloth) v. dta:m² huk⁶ ຕໍ່າຫູກ
we	pron. mi² how:³, puak⁵ how:³ ພວກເຮົາ, ພວກເຮົາ		n. baap⁶ pa⁶ ແບບຜ່າ
weak	adj. ohn² aa¹ ອ່ອນແອ		(bamboo) n. san⁴ ສານ
weaken	v. he:t² hay: ohn⁶ lo:ng³ ເຮັດໃຫ້ອ່ອນລົງ		(driving) v. ki² lo:t² bpay: ngo³ nge³ ຂີ່ລົດໄປໂງ່ງເງ່
wealth	(condition) n. kwam³ ha:ng³ mi² ຄວາມຮັ່ງມີ	weaver	n. ko:n³ dta:m² huk⁶ ຄົນຕໍ່າຫູກ
		web	n. nyay:³ ໄຍ
		wed	v. dtaang² dohng³ ແຕ່ງດອງ

	(common) v. dtaang $\overset{2}{}$
	ngán แต่ງງາມ $\overset{3}{}$
wedding	n. gan dtaang doìng $\overset{2}{}$
	ภามแต่ງอ9ງ
wedge	n. liːm $\overset{6}{}$ ทุ่ม $\overset{5}{}$
Wednesday	n. waìn puìt อันพุດ $\overset{3}{}$ $\overset{2}{}$
wee	(amount) adj. nǒy diâw $\overset{2}{}$
	น่อยດຽວ
	(size) adj. nǒy nǒy $\overset{5}{}$ $\overset{5}{}$
	น่อຍๆ
weed	(grass) n. nya ti boh mi $\overset{6}{}$ $\overset{2}{}$ $\overset{2}{}$ $\overset{3}{}$
	bpa nyot ຫຍາທີ່ບໍມີປະໂยด $\overset{3}{}$ $\overset{5}{}$
	(cigarette) n. gohk ya ภอกยา $\overset{6}{}$ $\overset{1}{}$
week	n. a tiːt ອาທิด $\overset{1}{}$
weekday	n. waìn heːt saː gan อันເຮັດภาม $\overset{3}{}$ $\overset{2}{}$ $\overset{2}{}$ $\overset{1}{}$
weekend	n. tay saːp bpaː da ท้ายสัปດา $\overset{5}{}$ $\overset{3}{}$ $\overset{3}{}$ $\overset{1}{}$
weekly	adv. tuːk tuːk a tiːt ทุกๆอาທิด $\overset{2}{}$ $\overset{2}{}$ $\overset{1}{}$ $\overset{2}{}$
	n. niːt dtaː nyaː sǎn lay saːp bpaː da มิตยะสาม ลายสัปດา $\overset{3}{}$ $\overset{3}{}$ $\overset{2}{}$ $\overset{4}{}$ $\overset{3}{}$ $\overset{3}{}$ $\overset{3}{}$ $\overset{1}{}$
weep	v. hohng hày ຮ้อງใຫ้ $\overset{5}{}$ $\overset{6}{}$
weight	n. naːm naːk น้ำพัภ $\overset{5}{}$ $\overset{3}{}$
	v. heːt hày naːk, mi naːm naːk ເຮັດใຫ้พัภ, มิน้ำพัภ $\overset{2}{}$ $\overset{6}{}$ $\overset{3}{}$ $\overset{3}{}$ $\overset{5}{}$ $\overset{3}{}$
weird	(strange) adj.bpaː lat ปลาถ $\overset{1}{}$
	(horrible) adj. bpeːn dta

	yǎn ເປ็มตาย้าม $\overset{5}{}$
welcome	intrj. nyiːn di dtohn $\overset{2}{}$ $\overset{1}{}$ $\overset{5}{}$
	laːp ยินถีຕ9มลับ $\overset{2}{}$
welfare	n. kwam uː doìm soːm bun, saː waːt di pap ถวามอุດมสมบูม, สะอัถถิพาย $\overset{3}{}$ $\overset{3}{}$ $\overset{1}{}$ $\overset{4}{}$ $\overset{1}{}$ $\overset{3}{}$ $\overset{3}{}$ $\overset{1}{}$ $\overset{5}{}$
well	(surprise) intrj. ho โຫ้ $\overset{6}{}$ $\overset{6}{}$
	(thinking) intrj. o โອ $\overset{5}{}$
	n. naːm sang น้ำส้าງ $\overset{5}{}$ $\overset{6}{}$
	adj. di ถิ $\overset{1}{}$
	adv. di ถิ $\overset{1}{}$
well-advised	adj. teuk náa naːm ถึกแมะมำถิ $\overset{4}{}$ $\overset{2}{}$ $\overset{3}{}$
well-done	(task) adj. ti saːm leːt loìng duay di ทิสำເรัດลิ้ງ ถอยถิ $\overset{2}{}$ $\overset{4}{}$ $\overset{2}{}$ $\overset{3}{}$ $\overset{5}{}$
	(meat) adj. suːk สุภ $\overset{3}{}$
well-known	adj. mi seu siang มิ่ชุสฺງ $\overset{3}{}$ $\overset{2}{}$ $\overset{4}{}$
well-neigh	adv. geuap ເຄือบ $\overset{6}{}$
well-off	(wealthy) haìng mi ຮັ่ງมิ $\overset{2}{}$ $\overset{3}{}$
	(without worry) boh mi leuang nyuìng chay ບໍ່ເຮ็9ງพยุ່ງใจ $\overset{2}{}$ $\overset{3}{}$ $\overset{3}{}$ $\overset{6}{}$ $\overset{1}{}$
well-to-do	haìng mi ຮັ่ງมิ $\overset{2}{}$ $\overset{3}{}$
west	adj. tang tiːt dta weːn $\overset{3}{}$ $\overset{3}{}$ $\overset{2}{}$ $\overset{3}{}$
	dtoːk ทาງทิດตะอันถิภ $\overset{1}{}$
	n. tiːt dta weːn dtoːk ทิດตะอันถิภ $\overset{3}{}$ $\overset{3}{}$ $\overset{3}{}$ $\overset{1}{}$
	n. pak dta weːn dtoːk พากตะເอันถิภ $\overset{5}{}$ $\overset{3}{}$ $\overset{3}{}$ $\overset{1}{}$

western	adj. tang³ tii:t² dta³ wē:n³ dto:k³ ทางทิดตะเว็นติก n. fiːm³ kow³ boy¹ ฝิมคาวบอย
westward	adv. tang³ tii:t² dta³ wē:n³ dto:k³ ทางทิดตะเว็นติก
wet	adj. bpiak¹ ปຽก v. heːt² hay:⁶ bpiak¹ เຮັດใຫ້ ปຽก
whale	n. bpa³ wǎn³ ปาวาม v. dteu:k⁶ bpa³ wǎn³ ตึกปา วาม
whale oil	n. naːm⁵ maːn³ bpa³ wǎn³ ม้ำมันปาวาม
whaling	n. gan¹ ha⁴ bpa³ wǎn³ ການ ຫາປາวาม
wharf	n. ta³ heua³ ທ່າເຮือ
what	adv. maan² nyaːng⁴ (ແມ່ນຫຍັງ adj. aːn¹ day: ອັນໃດ
whatever	adv. maan² nyaːng⁴ goh² dtam ແມ່ນຫยัງກໍຕາม adj. aːn¹ day: goh² dtam ອັນໃดกໍຕາม
wheat	n. kow: ba: le ເຂ້ายะเລ
wheel	(cart) n. go:ng³ gwian¹ ภ้อງอຽน (car) n. go:ng³ lo:t³ ภ้อງລົຖ
wheelbarrow	n. lo:t³ go:ng² diaw¹ ລົຖກ້อງອຽอ
when	(what time) conj. we³ la³ day: เอลาใด

	(what day?) conj. meua² day:¹ เมื่อใด
	(what part of day?) conj. nyaːm³ day: ยามใด
whenever	(any day)adv. meua² day: goh² dtam เมื่อใดກໍຕາม (any part of day) adv. nyaːm³ day: goh² dtam ยามใดกໍຕາม (anytime) adv. we³ la³ day: goh² dtam เอลาใดกໍຕາม
where	(general) conj. say:⁴ ใส? (specific) conj. bohn² day:¹ ຂ່ອมใด
whereabouts	n. bohn² yu³ ຂ່ອมຢ
wherever	adv. bohn² day: goh² dtam ຂ່ອมใดกໍຕາม
whereupon	adv. dtoh² chak⁶ naːn⁵ ຕຈากนั้ม
whether...or not	conj. leu³ boh⁴ ຖ2ບ
which	pron. seuing², ti² ຊึ່ງ, ຫ້ adj. aːn¹ day: ອັນໃດ
whichever	adj. aːn¹ day: goh² dtam ອັນໃดกໍຕາม
while	conj. nay³ ka: na: ti³ ในคมะທ้ beu:t³ diaw¹ ຍິຕຖ2ວ
whine	v. kang³ คาง
whip	n. may⁵ saa⁶ ไม้เສ (hit) v. kian⁶ dti¹ duay⁵ may⁵ ຂ2มຕิฉอยไม้

	(eggs) di (se:n kay:) ติ (เซิ่นไข่)
whirl	v. mun wian ໝຸນວຽນ
whirlpool	n. na:m wo:n ນ້ຳວົນ
whirlwind	n. lo:m ba mu ລົມບ້າໝູ
whiskers	(person) n. nuat dtay: kang ໜວດໃຕ້ຄາງ
	(cat) n. nuat maaw ໜວດແມວ
whiskey	n. low: wi:t sa: gi ເຫຼົ້າ ວິສກີ
whisper	n. gan seu:m ການຊຶ່ມ
	v. seu:m ຊຶ່ມ
whistle	n. mak wit ໝາກຫວິດ
	v. pi:w bpak ປິວປາກ
white	n. si kow ສີຂາວ
	adj. kow ຂາວ
who	pron. pu ti ຜູ້ທີ່
	(question word) pron. pay: ໃผ
whoever	pron. pay: goh dtam ໃผກໍຕາມ
whole	(thing) adj. mo:t ໝົດ
	(time) adj. dta: loht ຕລອດ
	(area) adj. ta:ng ທັງ
	n. ta:ng mo:t ທັງໝົດ
wholesale	adj. kay mow: ຂາຍເໝົາ
wholesome	adj. di ດີ
whom	pron. pay:, se:ng ໃผ, ເຊິ່ງ

whore	n. maa chang ແມ່ຈ້າງ
	(polite) n. nyi:ng so pe nй ຍິງໂສເພນี
whose	pron. kohng pay:, se:ng ຂອງໃผ, ເຊິ່ງ
why	adv. bpe:n nya:ng ເປັນຫຍັງ
wick	(candle) n. say: tian ໃສ້ທຽນ
	(lantern) n. say: kom ໃສ້ໂຄມ
wicked	adj. sua hay ຊົ່ວຮ້າຍ
wicker	n. way noy ຫວາຍນ້ອຍ
	adj. he:t duay way ເຮັດດ້ວຍຫວາຍ
wide	adj. guang ກວ້າງ
widely	adj. yang guang kuang ຢ່າງກວ້າງຂວາງ
widen	v. he:t hay: guang ohk ເຮັດໃຫ້ກວ້າງອອກ
widow	v. he:t hay: bpe:n naa may ເຮັດໃຫ້ເປັນແໝ່າຍ
	n. maa may ແໝ່າຍ
widower	n. poh may ໝ້າຍ
wield	(swing) v. gwaang gway: ແກວ່ງໄກວ
	(use) v. say: ໃຊ້
wife	n. mia ເມັຽ
wig	n. po:m bpohm ຜົມປອມ
wild	(savage) adj. bpa teuan ປ່າເຖື່ອນ
	(not tame) bpa ປ່າ

wildcat	(animal) n. seua maǎw	windstorm	n. loːm paˬ nyuˬ boh miˊ foːn
	ເສືອແມວ		ລົມພາຍບໍ່ມີຝົນ
	(person) n. koːn ti dtoh	windy	adj. loːm haáng ລົມແຮງ
	suˬ yang hot hiam ຄົນທີ່ຕໍ່	wine	n. loẃ waáng ເຫຼົ້າແວງ
	ຢ່າງໂຫດຫ້ຽມ	wing	n. bpik ປີກ
wilderness	n. bohn hoːk hang		v. biːn ບີນ
	ບ່ອນຮົກຮ້າງ	wink	v. nyiːp dta ຍິບຕາ
will	(intention) n. kwam dtang	winter	n. laˬ du now ລະດູໜາວ
	chaǐy ຄວາມຕັ້ງໃຈ		v. pan laˬ du now
	(testament) n. piˬ naǐyˬ		ຜານລະດູໜາວ
	gaːm ພິນັຍກັມ		
	(desire) v. yǎk daˬyˬ ຢາກໄດ້	wipe	v. seːt ເຊັດ
	(future) v. chǎ ຈະ	wipe out	v. taˬ laˊy ທຳລາຍ
	(would) v. koːng chǎ ຄົງຈະ	wire	v. dti saˊy ຕີສາຍ
	(bequeath) v. mohp piˬ naǐyˬ		n. seːn luǎt ເສັ້ນລວດ
	gaːm ມອບພິນັຍກັມ	wireless	adj. boh miˊ saˊy ບໍ່ມີສາຍ
willing	adj. dteːm chaˬy ເຕັມໃຈ		n. wiːt taˬ nyuˬ ວິທະຍຸ
willow	n. goːk maˊy naǎw neuːng	wisdom	n. kwam saˬ liǎw saˬ lat.
	ກົກໄມ້ແໜວໜຶ່ງ		bpaːn nya
wilt	v. nyuːp nyohp ຍຸບຍອບ		ຄວາມສະຫຼຽວສະຫຼາດ, ປັນຍາ
win	v. paá ແພ້	wise	adj. saˬ lat ສະຫຼາດ
	v. saˬ naˬ ຊະນະ	wish	n. kwam bpaˬ soˊng ຄວາມ
wind	(coil) v. paːn ohm ພັນອ້ອມ		ປະສົງ
	(clock) v. biːt mong		v. bpaˬ soˊng ປະສົງ
	ບິດໂມງ	wit	(ability) n. kwam saˬ lat
	n. loːm ລົມ		laˬk laám ຄວາມສະຫຼາດຫຼັກ
wind up	n. nyuˬ dtiˬ ຍຸຕິ		ແຫຼມ
window	n. bpohng yiam ປ່ອງຢ້ຽມ		(person) n. koːn saˬ mohng
windshield	n. gaˬ choːk naˊ loːt		saˬy ຄົນສະໝອງໄສ
	ກະຈົກໜ້າລົດ		n. kwam saˬ lat
			ຄວາມສະຫຼາດ

witch	n. maa mo:t ແມ່ມົດ
witchcraft	n. gan say: wet mo:n ການໄຊ້ເວດມົນ
witchery	n. mo:n ka ta ມົນຄາຖາ
with	prep. ga:p, na:m ກັບ, ນຳ
withdraw	(troops) v. tohy keun ຖອຍຄืນ
	(money) v. tohn ຖອນ
wither	v. haaw lo:ng ແຫ້ວລົງ
withhold	v. nya:p nyang ຢັບຢັງ
within	adv. pay nay: ພາຍໃນ
without	(outside) adv. pay nohk ພາຍນອກ
	(lacking) adv. bpa: sa: chak ປາສຈາກ
	conj. doy boh ໂດຍບໍ່
withstand	(endure) v. to:n dtoh ທົນຕໍ່
	(resist) v. yeun dtua dtoh ຍืນຕົວຕໍ່
witness	n. pa: nyan ພະຍານ
	v. bpe:n pa: nyan ເປັນພະຍານ
wizard	n. pu wi: set ຜູ້ວິເສດ
woe	n. kwam tu:k hohn ຄວາມທุກຮ້ອນ
wolf	n. ma opa ໝາປ່າ
woman	(women) n. maa nyi:ng ແມ່ຍิງ
wonder	n. kwam bpa: lat chay: ຄວາມປລາດໃຈ
	(doubt) n. so:ng say ສົງໄສ
	(want to know) v. yak hu wa ຢາກຮູ້ວ່າ
wonderful	adj. wi: set ວິເສດ
woo	v. gia gohm ເກี້ງກອມ
wood	n. may: ໄມ້
woods	n. bpa ປ່າ
wooden	(substance) adj. he:t duay may: ເຮັດດ້ວຍໄມ້
	(hard) adv. kaang keu may: ແຂງคืໄມ້
woodpecker	n. no:k say: ນົກໄສ້
woodwork	n. keuang may: ເคื່ອງໄມ້
wool	n. ko:n sa:t ຂົນສัດ
word for word	dtam kwam chi:ng, ka:m dto ka:m ຕາມຄວາມจิ່ງ, คำຕໍคำ
work	(usually labor) v. he:t wiak ເຮັດງูກ
	(usually office work) v. he:t gan ເຮັດການ
work out	(solve) gaa kay: ba:n ha da ແກ້ໄຂຍັນຫາໄດ້
work up	(develop) ka: nyay ohk ຂຍາຍອອກ he:t hay: di keun ເຮັດໃຫ້ดี້
worker	n. ga:m ma: gohn, ko:n ngan ກັມມະກອນ, คืນງານ
workman	n. sang fi meu ຊ່າງฝ่ມ
workout	(test) n. gan to:t sohp ການທົດສอย

(practice) n. gan feu:k aap ການຝຶກແອບ
(strenuous exercise) n. wiak gan ti say: ga:m la:ng ວຽກການທີ່ໃຊ້ກຳລັງ

world n. lok ໂລກ

worm (earthworm) n. ki ga: deuan ຂີ້ກະເດືອນ
(woodworm) n. duang ດ້ວງ

worn (clothes) adj. kat ຂາດ

worry (strong concern) v. ga:ng wo:n chay: ກັງວົນໃຈ
(mild concern) v. bpe:n huang ເປັນຫ່ວງ
(to bother) n. he:t hay: u:k chay: ເຮັດໃຫ້ອຶກໃຈ

worse adj. ki hay gua gow: ຂີ້ຮ້າຍກວ່າເກົ່າ

worship n. gan sa: daang kwam kow: lo:p ການສະແດງຄວາມເຄົາຣົບ
v. sa: daang kwam kow: lo:p ສະແດງຄວາມເຄົາຣົບ

worst adj. ki hay ti su:t ຂີ້ຮ້າຍທີ່ສຸດ
v. ow: sa: na: ເອົາຊະນະ

worth n. ka ຄ່າ
adj. mi ka ມີຄ່າ

worthy adj. so:m kuan day: la:p ສົມຄວນໄດ້ຮັບ

worthless adj. boh mi ka ບໍ່ມີຄ່າ

would (-'d) ko:ng cha: ຄົງຈະ

would rather yak he:t... lay gua ຢາກເຮັດ....ຫຼາຍກວ່າ

wound v. he:t hay: bat che:p ເຮັດໃຫ້ບາດເຈັບ
n. bat paa ບາດແຜ

wow! intrj. to! ໂທ້!

wrap n. keuang nu:ng nohk, seua ku:m ເຄື່ອງນຸ່ງນອກ, ເສື້ອຄຸມ

wrath n. kwam chay: hay ຄວາມໃຈຮ້າຍ

wreath n. dohk may: hoy ດອກໄມ້ຮ້ອຍ

wreck (ship) n. heua dtaak ເຮືອແຕກ
(auto n. lo:t ha:k ຣົດຫັກ
v. mang pe ມ້າງເພ

wrench n. ga: chaa kay: bu lohng ກະແຈໄຂບູລອງ
v. mun haang ໝູນແຮງ

wrestle v. bpa:m ປ້ຳ

wretch n. ko:n ti bpe:n dta ki diat ຄົນທີ່ເປັນຕາຂີ້ດຽດ

wring (twist) n. bi:t ບິດ
(wet clothes) v. bpa:n ປັ້ນ

wrinkle v. hiaw ຫ່ຽວ
n. hoy hiaw ຮອຍຫ່ຽວ

wrist n. koh meu ຂໍ້ມື

write v. kian ຂຽນ

write down v. cho:t way: ຈົດໄວ້

writer	n. na:k dtaang na:ng seu นักแต่งนั้งสี	yard	(measurement) n. la หຼๅ	
writhe	v. bi:t bpay: bi:t ma ยึดไปยืดมา		(lawn) n. dern ban เดินบ้าน	
writing	(action) n. gan kian การຂຽນ	yardstick	n. may: la ไม้ຫຼๅ	
	(handwriting) n. lay meu ลายมี	yarn	n. se:n day เສ้ນถาย	
	(book) n. bpeum ປື้ມ	yawn	v. how ຫาว	
writings	n. bo:t bpa: pa:n ບົດปะพัม	ye	pron. chow: ເຈ້า	
wrong	n. kwam pi:t ความผิด		pron. su ສ	
	(incorrect) adj. pi:t ຜິດ	yea	(vote) adv. ha:p hohng ow: ຮັບຮອງເຈ้า	
	(immoral) adj. pi:t si:n ta:m ผิดสีมตัม		(truly) adv. taa taa แต้ๆ	
		year	n. bpi ปี	
		yearly	adv. adj. bpa: cha:m bpi ปะจำปี	

X

x ray	n. sohng fay: fa สๆงไฟฟ้า n. fi:m e:k sa: le ฟิมເອ໊ກສະເເ	yearn	v. yak day: ยากไถ้	
		yeast	(liquor) n. seua low: ເຊื้อເຫຼๅ	
Xmas	(Fr.) n. bu:n no aan ขุมโมแอ๋ม		(bread) n. seua kow: chi ເຊื้อເຂๅจ	
	(Eng) n. bu:n kli:t sa: ma:t ขุมคริสมาถ	yell	v. hohng ຮ້ອງ	
xylophone	n. la: nat ຣะมาถ	yellow	n. si leuang สิ(ເຫຼືອງ)	
		yellow fever	n. kay: leuang ไຂ้(ເຫຼືອງ)	

Y

yacht	n. heua oay: tiaw ເຮือใบทๆว	yelp	v. hohng nge:ng nge:ng ຮ້ອງເຫ้าๆ n. sieng hohng nge:ng nge:ng สៀๆຮ້ອງເຫ้าๆ	
yak	n. ngua bpa meuang dti be วัอป่าເมือๆถิເย	yes	(intimate) intrj. er ເອ	
yankee	n. a: me li: ga:n ຈะເມริกัม		(respectful) intrj. doy ໂดย	

	(polite) intrj. chow:⁵ ເຈົ້າ
yesterday	n. meu⁵ wan³ ni⁵ ມື້ວານນີ້
yet	adv. nya:ng³ ຍັງ
yield	(concede)v. nyohm³ hay:⁶ ຍອມໃຫ້
	(produce) v. hay:⁶ po:n⁴ ໃຫ້ເພີ່ນ
	v. po:n⁴ ti⁵ day:⁵ la:p² ເພີ່ນທີ່ໄດ້ຮັບ
yoke	v. say:² aak⁶ ໃສ່ແອກ
	n. aak⁶ ແອກ
yon	adv. adj. pu:n³ ພຸ້ນ
yonder	adv. tang⁵ pu:n³ ທາງພຸ້ນ
you	(to superior) pron. tan² ທ່ານ
	(to equal) pron. chow:⁵ ເຈົ້າ
	(informal) pron. dto⁵ ໂຕ
	(intimate/same sex) pron. meu:ng³ ມຶງ
young	(person, animal) adj. nu:m² ໜຸ່ມ
	(plants) adj. ohn⁵ ອ່ອນ
youngster	n. de:k⁵ noy⁵ ເດັກນ້ອຍ
your	(superior) pron. kohng⁴ tan² ຂອງທ່ານ
	(equal) pron. kohng chow:⁵ ຂອງເຈົ້າ

	(informal) pron. kohng⁴ dto⁵ ຂອງໂຕ
	(intimate) pron. kohng⁴ meu:ng³ ຂອງມຶງ
you're welcome	intrj. boh⁵ bpe:n³ nya:ng⁴ ບໍ່ເປັນຫຍັງ
yourself	pron. dtua¹ chow:⁵ eng¹ ຕົວເຈົ້າເອງ
	pron. dtua¹ tan² eng¹ ຕົວທ່ານເອງ
youth	(period) n. way:⁴ nu:m² sow⁴ ໄວໜຸ່ມສາວ
	(person) n. nu:m² sow⁴ ໜຸ່ມສາວ
youthful	adj. ta² tang³ nu:m² ທ່າທາງໜຸ່ມ
youthfulness	n. kwam³ nu:m² naan⁵ ຄວາມໜຸ່ມແໜ້ນ

Z

zany	n. dtua¹ dta:³ lo:k² ມົວຕລົກ
zeal	n. gan¹ seua² pot⁵ ການເຊື່ອໂພດ
zealot	n. ba⁵ sat⁶ sai³ na³ ບາສາດສາມາ
zealous	adj. ma:n² ໝັ້ນ
zebra	n. ma⁵ lay³ ມ້າລາຍ
zenith	n. nyoht⁵ sung⁴ su:t³ ຍອດສູງສຸດ

zephyr	(west wind) n. lo:m dta we:n dto:k ລົມຕະເວັນຕົກ	zigzag	n. ko:t ko:t liaw liaw ຄົດຄົດລ້ຽວໆ
	(breeze) n. lo:m ohn ລົມອ່ອນ	zinc	n. sa:ng ga: si ສັງກະສີ
		zone	n. ket daan ເຂດແດນ
zeppelin	n. heua hoh: baap ban lo:ng ເຮືອເຫາະແບບບານລົງ	zoo	n. suan sa:t ສວນສັດ
zero	n. lek sun ເລກສູນ	zoological	adj. giaw ga:p sa:t ກ່ຽວກັບສັດ
zest	(enthusiasm) n. kwam so:n chay: a:n hnang ga ຄວາມ ສົນໃຈອັນແຮງກ້າ	zoologist	n. na:k ko:n kua tang sa:t ນັກຄົ້ນຄວາງສັດ
	(stimulant) n. si:ng ti ho:t hay: dteu:n dte:n ສ່ຽທເຮັດໃຫຕື່ນເຕັນ	zoology	n. wi sa giaw ga:p sa:t ວິຊາກ່ຽວກັບສັດ
		zoom	v. keun bpay: yang way: way: ຂຶ້ນໄປຢ່າງໄວໆ

ລາວ-ອັງກິດ
Lao-English

ໄກ່

ກະ	to estimate
ກະກຽມ	to expect, to prepare
ກະຈາຍ	to spread, scatter
ກະຈາຍສຽງ	to broadcast
ກະຈາດ	basket, pannier
ກະແຈ	key
ກະແຈມື	handcuffs
ກະຈົກ	mirror, glass
ກະໂຈມ	crown, to jump
ກະສິກັມ	agriculture
ກະສິກອນ	farmer
ກະສຸນປືນ	bullet
ກະເສດ	agriculture
ກະແສ	current
ກະສອບ	sack
ກະຊ້າ	hand basket
ກະຊຶບ	to whisper
ກະເຊີ	basket
ກະຊວງ	ministry
ກະດາດ (ເຈ້ຍ)	paper
ກະດາດຊຶບ	blotting paper
ກະດາດຂາຍ	sandpaper

ກະດານ	board
ກະດານດຳ	blackboard
ກະດິ່ງ (ກະດິ້ງ)	bells, chimes
ກະຕິ	monk's dwelling
ກະດຸມ	button
ກະດູກ	bone, skeleton
ກະດູກສັນຫຼັງ	vertebrae, spine
ກະເດັ້ງຂັ້ນ	to bounce
ກະແດ້ງ (ແຫ້ງ)	to dry
ກະດັນ	back of the neck
ກະໂດດ	to jump
ກະດອນ	to bounce
ກະໄດ (ຂັ້ນໄດ)	stairs, ladder
ກະຕັນຍູ	gratefulness
ກະຕ່າ	market basket
ກະຕ່າຍ	rabbit
ກະຕິກາ	rule, regulation
ກະຕິກ	can, tin
ກະແຕະ	bamboo tray
ກະຕ້	rattan ball
ກະຕັ້ງ	bucket
ກະໂຖມ	spittoon
ກະທະ	cooking pot
ກະທິ	coconut milk
ກະທິງ	wild ox
ກະທໍ	sack
ກະທ່ອມ (ຕູບ)	hut, cabin

ກະເທີຍ	travesty
ກະເທື່ອນ	to shake, agitate
ກະທຽມ	garlic
ກະບະ	trail
ກະບີ້	bayonet, monkey
ກະບື	buffalo
ກະບຸງ	pannier to carry paddy
ກະບົດ	to revolt, rebellion
ກະບອງ	torch
ກະບອຍ	coconut shell cup
ກະບວມແຫ່	procession
ກະປຸກ	pot
ກະປູ	crab, nail
ກະໂປະ	coconut shell
ກະໂປງ	european skirt
ກະປອງ	can
ກະປ່ອມ	lizard
ກະເປົາ	pocket
ກະເປົາເງິນ	wallet
ກະໂພກ	hip, firecracker
ກະຣຸນາ	kindly, please
ກະຣົດ	carrot
ກະລາດຳ	African, Negro
ກະລ່ຳປີ	cabbage
ກະໂຫຼກ	skull
ກະໂຫຼງ	"touque" lizard container
ກະຮອກ	squirrel

ກັກຂັງ	to imprison
ກັ້ງຮົ່ມ	to put out, umbrella
ກັດ	to bite
ກັດແຂວ	to grit teeth
ກັນ	each other
ກັນໂຊ້ນ	to absorb shock
ກັນດານ	dangerous
ກັນເຫງ	reasonable
ກັ່ນ	to distill
ກັ້ນກາງ	to prevent, to hinder
ກັບ	with, box, to come back
ກັບແກ້	gecko lizard
ກັບກອກຢາ	cigarette box
ກັບຂີດ	match
ກັບຄືນມາ	to return, come back
ກັບບ້ານ	to return home
ກັບໄຟ	match box
ກັມ	labor, act
ກັມມະການ	committee, council
ກັມມະການຕ່າມມວຍ	boxing referee
ກັມມະກອນ	laborer
ກັມເວນ	fate, destiny (usually bad)
ກາ	crow
ກາກະບາດ	sign of the cross
ກາຄຳຊອບ	medal
ກາໂຕລິກ	Catholic (religion)
ກາຕົມນ້ຳ	kettle for boiling water
ການ້ຳ	kettle

ກາເຟ	coffee	ການກິນ	eating
ກາລະໂລກ	pest, plague	ການກົງຕໍເວລາ	punctuality
ກ້າ	courageous, dare, seed	ການກ່ຽວເຂົ້າ	harvest
ກ້າກັ້ນ	brave	ການກ່ຽວສາວ	courtship
ກ້າແກມ, ຫວ່ານກ້າ	to sow	ການກວດເບິ່ງ	inspection
ກ້າຫານ	brave	ການກະຈາຍດ້ວຍໄຟຟ້າ	radio
ກາງ	central, middle, neutral	ການຂາຍຊາດ	treason
ກາງແກ (ແກງແກ)	pigeon	ການຂຶ້ນໃຈ້ກັບປາກ	recitation
ກາງຄືນ	night	ການແຂ່ງຂັນ	match
ກາງແຈ້ງ	in the open air	ການຂົນສົ່ງ	transport
ກາງແດດ	in the sun	ການຂຽນຮູບ	painting
ກາງຖຫນົນ	in the middle of the street	ການເຂົ້າໂຮງຮຽນ	school attendance
ກາງທະເລ	in the middle of the sea	ການຄ້າ	trade
ກາງທາງ	halfway	ການແຄ້ນໃຈ	resentment
ກາງນ້ຳ	in midstream	ການຄົ້ນຄວ້າ	research
ກາງປີກ	to spread the wings	ການງານ	work, labour
ກາງມຸ້ງ	to put up a mosquito net	ການສະແດງ	demonstration, show
ກາງແມ່ນ້ຳ	in the middle of the river	ການສັກຢາ	injection
ກາງເວັນ	daytime	ການເສັຽຫາຍ, ຄວາມເສັຽຫາຍ	damage
ກາງຮົ່ມ	to open an umbrella	ການສອບເສັ້ງ	examination
ກາງປ່າ	fishbone	ການສອບສວນ	investigation
ກາຍ	to pass	ການຊື້	purchasing
ກາຍຍາມ	pass the time	ການຍ່າງ	walking
ກາຍເປັນ	to become	ການເຕັ້ນ, ການໂດດ	jump
ກາຍໄປ	to pass	ການດ່າ	insult
ກ່າຍ	to copy	ການເດີນທາງ	travel
ການ	work, (noun maker)	ການດຳນາ	transplanting of rice
ການກ່າວຄຳປາໄສ	speech		

ການຕັດສຶມໃຈ	decision
ການຕາຍ	death
ການຕອບເລາໂຈດ	solution
ການຕິດຕໍ	communication
ການໄຕ້ໄຟ	turning on light
ການຖຽງວ່າກັນ	argument
ການທ່ອງທຽວ	voyage
ການທ່ວງຂໍແຜ	beg for alms
ການທ່າທາ	gesture, act
ການນອງເລືອດ	bloodshed
ການບັນທຸກ	transport
ການປະຊຸມ	meeting
ການປາດ (ການຜາຕັດ)	operation
ການປ້ານຝ່າຍ	irrigation
ການປຸກດົງ	agriculture
ການໄປກ່ຽວ	walk, promenade
ການຜ່າຕັດ	surgery
ການຕິດຖຽງວ່າກັນ	quarrel
ການຜຶກຫັດ	exercise, training
ການພະນັນ	gambling
ການຟ້ອນ	dance
ການເມືອງ	politics
ການລະມັດລະວັງ	precaution
ການປ່ຽມຍ່າມ	visit
ການຣຸກຮານ	aggression
ການແລ່ນ	running
ການລິ່ງເລກ	stargazing

ການເລືອກຕັ້ງ	election
ການກັດແຮງ	gymnastics
ການຫາປາ	hunting
ການໄຫ່ເນື້ອ	to flush out game
ການຫຼິ້ນ	play, games
ການອ່ານ	reading
ການໂອ່ຫຼວງ	deluxe
ການອອກ	act of taking out, letting out
ການອອກກສຽງສຳນຽງ	pronunciation
ການເຮັດສວນ	gardening
ການຮ້ອງເພັງ	singing
ການຮຽນ	study
ການຮຽນຄຳເວົ້າ	study of spoken language
ກ້ານ (ລຳ)	stem
ກ້ານຄໍ	neck
ກ້ານບໍ	anklet
ກ້ານພາວ	coconut frond
ກາບ	to bow in respect, palms together
ກາບໄມ້	tree bark
ກາບລາ	to leave a superior
ກາບອອຍ	sugarcane fiber
ກ້າມ (ເນື້ອ)	to harden, muscle
ກາວຂວັນ	to speak about
ກາວໂຈມຕິ	to attack verbally
ກາວຕູ	to accuse
ກາວໂທດ	to denounce
ກາວຫາ	to allege

ກ່າວຮ້າຍປ້າຍສີ	to accuse unjustly	ກິນຫຍ້າ	to graze
ກ້າວ	to step, step	ກິນອິ່ມ	to eat one's fill
ກ້າວຖອຍຫຼັງ	to step back	ກິ່ນ	smell, odor
ກ້າວໜ້າ	to progress, to advance	ກິ່ນຫອມ	aroma, fragrant
ກິຈການ	enterprise	ກິ່ນເໝັນ	bad smell
ກີນິນ	quinine	ກິລາ	sports, exercise
ກິຣິຍາ	action	ກິລາກາງແຈ້ງ	outdoor sports
ກິໂລ, ກິໂລກຣາມ	kilogram	ກີ່	weaving
ກິໂລແມັດ	kilometer	ກີບ	kip: Lao currency
ກິ່ງ	twig, branch	ກຶກຫຼາຍ	to think, many
ກິ່ງໄມ້	branch of tree	ກຳ	ພ tense
ກິ້ງ	to roll	ກຳຕາ	to stare
ກິດຊອກຢາ	cigarette butt	ກຳ	dumb
ກິດຕິມສັກ	honorary	ກືນ (ກືນລົງ)	to swallow
ກິນ	to eat	ກຸລີ	coolie
ກິນເຂົ້າເຈົ້າ (ກິນເຂົ້າງາຍ)	to have breakfast	ກຸຫຼາບ	rose
ກິນເຂົ້າແລງ	to have supper	ກຸກກວນ	to interfere
ກິນງາຍ	to have lunch	ກຸງ	capital city
ກິນແຊບ	to eat heartily	ກຸ້ງ	shrimp
ກິນຖິບ	to eat raw meat or fish	ກຸບ	farmer's conical hat
ກິນດອງ	to attend a wedding reception	ກຸ້ມໃຈ	to be restless
ກິນດ້ວຍຄວາມໂລພາ	to devour	ກູ	I (disrespectful or familiar)
ກິນຝິ່ນ	to take opium	ກູມິງ	you and I (familiar)
ກິນຢາ	to take medicine	ກູ້ເງິນ	to borrow money
ກິນແລງ	to have supper	ກູ້ຍືມ	to borrow money without interest
ກິນລ້ຽງ	to go to a party	ກຸດ	frizzled (hair)
ກິນລ້ຽງສົ່ງ	to go to a farewell party	ເກັດ	scale of animal or serpent

ເກັດປາ	fish scale	ເກາຍາບ	to confess one's sins
ເກັບ	to pick up	ເກາຍັນຫາ	to solve a problem
ເກັບກ່ຽວ	to harvest, to reap	ເກາຜ້າ	to undress
ເກັບພາສີ	to collect taxes	ແກງ	stew, soup
ເກ	unruly, skew	ແກງ	rapid
ເກງໃຈ	fearful	ແກງເຮັດ	to do on purpose
ເກສອນ	pollen	ແກນ	core
ເກນ	to recruit (soldiers)	ແກບເຂົ້າ	rice husk
ເກນທະຫານ	to conscript, draft	ແກ້ມ	cheek
ແກະ	sheep, to take off	ແກ້ມບ໋ອງ	dimple
ແກະສະຫລັກ	to carve	ແກວ	Vietnamese, Vietnam
ແກະລາຍ	to sculpt	ແກ້ວ (ກະຈົກ)	glass
ແກ	trumpet, horn (car)	ແກ້ວຕາ	pupil of eye
ແກ່	old	ກົກ	tree, trunk
ແກ່ຈົມເບື່ອຍ	overripe, almost rotting	ກົກຂາ	thigh
ແກ່ເຖົ້າ	old	ກົກແຂນ	upper arm
ແກ່ລາກ	drag	ກົກເສົາ	base of a column
ແກ້	to untie	ກົກຕານ	palm tree
ແກ້ໄຂ	to solve	ກົກໄມ້	tree
ແກ້ໄຂໃໝ່	to revise	ກົກລານ	palm tree
ແກ້ໄຂ	to cure a fever	ກົງ	straight, cage
ແກ້ຄະດີ	to defend oneself in court	ກົງກັນຂ້າມ	opposite
ແກ້ແຄມ	to avenge	ກົງກັບ	to correspond to
ແກ້ເສື້ອຜ້າ (ແກ້ເຄື່ອງນຸ່ງ) to undress		ກົງຂັງ	cage
ແກ້ເຊືອກ	to untie a cord	ກົງສຸນ	consul
ແກ້ຕົວ	to excuse oneself		
ແກ້ບະ	to reward when a vow is kept		

ກົງນົກ	bird cage	ກອກ	pipe (smoking)
ກົງລໍ້ (ກົງວຽນ)	wheel	ກອກຢາ	cigarette
ກົງພັດ	waterwheel, windmill	ກອກ	tap (liquids)
ກົງ	to bend	ກອກນ້ຳ	faucet
ກົດ	decree, to force, acid	ກອງ	drum, group, unit
ກົດເກນ	rule	ກອງກັນ	to point something behind
ກົດຂີ່	oppress	ກອງໂຈນ	a guerrilla unit
ກົດຈາລະຈອນ	traffic regulation	ກອງສອດແນມ	reconnaissance unit
ກົດຢິ່ງ	conceited	ກອງທະຫານ	a military unit
ກົດໝາຍ	law	ກອງທັບບົກ	infantry
ກົ້ນ	bottom	ກອງທັບອາກາດ	air force
ກົ້ນຂີ່	anus	ກອງວັນ	battalion
ກົ້ນຂວດ	bottom of bottle	ກອງຟືນ	a pile of wood
ກົບ	frog, carpenter's plane	ກອງຟອນ	funeral pyre
ກົມ	department, bureau	ກອງໄຟ	bonfire
ກົ້ມ	to bow the head	ກອງຮອຍ	military company
ກົ້ມຂາບ	to prostrate oneself	ກອງແລງ	the evening drum
ກົ້ມລົງ	to bend down	ກອງໜ້າ	vanguard
ໂກງ	to cheat	ກອງໜຸນ	reinforcements
ເກາະແໜນ	to fold one's arms	ກອງ	tube
ກໍ	also, then	ກອງແຂນ	bracelet
ກໍ່	to build a brick wall	ກອງສັກຢາ	syringe
ກໍ່ກວນ	to disturb, bother, annoy	ກອງສູບ	pump
ກໍ່ສ້າງ	to build, start	ກອງສອງ	binoculars
ກໍ່ຢ່າງ	it is the same to ...	ກອງສ່ອງຄາວ	telescope
ກໍ່ໄຟ	to build a fire	ກອງຖາຍຮູບ	camera
ກໍ່ອາດຈະເປັນໄດ້	it is possible	ກອງນ້ຳເປິກ	inkwell

ກອດ	to embrace	ກ້ງວເຂົ້າ	to reap rice
ກອດແຂນ	to cross the arms	ກ້ງວຕັດຫຍ້າ	to scythe weeds
ກອດຄໍ້	to hug	ເກຶອ	salt
ກອດແອວ	to hug the waist	ເກຶ່ອຍ	to draw water, help
ກອນ	before, first	ເກຶອບ	almost, nearly
ກອນ	pill, tablet	ເກຶອບຄໍ່	almost dark
ກອນຄຶມ	clod	ເກຶອບຈະ	about to, almost to do
ກອນເມກ	cloud	ເກຶອບສຳເຣັດ	almost complete
ກອນຫຶມ	small stone	ເກຶອບໄດ້	almost able to
ກອບ	scoop up	ເກຶອບບໍ	hardly
ກອບເຂົາ	to scoop up	ເກຶອບພໍດ	almost finished
ກອມນອນ	to sing to sleep	ກົວ	afraid
ເກຶ	to be astonished	ກົວ	lead (metal)
ເກຶດ	to be born	ກວຍ	bamboo pannier
ເກຶດຈາກ	to derive from	ກວຍ	to swing, squat
ເກຶດເຫດ	an event, occurance	ກວຍລ	to dig a ditch
ເກຶນ	too much	ກວຍ	banana
ເກຶນໄປ	too much	ກວດ	to investigate
ເກຶນກຳລັງ	beyond one's power	ກວດຕາ	to inspect
ເກຶນຄວນ	to take too much	ກວນ	to distrub
ເກຶບ	shoes	ກວນບ້ານ	village chief (archaic)
ເກັຽ	gear	ໃກ້	close, near
ກ້ວງ	smooth, clean	ໃກ້ຊິດກັນ	close together
ກງດ, ກງຼດ	honor	ໄກ	far
ກງຼມ (ຕງຼມ)	to prepare	ໄກເທົ່າໃດ	how far?
ກ້ງວ	to harvest	ໄກປານໃດ	how far?
ກ້ງວອັກຽ	concerning	ໄກປືນ	trigger

ໄກ່	chicken	ກຳໄລ	interest
ໄກ່ການມາຮຸ້ງ (ເປັດໄກ່)	poultry	ກຳລັງ	power
ໄກ່ໄຂ່	a laying hen	ກຳລັງກາຍ	physical strength
ໄກ່ຂັນ	cock crow	ກຳລັງຈະ	to be about to
ໄກ່ງວງ	turkey	ກຳລັງໃຈ	courage
ໄກ່ຕີ	fighting rooster	ກຳລັງທະຫານ	military power
ໄກ່ແມ່	hen	ກຳໄວ	to connect
ເກົາ	to scratch	ກ້ຳ	side
ເກົ່າ	old	ກຣາມ	gram, jaw
ເກົ້າ (໙)	nine (9)	ກວ່າ	more than
ເກົ້າຄົມ	to roll up the hair	ກວາງ	deer
ເກົ້າອີ້	chair without arms	ກວ້າງ	wide
ເກົ້າອີ້ມີແຂນເທົ້າ	armchair	ກວາດ	to sweep
ກຳ	to clench the fist	ກວາມບ້ານ	chief of village
ກຳກັບ	to direct, supervise	ກວຽມ	cart
ກຳຈັດ	to get rid of	ໄກວໄປໄກວມາ	to balance, swing
ກຳຍານ	benzoin		
ກຳນົດ	to limit		
ກຳນົດຣາຄາ	to set the price		
ກຳນົດວັນ	to fix a date for appoint- ment		
ກຳນົດ (ກຳພິດ)	to set		
ກຳນົດການ	to schedule work		
ກຳນົດເວລາ	to fix the time		
ກຳປັ່ນ	ship		
ກຳປັ້ນ	fist		
ກຳມີ	to clasp		
ກຳມະຫຍີ່	velvet		

ຂະເຈົ້າ	they
ຂຍາຍສຽງ	to amplify
ຂຍາຍຮູບ	to enlarge a picture
ຂຶ້	to rub, attack

ຂະນະ	time, period	ຂາເຄ	lame
ຂະນ້ອຍ	I, me (humble)	ຂາໂຂ	bent leg
ຂນາດ	size	ຂາໂຕ	thigh
ຂນາດໃຫຍ່	king-size	ຂານົກຍາງ	very long legs
ຂນົບທຳມງມ	custom	ຂາໄປ	departure, on the way
ຂນົມ	cake	ຂາລາຍ	tatooed leg, uneducated peasant
ຂະບວນຮົດໄຟ	cars of a train	ຂາລີບ	weak or shortened leg
ເຂມນ	Kampuchea	ຂາລ່ວຍ	paralyzed leg
ຂະໂມຍ	thief, burglar	ຂາ	root like ginger
ຂັງ	to lock up	ຂາ	to kill
ຂັງຄຸກ	to imprison	ຂາຕີ	to kill
ຂັດຂວງ	to oppose	ຂາຕົວເອງ	to commit suicide
ຂັດຄຳສັ່ງ	to disobey orders	ຂານ້ອຍ	I, me (to superiors)
ຂັດໃຈ	to offend	ຂາພະເຈົ້າ	I, me (formal)
ຂັນ	bowl	ຂາລາຊການ	functionary, civil servant
ຂັນເງິນ	silver chalice or bowl	ຂາງ	to melt, dry by fire
ຂັນລາງພາ	washbowl (never for feet)	ຂາງ	side
ຂັນ (ແຂກ)	to separate, stair	ຂາງຂວາ	righthand side
ຂັນໄດ	ladder	ຂາງຖນົນ	roadside
ຂັນທົດລອງ	experimental phase	ຂາງເທິງ	above
ຂັບ	to drive	ຂາງນັ້ນ	that side
ຂັບຣົດ	to drive a car	ຂາງຫຼັງ	behind, in back of, back
ຂັບໄລ່	to expel	ຂາງນອກ	outside, outdoors
ຂັບຮ້ອງ	to sing	ຂາງໃນ	inside, into, indoors
ຂາ	leg		
ຂາກັບ	on the way back		
ຂາກຸດ	amputated leg		

ຂ້າງລຸ່ມ	under	ຂາວຮ້າຍ	bad news
ຂ້າງໜ້າ	future	ຂີ່	to ride
ຂາຍ	to sell	ຂີ່ມ້າ	to ride a horse
ຂາຍຊາດ	to commit treason	ຂີ່ລົດ	to ride a vehicle
ຂາຍຍາກ	difficult to sell	ຂີ້	excrement, waste
ຂາຍໜ້າ	to lose face	ຂີ້ກະເດືອນ	earthworm
ຂາດ	torn	ຂີ້ກະດິກ	round worm
ຂາດຄວາມອົດທົນ	impatient	ຂີ້ກະດິກແປ	tapeworm
ຂາດຄວາມເຄົ່າລົບ	to be disrespectful	ຂີ້ກະຕອດ	wart
ຂາດເງິນ	to be broke (money)	ຂີ້ກະເທີ	phlegm
ຂາດໃຈ	to have a heart attack	ຂີ້ກາກ	skin disease
ຂາດທຶນ	to lose money	ຂີ້ແກບ	husk
ຂາດໂຮງຮຽນ	absent from school	ຂີ້ກົບ	wood shavings
ຂາມ	to cross, across	ຂີ້ກົ່ວ	lead (metal)
ຂາມຊັ້ນ	to skip a grade	ຂີ້ໄກ່	chicken droppings
ຂາມໄປ	to travel across	ຂີ້ຂ້າ	slave
ຂາມຟາກ	to cross a river	ຂີ້ເຂັບ	centipede
ຂາວ	white	ຂີ້ແຂວ	filth
ຂາວ	news	ຂີ້ຄ້ານ	lazy
ຂາວກິລາ	sports news	ຂີ້ຄຸຍ	haughty
ຂາວສັງຄົມ	society news	ຂີ້ໄຄ	dirt on body
ຂາວສຳຄັນ	headline news story	ຂີ້ໂງ່	idiot
ຂາວໃນປະເທດ	domestic news	ຂີ້ເຈ້ຍ	bat dung, saltpeter
ຂາວຜາຍ	illustrated news	ຂີ້ສູດ	beeswax
ຂາວມໍລະມະທັມ	necrology	ຂີ້ສໍ້	swindler
ຂາວດ່ວນ	urgent news	ຂີ້ຊາຍ	sand
ຂາວໃຫຍ່	important news	ຂີ້ຊື	resin

ຂີ້ໂຍຍ	weak, invalid	ຂີ້ຫົວ	dandruff
ຂີ້ດັງ	snot	ຂີ້ໄຫ້	cry baby
ຂີ້ຂຶ້	rascal	ຂີ້ເຫຍື້ອ	garbage
ຂີ້ກະດ	filthy	ຂີ້ໝຽງ	rust
ຂີ້ດິນ	soil	ຂີ້ໝິ້ນ	turmeric
ຂີ້ຕົມ	mud	ຂີ້ເຫຼົ້າ	drunkard
ຂີ້ຕົວະ	lie, to lie	ຂີ້ອ່ງ	haughty
ຂີ້ເຕົ່າ	B.O.	ຂີ້ເຮ້ະ (ຂີ້ຮ້າຍ)	ugly
ຂີ້ຖີ່	stingy	ຂີ້ເຫື່ອ	sweat
ຂີ້ທຸດ	leprosy	ຂີ້ເຮື້ອນ	leprosy
ຂີ້ເຜິ້ງ	beeswax	ຂີງ	ginger
ຂີ້ຝຸ່ນ	dust	ເຂີຍ	son-in-law
ຂີ້ມູກ	mucus	ຂີດ	to draw, to trace
ຂີ້ແມງວ້ນ	beauty spot	ຂີດຖອງ	to underline
ຂີ້ໂມ້	boastful	ຂີດຂາ	to cancel
ຂີ້ເມົາ	drunkard	ຂີດເສັ້ນ	to draw a line
ຂີ້ຢາ	opium addict	ຂີດເສັ້ນໄຕ້	to underline
ຂີ້ຢ້ານ	coward	ຂີດອອກ	to cross out
ຂີ້ລັກ	petty thief	ຂືນໃຈ	unwilling
ຂີ້ລາຍ	ugly, wicked	ຂືນຕາ	to offend the eyes
ຂີ້ໂລບ	greedy, fraud, dishonest	ຂືນຫູ	to offend the ears
ຂີ້ເລື່ອຍ	sawdust	ຂືວ	acrid, strong smell
ຂີ້ຫືດ	skin disease	ຂືມ	serious
ຂີ້ຫີນ	stone	ຂືມ	to rise, up
ຂີ້ຫຶງ	jealous	ຂືນໃຈ	to memorize by heart
ຂີ້ຫູ	ear wax	ຂືນສານ	to go to court
ຂີ້ຫຸດ	kaffir lime, skin disease	ຂືນສຸທາກາດ	to throw into the air

ຂຶ້ນສູງ	to rise up	ເຂັມ	needle
ຂຶ້ນສຽງ	to raise one's voice	ເຂັມຂັດ	belt
ຂຶ້ນຕົ້ນ	to begin, to start	ເຂັມສັກຢາ	syringe
ຂຶ້ນຕົ້ນໄມ້	to climb a tree	ເຂັມຊີ້ທິດ	compass
ຂຶ້ນທະບຽນ	to enroll, register	ເຂັມນາທີ	minute hand
ຂຶ້ນຂັ້ນໄດ	to climb the stairs	ເຂັມວິນາທີ	second hand
ຂຶ້ນບ້ານໃໝ່	to have a house-warming ceremony	ເຂັມຫຍິບຜ້າ	sewing needle
ຂຶ້ນໄປ	to go up	ເຂັມແຂງ	strong
ຂຶ້ນຝັ່ງ	to climb a river bank	ເຂັມງວດກວດຂັນ	strict
ຂຶ້ນພູ	to climb a mountain	ເຂດແດນ	border
ຂຶ້ນມາ	to come up	ເຂດທະຫານ	military region
ຂຶ້ນມ້າ	to mount a horse	ເຂດເທສບານ	city boundary
ຂຶ້ນລາຄາ	to raise the price	ແຂ້	crocodile
ຂຶ້ນລົດ	to get in a vehicle	ແຂກ	guest, Indian
ຂຶ້ນເຮືອນ	to go into a house	ແຂກດຳ	Negro
ຂື	beam	ແຂງ	hard
ຂຸດ	to dig	ແຂງແຮງ	strong
ຂຸດຄົ້ນ	to excavate	ແຂ່ງຂັນ	to compete
ຂຸດສົບ	to exhume	ແຂ່ງແດດ	to sunbathe
ຂຸດຕົ້ນໄມ້	to uproot a tree	ແຂ່ງຝົນ	to brave the rain
ຂຸມ	hole in ground	ແຂ່ງມ້າ	a horse race
ຂູ່	to threaten	ແຂ່ງເຮືອ	boat race
ຂູ່ເຂັນ	to threaten	ແຂນ	arm
ຂຸ່ຍ	flute	ແຂນກຸດ	armless
ຂູດຣີດ	to extort	ແຂນສອກ	elbow
ເຂັນຝ້າຍ (ປັ່ນ)	to spin thread	ແຂນເສື້ອ	sleeve
		ແຂນຫຼຸດ	dislocated arm

ແຂວ	tooth
ແຂວສັດ	fang
ແຂວຫຼຸ່ນ	teeth falling out
ຂົນ	body hair, feather, to transport
ຂົນແກະ	wool
ຂົນຄິ້ວ	eyebrow
ຂົນເຄື່ອງ	to transport things
ຂົນສັດ	animal hair, fur
ຂົນສົ່ງ	to transport
ຂົນສົ່ງທາງບົກ	to transport by land
ຂົນສົ່ງທາງອາກາດ	to transport by air
ຂົນສົ່ງທາງເຮືອ	to transport by water
ຂົນຕາ	eyelash
ຂົນນົກ	feather
ຂົນມ້າ	horsehair
ຂບ (ກັດ)	to bite
ຂບແຂວ	to grind one's teeth
ຂມ	bitter
ຂມຄູ່	to threaten
ຂົມຂືນ	to rape
ຂົມເຫັງ	to mistreat
ເຂາະ	cowbell
ຂໍ	to request
ຂໍກະແຈ	key
ຂໍເກາະ	hooked pole
ຂໍສເນີ	to propose
ຂໍສັບ	goad, pointed stick
ຂໍຊ້າງ	elephant goad
ຂໍຍອມ	to demand surrender
ຂໍແໄ	please give me ...
ຂໍຕົວ	excuse oneself
ຂໍຖາມ	to ask, let me ask
ຂໍທາງ	to ask someone to make way
ຂໍທານ	to beg for alms
ຂໍໂທດ	excuse me
ຂໍແຮງ	to ask for help
ຂໍພອນ	to ask for a blessing
ຂໍເມັຽ	to request to marry a girl
ຂໍຢືມ	to request to borrow
ຂໍລາ	to say good-bye
ຂໍອະໄພ	to apologize
ຂໍ້	principle, part of
ຂໍ້ກາວຫາ	accusation
ຂໍ້ຂວອງ	obstacle
ຂໍ້ແຂນ	wrist
ຂໍ້ຂວາງໃຈ	point of disagreement, doubt
ຂໍ້ຄິດເຫັນ	point of view
ຂໍ້ຄວາມ	text
ຂໍ້ສຳຄັນ	key point
ຂໍ້ສັງເກດ	remark
ຂໍ້ສັນຍາ	clause of treaty
ຂໍ້ສອບເສັ້ງ	examination question
ຂໍ້ສເນີ	proposal
ຂໍ້ຕກລົງ	point of agreement

ຂໍ້ໂຕ້ແຍ້ງ	argument	ຂອງບູດ	spoiled, rancid thing
ຂໍ້ຕໍ່	joint	ຂອງປອມ	counterfeit
ຂໍ້ຄາມ	question	ຂອງພື້ນເມືອງ	indigenous product
ຂໍ້ຜູກມັດ	obligation	ຂອງພວກເຮົາ	our, ours
ຂໍ້ມື	wrist	ຂອງມີຄ່າ	valuables
ຂອງ	reference	ຂອງລັກມາ	stolen object
ຂອງກິນ	food	ຂອງຫຼິ້ນ	toy, plaything
ຂອງເກົ່າ	antique	ຂອງຫລວງ	state property
ຂອງຂີ້ດຽດ	disgusting object	ຂອງໃຫລ່າໆ	gift, free
ຂອງແຂງ	solid thing	ຂອງຫວານ	dessert
ຂອງຂວັນ	gift for special occasions	ຂອງ	fishing reel, stuck
ຂອງຂອຍ	mine	ຂອຍ	I, me
ຂອງເຂົາ	their, theirs	ຂອງຄີ	skeleton
ຂອງຈິງ	the real thing, genuine	ຂອນໄມ້	tree trunk
ຂອງໂຈນ	stolen property	ຂອບ	edge
ຂອງເຈົ້າ	your, yours	ຂອບໃຈ	thank you
ຂອງຈຳເປັນ	necessity	ຂອບຟ້າ	horizon
ຂອງເສັງ	useless things	ຂຽງ	chopping board
ຂອງໃຊ້ສ່ວນຕົວ	personal effects	ຂຽງຂຍບຊີ້ນ	chopping board for meat
ຂອງດີ	magical object	ຂຽດ	frog
ຂອງຕົວຢ່າງ	example	ຂຽດໂມ້	braggart, boaster
ຂອງຖືກ	cheap article	ຂຽນ	to write
ຂອງເຖື່ອນ	contraband	ຂຽນຈົດໝາຍ	to write a letter
ຂອງທັມະດາ	ordinary articles	ຂຽນເຖິງ	to write to
ຂອງທານ	alms	ຂຽນທວາຍ	to dictate
ຂອງທ່ານ, ຂອງເພິ່ນ your, yours,		ຂ້ຽນ	to whip
	his, her, hers, their, theirs	ຂຽວ	green

ຂຽວອ່ອນ	light green	ໄຂ້ຫວັດ	head cold
ຂຽວ	to hurry	ໄຂ້ຫວັດໃຫຍ່	grippe, flu
ເຂື່ອນ	dam	ໄຂວ	cross
ຂົວ	bridge	ເຂົາ	they, them
ຂົ້ວ	to fry, cook	ເຂົາອາງາງ	deer antler
ຂົ້ວໃສ່ນ້ຳມັນ	to fry in fat	ເຂົາຄວາຍ	buffalo horn
ຂອງ	bad, evil omen	ເຂົ່າ	knee
ຂວດ	bottle	ເຂົ້າ	rice, to enter
ຂວັ້ມນົມ	nipple	ເຂົ້າກັນ	to get along together
ໄຂ	to open, fat	ເຂົ້າກັນ	to go through ordeal
ໄຂອອກ	to open	ເຂົ້າກ້າ	seed rice
ໄຂ່	egg, to lay eggs	ເຂົ້າເກັ້ງ	to put into gear
ໄຂ່ໄກ່	chicken egg	ເຂົ້າກ້ວງຂວງ	to intervene
ໄຂ່ຂາວ	egg white, albumen	ເຂົ້າໄກ້	to approach
ໄຂ່ດາວ	sunny-side up	ເຂົ້າເຂົ້າກັນ (ເຂົ້າກັນ)	to agree
ໄຂ່ຈືນ	fried egg	ເຂົ້າຂ້າງ	to side with
ໄຂ່ຕົ້ມ	hard boiled egg	ເຂົ້າຂອງ	to load, materials
ໄຂ່ມຸກ	pearl	ເຂົ້າຂູບ	rice dumpling
ໄຂ່ລວກ	soft boiled egg	ເຂົ້າຈາວ	non-glutinous rice
ໄຂ່ຫຳ	testicle	ເຂົ້າຈີ່	bread
ໄຂ່ເນົ່າ	rotten egg	ເຂົ້າໂຈມຕີ	to assault
ໄຂ່ຫຼ້ງ	kidney	ເຂົ້າໃຈ	to understand
ໄຂ້	fever	ເຂົ້າໃຈກັນດີ	to understand mutually
ໄຂ້ສັ້ນ	malaria	ເຂົ້າໃຈຜິດ	to misunderstand
ໄຂ້ທະລະພິດ	smallpox	ເຂົ້າເຈົ້າ	they
ໄຂ້ປ່າ	malaria	ເຂົ້າສະມາທິ	to meditate
ໄຂ້ຫດ	measles	ເຂົ້າສັງຄະຫຍາ	rice with custard

ເຂົ້າສາລີ	corn	ເຂົ້າປຸ້ນ	Lao spaghetti
ເຂົ້າສາສນາ	to be converted	ເຂົ້າປູກ	seed rice
ເຂົ້າສານ	polished rice, hulled rice	ເຂົ້າເປັນສະມາຊິກ	to become a member
ເຂົ້າສຸກ	ripe rice, cooked rice	ເຂົ້າແປ້ງ	rice flour, face powder
ເຂົ້າເສັ້ງຖ້າມ	to compete	ເຂົ້າປຽກ	rice congee
ເຂົ້າເຊົ້າ	breakfast	ເຂົ້າເປືອກ	paddy, unhusked rice
ເຂົ້າດໍ	three-month rice	ເຂົ້າໄປ	to go in
ເຂົ້າຕົ້ມ	glutinous rice cake	ເຂົ້າໄປເຖິງ	to attain
ເຂົ້າຕອກແຕກ	puffed rice	ເຂົ້າຜັດ	fried rice
ເຂົ້າຕິ້ວ	travel ration	ເຂົ້າພັກໂຮງເຕັ້ມ	to stay in a hotel
ເຂົ້າທໍາ	to make sense	ເຂົ້າເພນ	pre-noon meal for bonzes
ເຂົ້າທຶ່ມ	to become a partner in	ເຂົ້າພົບ	to pay a visit
ເຂົ້າແທມທີ	to replace	ເຂົ້າຟ່າງ	sorghum
ເຂົ້ານາແຊງ	dry season rice	ເຂົ້າມາ	to enter, to come in
ເຂົ້າແນວ	seed rice	ເຂົ້າມານ	young rice
ເຂົ້ານອນ	to go to bed	ເຂົ້າມອບຕົວ	to come to surrender
ເຂົ້າໃນ	to enter into	ເຂົ້າເມືອງ	to immigrate, enter city
ເຂົ້າບ້ານ	to enter a house	ເຂົ້າຮັບຕໍາແໜ່ງ	to enter into a position
ເຂົ້າບູດ	moldy rice	ເຂົ້າຮັບໜ້າທີ	to take over the duty
ເຂົ້າບາເລ	wheat, corn	ເຂົ້າລອດຊ່ອງ	noodle-like rice cake in coconut milk
ເຂົ້າບໍໄດ້	no admittance	ເຂົ້າຫຸງ	cooked white rice
ເຂົ້າເບຶ	soaked and powdered rice	ເຂົ້າໜຶ້ງ	steamed rice
ເຂົ້າປະກວດ	to enter a contest	ເຂົ້າໜົມ	cake, candy, cookie
ເຂົ້າປະດັບດິນ	festival to the dead	ເຂົ້າໜົມຄົກ	coconut rice candy
ເຂົ້າປະຕູ	to enter a doorway	ເຂົ້າໜຽວ	sticky rice
ເຂົ້າປາຍ	broken rice	ເຂົ້າໝ່າ	soaked sticky rice

ເຂົ້າຫຼາມ	sticky rice cooked in bamboo
ເຂົ້າອູ່	to dry-dock for repair
ເຂົ້າຮູ	to enter a hole
ເຂົ້າຮູບ	to fit well
ເຂົ້າເຮືອນ	to enter the house
ເຂົ້າຮ່ວມ	to join
ຂວັນ	soul
ຂວາ	right (side)
ຂວາງ	to bar, hazzard
ຂວາງທາງ	to block the way
ຂວານ	axe
ແຂວງ	province
ແຂວນ	to be hanged
ໄຂວ່	to cross (legs)
ຂວ້ຳລົງ	to press

ຄວາຍ

ຄະດີອາຍາ	criminal case
ຄະນະ	group
ຄະນະກັມມະການ	committee, board
ຄະນະກັມມະການອຳນວຍການ	board of directors

ຄະນະກັມມະທິການ	commission
ຄະນະຂ້າຮາຍການ	official staff
ຄະນະທະຫານ	military team
ຄະນະທູດານຸທູດ	diplomatic corps
ຄະນະທູດສັມທະວະໄມຕີ	goodwill mission
ຄະນະທູດທະຫານ	military mission
ຄະນະທ່ອງທ່ຽວ	tourist group
ຄະນະປະຕິວັດ	revolutionary party
ຄະນະແພດສາດ	faculty of medicine
ຄະນະຣັຖບານ	cabinet of ministers
ຄະແນນ	score, grade
ຄະແນນສຽງ	vote
ຄະນອງ	in great joy
ຄັກ	clear(ly), exact(ly)
ຄັກແມ່	sure
ຄັກຊີ້	perfect
ຄັງ	warehouse, treasury
ຄັງກະສຸນ	arsenal
ຄັງເງິນ	treasury
ຄັງກ່ອນ	in former times
ຄັງສຸດທ້າຍ	last time
ຄັງທຳອິດ	first time
ຄັງແຮກ	first time
ຄັດ (ກ່າຍ)	to copy
ຄັດຄ້ານ	to disagree, to protest
ຄັດເລືອກ	to select
ຄັດເລືອດ	to stop the flow of blood

ຄົມ	itch
ຄົມຄາກ	toad
ຄົມຈອງ	umbrella handle
ຄົມໄດ	stairs, ladder
ຄົມໄຖ	plough handle
ຄົມມາ	ricefield dike
ຄົມເບັດ	fishing rod
ຄົມປາກກາ	pen holder
ຄົມຮົ່ມ	umbrella rod
ຄົ້ມ	to squeeze
ຄັ້ມຄໍ	to strangle
ຄັ້ມບີບ	to squeeze
ຄັບ	narrow
ຄັບແຄບ	narrow
ຄັບອົກຄັບໃຈ	unhappy, distressed
ຄາຕະກັມ	murder
ຄາຕະກອນ	murderer
ຄາຖາ	magic formula
ຄາມື	clenched hand, handful
ຄາຢູ່	caught in
ຄາຣະວະ	respect
ຄາວຽກ	busy, tied up by work
ຄ່າ	value, cost
ຄ່າຂົນສ່ອງ	delivery charge, tip
ຄ່າຄອງຊີບ	cost of living
ຄ່າຈ້າງ	wage
ຄ່າຈອດລົດ	parking fee

ຄ່າສິນຜອດ	bride price
ຄ່າເສັງຫາຍ	compensation
ຄ່າໃຊ້ຈ່າຍ	expenses
ຄ່າເຊົ່າ	rent
ຄ່າເຊົ່າທີ່ດິນ	land rent
ຄ່າດານ	duty, tariff
ຄ່າຕອບແທນ	compensation
ຄ່າທົດຂ້ວນ	indemnity
ຄ່າມາ	rent of ricefield
ຄ່ານາຍຜ້າ	brokerage
ຄ່າບຳນງ	pension
ຄ່າປະກັນ	bail, security
ຄ່າຜ່ານຂົວ	bridge toll
ຄ່າຣົດ	fare
ຄ່າຮຽນ	tuition
ຄ່າແຮງ	cost of labor
ຄ້າ	trade
ຄ້າຂາຍ	to do business
ຄ້າເຖື່ອນ	contraband trade
ຄາງ	chin
ຄາງກະໄຕ	jaw
ຄ່າງ	kind of monkey
ຄ້າງ	stuck
ຄ້າງຄ່າເຊົ່າ	back rent
ຄ້າງຄືນ	to spend the night
ຄາຍ	camp
ຄ້າຍກັນ	similar

ຄ້າຍກັບວ່າ	as if	ຄີງ	body
ຄາດ	expectant, to expect	ຄິດ	to separate
ຄາດຕະກອນ	murderer	ຄີມ	pliers
ຄາດນາ	to harrow a ricefield	ຄີມຄີບ	tongs
ຄາດຍໍ່ຖິ່ງ	unexpected	ຄີມເຄົ້າ	iron pincers
ຄານ	to crawl	ຄິ້ວ	eyebrow
ຄ້ານ	lazy	ຄິ້ວກົ່ງ	arched eyebrow
ຄາບ	to bite	ຄິ້ວບາງ	sparse eyebrows
ຄາວ	occasion, raw or fresh odor	ຄຶດ	to think
ຄາວກ່ອນ	last time, before	ຄຶດຄຸກ	discontented
ຄາວຊິ້ນ	raw meat odor	ຄຶດພິຈາຣະນາ	to consider
ຄາວດຽວ	once	ຄຶດໃຫ້ຄັກ	to consider carefully
ຄາວປາ	smell of raw fish	ຄຶດຮອດ	to think of
		ຄຶດຍາກ	difficult to think of
ຄິດ	to think	ຄື	to resemble, similar
ຄິດຄ່າບ່ອຍການ	to fix the fee	ຄືກັນ	same
ຄິດຄົ້ນ	to research	ຄືກັນກັບ	similar to
ຄິດວ່າ	to think that ...	ຄືເກົ່າ	as before
ຄິດສະເລ່ຍ	to average	ຄືຊິ	perhaps
ຄິດເລກ	to caculate	ຄືນ	night, give back
ຄິດເຖິງ	to think of	ຄືນກ່ອນ	the night before
ຄິດເຖິງເຮືອນ	homesick	ຄືນເງິນ	to refund
ຄິດທໍຣະຍົດ	to conspire against	ຄືນດີ	to reconcile
ຄິດບໍ່ອອກ	to be unable to figure it out	ຄືນດີກັນໄດ້	reconcilable
ຄິດໄປຄິດມາ	to ponder	ຄືນດີກັນບໍ່ໄດ້	irreconcilable
ຄີໄຟ	earthen stove base, kitchen	ຄືນນີ້	last night
ຄີກ	odd	ຄືນມາ	to come back

ຄືນວານນີ້	night before last	ຄູ່	in pairs
ຄືບໜ້າ	to progress	ຄູ່ກັນ	the same
ຄ	pail	ຄູ່ແຂງ	worthy, on the same level
ຄຸເຂົ່າ	to kneel	ຄູ່ຄວນ	worthy
ຄຕັກນ້ຳ	water bucket	ຄູ່ສົມລົດ	spouse (legal term)
ຄຸກ	prison, jail	ຄູ່ຊີວິດ	partners for life
ຄຸກມືດ	unlighted prison cell	ຄູ່ຕໍ່ສູ້	opponent
ຄຸງ	to reach, too close	ຄູ່ມື	manual, handbook
ຄຸດ	legendary birdman, Garuda	ຄູ່ໝັ້ນ	fiancé or fiancée
ຄຸນຄ່າ	value, worth	ຄູ່ອາຄາດ	adversaries
ຄຸນຄວາມດີ	goodness, merit	ຄູ່ຮັກ	lovers
ຄຸນນະສົມບັດ	quality, qualification	ຄຸເຄົ່າ, ຄຸເຊົ່າ	to bend one's knees
ຄຸນນະພາບ	quality	ຄູ້ແຂນ	to fold one's arms
ຄຸນພໍ່	catholic priest, father	ຄຸຍກັນ	to chat
ຄຸນແມ່	catholic nun, sister	ຄຸຍໂມ້	to boast
ຄຸບ	to snatch	ຄູດ	to drag, plane
ຄຸມ	to guard	ຄູນເລກ	to multiply
ຄຸມຂັງ	to imprison	ເຄັ່ງ	taut, tense
ຄຸມຕົວ	be watchful	ເຄັມ	salty
ຄຸມເນົາ	to cover with warm clothes	ເຄ	lame
ຄຸ້ມ	section of town or village	ແຄນ	khene, Lao wind instrument
ຄຸ້ມກັນ	out of danger	ແຄນ	to be hurt emotionally
ຄຸ້ມຄ່າຈ້າງ	reasonable (wage)	ແຄນໃຈ	fretful
ຄຸ້ມນາ	boundary of ricefield	ເຄຍ	narrow
ຄູສອນ	teacher	ແຄມ	edge
ຄຸບາ	priest		
ຄູໃຫຍ່	principal of school		

ແຄມຂອງ	beside the Mekong River	ຄົນຄົດໂກງ	dishonest person
ແຄມນ້ຳ	on the river bank	ຄົນງານ	laborer, workman
ຄກ	mortar	ຄົນໂງ່	fool, stupid person
ຄกตำเຂ้า	rice mortar	ຄົນງອຍ	paralytic
ຄືງຈະ	probably	ຄົນເຈັບ	sick person
ຄືງຊິ	may be	ຄົນຈົນ	poor people
ຄືງເຫຼືອ	to remain	ຄົນເຈົາຊູ	lover
ຄົດ	to bend	ຄົນຂຸນຕຳ	proletariat
ຄົນ	person, man, to mix	ຄົນຊຸຍທ່ຽວ	traveller, playboy
ຄົນກ້າຫານ	a brave man	ຄົນຊຸຍເວົ້າຂ້ວມ	gossip
ຄົນກິນຫຼາຍ	glutton	ຄົນຍ່າງ	pedestrian
ຄົນເກັບເງິນ	money collector	ຄົນຍາມ	watchman
ຄົນໃກ້ຄຽງ	neighbor	ຄົນດີ	good man
ຄົນກວາດຖນົນ	street sweeper	ຄົນໂດຍສານ	passenger
ຄົນຂາຍຊີ້ນ	butcher	ຄົນເດີນທາງ	traveller
ຄົນຂີ່ມ້າ	cowboy, horse rider	ຄົນເດີນເຮືອ	navigator
ຄົນຂີ່ຣົດຖີບ	cyclist	ຄົນດຽວ	one person, alone
ຄົນຂີ້ຄ້ານ	lazy person	ຄົນໃດ	who?
ຄົນຂີ້ຕົວະ	liar	ຄົນໃດຄົນນຶ່ງ	anyone, someone
ຄົນຂີ້ທູດ	leper	ຄົນຕັກນ້ຳ	water vendor
ຄົນຂີ້ລັກ	robber	ຄົນຕັດຟືນ	woodcutter
ຄົນຂີ້ໂລບ	greedy person	ຄົນຕະລົກ, ຄົນຕລົກ	comedian
ຄົນຂີ້ຢ້ານ	coward	ຄົນດັບໄຟ	firefighter
ຄົນຂີ້ຖີ່	stingy person	ຄົນຕ່າງຊາດ	alien, foreigner
ຄົນຂີ້ເຫຼົ້າ	drunkard	ຄົນຕ່າງຖິ່ນ	stranger
ຄົນຂໍທານ	beggar	ຄົນຕາບອດ	blind man
ຄົນຄົງ	invulnerable person	ຄົນຕິດຝິ່ນ	opium addict

ຄົນຕີກອງ	drummer	ຄົນໂລບ	greedy person
ຄົນຖຶກເນຣະເທດ	exile	ຄົນລ້ຽງແກະ	shepherd
ຄົນທ້າມະດາ	average person	ຄົນລ້ຽງຄວາຍ	buffalo boy
ຄົນທຸກ	poor man	ຄົນລ້ຽງເດັກນ້ອຍ	governess
ຄົນໂທດ	prisoner	ຄົນລວງກະເປົ໋າ	pickpocket
ຄົນໄທ	Thai	ຄົນເວົ້າຫຼາຍ	gossiper
ຄົນນອກ	stranger	ຄົນຫາປາ	fisherman
ຄົນນອກກົດໝາຍ	outlaw	ຄົນຫຍາບຊ້າ	brute
ຄົນໃນເມືອງ	city dweller	ຄົນຫຼິ້ນກິນ	juggler
ຄົນນຳທຽວ	guide	ຄົນຮັກ	beloved
ຄົນບ້າ	madman	ຄົນຮ້າຍ	criminal
ຄົນບາບ	sinner	ຄົນຮູ້	docile person
ຄົນປ່າ	forest dweller	ຄົ້ນ	to search for
ຄົນປາກກືກ	mute	ຄົ້ນຄວ້າ	to research
ຄົນເປັຽ	invalid	ຄົ້ນພົບ	to discover, to find
ຄົນປ່ວຽ	solitary person, bachelor	ຄົ້ນຫາ	to explore
ຄົນປອມ	charlatan	ຄົ້ນຫາຄວາມຈິງ	to seek the truth
ຄົນເຝົ້າປະຕູ	doorman	ຄົມ	sharp
ຄົນຜານ	mischievous person	ໂຄ	cow
ຄົນພາຍເຮືອ	boatman	ໂຄສະນາ	advertising
ຄົນພື້ນເມືອງ	native	ໂຄສະນາການ	propaganda
ຄົນຟັງ	listener, audience	ໂຄສະນາຊວນເຊື່ອ	propaganda
ຄົນມັກຫຼິ້ນມັກກິນ	playboy	ໂຄສະນາຫາສຽງ	political campaign
ຄົນມີ	rich man	ໂຄສົກ	announcer, spokesman
ຄົນມອດໄຟ	fireman	ໂຄຣົບ	to respect
ຄົນລັຽຈ້າງ	hired man	ໂຄກ	mound
ຄົນລາວ	Lao person, Laotian	ໂຄງການ	project, program

ໂຄງການກໍ່ສ້າງ	construction project
ໂຄ່ງເຄ່ງ	huge, big
ໂຄດ	ancestor
ໂຄນ	base of tree
ໂຄນລົ້ມ	to fall down
ໂຄມຕັ້ງ	table lamp
ໂຄມຍິບ	flashlight
ໂຄມແພະຍຸ	gas lantern
ໂຄມໄຟ	electric light
ໂຄມຣົຖຍົນ	headlights
ເຄາະ	to knock, luck
ເຄາະຮ້າຍ	bad luck
ຄໍ	neck
ຄໍເສື້ອ	collar
ຄໍເປັນແພງງ	goiter
ຄໍແຫບ	laryngitis
ຄອກ	pen
ຄອກງົວ	cowshed
ຄອກມ້າ	stable
ຄອກຫມູ	pigsty
ຄອງຄວາມເປັນໃຫຍ່	dominate
ຄອງຄວາມເປັນໂສດ	to remain a bachelor
ຄອງຊີບ	to earn a living, to subsist
ຄອງຮັກ	to be faithful
ຄອງ	gong
ຄອຍຖ້າ	to wait for
ຄອຍເອົາໃຈ	to try to please someone

ຄອຍ	gentle
ຄອຍຍັງຊົວ	improving in health
ຄອຍຍ່າງ	to walk slowly
ຄອຍຄືນ	convalescing
ຄອຍຍຸຄອຍທີມ	so so
ຄອຍ	slope
ຄອນ	stick
ຄອນຕີ	hammer
ຄອນຕອກກຂໍ້	mallet
ຄອນໄມ້	wooden mallet
ຄອຍຄົວ	family
ເຄິ່ງ	half
ເຄິ່ງເດືອນ	half a month
ເຄິ່ງທາງ	halfway
ເຄິ່ງຣາຄາ	half price
ເຄິ່ງເວລາ	half of the day
ເຄີຍ	ever
ເຄີຍກິນ	accustomed to eat
ເຄີຍໄປ	used to go
ເຄີຍຢູ່	used to live
ຄຽງກັນ	side by side
ຄຽດ	to resent, angry with
ຄຽດແຄ້ນ	to resent
ຄຽດໃສ່	to be angry with
ຄ້ຽວ	to chew
ຄ້ຽວຢາ	to chew tobacco
ຄ້ຽວຫມາກ	to chew betel

ເຄື່ອງ	vine
ເຄື່ອຫວ້ອຍ	bunch of bananas
ເຄື່ອເຂົາ	jungle vine
ເຄື່ອຈັກກະພັບ	commonwealth
ເຄືອງ	to offend
ເຄື່ອງຕາ	unpleasant to see
ເຄື່ອງຫູ	unpleasant to hear
ເຄື່ອງ	article, thing, clothing
ເຄື່ອງກະຈາຍສຽງ	record player
ເຄື່ອງກະປ໋ອງ	canned food
ເຄື່ອງກັນຜີ	amulet against evil spirits
ເຄື່ອງກິລາ	sports equipment
ເຄື່ອງກິນ	food
ເຄື່ອງແກ້ມ	snack served with alcohol
ເຄື່ອງກິນ	machine
ເຄື່ອງກອງນ້ຳ	filter
ເຄື່ອງກວດຮ່າງກາຍ	stethoscope
ເຄື່ອງຂຽນ	stationery
ເຄື່ອງຄິດເລກ	calculating machine
ເຄື່ອງເຄືອບ	porcelain
ເຄື່ອງຈັກ	machine, machinery
ເຄື່ອງເຈາະ	drill
ເຄື່ອງສາຍພັງ	movie projector
ເຄື່ອງສິດຢາ	hypodermic syringe
ເຄື່ອງເສບ	musical instruments
ເຄື່ອງສົ່ງ	transmitter

ເຄື່ອງຊັກຜ້າ	washing machine
ເຄື່ອງຊັ່ງ	scales, balance
ເຄື່ອງຊັ່ງນ້ຳພັກຄົນ	scales for weighing people
ເຄື່ອງຊຸມຶ່ງ	suit of clothes, set of tools
ເຄື່ອງໃຊ	utensil, instrument, facilities
ເຄື່ອງໃຊ້ສ່ວນຕົວ	personal effects
ເຄື່ອງຕັດຈ້ຽ	paper cutter
ເຄື່ອງຕັດຫຍ້າ	lawn mower
ເຄື່ອງດັບເພີງ	fire extinguisher
ເຄື່ອງດູດຝຸ່ນ	vacuum sweeper
ເຄື່ອງດື່ມ	drink
ເຄື່ອງດົນຕຣີ	musical instrument
ເຄື່ອງຕົກແຕ່ງ	ornament
ເຄື່ອງຕອນ	gift
ເຄື່ອງຖ້ວຍຊາມ	dishware
ເຄື່ອງທີວີ	television (TV)
ເຄື່ອງໂທຣະສັບ	telephone receiver
ເຄື່ອງໂທຣະເລກ	telegraph
ເຄື່ອງນຸ່ງ	clothing
ເຄື່ອງບັນທຶກສຽງ	tape recorder
ເຄື່ອງບິນ	airplane
ເຄື່ອງບິນໂດຍສານ	commercial aircraft
ເຄື່ອງບິນຖິ້ມລະເບີດ	bomber
ເຄື່ອງບິນໄອພົ່ນ	jet plane
ເຄື່ອງແບບ	uniform
ເຄື່ອງພິມດີດ	typewriter
ເຄື່ອງປັ່ນມ້າ	pulverizer

ເຄື່ອງຟັກໄຂ່	incubator
ເຄື່ອງມືຫາປາ	fishing equipment
ເຄື່ອງມຸດນ້ຳ	scuba equipment
ເຄື່ອງລັບອິທະຍຸ	radio receiver
ເຄື່ອງວັດຄວາມໄວ	speedometer
ເຄື່ອງວັດຄວາມຮ້ອນເຢັນ	thermometer
ເຄື່ອງວັດນ້ຳຝົນ	rainfall gauge
ເຄື່ອງພາຍການຄ້າ	trademark
ເຄື່ອງພາຍ	sign, mark
ເຄື່ອງຫຼິ້ນຈານສຽງ	record player
ເຄື່ອງຫຼິ້ນເດັກນ້ອຍ	toys
ເຄື່ອງຫຼິ້ນແຜນສຽງ	record player
ເຄື່ອງເຫຼົາມສໍ	pencil sharpener
ເຄື່ອງອັດສຳເນົາ	duplicator
ເຄື່ອງອັດສຽງ	tape recorder
ເຄື່ອງອາໄລ	spare part
ເຄື່ອງແຕ່ງ	ornament
ເຄື່ອງເຮືອນ	furniture, household articles
ເຄື່ອນ	to move
ເຄື່ອນຍ້າຍ	to transfer
ຄົວ	kitchen
ຄົວກິນ	to cook
ຄວງ	to twirl
ຄວນ	ought to
ຄວນຈະ	ought
ຄວບຄຸມ	to control
ໃຄຂຶ້ນ	to swell up

ໄຄ	to become better
ໄຄແຕ່	to recover
ເຄົາລົບ	respect
ເຄົາລົບກົດໝາຍ	to respect the law
ເຄົາລົບໃນຕົວເອງ	self-respect
ເຄົາລົບຢຳເກງ	to respect with awe
ເຄົ້າແມວ	screech owl
ຄຳ	word, gold, to feel with hand
ຄຳກ່າວຫາ	accusation
ຄຳກອນ	poem
ຄຳຂາວ	platinum
ຄຳຂໍ	request
ຄຳຄັດຄ້ານ	objection
ຄຳສະເໜີ	proposal
ຄຳສັ່ງ	order
ຄຳສັ່ງສານ	court decision
ຄຳສັ່ງສອນ	preach
ຄຳສັ່ງສອນຂອງພະພຸດເຈົ້າ	the teachings of Buddha
ຄຳສອນ	preach
ຄຳສາບານ	oath
ຄຳສາລະພາບ	confession
ຄຳຊີ້ແຈງ	explanation
ຄຳອວຍໄຊ	congratulations
ຄຳຕັກເຕືອນ	warning
ຄຳເຕືອນ	advice
ຄຳຕັດສິນ	judgement
ຄຳຕອບ	answer

ຄຳຖາມ	question	ຄ້ວດ	to chisel out, to sculpt
ຄຳແນະນຳ	introduction	ຄ້ວດດອກ	to carve a flower
ຄຳນວນ	to calculate	ຄ້ວດລາຍ	to carve a design
ຄຳປາໄສ	speech	ຄ້ວດຫູ	to pick one's ears
ຄຳແປ	translation, explanation	ຄ້ວມ	smoke
ຄຳພິພາກສາ	judgement, verdict, decision	ຄ້ວມທາງກຍ່າ	cigarette smoke
ຄຳຜິດ	fault, error	ຄ້ວມໄຟ	smoke
ຄຳຝັນ	dream	ຄ້ວມຊ້າງ	mahout, elephant trainer
ຄຳຟ້ອງ	accusation	ຄວາ	to try to get
ຄຳເວົ້າ	word	ຄວາໃສ່	to grab hastily
ຄຳໃຫ້ການ	interrogation, proceedings	ຄວາຍ	buffalo
ຄຳຫມັ້ນສັນຍາ	agreement, contract	ຄວານມ້າ	horse trainer
ຄຳອະທິບາຍ	explanation	ຄວານຊ້າງ	mahout, elephant trainer
ຄຳອຸທິດ	dedication	ຄວາມ	word, case
ຄຳອຳລາ	farewell	ຄວາມກະລຸນາ	kindness
ຄຳອ້ອນວອນ	supplication	ຄວາມກ້າຫານ	bravery
ຄຳອວຍພອນ	wish	ຄວາມກິ້ກກ້ອງ	reflection
ຄຳອວຍພອນປີໃຫມ່	New Year's greetings	ຄວາມກົດຂີ່	oppression
ຄຳຣູ້	wise, well-behaved	ຄວາມກົດດັນ	pressure
ຄຳຮ້ອງຂໍ	request, application	ຄວາມໃກ້ຊິດ	intimacy
ຄຳຫມາກ	quid of betel nut	ຄວາມເກົ່າມາເລົ່າໃຫມ່	the same old story
ຄຳ	night	ຄວາມເຂັ້ມແຂງ	strength, force
ຄຳນີ້	tonight	ຄວາມຄິດ	idea, concept
ຄຳມືດ	nightfall	ຄວາມຄິດຝັນ	vision
ຄ້ຳປະກັນ	surety	ຄວາມຄິດເຫັນ	opinion
ຄຣູ	teacher	ຄວາມຄຶດ	thought
ຄຣູບາ	monk		

ຄວາມໂຄຣິບໂມຍຖີ	reward		ຄວາມສຳຄັນ	importance
ຄວາມຄຸດແຄ້ມ	tension		ຄວາມສຳພັນ	relationship
ຄວາມໂງ່	ignorance		ຄວາມຊ່າລື	rumor
ຄວາມງງຍ	silence		ຄວາມຊ້າ	slowness
ຄວາມຈະເຣີນ	prosperity		ຄວາມຊື່	honesty
ຄວາມຈິງ	truth		ຄວາມຊື່ນໃຈ	pleasure, amusement
ຄວາມຈິບຫາຍ	disaster		ຄວາມຄຸນ	merit
ຄວາມເຈັບ	pain, agony		ຄວາມເຊື່ອ	belief
ຄວາມຈົບງາມ	neatness		ຄວາມຊົວ	evil
ຄວາມຈຳເປັນ	necessity		ຄວາມຊ່ວຍເຫຼືອ	aid
ຄວາມສະອາດ	cleanliness		ຄວາມຊຳນານ	experience
ຄວາມສະງ່າ	grandeur		ຄວາມດັນໂລຫິດ	blood pressure
ຄວາມສັນธะເສີມ	congratulations		ຄວາມດ່າ	insult
ຄວາມສງົບ	peace, calm		ຄວາມດີ	virtue, goodness, merit
ຄວາມສະດວກ	convenience		ຄວາມດີຄວາມຄຸນ	meritorious action
ຄວາມສລາດ	intelligence		ຄວາມເດືອດຮ້ອນ	penalty, trouble
ຄວາມສັຕຊື່	loyalty		ຄວາມຕັ້ງໃຈ	willingness
ຄວາມສາມາດ	ability		ຄວາມຕ່າງ	strangeness
ຄວາມສິບຫາຍ	disaster		ຄວາມແຕກຕ່າງ	difference
ຄວາມສຸພາບ	politeness		ຄວາມຕອງການ	need
ຄວາມສຸກ	happiness		ຄວາມຕຳຊ້າ	evil
ຄວາມສູງ	height		ຄວາມຕຶກຕອງປ່ອງງອງ	solidarity
ຄວາມແສບຮ້ອນ	torture		ຄວາມທາຍ	prediction
ຄວາມເສົ້າໃຈ	sorrow		ຄວາມທົນທານ	endurance
ຄວາມເສັຍສລະ	devotion		ຄວາມທຸກ	suffering
ຄວາມເສັຍຫາຍ	damage		ຄວາມທຸກຍາກ	poverty, misery
ຄວາມສົມບູນ	perfection			

ຄວາມໄທ	Thai words	ຄວາມລຳບາກ	difficulty
ຄວາມນ້ອຍໃຈ	inferiority	ຄວາມໄວ	speed
ຄວາມບໍ່ສຸພາບ	impoliteness	ຄວາມໄວ້ວາງໃຈ	confidence
ຄວາມບົກຜ່ອງ	deficiency	ຄວາມອິດົກ	anguish
ຄວາມປະມາດ	negligence	ຄວາມເວົ້າ	conversation
ຄວາມເປັນກາງ	neutrality	ຄວາມເວົ້າຫຼິ້ນ	joke
ຄວາມເປັນສັດຕຣູ	enmity	ຄວາມເຫັນ	opinion
ຄວາມເປັນລະບຽບ	order	ຄວາມເຫັນແກ່ຕົວ	selfishness
ຄວາມເປັນໃຫຍ່	grandeur	ຄວາມຫຍຸ້ງຍາກ	difficulty
ຄວາມເປັນອິສຣະ	freedom	ຄວາມໝັ້ນຄົງ	permanence
ຄວາມປາຖມາ	wish	ຄວາມຫຼັງ	the past
ຄວາມປອດໄພ	safety	ຄວາມຫວັງ	hope
ຄວາມປຽບທຽບ	comparison	ຄວາມຫວັງດີ	good intentions
ຄວາມຜິດ	mistake	ຄວາມອັບອາຍ	shame
ຄວາມຝັນ	dream	ຄວາມອາຍ	shame
ຄວາມພະຍາຍາມ	endeavor	ຄວາມສົງສານ	pity
ຄວາມພະຍາບາດ	vengeance, malice	ຄວາມສີ່ເໝື່ອຍ	weariness
ຄວາມພຽງພໍ	enough	ຄວາມສູງ	pride
ຄວາມຮັກ	love	ຄວາມອົດທົນ	patience
ຄວາມມັກໃຫຍ່ໄຝ່ສູງ	ambition	ຄວາມອ່ອນຫວານ	gentleness
ຄວາມມິດ	silence	ຄວາມອ່ອນແອ	weakness
ຄວາມມຸ້ງໝາຍ	objective	ຄວາມຮັກ	love
ຄວາມໂມໂຫໂທໂສ	tantrum	ຄວາມຮັ່ງມີ	wealth
ຄວາມລະວັງ	precaution	ຄວາມຮູ້	knowledge
ຄວາມລະມັດລະວັງ	caution, care	ຄວາມຮູ້ສຶກ	feeling
ຄວາມລັບ	secret	ຄວາມຮ້ອນ	heat
ຄວາມໂລບ	cupidity		

ງະ	open
ງັດ	to pry open
ງັນ	all night vigil, wake
ງັນກຳ	all night gathering for child birth
ງັບ	to half close, shut
ງັບສົບ	shut up (insulting)
ງັບປະຕູ	to half close the door
ງັບປາກ	to close one's mouth
ງາ	tusk
ງາຊ້າງ	ivory
ງ່າໄມ້	tree branch
ງ້າວ	to force open
ງ້າງປືນ	to cock a gun
ງ້າງອອກ	to open up
ງາຍ (ກິນງາຍ)	lunch
ງ່າຍ	easy, simple
ງານ	job, business, party
ງານຂຶ້ນເຮືອນໃໝ່	housewarming
ງານສົບ	cremation, funeral
ງານສ່ວນຕົວ	private business
ງານຍາກ	heavy labor

ງານວັນເກີດ	birthday party
ງາມ	beautiful, pretty
ງາມຫລາ (ງາມຍິ່ງ)	pretty
ງ່າມປູ	crab claw
ງິ້ວ	Chinese theater, kapok
ງຶດ	to consent, salute with head
ງູ	snake
ງູຈົງອາງ	king cobra
ງູພິດກັດບໍ່ມີພິດ	venomous snakes
ງູເຫົ່າ	cobra
ແງະ	to take off
ແງມ	to crave
ງົ່ວ	numb
ງົດງາມ	very beautiful
ງົບປມານ	budget
ໂງ່	ignorant, stupid
ໂງ່ (ໃຈບຶກ)	ignorant, stupid
ໂງ້ງ	curved
ເງາະ	rambutan
ງໍ	crooked, bent
ງຶ	to bother about, surprise
ງອນ	to pretend, touchy, liable
ງອນຄໍ	nape
ງອມ	very ripe
ເງິນ	money, silver
ເງິນສົດ	cash
ເງິນເດືອນ	monthly, salary
ເງິນບຳນານ	pension

ເຈ້ຍປອມ	counterfeit money
ເຈ້ຍຫຼຸນ (ເຈ້ຍຍ່ອຍ)	small change
ເຈ້ຽ	to straighten up
ວ້າວ (ວ່າງວ່າ)	fin
ງຽບ (ມິດ)	silent
ເຈືອກ	dragon
ເຈື່ອນໄຂ	condition, term
ງົວ	steer, cow, beef
ງົວເຖິກ	bull
ງວງ	proboscis
ງວງຊ້າງ	elephant's trunk
ງ່ວງນອນ	to feel sleepy
ງວມ	covered
ໄງ່	dust
ເງົາ	shadow
ງອກໄປ	to turn, turn around

ຈະ	shall, will
ຈະແຈ້ງ	will be clear
ຈະບໍ	will not

ຈະລາຈອນ	traffic
ຈະເຣີນ	prosperity
ຈະຣວດ	rocket
ຈັກ	how many?
ຈັກ (ເຄື່ອງຈັກ)	machine
ຈັກຍິບເຄື່ອງ	sewing machine
ຈັກຕອກ	to cut bamboo strips
ຈັກເທື່ອ	how often?
ຈັກເທົ່າໃດ	how many?
ຈັກນ້ອຍ (ຈັກໜ່ອຍ)	a little while
ຈັກຢ່າງ	how many kinds?
ຈັກກິໂລ	how many kilometers?
ຈັກອັນ	how many pieces?
ຈັງໄຣ	unmannerly
ຈັງຫວະ	rhythm
ຈັດ	to arrange
ຈັດການ (ຈັດວຽກ)	to manage to do
ຈັດແຈງ	to prepare
ຈັດແຖວ	to line up
ຈັດຣາຍການ	to launch a program
ຈັດໃຫ້	to serve
ຈັດວາ	plus sign, of fourth gr
ຈັນເພັງ	full moon
ຈັ່ມ	fishtrap
ຈັບ	to take, to touch
ຈັບກຸມ	to arrest
ຈັບຂະໂມຍ	to arrest a robber

ຈັບໃຈ	interesting
ຈັບສລາກ	to draw lots
ຈັບຕາຍ	to capture dead
ຈັບມື	to shake hands
ຈັບເວລາ	to time
ຈັບໄວ້ (ຈັບເຈົ້າ)	to seize and hold
ຈາ	chief
ຈາຍົມພິຍາມ	the rulers of hell
ຈາກ	from, to leave
ຈາກກັນ	to separate from each other
ຈາກນີ້ເຖິງນັ້ນ	from here to there
ຈາກໄປ	to go away
ຈາງ	saltless, tasteless
ຈາງ	to hire
ຈາຍ	to spend
ຈາຍເກີນ	to overpay
ຈາຍຄ່າອາຫານ	to pay for food
ຈາຍເງິນ	to pay money
ຈາຍເງິນເດືອນ	to pay salaries
ຈາຍແລ້ວ	paid
ຈານ	plate
ຈານສຽງ	record (music)
ຈາມ	to sneeze
ຈາວ	even
ຈາວກັນ	even, tie score
ຈາວ	to advertise for sale
ຈາວຂາຍ	to advertise and sell
ຈິ້ງຈຸ່ມ	lizard
ຈິຕວິທຍາ	psychology
ຈິກ	to pick, press to get resin
ຈິງ	true
ຈິງໃຈ	sincere(ly)
ຈິຕບໍ່	feebleminded
ຈິບ	to sip
ຈິບຫາຍ	to ruin
ຈິມາຍ	field cricket
ຈີກ	to tear
ຈີ່	to roast
ຈີ່ເຂົ້າ	to bake rice bread
ຈີ້	to point, poke at
ຈີນ	China
ຈີນປະຊາຊົນ	People's Republic of China
ຈີມແຂ້ວ	to pick the teeth
ຈິງ (ຈຶ່ງ)	so, then
ຈື່	to remember
ຈື່ດີ	to remember well
ຈື່ໄວ້	to hold in memory
ຈືດ	tasteless, insipid, barely seasoned
ຈືນ	to fry, fried
ຈຸ	to come very close to
ຈຸກ	to have a stomach ache
ຈຸດ	point, spot
ຈຸດສຳຄັນ	key point

ຈຸດບົກພ້ອງ	weak point, bad point	ເຈັບຫົວເຈີກ	chest illness
ຈຸດປະສົງ	objective	ເຈັບແອວ	lumbago
ຈຸດໄຟ	to light	ເຈລະຈາ	to negotiate
ຈຸດໝາຍ	destination	ແຈ	corner
ຈຸຕິ	death (of monks)	ແຈກັນ	flower vase
ຈຸບ	to soak	ແຈກ	to distribute
ຈຸມນ້ຳ	to soak	ແຈກຢາຍ	to distribute
ຈຸມ	group	ແຈກຣາງວັນ	to distribute prizes
ຈູງ	to lead	ແຈ້ງ	clear, bright
ຈູງມ້າ	to lead a horse	ແຈ້ງຂໍຫາ	to complain against
ຈູດ	to burn	ແຈ້ງຄວາມ	to announce, inform
ຈູດທຸບ	to light incense	ແຈ້ງຜົນ	to publish the results
ຈູບ	to kiss	ແຈ້ງຣາຄາ	to declare the price
ຈູບຫອຍ	to suck a snail from shell	ແຈ້ງຣາຍລະອຽດ	to report the details
ເຈັກ	Chinese	ແຈບ	well fitting
ເຈັດ (ງ)	seven (7)	ແຈ່ມໃສ	clear
ເຈັດສິບ(ງ໐)	seventy (70)	ແຈວ	pepper sauce, condiments
ເຈັບ	sick, ill	ຈົກ	hoe
ເຈັບແຂ້ວ	toothache	ຈົກສລາກ	to draw lots
ເຈັບຄໍ	sore throat	ຈົງຮັກພັກດີ	loyal
ເຈັບຄິງ	to ache all over	ຈົງອາງ	king cobra
ເຈັບໃຈ	resentful, to vex	ຈົງ	be, must, should
ເຈັບທ້ອງ	stomach ache	ຈົດ	to note
ເຈັບຕາ	conjunctivitis	ຈົດຈຳ	to remember
ເຈັບປ່ວຍ	ill	ຈົດຊື່	to write one's name
ເຈັບຫົວ	headache	ຈົດທະບຽນ	to register
ເຈັບໜັກ	seriously ill, wounded	ຈົດທະບຽນການຄ້າ	to patent

ຈົດບັນຊີ	to enter accounts
ຈົດບັນທຶກ	to note
ຈົດໝາຍ	letter
ຈົດໝາຍດ່ວນ	special delivery letter
ຈົນ	poor
ຈົນຄົນສຸດທ້າຍ	to the last man
ຈົນສຸດ	utmost
ຈົນສຸດຄວາມສາມາດ	to the best of one's ability
ຈົນໄດ້	until success
ຈົນຕາຍ	until death
ຈົນຕລອດຊີວິດ	for life
ຈົນນາທີສຸດທ້າຍ	to the last minute
ຈົນວ່າ	until
ຈົນຮອດ	until (distance)
ຈົນເຖິງ	until
ຈົບ	good, to end
ຈົບງາມ	gracious
ຈົບຈາກໂຮງຮຽນ	to complete school
ຈົບແລ້ວ	to finish something
ຈົບຫຼາຍ	very good
ຈົມນ້ຳ	to drown
ຈົມລົງ	to sink
ຈົມ	to grumble
ຈົມດ່າ	to grumble about
ຈົມຫາ	to miss
ຈົມພືງສີ	to recite aloud
ໂຈດ (ໂຈດເລກ)	mathematical problem
ໂຈນ	thief
ໂຈນຜູ້ຮ້າຍ	criminal
ໂຈມ	to lift in one's arms
ໂຈມຕີ	to attack
ໂຈມຕີຢ່າງໂຈ້ງໂຈ້ງ	surprise attack
ເຈາະ	to pierce
ຈໍ	screen
ຈໍ	to sprout
ຈົມວຍ	on guard in boxing
ຈອກ	glass
ຈອກແກ້ວ	glass
ຈອງ	to reserve
ຈອງຫອງ	bad mannered
ຈອງ	parasol
ຈອຍ	thin
ຈອຍລົງ	to become thin
ຈອດເຊື່ອມ	to solder, to weld
ຈອບ	to set ambush
ຈອບເບິ່ງ	to watch secretly
ຈອບຟັງ	to eavesdrop
ຈອມ	top
ຈອມພູ	mountain top
ຈອມພົນ	marshal
ຈອມ	pointed, conical
ເຈື	to meet

ເຈີດ	to glide	ใจร้าย	angry
ເຈັ້ງ	bat	ใจร้อม	impatient
ເຈັ້ງ	to carry on one's back	ເຈົ້າ	yes, you, your, person of royal family
ເຈັ້ງລູກ	to carry a child on one's back	ເຈົ້າຂອງ	owner
ເຈັ້ງ	paper	ເຈົ້າແຂວງ	provincial governor
ຈຸມ	humble	ເຈົ້າສາວ	bride
ຈຸມໃຈ	to think of others first, meek	ເຈົ້າຊີວິດ	king
ຈົວ	Buddhist novice	ເຈົ້າຊູ້	Don Juan
ຈົວນ້ອຍ	young novice	ເຈົ້າຍິງ	princess
ໃຈ	heart	ເຈົ້ານາຍ	dignitary
ໃຈກ້າ	brave	ເຈົ້າບ່າວ	groom
ໃຈຄໍ	disposition	ເຈົ້າພາຍ	host
ໃຈແຄບ	mean	ເຈົ້າຟ້າ	crown prince
ໃຈຄວາມ	essence of a story	ເຈົ້າມື	banker for gambling
ໃຈງ່າຍ	credulous	ເຈົ້າວັດ	abbot
ໃຈສມັກ	voluntary	ເຈົ້າທິວ	bonze
ໃຈດີ	good hearted	ເຈົ້າພາທຳ	officer
ໃຈເດັດ	decisive	ເຈົ້າອະທິການ	abbot
ໃຈດຳ	evil hearted	ຈຳ	to remember, pawn, mortgage
ໃຈນ້ອຍ	narrow minded	ຈຳຄຸກ	to imprison
ໃຈບຸນ	generous	ຈຳຄຸກຕລອດຊີວິດ	to imprison for life
ໃຈບືກ	stupid, bigoted	ຈຳໃຈ	to be constrained, obliged
ໃຈເຢັນ	imperturbable	ຈຳໄດ້	to remember
ໃຈໃຫຍ່	magnanimous	ຈຳໄດ້ດີ	to remember well
ໃຈອົດທົນ	patient	ຈຳນວນ	number of items
ໃຈອ່ອນ	sensitive	ຈຳເປັນ	necessary
ໃຈອຳມະຫິດ	savage, cruel	ຈຳພວກ	kind

ຈຳເພາະ — especially
ຈຳວັດສາ — to pass Buddhist lent
ຈຳໄວ້ — to memorize
ຈ້ຳ — to mark, sorcerer

ເສືອ

ສະກັດ — to blockade
ສະເກັດ (ສເກັດ) — pieces, bits
ສະເກັດຈະເບີດ — shell fragment
ສະກຸນສູງ — noble family
ສະກົດຕາມຮອຍ — to trail
ສະວ່າ (ສະຫວ່າ) — pretty
ສະວ່າງງາມ — splendid
ສະຫວ່າຜ່າເຜື່ອ — prosperous
ສວິ່ງງຽບ — quiet
ສະສາງ — to clean up
ສະສົມ — to collect
ສະສົມກາຳລັງ — to reinforce the army
ສະສົມອາວຸດ — to stock weapons
ສະສົມອາຫານ — to stock food
ສະແດງ (ສແດງ) — to show
ສະແດງກິຣິຍາ — to act politely
ສະແດງກົນ — to dupe

ສະແດງຄວາມຍິນດີ — to compliment
ສະແດງທັມ — to preach
ສະແດງບົດຍາດ — to play a role
ສະແດງລະຄອນ — to act (drama)
ສະແດງເຫດຜົນ — to show the results of
ສະດຸດ — to stumble
ສະເດັດເຈົ້າ — prince
ສະເດັດປະພາດ — to take a trip (formal)
ສະດວກບົວ — lotus pond
ສະດວກ (ສດວກ) — convenient
ສະຕິ — conscious
ສະຕິປັນຍາ — intelligence
ສະແຕມ — postage stamp
ສະຕຣີ — woman
ສະຖານ — place, premise
ສະຖານະການ — situation
ສະຖານີ — station
ສະຖາບັນ — institution
ສະຖານທີ່ເກີດເຫດ — scene of action
ສະຖານທີ່ຕາກອາກາດ — vacation spot
ສະຖານທູດ — embassy
ສະຖານພະຍາບານ — infirmary
ສະເທືອນ — to shake
ສັນຍມີ — boxing gloves
ສນາມ — field
ສນາມກິລາ — stadium, athletic field
ສນາມກິລາແຫ່ງຊາດ — national stadium

ສນາມກອຟ	golf course	ສມັກງານ	to apply for a job
ສນາມເຕະບານ	soccer field	ສມັກໃຈ	willing, voluntarily
ສນາມເຕນນິສ	tennis court	ສະມາຄົມ	association
ສນາມບິນ	airport	ສະມາຊິກ	member
ສນາມມ້າ	race track	ສມຸດ	notebook
ສນາມມວຍ	boxing arena	ສຸມດຄູ່ມື	manual
ສນາມຣົບ	battlefield	ສມຸດບັນທຶກ	book
ສນາມຫຍ້າ	lawn	ສອງ	to return (a kindness)
ສນາມຫຼິ້ນ	playground	ສມໍ	anchor
ສນຸກ	fun, happy	ສມອງ	brain, mind, intelligence
ສເນ	to charm	ສເມີ	equal, level, always
ສັນນ	therefore	ສມຽນ	secretary
ສັນຍສນຸນ	to support	ສໄມ	period of time
ສະນ້ຳ	pond	ສໄມກ່ອນ	in old times, before
ສະບາຍ (ສບາຍ)	comfortable, happy	ສໄມນີ້	the present
ສະບາຍໃຈ	at ease	ສໄມປະຈຸບັນ	at present
ສະບາຍດີ (ມື້ເຊົ້າ)	good morning	ສໄມໃໝ່	modern
ສະບາຍດີ (ມື້ແລງ)	good evening	ສມ່ຳສເມີ	even, equal
ສະບາຍຖືບ	how do you do?	ສຣະ	well
ສະບູ	soap	ສຣຸບ	to summarise, conclude
ສະບູຫອມ	perfumed soap	ສເຣີມສລອງ	to celebrate
ສະພາແຫ່ງຊາດ	National Assembly	ສະລະຊີວິດ (ສະລະຊີບ)	to sacrifice one's life
ສະພານ	bridge	ສະລະຖິ້ມ	to abandon
ສະເພາະ	specifically	ສລັກ	to sculpture, carve
ສະເພົາ	sampan	ສລັບ	to alternate
ສມັກ	to volunteer	ສລັບກັນ	to alternate
ສມັກແຂ່ງຂັນ	to enter contest	ສລັບສີ	to paint stripes
		ສລາກ	lottery ticket
		ສລາດ	intelligent, smart, clever

ສລາມ	shark
ສລຸບ	summary
ສລອກກອກ	sly, funny
ສລອງ	to celebrate
ສເລີມສລອງ	celebration
ສວັນ	paradise, heaven
ສວ່າງແຈ້ງ	bright, sunrise
ສວ່າງເທ່ວົ້າ	escape from a calamity, to get out of difficulty
ສວາຍ	noon
ສະອິດໄຟ	electric switch
ສເວີຍ	to eat (for monks)
ສະຫະກອນ	cooperative association
ສະຫະປະຊາຊາດ	United Nations
ສະຫະລັດອະເມຣິກາ	United States of America
ສະຫາຍ	friend, comrade
ສະຫົວ	to wash one's hair
ສະອາດ	clean
ສະອາບນ້ຳ	wash basin, bathtub
ສະເອິະ (ສະເອິ)	to hiccup
ສັກກາຣະບູຊາ	to worship
ສັກຢາ	injection
ສັງກະສີ	zinc, corrugated zinc
ສັງເກດ	to observe
ສັງເກດເຫັນ	to notice
ສັງຄະຮາດ	chief priest, patriarch

ສັງຄົມ	society
ສັ່ງ	to command, to order
ສັ່ງຂ້າ	to order to kill
ສັ່ງຂີ້ມູກ	to blow one's nose
ສັ່ງເຄອງ	to order goods
ສັ່ງເຄອງກິນ	to order a meal
ສັ່ງເຄອງຈາກນອກ	to import
ສັ່ງສອນ	to teach
ສັ່ງຊື້ເຄອງ	to order goods
ສັ່ງປ່ອຍ	to order release
ສັ່ງພັກຣາຊການ	to suspend an official
ສັ່ງຢາ	to prescribe medicine
ສັ່ງຫ້າມ	to prohibit
ສັດ	animal
ສັດຊື່	honest, loyal, sincere
ສັດຕຣູ	enemy
ສັດນ້ຳ	water animal
ສັດປ່າ	wild animal
ສັດຮ້າຍ	ferocious animal
ສັນ	to eat (for monks)
ສັນຊາດ	nationality
ສັນຍາ	treaty
ສັນຍາຊື້ຂາຍ	sales contract
ສັນຍາເຊົ່າ	lease
ສັນຍານໄພ	alarm
ສັນຍານໄຟໄໝ້	fire alarm

ສົມດານ	character
ສົມດານຊົວ	incorrigible
ສັນຕິ	peace
ສັນຣະເສີນ	to congratulate
ສັນຣະເສີນຍ້ອງຍໍ	to praise
ສັ່ນ	to tremble
ສັ່ນກະດິງ	to ring a bell
ສັນສະເທືອນ	to agitate
ສັ່ນເງິ້ມ	to tremble
ສັ່ນຫົວ	to nod
ສັ້ນ	short, brief
ສັບ	to mince
ສັມຜັດມື	to shake hands
ສັມພັນທະໄມຕຣີ	friendly relations
ສັມພາດ	to interview
ສາສນາ	religion
ສາສນາພຸດ	Buddhism
ສາທາຣະນະສຸກ	public health
ສາບານ	to swear
ສາບານຕົວ	to swear in
ສາບານວ່າ	to swear that...
ສາມະເນນ	novice
ສາມັກຄີ	solidarity
ສາມາດ (ສາມາຖ)	can, to be able
ສາຣະພາບ	to confess
ສາຣະວັດ	inspector, police
ສາລີ	corn

ສາກ	pestle
ສາກກະເບືອ	large kitchen pestle
ສາງ ໄພ່	to shuffle cards
ສາງ	granary, warehouse
ສາງຂຶ້ນ	to rise, arise
ສາງຊາດ	to build the nation
ສາງຊື່ສຽງ	to become popular
ສາສດາ	professor, academic
ສາຍ	wire
ສາຍໂສ້	chain
ສາຍສ້ອຍຄໍ	necklace
ສາຍຈະມວນ	fuse for rocket
ສາຍຕາ	sight
ສາຍຕາສັ້ນ	nearsighted
ສາຍຕາຍາວ	farsighted
ສາຍໄຟຟ້າ	electric wire
ສາຍອາກາດ	antenna
ສາຍແອວ	belt
ສາຍຮັດແອວ	belt
ສາດ	mat
ສາດສນາ	religion
ສາດສະນາພຸດ	Buddhism
ສາດນ້ຳ	to splash water
ສານ	to weave (a basket)
ສາບ	to patch up, stinking
ສານ(ມ໌)	three (3)

ສາມເທົ້າ	triple	ສີແສດ	vermilion
ສາມລ່ຽມ	triangle	ສີຊົມພູ	pink
ສາມລໍ້	"samloh," tricycle-taxi	ສີສົ້ມ	orange color
ສາວ	girl, to draw wire	ສີຊໍ	to play the violin
ສາວໂທ່ຍ	spinster	ສີຍັງແຫ້ງ	wet paint!
ສຶກ	to leave the priesthood	ສີດາ	guava
ສິງ	lion	ສີແດງ	red
ສິ່ງຂອງ	things	ສີດຳ	black
ສິດຖິ	rights by law	ສີຕາ	to rub the eyes
ສິບ (໑໐)	ten (10)	ສີເທົາ	gray
ສິບເອັດ (໑໑)	eleven (11)	ສີນ້ຳ	water colors
ສີ	to rub, color	ສີນ້ຳເງີນ	blue
ສີກາກີ	kaki	ສີນ້ຳຕານ	brown
ສີກຸຫລາບ	rose colored	ສີນ້ຳມັນ	oil paint
ສີເຂັ້ມ	dark in color	ສີຟ້າ	sky blue
ສີກົມມະທຳ	navy blue	ສີມ່ວງ	purple
ສີຂາວ	white	ສີເຫລືອງ	yellow
ສີແຂ້ວ	to brush one's teeth	ສີອ່ອນ	light or pale in color
ສີເຂັ້ມ	dark in color	ສີ່ (໔)	four (4)
ສີຂຽວ	green	ສີ່ແຍກ	crossroads, intersection
ສີຂຽວເຂົ້າ	dark green	ສີ່ຫີດ	the four cardinal directions
ສີເຂົ້າ	to husk rice	ສີ່ສິບ (໔໐)	fourty (40)
ສີຄາມ	indigo	ສີ່ກຸ່ງມ	quadrangle, quadrilateral
ສີຈາງ	light colored	ສີ່ກຸ່ງມມິນທີນ	square
ສີເຈັບໆ	slight pain	ສີ້	to have intercourse
ສີສະ	head	ສີກັນ	to copulate

ສີກ	to tear apart	ສຸດ	end
ສີດຢາ	to give injection	ສຸດຄວາມຊາມາດ	to the best of one's ability
ສີດພົ່ນ	to spray	ສຸດຈະຮິດ	honest, faithful
ສິນຄ້າ	merchandise	ສຸດທ້າຍ	final
ສິນຄ້າໜິດສີ	contraband, smuggled goods	ສຸບ	to put on
ສິນບົນ	bribe	ສຸບເກີບ	to put on shoes
ສິນລະທັມ (ສິລທັມ)	morale	ສຸບໃສ່	to put something on
ສິນລະປະ	art	ສູບນ້ຳ	to pump water
ສິ້ນ	Lao skirt	ສຸບໝວກ	to put a hat on
ສິ້ນຍ່ອນ	petticoat	ສຸມໄຟ	to build a fire
ສິ້ນສຸດລົງ	end	ສຸຣາ	liquor
ສິມ	temple, sanctuary	ສູ	you (children)
ສິວ	pimple	ສູ	all, every
ສິວ	chisel	ສູຂ້ວນ	Lao ceremony, rite
ສິກສາ	education	ສູ	to fight against
ສື່ມພັນ	medium	ສູກັນຕົວຕໍ່ຕົວ	to fight man to man
ສືບຂ່າວ	to ask about, cover (news)	ສູຄວາມ	to make something clear
ສືບຖາມ	to inquire	ສູຄວາມຕາຍ	to brave death
ສືບສວນ	to interrogate	ສູຕາຍ	to fight to the death
ສືບພັນ	to engender	ສູງ	high, tall
ສຸ	to rub	ສູງພຽງຫົວເຂົ່າ	knee-high
ສຸພາບຮຽບຮ້ອຍ	polite	ສູດ	to pray, sutra
ສຸກ	ripe, cooked	ສູດມົນ	to pray
ສຸກະພາບ	health	ສູນ (0)	angry, zero (0)
ສຸກສະບາຍ	happy	ສູນກາງ	center
		ສູບ	to smoke
		ສູບຝິ່ນ	to smoke opium

ສູບຢາ	to smoke tobacco	ແສບຄໍ	to have a sore throat
ສູບຢາງຣົດ	to pump up a tire	ແສບທ້ອງ	hungry
ສູບລົມ	to pump up a tire	ແຟບລິ້ນ	to have a burned tongue
ເສັ່ງ	to compete, exam	ສົງ	monk
ເສັ່ງກັນ	to take an exam together	ສົງການ	Lao New Year (April), the Water Festival
ເສັ່ງໄດ້	to pass an exam	ສົງຄາມ	war, battle
ເສັ່ງຕົກ	to fail an exam	ສົງສານ	to pity
ເສັດ	ended, finished	ສົງໄສ	to suspect
ເສັ້ນ	line	ສົ່ງ	to send
ເສັ້ນປະສາດ	nerve	ສົ່ງໃຫ້	to hand over
ເສັ້ນໝີ່ (ເສັ້ນເຂົາປຸ່ນ)	noodles	ສົ່ງຂາວ	to send a message
ເສັ້ນເລືອດ	vein	ສົ່ງຄືນ	to give back, return
ເສຣີ	free, independent	ສົ່ງສຽງ	to cry out
ເສຣີພາບ	freedom	ສົ່ງເສີມ	to support, to favor
ເສຣີພາບໃນການຮຽນ	freedom of learning	ສົ້ງ	pants, trousers
ເສຣີພາບໃນການເວົ້າ	freedom of speech	ສົ້ງຂາສັ້ນ	shorts
ເສດ	to be left over	ສົ້ງຂາຍາວ	trousers
ເສດຖີ	rich person	ສົ້ງເສື້ອ	clothing
ເສບ	to play music	ສົ້ງຊ້ອນ	underwear
ເສົາ	rod	ສົດ	fresh
ແສງ	light	ສົດຊື່ນ	refreshing
ແສງໄຟ	firelight	ສົນ	mix-up
ແສງມົວ	weak light	ສົນກັນ	to confuse
ແສງອາທິດ	sunlight	ສົນ	tip, trace
ແສດ	orange (color)	ສົ້ນຕີນ	heel (foot)
ແສນ	hundred thousand (100,000)	ສົ້ນເກີບ	heel (shoe)
ແສບ	to feel pain	ສົບມົກ	bill, beak

ສົມ	to be fit	ສໍສີ	colored pencil, crayon
ສົມກາງດ	honorable	ສໍດຳ	lead pencil
ສົມກັນ	to fit together	ສໍ້	to interrogate
ສົມຄ່າຈ້າງ	to earn one's pay	ສໍ້ໂກງ	to cheat
ສົມຄວນ	appropriate	ສໍ້ຫຼ	sly, flattering
ສົມຍອມ	to admit	ສອກ	elbow, unit of length
ສົມເດັດພະເຈົ້າມະຫາຊີວິດ	the King (Lord of life)	ສອງ (໒)	two (2)
ສົມເດັດພະສັງຄະຣາດ	patriarch	ສອງຈິດສອງໃຈ	to hesitate
ສົມບັດ	property	ສອງສາມ	a few, two or three
ສົມບູນ (ສົມບຸນ)	healthy, perfect, complete	ສອງຕໍ່ (ສອງເທົ່າ)	double
ສົມມຸດ	to suppose, if	ສອງໃນສາມ	two-thirds (2/3)
ສົມຣາຄາ	to be worth its price	ສ່ອງ	to see through
ສົມທ້ວງ	just as you hoped, your wish come true	ສ່ອງກະຈົກ	to look in a mirror
ສົ້ມ	sour, orange	ສ່ອງກ້ອງ	to look through binoculars
ສົ້ມຕຳ	sour papaya dish	ສ່ອງເບິ່ງ	to look at
ສົ້ມຜັກ	fermented vegetable	ສ່ອງໄພ້ຟ້າ	to x-ray
ໂສມັນ	to discuss, argue	ສ້ອຍ (ຄໍ)	necklace
ໂສໂຄກ	dirty	ສ້ອຍແຂນ	bracelet
ໂສໄດ້ໂສເສັ້ງ	to risk	ສອດ	to insert
ໂສຕາຍ	to risk one's life	ສອນ	to teach, arrow
ໂສ້	chain	ສອນພິເສດ	to tutor, coach
ໂສມາເສົ້າ	sad	ສ່ອນ	to begin to ripen, cataract (eye)
ໂສ້ງ	trousers	ສອບ	to test
ໂສ້ງຂາສັ້ນ	shorts	ສອບແກ້ໂຕ	to pass a re-examination
ໂສດ	single	ສອບຂຽນ	written examination
ສໍ	pencil	ສອບເຂົາ	to pass entrance exam
ສໍຂາວ	chalk	ສອບຄວາມຣູ້	I.Q. test

ສອບເສັງ	to take an exam	ເສັງຜາສີ	to pay taxes
ສອບສວນ	to interrogate	ເສັ່ງແພງໂພດ	to pay too much
ສອບໄດ້	to pass exam	ເສັ່ງລ້າໆ	to lose for nothing
ສອບຕົກ	to fail an exam	ເສັ່ງເວລາ	to waste time
ສອບປາກເປົ່າ	oral examination	ເສັ່ງໜ້າເສັ່ງຕາ	to lose one's reputation
ສອມ	fork	ເສັ່ງຫຼຽມ	outsmarted
ເສິກ	war	ເສັ່ງຫາຍ	to lose, damage
ເສີມສອຍ	to make up	ເສັ່ງອັງຄະ	disabled, lame
ເສັ່ງ	to lose, pay	ເສັ່ງໂອກາດ	to miss an opportunity
ເສັ່ງກິລິຍາ	impolite	ສງງ	sound, voice, tone
ເສັ່ງກຳລັງໃຈ	to be discouraged	ສງງກອງ	echo
ເສັ່ງກຽດ	to lose honor	ສງງແຂງ	bold voice
ເສັ່ງຄ່າທຳນຽມ	to pay fee	ສງງຄ້ອງ	sound of gong
ເສັ່ງຄີມ	to degrade oneself	ສງງສູງ	high voice
ເສັ່ງເຄາະ	to accept misfortune	ສງງດັງ	noisy
ເສັ່ງເຄີມ	to cost	ສງງຕົບມື	applause
ເສັ່ງໃຈ	to be sorry	ສງງປະສານ	harmony of voices
ເສັ່ງໄປ	to lose, lost	ສງງຟ້າຮ້ອງ	thunder
ເສັ່ງສລະ	to sacrifice	ສງງແຫບ	hoarse voice
ເສັ່ງສາວ	to lose one's virginity	ສງງຫົວ	laughter
ເສັ່ງຊາດ	unworthy of one's race	ສງງຮ້ອງ	appeal
ເສັ່ງຊື່	to lose one's reputation	ສງງເອີ້ນ	cry for help
ເສັ່ງຊົງ	deformed	ສ່ງງ	to try risk
ເສັ່ງດາຍ	pity, to regret	ສງງໂຊກ	to take a chance, to try one's luck
ເສັ່ງເດັກນ້ອຍ	to spoil a child	ສງມ	thorn
ເສັ່ງດອກເບ້ຍ	to pay interest	ສງມ	small spade
ເສັ່ງຕາ	to become blind or near-sighted	ເສື່ອ (ໂຕ໌ງ)	tiger
ເສັ່ງປຽບ	to be at a disadvantage		

ເສືອດາວ	leopard	ສວນທາງ	to pass each other
ເສືອດໍາ	panther	ສວນຜັກ	vegetable garden
ເສື່ອ	mattress	ສວນ	part
ເສື່ອສາດ	mat	ສວນດຽວ	one part only
ເສື້ອ	blouse, shirt	ສວນຄົວ	private
ເສື້ອກັນຝົນ	raincoat	ສວນຫຼາຍ	majority
ເສື້ອກັນພາວ	overcoat	ສອຍ	to snap at
ເສື້ອກ້າມ	undershirt	ສວມ	to put on
ເສື້ອຊ້ອນ	underwear	ໃສ	clear, bright, light
ເສື້ອຍົກຊົງ	bra	ໃສ່	to wear, to put on
ເສື້ອຢືດ	elastic underwear, T-shirt	ໃສກະແຈ	to lock
ເສື້ອນອນ	pajamas	ໃສ່ເສື້ອຜ້າ	to dress
ເສື້ອຜ້າ	clothes	ໃສ່ຊື່	to sign the register
ເສື້ອຜູ້ຍິງ	blouse	ໃສ່ໂທດ	to determine the punishment
ເສື້ອຝົນ	raincoat	ໃສນ້ຳຫອມ	to perfume
ເສື້ອໃຫຍ່	coat	ໃສ່ບ່າ	to put on one's shoulder
ເສື້ອໄໝ	silk garment	ໃສຢາ	to apply ointment
ເສື້ອດຕາເບິ່ງ	to glance at	ໃສແວ່ນຕາ	to wear glasses
ສອຍ	late in the day	ໄສ (ໄສກົບ)	to plane
ສວຍ	to wipe one's face	ໄສ້	intestine, tube, cord
ສອດມົນ	to chant a prayer	ໄສ້ກອກ	Chinese spiced sausage
ສວນ	garden	ໄສ້ໄກ່	chicken entrails
ສວນຄົວ	family garden	ໄສ້ຕະກຽງ	lamp wick
ສວນສະໜາມ	military review, parade	ໄສ້ຕິ່ງ	appendix
ສວນສະໜຸກ	playground	ໄສ້ອົ່ວ	sausage

ເສົາ	post, column	ຢະມັດ	to shiver
ເສົາທຸງ	flag pole	ຢະລາ (ຢະຊາ)	old, aged, senile
ເສົ້າ	short of breath	ຢະແລງ	crowbar, lever
ເສົ້າ	sad	ຢະເລຶຍເສິກ	prisoner of war (P.O.W.)
ສຳຄັນ	important	ຢ້າກ	to wash
ສຳລັບ	for	ຢ້າກ	to draw, dip, raise
ສຳນຽງ	accent, pronunciation	ຢ້າກເຄື່ອງ	to wash clothes
ສຳມະໂນຄົວ	census	ຢ້າກຈູງ	to lead, to guide
ສຳຣວດ	to inspect	ຢ້າກຊາ	to delay
ສຳຣວດສຳມະໂນຄົວ to take a census		ຢ້າກຢວມ	to urge on
ສຳເຣັດ	to complete, succeed	ຢ້າກເຕຶອນ	to warn
ສັ້ງ	way, like, manner	ຢ້າກຕົວຢ່າງ	to illustrate, exemplify
		ຢ້າກຖາມ	to question
		ຢ້າກທຸງ	to raise a flag
		ຢ້າກປຶນ	to draw a gun
		ຢ້າກແຫ້ງ	to dry clean
		ຢ້າກອານິຈາ	to pray at a funeral
		ຢ້າກຮູບ	to develop a photograph

		ຊັງ	to hate
		ຊັງກັນ	to hate each other
		ຊັງນ້ຳຫນ້າ	to loathe
		ຊັ່ງ	to weight
ຢະໝັກ	to halt	ຊັ່ງຕິແມດ	centimeter
ຢະດຸກ	to stumble	ຊັ້ນ	to tremble
ຢະຕາກັມ	fate destiny	ຊັ້ນ	floor, story, grade, rank
ຢະຕາຂຶ້ມ	prosperity, luck	ຊັ້ນທຳອາງ	first grade, primary course
ຢະນິດ (ຢນິດ)	kind, sort	ຊັ້ນຈັດຕະວາ	fourth grade
ຢະນີ	gibbon		

ຊັ້ນສູງ	high-ranking	ຊາງ	childhood dysentery
ຊັ້ນຕີ	third grade	ຊ່າງ	craftsman, artisan
ຊັ້ນຕ່ຳ	low-ranking	ຊ່າງກໍ່	mason
ຊັ້ນຕົ້ນ	first stage	ຊ່າງເກີບ	shoemaker
ຊັ້ນໂທ	second grade	ຊ່າງຄຳ	jeweler, goldsmith
ຊັ້ນເທິງ	upstairs	ຊ່າງຈັກ	mechanic
ຊັ້ນນອກ	outer layer, outside, right side of fabric	ຊ່າງຊັກເຄື່ອງ	launderer
ຊັ້ນໃນ	inside	ຊ່າງຍິບເຄື່ອງ	tailor, seamstress
ຊັ້ນພິເສດ	special grade	ຊ່າງຕັດເຄື່ອງ, ຕັດເສື້ອ	tailor, dressmaker
ຊັ້ນລຸ່ມ	ground floor, downstairs	ຊ່າງຕັດຜົມ	barber, coiffeur
ຊັ້ນວັນນະ	caste, class	ຊ່າງຕີຄຳ	jeweler
ຊັ້ນເອກ	top grade	ຊ່າງຕີເຫຼັກ	blacksmith
ຊັບສິນ	property	ຊ່າງແຕ້ມ	painter, artist
ຊັບສິນບັດ	property	ຊ່າງຕ່ຳຜ້າ (ຊ່າງຕ່ຳຫູກ)	weaver
ຊັບທັມມະຊາດ	natural resources	ຊ່າງຖ່າຍຮູບ	photographer
ຊາ	tea	ຊ່າງທາສີ	painter
ຊາຕາ	luck	ຊ່າງປັ້ນ	potter
ຊາ	rumor	ຊ່າງແປງແຂ້ວ	dentist
ຊາລື	well-known	ຊ່າງໄຟຟ້າ	electrician
ຊາ	basket, pannier, slow	ຊ່າງໄມ້	carpenter
ຊາໆ	slowly	ຊ່າງຍິບຜູ້ຍິງ	**seamstress, needle woman**
ຊານານ	delay, long time	ຊ້າງ	elephant
ຊາກ	corpse	ຊ້າງສານ	adult elephant
ຊາກຄິນຕາຍ	corpse	ຊ້າງກໍ	tuskless elephant
ຊາກຈອຍ	occasionally	ຊ້າງເຜືອກ	white elephant
ຊາກຜີ	corpse	ຊ້າງພາຍ	tusked elephant (male)
ຊາກຜີຕາຍ	corpse	ຊາຍ	male, man

ຊາຍສະກ້ານ	able-bodied man	ຊາວວຽດນາມ	Vietnam, Vietnamese
ຊາຍໂສດ	bachelor	ຊາວເອັດ (໒໑)	twenty-one (21)
ຊາຍຊູ້	Don Juan, lover	ຊາວເອີຣົບ	European
ຊາຍຍິງ	men and women	ຊາວອຳນາດ	people who have power
ຊາຍປ່າ	jungle perimeter (edge of jungle)	ຊາວ	to clear land
ຊ້າຍ	left (side)	ຊີເນມາ	movies
ຊາດ	race, nation	ຊີ່ງ	balance, scale
ຊາດກ່ອນ	previous life	ຊີກິໂລ	kilogram scale
ຊາດນີ້	this incarnation	ຊີ	drill
ຊາດຜິວຂາວ	white race, European	ຊີວາ	life
ຊານ	outside balcony, back porch	ຊີວິດ	life
ຊານ	deep plate	ຊີວິດປະຈຳວັນ	daily life
ຊານລ້າງໜ້າ	wash basin	ຊີກາຢາ (ກາຍປ່າ)	nicotine
ຊາວ (໒໐) twenty (20), category of people		ຊີມັງ	cement
ຊາວຈີນ	Chinese	ຊີ້ຍອກ	to indicate, point out
ຊາວສວນ	gardener	ຊີຂາດ	to decide
ຊາວຕະເວັນຕົກ	westerner	ຊີ້ແຈງ	to explain, describe
ຊາວຕະເວັນອອກ	easterner	ຊີຕິ່ນຊີ້	to gesticulate
ຊາວຕ່າງປະເທດ	foreigner	ຊີ້ຕົວ	to identify
ຊາວນາ	farmer	ຊີມື	to raise the hand
ຊາວມິຄົນ	settler	ຊີໜ້າ	to point at somebody
ຊາວບ້ານ	villager	ຊີໜ້າຊີ້ຕາ	to point at somebody
ຊາວບ້ານນອກ	rural people	ຊີກ	piece
ຊາວປ່າ	forest people	ຊີງ	to dispute, wrangle
ຊາວພຸດ	Buddhist	ຊີ້ນ	meat, flesh
ຊາວເມືອງ	city dweller	ຊີ້ນຢ່າງ (ຊີ້ນປິ້ງ)	smoked meat
ຊາວລາວ	Lao, Laotian	ຊີ້ນໝູ	pork

ຊີມ (ຊີມຣົດ)	to taste	ຊຸດອາບນ້ຳ	bathing suit
ຊິງ	rice steamer	ຊຸບມິດ	to temper a knife
ຊິງລິງ	(sit, stand) still	ຊຸບລ້ງ	to support, guard
ຊິ່ງ	that, which	ຊຸມ	meeting
ຊື່ນ	gay, vivacious	ຊຸມເຂົ້າ	to banquet
ຊື່ນໃຈ	delighted, gay	ຊຸມແຊວ	to visit and talk
ຊື່ນຊົມຍິນດີ	to appreciate	ຊຸ່ມ	humid
ຊື່ນບານ	happy, joyful	ຊຸ່ມຊື່ນ	wet
ຊື່ນມ່ວນ	happy, joyful, pleasant	ຊູໃຈ	to encourage
ຊືມ	to absorb	ຊູຊີ	to continue obstinately
ຊື່	name, straight	ຊູແຫ	to weight a fishing net
ຊື່ວ່າ	name is	ຊຸ	every
ຊື່ສັດ	honest	ຊຸຍາມ	every moment
ຊື່ສຽງ	reputation, fame	ຊຸເທື່ອ	every time
ຊື່ ໆ	straight, do nothing	ຊຸແນວ	everything
ຊື້	to buy, purchase	ຊຸມື້	every day
ຊື້ເຄື່ອງ	to shop	ຊູ້	lover
ຊື້ຂາຍ	to do business	ຊູ້ສາວ	mistress
ຊື້ມາ	to bring in	ຊູ້ແພງ	beloved
ຊື້ຍູ້ຊື້ກິນ	to buy necessities	ຊຸດໂຊມລົງ	to deteriorate
ຊຸເຊື່ອງ	to hide	ຊູມ	to touch
ຊຸຢເຍ	July	ເຊະ	go away! (to dogs)
ຊຸດ	suit, set	ເຊັດ	to wipe dry
ຊຸດໂຊມ	to worsen, decayed	ເຊັດຕົວ	to dry oneself
		ເຊັນ	to sign
		ເຊັນສັນຍາ	to sign an agreement

ເຊັນຊື່	signature, to sign	ໂຊໂກລາ	chocolate
ເຊັ້ນຢ້ານ	to tremble from fear	ໂຊດາ	soda
ເຊັ່ນ	such as	ໂຊກ	luck
ເຊ	to lurch	ໂຊກຊາຕາ	destiny, fate
ແຊກ	to penetrate	ໂຊກໄຊ	good luck
ແຊກຊຶມ	to infiltrate	ໂຊກຮ້າຍ	bad luck, misfortune
ແຊກແຊງ	to interfere	ຊໍ	violin
ແຊງ	to butt in	ຊໍອູ້	string violin
ແຊບ	delicious	ຊໍດຶງ	banjo
ແຊບຊ້ອຍ	very delicious	ຊໍດອກໄມ້	inflorescence
ແຊມ	to be overloaded	ຊອກ	to seek search
ແຊວ	noisy	ຊອກກິນ	to make a living
ຊົກ	to fist fight	ຊອກຫາ	to seek, look for
ຊົກມວຍ	to box, boxing	ຊອງ	envelope
ຊົງຂະເດັດ	to go (high)	ຊອງຢາຊອງ	pack of cigarette
ຊົງປະທັບ	to stay (high)	ຊອງຟັງສີ	envelope
ຊົງໂປດເກົ້າໂປດກະຫມອມ	to permit (high)	ຊອງທາງ	means
ຊົດຊ່ວຍ	to help	ຊອຍ	to help
ຊົນ	to collide	ຊອດ	half-breed, until
ຊົນນະບົດ	countryside	ຊອດແຈ້ງ	until morning
ຊົນບົດ	countryside	ຊອດຫູ	to reach one's ears (news)
ຊົມ	to prise, to admire	ຊອນ	to pile up
ຊົມຊື່ນ	happy, joyful	ຊອນຮ້ດ	two persons ride on one bike
ຊົມຊື່ນຍິນດີ	overjoyed	ຊອບ	to like, satisfied
ຊົມເຊີຍ	to prise, to admire	ຊອບໃຈ	satisfied
ໂຊະ	out of order, old	ຊອບທຳ	righteous, ethical
ໂຊ	go away! (to chickens), invalid		

ຊອມ	to observe, spy, peep	ເຊື້ອໂລກ (ເຊື້ອໂຣກ) germs	
ຊອມເບິ່ງ	to watch, spy on	ເຊືອກ	rope, string, cord
ຊອມຮົບ	military exercise	ເຊືອບ	to fall asleep, nap
ເຊິ່ງ	which, that	ເຊື່ອມ	to lose, absorbed, melt
ເຊິ່ງກັນແລະກັນ	mutual	ຊົ່ວ	bad, vile
ເຊີ່	to be surprised, faint	ຊົ່ວຄາວ	temporary
ເຊີ້ງ	to sing bawdy festival songs	ຊົ່ວຄົນ	generation (time)
ເຊີດຊູ	to admire, exalt	ຊົ່ວຊ້າຜ່າມາມ	vile, base
ເຊີດເບິ່ອ	to go hunting	ຊົ່ວໂມງ	hour
ເຊີນ	to invite, please	ຊົ່ວອາຍຸ	lifetime
ເຊີນເຂົ້າມາ	please come in!	ຊົ່ວຮ້າຍ	evil
ເຊີນເດີ່	to your health!	ຊ່ວງ	to race
ຊວງ	ex-monk, town	ຊ່ວງມ້າ	horse race
ຊວງມິງ	Lao folk hero, a punster	ຊ່ວງເຮືອ	boat race
ເຊື່ອ	to believe, to trust	ຊ່ວຍ	aid, assist
ເຊື່ອຖື	to believe in, worship	ຊ່ວຍກັນ	to help each other
ເຊື່ອຖວຍຟັງຄວາມ	to obey	ຊ່ວຍຊີວິດ	to save a life
ເຊື່ອຟັງ	to obey	ຊ່ວຍເຫຼືອ	to help
ເຊື່ອໝັ້ນ	to believe firmly	ຊ່ວຍແຮງ	to help out
ເຊື່ອຖືເຊື່ອໃຈ	to have confidence in	ຊວດຫລວດ	to defy, impudent, brazen
ເຊື້ອ	ancestry, family	ຊວນ	to persuade, urge
ເຊື້ອກະສັດ	of royal blood	ຊວນເຊື່ອ	to pretend, convince someone to believe
ເຊື້ອເຈົ້າ	of noble lineage	ໄຊ	bamboo fish trap
ເຊື້ອສາຍ	ancestry	ໄຊຊະມະ	victory
ເຊື້ອຊັ້ນວັນນະ	class, caste	ໄຊຍະບູລີ	Sainyaburi, province in Laos
ເຊື້ອຖື	to rely	ໄຊໂຍ	victory!
ເຊື້ອແນວ	lineage	ໃຊ້	to spend, use, serve

ໃຊ້ກົມ	to suffer consequences
ໃຊ້ຄ່າເສັຽຫາຍ	to reimburse for loss
ໃຊ້ເງິນ	to pay money
ໃຊ້ຈ່າຍ	expense
ໃຊ້ສອຍ	to aid, serve
ໃຊ້ເວນ	to pay for sins of former life
ໃຊ້ໄວ້	used for
ໃຊ້ຫົວຄິດ	to use one's brain
ໃຊ້ໜີ້	to pay a debt
ໃຊ້ອຳນາດບັງຄັບ	to coerce
ໃຊ້ເຂົາ	to winnow rice
ເຊົາ	to cease, stop
ເຊົາເສິກ	cease fire, to end war
ເຊົານົມ	to wean
ເຊົາເມື່ອຍ	to rest
ເຊົາວະເລກ	shorthand
ເຊົ່າ	to rent
ເຊົ່າເຮືອນ	to rent a house
ເຊົ້າ	morning, early
ເຊົ້າມືດ	dawn
ຊົ່ວຄາ	temporary
ຊຳນານ	experience, skilled
ຊຳນິຊຳນານ	experienced, skillful
ຊຳດຽວກັນ	of same
ຊຳໃດ	how big?
ຊຳນັ້ນ	about that size
ຊ້ຳ	dark (color), to repeat

ຊ້ຳໃຈ	to feel hurt
ຊ້ຳຊາກ	repeatedly
ຊ້ຳທ້າຍ	to finish
ຊ້ຳບໍ່ພໍ	and that's not all

ຍະ	to separate, open
ຍະອອກ	to spread apart
ຍັກ	giant
ຍັກຂິນີ	giantess
ຍັກຍອກ	to embezzle
ຍັງ	not yet
ຍັງມີ	to have something left
ຍັດ	to stuff in, to pack tight
ຍັດໃສ່	to cram, stuff
ຍັດປືນ	to load a gun
ຍັ່ມລົງ	to press down
ຍັບ	stealthly
ຍັບເຂົາ	slowly
ຍາ	honorific

ยาคຸ	monk	ຍິ່ງ	extreme, supreme
ຍ່າ	paternal grandmother	ຍິ່ງກວ່າ	more
ยาก	difficult	ຍິ່ງກວ່ານັ້ນ	more than that
ยากแคๆ	in poverty	ຍິ່ງກວ່ານີ້	more than this
ยากจิ๊ม	impoverished	ຍິ່ງໃຫຍ່	great(ly)
ยากใจ	in difficulty	ຍິນ	to hear
ยากຊา	difficult	ຍິນຍອມ	to consent
ยากลຳบาก	distress	ຍິນດີ	to be glad
ยาๆ (ไม้)	hardwood tree	ຍິນດີຊົມຊື່ນ	gratified
ยาๆไก่	portable chicken cage	ຍິນດີຕ້ອນຮັບ	to be glad to meet someone
ຍ່າງ	to walk	ຍິ້ມ	to smile
ຍ້າຍ	to move houses	ຍິ້ມແຍ້ມແຈ່ມໃສ	delight
ยาด	to snatch	ຍີ່	second lunar month (Jan.)
ยาดแย่ๆ	to take by force	ຍີ່ປຸ່ນ	Japan
ยาดโยม	lay people	ຍີ່ຫໍ	trademark
ยาดติ	relative	ຍຶດ	to take away
ยาดติกา	relative	ຍຶດຄອງ	to occupy
ยามบิ๊ม	motor vehicle	ຍຶດຖື	to believe in
ยามพาทะมะ	vehicle	ຍຶດໝັ້ນ	to hold fast
ยาม	watchman, guard, period of time	ຍຶດອອກ	to stretch out
ยามเมื๊อ	when	ຍຶດເອົາ	to take
ยาว	long	ຍຶດຍາວ	lengthy
ยาวมาม	long time	ຍຶດ ๆ	to follow (successively)
ยิก	to pinch, twitch	ຍືນຍັນ	to assert
ยิๆ	to shoot , female	ຍື່ນຄຳຟ້ອງ	to submit a complaint (legal)
ยิๆเมื๊อ	to go hunting	ຍື່ນຄຳຮ້ອງຂໍ	to submit a request
ยิๆยิม	to shoot		

ยื่นคำร้องๆษฺทุ	to submit a complaint	ยกทัสัวงยึมบก	military landing
ยื่นรายงาน	to submit a report	ยกขึ้น	to lift up
ยื่นใท้	to hand to	ยกย้าย	to move
ยุแย	to incite	ยกยอง	to congratulate
ยุยิ้ง	to exhort	ยกโทด	to pardon, forgive
ยุติ	to end, stop	ยกเอ้ม	except
ยุติทัม	justice	ยกเลิก	to cancel
ยุง	mosquito	ยกใท้	to hand over
ยุดทะสาด	strategic	ยิง	to praise
ยุดทะวิธี	tactic	ยด	honor
ยุมสิบ	to pucker up	ยดสัก	title, rank
ยุมทิว	a smile (wry)	ยิม	airplane, engine
ยู	broom	ยิม	a kind of tree
ยู้	to push	ยิมผียาม	guardians of the underwor
ยูง	peacock	ยิมมะราด	king of the underworld
เยสุ	Jesus	โยทา	public works
แยก	to separate	โยง	to jump
แยกกัม	to separate	โยน	to throw, sway
แยกย้าย	to separate	โยมวัด	Buddhist followers in Wat
แยกออก	to divide	เยาะเย้ย	to deride
แยง	to look in a mirror	ยู	to lift, a kind of plant
แยงกะจก	to look into a large mirror	ยูใท้	to offer
แย่วชิ้ง	snatch and run	ยมิมิบ (ยมิไทว)	to salute, to wave to
โยะยาม	to give time		
ยก	to lift	ยยุ้ม	meat paste
ยกทองทับ	to move an army		

ย์แย	weak
ย์	Lao-Thai tribe of upper Mekong
ย์เยิ้ม	to mock
ย์ท	discouraged, tired
ยอก	to shake
ยอง	ruminant animal
ยองฝ้าย	carded cotton
ยอง	to praise
ยองย์	to flatter
ยอย	small piece
ยอย	to drip, trickle
ยอด	top
ยอดอุฝ้า	roof ornaments of a pagoda
ยอดปะมุก	chief of state
ยอดห้วย	source of stream
ยอม	due to
ยอมว่า	because
ยอม	to surrender, yield, submit
ยอมจำนิม	to surrender
ยอมตาย	to accept the conditions
ยอมรับ	to surrender
ยอมรับผิด	to admit guilt
ยอมรับรู้	to recognize (political)
ยอม	to dye
ยอมใจ	to encourage
ยอมสี	to dye
เย์ม	vast, enduring

เยื่อย	disconnected
ย์อะ	to trick
ย์อะเย์า	cheating
ยอเยาม	vehicle
ไย	fibre, filament
เย์าอะอุ้ม	youth
ย์ยี	to stamp, ravage

ก เด็ก

ถักสะกัด	to ambush
ถัว	nose, to sound
ถัวขึ้ม	to make louder, to build a fire
ถัววอง	long nosed
ถัวไฟ	to heat
ถัวโม	hooked nose
ถัวแฟบ	flat nosed
ถั่ว	as, like
ถั่วท่าอ้าวอิม	as mentioned above
ถั่วเท่า	as before
ถั่วใจ	as wished

ຕົ້ວດງວ	same	ຕາງ	net
ຕົ້ວດງວກັນ	just like	ຕາງແຫ	fishing net
ຕົ້ວຕໍ່ໄປນີ້	as follows:	ຕ່າງ	spotted
ຕົ້ວທີ່ທ່າວມານີ້	as has been stated	ຕາຍ	thread
ຕົ້ວນີ້	like this	ຕ່ານ	post, checkpoint
ຕົ້ວນັ້ນ	like that	ຕ່ານກວດຄົນເຂົ້າເມືອງ	immigration office
ຕົ້ວປາຖມາ	as wished	ຕ່ານຕຳຣວດ	police station
ຕົ້ວໝາຍ	as intended, meant	ຕ່ານພາສີ	customs house
ຕົ້ວລຸ່ມນີ້	as below, follows	ຕານ	side, hardened
ຕົ້ວເຕີມ	as before, in old times	ຕ່ານການເມືອງ	the political domain
ຕັດສັນດານ	to reform	ຕ່ານຂ້າງ	the side of
ຕັດແປງ	to alter	ຕ່ານຊ້າຍ	on the left
ຕັດຜົມ	to wave hair	ຕ່ານທະຫານ	the military aspect
ຕັບ	to extinguish	ຕ່ານໜ້າ	at the front
ຕັບສູນ	to die, disappear	ຕ່ານຫຼັງ	at the rear, at the back
ຕັບຊີວິດ	to die	ຕາບ	sword
ຕັບໄຟຟ້າ	to turn out the light	ຕາບກະຍະສິດ	magic sword
ຕັບອາຍ	to ruin	ຕ່າມ	handle, hilt
ດາຣາ	star	ດາວ	star
ດາຣາສາດ	astronomy	ດາວເຄາະ	planet
ດາຣາຮູບເງົາ	movie star	ດາວຄ້ອມ	comet
ດ່າແຫ	to ready a casting net	ດາວຊະເດົດ	shooting star, meteor
ດ່າ	to scold	ດາວຊ້າງ	North star
ດ່າກັນ	to insult each other	ດາວໜມູນ	man-made satellite
ດ່າແຊ່ງ	to curse	ດາວພະສຸກ	Venus
ດ່າປ້ອຍ	to insult, to curse	ດາວພະເສົາ	Saturn
ດ່າກ	anus, rectum	ດາວພະພຸດ	Mercury

ດາວພະຫັດ	Jupiter	ດິດພິນ	to play the harp
ດາວພະອັງຄານ	Mars	ດິເລກຄິດ	to calculate on an abacus
ດາວເຜັດ	morning star	ດິເຫຼືອກ	to flip away
ດາວຫຼູ	constellation	ດິ້ນອອກ	to wriggle out
ດິນ	earth, soil, land	ດຶງ	to pull
ດິນຂໍ	tile	ດຶງອອກ	to extract, pull away, out
ດິນຈີ່	brick	ດື້	obstinate
ດິນສໍ	pencil	ດື່ມ	to drink
ດິນຊີມັງ	cement	ດື່ມຖວາຍພອນ	to drink to someone
ດິນຊາຍ	sand	ດື່ມອວຍພອນ	to drink a toast
ດິນຕາກ	clay	ດຸ	diligent
ດິນແດນ	territory	ດຸເດືອດ	fierce, serious
ດິນໂປ່ງ	salty earth	ດຸລິຍາງ	band
ດິນຟ້າອາກາດ	climate	ດຸໝັ່ນ	hard working
ດິນລະເບີດ	dynamite	ດຸດ	to pull out, dig
ດິນຫຼົມ	mud	ດຸມ	button
ດິນໄຫວ	earthquake	ດຸມກົງ	wheel hub
ດິບ	raw	ດູ	look
ດີ	good	ດູຖູກ	to look down on
ດີກວ່າ	better	ດູໝໍ	to consult a fortune teller
ດີທີ່ສຸດ	best	ດູແລ	to guard, to look after
ດີໃຈ	happy, glad	ດູໝິ່ນ	to disdain
ດີພໍໃຊ້ໄດ້	not too bad	ດູກ	bone
ດີຫຼາຍ	very good	ດູກຂ້າງ	rib
ດີເລີດ	excellent	ດູກເສື້ອ	seam of clothes
ດີອົກດີໃຈ	glad	ດູກສັນຫຼັງ	spine
ດິດຝ້າຍ	to card cotton	ດູກຕໍ່	bone articulation

ດູດ	to suck
ດູດກອກ	to smoke a pipe
ດູດກືນ	to suck
ດູດດຶງ	to draw, pull, attract
ດູດນ້ຳ	to suck water
ດູດຢາ	to smoke tobacco
ດູດເອົາ	to suck
ເດັກ	child
ເດັກເກີດໃໝ່	new born child
ເດັກກຳພ້າ	orphan
ເດັກນ້ອຍ	child
ເດັກນ້ອຍໂລເລ	good for nothing, brat
ເດັກຜູ້ຊາຍ	boy
ເດັກຜູ້ຍິງ	girl
ເດັກຮຸ	obedient child
ເດັດ	to pluck, pick, strict
ເດັດຂາດ	absolute (ly)
ເດັດດອກໄມ້	to pick flowers
ເດັດດ່ຽວ	resolute (ly)
ເດັດເອົາ	to pick
ເດຊະບຸນ	luck
ເດຊານຸພາບ	power (high)
ເດຊີແມດ	decimeter
ເດ	to protrude, stretch
ເດມື	to extend the hand
ເດນ	garbage, waste
ແດ	(sentence final element of request)
ແດງ	red
ແດງຊາຍ	red ant
ແດດ	sunshine
ແດດສ່ອງ	sunlight
ແດດອອກ	the sun shines
ແດດຮ້ອນ	hot weather
ແດດຮ້ອນແດດເຜົ້າ	boiling hot
ແດນ	border
ແດນດິນ	land
ແດນຕໍ່ແດນ	boundary to boundary
ດົກ	abundant
ດົງ	jungle, village
ດົງ	flat bamboo basket
ດົງຝັດ	winnowing rice
ດົນ	long time
ດົນຕຣີ	music
ດົນເຕີຍ	for a little while
ດົນປານໃດ	how long, when
ດົນນານ	a long time ago
ດົນແລ້ວ	a long time since
ດົນເມີນ	firewood
ດົມ	to smell
ດົມກິ່ນ	to sniff
ດົມເຫັມ	to kiss (usually on cheek)
ໂດ	red fish
ໂດລາ	dollar
ໂດຍ	by means of

ໂດຍກົງ	directly	ດອກຂີ້	bamboo flower
ໂດຍຂ້ອຍ	yes (polite)	ດອມເຮືອຍ້າ	loudspeaker
ໂດຍງ່າຍ	easily	ດອກງິ້ວ	kapok flower
ໂດຍເຈຕນາ	intentionally	ດອກຈຳປາ	national flower (white jasmine frangipani)
ໂດຍສະເພາະ	especially	ດອກຈຳປີ	red jasmine
ໂດຍສະເພາະຢ່າງຍິ່ງ	particularly	ດອກດາວເຮືອງ	marigold
ໂດຍສັດຊື່	honestly	ດອກເບ້ຍ	interest on loan
ໂດຍສານ	to travel, taxi	ດອກບົວ	lotus
ໂດຍສຸຈະຣິດ	in good faith	ດອກບົວຂີ້ແຫ້	water lily
ໂດຍດີ (ໂດຍຄັກແໜ)	fairly	ດອກບົວທອງ	lotus
ໂດຍເໜ່ອມ	urgently	ດອກຝ້າຍ	cotton ball
ໂດຍທັນທີ	instantly	ດອກໄຟຟ້າ	lightbulb
ໂດຍທາງອ້ອມ	indirectly	ດອກມາລາ	garland of flowers
ໂດຍທົ່ວໄປ	generally	ດອກໄມ້	flower
ໂດຍເປີດເຜີຍ	openly	ດອກເອື້ອງ	orchid
ໂດຍຜ່ານ	through, in care of	ດອງ	to pickle
ໂດຍມາກ	mostly	ດອຍ	mountain
ໂດຍຮຽບຮ້ອຍ	in good order	ດອນ	island
ໂດຍລຳພັງ	by one's self	ເດີກເຣ	degree (temp.)
ໂດຍອາຈາ	verbally	ເດີນ	to walk
ໂດດ	to jump	ເດີນຂະບວນ	to parade
ໂດດຈ້ອງ	to parachute	ເດີນທາງ	trip
ໂດດດ່ຽວ	isolated, only one	ເດີນໄປ	to go
ໂດດໜີ	to run away	ເດີນໄປເດີນມາ	to go and return
ໂດມ	to hit, collide	ເດີນໜ້າ	to walk forward
ດອກ (ດອກໄມ້)	flower	ເດີນເຮືອ	to navigate
ດອກກຸຫຼາບ	rose	ເດີ່ນ	field, court

ເດີ່ນກິລາ	stadium	ເດືອນອ້າຍ	first lunar month (Dec.)
ເດີ່ນຍິນ	airport	ເດືອນອອກໃໝ່	new moon
ເດີ່ນເຕະບານ	football field	ເດືອນແຮມ	the declining or waning moon
ເດີມ	before, once	ດວງ	(classifier: astro.....)
ເດີມພັນ	stakes in gambling	ດວງຈັນ	moon
ເດຍລະດາດ	in disorder, scattered	ດວງໃຈ	heart
ດຸນ	tickle	ດວງວິນຍານ	soul
ດຸນຄີງ	tickle	ດວງອາທິດ	sun
ດຸນມີ	to be shocked by touching	ດວງ	larva
ດຽວ	single, one	ດວຍ	with
ດຽວກັນ	the same	ດວຍວ່າ	because
ດຽວນີ້	now, immediately	ດວຍເຫດນີ້	for this reason
ດ່ຽວ	isolated	ດວຍຮັກ	with love
ເດືອ	rooster's spur	ດວນ	urgent
ເດືອຍ	rooster's spur	ດວນທີ່ສຸດ	most urgent
ເດືອດຮ້ອນ	trouble	ໃດ	which, any, each
ເດືອນ	moon, month	ໄດ້	to get, obtain, past tense
ເດືອນກ່ອນ	last month, the month before last	ໄດ້ສ່ວນ	well-proportioned
ເດືອນຂຶ້ນ	the rising or waxing moon	ໂດຍວນ	willing, thanks to, due to
ເດືອນຈງງ	first lunar month (Dec.)	ໄດ້ຍິນ	to hear
ເດືອນຍີ່	second lunar month (Jan.)	ໄດ້ດິບໄດ້ດີ	to gain rank
ເດືອນດັບ	the setting of the moon, last day of a lunar month	ໄດ້ເດີມ	to develop bad habits
ເດືອນຕົກ	the moon sets	ໄດ້ທາ	to have a chance
ເດືອນແລ້ວນ	last month	ໄດ້ບຸນ	to acquire merit
ເດືອນເພັງ	full moon	ໄດ້ປ່ຽບ	to get the advantage
ເດືອນມືດ	dark part of the moon	ໄດ້ຜົນ	to succeed
ເດືອນທງາຍ	moonlight	ໄດ້ຜົນດີ	to be effective

ໄດ້ມູນ	to inherit
ໄດ້ຮັບມອບຜາຍ	to be given
ໄພຫາໄດ້ຕາ	to win recognition
ເດົາ	to guess
ເດົາຖືກ	to guess correctly
ເດົາ	to move up and down
ດຳ	black
ດຳນາ	to transplant rice
ດຳເນີນ	to carry on
ດຳເນີນຄະດີ	to put on trial
ດຳເນີນງານ	to manage
ດຳເນີນຊີວິດ	to earn a livelihood
ດຳນ້ຳ	to plunge into the water
ດຳຣົງໄວ້	to maintain

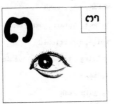

ຕະກຸນ	family
ຕະກຽງ	lamp
ຕະຂອງ	club, stick
ຕະຂອງເຜັດ	cactus
ຕະໄບ	file
ຕະປູ	nail

ຕະໂພນ	a two-face drum
ຕະລາການ	judge
ຕະລ້າງ	space under house on stilts
ຕລາດ	market
ຕລາດນັດ	fair
ຕລາດເມືດ	black market
ຕລິ່ງ	river bank
ຕລົກ	comic
ຕລອດ	through out, all
ຕລອດການ	perpetual
ຕລອດຄືນ	all night long
ຕລອດເຖິງ	together with
ຕລອດປີ	the whole year, forever
ຕລອດໄປ	for a long time (to come)
ຕລອດມາ	for a long time (already)
ຕລອດເມື່ອ (ຕລອດເວລາ)	all the time
ຕລອດວັນ	all day
ຕະວັນ	sun
ຕະເວັນ	patrol
ຕະຫຼົກ	to joke
ຕັກແຕນ	grasshopper
ຕັກເຕືອນ	to warn
ຕັກບາດ	to give alms
ຕ້ງກະຕົ້ວ	rubber
ຕັ່ງ	chair, sofa, stool
ຕັ່ງຍາວ	bench
ຕັ່ງຊີ	armchair

ຕັ້ງ	to set up
ຕັ້ງກະຕິກາ	to establish rules
ຕັ້ງກົກ	to begin
ຕັ້ງຂຶ້ນ	to establish
ຕັ້ງຂຶ້ນໄວ້	to set up
ຕັ້ງສັງເກດ	to observe
ຕັ້ງໄຂ	to stand (baby)
ຕັ້ງຄາຍ	to set up fort
ຕັ້ງຄຳຖາມ	to raise a question
ຕັ້ງຈິດຕັ້ງໃຈ	to listen intently
ຕັ້ງຊື່	to name
ຕັ້ງແຕ່	from, since
ຕັ້ງແຕ່ໃດຫນາ	long since
ຕັ້ງແຕ່ນັ້ນມາ	from then on
ຕັ້ງແຕ່ນີ້ໄປ	from now on
ຕັ້ງແຕ່ແຣກ	from the very beginning
ຕັ້ງແຕ່ເລັກແຕ່ນ້ອຍ	from childhood
ຕັ້ງຕົ້ນ	to begin
ຕັ້ງໂຕະ	to set the table
ຕັ້ງຕົວ	to establish oneself
ຕັ້ງຕົວຂຶ້ນ	to stand alone
ຕັ້ງແຖວ	to stand in a row
ຕັ້ງແທນ	to appoint a representative
ຕັ້ງບໍຣັກ຦ທບ຋ຍ	don't know anything
ຕັ້ງປ່ອນສູ້	to fight against
ຕັ້ງປ່ອນຍິງ	to set up a firing position
ຕັ້ງໂມງ	to set a clock, a watch
ຕັ້ງເມືອງ	to establish a city
ຕັ້ງຢູ່	to be located
ຕັ້ງຢືນ	to be vertical
ຕັ້ງໄວ້	to place, to install
ຕັ້ງໜາ	to be determined
ຕັ້ງໜາຄອຍ	to keep on waiting
ຕັ້ງໝັ້ນ	to stand firmly
ຕັ້ງຫມັ້ຖານ	to lay foundation
ຕັ້ງຫາຍວັນ	for many days now
ຕັ້ງອົກຕັ້ງໃຈ	to pay attention to
ຕັ້ງເຣັດ	to do on purpose
ຕັດ	to cut
ຕັດຂາດ	to break off
ຕັດຄໍ	to behead, to decapitate
ຕັດຄວາມເວົ້າ	to interrupt
ຕັດເງິນເຖືນ	to cut one's salary
ຕັດໃຈ	to decide in spite of
ຕັດສະບຽງ	to cut off food supply
ຕັດສິດ	to deprive of civil rights
ຕັດສິນ	to judge
ຕັດສິນໃຈ	to decide
ຕັດຊີ້ຂາດ	call attention, advise
ຕັດເສື້ອ	to make or order clothes
ຕັດສຳພັນ	to sever relation
ຕັດຍາດພີ່ນ້ອງ	to forsake one's relatives
ຕັດເດັດຂາດ	to break off, permanently
ຕັດທາງ	to bar the way

ຕັດຜົມ	haircut	ຕາຊັ່ງ	marking on scales
ຕັດໄມຕີ	to end a friendship	ຕາເຊື່	bleary eyed, dim sighted
ຕັດໄມ້	to cut wood	ຕາດິນ	registered deed to land
ຕັດຫົນທາງ	to preclude	ຕາຕະຮາງ	lines on schedule
ຕັດຫົວ	to behead, to decapitate	ຕາທິບ	clairvoyant
ຕັດອອກ	omit, to cut off	ຕານາ	title or deed of a ricefield
ຕັນໃຈ	slow witted, obtuse	ຕາຍອດ	blind
ຕັນດັງ	stuffed nose	ຕາໂປ	swollen eyes
ຕັນທາງ	to block a road	ຕາປຸກ	trachoma
ຕັນປັນຍາ	at one's wits end	ຕາໄປສະນີ	postage stamp
ຕັນຫາ	lust	ຕາເປົ່າ	empty eyes
ຕັນຫາຮອມ	lust	ຕາຝັ່ງ	shore
ຕັບ	liver	ຕາຝາງ	near sighted
ຕັບເຈ້ຍ	stack of paper	ຕາຮາງ	numerical table, schedule
ຕັບລູກປືນ	stack of cartridges	ຕາລ່າງ	area under the house
ຕາ	eye	ຕາໂລ້	protruding eyes
ຕາກ້າ	rice seed bed	ຕາລໍ	blind in one eye
ຕາກົດໝາຍ	to seal legally	ຕາວັນ	sun
ຕາໂກນ	sunken eyes	ຕາວັນຂຶ້ນ	sunrise
ຕາກໍ່	angry eyes	ຕາວັນຕົກ	West, occident, sunset
ຕາຂາວ	cowardly, white of the eye	ຕາວັນອອກ	East, orient, sunrise
ຕາຄົມ	sharp eyes	ຕາທິບ	slit eyes
ຕາຄຳຮ້ອຍ (ກາຄຳຮ້ອຍ)	medal	ຕາແຫ	net
ຕາສິນຄ້າ	brand, trademark	ຕາໜ່າຍ	dislikeable
ຕາແສງ	district (Tasseng)	ຕາຫຼິ່ງ	bank
ຕາຊັ່ງ	detestful	ຕາຫຼີວ	squint
ຕາຊັ່ງ	marking on scales, weight		

ຕາເບິ່ອກ	eyes which appear to be looking up	ຕາຍໂຕ	stable, net, fixed
ຕາຮ້າຍ	evil eye	ຕາຍຕິວ	permanent
ຕາກ (ຕາກແຄຄ)	exposed to the sun	ຕາຍຜາຍ	to die in childbirth
ຕາງຫຼວງຕາງຕາ	to act for	ຕາຍຜ່າແລ້ງ	to die of drought
ຕາງໜ້າ	deputy, agent, representative	ຕາຍທຸງ (ຕາຍໂທງ)	to die accidently
ຕ່າງ	strange, alien foreign	ຕາຍຮາ	die unnaturally (no reincarnation)
ຕ່າງກັນ	different	ຕາຍຮາແຊວ	oh, my god! (swear word)
ຕ່າງເຄື່ອງ	to load	ຕາມ	palm
ຕ່າງດ່າວ	alien	ຕານ	to resist
ຕ່າງຕາ	different in appearance	ຕານທານ	to resist, invent
ຕ່າງໆ	various, different, diverse	ຕານຍັນ	to resist
ຕ່າງໆ ນາໆ	various, of all sorts	ຕາບ	to patch, scar, until
ຕ່າງທ້ອງ	by a different mother	ຕາບຊາຍ	loose
ຕ່າງປະເທດ	foreign country	ຕາບໃດ	so long as
ຕ່າງປະຫຼາດ	strange, odd	ຕາມ	to follow, according to...., as....
ຕ່າງຫາກ	separately, not that way, but	ຕາມກັນ	to follow others
ຕ່າງໜ້າ	stranger	ຕາມເຄີຍ	as usual
ຕ່າງ	earrings	ຕາມຄວນ	as proper, fitting
ຕາຍ	to die	ຕາມໃຈສະມັກ	at will
ຕາຍກະດ່າງ	not afraid of death, disobedient	ຕາມໃຈຕົນເອງ	by one's own will
ຕາຍຄາທີ່	to die immediately	ຕາມໃຈມັກ	as one wishes
ຕາຍຄືນ	to come back to life	ຕາມສະບາຍ	at home
ຕາຍໃຈ	to trust implicitly	ຕາມສະໄໝ	up to date
ຕາຍໄປ	dead	ຕາມສົມຄວນ	reasonably
ຕາຍສ້ຽງ	to die to the last one	ຕາມສ່ວນ	proportionately
ຕາຍຫັຍ	to perish	ຕາມຢ່າງ	whatever it is
ຕາຍຕິກນ້ຳ	to drown	ຕາມເດີມ	as before, as usual

ຕາມ ໆ ກັນ	one after another	ຕິດຊັດ	to meet an obstacle
ຕາມແຕ່	to depend on	ຕິດເງິນ	to owe money
ຕາມທາງກວ້າງ	crosswise	ຕິດໃຈ	to be fascinated by
ຕາມທາງຍາວ	lengthwise, along	ຕິດສາວ	to fall in love with a girl
ຕາມນ້ຳ	downstream	ຕິດຕັ້ງ	to install, to set up
ຕາມບຸນ	happy-go-lucky	ຕິດຕາມ	to follow
ຕາມບຸນຕາມກັມ	at random, haphazardly	ຕິດກັນ	successively
ຕາມເບັດ	to bait a hook	ຕິດຕົວ	on one's person
ຕາມແບບ	according to pattern	ຕິດຕໍ່	to communicate
ຕາມປົກກະຕິ	as usual	ຕິດຕໍ່ກັນ	continuously, to contact
ຕາມພາສາ	in the guise of	ຕິດຕໍ່ມາ	to have carried on
ຕາມທັມມະດາ	as usual	ຕິດຕໍ່ຢູ່ນຳ	to be related to
ຕາມມີ	according to reality	ຕິດທຸລະ	to be busy
ຕາມມີຕາມເກີດ	with what one has	ຕິດແປດ	to contaminate, to stick to, to get sick
ຕາມເຮັ້ງຕາມຮາວ	as best one can	ຕິດຝິ່ນ	to be addicted to opium
ຕາມລາຍງານ	according to reports	ຕິດໜີ້	in debt
ຕາມລຳດັບ	in order	ຕິດໝູ່	to join a group of friends
ຕາມລຳພັງ	alone	ຕິບ	small container for boiled rice
ຕາມເວັນຕາມກັມ	as fate decrees	ຕີ	to hit, beat, strike
ຕາມອຳເພີໃຈ	of one's own choice	ຕີກາ	to seal
ຕ່າວຄືນ	to return, come back	ຕີກັນ	to beat, to thrash
ຕ່າວເມືອ	to come back	ຕີຮາຄາ	to set a price
ຕິ	to blame	ຕີຄິ້ວ	to wink at someone
ຕິຕຽນ	to blame	ຕີຄືນ	to hit against, repel, drive back
ຕິດ	to paste, to stick	ຕີຄວາມພາຍ	to interpret
ຕິດກັນ	stuck, related	ຕີຈັກ	to type
ຕິດກາວ	to glue on	ຕີຊຸ້ຫ້າຍ	to do at the last minute

ຕິຕາ	to seal
ຕິໂຕ້	to fight back
ຕິງາໜັກ	to guess a weight, weigh
ຕິຍາມ	to play ball
ຕິເຕັຽກ	to set fish trap
ຕິພິມ	to print
ຕິເພນ	to strike noon gong for monks
ຕິມວຍ	to box
ຕິຣາຄາ	to fix a price
ຕິລັງກາ	to turn a somersault
ຕິເຫັກ	blacksmithing, to forge metal
ຕິ້ງ	to budge, sway
ຕີນ	foot, tire (vehicle)
ຕີນກາ	cross mark (+), plus
ຕີນສັຕ	paw, leg, feet (animal)
ຕີນທຳ	to push with foot
ຕີນເປົ່າ	barefoot
ຕີນພູ	foothills
ຕີບ	narrow
ຕີກ	building, to fish
ຕຶກຕອງ	to think
ຕຶກຕອງເບິ່ງ	to consider, think over
ຕຶງ	tight
ຕຶງຂຶ້ນ	to swell up
ຕຶງຄຽດ	sulky
ຕຶບ	overgrown
ຕື້	one billion (1,000,000,000)

ຕື່ນ	to awake
ຕື່ນຂ່າວ	to get excited about the news
ຕື່ນຂຶ້ນ	to get up, arise
ຕື່ນໃຈ	to be excited about
ຕື່ນເຕັ້ນ	to be excited
ຕື່ນຕົວ	alert
ຕື້ນ	shallow
ຕື່ມຕັນຄໍຫອຍ	choking
ຕື່ມ	to add to, additional
ຕື່ມຂຶ້ນ	to increase
ຕື່ມອີກ	to add up
ຕື່ມແຮງ	to help out, to reinforce
ຕຸກະຕາ	doll
ຕຸ້ຍ	fat (person)
ຕຸຍແກ້ມ	to touch a girl's cheek
ຕຸດສົງການ	new year vacation
ຕຸ່ນ	mole
ຕຸ້ມຫູ	earrings
ຕຸລາ	balance, scales, October
ຕຸລາການ	judge
ຕູ່	to accuse falsely
ຕູ້	wardrobe, cabinet, breast
ຕູ້ພັບ	bookcase
ຕູບ	hut
ຕູບຕອງ	leaf-roofed hut
ຕູມ	bael fruit tree
ຕູມ	cage, trap, to look after

ຕຸ້ມບ່າວໄພ່	to protect the people	ແຕ່ນີ້, ມື້ຍພາ	from now on
ເຕະ	to kick	ແຕເຄົ້າ	from the beginning
ເຕະກະຕໍ້	to play soccer with a rattan ball	ແຕເຊິ່ມ	long since
ເຕະບານ	soccer	ແຕເຊົ້າຈົນຄໍ່າ	from morning to night
ເຕັ້ນລົງ	to press down on	ແຕເຊົ້າ	very early morning
ເຕິງ	to put on top of	ແຕເຕີນ	from the beginning
ເຕັ້ນ	to jump, to dance	ແຕໃດໆມາ	it has always been so, before
ເຕັ້ນຂ້າມ	to jump over	ແຕເຕົ້ນ	from the beginning
ເຕັ້ນໂຍ່ງ	to jump straight up	ແຕເຕັ້ນຈົນຮອດປາຍ	from beginning to end
ເຕັ້ນເຕາະເຕັ້ນດ່າງ	to jump for joy	ແຕເຖິງຢ່າງໃດກໍ່ຕາມ	however, anyway
ເຕັ້ນລະບຳ	to dance western style	ແຕທໍ່ນີ້ໄປ	from now on only
ເຕັ້ນລຳ	to dance Lao style	ແຕນີ້ໄປ	from now on
ເຕັ້ນແຮ່ງເຕະກາ	to jump with delight	ແຕນັ້ນມາ	from then on
ເຕັມ	full	ແຕນ້ອຍ	from childhood
ເຕັມໃຈ	to be satisfied	ແຕປະການໃດເລີຍ	what so ever
ເຕັມມ້ອມ	entirely	ແຕບູຮານມະການ	since antiquity
ເຕັມໂຕ	all over the body	ແຕຜູ້ງ່ວສັ້ນໆ	in a few words
ເຕັມຕົວ	to the limit of one's strength	ແຕຢ່າງງໃດ	however, in any way
ເຕັມຕຶມ	at full speed	ແຕລະ	each
ເຕັມທີ່	utmost	ແຕລະຂັ້ນ	step by step
ເຕັມຍ່ມ	full to the brim	ແຕເລັກແຕນ້ອຍ	ever since childhood
ເຕັມໄປດ້ວຍ	to be full of	ແຕວ່າ	but
ເຕັມອັດຕຣາເສີກ	fully armed	ແຕທາກວ່າ	but
ແຕະດ່າງ	to tap lightly, to touch	ແຕດົນນານ	for a long time
ແຕະຢ່າ	tobacco drying rack	ແຕເໜືອຕລອດໃຕ້	from North to South
ແຕ່	but	ແຕແຮກ	at first
ແຕທີ່ (ແຕກ່ອນ)	before	ແຕຣຸ່ງ	since dawn

ແຕກ	to break
ແຕກກະຈາຍ	to be scattered
ແຕກແຍກ	to separate
ແຕກຕ່າງ	different
ແຕກຕື່ນ	to panic and run away
ແຕກທະລາຍລົງ	to fall apart
ແຕກທັບ	separated from the main unit
ແຕກໃບ	to put out leaves
ແຕກພັກແຕກພວກ	to leave a party
ແຕກພວກ	to break off from one's group
ແຕກເມແຜລູກ	to multiply
ແຕກຫັກ	to be broken
ແຕກແຫງ	split, cracked
ແຕກຫນີ	to flee
ແຕກໜໍ	to germinate
ແຕກອອກ	to split away, open
ແຕງ	cucumber
ແຕງໄທ	cantaloupe
ແຕ່ງ	to decorate, dress, prepare
ແຕ່ງກາຍ	to dress one's self
ແຕ່ງກົນອຸບາຍ	to prepare a dirty trick
ແຕ່ງກອນ	to write poetry
ແຕ່ງໂຄງ	to compose poetry
ແຕ່ງຄົມໄນ	to send someone
ແຕ່ງຄຳຟ້ອງ	to draw up an indictment
ແຕ່ງງານ	marriage, wedding
ແຕ່ງດອງ	marriage

ແຕ່ງຕັ້ງ	to appoint, to set up
ແຕ່ງຕົວ	to dress
ແຕ່ງໂຕະ (ໂຕະ)	to set the table
ແຕ່ງເຜດ	to pretty up
ແຕ່ງເຣື່ອງ	to write a story
ແຕ່ງເລັບ	to manicure
ແຕມ	tree wasp
ແຕມ	to draw (pictures)
ແຕມສີ	to paint
ແຕມປູມ	to prepare betel
ແຕມພິງສີ	to write carefully
ແຕມຮູບ	to paint a picture
ຕົກ	to fall
ຕົກກ້າ	to sow seed
ຕົກໃຈ	to be freightened
ຕົກສະເງິ້	to gape, dumbfounded
ຕົກຕາດ	waterfall
ຕົກແຕ່ງ	to arrange
ຕົກຕ່ຳ	to degrade
ຕົກມະຮົກ	to go to hell
ຕົກລົງໃຈ	to decide, agree
ຕົກເທິນ	to fall off a precipice
ຕົກອົກຕົກໃຈ	to be frightened
ຕົງ	rafter, house percentage in gambling
ຕົງຕໍເວລາ	punctual on time
ຕົດ	to fart, to pass gas
ຕົດແຕກ	involuntary fart
ຕົມ	oneself, one's own

ຕົມເອງ	one's self		
ຕົມ	trunk, tree, beginning		
ຕົມກາເຟ	coffee tree	ຕົບມື	to applaud
ຕົມກາວ	balsam	ຕົບຫົວ	to pat on the head
ຕົມກ້ຽງ	rose-apple tree	ຕົມ	mud, dirt
ຕົມຄ	a kind of palm tree	ຕົມ	to boil
ຕົມຈັນ	sandalwood tree	ໂຕະ	table, desk
ຕົມສະບັບ	manuscript (original)	ໂຕເລກ	number
ຕົມສົມ	pine tree	ໂຕເອງ	self
ຕົມຊາ	tea bush	ໂຕໜັງສື	letter (character)
ຕົມຕານ	sugar palm tree	ໂຕ	body
ຕົມທຶນ	capital, assets	ໂຕ	to reply, rebut
ຕົມປີ	beginning of year	ໂຕແຍ້ງ	to dispute
ຕົມຜ້າງ	flame tree, poinciana	ໂຕຕອບ	to correspond
ຕົມໄຜ	banyan tree	ໂຕຖຽງ	to argue
ຕົມມີ່	jackfruit tree	ໂຕອາທິ	to debate
ຕົມມ່ວງ	mango tree	ໂຕ່ງເຕ່ງ	swaying
ຕົມໄມ້	tree	ໂຕມ	metric ton, to lump down esc
ຕົມເຫດ	cause	ໂຕມຈ້ອງ	to jump with parachute
ຕົມຫຸ່ງ	papaya tree	ໂຕມຄາຍ	to desert one's post
ຕົມອ້ອຍ	sugarcane	ໂຕມຕາດ	waterfall
ຕົບ	to clap	ໂຕມອອກ	to escape
ຕົບແກ້ມ	to slap the cheek	ຕໍ	stump
ຕົບແສ່ງ	to strike cymbols	ຕໍ	to add, to link
ຕົບຕາ	to deceive	ຕໍ່ກັນ	to attach to, next to
ຕົບແຕ່ງ	to decorate	ຕໍ່ໄກ່	to decoy wild chickens
ຕົບປີກ	to flap the wings	ຕໍ່ກັນ	to follow

ຕໍ່ທອດກຢາ	to light one cigarette from another	ຕອກຕະປູ	to nail
ຕໍ່ຈາກ	continued from	ຕອກແຕກ	pop-corn
ຕໍ່ຈາກນີ້ໄປ	from now on	ຕອກເໝາ	to speak frankly
ຕໍ່ແຕ່ນັ້ນມາ	thereafter	ຕອກຫຼັກ	to drive a stake
ຕໍ່ສັນຍາ	to renew a contract	ຕອງ	to filter
ຕໍ່ສູ້	to fight with	ຕອງກວຍ	banana leaf
ຕໍ່ເຊືອກ	to tie up	ຕອງນ້ຳ	to filter water
ຕໍ່ຕານ	to resist, defend, attack	ຕອງເຫຼືອງ	mountain nomad tribe, "Yellow Leaves"
ຕໍ່ໆ ໄປ	etcetera (etc.)	ຕອງແຕງ	harness crossbar of plow
ຕໍ່ເຕີມ	to add	ຕອງ	to touch, must
ຕໍ່ໄປນີ້	from now on	ຕອງການ	to need
ຕໍ່ນີ້ເມື່ອໜ້າ	from now on	ຕອງຄະດີ	to be persecuted
ຕໍ່ນົກ	to catch birds by decoy	ຕອງໃຈ	to be pleased
ຕໍ່ເນື່ອງກັນມາ	continuously	ຕອງຊຸມ	to touch lightly
ຕໍ່ປີ	per year	ຕອງຕາ	pleasing to the eye
ຕໍ່ປາກ	to quote, cite	ຕອງຕິ	to criticize
ຕໍ່ມາ	later on, afterwards	ຕອງຖືກ	to touch, must be correct
ຕໍ່ມາຄາວໜຶ່ງ	a little later	ຕອງໂທດ	to be penalized
ຕໍ່ມາຍາຍນານມາ	not long after	ຕອງຫາ	to be accused
ຕໍ່ຣາຄາ	to bargain	ຕອງຫ້າມ	to be forbidden, prohibited
ຕໍ່ວ່າ	to protest	ຕອຍ	to punch
ຕໍ່ວ່າຕໍ່ຂານ	to protest	ຕອຍເຫຼັກໄຟ	to strike a flint
ຕໍ່ໜ້າ	in front of	ຕອດ	to bite, peck
ຕໍ່ໃໝ່	to renew	ຕອນ	time
ຕໍ່ອິກ	to continue	ຕອນຂາກັບ	on the way back
ຕໍ່ເຮືອ	to build a boat	ຕອນຂາກັບໄປ	on the way there
ຕອກ	bamboo strips	ຕອນຈົບ	ending, final part

ຕອນສຸດທ້າຍ	finally	ຕຽມ	to criticize
ຕອນເດິກ	late at night	ຕຽມ	to prepare
ຕອນຕົ້ນ	in at the beginning	ຕຽມຕົວ	to get ready
ຕອນທ້າຍ	at the end	ຕຽມພ້ອມ	to be alert
ຕອນບ່າຍ	afternoon	ຕຽມໃຈ	to be ready for
ຕອນປາຍ	nearly at the end	ເຕີ່ຍ	hanging
ຕອນແຮກ	at first	ເຕືອນ	to remind, warn
ຕອນຫຼັງໆ	lately	ເຕືອນຈິດເຕືອນໃຈ	to remind
ຕອນ	piece (classifier: cloth)	ເຕືອນໃຫ້	to remind of
ຕອນ	to welcome, entertain	ຕົວະ	to lie
ຕອນຮັບ	to welcome	ຕົວະຍົວະ	to deceive
ຕອນຮັບແຂກ	to receive guests	ຕົວ	body, letter of alphabet
ຕອບ	to answer	ຕົວການ	main culprit, principal defender
ຕອບຄຸນ	to repay a favor	ຕົວຂ້ອຍ	myself
ຕອບຄວາມ	to answer a question	ຕົວຂອມ	Khmer Buddhist script
ຕອບສະໜອງ	to respond	ຕົວເງືອກ	water dragon
ຕອບໂຕ້	to argue	ຕົວຈິງ	actual, real
ຕອບບຸນແທນຄຸນ	to repay kindness	ຕົວສະກົດ	letter spelling
ຕອບມື	to hit back	ຕົວຕລົກ	clown
ຕອມ	to gather	ຕົວຕັ້ງຕົວຕີ	principal
ຕອມໂຮມ	to collect	ຕົວຕໍ່ຕົວ	one to one
ເຕີບ	very much	ຕົວເຕົ່າ	turtle
ເຕີມ	to add	ຕົວທັມ	Burmese Pali alphabet
ເຕີມນ້ຳມັນ	to refuel	ຕົວທ່ານເອງ	yourself
ເຕັ້ຍ	dwarf	ຕົວແທນ	representative, agent
ເຕັ້ຍໆ	very low, short	ຕົວແບບ	model
ຕຽງ	bed	ຕົວເພະຍາດ	germ or bacteria

ຕົວພິມ	type for printing
ຕົວແມ່	female
ຕົວຢ່າງ	example
ຕົວລະຄອນ	player, actor
ຕົວລູກຮອກ	tadpole
ຕົວເລກ	number, numeral
ຕົວໜັງສື	letters of alphabet
ຕວງ	to measure
ຕວດ	to inspect
ໄຕປິດົກ	Buddhist canons
ໄຕ່	to crawl on
ໄຕ່ສວນ	to investigate
ໄຕ່ເຊືອກ	tightrope walking
ໄຕ່ຕາມທາງ	to follow a road
ໄຕ່ຖາມ	to inquire
ໄຕ້	to light
ໄຕ້ໂຄມ	to light a lamp
ໄຕ້ໄຟ	to light a fire, to turn on light
ໄຕ້ໄຟຟ້າ	to turn on an electric light
ໃຕ	viscera, spleen
ໃຕ້	under, South
ໃຕ້ດິນ	underground
ໃຕ້ເທົ້າ	your excellency, majesty
ໃຕ້ນ້ຳ	submarine
ໃຕ້ລ່າງ	under
ໃຕ້ລຸ່ມຟ້າ	under heaven, on earth
ເຕົາ	stove
ເຕົາສູບ	bellows
ເຕົາຖ່ານ	charcoal kiln
ເຕົາເຜົາ	kiln, crematorium
ເຕົາໄຟ	stove
ເຕົາລໍ່	metal melting furnace
ເຕົາອົບ	oven
ເຕົາຣີດ	iron
ເຕົ່າ	turtle
ເຕົ້າ	to assemble, jar
ເຕົ້າກັນ	assemble in a group
ເຕົ້ານົມ	breast
ເຕົ້ານ້ຳ	waterjar
ເຕົ້ານ້ຳຊາ	teapot
ເຕົ້າຮູ້	bean curd
ເຕົ້າໂຮມ	to assemble
ຕຳ	to hit, to pound (rice, etc.)
ຕຳກັນ	to crash
ຕຳນານ	legend, story
ຕຳຣາ	formula
ຕຳຣວດ (ຕຳຣວຈ, ຕຳຫຼວດ)	police
ຕຳແໜ່ງ	position
ຕ່ຳ	low, to weave
ຕ່ຳໃຈ	to be depressed
ຕ່ຳເຕ້ຍ	dwarfish
ຕ່ຳຕ້ອຍ	inferior
ຕ່ຳຜ້າ	to weave cloth
ຕ່ຳແພ	to weave silk cloth
ຕ່ຳແໜ່ງ	position

ຕຣາຕັ້ງ   credentials

ໄຕ

ຖນົນ   road

ຖນົນຫຼວງ   public road, highway, main road

ຖນອມ (ຖະໜອມ)   to take care of

ຖນອມຮັກ   to embrace, cherish, love

ຖວາຍ   to offer (religious)

ຖວາຍຊີວິດ   to offer one's self

ຖວາຍບູຊາ   to give offerings

ຖັກລູກໄມ   to crochet

ຖັງ   bucket

ຖັງຂີ້ເຫຍື້ອ   dust bin

ຖັງນ້ຳມັນ   gas tank

ຖານະ   position, status

ຖາວອນ   permanent

ຖ້າ   if, to wait for

ຖ້າຈະ   if

ຖ້າຍັດຖ້ງ   wait a minute

ຖ້າເປັນຂ້ອຍ   if I were you

ຖ້າຢ່າງນັ້ນ   in that case

ຖ້າວ່າ   if

ຖ້າຫາກ   if

ຖາກ   to trim

ຖາກໄມ້   to trim a tree

ຖາງ   to clear (land)

ຖາງປ່າ   to clear the forest

ຖາງຫຍ້າ   to clear away grass

ຖາງໄຮ່   to clear land for upland rice

ຖ່າຍ   to change

ຖ່າຍເຄື່ອງນຸ່ງ   to change clothes

ຖ່າຍເສື້ອ   to change shirt

ຖ່າຍທອງ   to take a laxative

ຖ່າຍທອດສຽງ   to broadcast (relay)

ຖ່າຍຢາ   to purge with drugs

ຖ່າຍເບົາ   to piss

ຖ່າຍຮູບ   to photograph

ຖ່ານ   charcoal

ຖ່ານໄຟສາຍ   dry cell battery

ຖ່ານຫິນ   coal

ຖາມ   to ask, question

ຖາມຂ່າວ   to ask about the news

ຖາມຄວາມເຫັນ   to ask for an opinion

ຖາມເຖິງ   to ask about

ຖາມໄປຖາມມາ   to interrogate

ຖາມຫາ   to ask about

ຖາມໜີ້   to ask payment of a debt

ຄຸ້ມ	place, premise	ຖືກຕີ	to be hit
ຄຸ	close together, stingy	ຖືກຕົມ	to be duped
ຄືບ	to pedal	ຖືກໂທດ	to be punished
ຄືບຣົດ	to pedal a bicycle	ຖືກປັບໃໝ	to be fined
ຄົ້ມ	to throw away	ຖືກປາກ	to please the taste
ຄົ້ມໂທດໃສ່	to lay the blame on	ຖືກຟ້ອງ	accused, sued
ຄົ້ມວຽກ	to quit a job	ຖືກແລ້ວ	that's right, ok!
ຖື	to hold	ຖືກເວລາ	on time
ຖືງຸດ	to respect, pride	ຖືກຫູ	pleasing to the ear
ຖືສາດສະນາ	to adher to a religion	ຖືກອກຖືກໃຈ	well-liked
ຖືສິນ	to obey precepts	ຖືກແຮ້ວ	caught in a snare
ຖືໂຕ	to be conceited	ຖຸມ	to smoke
ຖືຕົວ	aloof	ຖຸມຢາ	to smoke tobacco
ຖືປະເພນີ	to follow custom	ຖຸ	to rub
ຖືເປັນຄວາມລັບ	to keep a secret	ຖຸພື້ນເຮືອນ	to clean the floor
ຖືປືນ	to carry a gun	ແຖ	to shave
ຖືພາມານ	to be pregnant	ແຖໜວດ	to shave the beard
ຖືໂອກາດ	to take the opportunity	ແຖບ	region
ຖືກ	cheap	ແຖມໃຫ້	to give something extra
ຖືກກັນ	to get along well	ແຖວ	row, line
ຖືກກວ່າ	cheaper than	ແຖວໜັງສື	line or column of writing
ຖືກຂັງ	to have been arrested	ໂຖ	vase
ຖືກຄຸກ	to be imprisoned	ໂຖດອກໄມ້	vase, flower pot
ຖືກຕ້ອງ	correct	ໂຖນ້ຳເຮືອນ	water jar
ຖືກຈັບ	to be arrested	ຖີບ	to raise a foot to step
ຖືກໃຈ	satisfied, to like	ຖີບຖຽງ	to discuss
ຖືກຕາ	to please the eye	ຖົງ	sack

ຖົງເຂົ້າ	rice sack
ຖົງເສື້ອ	shirt pocket
ຖົງຍ່າມ	sack with shoulder strap
ຖົງຕີນ	socks
ຖົງມື	glove
ຖົມ	to fill up
ຖົມດິນ	to fill up with earth
ຖົ່ມ	to spit
ຖົ່ມນ້ຳລາຍ	to spit
ຖອກ	to pour
ຖອກທ້ອງ	diarrhea
ຖອຍ	to withdraw
ຖອຍຫຼັງ	to retreat
ຖ້ອຍ	naughty
ຖອດ	to take out
ຖອດອອກ	to draw out
ຖອນ	to withdraw
ຖອນແຂ້ວ	to pull out a tooth
ຖອນຕະປູ	to pull out a nail
ຖອນອອກ	to pull out
ຖ່ອມໂຕ, ຕົວ	to humiliate oneself
ເຖິງ	to arrive
ເຖິງແກ່ກັມ	to die (ordinary person)
ເຖິງແກ່ມໍລະນະພາບ	to die (monk)
ເຖິງຈະ	even if

ເຖິງດຽວນີ້	until now
ເຖິງແມ່ວ່າ	although
ເຖິງຢ່າງໃດກໍດີ	however
ເຖິງຢ່າງໃດກໍຕາມ	nevertheless
ເຖິງວ່າ	although
ຖຽງ	to argue, hut
ຖຽງກັນ	to quarrel
ຖຽງນາ	hut for watching ricefield
ຖ້ຽວ	to wander, to stroll
ຖ້ຽວຫຼິ້ນ	to go for a walk
ເຖື່ອນ	outlaw, illegal
ຖົ່ວ	bean, gambling game
ຖົ່ວຂຽວ	green pea
ຖົ່ວງອກ	bean sprout
ຖົ່ວດິນ	peanut
ຖົ່ວພັກຍາວ (ຖົ່ວຍາວ)	cowpea
ຖົ່ວເຫຼືອງ	soybean
ຖ້ວຍ	bowl
ຖ້ວຍຊາມ	cookingware, dishes
ຖ້ວມ	to flood
ໄຖ	to plow
ໄຖວົວ	to plow with oxen
ໄຖດິນ	to plough the soil
ໄຖ່	to redeem
ໄຖ່ເຄື່ອງ	to redeem goods
ເຖົາ	vine

ເຖົ້າ   old

ຖ້ຳ   cave

ທະນະບັດ   paper money, bank note

ທະນາຍ   attorney

ທະນາຍຄວາມ   lawyer, defender

ທະບຽນ   register

ທະບຽນການຄ້າ   sales license

ທະລາຍ   in ruin

ທະເລ   sea

ທະເລຊາຍ   desert

ທະເລເລິກ   high seas

ທວາຍ   to estimate, guess

ທະວີບ   continent

ທະຫານ   soldier

ທະຫານຍາມ   sentry

ທະຫານບ້ານ   village guard

ທະຫານປືນໃຫຍ່   artillery

ທະຫານມ້າ   cavalry

ທະຫານອາກາດ   air force

ທະຫານອາສາ   volunteer soldier

ທັກ   to greet

ທັກທາຍ   to address, greet

ທັກທາຍປາໃສ   to exchange greetings

ທັງຊ້ມທັງລິງ   both ways, anyway

ທັງຈິດທັງໃຈ   with all one's heart

ທັງສິ້ນ   all, every

ທັງສິ້ນທັງຢ້ນ   trembling with fear

ທັງສອງ   both

ທັງຊາດ   the whole nation, national(ly)

ທັງມົນ   all

ທັງຫຼາຍ   all

ທັສນາຈອນ   sight-seeing, excursion

ທັງ ໆ ທີ່   although

ທັງນີ້   all this

ທັງນີ້ກໍເພາະວ່າ   this is because

ທັງປະເທດ   throughout the country

ທັງມວນ   entirely, all

ທັງຫມູ່   all the group

ທັງຫມົດ   all together, everything

ທັນ   to overtake, to be in time

ທັນໃຈ   quickly, promptly

ທັນສໄມ   current, up-to-date

ທັນທີ   suddenly

ທັນໃດ   suddenly

ທັນໂມງ   on time

ທັນເວລາ	on time	ທາງຂວາ	right side
ທັນອົກທັນໃຈ	satisfactorily	ທາງຂວາງ	horizontally, width
ໄຫ	to smash, army	ທາງຄົດ	winding road
ໄຫເອົາ	to conquer and seize	ທາງຄົມຍ່າງ	sidewalk
ໍຫມ (ທັມມະ)	morality, Buddhist law, justice	ທາງແຄບ	narrow road
ທັມມະນູນ	custom	ທາງຄົບ	crossroads
ທັມມະຊາດ	nature	ທາງໂວ້ງ	detour
ທັມມະດາ	ordinary	ທາງສະດວກ	convenient road
ທັມມະນູນ	constitution	ທາງສັງຄົມ	socially
ທາ (ທາສີ)	to paint	ທາງສັດຊື່	honestly
ທານ້ຳຫອມ	to perfume	ທາງສຸຈິດ	honestly
ທາບາດ	to paint a wound	ທາງເໝັນໃດ	which way?
ທາປູນ	to whitewash	ທາງຊ້າຍ	left side
ທາຣຸນ	rough, cruel	ທາງຊື່	straight road
ທ່າ	waterfront	ທາງຍຸບ	properly, rightly
ທ່າທາງ	attitude	ທາງດິນ	dirt road
ທ່ານ້ຳ	waterfront	ທາງດຽວ	one way
ທ່າເຮືອ	harbor, dock, port	ທາງໃດ	which way?
ທ້າ	to challenge	ທາງຕັ້ງ	vertically
ທ້າພະນັນ	to bet, to gamble	ທາງໃຕ້	downward, southward
ທາງ	road, trail, path, street, way	ທາງຖືກ	in the right direction
ທາງກາງ	middle	ທາງທຸຣະຈິດ	dishonestly
ທາງການ	officially, formally	ທາງເທິງ	upstairs, above
ທາງໄກ	long way, far	ທາງທຽວ	well used road
ທາງໃກ້	short way	ທາງນີ້	this way
ທາງຂ້າງ	side	ທາງນອກ	outside, outdoors, externally
ທາງເຂົ້າ	entrance	ທາງນອຍ	path, walk, drive

ທາງໃນ	inside, interior, internally	ທາຍປີ	end of the year
ທາງນ້ຳ	by water, waterway	ທາຍປືນ	butt of gun stock
ທາງບົກ	by land, land route	ທາຍເຮືອ	stern of boat
ທາງແຍກ	forked road	ທາດ	pagoda, stupa
ທາງບ້ານ	home	ທານ	to give alms
ທາງປິ້ນ	reverse side	ທ່ານ	sir (officials), you, he
ທາງຜ່ານ	passage way	ທາວ	sir (polite), Mr.
ທາງຜິດ	wrong way	ທິດ	ex-Buddhist monk, direction
ທາງພູ	in the mountains	ທິດຕະວັນຕົກ	West
ທາງພຸ້ນ	over there	ທິດຕະວັນອອກ	East
ທາງມົນ	slippery road	ທິດໃຕ້	South
ທາງລັດ	short cut	ທິດເໜືອ	North
ທາງລຸ່ມ	downstairs, below, under	ທີ	time
ທາງແລ່ນຂຶ້ນລົງ	runway	ທີດງວ	at once
ທາງໜ້າ	ahead, forward	ທີນຶ່ງ	first time, once
ທາງເໜືອ	north	ທີລະໜ້ອຍ	little by little
ທາງຫຼັງ	behind, backwards	ທີຫຼັງ	later
ທາງຫຼວງ	highway, main road	ທີ່	place, thing, that
ທາງອາກາດ	by air, air route	ທີ່ເກີດ	birthplace
ທາງອອກ	transit, outlet, exit	ທີ່ຫຼົບຫຼີກ	hiding place
ທາງອ້ອມ	detour	ທີ່ຈິງ	truly
ທາງຮົກ	overgrown road	ທີ່ຈອດ	parking area
ທາງເຮືອ	by boat, waterway	ທີ່ສູງ	plateau
ທາງຮ່ວມ	way, road	ທີ່ສຸດ	the most, superlative degree
ທາຍ	back, tail, rear, end	ທີ່ດີກວ່າໝູ່	the best
ທາຍເດືອນ	end of the month	ທີ່ດິນ	land, ground
		ທີ່ຕັ້ງ	site, location

ທີ່ຕ່ຳ	lowland	ທຸກໃຈ	unfortunate, unhappy
ທີ່ແທ້	really	ທຸກສິ່ງທຸກຢ່າງ	everything
ທີ່ນັ່ງ	seat	ທຸກຊະນິດ	every kind, type
ທີ່ນັ້ນ	there	ທຸກຊາດ	every country, every race
ທີ່ນິຍົມ	preferred	ທຸກທາງ	everywhere
ທີ່ນີ້	here	ທຸກທີ່ (ທຸກບ່ອນ)	everywhere, every place
ທີ່ນື່ງ	the first	ທຸກທິດທຸກທາງ	every direction
ທີ່ປະຊຸມ	conference room	ທຸກ ໆມື້	everyday
ທີ່ແປນ	clearing	ທຸກເວລາ	every time
ທີ່ປຽດໄພ	refuge, shelter	ທຸກເທື່ອ	always, each time
ທີ່ຝັ່ງສົບ	cemetery	ທຸກບ້ານ	everywhere, every village
ທີ່ພັກ	dwelling, residence	ທຸກປະການ	everything
ທີ່ເພິ່ງ	prop, support	ທຸກພະແນກ	all, all sections
ທີ່ຢູ່	address	ທຸກມື້	everyday
ທີ່ແຮກ	first time, at first	ທຸກຢ່າງ	everything
ທີ່ລະລຶກ (ທີ່ລະລຶກ)	memory, souvenir	ທຸກລະຍະ	always
ທີ່ໝັ້ນ	stronghold	ທຸກເວລາ	always, every time
ທີ່ເວົ້າເປົ່າ	vacancy, empty space	ທຸກໂອກາດ	occasionally,
ທີ່ມົນຊັບ	capital money, budget		at every opportunity
ທຶບ	covered, deep (jungle, forest)	ທຸງ	flag
ທຸຣະ	business, work	ທຸບ	to smash, hammer
ທຸຣະສ່ວນຕົວ	personal business	ທຸບຕີ	to beat
ທຸກ	every, all, each	ທູດ (ທູຕ)	ambassador, representative
ທຸກຂ໌	suffering, misery, poverty	ທູບ	incense stick
ທຸກຍາກ	hardship, poverty	ທູບທຽນ	incense stick and candle
ທຸກຄົນ	everyone	ທູບຫອມ	incense
ທຸກເຮືນ	poor	ເທ	pour

ເທນ້ຳ	to pour water
ເທດ	sermon
ເທສນາ	sermon
ເທສບານ	municipal
ເທບຊັດສຽງ	recording tape
ແທ້	truely, indeed certainly
ແທ້ຈິງ	really, truely
ແທ້ຫວບ	really?
ແທ້ນາ	really!
ແທ້ນໍ	truely?
ແທ້ແລວ	yes, it is!
ແທກ	to measure
ແທງ	to stab
ແທງຈິມຊຸດ	to pierce, stab
ແທງຈິມຕາຍ	to stab to death
ແທງດອຍມິດ	to stab with a knife
ແທງຄີວ	to bet on odd and even
ແທງເບ	to buy illegal lottery tickets
ແທງມາ	to bet on a horse
ແທງ	(classifier: bar, block)
ແທງເງິນ	silver ingot
ແທງເຫຼັກ	piece of steel
ແທນ	to replace, substitute, instead of
ແທນທີ່	instead of, to take place of
ແທນ	a stand, holder
ແທນພິມ	printing press
ທງ	field, meadow
ທົງນາ	rice field
ທິດ	irrigate
ທິດສອບ	to test
ທິດແທນ	to compensate
ທິດນ້ຳ	to irrigate
ທິດລອງ	to test, experiment
ທິນ	to endure, suffer
ທິນແດດທິນຝົນ	to experience bad weather
ທິນທໍຣະນານ	to suffer from torture
ທິນທື	to endure hunger
ທບ	to fold, double
ທບທວນ	repeatedly
ໂທ	oh!, of second grade
ໂທຣະຄົມມະນາຄົມ	telecommunications
ໂທຣະສັບ	telephone
ໂທຣະທັດ	telescope
ໂທຣະພາຍ (ທີວີ)	television (TV)
ໂທຣະເລກ	telegraph, telegram
ໂທດ	punishment, penalty
ໂທດປະຫານຊີວິດ	capital punishment
ໂທມ	lonely
ທໍ	basket, to crash
ທໍຣະນີ (ປະຖຶເຮືອນ)	threshold
ທໍຣະຍົດ	to betray, wickedness
ທໍຣະພີ	Lao Oedipus
ທໍຣະນານ	to torture, oppress
ທໍ	tube, pipe, how much?

ທຫ້ານ	equally	ທອມເງິນ	to save money
ທໍໃດ	how much?, how many?	ທອມສະແຕມ	to collect stamps
ທໝນ	that much, that's all	ທອມໂຮມ	to centralize, assemble, unite
ທໍນ້ຳ	water pipe	ເທິງ	upper, above, on top of, up
ທໍຢາງ	rubber tube	ເທິງສ້ວນ	in heaven
ທອງ	copper, gold (less used)	ເທິງພູ	on the mountain
ທອງຄຳຊ່ອຍ	gold plated	ເທິງຟ້າ	in the sky, in heaven
ທອງແດງ	copper	ເທິງນັ້ນ	up there
ທອງແທ່ງ	gold ingot	ເທິງຫົວ	on the head
ທອງນາກ	gold-copper alloy	ເທິງຫຼັງຄາ	on the roof
ທ່ອງທຽວ	to travel, tour	ເທິງເຮືອ	on board boat
ທ່ອງບົດຮຽນ	to memorize a lesson	ເທິງເຮືອນ	in the house
ທອງ	belly, interior	ເທິບ	lean-to roof
ທອງຂື້ລາກ	cholera	ທ່ຽງ	noon, straight, accurate
ທອງຖິ່ນ	rural	ທ່ຽງກົງ	exact, accurate
ທອງນ້ອຍ	lower abdomen	ທ່ຽງຄືນ	midnight
ທອງບິດ	dysentery	ທ່ຽງທັນ	honest, just
ທອງບໍ່ດີ	indigestion	ທຽນ	wax candle, candle
ທອງປ່ອງ	pot bellied	ທຽນໄຂ	candle
ທອງແຜນ	constipation	ທຽບ	to compare
ທອງເຮືອ	bottom of a boat	ທ່ຽວ	to go back and forth
ທອດກະຖິ່ນ	to give alms to monks	ທ່ຽວ	to travel, seek pleasure, fast
ທອນ	to change money	ທ່ຽວກາງຄືນ	to go out at night
ທອນເງິນ	to give change, refund money	ທ່ຽວໄປ	to wander
ທ່ອນ	section, part, segment	ທ່ຽວໄປທ່ຽວມາ	to go back and forth (quickly)
ທ່ອນໄມ້	a piece of wood	ທ່ຽວຫຼິ້ນ	to stroll, to seek pleasure
ທອມ	to save	ເທື່ອ	times

ເທື່ອກ່ອນ	time before
ເທື່ອທໍາອິດ	the first time
ເທື່ອນີ້	this time
ເທື່ອລະ	each time, every time
ເທື່ອລະຄໍາ	word by word
ເທື່ອລະນ້ອຍ	little by little
ເທື່ອໜ້າ	next time
ເທື່ອໜ້າເທື່ອໃໝ	next time
ທົ່ວ	everywhere, all over
ທົ່ວເຖິງກັນ	entirely
ທົ່ວທັງໂຕ	all over the body
ທົ່ວປະເທດ	nationwide
ທົ່ວໄປ	generally
ທວງຖາມ	to repeat a request
ທວງຖາມ	to question, denounce
ທວຍ	people
ທວນ	to return
ໄທ	Thai, people
ໄທດໍາ	Black Thai tribe
ໄທບ້ານ	villager
ໄທບ້ານນອກ	villager, peasant
ໄທແມ້ວ	Meo tribe (Hmong)
ໄທເມືອງ	citizen, city dweller
ໄທຢ້າວ	Yao tribe
ໄທລາວ	Laotian, Lao
ໄທລື້	Thai Lu tribe
ໄທເຮືອນ	household

ເທົາ	grey
ເທົ່າ	**quantity**, much
ເທົ່າກັນ	equal
ເທົ່າກັບ	to equal, be equal to
ເທົ່າໃດ	how much?, many? to what extent?
ເທົ້າ	feet
ທໍາ	to do
ທໍາງານ	to work
ທໍາສັນຍາ	to make a contract
ທໍາຊົ່ວ	to do evil, badly made
ທໍາດີທີ່ສຸດ	to do one's best
ທໍາຕາມຄໍາສັ່ງ	to follow orders
ທໍາຖືກ	to do right
ທໍາຕາມໃຈຊ່ອງ	to do as you like
ທໍາທ່າ	to act, pretend
ທໍາທ່າບໍໄດ້ຍິນ	to turn deaf ear to
ທໍາແທນ	to substitute
ທໍາໂທດ	to punish
ທໍານາຍ	to foretell, predict
...າຍຝັນ	to interpret dreams
ມຽງ	manner, sort
ເນ຺ຍມ	custom
...ບຸນ	to earn merit, hold a festival
...ບຸນທາຜູ້ຕາຍ	ceremony for the dead
ທໍາມາຫາກິນ	to earn a living
ທໍາລາຍ	destroy

ຫຼາຍກຸດ	to dishonor
ຫ້ໃຫ້	to cause, bring about
ຫ້ພາທີ	to do one's duty
ຫ້ຊິດ	at first
ຫ້ຮ້າຍ	to assault
ຫ້ຮ້າຍຮ່າງກາຍ	to assault

ນ | ນັກ

ນະຄອນ	city
ນະຄອນຫຼວງ	capital
ນະໂຍບາຍ	policy
ນະມັສການ	to pay homage to Buddha
ນະຮົກ	hell
ນັກ	professional, expert
ນັກກະວີ	poet
ນັກການທູດ	diplomat
ນັກການເມືອງ	politician
ນັກກິລາ	althlete, sportsman
ນັກເຊຍ	musician of an orchestra
ນັກກົດໝາຍ	lawyer
ນັກຂຽນ	writer
ນັກຄຳນວນ	mathematician
ນັກສື່ຂ່າວ	newspaper reporter
ນັກສຶກສາ	student
ນັກສືບ	detective
ນັກດົນຕຣີ	musician
ນັກເຕັ້ນລຳ	dancer (Lao style)
ນັກໂທດ	prisoner, convict
ນັກໂທດການເມືອງ	political prisoner
ນັກໂທດເຖິງຕາຍ	condemned prisoner
ນັກບິນ	pilot
ນັກບວດ	clergyman, monk

ມັກໂບຣານຄະຕິ	archaeologist	ນັ່ງຍ່ອງຢໍ້	to squat
ມັກປະພັນ	author, writer	ນັ່ງລົງ	to sit down
ມັກພາສາ	linguist, interpreter	ນັ່ງໄຫວ້	to sit in respect for dignitary
ມັກພູມິສາດ	geographer	ນັດ	to make an appointment, pineapple
ມັກຟ້ອນ	dancer		
ມັກມວຍ	boxer	ນັດດຶ່ງ	one shot
ມັກເລງ	debaucher, gangster	ນັດໂມງ	to set a time
ມັກວິຊຸະອະກອນ	engineer	ນັນ	noisy
ມັກວິທຍາສາດ	scientist	ນັນ	that
ມັກເວົ້າ	orator	ນັບ	to count
ມັກໜັງສືພິມ	newspaperman	ນັບຖື	to respect, worship
ມັກອາວະກາດ	astronaut	ນັບບໍ່ຖວນ	countless
ມັກຮຽນ (ລູກສິດ)	student	ນັບມື້ນັບຫຼາຍ	to increase daily
ມັກຮຽນນາຍຮອຍ	cadet	ນັບວ່າ	it is regarded as
ມັກຮຽນອຶທຍາໄລ	high school student	ນັບໃໝ່	to recount
ນັ່ງ	to sit	ນາ	rice field
ນັ່ງທ່າຍຕົ້ນ	to sit with feet outstretched	ນາເກືອ	salt mine
ນັ່ງຂັດຖະຫຼາດ	to sit cross-legged	ນາແຢງ	dry season ricefield
ນັ່ງໄຂວ່ຫ້າງ	to across legs	ນາຍກັຣັຖມົນຕຣີ	prime minister
ນັ່ງຄອຍ	to sit and wait	ນາຕະສິນ	traditional dance
ນັ່ງຕັກ	to sit on someone's lap	ນາທີ	minute
ນັ່ງຕັ່ງ	to sit on a chair	ນາຜຼງ	flat field
ນັ່ງທຣງມ	to sit as a spirit medium	ນາລິກາ	clock
ນັ່ງເທ້າແກ້ມ	to sit with head in hands	ນາວາ	ship, navy
ນັ່ງພັກ	to sit and rest	ນາວາກີ	sailor
ນັ່ງຢູ່	to be sitting	ນາວອາອາກາດ	airplane, air force

ນາວີ	ship	ນາຍພະຄັງ	royal treasurer
ນະລົກ	hell	ນາຍພາສາ	interpreter, translator
ນ້າ	younger aunt or uncle	ນາຍພານ	hunter
ນ້າສາວ	maternal younger aunt	ນາຍພົນ	general
ນ້າບ່າວ	maternal younger uncle	ນາຍຫ້າງ	store owner
ນ້າໄພ້	younger aunt in-law	ນາຍໝໍ	doctor
ນາກ	otter, Naga	ນາຍຮ້ອຍ	company officer, merchant
ນາງ	lady, Mrs.	ນາມສະກຸນ	family name
ນາງກໍ່ລັກ	girl pendant which brings luck	ນິຍົມ	popular, prefer, to like
ນາງງາມ	beauty queen	ນິທານ	fable, story, tale
ນາງເງືອກ	mermaid	ນິໄສ	habit, custom
ນາງສາວ	Miss	ນິນທາ	to slander, gossip, criticism
ນາງທຽມ	female spirit medium	ນິພານ	to die, enter nirvana
ນາງແບບ	artist's model	ນິ່ງ	still, motionless
ນາງເຜິ້ງ	queen bee	ນິ່ງເສຍ	to remain silent
ນາງພະຍາບານ	nurse	ນິ້ວ	finger, inch
ນາງພະດຸ່ງຄັມ	midwife	ນິ້ວກາງ	middle finger
ນາງຟ້າ	fairy	ນິ້ວກ້ອຍ	little finger
ນາງໝໍ	nurse	ນິ້ວຊີ້	index finger
ນາງເອກ	heroine	ນິ້ວຕີນ	toe
ນາຍ	chief, boss	ນິ້ວໂປ້	thumb, big toe
ນາຍຄູ	teacher	ນິ້ວນາງ	ring finger
ນາຍຊ່າງ	mechanic, engineer	ນິ້ວມື	finger
ນາຍດ່ານ	custom house chief	ນີ້ (ຢ່າງນີ້)	this
ນາຍຕຳຣວຈ	police officer	ນີ້ມາ (ຢູ່ນີ້)	here
ນາຍທະຫານ	army officer		
ນາຍທຶນ	capitalist		

ນີ້ເນ (ນີ້ເດ)	here it is
ນຶກ	to think
ນຶກເຖິງ	to think of
ນຶກວ່າ	to think that
ນຶ່ງ (໑)	one (1)
ນຶກ	to think
ນຸ່ງ	to put on, wear
ນຸ່ງເຄື່ອງ	to dress
ນຸ່ງຫົ່ມ	to wear clothes
ນຸນ	swollen, rotten
ເນຣະຄຸນ	ungrateful
ເນຣະເທດ	to exile
ເນນ	Buddhist novice
ແນະນຳ	to introduce
ແນະນຳໃຫ້ຮູ້ຈັກ	to introduce, present
ແນປືນ	to aim a gun
ແນ່	surely
ແນ່ໃຈ	sure, confident
ແນວ	kind, way
ແນວຄວາມຄິດ	idea
ແນວໃດ	in what way, how
ແນວ (ແຖວ)	row, line
ແນວນັ້ນ	that kind
ແນວນັ້ນແນວນີ້	in every way, in any way
ແນວຣົບ	battle line, front
ແນວໜ້າ	front

ນົກ	bird
ນົກກະສາ	crane
ນົກກະທາ	quail, partridge
ນົກຄານນ້ຳ	marsh hen
ນົກກາເວົາ	blackbird
ນົກກາງແກ	pigeon
ນົກກາງເຂນ	robin
ນົກແກວ	parrot
ນົກຂະນີມ	oriole
ນົກຂີກະເຕືນ	snipe
ນົກຂຸມ	quail
ນົກເຂົາ	dove
ນົກຄຸມ	pet bird
ນົກເຄົາ	owl
ນົກຈາບ	rice bird
ນົກຈີບ	pink warbler
ນົກຈອກ	sparrow
ນົກເຈ່າ	heron
ນົກສອງທົວ	servant of two masters
ນົກໄຊ	woodpecker
ນົກຍາງ	stork, crane
ນົກຍຸງ	peacock
ນົກຕໍ	bird decoy
ນົກເຕີນ	king fisher
ນົກທາ	partridge
ນົກມາງມອນ	gull
ນົກເປັດນ້ຳ	teal

ນົກປືນ	flintlock rifle, hammer of gun	ນອກນັ້ນ	besides that
ນົກເຊ່ງ	pet bird	ນອກເຝັ່ງ	offshore
ນົກຕິງ	swan	ນອກເຮື່ອງ	irrelevant
ນົກທີ່ຂວານ	woodpecker	ນອກຮີດ	immoral
ນົກແອ່ນ	swallow	ນ້ອງ	younger brother or sister
ນົກຮ້ອງ	singing mina	ນ້ອງເຂີຍ	younger brother-in-law
ນົກແຮ້ງ	vulture	ນ້ອງສາວ	younger sister
ນົບ	to pray, greet respectfully	ນ້ອງຊາຍ	younger brother
ນົບໄຫວ້	to pray	ນ້ອງຜົວ	younger brother or sister-in-law
ນົມ	breast	ນ້ອງໃພ	younger sister-in-law
ນົມງົວ	cow milk	ນ້ອຍ	little, small
ນົມຍານ	drooping breasts	ນ້ອຍກວ່າ	less
ໂນ	to swell up	ນ້ອຍໃຈ	to feel disparaged, timid
ໂນນ	highland	ນ້ອຍນິ່ງ	a little
ນໍ	horn	ນອນ	to sleep
ນໍແຮດ	rhinoceros horn	ນອນກົ້ມ	to settle at the bottom, dregs, lees
ນໍ	question word to beg agreement	ນອນສລອຍ	siesta, to take a nap
ນອກ	out, outside	ນອນເດິກ	to go to bed late
ນອກກົດໝາຍ	outlaw	ນອນຕາຍ	to lie dead
ນອກເຂດ	beyond the bounds of	ນອນຕື່ນ	to wake up
ນອກຈາກ	except	ນອນແຕ່ຫົວຄ່ຳ	early to bed
ນອກຈາກນັ້ນ	besides that	ນອນບໍ່ຫລັບ	cannot sleep
ນອກຈາກນີ້	also, besides	ນອນເວີມ	siesta, nap
ນອກໃຈ	unfaithful	ນອນຫງາຍ	to lie face up
ນອກຈາກວ່າ	unless	ນອນຫລັບ	to sleep deeply
ນອກຊານ	porch	ນ້ຽງ	to be slanted, to lean
ນອກທາງ	out of the way	ນ້ຽງຫົວລົງ	to bow the head

ເມີຍ	cheese	ໃນບໍຣິເວນ	in the vicinity of, near
ເນື້ອ	flesh, meat	ໃນຂັດຈຸບັນ	at present
ເນື້ອຄວາມ	gist, content	ໃນເມືອງ	urban, downtown
ເນື້ອເລື່ອງ	theme	ໃນຣະຍະນີ້	at this time
ເນື້ອງຈາກ	due to, because of	ໃນຣະຫວ່າງ	between, among, approximately, about
ມ້ວ	delicious, tasty	ໃນໂລກ	in the world
ມວດ	to massage	ໃນເວລາດຽວກັນ	at the same time
ມວນ	of beautiful color, elegant	ໃນເວລາທີ່	during the time of
ມວນ	to quilt, wad	ໃນເວລາອັນຄວນ	in due time
ໃນ	in, seed	ໃນໄວໆ ນີ້	very soon
ໃນຂນະນັ້ນ	justly, at that time	ໃນມໍ່ໆ ນີ້	soon, presently
ໃນຂັ້ນສຸດທ້າຍ	finally	ເນົ່າ	spoiled, rotten
ໃນຂັ້ນຕໍ່ໄປ	after that	ເນົ່າຍຸດ	mouldy and spoiled
ໃນຂັ້ນນີ້	at this stage	ເນົ່າເໝັນ	stinking
ໃນເຂດ	within bounds of	ນຳ	to lead, with together
ໃນໃຈ	mental, emotional, at heart	ນຳກັນ	together, with
ໃນຈຳນວນ	in the number of	ນຳກັນ	to follow after
ໃນສໄໝນີ້	nowadays	ນຳທັນ	to catch up with
ໃນສໄໝກ່ອນ	in former days	ນຳທາງ	to lead the way, guide
ໃນຕອນສຸດທ້າຍ	at the end of (time)	ນຳພາ້ວ	to guide
ໃນຍາມທຸກຍາກ	in hard times	ນຳໄປ	to follow, lead
ໃນທັນໃດ	immediately	ນຳພາ	to take the lead
ໃນທັນທີ	immediately	ນຳຫຼັ້ວ	to follow after
ໃນທາງກົງກັນຂ້າມ	on the contrary	ນຳອອກເຜີຍແຜ່	to disseminate
ໃນທີ່ສຸດ	at last	ນ້ຳ	to beat, repeat
ໃນນັ້ນ	inside, among those	ນ້ຳ	water, liquid
ໃນບໍ່ຊ້ານີ້	soon	ນ້ຳກະທິ	coconut milk

ນ້ຳກັ່ນ	distilled water	ນ້ຳຍ່ຽວ	urine
ນ້ຳຄາວ	gum	ນ້ຳຕາ	tears
ນ້ຳດື່ມ	drinking water	ນ້ຳເຕົ້າ	bottle, gourd
ນ້ຳແກງ	soup	ນ້ຳຕານ	sugar
ນ້ຳແຕ້ວ	flood	ນ້ຳຕານກ້ອນ	lump sugar
ນ້ຳກົດ	acid	ນ້ຳຕານຂາວ	white sugar
ນ້ຳກອກ	tap water	ນ້ຳຕານແດງ	brown sugar
ນ້ຳກ້ອນ	ice	ນ້ຳຕານປີບ	lump palm sugar
ນ້ຳກຸງ	lacquer	ນ້ຳຕື້ນ	shallow water
ນ້ຳຂຶ້ນ	river water rises	ນ້ຳຕົກ	waterfall
ນ້ຳຂຸ່ນ	turbulent water	ນ້ຳຕົ້ມ	boiled water
ນ້ຳຂອງ	Mekong River	ນ້ຳຕອງ	filtered water
ນ້ຳເຂົ້າ	rice water	ນ້ຳຖ້ວມ	flood
ນ້ຳຄ້າງ	dew	ນ້ຳທະເລ	sea
ນ້ຳຄຳ	golden color, real meaning of a word	ນ້ຳນົມ	milk
ນ້ຳງື່ມ	Nam Ngum River	ນ້ຳນົມຂຸ້ນ	condensed milk
ນ້ຳຈິດ	fresh water	ນ້ຳບາຫຼອດ	thermometer
ນ້ຳແຈ່ວ	pepper sauce	ນ້ຳບີ	bile
ນ້ຳສ້າງ	well	ນ້ຳແບ້ມ	semen, sperm
ນ້ຳສີ	paint	ນ້ຳເບີ້	number
ນ້ຳສົ້ມ	vinegar	ນ້ຳບິກ	receding water
ນ້ຳໂສດາ	soda	ນ້ຳບວກ	puddle, water buff wal
ນ້ຳໃສ	pure, clear water	ນ້ຳປາ	fish sauce
ນ້ຳຊາ	tea	ນ້ຳຕົ້ມໄມ້	fruit juice
ນ້ຳຊຸ້ນ	gravy	ນ້ຳເຜິ້ງ	honey
ນ້ຳຍ້ອມ	dye	ນ້ຳຝົນ	rainwater
		ນ້ຳໝາກ	hot sauce

ນ້ຳພຸ	fountain
ນ້ຳມັນ	oil, petroleum products
ນ້ຳມັນກ໊າດ	kerosene
ນ້ຳມັນຂຽວ	green medicinal oil
ນ້ຳມັນເຄື່ອຍສີ	lacquer
ນ້ຳມັນງາ	sesame oil
ນ້ຳມັນສລັດ	salad oil
ນ້ຳມັນຕັບປາ	codliver oil
ນ້ຳມັນທາຜົມ	hair oil
ນ້ຳມັນເບີ	butter
ນ້ຳມັນຍາງ, ຍໍສີ	resin
ນ້ຳມັນໝູ	lard
ນ້ຳມັນແອດຊັ້ງ	gasoline
ນ້ຳມຶກ	ink
ນ້ຳມົນ	lustral water
ນ້ຳມອດໄຟ	fire engine
ນ້ຳຢາ	liquid medicine, soup
ນ້ຳເຢັນ	cold water
ນ້ຳລ້າ	plain water
ນ້ຳລາຍ	saliva
ນ້ຳເລິກ	deep water
ນ້ຳເຊິມ	cross current
ນ້ຳວົນ	whirlpool
ນ້ຳແຫ້ງ	dry riverbed
ນ້ຳທໍ່ເຜິ້ງ	honey
ນ້ຳທອມ	perfume

ນ້ຳໜັກ	weight
ນ້ຳໜອງ	pus
ນ້ຳໝາກ	betel expectorant
ນ້ຳໝາກນາວ	lemonade
ນ້ຳໝາກພ້າວ	coconut water
ນ້ຳໝາກໄມ້	fruit juice
ນ້ຳໝອກ	fog
ນ້ຳຫວານ	soft drink
ນ້ຳອັດລົມ	bottled drinks
ນ້ຳອາບ	bath water
ນ້ຳອົບ	perfume
ນ້ຳອ້ອຍ	sugarcane juice

ຂ ເຂັດ

ບັກ	master, boy	ບັນໄດ	ladder
ບັງ	to hide	ບັນທິດ	to note
ບັງເກີດ	to happen	ບັນທຶກການສອນ	lesson notes
ບັງຄັບ	to control	ບັນທຸກ	to load, transport
ບັງຄັບບັງເຕິງ	to threaten, oppress	ບັນເທິງ	to amuse
ບັງຄັບບັນຊາ	to command, control	ບັນນາທິການ	editor
ບັງບວດ	to oppress	ບັນຣະຍາຍ	to explain, lecture
ບັງອາດ	to dare, indiscreet	ບັນລັງ	throne
ບັງເອີນ	to happen by chance	ບັນລຸ	to attain
ບັງ	tube, cylinder	ບັນລຸຜົນ	to succeed
ບັງສູບ	pump	ບັນຫາ	problem
ບັງສຸກ	multiplication table	ບັນຫາການເມືອງ	political problem
ບັງສູບ	bellows	ບັນຫາສຳຄັນ	important problem
ບັງນ້ຳ	bamboo tube for water	ບັ່ມ	to divide in pieces
ບັງໄຟ	rocket	ບັ່ມຟືນ	to cut firewood
ບັງໄຟດອກ	roman candle, firecracker on a tree	ບ່ມ	part
ບັງໄມ້ເອ້	long bamboo tube	ບ່ມກ່ກ	first part
ບັດເຊີນ	invitation card	ບ່ມປາຍ	final part
ບັດນີ້	now	ບາສີ	Lao communal ceremony
ບັດປະຈຳຕົວ	identification card	ບາທລອດ	thermometer
ບັດຜ່ານປະຕູ	ticket of admission	ບ່າ	shoulder
ບັດລາຍຊື່ອງກິນ	menu	ບ່າໄຫ່	shoulder
ບັນຈຸ	to contain, insert	ບ້າ	crazy
ບັນຈຸປືນ	to load a gun	ບ້າສົງຄາມ	warmonger
ບັນຊາ	to command	ບ້າຕັນຫາ	lustful man
ບັນຊາການ	to command, commanding	ບ້າມກ້ລາຍ	carrulous
ບັນຊາການສູງສຸດ	supreme command	ບ້າເລືອດ	bloodthirsty

ບາພຸ	epilepsy	ບານໃກ້ບານໄກ	near and far
ບາກບົມ	to persevere	ບານເກົ່າ	homeland
ບາງ	thin, some	ບານເດີມ	original home
ບາງຄົນ	someone, somebody	ບານນາ	countryside
ບາງຄຶງ	sometimes	ບານນອກ	rural, the sticks
ບາງສິ່ງ	something	ບານນອກຂອງນາ	countryside
ບາງທີ (ບາງເທື)	maybe	ບານພັກ	residence
ບາງເທື່ອ	sometimes	ບານເມືອງ	country
ບາງບ່ອນ	someplace	ບານຮ້າງ	deserted village
ບາງພວກ	some people, some groups	ບານເຮືອນ	home
ບາງຢ່າງ	something, some kinds	ບາບ	sin
ບາງແຫ່ງ	somewhere	ບາບກັມ	sin
ບາຍ	to touch	ບາບໜັກ	grave offense
ບາຍ	afternoon, to spread food on rice	ບ່າວ	youth
ບ່າຍເຂົາ	to have a snack	ບ່າວສາວ	youth and maidens
ບາດ	wound	ບ່າວໄພ່	common people
ບາດເຈັບ	wounded	ບ່າວແອວ	teenage boy
ບາດໃຈ	grieved	ບ່າວຮານ	young man
ບາດຍ່າງ	step	ບີ	to divide
ບາດຕາ	ugly	ບີດາ	father
ບາດແຜ	wound	ບີດແຂນ	to twist the arm
ບານ	to bloom	ບີດຄິ້ງ	to stretch, physically
ບານປະຕູ	panel	ບີດຄໍ	to wring the neck
ບານພັບ	hinge	ບິນ	to fly
ບານ	home	ບິນທະບາດ	to beg alms
ບານເກີດ	birthplace	ບີບ	to squeeze
ບານເກີດເມືອງນອນ	home town	ບິບເເຖາ	to sound a horn

ຍືບນ້ຳນົມ	to milk	ບູຊາ	to venerate, give off
ຍືບບ້ວຄັບ	to oppress	ເບັ່ງ	to swell, swollen
ຍືບບີ້	oppress	ເບັ່ງທ້ອງ	swollen abdomen
ຍືບມື	to squeeze one's hand	ເບິ່ງ	to push away
ຍືບເຊັ່ນ	to massage	ເບັດ	fishhook
ຍືກຍືນ	stubborn	ເບັ້ງ	beer
ຍຶງ	pond	ເບັ້ງບຳນານ	pension
ຍຶດຄງວ (ຍຶດນຶ່ງ)	an instant	ເບັ້ງມື້	per diem
ບຸປ່າ	to treck thru the forest	ແບມື	to open one's hand
ບຸຣະມະ	to restore	ແບ	goat
ບຸຣຸດ	person, man	ແບເຖິກ (ແກ່)	billy goat
ບຸກ	to invade	ແບແມ	nanny goat
ບຸກຄິມສຳຄັນ	prominent personality	ແບກ	to carry on shoulder
ບຸກໂຈມຕີ	to attack	ແບກປືນ	to shoulder a gun
ບຸກລຸກ	to invade	ແບ່ງ	to divide
ບຸກລຸກເອົາ	to take over	ແບ່ງກັນ	to divide up
ບຸງ	paddy basket	ແບ່ງແຍກ	to separate
ບຸນ	festival, merit	ແບນ	flat
ບຸນຊ່ວງເຮືອ	boat race festival	ແບນມື	to open one's hand
ບຸນຕັກບາດ	ceremony of bonzes	ແບນ	to throw
ບຸນປີໃໝ່	New Year festival	ແບນຫີນ	to throw stones
ບຸນມາຄະບຸຊາ	Festival celebrating the teachings of the Buddha	ແບນ	penis
ບຸນວິສາຂະບຸຊາ	Festival celebrating the birth, death & attainment of Buddha	ແບບ	model
ບຸນຕົກນ້ຳ	Water festival	ແບບສອນອ່ານ	reader
ບຸນຕ່ເຂົາສະລາກ	Ancestor festival	ແບບແຜນ	model, plan
ບຸນຕ່ເຂົາປະດັບດິນ	Rice growing festival	ແບບພິມ	proof copy
ບຸບ	to beat	ແບບຢ່າງ	**example**

ແບບຮຽນ	textbook	ບໍລິຈາກ	donation
ບົກ	land, dry	ບໍລິສັດ	company
ບົກພ່ອງ	deficiency	ບໍລິສັດຂົນສົ່ງ	transport company
ບົງການ	to direct	ບໍລິສຸດ	pure, virgin
ບົງໜາມ	to pull out a thorn	ບໍລິສຸດໃຈ	pure in heart
ບົງຝຶ່ງ	to pierce an abscess	ບໍລິບູນ	complete
ບົງ	caterpillar	ບໍລິໂພກ	to consume
ບົ້ງກີ້	millipede	ບໍລິວານ	followers
ບົດ	to grind, writing	ບໍລິເວນ	area
ບົດຄວາມ	text	ບໍລິຫານ	to execute, manage
ບົດນຳ	preface	ບໍ່	(negative or question word particle), source
ບົດບັນນາທິການ	editorial	ບໍ່ກາ	not dare to
ບົດບາດ	role	ບໍ່ກາຄັດຄ້ານ	not dare to oppose
ບົດຝາວະນາ	devotional lesson	ບໍ່ເກີດ	original place
ບົດເພງ (ບົດຮ້ອງ)	song	ບໍ່ເກືອ	salt mine
ບົດລະຄອນ	play, script	ບໍ່ກວ່າ	nothing better than
ບົດວິຈານ	commentary	ບໍ່ຂາດນີ້	without a crack
ບົດຮຽນ	lesson	ບໍ່ຂືນ	not to refuse
ບົມ	top, to bribe	ບໍ່ຂືນເທົ່າໃຜ	independent
ບົມສ້ວນ	in heaven	ບໍ່ແຂງແຮງ	weak
ບົມເອທາ	in the air	ບໍ່ເຄີຍ	never, not usually
ບົມ	bomb	ບໍ່ຄຳ	gold mine
ບົ່ມ	to ripen	ບໍ່ຄວນ	ought not
ໂບກທຸງ	to wave a flag	ບໍ່ງ	not to care about
ໂບກປູນ	to plaster	ບໍ່ເງິນ	silver mine
ໂບກມື	to wave one's hand	ບໍ່ລື	to forget
ເບາະ	cushion, is that so?	ບໍ່ຈຳ	to forget, no matter

ບໍ່ຈຳກັດ	unlimited	ບໍ່ນ້ຳ	well
ບໍ່ສະດວກ	inconvenient	ບໍ່ນ້ຳມັນ	oil well
ບໍ່ສະບາຍ	unhappy, sick	ບໍ່ນ້ຳມຶກ	inkwell
ບໍ່ສະອາດ	dirty	ບໍ່ນ້ຳຮ້ອນ	hot spring
ບໍ່ສັດຊື່	dishonest	ບໍ່ບໍລິສຸດ	impure
ບໍ່ສຸພາບ	impolite, rude	ບໍ່ປານ	unequal to
ບໍ່ສິ້ນສຸດ	eternal	ບໍ່ເປັນຫຍັງ	so what, never mind, it doesn't matter, you're welcome
ບໍ່ສົນໃຈ	uninterested	ບໍ່ແຜ	unbreakable
ບໍ່ຊ້າກໍໄວ	sooner or later	ບໍ່ຜາກຳນົດ	indefinite
ບໍ່ເຊື່ອ	to doubt	ບໍ່ມີ	don't have
ບໍ່ຊຳນານ	inexperienced	ບໍ່ມີະບຽບ	disorderly
ບໍ່ເຊົາ	incessant	ບໍ່ມີວຽກເຮັດ	unemployed
ບໍ່ຍອມຟັງເຫດຜົນ	deaf to reason	ບໍ່ມີຫຍັງໄດ (ບໍ່ມີຫຍັງ)	nothing at all
ບໍ່ດີ	bad	ບໍ່ສ້ຽງນີ້	not so, usually no
ບໍ່ດີໃຈ	unhappy	ບໍ່ເຫັນແກ່ຕົວ	selfless, unselfish
ບໍ່ເດືອດຮ້ອນ	carefree	ບໍ່ໜ້າເຊື່ອ	incredible, fantastic
ບໍ່ດົນ	not long	ບໍ່ໜ້າເປັນໄປໄດ	improbable, unlikely
ບໍ່ໄດ	impossible, not able to	ບໍ່ໜານ	unlucky
ບໍ່ເຕັມໃຈ	unwilling	ບໍ່ໃຫ	not give anything
ບໍ່ຕົກລົງ	to disagree	ບໍ່ເອົາໃຈກັນ	unobliging
ບໍ່ຕອງ	forget about it, must not	ບໍ່ອຶດຢາກ	to have enough, lack nothing
ບໍ່ຖ່ານຫີນ	coal mine	ບໍ່ອຶ່ມ	unsatiated, never have enough
ບໍ່ຖຶກ	incorrect	ບໍ່ຕາຍ	immortal
ບໍ່ທັນ	not on time	ບໍ່ຮູ້ເນື້ອ	to lose consciousness
ບໍ່ທອງແດງ	copper mine	ບໍ່ຮແລວ	unfinished
ບໍ່ນຶກຝັນ	unexpected	ບໍ່ຮແລວຈັກເທື່ອ	unending, endless
ບໍ່ແຈ	unclear	ບໍ່ຮຫັຍວຈັກຄີ	nothing
		ບໍ່ຮອາຍ	shameless

ບໍ່ແຮ່	mine	ຂອນຢູ່ບ່ອນເຊົາ	residence (home)
ບອກ	to tell	ຂອນຢູ່ບ່ອນນອນ	lodging
ບອກຂ່າວ	tell the news	ຂອນລີໄພ	shelter, place of refuge
ບອກສອນ	to teach	ຂອນເຊົາໄສ	shelter
ບອກຊື່	to tell name	ຂອນຮົ່ມ	shady spot
ບອກຍາກ	naughty, difficult to say	ເບີກຂອງ	to distribute goods
ບອກວ່າ	to tell that...	ເບີກເງິນ	to pay money
ບອກໃຫ້ຮູ້	to inform	ເບີກເງິນເດືອນ	to pay salaries
ບອງ	to put in water	ເບີກທາງ	to break through, find a way out
ບ່ວງຫູ	to pierce the ears	ເບີກບານ	be happy
ບອດ	blind	ເບີກບານມ່ວນຊື່ນ	to be happy
ບ່ອນ	place	ເບິ່ງ	to watch, to look at
ບ່ອນກັກຂັງ	prison	ເບິ່ງແຍງ	to look after
ບ່ອນເກີດ	birthplace	ເບິ່ງຖຸ	to look at, Look!
ບ່ອນໄກ	place far away	ເບິ່ງໜັງສື	to read books
ບ່ອນຂັງນ້ຳ	reservoir	ເບຍລົມ	to expose to wind
ບ່ອນຂາຍປີ້	ticket office	ບຽດບຽນ	to mistreat
ບ່ອນຄົວກິນ	kitchen	ບ້ວງ	twisted
ບ່ອນຈອດ	landing place, parking area	ເບື່ອ	sick and tired of, poisone
ບ່ອນສາທາລະນະ	public place	ເບື່ອຕາ	tired of seeing
ບ່ອນສູງ	highland	ເບື່ອໂລກ	to be disgruntled
ບ່ອນດີ	comfortable place	ເບື່ອຫູ	monotonous sound
ບ່ອນໃດ	where	ເບື່ອອາຫານ	to lose one's appetite
ບ່ອນຕາກອາກາດ	health resort	ເບື້ອງ	side
ບ່ອນນີ້	here	ເບື້ອງຂວາ	right side
ບ່ອນນອນ	bedroom	ເບື້ອງຊ້າຍ	left side
ບ່ອນຢູ່	location, where one stays	ເບື້ອງຕົ້ນ	preliminary

ເບື້ອງໜ້າ	front	ໃບມີດແຖ	razor blade
ເບື້ອງຫຼັງ	behind	ໃບມອນ	mulberry leaf
ບົວ	lotus	ໃບປ່ຽມ	certificate
ບົວເງິນ	silver lotus	ໃບປ່າ	tobacco leaf
ບົວຫຼວງ	lotus	ໃບລັບ	receipt
ບົວແບ້	small lotus	ໃບລັບສົ່ງຄ້າ	bill of lading
ບົວຣະບັດ	to look after	ໃບລາ	resignation, permission
ບວກ	to add	ໃບລານ	palm leaves for writing
ບວກຄວາຍ	buffalo wallow	ໃບຫູ	earlobe
ບວກນ້ຳ	puddle	ໃບໜ້າ	feature
ບ່ວງ	spoon	ໃບຫຍ້າ	blade of grass
ບວດ	to enter the priesthood	ໃບອະນຸຍາດ	license
ບ່ວມ	swollen	ໃບຮູບປະພັນສັດ	animal certificate
ໃບ	leaf, paper	ໄບ່	talk in sleep
ໃບຂັບຂີ່	driving license	ໄບ້	dumb, stupid
ໃບສມັກ	application form	ເບົາ	light, not heavy
ໃບຊາ	tea leaf	ເບົາໃຈ	relieved
ໃບຊາຕາ	birth certificate	ເບົາບາງ	sparse
ໃບແຊກ	primary school certificate	ເບົາໄປ	to diminish
ໃບເດີນທາງ	permission to travel	ເບົາມື	to be relieved of work
ໃບຕອງ	banana leaves	ເບົາແຮງ	to be relieved
ໃບປະກັນ	warrant	ເບົາຕາ	eye socket
ໃບປົກ	cover, binding	ບຳເພັນສິນ	to observe religious precepts
ໃບຝາກເງິນ	deposit slip	ບຳຣຸງ	to be helpful, nourish
ໃບພັດ	propeller	ບຳເໜັດ	commission, bonus
ໃບພັດລົມ	fan		
ໃບໄມ້	tree leaf		

ປະກົດຜົນ   to obtain a result

ປະກວດ   contest

ປະກວດນາງງາມ   beauty contest

ປະຈຸບັນ   now, the present

ປະຈຳ   permanent, fixed, attached

ປະຈຳການ   in service

ປະຈຳເດືອນ   monthly

ປະຈຳປີ   annual

ປະຈຳມື້   daily

ປະຈຳຢູ່   to be situated at

ປະສາດ   nerve

ປະສັດ   cattle, domestic animal

ປະສົມ   mixed

ປະສົມພັນ   to cross-breed, hybridize

ປະເສີດ   excellent

ປະຊາຊົນ   population

ປະຊຸມ   to meet, assemble

ປະຊຸມລັບ   secret meeting

ປະໂຍດ   useful

ປະດິດ   to invent, to found

ປະຕັວ   patent

ປະຕິທິນ   calendar

ປະຕິບັດ   to act

ປະຕິບັດງານ   to operate, carry on

ປະຕິບັດຕາມ   to do as recommended

ປະຕູ   door

ປະຖົມ   elementary

ປະ   to divorce, to abandon

ປະກັນຊີວິດ   life insurance

ປະກັນໄຟ   fire insurance

ປະກາສະນີຍະບັດ   certificate

ປະກາດ   to announce, declare

ປະກາດໂຄສະນາ   to advertise

ປະກົດ   to appear, seem

ປະຖົມສຶກສາ	elementary education	ປັດເຮືອນ	to sweep out the house
ປະຖົມມະເລີກ	first time	ປັນ	to divide, distribute, share
ປະທັບໃຈ	to impress	ປັນຍາ	common sense
ປະທັບຕາ	to seal	ປັນຫາ	problem
ປະທານາທິບໍດີ	president	ປັ້ນ	to spin
ປະທານ	chairman	ປັ້ນຝ້າຍ	to spin cotton
ປະເທດ	country	ປັ້ນເຂົ້າ	to eat breakfast
ປະເທດລາວ	Laos	ປັ້ນຮູບ	to make clay images
ປະທ້ວງ	to protest	ປັ້ນໝໍ້	to make pots
ປະເປືອຍ	naked	ປັບປຸງ	to improve
ປະເພນີ	tradition	ປັບປຸງຊົນນະບົດ	to develop rural area
ປະພຶດ	to behave	ປາ	fish
ປະພຶດຕົນ	to behave	ປາກະປ໋ອງ	canned fish
ປະມາດ	to be careless, underestimate	ປາກັດ	fighting fish
ປະມານ	to estimate, approximately	ປາກົດ	small catfish, to seem cle
ປະມູນ	to propose	ປາກົດວ່າ	to seem clear that ...
ປະມູນລາຄາ	to bid	ປາຂາວ	fish for "padek"
ປະວັດ	history	ປາເຂັ້ງ	perch
ປະຫານຊີວິດ	to execute	ປາເຄັມ	salted fish
ປະຫຍັດເງິນ	to save money	ປາຄຳ	goldfish
ປະຫຍັດເວລາ	to save time	ປາສາດ	castle
ປະພັກຜື	to take time off	ປາສະລາມ	shark
ປັກ	to stick, sting	ປາສະລິດ	pilot fish
ປັດ	to brush, sweep	ປາສົດ	fresh fish
ປັດຈຸບັນ	the present	ປາສ້ອຍ	fish for "padek"
ປັດຍອນນອນ	to make a bed	ປາຮິວ	tiny carp
ປັດຝຸ່ນ	to dust	ປາດຸກ	catfish

ປາແຄກ	"padek," fermented fish in sauce	ປາງກ່ອນ	last world
ປ່າຉະນາ	wish	ປາຍ	end
ປາທະກະຖາ	speech, preach	ປາຍທາງ	end of a path
ປາກຸ	mackerel	ປາຍນ້ຶວມຶ	finger tip
ປາໄນ	chinese carp	ປາຍປາກກາ	pen point
ປາບຶກ	giant catfish	ປາຍມິດ	knife point
ປາຍູ່	guppy	ປາຍລຶ້ນ	tip of tongue
ປາຢ່າງ	smoked fish	ປ້າຍ	signboard, sign label
ປາເສຶມ	large catfish	ປ້າຍໂຄສະນາ	billboard
ປາວານ	whale	ປ້າຍຕິດປະກາດ	bulletin board
ປາແຫ້ວ	dried fish	ປາດ	to slice, operate
ປາໝໍ	climbing fish	ປາດຄໍ	to cut the throat
ປາລຸດ	scorpion fish	ປາຖນາ	desire
ປາໄຫຼ	eel	ປານ	as, like, Mongalian macula
ປ່າ	forest	ປານດິວ	skin disease
ປ່າສູງ	high forest	ປານໃດ	when
ປ່າຊາ	cemetery	ປານວ່າ	as if, as
ປ່າໄຜ່	bamboo grove	ປ່ານ	jute
ປ່າໄມ້	forestry	ປ້ານ	to irrigate, to bar
ປ້າ	aunt	ປ້ານຄູ	to dike, dam
ປາກ	mouth, to speak	ປ້ານນ້ຳ	to irrigate
ປາກກາ	pen	ປ້ານລົມ	wood to stop roof-thatch from falling down
ປາກກຶກ	mute	ປາບ	to put under one's control
ປາກຂອດ	to speak clearly	ປາບກະບົດ	to suppress a rebellion
ປາກເປົ່າ	oral	ປ່າວ	to inform
ປາກແຫວ່ງ	harelip	ປ່າວເຕືອນ	to warn, publicize
ປາກຮ້າຍ	to curse		

ຍົດຍົມດົ	to appreciate	ຍົ້ນ	to change mind, rotate
ຍົດ	to stop, close, pick	ຍົ້ນໄປຍົ້ນມາ	to vaciliate
ຍົດທາງເດີນ	to block the way	ຍົກສາ	to consult
ຍົດປະກາດ	to stop informing	ຍົນ	gun
ຍົດປະຊຸມ	to close a meeting	ຍົນກົນເບົາ	light machine gun
ຍົດບັງ	to hide the truth	ຍົນຍາວ	rifle
ຍົດບັນຊີ	to close an account	ຍົນຖີບ	gun recoil
ຍົດປາກ	shut up!	ຍົນເຖື່ອນ	illicit firearms
ຍົ້ນ	to spin, turn, bake	ຍົນແຝດ	double-barrel shotgun
ຍົ້ນປວຍວິอຣະຂັດ	to care for	ຍົນໝັ້ນ	pistol
ຍົວ	blowing in the breeze, flying	ຍົນໃຫຍ່	artillery, cannon
ປີ	year, banana flower	ປຶ້ນ	book
ປີກາຍນີ້	last year	ປຶ້ນອ່ານ	reading book
ປີກ່ອນ	year before last	ປຶ້ນຂຽນ	exercise book
ປີສາດ	devil	ປຸກ	to build
ປີໜ້າ	next year	ປຸກໃຈ	to arouse, incite
ປີໃໝ່	new year's day	ປຸກໃຫ້ຕື່ນ	to wake up there
ປີ່	flute	ປຸກເຮືອນ	to build a house
ປີ້	ticket	ປຸຍ	hairy
ປີ້ບິນ	airplane ticket	ປຸ໋ຍ	fertilizer
ປີກ	wing	ປຸ້ນ	to plunder
ປີກນົກ	bird wing	ປຸ່ມທ້ອງ	to feel nauseous
ປົງ	leech	ປູ	crab, to spread
ປີ້ງ	to grill	ປູເຄັມ	pickled crab
ປີນ	to climb by crawling	ປູສາດ	to spread out a mattress
ປີນກກໄມ້	to climb a tree	ປູ່ເຍີ ຍ່າເຍີ	two string-covered New Year spirits in Luang Prabai
ປີນຂຶ້ນ	to go up, mount	ປູໂຕະ	to spread a table cloth

ປູທະເລ	salt water crab
ປູນາ	land crab
ປູຜ້າ	to spread a cloth
ປູຜົມ	to lay a carpet
ປູຍ່າງ	to asphalt a road surface
ປູ	worn out, dull
ປູກ	to grow
ປູກຜັກ	to grow vegetables
ປູກຝີ	to vaccinate
ປູກຝັງ	agriculture
ປູກຍາ	to plant tobacco
ປູນ	lime
ປູນຂາວ	lime
ປູນຊີມັງ	cement
ເປັດ	duck
ເປັດໄກ່	poultry
ເປັດນ້ຳ	wild duck, teal
ເປັນ	to be
ເປັນກະບົດ	to rebel
ເປັນກັນເອງ	informal, cordial
ເປັນກາງ	to be neutral, neutrality
ເປັນກຸນເຈົ້າ	in honor of
ເປັນຂະບົດ	in rebellion
ເປັນຂ້ອຍ	to be servant or slave
ເປັນໄຂ້	to have a fever
ເປັນຄູ່	in pairs
ເປັນໂສດ	single, bachelor
ເປັນສ່ອນ	in parts
ເປັນຕາຊິດ	amazing
ເປັນຕາເສ້ຍດາຍ	pity
ເປັນຕາເມື່ອຍ	tiring
ເປັນຕາຊັງ	odious, hateful
ເປັນຕາເບິ່ງ	good to look at
ເປັນຕົ້ນ	for example, and others also
ເປັນຕົ້ນມາ	from then until now
ເປັນຕົມ	muddy
ເປັນແຕ່ກຸນ	happy-go-lucky
ເປັນແຖວ	lined up
ເປັນຕໍ່	in a good position
ເປັນທາງການ	to be official
ເປັນທີ່ນິຍົມ	popular
ເປັນໂທສ	guilty
ເປັນປະຈຳ	habitually, regularly
ເປັນປະໂຍດ	useful
ເປັນປະທານ	to preside over
ເປັນບ້າ	insane, crazy
ເປັນບາດ	wounded
ເປັນບ່າວ	to reach manhood
ເປັນປາກສຽງ	to quarrel
ເປັນປາກເປັນສຽງກັນ	to quarrel
ເປັນປານ	to have a birthmark
ເປັນຜອບ	possessed by evil spirit
ເປັນໄປຕາມສໄມ	changeable, following the fashion
ເປັນໄປບໍ່ໄດ້	impossible

ເປັນຜົນສຳເຣັດ	to be successful	ແປ້ງຍົມ	cake flour
ເປັນຜະຍາດ	to be sick	ແປ້ງສາລິ	corn flour
ເປັນພະຍານ	to be a witness	ແປ້ງຜັດໜ້າ	face powder
ເປັນພິດ	venomous, toxic	ແປ້ງເຫົ້າ	yeast
ເປັນລົມ	to faint, swoon	ແປມ	smooth
ເປັນວ້າ	rabid	ແປ້ນ	panel, plank, board
ເປັນຫ່ວງ	to worry	ແປ້ນກະດານ	board
ເປັນເຫດ	to happen	ແປ້ນນັ່ງ	bench
ເປັນຫຍັງ	what's the matter?	ແປ່ຍນໍ້າ	water pipe
ເປັນໜີ້	in debt	ແປອ	flow
ເປັນໜອງ	full of pus	ແປອໄຟ	flame
ເປັນໜອນ	to have worms	ປົກ	to cover
ເປັນໝູ່	in groups	ປົກກະຕິ	normal
ເປັນຫວັດ	to have a head cold	ປົກຄອງ	to govern
ເປ	hammock	ປົກຍິດ	to hide
ເປ່ງ	to open, speak out	ປົກປ້ອງ	to protect
ແປະ	close to	ປ່ຽ	to let
ແປະໃສ່	to put on, apply	ປ່ຽວດອກ	to bloom
ແປ	flat, to translate	ປົດ	to remove
ແປຕາມຕົວອັກສອນ	to translate literally	ປົດປ່ອຍ	to free, liberate
ແປວ່າ	to mean	ປົ້ນ	to grind, crash
ແປເຮືອນ	top beam of the house	ປົບ	to hit, escape
ແປກປະຫຼາດ	odd	ໂປ	swollen
ແປງ	to repair, brush	ໄປ້	big, chief
ແປງປັດຕົມ	hair brush	ປອກ	to peel, ring
ແປງຜັດແຂ້ວ	tooth brush	ປອກແຂນ	bracelet
ແປ້ງ	flour	ປອກຄໍ	necklace
		ປອກເປືອກ	to peel

ປອກນີ້	thimble	ເປີດກ໊ອກນ້ຳ	to turn on the water faucet
ປອກໝອນ	pillow case	ເປີດປະຊຸມ	to open a meeting
ປອງ	to aim, to be after	ເປີດປ້າຍ	to unveil a sign
ປ່ອງ	hole	ເປີດເຜີຍ	to reveal
ປ່ອງຢ້ຽມ	window	ເປີດພິທີ	to inaugurate
ປ້ອງກັນ	to protect, prevent	ເປີດໜ່າຍ	to be tired of, fed up
ປ້ອງກັນປະເທດ	to defend nation	ເປັ້ງ	to beat, hurried
ປ່ອຍ	to release, free	ເປັ້ງ	paralyzed, lame
ປ່ອຍຄົນໂທດ	to release a prisoner	ປຽກ	wet
ປ່ອຍຖິ້ມ	to omit	ປ່ຽງ	piece
ປ້ອຍ	to curse	ປ່ຽນ	to change
ປອດ	lungs, intact	ປ່ຽນກັນ	to exchange
ປອດໄພ	safety	ປ່ຽນໃຈ	to change one's mind
ປອດແຕ້ວ	tuberculosis	ປ່ຽນຕົວ	to substitute
ປ່ອນ	to send down to, to put in	ປ່ຽນທາງ	to change one's course
ປ່ອນບັດ	to vote	ປ່ຽນແປງ	to change
ປ້ອນ	to feed (food)	ປຽບ	to compare
ປ້ອນລູກ	to feed a child	ປຽບທຽບ	to compare
ປອບ	to soothe, evil spirit	ປ່ຽວ	alone
ປອບໃຈ	to calm oneself	ປ່ຽວໃຈ	lonely
ປອມ	false	ເປືອກ	bark, shell
ປອມຕົວ	to disguise	ເປືອກເຂົ້າ	husk of rice
ປອມແປງ	to falsify	ເປືອກໄມ້	bark of tree
ປອມລາຍມື	forgery	ເປືອກໝາກພ້າວ	coconut husk
ປອມຕົວສ໌	to forge a document	ເປືອງ	to cost too much
ເປີດ	to open	ເປືອງເງິນ	to cost money
		ເປືອງທີ່	to waste space

ເຂື່ງຍຂ່ອມ	to waste space	ໄປໃນເມືອງ	to go downtown
ເຂື່ງຍເວລາ	to waste time	ໄປພຸ້ນ	to go over there
ເຍືຍ	naked	ໄປຢາມ	to visit someone
ເປືຍກາຍ	naked	ໄປຣັບ	to go meet
ເບື່ອຍ	to rot	ໄປລາດຕະເວນ	to go on patrol
ເບື້ອນ	dirty	ໄປຖົດ	to defecate (polite)
ເປື້ອນເປີ	to stain	ໄປຕາ	to go see
ປົວ	to cure	ໄປຫາໝໍ	to see a doctor
ປວກ	termite	ໄປຫຼິ້ນ	to go out for pleasure
ປວງ	all	ເປົາ	sack
ປ່ວງ	to be insane	ເປົ່າ	empty, to blow
ປ່ວຍ	ill, sick	ເປົ່າແຄນ (ເປົ່າຄຸຍ)	to plan the khene (khɛ̀ɛ̀n)
ປວດ	to ache	ເປົ່າຕ່ວາງ	vacant
ປວດຄີງ	to ache all over the body	ເປົ້າ	target
ໄປ	to go	ເປົ້າສາຍຕາ	pupil of the eyes
ໄປສະນີ	post office	ເປົ້າພາຍ	target
ໄປຊື່ໆ	to go straight ahead	ປ້ຳ	to wrestle
ໄປໃສ	Where are you going?	ປ້ຳກັນ	to wrestle together
ໄປໃສມາ	Where have you been?		
ໄປຕາກອາກາດ	to take a vacation		
ໄປຕ້ອມ	to go to meet		
ໄປເຖິງ	to arrive		
ໄປທຸຣະ	to go on business		
ໄປຫຼ່ຽວ	to take a walk around		
ໄປນອກ	to go abroad		
ໄປນອນ	to go to bed		

ຂະຈິມໄພ	adventure
ຂະສົມ	mixed, to mix
ຂຍາ	wisdom
ຂະແນກ	division, section
ຂະແນກການ (ຂະແນກງານ)	office
ຜັກ	vegetable
ຜັກກະລ່ຳປີ	cabbage
ຜັກກະລ່ຳປີດອກ	cauliflower
ຜັກກາດ	Chinese cabbage
ຜັກກາດຂຽວ	Chinese mustard
ຜັກກາດແດງ	carrot
ຜັກກາດຂໍ	Chinese cabbage
ຜັກກາດຫົວ	turnip
ຜັກກູດ	edible bracken
ຜັກສະຫຼັດ	lettuce
ຜັກດອງ	pickled vegetable
ຜັກບົ່ວ	onion, scallion
ຜັກບົ້ງ	morning glory
ຂັດ	to polish
ຂັດເກີບ	to shine shoes
ຂັດແຂ້ວ	to brush one's teeth
ຂັດແປ້ງ	to powder
ຜາ	cliff
ຜາສາດ	palace
ຜ່າ	to cut
ຜ່າຟືນ	to split firewood
ຜ່າໄມ້	to split wood

ຜ້າ	cloth
ຜ້າກັ້ງ	curtain
ຜ້າກັນເບື້ອນ	apron
ຜ້າຂາດ	rag
ຜ້າຂົນສັດ	woolen cloth
ຜ້າສະໝຼຽງ	men's silk skirt
ຜ້າສຳລີ	cotton lint
ຜ້າເຊັດຖ້ວຍ	dish cloth
ຜ້າເຊັດຕົວ	towel
ຜ້າເຊັດມື	napkin
ຜ້າເຊັດໜ້າ	face towel
ຜ້ານວມ	quilt
ຜ້າປູບ່ອນນອນ	bed sheet
ຜ້າປູໂຕະ	table cloth
ຜ້າພັນຄໍ	scarf
ຜ້າພັນບາດ	gauze, bandage
ຜ້າແພນີ້	handerchief
ຜ້າຝ້າ	cotton blanket, quilt
ຜ້າຫົ່ມ	blanket
ຜ້າອ້ອມ	diaper
ຜ່ານ	to pass
ຜ່ານໄປ	to go via
ຜາຍແພ້	to conquer
ຜິດ	wrong
ຜິດກັນ	to quarrel, in discord
ຜິດກົດໝາຍ	illegal
ຜິດໃຈ	to vex, vexed

ຜິດສັນຍາ	to break a promise	ຜູ້ຂາຍ	vendor
ຜິດຖຽງ	to quarrel	ຜູ້ຄຸມຄົນໂທດ	jailer
ຜິດຖຽງກັນ	to quarrel	ຜູ້ຈັດການ	manager
ຜິດທັມມະດາ	unusual	ຜູ້ສໍາເຣັດຕ່າງຽການ	governor general
ຜິດນັດ	to miss an appointment	ຜູ້ສມັກ	applicant
ຜິດປະເພນີ	against custom	ຜູ້ສາວ	young woman
ຜິດປົກກະຕິ	abnormal	ຜູ້ສືບ	spy
ຜິດຄອງ	to go against a tradition	ຜູ້ສືບຣາຊບັນລັງ	successor to the throne
ຜິດຜົວ	to commit adultery (female)	ຜູ້ສົມຮ່ວມຄິດ	accomplice
ຜິດເມັຽ	to commit adultery (male)	ຜູ້ສອນ	teacher
ຜິດຣະບຽບ	not in order	ຜູ້ຊະນະ	winner
ຜິດຫວັງ	disappointed	ຜູ້ຊາຍ	man
ຜິວ	skin	ຜູ້ຊື່ຂ່າວ, ຜູ້ສື່ຂ່າວ	reporter
ຜີ	ghost	ຜູ້ຊື້	purchaser
ຜີກອງກ້າຍ	an evil forest spirit	ຜູ້ຊ່ວຍ	assistant
ຜີສິງ	haunted	ຜູ້ເຊົ່າ	tenant
ຜີດິບ	vampire	ຜູ້ຊໍານານ	expert
ຜີບ້າ	silly	ຜູ້ຍິງ	woman
ຜີປອບ	an evil spirit which possesses one completely	ຜູ້ດີ	high-class people
ຜີເຜດ	demon	ຜູ້ຄຸມແລ	superintendent
ຜີຫຼອກ	ghost, phantom	ຜູ້ໃດ	who
ຜີອໍາ	to be stuck dumb by a spirit	ຜູ້ໂດຍສານ	passenger
ຜີກ	to evade	ຜູ້ດຽວ	alone
ຜິວ	skin	ຜູ້ຕັດສິນ	judge, decision maker
ຜຸ	decay	ຜູ້ຕາງໜ້າ	representative
ຜູ້	person, male	ຜູ້ແຕ່ງ	author
ຜູ້ແຂ່ງຂັນ	candidate	ຜູ້ເຖົ້າຜູ້ເຖົ້າ	elders

ຜູ້ແທນຣາດສະດອນ	member of parliament
ຜູ້ທະຣະຍົດຊາດ	traitor
ຜູ້ນຳ	leader
ຜູ້ນື່ງ	one person
ຜູ້ນັ້ນ	that person
ຜູ້ບາວ	young man
ຜູ້ຜິດ	criminal
ຜູ້ພິມ	publisher
ຜູ້ຟັງ	listener
ຜູ້ຮັກສາ	keeper
ຜູ້ຮັບເໝົາ	contractor
ຜູ້ລີ້ໄພ	refugee
ຜູ້ໃຫຍ່	adult, V.I.P.
ຜູ້ອ້ອຍພະຍົກ	refugee, displaced person
ຜູ້ອື່ນ	others
ຜູ້ອອກແບບ	designer
ຜູ້ອຳນວຍການ	administrator
ຜູ້ຮ້າຍຂ້າຄົນ	murderer
ຜູກ	to tie
ຜູກຄໍຕາຍ	to hang
ເຜັດ	hot, peppery
ເຜັດຮ້ອນ	hot, peppery
ແຜ	wound
ແຜ່	to distribute, spread
ແຜ່ສາຍ	to propagate
ແຜນ	plan
ແຜນການ	program, plan

ແຜນທີ່	map
ແຜນຕັ້ງ	plan, planning
ແຜນ	sheet
ແຜນກະດານ	board
ແຜນເຈ້ຍ	sheet of paper
ແຜນສຽງ	record (music)
ແຜນດິນ	ground, reign
ແຜນດິນໄຫວ	earthquake
ແຜນທີ່	map
ແຜນທອງ	gold leaf
ຜົນ (ຜົລ)	result
ຜົນສຸດທ້າຍ	final result
ຜົນເສັ້ງຫາຍ	loss damage
ຜົນສຳເຣັດ	success
ຜົລທີ່ສຸດ	after all
ຜົລປະໂຍດ	advantage
ຜົມ	hair
ຜົມກ່ຽກ	curly hair
ຜົມວໍ່	curly hair
ຜົມຄັ້ວ	thick hair
ຜົມແບ່ງ	part in one's hair
ຜົມປອມ	wig
ຜົມຍິກ	curly hair
ຜົມຫງອກ	gray hair
ຜົມຫຍຸ້ງ	ruffled hair
ຜົມທຍອງ	wavy hair

ຜອມ	thin
ຜອມໂຊ	emaciated
ເຜີ	to forget one's self
ເຜິ້ງ	bee
ເຜີຍແຜ່	to spread
ຜູກ	taut cord or wire
ຜູກຕາກຜ້າ	clothes line
ຜູກເບັດ	fish trap line
ຜົວ	husband
ຜົວເມັຽ	husband and wife
ໃຜ	who
ໃຜກໍຕາມ	whoever
ໃຜກໍຢ່າ	whoever
ໃຜຕໍໃຜ	everybody
ໃຜລາວ	(of) them, (of) that person
ເຜົາ	to burn
ເຜົາດິນຈີ່	to burn bricks
ເຜົາຖ່ານ	to make charcoal
ເຜົາປູນ	to burn lime
ເຜົາຜີ	to cremate a corpse

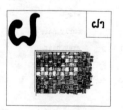

ຝ | ຝາ

ຝຣັ່ງ	French
ຝັກ	sheath
ຝັກດາບ	scabbard
ຝັງ	to bury
ຝັງຄາຍ	to bury an animal corpse
ຝັງສົບ	to bury a body
ຝັງເພັດ	to set a diamond
ຝັ່ງ	river bank
ຝັນ	to dream
ຝັນເຫັນ	to dream about
ຝັ້ນເຊົາ	to twist
ຝັ້ນເຊືອກ	to braid a rope
ຝາ	wall, lid, cover
ຝາກັ້ນຫ້ອງ	partition, wall
ຝາຕຶກ	wall of building
ຝາແຝດ	twin
ຝາເຮືອນ	sliding wall
ຝ່າ	to go through, palm, sole
ຝ່າຕິນ	sole (foot)
ຝ່າມື	palm (hand)
ຝ້າ	cloud, blemish (face)
ຝາກ	to entrust, deposit
ຝາກໄປ	to send, transmit
ຝາກຝັງ	to entrust in someone's care
ຝາກຝັງໃຈ	to leave, consign
ຝາກໄວ້	to leave something
ຝາກຫ້ວສີ	to mail a letter

ຝາກຫັວ	to give one's heart to
ຝາຍ	dam
ຝ່າຍ	part
ຝ້າຍ	cotton
ຝາດ	astringent taste
ຝິ່ນ	opium
ຝີ	infection
ຝີມື	dexterity, skill
ຝີພາກມ່ວງ	syphilis
ຝຶກ (ເຝິກ)	to train, teach
ຝຶກສອນ	to train, instruct
ຝຶກຝົນ	to train
ຝຶກຫັດ	to practice
ຝືດ	out of order
ຝືນໃຈ	to be constrained
ຝົ້ນ	goose pimples
ຝຸ່ນ	dust
ຝູງ	crowd
ແຝງ	to hug, intertwine
ແຝດ	twin
ຝົນ	rain
ຝົນຕົກ	to rain
ຝົນມີດ	to sharpen a knife
ຝອຍ (ຂີ້ຝອຍ)	sawdust
ເຝີກແຫຍ	to drill
ເຝິກຫັດ	to practice
ເຝີ	noodle soup

ເຝືອ	cloud
ເຝົ້າ	to protect, defend, guard

ພະແກ້ວ	Emerald Buddha
ພະສາດ	palace
ພຍາຍາມ	to endeavour
ພະຍາດ	disease
ພະຍາດປອດແຫ້ງ	tuberculosis
ພະຍານ	witness
ພະຍານຫຼັກຖານ	evidence
ພະຍຸ	storm
ພະຍຸຝົນ	rain storm
ພະຍຸຫິມະ	snow storm
ພະນະທ່ານ	excellency
ພະນັກງານ	civil official, employee
ພະເປັນເຈົ້າ	god, king
ພະພຸທທະເຈົ້າ	Buddha
ພະພຸທທະສາສນາ	Buddhism
ພະພຸທຮຼປ	image of Buddha

ພະມ້າ	Burma
ພະຮາຊວັງ	royal palace
ພະຮາຊວົງ	royal family
ພະຮາຊອານາຈັກ	kingdom
ພະຮາຊິນີ	queen
ພະຣືສີ	hermit
ພະຣັຕນະໄຕ	Three Gems of Buddhism: Buddha, teaching and Buddhist clergy
ພະລະຍາ	wife
ພະອາທິດ	sun
ພະເອກ	hero (actor)
ພະອົງ	king, prince
ພັກ	to rest
ພັກເຊົາ	to rest
ພັກຢູ່ຫ້ວຍ	to stay with
ພັກຜ່ອນ	to recess
ພັກການ	to be laid off work
ພັກໂຮງຮຽນ	school vacation
ພັງ	to destroy
ພັງເຂົາໄປ	to break open
ພັງປະຕູ	to force open a door
ພັງພິນາດ	to smash
ພັງພິນາສ	to destroy
ພັງເຮືອນ	to pull down a house
ພັດ	to blow, leave
ພັດທະນາ, ພັທນາ	development
ພັດພາກຈາກກັນ	to be separated
ພັດລົມ	electric fan

ພັນ	one thousand, colonel, to roll
ພັນແຜ	to bandage a wound
ພັບ	book, to close
ພັບຂຽນ	notebook
ພັບຕາ	to blink
ພາ	lead, tray
ພາເຂົ້າ	tray for meal
ພາສາ	language
ພາສາກາງ	standard language
ພາສາຕ່າງປະເທດ	foreign language
ພາສາພື້ນເມືອງ	local language, dialect
ພາສີ	tax
ພາສີການຄ້າ	business tax
ພາສີສິນຄ້າເຂົ້າ	import duty
ພາສີສິນຄ້າອອກ	export tax
ພາສີລາຍໄດ້	income tax
ພາສີອາກອນ	customs duty
ພາສິດ	proverb
ພາຍຸ	storm
ພາໄປ	to take, lead
ພາໄປທ່ຽວ	to date someone
ພາໂລ	capricious, to annoy
ພາວະນາ	to pray, meditate
ພ້າ	knife
ພາກ	version, part
ພາກໃຕ້	southern region

ພາກນີ້	on this side	ພິທີການ	protocol
ພາກພຽມ	to try	ພິທີແຕ່ງງານ	marriage ceremony
ພາກເໜືອ	northern region	ພິທີບວດ	ordination ceremony
ພາຍ (ພາຍແຈວ)	to row	ພິທີເຜົາສົບ	cremation
ພາຍປືນ	to carry rifle in a sling	ພິທີຝັງສົບ	burial service
ພາຍລຸນ	afterwards	ພິທີໂນຍ	transfer ceremony
ພາຍໜ້າ	in the future	ພິໄນກັມ	testament
ພາຍຫຼັງ	afterward	ພິພິທະພັນ	museum
ພ່າຍ	to flee	ພິລຶກ	strange
ພ່າຍແພ້	to be defeated	ພິລຶກພິລັ່	exggerated, excessive
ພາດທ່າ	to make a false move	ພິດ	venom, poison
ພາດບ່າ	to shoulder	ພິດໄຂ້	virulence of fever
ພາດຫົວເຣື່ອງ	headline	ພິດງູ	snake venom
ພານ	hunter, to look for trouble	ພິມດີດ	to type, typing
ພານຫາເຣື່ອງ	to look for trouble	ພິມຜິດ	to misprint
ພາບ	picture	ພີ	fat
ພາບແຕ້ມ	painting	ພີຂຶ້ນ	to get fatter
ພາບຖ່າຍ	photograph	ພີ້ນ້ອງ	relatives
ພາບພະຍັນ	cinema, movie	ພີ້	here
ພານ	Brahmin	ພື	to spread out
ພິການ	deformed	ພື້ນ	floor
ພິຈາຣະນາ	to consider	ພື້ນດິນ	plot of land, ground
ພິຂຸ	monk	ພື້ນທີ່	area
ພິສຸດ	to prove	ພື້ນແປ້ນ	floor of planks
ພິສວົງ (ແປກປລາດ)	strange, to doubt	ພື້ນເມືອງ	indigenous, native
ພິເສດ	special, extra	ພື້ນເຣືອນ	floor
ພິທີ	ceremony	ພຸງ	stomach

ຜຸ່ງ	to dart	ແຜ່ລູກ	to reproduce (animal)
ຜຸງອອກ	to gush out	ແຜ້	to win
ຜຸດທະສັກກະຣາດ (ພ.ສ.) Buddhist Era (B.E.)		ແຜປຽບ	to win the advantage
ຜຸ້ນ	there, over there	ແພງ	expensive
ພູ	hill	ແພດ	physician
ພູເຂົາ	mountain	ພິກ	pocket, sack
ພູເຂົາໄຟ	volcano	ພິກຍ່ຽວ	bladder
ພູມິສາດ	geography	ພິນ	first military or police rank
ພູມິປະເທດ	terrain	ພິນລະເມືອງ (ພົລເມືອງ)	population, inhabitants
ເພັງ	song	ພິນລະເຮືອນ	civilian
ເພັງສາກົນ	foreign song	ພົມ	to spray
ເພັງຊາດ	national anthem	ພົມຄວັນ	to blow smoke
ເພັງເດີນ	marching song	ພົມສີ	to spray paint
ເພັງພື້ນເມືອງ	folk song	ພົມກ່າມິດ	to expire
ເພັດ	diamond	ພົມຈາກ	to be free from.....
ເພ	to demolish	ພົມທຸກ	to be free from misery
ເພພັງ	to tear down	ພົມໄພ	out of danger
ເພດານ	ceiling	ພົບກັບ	to meet with
ເພດ (ເພສ)	sex	ພົບກາງທາງ	to meet en route
ເພດຊາຍ	masculine, male	ພົບຫັນ	to find
ເພດຍິງ	feminine, female	ພົມ	to sprinkle to moisten, carpe
ແພະ	goat	ໂພງ	to bloat, inflated
ແພ	raft, cloth	ໂພດ	too much
ແພປູຍ່ອນ	bed sheet	ໂພມ	mound
ແພມິນ	handkerchief	ໂພມປວກ	termite mound
ແພ່	to spread	ເພາະ	because
		ເພາະວ່າ	because

ເພາະສະນັ້ນ	therefore	ພ້ອມ	together
ເພາະປູກ	plant	ພ້ອມກັນ	together with
ພໍ	adequate, enough, sufficient	ພ້ອມກັນນີ້	herewith
ພໍໃຈ	to be satisfied	ພ້ອມໃຈ	with one heart
ພໍດີ	just right, good enough	ພ້ອມໃຈກັນ	unanimous
ພໍຢູ່ພໍກິນ	to have enough to live on	ພ້ອມພຽງ	united
ພໍຮ້າພໍໃຈ	satisfied	ພ້ອມອົກພ້ອມໃຈ	with united will
ພໍ່	father	ເພິ່ນ	he
ພໍຄ້າ	merchant	ເພີ້ຝັນ	to dream
ພໍຄົວ	cook	ເພິ່ງ	to shelter
ພໍສ່ຽວ	friend (adult)	ເພີ່ມ	to add
ພໍສ່ຽວແພ່ສ່ຽວ	friends of the family	ເພີ່ມກຳລັງ	to reinforce
ພໍຕາ	maternal grandfather or uncle	ເພີ່ມເຕີມ	to increase
ພໍຕູ້	grandfather	ເພີ່ມເຕີມ	to supplement, to add
ພໍເຖົ້າ	maternal grandfather, father-in-law	ພຽງ	level, only
ພໍນາ	farmer	ພຽງຄັ້ງດຽວ	only one time
ພໍນ້າ	stepfather	ພຽງໃດ	how?, to what extent
ພໍບ້ານ	village chief	ພຽງພໍ	sufficient
ພໍຜົວ	father of husband	ພຽມ	to be attentive, try
ພໍແມ່	father and mother	ເພື່ອ	in order to
ພໍເມັຍ	father of wife	ເພື່ອຈະ	in order to
ພໍລ້ຽງ	foster father	ເພື່ອຕົວຂອງມັນເອງ	for it's own sake
ພໍຫມ້າຍ	widower	ເພື່ອເປັນກຽດ	in honor of
ພໍຮ້າງ	divorced man	ເພື່ອວ່າ	so that
ພໍເຮືອນ	head of family	ເພື່ອເຫັນແກ່	for the sake of
ພໍ້	to meet	ເພື່ອໃຫ້	in order to
ພອນ	blessing	ເພື່ອນ	friend
		ເພື່ອນເຈົ້າສາວ	bride's maid

ເພື່ອນເຈົ້າບ່າວ	best man
ເພື່ອນຊຸມິດ	intimate friend
ເພື່ອນຕາຍ	friend in need, true friend
ເພື່ອນຫຼິ້ນມ່ານ	playmate
ເພື່ອນຮ່ວມງານ	fellow worker
ພິອພັນ	to be related
ພວກ	group, side
ພວກຂະບົດ	rebels
ພວກເຂົາ	they
ພວກເຈົ້າ	you (plural)
ພວກດຽວກັນ	of the same group
ພວກເຕັກນິກ	technical mission
ພວກເຖົ້າເຝົ່າ	old people
ພວກທ່ານ	you (plural), gentlemen
ພວກມັນ	they, them
ພວກໜຸ່ມໆ ສາວໆ	young people
ພວກອັກສອນ	consonant group
ພວກເຮົາ	we, us
ພວກເຮົາບາງວຄົນ	some of us
ພວງ	garland
ພວງດອກໄມ້	bouquet of flowers
ພວງໝາກໄມ້	garland of fruit
ພວມ	in the middle of doing something
ໄພ້ (ລູກໄພ້)	female (daughter)-in-law
ພຣະ	monk
ພຣະຈັນ	the moon

ພຣະສາສດາ	Buddha
ພຣະສົງ	monk
ພຣະທັມ	teaching of Buddha
ພຣະທາດຫຼວງ	That Luang (national shrine)
ພຣະນາງ	queen
ພຣະພຸດ	Buddha
ພຣະພຸທຣຸບ	Buddha statue
ພຣະຣັຕນະໄຕ	Three Gems
ພຣະອາທິດ	the sun

ຟັກໄຂ່	to hatch
ຟັກລາບ	to chop meat for making "Lap"
ຟັງ	to listen
ຟັງຄວາມ	to obey
ຟັງເທດ	to listen to a sermon
ຟັນ	to cut, slice
ຟັນດາບ	to do sword-play
ຟ້າ (ຜ້າຟ້າ)	a cloth covering
ຟ້າ (ສີຟ້າ)	sky, blue
ຟ້າຄຶ້ມ	sky is covered
ຟ້າຕ່າ	to thunder
ຟ້າມືດ	sky is dark
ຟ້າແມບເຫຼື້ອມ	lightning
ຟ້າລົມ (ຟ້າລົມຝົນຕົກ)	wind blows before rain
ຟ້າເຫຼື້ອມ	lightning
ຟ້າຮ້ອງ	to thunder
ຟາກ	bank, side
ຟາກນີ້	this side
ຟາດ	to beat
ຟາດເຂົ້າ	to thresh paddy
ຟານ	muntjak deer
ຟ້າວ	quick
ຟິວ	fuse
ຟືນ	wood
ຟື້ນ	to recover, to get well
ຟິມ	film
ຟຸດບານ	football

ຟູ	to float
ຟູຂຶ້ນ	to float up
ຟອກ	to wash
ຟອງ	bubble
ຟອງສາບູ	soap bubble
ຟອງນ້ຳ	sponge
ຟ້ອງ	to bring law suit against someone, indict
ຟ້ອງຄະດີແພ່ງ	to take civil action against someone
ຟ້ອງຮ້ອງ	to make a complaint against
ຟອຍ	broom
ຟອຍຂັດແຂ້ວ	toothbrush
ຟ້ອນ	to dance
ເຟືອງເຂົ້າ	rice straw
ໄຟ	fire
ໄຟສາຍ	flashlight, torch
ໄຟຟ້າ	electricity
ໄຟຟ້າຫຼອດ	a neon lamp
ໄຟລາມ	fire is spreading
ໄຟໄໝ້	fire

ມ ມ້າ

ມະຫາ	great (monk's title)	ມາຈາກ	to come from
ມະຫາກະສັດ	king	ມາຈົນເຖິງ	to arrive at, until
ມະຫາສະໝຸດ	ocean	ມາດາ	mother
ມະຫາໄພ	great danger	ມາເຖິງ	to arrive at
ມະຫາດໄທ	interior (ministry)	ມາທັນ	to arrive on time
ມະເຫສີ	queen	ມານີ້	to come here
ມັກ	to like, to love, to want	ມາບ້ານ	to come home
ມັກກິນ	greedy, gluttonous	ມາບໍ່ທັນ	to miss, to be late
ມັກຄຸຍ	to brag, boast	ມາພີ້	to come here
ມັກງ່າຍ	lazy	ມາພໍ້	to meet
ມັກມ່ວນ	fun-loving	ມາເພິ່ງ	to ask for help
ມັກໃຫຍ່	to be ambitious	ມາຢາມ	to visit
ມັກເຫລົ້າ	drunkard	ມາຍ້ຽມ	to visit
ມັກຫຼິ້ນ	fun-loving	ມາຫາ	to come see
ມັງກອນ	dragon	ມາຮອດ	to arrive, until
ມັດ	to tie, to attach	ມ້າ	horse
ມັດເຂົ້າ	sheaf of rice	ມ້າກາຍກ້ວຍ	toy horse
ມັດທະຍົມ (ມັດຍັດ) high school		ມ້ານັ່ງ	bench
ມັດທະຍົມສຶກສາ	secondary education	ມາກ	very
ມັດຟືນ	faggot of firewood	ມາກມາຍ	a lot
ມັນ	fat, nut taste, it	ມ້າງ	to take apart, to break down
ມັນຄ້າງ	sweet potato	ມ້າງເພ	to break up
ມັນຕົນ	manioc for topioca	ມ້າຍອອກ	to unroll, unwind
ມັນຝລັ່ງ	potato	ມານ	to be pregnant, (classifier: ear of grain)
ມັນເພົາ	yam bean	ມານເຂົ້າ	ear of rice
ມາ	to come	ມານສາລີ	ear of corn

ບ້ານ	faded, pale		
ມານະອົດທົນ	patience	ມີຍົດ	honored
ມິດ	quiet, silent	ມີທ່າ	in a good position
ມິດຕະພາບ (ມິດພາບ)	friendship	ມີທຸຣະ	busy
ມີ	to have, possess, own, there is, there are	ມີແທ້	truly, really exist
ມີກຸດ	to have prestige	ມີໂທດ	guilty
ມີກຳໄລ	profitable	ມີບຸນ	virtuous
ມີຂົນ	hairy	ມີພິດ	poisonous
ມີຂອບເຂດ	limited	ມີຢູ່	have got, really have
ມີຄ່າ	valuable, precious	ມີຣາຄາ	valuable
ມີຄຸນ	to be grateful	ມີລາບ	lucky
ມີຄູ່	engaged	ມີວາດ	polite
ມີຄວາມສຸກ	happy	ມີເວນ	unfortunate because of sin in last life
ມີຄວາມສົນໃຈ	to be interested in	ມີເຫດຜົນ	reasonable
ມີຄວາມຮູ້	knowledge	ມີໜ້ານີຕາ	to be respected
ມີຄວາມໝາຍ	meaningful	ມີຫຼາຍແນວ	of many kinds
ມີໃຈ	to pay attention, to have will	ມີຫວັງ	to be hopeful
ມີໃຈໄສ	to look after someone	ມີອາຊີບ	to have a job
ມີສະຕິ	to be conscious of	ມີ່	yellow egg noodles
ມີສະເນ່	charming	ມີດ	knife
ມີສິດ	to have a right	ມີດຕັດ	scissors
ມີສິດແຕ່ຜູ້ດຽວ	to have an exclusive patent or copyright	ມີດແຖ	razor
ມີສຽງ	to argue	ມີດພ້າ	knife
ມີສ່ວນ	to have a part	ມີດແທງ	dagger
ມີຊີວິດ	alive, living	ມຶງ	you (impolite)
ມີຊື່ສຽງ	well-known, famous	ມຶນເມົ່າ	intoxicate
ມີໂຊກ	good luck, to be lucky	ມື	hand
ມີໄຊ	to be victorious	ມີກ່າຍພາຜາກ	to worry at a loss

ມືງ່ອຍ	paralyzed hand
ມືເທົາເທົ້າ	to cradle one's cheek in one's palm
ມືເປົ່າ	empty-handed
ມືນົບໜ້າ	to hide one's face in one's hands
ມືໄວ	pickpocket
ມື້	day
ມື້ກີ້	just now
ມື້ກຶ້ນີ້	a moment ago
ມື້ກອນ	day before yesterday, the other day
ມື້ແຂ່ງຂັນ	day of a competition
ມື້ຄືນ	night
ມື້ຄືນນີ້	last night
ມື້ຄືນວານນີ້	night before last
ມື້ສວຍ	daytime
ມື້ຊື້ນ	day before yesterday
ມື້ເຊົ້າ	morning
ມື້ໄດ	what day?
ມື້ໃດໜຶ່ງ	someday, anyday
ມື້ທີ່ລະລຶກ	memorial day
ມື້ນັດ	appointment date
ມື້ນີ້	today
ມື້ພັກ	holiday, day off
ມື້ລະ	per day
ມື້ແລງ	evening
ມື້ແລງນີ້	tonight
ມື້ວານນີ້	yesterday

ມື້ເວັ້ມ	daytime
ມື້ໜາໆ	one of these days
ມື້ອື່ນ	tomorrow
ມື້ຮື	day after tomorrow
ມືດ	dark
ມືດແລ້ວ	nightfall
ມືກຂັ້ນ	dense crowd
ມືນ	to open one's eyes
ມືນຕາ	to open one's eyes
ມື່ນ	slippery
ມຸງ	to roof
ມຸງກຸດ	crown
ມຸງກຸດຣາຊກຸມານ	crown prince
ມຸງສັງກະສີ	to roof with galvanized iron s.
ມຸ້ງ	mosquito net
ມຸສາ	tricky, false
ມຸດນ້ຳ	to dive into water
ມຸນ	powdered, to fragment
ມູນມັງ	heritage
ເມກ	cloud
ເມັດ	grain, pill
ເມັດກາເຟ	coffee bean
ເມັດເຂົ້າ	kernel of rice
ເມັດງາ	sesame seed
ເມັດຊາຍ	grain of sand
ເມັນ	louse (lice)
ເມດຕາ	mercy

ແມ່	mother	ແມ່ເລັກ	magnet
ແມ່ໄກ່	hen	ແມ່ເລັ້ວ	playgirl
ແມຂາວ	nun	ແມລ້ງ	fostermother
ແມຄາ	female merchant	ແມອອກ	woman (monks' language)
ແມ່ຄົວ	female cook	ແມ່ຣັກ	dear mother, adoptive mother
ແມຈາງ	prostitute	ແມຮ້າງ	divorced wife
ແມສື່	female go-between	ແມ່ເຮືອນ	housewife
ແມຍາ	paternal grandmother, mother of husband	ແມງ	insect, bug
ແມຍາຍ	maternal grandmother, mother of wife	ແມງກະບີ້	silk moth
ແມ່ຍິງ	woman (women), girl	ແມງກະເບື້ອ	butterfly, moth
ແມຕູ	maternal grandmother	ແມງຂີ້ເຂັຍ	large centipede
ແມຕຳແຍ	midwife	ແມງແຄງ	stink bug
ແມ່ເຖົ້າ	maternal grandmother, mother of wife	ແມງງອດ	scorpion
ແມນາ	stepmother	ແມງເງົາ	scorpion
ແມ່ນ້ຳ	river	ແມງຈິ້ມາຍ	cricket
ແມ່ນ້ຳຂອງ	Mekong River	ແມງສາບ	cockroach
ແມບານ	housewife	ແມງຊອນ	mole cricket
ແມປ້າ	aunt	ແມງດາ	horseshoe crab, water bug
ແມປານສາວ	female relatives, womenfolk	ແມງຕັກແຕນ	grasshopper
ແມ່ເຜິ້ງ	bee	ແມງຕັບເຕົ້າ	water beetle
ແມ່ພະຍາດ	disease, germ	ແມງຕໍ	wasp
ແມ່ພິມ	mould	ແມງບົງ	caterpillar
ແມມາຍ	widow	ແມງບົ້ງກື້	millipede
ແມ່ມານ	pregnant woman	ແມງປໍ	dragonfly
ແມ່ມື	thumb	ແມງເຜິ້ງ	bee
ແມ່ເມັຽ	mother of wife	ແມງມີ້	gnat
ແມ່ລູກອອນ	mother of a baby		

ແມງມຸມ	spider
ແມງມອດ	weevil
ແມງໄມ້	bug, insect
ແມງເນົ້າ	nun moth, Tussock moth
ແມງວັນ	fly
ແມງວີ່	fruit fly
ແມງຫິ່ງຫ້ອຍ	firefly
ແມັດ	meter
ແມນ	yes it is
ແມນແທ້	true, indeed
ແມນໃຜ	who? who is it?
ແມນໃຜຮັບໂທຣະສັບ	who is speaking?
ແມນແລ້ວ	that's right
ແມນວ່າ	if
ແມນຫຍັງ	what?
ແມບລີ້ນ	to stick out one's tongue
ແມວ	cat
ແມ້ວ	the Meo tribe (Hmong)
ມົງກຸດ	crown
ມົດ	ant
ມົດສົ້ມ	red ant
ມົນ	round
ມົນ	gray
ມົບ	to hide with one's hand
ມົບໜ້າ	to hide one's face
ໂມ້	to brag, boast, grindstone
ໂມໂຫ	angry

ໂມໂຕງ່າຍ	easy to anger, irascible
ໂມງ	clock, watch, hour, o'clock
ໂມງປຸກ	alarm clock
ໂມງມັດແຂນ	wrist watch
ເໝາະສົມ	suitable
ມໍດູ	fortune telling, divination
ມໍລະສຸມ	monsoon, storm
ມໍລະດົກ	inheritance
ມໍລະນະກ້ານ	death, to die
ມໍລະນະພາບ	to die
ໝໍ້	close, near
ໝໍ້ໆ ນີ້	soon, coming soon
ມອງ	fishing net, to look at
ມອງຕີກປາ	fish net
ມອດ	to turn off, to extinguish
ມອດໄຟ	to turn out the light
ມອບ	to give, to hand over
ມອບສິດ	to give the right to
ມອບສົມບັດ	to bequeath
ມອບໂຕ, ມອບຕົວ	to turn oneself in, to give oneself up
ມອບໃຫ້	to give, to hand over, to transfer to
ເມັຽ	wife
ເມັຽນ້ອຍ	concubine, second wife
ເມັຽລັບ	mistress
ເມັຽໃຫຍ່	legal wife
ເມັຽຫຼວງ	legal wife
ມຽມ	to arrange, tidy up

ມູມເຄື່ອງ	to put things away	ເມື່ອຍ	tired
ມູມຄາຍ	to bury animal remains corpse	ມົວ	dim
ເມືອ	to go back, to return	ມົວຕາ	to see indistinctly
ເມືອນໍາ	to return with	ມົວເມົາ	drunk, addicted
ເມືອບ້ານ	to go back home, to return home	ມົວໝອງ	blurred, stained
ເມືອເຮືອນ	to go back home, to return home	ມອຍ	to box, boxing
ເມື່ອ	day, (classifier, time)	ມອຍປ້ຳ	wrestling
ເມື່ອກີ້	just a moment ago, just then	ມ່ອນ	happy, joyous
ເມື່ອກ່ອນ	formerly	ມ່ອນຊື່ນ	happy
ເມື່ອໃດ	when?	ມ້ອນເຊືອກ	to coil rope
ເມື່ອໃດກໍຕາມ	whenever	ໄມ	mile
ເມື່ອຕະກີ້	just now	ໄມຕຣີ (ໄມຕີ)	friendship
ເມື່ອວານນີ້	yesterday	ໄມຕຣີຈິດ	friendship
ເມື່ອວານານີ້	lately	ໄມ້	tree, wood
ເມືອກ	slimy, humid	ໄມ້ກະດານ	plank, board
ເມືອງ	city, town, country, district	ໄມ້ຕະຄານ	spatula
ເມືອງຂະເໝັນ	Kampuchea	ໄມ້ຕ້ວ	rice threshing bamboo poles
ເມືອງຍີ່ປຸ່ນ	Japan	ໄມ້ຕໍ້ມ	vowel, letter (x̄x)
ເມືອງໄທ	Thailand	ໄມ້ຕ້ວ	vowel, letter (x̂x)
ເມືອງນອກ	foreign land		
ເມືອງຜີ	spirit world, hell	ໄມ້ກວາດ	broom
ເມືອງຝຣັ່ງ	France	ໄມ້ຂີດໄຟ	match
ເມືອງລາວ	Laos	ໄມ້ຄໍ້	wooden support
ເມືອງຫຼວງ	Luang Prabang, capital of Laos	ໄມ້ຄົດ	warped piece of wood
ເມືອງອຸດສາຫະກັມ	industrial city	ໄມ້ຄອນ	a piece of wood
ເມືອງເອກ	capital	ໄມ້ຄອນເທົ້າ	cane, walking stick
ເມືອງຮ້ອນ	tropical country	ໄມ້ຄ້ວັກຫູ	ear pick
		ໄມ້ສັກ	teak

ໄມ້ສາວ	fruit picking stick	ເມົາຝິ່ນ	opium-intoxicated
ໄມ້ແສ້	whip	ເມົາຢາ	drugged
ໄມ້ຊາງ	thornless bamboo, blowgun	ເມົາເຫຼົ້າ	drunk with alcohol
ໄມ້ຈັຕະວາ	(×) mai: cha:t dta: wa tone mark		
ໄມ້ຢາງ	Yang tree		
ໄມ້ຄາມ	spatula, handle		
ໄມ້ດິບ	green wood		
ໄມ້ໂກກ	rotten, crumbling wood		
ໄມ້ຕີ	(×) mai: dti tone mark		
ໄມ້ຕີກອງ	drumstick		
ໄມ້ຖູ	chopsticks		
ໄມ້ໂທ	(×) mai: tho tone mark		

ໄມ້ເທົາ	cane, crutch	ຍິ້ງ	to measure depth
ໄມ້ບັນທັດ	ruler, straightedge	ຍິ້ງນ້ຳ	to sound depth of water
ໄມ້ປີ້ງ	stick for roasting	ຢາ	medicine, drug
ໄມ້ແປ້ນ	lumber	ຢາຄີນິນ	quinine
ໄມ້ໄຜ່	bamboo	ຢາຂ້າແມງ	insecticide
ໄມ້ຕັ້ມສງງ	tone marks	ຢາສູບ (ຢາຖຸ)	tobacco
ໄມ້ພາຍ	oar, paddle	ຢາຖ່າຍ	laxative
ໄມ້ມະລາຍ	(ไ×) mai: ma: lai vowel sign	ຢານອນຫຼັບ	sleeping potion
ໄມ້ເມດ	yardstick	ຢາເບື່ອ	poison
ໄມ້ມວນ	(ไ×) mai: muan vowel sign	ຢາຂັດແຂ້ວ	toothpaste
ໄມ້ເອກ	(×) mai: ek tone mark	ຢາໄອ	cough medicine
ໄມ້ອັດ	stopper	ຢາຮາກໄມ້	medicinal root, herbs
ໄມ່ອ	kind of reed	ຢ່າ	don't . . .
ເມົາ	drunk	ຢ່າຟ້າວ	don't hurry
ເມົາຍົນ	airsick	ຢາກ	to want

ຢາກເຂົ້າ	to be hungry	ຢືນຂຶ້ນ	to stand up
ຢາກໄດ້	to want	ຢືນຢັນ	to attest
ຢາກນອນ	to be sleepy	ຢືມ	to borrow
ຢາກນ້ຳ	to be thirsty	ຢືມເງິນ	to borrow money
ຢາກຮາກ	to feel nauseated	ຢຸດ	stop
ຢາກຮູ້	to be curious	ຢຸດງານ	to go on strike
ຢາກຮູ້ຢາກເຫັນ	to be curious	ຢຸດພັກ	to rest
ຢາງ	rubber	ຢູ່	to stay, to be (location)
ຢາງທາວ	glue	ຢູ່ກັບ	to stay with
ຢາງປຸທາງ	road asphalt	ຢູ່ໃກ້	near
ຢາງລຶບ	eraser	ຢູ່ໄກ	far
ຢ່າງ	type, kind	ຢູ່ກຳ	fasting after childbirth
ຢ່າງກັນເອງ	informally	ຢູ່ໃສ	where?
ຢ່າງວ່າຍໆ	simply	ຢູ່ເທິງ	above, upstairs
ຢ່າງສູງສຸດ	in the highest degree	ຢູ່ນີ້	here
ຢ່າງຈາ	slowly	ຢູ່ໃນ	in
ຢ່າງດີ	good quality	ຢູ່ນຳ	to live with
ຢ່າງເດັດຂາດ	absolutely	ຢູ່ບ້ານ	at home
ຢ່າງໃດ	how?, what kind	ຢູ່ພຸ້	here, there
ຢ່າງ	to roast	ຢູ່ເຮືອນ	at home
ຢ່າງຊີ້ນ	to roast meat	ເຢັນ	cool
ຢາຍ	to distribute	ຢອກ	to tease, joke
ຢ້ານ	to be afraid	ຢອກກັນ	to have fun
ຢ້ານຜິດ	afraid of error	ຢອກຫຼິ້ນ	to play
ຢາມ	to visit a person	ຢອງ	to put on top of
ຢືນ	to stand up	ຢອດ	to drop, thin
ຢືນກົງ	to stand up straight	ຢຽດ	to stretch out (body)

ປຸດຂາ	to stretch one's legs
ປ່ວຍ	to run over, to step on
ຢ້ຽມ	to visit

ຣ ຣົດ

ຣະກາ	chicken (of 12 horary signs)
ຣະຍະ	period
ຣະດັບ	level
ຣະດູ	season
ຣະດູໃບໄມ້ປົ່ງ	spring
ຣະດູໃບໄມ້ຫລົ່ງ	fall
ຣະດູຝົນ	rainy season
ຣະດູແລ້ງ	dry season
ຣະດູຫນາວ	winter
ຣະດູຮ້ອນ	summer
ຣະບາດ	to spread far and wide
ຣະບຽງ	balcony
ຣະບຽບ	order, rules
ຣະບຽບວິໄນ	discipline

ຣະມັດຣະວັງ	alert, careful
ຣະລຶກ	to remember, souvenir
ຣະວັງ	Watch out!, to pay attention
ຣະວັງຕົວ	to watch out
ຣະແວງ	to suspect
ຣະແວງສົງໄສ	to suspect
ຣະຫວ່າງ	among
ຣະຫວ່າງຊາດ	international
ຣະຫວ່າງປະເທດ	international
ຣັກສາ	to protect
ຣັຕນະໄຕ	Three Gems of Buddhism: Buddha, teaching, the priesthood
ຣັຖ	state
ຣັຖສະພາ	parliament
ຣັຖທັມມະນຸນ	constitution
ຣັຖບານ	government
ຣັຖປະຫານ	coup d'etat
ຣັຖມົນຕຣີ (ຣັຖມົນຕີ)	cabinet minister
ຣັຖມົນຕຣີຊ່ວຍວ່າການ	deputy minister
ຣາຄາ	price
ຣາຄາຂາຍ	sale price
ຣາຄາຂາຍສົ່ງ	wholesale price
ຣາຄາຂາຍຍ່ອຍ	retail price
ຣາຄາຊື້	purchase price
ຣາຄາຕະລາດ (ຣາຄາຫລາດ)	market price
ຣາວວັນ	reward
ຣາສຕອນ	the people
ຣາຊຸສັບ	court language

ຣາຊສໍານັກ	royal court	ຣົຖປະຈໍາທາງ	bus
ຣາຊການ	public administration (royal)	ຣົຖພະຍາບານ	ambulance
ຣາຊສີ	lion king	ຣົຖພະຫີນີ້ງ	royal carriage
ຣາຊບັນລັງ	throne	ຣົຖພວງ	trailer
ຣາຊບຸດ	prince	ຣົຖມ້າ	horse cart
ຣາຊບຸດຕີ	princess	ຣົຖລາກ	rickshaw
ຣາຊວັງ	royal palace	ຣົຖລາງ	tram
ຣາຊວົງ	dynasty	ຣົບ (ລົບ)	to fight
ຣາຊອານາຈັກ	kingdom	ຣົບລາຂ້າຟັນ	pitched battle
ຣາຊໂອງການ	royal decrees	ຣົບເຣອ	to combat
ຣາຍການ	list	ໂຣກ	disease
ຣຊີ	hermit	ໂຣກຄໍຕີບ	diphteria
ຣົດ	taste	ໂຣກຕິດຕໍ່	contagious disease
ຣົຖ	vehicle	ໂຣກຂີ້ຮາກ	diarrhea
ຣົຖເກ໋ງ	sedan	ໂຣກບິດ	dysentery
ຣົຖຈັກ	motorcycle	ໂຣກລະບາດ	epidemic
ຣົຖສາມລໍ້	"samloh," tricycle-pedicab	ໂຣກຫືດ	asthma
ຣົຖຍົນ	automobile	ໂຣກຫົວໃຈ	heart disease
ຣົຖໂດຍສານ	taxi	ໂຣກໜອງໃນ	gonorrhea
ຣົຖດ່ວນ	express	ໂຣກພາວ້	rabies
ຣົຖຫັກຊີ	taxi	ໂຣກອະຫິວາ	cholera
ຣົຖໃຕ້ດິນ	subway	ໂຣກເຮື້ອນ	leprosy
ຣົຖຖີບ	bicycle	ໂຣງງານ	factory
ຣົຖຫົວ	tank	ໂຣງຮຽນ	school
ຣົຖທັບຍທາງ	roadroller		
ຣົຖບັນທຸກ	truck	ເຣີ່ມ(ລົງມື)	to start to do, to begin
ຣົຖບົດຖນົມ	steamroller	ເຣື່ອງ	story
		ເຣື່ອງນີ້	this matter

ເຣື່ອງໃຫຍ່	important affair
ຮວມ (ຮວມ)	to combine , to join, to collect
ຮວມມື	to collaborate
ຮວມໃນຮວມມື	to cooperate

ລິງ

ລະຄັງ	bell
ລະຄອນ	play
ລະຄອນສັດ	circus
ລະຄອນໂສກ	tragedy
ລະຄອນຕະຫລົກ	comedy
ລະຍະ	period
ລະດັບ	level
ລະບາຍນ້ຳ	to drain water out
ລະບາຍອາກາດ	to ventilate
ລະບາດ	to spread
ລະເບີດ	to explode
ລະບົບ	system
ລະບຽງ	porch
ລະບຳ	Westernized dance

ລະເມີ	to wander, talk in one's sleep
ລະລາຍ	to dissolve, melt
ລະລຶກ	to remember
ລະຫວ່າງ	between
ລະອາຍ	to be ashamed
ລະອຽດ	elaborate, detailed
ລັກ	to steal
ລັກລອບມາ	to smuggle in
ລັກຫນີ	to sneak away
ລັກເອົາ	to steal
ລັກເຮັດ	to do secretly
ລັງກຽດ	to abhor, to detest
ລັ່ງຄັ່ງ	bell
ລັ່ງເລ	to hestitate, to be uncertain
ລັດ	to take a short cut
ລັດທາງ	to take a short cut
ລັດທິ	doctrine, ideology
ລັດທິຄອມມິວນິດ	communism
ລັດຈັກກະພັດນິຍົມ	imperialism
ລັດປ່າ	to go through the woods
ລັ່ນໄກ	to pull the trigger
ລັ່ນປືນ	to shoot a gun
ລັບ	to receive
ລັບແຂກ	to receive guests
ລັບເງິນເດືອນ	to receive pay
ລັບຈ້າງ	to be employed
ລັບສາຣະພາບ	to confess

ລັບສິນບົນ	to take a bribe	ລາຍການປະຊຸມ	proceedings
ລັບຜິດຊອບ	to accept responsibility	ລາຍງານ	account, report
ລາ	good-bye	ລາຍຈ່າຍ	expenses
ລາກ່ອນ	good-bye (staying person)	ລາຍຊື່	list
ລາຄາ	price	ລາຍເຊັ້ນ	signature
ລາໄປ	to depart	ລາຍໄດ້	income, revenue
ລາອອກ	to resign	ລາຍຕາ	dazzling, dizzy
ລ່າສັດ	to hunt	ລາດ	slope, to pave, spread
ລ່າທີ່ສຸດ	latest	ລາດຢາງ	to pave with asphalt
ລ້າສມັຍ	old-fashined, out-of-date	ລານເຂົ້າ	rice threshing floor
ລ້າ	free, only	ລານໂມງ	watch spring
ລາກ	to pull, to drag	ລາບ	spiced, minced meat dish
ລາກໄມ້	to haul logs	ລ້ານ	bald, million
ລາງ	some, track	ລ້ານຊ້າງ	old Laos: land of a million elephants
ລາງຄົນ	somebody, some people	ລາມ	to spread (fire)
ລາງເທື່ອ	sometimes	ລ່າມ	to tie up, interpreter
ລາງແນວ	some kind	ລ່າມໂສ້	to chain , to put into irons
ລາງບ່ອນ	someplace or places	ລາວ	he, him, she, her, Laos
ລາງພວກ	some groups	ລິເກ	popular theater
ລາງຢ່າງ	something	ລີ້	to hide
ລາງรິດໄມ	railroad track	ລີ້ຊ່ອນ	to hide
ລ້າງ	to wash, to scrub, to clean	ລີ້ໄພ	to take refuge
ລ້າງແຄ້ນ	to avenge, revenge	ລິງ	monkey
ລ້າງບາບ	to baptise	ລິດ	liter
ລ້າງຮູບ	to develop a photograph	ລີ້ນ	tongue
ລາຍ	stripe	ລີ້ນຊັກ	drawer
ລາຍການ	program, item, menu	ລິ້ມປີ່	reed (musical)

ລຶ້ງ	accustomed to	ລູກຄິດ	abacus
ລຶ້ງເຄີຍ	to be acquainted with	ລູກເຄິ່ງ	half blood
ລື່ມ	to pass, skid (car)	ລູກສາວ	daughter
ລືຊາ	well known	ລູກສິດ	pupil, student
ລືມ	to forget	ລູກສູບ	piston, cylinder
ລືມຕົວ	to forget oneself, day dream	ລູກສອນ	arrow
ລຶບ	to erase	ລູກເສືອ	boy scout
ລຸຫຼອງ	to miscarriage	ລູກຊາຍ	son
ລຸກ	to arise, to get up	ລູກຊີ້ນ	meatball
ລຸກຂຶ້ນ	to arise, to get up	ລູກຊອດ	half-breed
ລຸກແຕ່ເຊົ້າ	to get up early	ລູກແຕກ	hand grenade
ລຸກໄປ	to get up and go	ລູກແຕກປາຣະມະນູ	atomic bomb
ລຸກມາ	to come from	ລູກນ້ອງ	subordinate, nephew
ລຸກລາມ	to invade, to spread over	ລູກບ້ານ	villagers
ລຸວລົວ	to disturb	ລູກປືນ	bullet
ລຸຍ	to wade, splash in the mud	ລູກຝາແຝດ	twin
ລຸມ	last, late coming	ລູກໄພ້	daughter-in-law
ລຸມຫຼັງ	after	ລູກໄມ້	lace, bamboo shoot
ລຸ່ມ	below, under, low, downstairs	ລູກລະເບີດ	bomb, grenade
ລູກ	baby, child	ລູກຫົວສາວ	first-born child
ລູກກະແຈ	key	ລູກຫຼ້າ	youngest child
ລູກກົກ	oldest child	ລູກຊາຍລູກນ້ອງ	cousins
ລູກໄກ່	chick	ລຸງ	uncle
ລູກກຳພ້າ	orphan	ລູບ	to rub, feel
ລູກຂັ້ນໄດ	step, rung, stair	ເລຂາ	secretary
ລູກເຂີຍ	son-in-law	ເລຂານຸການ	secretary
ລູກຄ້າ	customer	ເລຫຼັງ	to auction

ເລ້ກົນ	trick
ເລກ	number, math
ເລກອະນຶດ	arithmetic
ເລກຄູນ	multiplication
ເລກສູນ	zero
ເລກສົມ	addition
ເລກທີ	(numeral) the ___ th
ເລກລົບ	subtraction
ເລກຫານ	division
ເລັບ	nail, claw, hoof
ເລັບຕີນ	toenail
ເລັບມື	fingernail
ເລາະ	to fight, to insult
ເລາະກັນ	to fight
ແລະ	and
ແລກ	to exchange
ແລກປ່ຽນສິນຄ້າ	to barter
ແລງ	evening
ແລ້ງ	dry
ແລ່ນ	to run
ແລ່ນໜີ	to run away, to flee
ແລບ	to stick out
ແລບລີ້ນ	to stick out one's tongue
ແລວ	finished, already, then
ລ້າໄກ່	chicken coop
ລົງ	to decend, to go down

ລົງຄະແນນສຽງ	to vote
ລົງຄ້ອຍ	down slope, down the coast
ລົງຄວາມເຫັນ	to be of an opinion
ລົງເງິນ	to bet money
ລົງຊື່	to sign one's name
ລົງທະບຽນ	to enroll, to register
ລົງທ້າຍ	to end, to finish
ລົງໂທດ	to punish
ລົງໄປ	to descend
ລົງມາ	to come down
ລົງມື	to begin to work
ລົງເຮືອ	to embark
ລົດຄ່າຈ້າງ	to reduce wages
ລົດຣາຄາ	to reduce price
ລົມ	to expose to flame
ລົມໄຟ	to expose to fire
ລົບ	to subtract, erase, delete
ລົມ	wind, to talk
ລົມກັນ	to discuss, talk together
ລົມຍ່າວ	to flirt with a boy
ລົມຜູ້ສາວ	to court a girl
ລົມຝົນ	wind and rain
ລົມພາຍຸ	storm
ລົມອ່ອນ	breeze
ລົ້ມ	to stumble, faint
ລົ້ມລະລາຍ	to go bankrupt, ruin
ໂລເລ	fickle, unreliable

ໂລພາ	greedy	ລອຍກະໂຖງ	ceremony of floating boats (sin) away
ໂລຫະ	metal	ລອຍນ້ຳ	to swim
ໂລ່	shield, to flow out	ລອດ	to pass through
ໂລກ	world	ລອດຈ່ອງ	rice candy
ໂລກພະຈັນ	the moon	ລອດບ້ວງ	to escape from a trap
ໂລງ	coffin	ລອບຄອບ	careful
ໂລດ	immediately, straight-forwardly	ລ້ອມ	to surround
ໂລບ	greedy, greed	ລ້ອມຮົ້ວ	to fence in
ໂລບມາກ	very greedy	ເລິກ	deep, profound
ເລາະ	to walk round, coast	ເລິກລັບ	mysterious, secret
ເລາະຫຼິ້ນ	to walk for pleasure	ເລີກ	to roll up, stop
ລໍ	to wait	ເລີກການ	to stop work
ລໍຈັງຫວະ	to wait for the right moment	ເລີກບຸນ	end of festival
ລໍຖ້າ	to wait for	ເລີຍ	pass by, beyond
ລໍໂອກາດ	to wait for an opportunity	ເລີດ	excellent, champion
ລໍ້	to tempt, tease, wheel	ເລັ້ງກິນ	to lick up
ລໍ້ຝ້າຍ	to card cotton	ລຽງ	to put in order, pure
ລໍ້ລວງ	to deceive	ລ້ຽງ	to feed, feast
ລໍ້ຫຼິ້ນ	to joke, tease	ລ້ຽງເກື່ອ	to pay for someone
ລອກ	to peel, photocopy	ລ້ຽງສັດ	to breed animals
ລອງ	to try, test	ລ້ຽງສົ່ງ	farewell party
ລອງໃຈ	to test another's motive	ລ້ຽງຊີບ	to earn a living
ລອງຍິງປືນ	to practice shooting	ລ້ຽງຕ້ອນຮັບ	welcoming party
ລອງເຕົາ	stockings, socks	ລຽມ	to line up
ລອງເບິ່ງ	to try, to try to see	ລຽມແຖວ	to put in line
ລອງແພ	to float raft	ລ້ຽວ	to turn, winding, twisting
ລອຍ	to float, swim	ເລືອ	to creep, crawl

ເລືອກ	to choose, elect	ໄລ່	to chase
ເລືອກຕັ້ງ	election	ໄລ່ຕາມ	to pursue
ເລື່ອຍ	to saw	ໄລ່ທັນ	to overtake
ເລື້ອຍໆ	always	ໄລ່ຜີ	to exorcise a spirit
ເລືອດ	blood	ໄລ່ເລກ	to calculate
ເລືອດຂຶ້ນໜ້າ	to blush	ໄລ່ອອກ	to expel
ເລືອດຂຸ້	blood clot	ໄລ່ອອກກການ	to discharge, to dismiss
ເລືອດອອກ	to bleed	ໄລ່ອອກຈາກການ	to discharge
ເລື່ອນ	to slide, postpone	ໄລ່ອອກຈາກປະເທດ	to exile
ເລື່ອນການປະຊຸມ	to postpone a meeting	ໄລ່ອອກຈາກໂຮງຮຽນ	to expel from school
ເລື່ອນຂັ້ນ	to promote in rank	ເລົາ	reed, tube
ເລື່ອນຍົດ	to be promoted in rank	ເລົາຄິງ	body (tool, instrument)
ເລື່ອນລອຍ	to drift	ເລົາບັ້ງໄຟ	rocket tube
ລວກໄຂ່	to soft-boil an egg	ເລົາປືນ	gun barrel
ລວງກວ້າງ	width	ເລົ່າ	to tell, recite
ລວງສູງ	height	ເລົ່ານິທານ	to tell a story
ລວງ	to offend	ເລົ່າບົດຮຽນ	to memorize a lesson
ລວງກະເປົ໋າ	to pick pocket	ເລົ່າເຣື່ອງ	to narrate
ລວງເກີນ	to take advantage of	ເລົ້າ	storehouse, granary
ລວງເຂດ	to trespass	ເລົ້າໄກ່	chicken coop
ລວງໜ້າ	in advance	ລຳ	folksong, to sing, trunk
ລວຍ	to be rich	ລຳໄດັບ	level
ລວດ	wire	ລຳຕົ້ນ	stem, stalk, trunk
ລວດລາຍ	decorative design	ລຳຄານ	annoyed
ລວດໜາມ	barbed wire	ລຳຕັດ	humorous bawdy song
ໄລ (ລັຍ)	latch	ລຳນ້ຳ	water~~-~~way
ໄລຍະ	period	ລຳບາກ	difficulty

ລຳໂພງ	loudspeaker
ລຳໄລ	to talk on and on
ລຳວົງ	Lao circle dance

ວົງ	king's palace
ວັດ	wat, temple
ວັດຄຸນພໍ	Christian church
ວັດຖຸເຂົ້າຂອງ	material
ວັດແທກ	to measure
ວັດຮ້າງ	deserted temple
ວັນ	day
ວັນເກີດ	birthday
ວັນຈັນ	Monday
ວັນສິນ	day of fasting
ວັນສຸກ	Friday
ວັນສລອງ	anniversary
ວັນເສົາ	Saturday
ວັນຊາດ	National Day
ວັນຕາຍ	doomsday

ວັນທີ	(date) the ___ th
ວັນມະຄະຖີ	literature
ວັນມະໂລກ	tuberculosis
ວັນພະຫັດ	Thursday
ວັນພັກ	day off
ວັນພັກການ	holiday
ວັນພຸດ	Wednesday
ວັນເພງ	full moon day
ວັນຣະລຶກ	Memorial Day
ວັນນຶ່ງ	one day
ວັນອາທິດ	Sunday
ວັນອັງຄານ	Tuesday
ວາ	linear measure using body as ruler
ວາແຂນອອກ	to extend the arms
ວາຈາ	word
ວ່າ	to say, that
ວ່າການ	to administer
ວາງ	to put down
ວາງໂຄງການ	to plan
ວາງໃຈ	to rely on, trust
ວາງຍາມ	to station sentries
ວ່າງ	free, vacant
ວານນີ້	yesterday
ວ່າວ	kite
ວິເສດ	exceptional
ວິຊາ	subject of study
ວິຊາການ	technology, know-how

ວິຊາຄູ	pedagogy
ວິດ	toilet
ວິທະຍຸ	radio
ວິທີ	method
ວິໄນ	discipline
ວິນາທີ	second, instant
ວິທຍາສາດ	science
ວິທຍາໄລ	college
ວິນ	to be dizzy
ວິນຍານ	spirit
ວິນຕົວ	to be dizzy
ວີ	fan, to fan
ວຸ້ນວາຍ	to riot
ເວັ້ນ	to avoid
ເວັ້ນຈາກ	to except
ເວັ້ນແຕ່	except
ເວັ້ນໄວ້	except
ເວທີ	stage
ເວທີມວຍ	boxing arena
ເວລາ	time
ເວລາກາງຄືນ	night time
ເວລາກາງວັນ	daytime
ເວລາຄ່ຳ	night time
ເວລາເຊົ້າ	morning
ເວລາໃດ	when
ເວລາທ່ຽງ	noon

ເວລາທ່ຽງຄືນ	midnight
ເວລານອນ	bedtime
ເວລາບ່າຍ	afternoon
ເວລາວ່າງ	leisure, free time
ເວລາຫຼິ້ນ	playtime
ເວມກັມ	fate
ແວະ	to rest, drop in
ແວ່	to stop on route
ແວ່ນ	mirror
ແວ່ນຂະຍາຍ	magnifying glass
ແວ່ນສ່ອງ	lens
ແວ່ນແຍງ	mirror
ແວ່ນຕາ	eye glasses
ແວ່ນຕາກັນແດດ	sun glasses
ແວວຕາ	light in the eyes
ໂວລເລຍນາມ	volleyball
ວົງ	round, circle
ວົງກົມ	circle
ວົງດົນຕຣີ	musical band
ວົງມົນ	circle
ວົງເລັບ	parentheses
ວົນ	to revolve
ວົນທາ	to beseech
ວໍ	rabid
ວອດວາຍ	to ruin, disappear, dead
ເວີນ	whirlpool
ອງກ	work

ອງການານ	function, occupation	ຫັກ	to break
ໄວ	quick	ຫັກໄມ້	to break wood in fortune telling
ໄວຍາກອນ	grammar	ຫັດຂຽນ	to practice writing
ໄວໄຟ	inflammable	ຫັດງ່າຍ	easy to train
ໄວມື	quick with one's hand	ຫັນ	to turn
ໄວ້ໃຈ	to trust	ຫັນໃຈ	to breathe
ໄວ້ໃຈໄດ້	trustworthy	ຫັນໃຈຍາກ	to breathe with difficulty
ໄວ້ທຸກ	to wear clothes of mourning	ຫັນຫົວ	to turn one's head
ໄວ້ເນື້ອເຊື່ອໃຈ	trustworthy	ຫັນເມ	there, I told you!
ໄວ້ວາງໃຈ	to confide in	ຫາ	to search, for, to
ໄວ້ຫນ້າ	to save face	ຫາກິນ	to earn a living
ໄວ້ອາໄລ	to miss	ຫາກໍ	just
ເວົ້າ	to talk	ຫາກໍເກີດ	just born
ເວົ້າເກີນຄວາມຈິງ	to exaggerate	ຫາເງິນ	to make money
ເວົ້າຂວັນ	to speak ill of	ຫາສຽງ	to canvass
ເວົ້າຄືນ	to repeat	ຫາເຈົ້າກິນຄ່ຳ	to subsist, to live hand to mouth
ເວົ້າຊ້າໆ	to speak slowly	ຫາຍາກ	rare
ເວົ້າຊັດ	to speak fluently	ຫາປາ	to fish
ເວົ້າຊ້ຳ	to repeat	ຫ້າ (໕)	five (5)
ເວົ້າຍອງ	to praise	ຫາງ	tail
ເວົ້າຕົວະ	to tell a lie	ຫາງຕາ	corner of the eye
		ຫາງເຕົ່າ	hair at the nape
		ຫ່າງໄກ	far away
		ຫ່າງຈາກ	far from
		ຫາງ	store, to get ready
		ຫາງປືນ	to load a gun
		ຫາງໄວ້	to prepare

ຫ ໄຫ

ທາງແຮ້ວ	to set a trap	ຫິນຜາ	rocks
ທາຍໃຈ	to breathe	ຫິນລັບມິດ	whetstone
ທາຍໃຈເຂົ້າ	to inhale	ຫິນເຫີບ	Hin Heup, birthplace of neutral Laos (place name)
ທາຍໃຈຍາວ	to breathe deeply	ຫິນແຫ່	gravel
ທາຍພະຍາດ	cured	ທີ	womb
ທາດຊາຍ	beach	ທີບ	box, suitcase
ທານ	to divide	ທີບຄົນຕາຍ	coffin
ທານ	goose	ທີບສຽງ	phonograph
ທານຜູ້	gander	ທິດ	asthma
ທານ	to carry on one-man shoulder pole	ທຸງ	to boil, steam
ທານ	to carry on a two-man shoulder pole	ທຸງເຂົ້າ	to steam rice
ທານ	to forbid	ທຸນສ່ວນ	partnership
ທານຍ່ງມ	no visitors allowed	ທຸນ	to cover all
ທາວ	to yawn	ທຸນເກາະ	armored
ທາວງອນ	to yawn	ຫູ	ear
ທາວ	to exult, bursting	ຫູຜ້າກັ້ງ	curtain ring
ຫິມະ	snow	ຫູມຸງ	mosquito net ring
ຫິ່ງຫ້ອຍ	firefly	ຫູໜວກ	completely deaf
ຫິ້ງ	shelf	ຫູໜອງ	ear infection
ຫິດ	scabies	ຫູດ	Kafir lime
ຫິວ	hungry	ຫຸບ	to spoon up, suck in
ຫິວເຂົ້າ	hungry	ຫຸບແກງ	to spoon up soup
ຫິວງອນ	sleepy	ເຫັດ	mushroom
ຫິວນ້ຳ	thirsty	ເຫັດໂຄມ	white mushroom
ຫິນ	stone	ເຫັດແສງ	poisonous mushroom
ຫິນຊາຍ	gravel	ເຫັດປວກ	white-ant mushroom
ຫິນປູນ	limestone	ເຫັດເຫຼື້ງ	large yellow mushroom

ເຫັດເຜື່ອງ	white mushroom	ຫົກ (໖)	six (6)
ເຫັດເຍາະ	puffball	ຫົກສິບ (໖໐)	sixty (60)
ເຫັນ	to see	ຫົກນັດ	six shooter, pistol
ເຫັນກັບຕາ	to see with one's own eyes	ຫົກຫຼ່ຽມ	hexagonal
ເຫັນແກ່ຕົວເອງ	selfish	ຫົງ	swan
ເຫັນໃຈ	sympathetic	ຫົດ	to shrink, sprinkle
ເຫັນດີ	to agree	ຫົດສວນ	to water the graden
ເຫັນດີນຳ	to agree	ຫົດນ້ຳ	to sprinkle with water
ເຫັນວ່າ	to think that ...	ຫົນທາງ	way
ເຫັນອົກເຫັນໃຈ	to sympathize	ຫົນຫວາຍ	anxious, uneasy
ເຫັບ	tick	ຫົ່ມ	to cover with a blanket
ເຫດການ	event	ຫົ່ມຜ້າ	to cover with a cloth
ເຫດໃດ	why	ໄຫ	to hunt
ເຫນ	civet	ໄຫ່ເນື້ອ	to hunt
ເຫວ	cliff	ເຫາະ	to fly
ແຫ	fishnet	ຫໍສະມຸດ	library
ແຫ່	to go in procession	ທຳມມາດ	pulpit
ແຫ່ຂະບວນ	procession	ຫໍຜີ	spirit house
ແຫ່ຕາມ	to crowd after	ຫໍ່	to wrap up
ແຫ່ຜາສາດ	procession of religious images	ຫໍ່ເຂົ້າ	to prepare a wrapped lun
ແຫກຄຸກ	to break out of jail	ຫອກ	spear
ແຫ່ງນຶ່ງ	one place	ຫ້ອງ	room
ແຫ້ງ	dry	ຫ້ອງການ	office
ແຫະ	to gnaw	ຫ້ອງກິນເຂົ້າ	dining room
ແຫະກະດູກ	to gnaw a bone	ຫ້ອງເກັບຂອງ	store room
ແຫບ	hoarse (voice)	ຫ້ອງຄົນເຈັບ	sick room
ແຫບຄໍ	hoarse, husky	ຫ້ອງສູບຢາ	smoking room

ຫ້ອງແຕ່ງຕົວ	dressing room	ຫົວໃຈ	heart
ຫ້ອງໃຕ້ດິນ	cellar	ຫົວຊາ	to take care of
ຫ້ອງນອນ	bedroom	ຫົວຍິ້ມ	to smile
ຫ້ອງນ້ຳ	bathroom, restroom	ຫົວທຍຸ້	wind blown, unkempt
ຫ້ອງປະຊຸມ	conference room	ຫົວນົມ	nipple
ຫ້ອງເປົ່າ	empty room	ຫົວຜັກທຽມ	garlic
ຫ້ອງຜ່າຕັດ	hospital operating room	ຫົວຜັກບົ່ວ	onion
ຫ້ອງຮັບແຂກ	parlor, living room	ຫົວເຜືອກ	taro
ຫ້ອງຮຽນ	classroom	ຫົວລ້ານ	bald
ຫອຍ	shell	ຫົວໂລ້ນ	shaved head
ຫອຍແຄງ	cockle	ຫົວຫງອກ	gray hair
ຫອຍສັງ	conch shell	ຫົວໜ້າ	chief
ຫອຍນາງລົ້ມ	oyster	ຫວງ	to retain, monopolize
ຫອຍ	to hang	ຫວງແຫນ	to guard, watch over
ຫງນໄກ່	cock's comb	ຫວງ	anxious for
ຫອຍ	to carry in the arms	ຫວຍ	stream
ຫອມ	good smell	ຫວດເຂົ້າ	basket for steaming rice
ເຫິງນານ	a long time	ໃຫ້	to give
ຫ່ຽວແຫ້ວ	to parch, wither	ໃຫ້ງຸດເແກ່	to honor
ເຫື່ອ	perspiration, sweat	ໃຫ້ຄວາມສະດວກ	to facilitate
ຫົວ	head, to laugh, classifier: book	ໃຫ້ສິນບົນ	to bribe
ຫົວກະທິ	the best of the lot	ໃຫ້ເຊົ່າ	to rent
ຫົວຂວັນ	to laugh, mock	ໃຫ້ທັນເວລາ	to be on time
ຫົວແຂງ	stubborn	ໃຫ້ເຜີນ	to produce
ຫົວເຂົ່າ	knee	ໃຫ້ພອນ	to bless
ຫົວຄິດ	thought, idea	ໃຫ້ຢືມ	to loan, lend
ຫົວຄ່ຳ	early evening	ໃຫ້ຮາງວັນ	to reward

ໃຫ້ໄວທີ່ສຸດທີ່ຈະໄວໄດ້	to do as soon as possible	ໃຫຍ່	big, large
ໃຫ້ອາໄພ	to forgive	ຫຍ້ຳ	to chew
ໃຫ້ຊູ	to inform	ຫັກ	heavy
ໄຫ	pot, jar	ຫັກຫ່ວງ	worried
ໄຫ້	to cry	ຫັງ	skin
ເຫົາ	head lice	ຫັງແກະ	skin of a sheep
ເຫົາ	to bark	ຫັງສັດ	leather
ຫາໂປ່ງ	hernia	ຫັງສື	book
ຫງາຍ	to turn face up	ຫັງສືຄູ່ມື	handbook
ຫງາຍຂື້ນ	to reassume a post	ຫັງສືສັນຍາ	contract
ແຫງນ	to lift up one's head	ຫັງສືເດີນທາງ	travel document, pass
ແຫງນຄໍ	to look up	ຫັງສືນິຍາຍ	romance, novel
ຫງອກ	white hair or fur	ຫັງສືນຳທ່ຽວ	guidebook
ເຫງົາ	lonesome	ຫັງສືຜ່ານແດນ	passport, laisser-pas
ເຫງົານອນ	to be sleepy	ຫັງສືພິມ	newspaper
ຫຍັງ	what? why?	ຫັງສືວັນນະຄະດີ	literary work
ຫຍັບເຂົ້າ	to move closer	ຫັງສືວິທຍາການ	scientific work
ຫຍ້າ	grass	ຫັງສືວຽນ	circular, bulletin
ຫຍາບ	tough, hard	ຫັງຕາ	eyelid
ຫຍາບຊ້າ	stupid	ຫນາ	thick
ຫຍິບ	to sew	ຫນາຂື້ນ	to thicken
ຫຍຸ້ງ	confused, difficult	ຫນາແໜນ	dense
ຫຍຸ້ງໃຈ	anxious	ຫນ້າ	face, in front of, se
ຫຍຸ້ງຍາກ	troublesome	ຫນ້າກາກ	mask
ຫຍຸ້ງວຽກ	very busy	ຫນ້າເກັບກ່ຽວ	harvest season
ແຫຍເຂັມ	to thread a needle	ຫນ້າຂື້ນ	taciturne
ຫຍໍ້	to abbreviate	ຫນ້າໂຍນ	face mask for drama
ຫຍໍ້ຄວາມ	to abridge contents		
ເຫຍື່ອ, ເຍື່ອ	bait, feed		

ພາເສັ່ງດາຍ	regretable
ພາດຄານ	shameless
ພາທີ່ການ	function, duty
ພາຍບ້ານ	in front of the house
ພາບູດ	frown, scowl face
ພາຜາ	cliff
ພາຜາກ	forehead
ພາຢາກທິວ	comic, amusing, funny
ພາຢ່ານ	dreadful
ພາມອດ	pockmarked
ພາພອງ	poisoned arrow
ຫາໝາ	dog-face (rude)
ພາອາຍ	ashamed
ພາເອິກ	chest (body)
ພາຮັກ	lovable
ພາຮາຍ	evil face
ພ້າຍ	to disgust
ໝອຍ	(classifier: cloud, fruit, units)
ພານຜັກ	vegetable garden
ພານ	thorn
ພາວ	cold (temperature)
ພາວໄຂ້	chills and fever
ພິ	to escape
ພິຈາກ	to flee from
ພິຍພົ້ນ	to fail to escape
ພົ້ນ	to escape from danger
ພີ້	debt
ຟົ້ວ	bladder inflamation
ຟື່ງ	variant form of ໜຶ່ງ
	the number one (1)
ຟື່ງໃນສາມ	one third (1/3)
ຟື່ງ	to steam food
ໝຸ່	young, youth
ໝູ	mouse, rat
ໝູທ່ອງຂາງ	white rat
ໝຸໝາ	brown rat
ເຟິງ	to move
ເຟິວຕິວ	to move
ເຟິບ	to jab, insinuate
ເຟິບໃສ່	to insert
ເຟິບຽາ	beri-beri
ເຟງ	to feel vexed
ເຟງງຳນ່າຍ	disgusted
ເຟມ	tight
ເຟມຍ	bar spring
ເຟມຍຄີບ	to pinch
ເຟມ	sour pork dish
ໜໍ່	sprout, shoot
ໜໍກ້ວຍ	banana shoot
ໜໍໄມ້	bamboo sprout
ໜໍໄມ້ຝຣັ່ງ	asparagus
ໝອງ	gonorrhea, lake
ໝອງໃນ	gonorrhea
ໝອຍ, ໝອຍນຶ່ງ	a little
ໝອນ	larva

ໝຽງ	sticky	ໝາກເກືອ	ebony fruit
ເໜືອ	north	ໝາກກ້ວຍ	banana
ໝວກ	deaf	ໝາກຂາມ	tamarind
ໝວກຫູ	too noisy	ໝາກຄ້ວ	hardwood tree fruit
ໝ່ວຍ	unit, fruit	ໝາກແຄ້ວ	eggplant
ໝວດ	mustache	ໝາກງາ	sesame
ໝໍ່	viril	ໝາກແງວ	lichi
ໝັນ	diligent, often	ໝາກເງາະ	rambutan
ໝັນຮຽນ	studious	ໝາກຂ່າງ	toy top
ໝັ້ນ	steady, engaged	ໝາກຂີ້ຫູດ	Kaffir lime
ໝາ	dog	ໝາກຂຽບ	custard apple
ໝາຂີ້ເຮື້ອນ	cur dog	ໝາກເຂືອ	eggplant (generic)
ໝາຈອກ	fox	ໝາກເຂືອຂົມ	small wild eggplant
ໝາຍຍູ່	long-haired dog	ໝາກເຂືອເຄືອ	cherry tomato
ໝານ້ອຍ	puppy	ໝາກເຂືອຂ່າ	datura
ໝາໄມ	Malay wild dog	ໝາກເຂືອທໍ້ນ້ຳ	eggplant
ໝາປ່າ	wolf	ໝາກຈັບ	water chestnut
ໝາຫານ	hunting dog	ໝາກສີດາ	guava
ໝາແມ່	bitch	ໝາກຫຸກ ໝາກໄສ	small pox, chicken pox
ໝາວ້	mad dog, rabid dog	ໝາກໄລ່ໄຖ	plowshare
ໝ່າ	to soak rice	ໝາກສົ້ມ	citrus (generic)
ໝ່າເຂົ້າ	to soak rice	ໝາກສົ້ມໂຮງ	kind of almond
ໝາກ	areca nut, fruit	ໝາກຍົມ	star gooseberry
ໝາກກະດຸນ	button	ໝາກຍ່ຳໄຍ	longan
ໝາກກອກ	hogplum	ໝາກເດັ້ມ	tomato
ໝາກກຸງ	rose apple	ໝາກເດື່ອ	ficus
ໝາກກຽງ	orange	ໝາກເດືອຍ	job's tears (fruit)

ໝາກຕານ	sugar palm fruit	ໝາກພ້າວ	coconut
ໝາກຕູມ	bael fruit	ໝາກພີລາ	pomegranate
ໝາກແຕງ	melon, cucumber	ໝາກພິກໄທ	pepper
ໝາກແຕງໂມ	watermelon	ໝາກຟັກ	pumpkin
ໝາກແຕງອ່ອນ	cucumber	ໝາກເຟືອງ	carambola
ໝາກໂຕນ	large gourd	ໝາກໄຟ	sour berry
ໝາກຕ້ອງ	type of mangosteen	ໝາກມັງຄຸດ	mangosteen
ໝາກຖົ່ວ	bean	ໝາກມີ້	jackfruit
ໝາກຖົ່ວຂຽວ	green bean	ໝາກໂມ	watermelon
ໝາກຖົ່ວງອກ	bean sprout	ໝາກມ່ວງ	mango
ໝາກຖົ່ວຍາວ	long bean	ໝາກມ່ວງຫິມະພານ	cashew nut
ໝາກຖົ່ວດິນ	peanut	ໝາກໄມ້	fruit
ໝາກຖົ່ວແຕ	pigeon pea	ໝາກລິ້ນຈີ່	lichi
ໝາກທັນ	jujube	ໝາກທິວໃຈ	the heart
ໝາກທຸຣຽນ	durian	ໝາກເຮັຍ	hailstone
ໝາກມັດ	pineapple	ໝາກອາງຸ່ນ	grape
ໝາກມາວ	lime, lemon	ໝາກອຶ	pumpkin
ໝາກມອຍ	type of gourd	ໝາກຫຸ່ງ	papaya
ໝາກນ້ຳ	type of squash	ໝາຍ	to mean
ໝາກຍາມ	football	ໝາຍເກາະ	summons
ໝາກບົກ	type of almond	ໝາຍຄວາມ	to mean
ໝາກບົວ	lotus	ໝາຍຄວາມວ່າ	to mean that
ໝາກບວບ	gourd	ໝາຍຈະ	expecting
ໝາກປີ	banana flower	ໝາຍເຖິງ	to mean
ໝາກຜາງ	marian plum	ໝີ	bear
ໝາກເຜັດ	hot pepper	ໝີຂາວ	polar bear
ໝາກເຜັດແຫ້ງ	dried pepper	ໝີຄວາຍ	black bear

ຜົ້ນ້ຳ	noodle soup	ໝໍ	fortune-teller
ຝຸ່	gunpowder	ໝໍຢາ	herb doctor
ໝູ	pig	ໝໍລຳ	singer of Lam folksong
ໝູປ່າ	wild boar	ໝໍ້	pot
ໝູ່	friend, (classifier: group)	ໝໍ້ກະທະ	semi-spherical cast-iron
ໝູ່	friend	ໝໍ້ກາເຟ	coffee pot
ໝູ່ບ້ານ	village	ໝໍ້ແກງ	stew pot
ໝູ່ເຮົາ	we	ໝໍ້ຕອງ	filter
ໝູນວຽນ	to revolve around	ໝໍ້ຢາງ	cast iron pot
ໝູບ	to crouch	ໝໍ້ເຂົ້າ	rice pot
ເໝັນ	to stink	ໝໍ້ນຶ້ງ	rice steamer
ເໝັນຄາວ	rotten smelling	ໝໍ້ໄຟ	battery
ໝກໄຟ	to cook in ashes or in banana leaf wrapping	ໝອກ	fog
ໝກມັນ	to cook yams in ashes	ໝອງ	sad
ໝົດ	finished, all	ໝອງໃຈ	sullen
ໝົດທຸກມວນ	entirely	ໝອຍ	pubic hair
ໝົດມື້	all day long	ໝອນ	pillow
ໝົດແລ້ວ	finished	ໝອນຂ້າງ	bolster
ໝົດເວລາ	time is up	ໝອບ	to crouch
ໝົ່ນ	grey	ເໝືອນ	like
ເໝາະ	fit	ເໝືອນກັນ	same
ເໝາະສົມ	suitable	ເໝືອນກັບ	similar to
ໝໍ	doctor, expert	ໝວກ	hat
ໝໍແຄນ	khene-player	ໝວກເບ້ຍ	cap
ໝໍດູ	fortune-teller	ໝວກເຫຼັກ	helmet
ໝໍນວດ	masseur	ໃໝ່	new
ໝໍຜ່າຕັດ	surgeon	ໄໝ	silk, to fine

ໄໝຄຳ	silkshot with gold	ຫຼາຍໃຈ	uncertain, divided in heart
ໄໝຫຍິບ	thread	ຫຼາຍເທື່ອ	often
ໄໝ້	to burn	ຫຼາຍເທົ່າ	many times
ຫຼຽນ	coin, medal	ຫຼາຍແນວ	many kinds
ຫຼັກ	pole	ຫຼາຍໂພດ	too much
ຫຼັກການ	principle	ຫຼາຍໆ	very much
ຫຼັກສູດ	curriculum	ຫຼານ	grandchild, nephew, niece
ຫຼັກຖານ	evidence	ຫຼານເຂີຍ	husband of niece or granddaughter
ຫຼັກວິຊາ	theory	ຫຼານສາວ	niece
ຫຼັງ	after	ຫຼານຊາຍ	nephew
ຫຼັງໂກ່ງ	hunchback	ຫຼານໃພ້	wife of nephew or grandson
ຫຼັງຄາ	roof	ຫຼາວ	lance, stake
ຫຼັງຄາເຮືອນ	roof	ຫຼາວເຫຼັກ	rod, spear or iron
ຫຼັງຈາກ	after ...ing	ຫຼິ້ນ	to play, gamble
ຫຼັງຈາກນັ້ນມາ	later on, afterwards	ຫຼິ້ນກົນ	to play a trick
ຫຼັງເຮືອນ	behind the house	ຫຼິ້ນສາວ	fornication, to court a girl
ຫຼັງມື	the back of one's hand	ຫຼິ້ນຊູ້	adultery, to court
ຫຼັງແອ່ນ	with the back arched backward	ຫຼິ້ນຄວ	to play the shell game
ຫຼັບ	to sleep	ຫຼິ້ນບານ	to play soccer (football)
ຫຼັບຕາ	to close one's eyes, blink	ຫຼິ້ນໄພ່	to play cards
ຫຼັບຕາຈ້ວ	to squint in displeasure	ຫຼິ້ນລະຄອນ	to perform a play
ຫຼາ	yard (measure)	ຫຼິ້ນພານາບ້າ	game of bacci with dried fruit
ຫຼາສໄມ	out-of-date	ຫຼິ້ນພານລີ້	game of hide-and-seek
ຫຼາສຸດ	latest	ຫຼີກ	to deviate, avert
ຫຼາຍ	many	ຫຼີກເວັ້ນ	to avoid
ຫຼາຍກວ່າ	more than	ຫຼີກຫຼີ	to dodge
ຫຼາຍຄົນ	many people	ຫຼື	or

ທຸລາ	to miscarry	ຫຼອກຫຼິ້ນ	to joke
ທຸດ	to undo	ຫຼອດລົມ	windpipe, tube
ທຸດຮາຄາ	to lower the price	ຫຼອດວິທະຍຸ	radio tube
ທຸດຜົ້ນ	to escape from	ຫຼານ	to surprise, great-grandchild
ທຸດມື	to drop from hands	ເຫຼີ	to shout in sleep, nightmare
ທຸດລົງ	to lessen	ຫຼຽວ	to turn one's head to see
ທຸດອອກ	to slip out, come undone	ຫຼຽວຊ້າຍຫຼຽວຂວາ	to turn left and right
ທຸນ	ditch, hole	ຫຼຽວເບິ່ງ	to turn to look at
ເຫຼັກ	iron, metal	ຫຼຽວໄປ	to turn
ເຫຼັກກ້າ	steel	ຫຼຽວເຫັນ	to glimpse, catch sight of
ເຫຼັກໄຂຄວງ	screwdriver	ຫຼຽວພ້າ	to look around
ເຫຼັກຕາປູ	metal nail	ຫຼຽວຫຼັງ	to look back
ເຫຼັກໄຫຼ	magic invulnerability stone	ເຫຼືອ	to be left over, remain
ແຫຼ	to stain, blackened	ເຫຼືອງ	yellow
ແຫຼວ	eagle	ເຫຼື້ອມ	to dazzle, brilliant
ແຫຼວນົກເຂົ້າ	falcon	ຫຼວງ	public, great, royal
ຫຼົງ	to make a mistake	ໄຫຼ	to flow
ຫຼົງທາງ	to take the wrong road	ໄຫຼແຮງ	to flow rapidly
ຫຼົງລືມ	to forget	ເຫຼົາ	to carve, sharpen
ຫຼົບ	to escape, hide	ເຫຼົ່າ	plural word
ຫຼົບຫນີ	to sneak away	ເຫຼົ່ານັ້ນ	those
ຫຼົ້ມ	to get muddy, stuck	ເຫຼົ່ານີ້	these
ຫຼົ່ມ	to sink, turn over	ເຫຼົ້າ	alcohol
ໂຫຼ	dozen	ເຫຼົ້າແວງ	wine
ຫຼໍ່	to cast metal	ຫວັງ	hope
ຫຼອກ	to fool, joke	ຫວັງດີ	to mean well
ຫຼອກລວງ	to defraud	ຫວັດ	sick with a cold

ທ່ວາງ	between	ຊະມາຄິດ	the future
ທ່ວາງກາງ	between	ຊະມາໄນ, ຊນາໄນ	public health
ທ່ວາງພູເຂົາ	valley	ຊະມຸສອນ	souvenir
ທ່ວາງມໍ່ນີ້	in the recent past	ຊະໄພ	to forgive
ທ່ວງພີ້ນນີ້	in a little while	ຊະໄພໂທດ	amnesty
ທວານ	sweet	ຊະເມຣິກາ	America, (Yankee)
ທ່ວານ	to sow broadcast	ຊະທືວາ	cholera
ທ່ວານກ້າ	to broadcast rice seed	ຊະໄຫ່	spare part
ທ້ວານ	vine	ຊິດ	to close
ທວີ	to comb, comb	ຊັນຕຣາຍ	danger
ທວີກ້ວຍ	bunch of bananas	ຊັນໃດ (ຜູ້ໃດ)	what, which, (who)
ທວີຫົວ	to comb one's hair	ຊັນນີ້	this
ແທວນ	ring (jewelry)	ຊັນນັ້ນ	that
ໄທ້ວ	to pay respects to	ຊັນລະ	each
ທວ່າ	suddenly to come bruskly, gone	ຊາກາດ	air, weather
		ຊາການ	plight
		ຊາດຈະ	possibly, probably
		ຊາ	paternal younger aunt
		ຊາຈານ	professor
		ຊາໄສ	to rely upon

ຊະກະຕັນຍູ	(un)grateful	ຊາໄສຢູ່	to dwell
ຊະຖີຄ	past, ex- ...	ຊາຊີວະສືກສາ	vocational training
ຊະທີບດີ	director	ຊາຊີ	Asia
ຊະທີບາຍ	to explain	ຊາຊີບ	occupation
		ຊາຍຸ	age
		ຊາຍຸເຖົາ	old age
		ຊາຍຍືນ	longevity

ອາທິດແລ້ວ	last week	ອິດຕົມ	to pity
ອາທິດໜ້າ	next week	ອິກ	also, again
ອານາຄົດ	future	ອິ່ມ	full, satisfied
ອາຮີອາຣຍ	mercy, kindness	ອິ່ມແລ້ວ	to be full
ອາລົມດີ	good temper	ອິດຫຍນອນ	to want to sleep
ອາຣົມຮ້າຍ	bad temper	ອິດຢາກ	to be short of, wanting
ອາວຸດ	weapon	ອື່ມ	humid
ອາຫານ	food	ອື່ນ	other
ອ່າງ	basin	ອຸບັດເຫດ	accident
ອາຍ	bashful, shy, vapor	ອຸດສາຫະກັມ	industry
ອາຍນ້ຳ	water vapor	ອຸດົມສົມບູນ	plenty, prosperity
ອ້າຍ	older brother	ອຸປກອນ	equipment
ອ້າຍກົກ	oldest brother	ອຸ່ນ	warm
ອ້າຍເຂີຍ	older sister's husband	ອູ່	cradle, garage, car repair shop
ອ້າຍເມັຍ	wife's older brother	ອູບເງິນ	silver box
ອານ	saddle	ອູບຢາ	tobacco box
ອານມ້າ	saddle	ອູ້ມ	to carry in arms
ອ່ານ	read	ອູ້ມລູກ	to hold a child in arms
ອ່ານໃນໃຈ	silent reading	ເອະອະ	noisy
ອ່ານບໍ່ອອກ	illegible	ເອ	to decorate
ອ່ານອອກ	legible	ເອກະຊົນ	private, individual
ອາບ	to bathe	ເອກ	of first grade
ອາບແດດ	to sunbathe	ແອກ	yoke
ອາບນ້ຳ	to take a bath		
ອາບນ້ຳທະເລ	sea-bathing	ແອກຄາດ	yoke of the harrow
ອາວ	paternal younger uncle	ແອກໄຖ	yoke of the plow
ອີງ	to lean on	ແອບ	to exercise
ອິດສາ	to envy	ແອ້ມ	to enclose by walls
ອິດເມື່ອຍ	weary, tired	ແອ້ມແປ້ນ	to enclose with planks

ແອວ	waist
ແອວກິ້ວ	slender waist
ແອວກົມ	rounded waist
ແອວບາງ	slender waist
ອົກ	chest (body)
ອົດຕາຍ	to starve to death
ອົດຢາກ	to starve
ອົດທົນ	patient
ອົບ	to bake, fragrant
ອົບພະຍົກ	to evacuate
ອົບລົມ	to train
ອົບອຸ່ນ	warm
ອົມ	to suck
ໂອ	oh! (surprise)
ໂອໂຕ	car
ໂອຍ	oh! (pain)
ໂອຍ	to surround, embrace
ເອາະ	thick soup of North Laos
ອອກ	out
ອອກຖແລງ	to issue a statement
ອອກໄປ	to go out
ອອກຈາກ	to come out from, leave
ອວງມື	back of the hand
ອອຍ	to console
ອອຍໃຈ	to console
ອ້ອຍ	sugarcane
ອວນຫວານ	pleasant, melodious
ອ່ອນ	soft, light (color)

ອ່ອນໃຈ	to become discouraged
ອ່ອນແຮງ	weak
ອອມຊົມ	to save (money), saving
ເອ	yes
ເອີ້ນ	to call
ງຽງ	to move to oneside, leaning
ເອື້ອຍ	older sister
ເອື້ອຍນ້ອງ	sisters
ເອື້ອຍຕົວ	husband's older sister
ເອື້ອຍໃພ້	older sister-in-law
ອວຍ	to offer
ອວຍໄຊ	to wish victory
ອວດ	to show off
ອວດດີ	conceited
ອວດອ້າງ	to boast
ເອົາ	to get
ເອົາໄປ	to take
ເອົາມາ	to bring
ອຳນາດ	power
9ຳລາ	to say good-bye

5 ເຮືອ

ຮັກ	to love	ຮ່າງກາຍ	body
ຮັກກັນ	to love each other	ຮ່າງຄິງ	body
ຮັກຄວາມສງົບ	peace-loving	ຮ້າງ	to desert
ຮັກສາ	to take care of	ຮ້າງເມັຽ	to divorce one's wife
ຮັກສາຄຳໝັ້ນ	to keep a promise	ຮາຍ	bad, wicked, to yell
ຮັກສາຕົວ	to protect one's self	ຮ້ານ	booth, shop, store
ຮັກສາລະບຽບ	to observe the rules	ຮ້ານກາເຟ	coffee shop
ຮັກສາອິສສະຣະພາບ	to maintain independence	ຮ້ານຂາຍປຶ້ມ	bookstore
ຮັກສາເອກກະລາດ	to maintain independence	ຮ້ານຂາຍຜ້າ	cloth merchant's shop
ຮັກຊາດ	patriotic	ຮ້ານຂາຍຢາ	pharmacy
ຮັກແພງ	to love, respect	ຮ້ານອາຫານ	restaurant
ຮັກທອມ	to love	ຮາວຕາກຜ້າ	clothes line
ຮັງ	nest	ຮາວຮົ້ວ	fence
ຮັ່ງ	rich	ຮ່ມຕອງ	to consider well
ຮັ່ງມີ	rich	ຮ່ມຕອງໃຫ້ຖີ່ຖ້ວນ	to consider very carefully
ຮັດ	to tie, fasten	ຮີມ	edge
ຮາວີ	to try to damage, hostile	ຮີມຕາ	eyelid
ຮ່າ	epidemic	ຮີມນ້ຳ	bank
ຮາກ	to vomit, root, origin	ຮີມຍີປາກ	lips
ຮາກແກ້ວ	taproot	ຮີມຝັ່ງ	shore
ຮາກໄມ້	tree root	ຮີມແມ່ນ້ຳ	river bank
ຮາກຢາ	root medicine	ຮີດເຄື່ອງ	to iron clothes
ຮາກເລືອດ	to vomit blood	ຮີບ	hurry
ຮາກອອກ	to vomit	ຮີບດ່ວນ	urgent
ຮາງຮິນ	gutter	ຮີບໄປ	to go in a hurry
ຮາງໝູ	pig's trough	ຮີບມາ	to come in a hurry
ຮ່າງ	body	ຮື້	to carry off, raise

ຣູກ	to rub	ຣຸງຂື້ນ	sunrise
ຣຸງກິນນ້ຳ	rainbow	ຣຸງແຈ້ງ	daylight
ຣຸງ	light, papaya	ຣຸງເຊົ້າ	daybreak
ຣຸງ	dragon	ຣຸບ	picture
ຣຸນ	the same age, generation	ຣຸບຂຽນ	sketch
ຣຸນ	stock, share of invested capital	ຣຸບຄັດ	engraving
ຣຸ	hole	ຣຸບຖ່າຍ	photograph
ຣຸກະແຈ	key hole	ເຣົ່ງ	lucky
ຣຸຂີ້	anus	ເຣັດ	to do, to make
ຣຸດັງ	nostril	ເຣັດການ	to work
ຣຸປືນ	gun bore	ເຣັດກິນ	to cook
ຣຸຫູ	earduct	ເຣັດເງິນປອມ	to counterfeit money
ຣຸໜູ	rat hole	ເຣັດສວນ	to garden, farm (vegetables)
ຣຸພາກກະດຸມ	buttonhole	ເຣັດຊົ່ວ	to behave badly
ຣູ້	to know	ເຣັດດີ	to do well
ຣູ້ຄວາມຄົມ	to be smart, wise	ເຣັດດອງ	to prepare for wedding
ຣູ້ຈັກ	to know	ເຣັດແຕກ	to break
ຣູ້ສຶກ	to feel	ເຣັດຕົກ	to make fall
ຣູ້ສຶກເສັງໃຈ	to repent	ເຣັດທານ	to give alms for the dead
ຣູ້ສຶກສົງສານ	to feel sorry for	ເຣັດນາ	to farm (wet paddy)
ຣູ້ສຶກລະອາຍໃຈ	to feel ashamed	ເຣັດບຸນ	to have a festival, make merit
ຣູ້ຕົວ	to be conscious of	ເຣັດຜິດ	to make a mistake, to do wrong
ຣູ້ແທ້	to know for sure	ເຣັດວຽກ	to work, to be employed
ຣູ້ເມື່ອຄີງ	to regain consciousness	ເຣັດໄຮ່ເຣັດນາ	to farm
ຣູ້ເຣື່ອງ	to know about	ແຮງ	power
ຣູ້ວ່າ	to know that	ແຮງກວ່າ	stronger than
ຣູ້	bright	ແຮງງານ	labor

ແຮງມ້າ	horsepower	ໂຮງເຮັດນ້ຳຕານ	sugar mill
ແຮ້ງ	vulture	ໂຮງຮຽນ	school
ຣົກ	overgrown, to overflow	ໂຮງຮຽນຄຸນແມ່	girl's Catholic school
ຣົມອາຍຢາ	to apply medicinal steam	ໂຮງຮຽນສິນລະປະກອນ	school of fine arts
ຣົມ	shade	ໂຮງຮຽນຊັ້ນປະຖົມ	primary school
ຣົມໄມ້	tree shade	ໂຮງຮຽນດັດສັນດານ	reform school
ຣົມເຢັນ	to stay happy	ໂຮງຮຽນມັດທະຍົມ	secondary school
ໂຣ	to cheer	ໂຮງຮຽນອຸດທະຍາໄລ	college
ໂຣຣອງ	to cheer	ໂຮງຮຽນວັດ	temple school
ໂຮງການ	office	ໂຮງຮຽນອະນຸບານ	kindergarten
ໂຮງຂ້າສັດ	slaughter house	ໂຮມກັນ	together
ໂຮງງານ	factory	ຮອງ	deputy
ໂຮງສາຍ	post office	ຮອງເທົ້າ	socks
ໂຮງສີ	mill	ຮອງນາຍົກລັດຖມົນຕຣີ	deputy prime minister
ໂຮງສີເຂົ້າ	rice mill	ຮອງປະທານາທິບໍດີ	vice president
ໂຮງສີເມກາ	movie theatre	ຮອງ	ditch
ໂຮງຕີເຫລັກ	blacksmith shop	ຮອງນ້ຳ	channel
ໂຮງຕົ້ມເຫລົ້າ	distillery	ຮອງຮອຍ	clue
ໂຮງພະຍາບານ	hospital	ຮອງ	to call
ໂຮງພິມ	printing house	ຮອງຂໍ	to request
ໂຮງໄຟຟ້າ	power station	ຮອງຮ້ອງ	to shout
ໂຮງເຢັນ	morgue	ຮອງທຸກ	to complain
ໂຮງເລື່ອຍ	sawmill	ຮອງເພ້ງ	to sing
ໂຮງແຮມ	hotel	ຮອງໄຫ້	to cry
ໂຮງໝໍ	hospital	ຮອງໂຣ	to cheer
ໂຮງໝໍນ້ອຍ	dispensary	ຮອງຮຽນ	to complain about
ໂຮງເຮັດນ້ຳກ້ອນ	ice plant	ຮອຍ	trace, to seem

ຮອຍຕີນ	footprint	ຮຽງກ້ຳ	to place side by side
ຮອຍແຕກ	fracture	ຮຽງແຖວ	to line up
ຮອຍໄຄ	harrow	ຮຽນ	to study, to learn
ຮອຍເບື້ອມ	stain	ຮຽນດ້ວຍຕົນເອງ	self-taught
ຮອຍພະພຸດທະບາດ	Buddha's footprint	ຮຽນຜັງສີ	to study
ຮອຍມື	fingerprint	ເຮືອ	boat
ຮອຍເລືອດ	blood stain	ເຮືອຈັກ	motorboat
ຮອຍ (900)	one hundred (100)	ເຮືອຈ້າງ	ferry boat
ຮອຍດອກໄມ້	to string a garland	ເຮືອສຳເພົາ	junk
ຮອດ	to arrive	ເຮືອດຳນ້ຳ	submarine
ຮອດຍາມ	the time has come	ເຮືອແຕກ	shipwreck
ຮອດຫູ	to hear, know	ເຮືອໃບ	sailboat
ຮອນ	hot (temperature)	ເຮືອບິນ	airplace
ຮອນອົກຮອນໃຈ	to be worried	ເຮືອບິນໄອພົ່ນ	jet plane
ຮອນຮິນ	to worried	ເຮືອຮົບ	warship
ຮອບຄອບ	carefully, thoroughly	ເຮືອລາດຕະເວນ	cruiser
ຮອບປະຖົມມະເລິກ	the first round	ເຮືອງ	light
ຮອບໂລກ	around the world	ເຮືອດ	bedbug
ຮອມພູ	valley	ເຮືອນ	house, home
ເຮັ່	to lose way, lost	ເຮືອນຄົວ	kitchen
ຮງກ	to call	ເຮືອນສອງຊັ້ນ	two-story house
ຮງກຊື່	to name	ເຮືອນຊັ້ນດຽວ	one-story house
ຮງກປະຊຸມ	to call a meeting	ເຮືອນດີ	funeral house
ຮງກວ່າ	to be called	ເຮືອນດອງ	wedding house
ຮງກຫາ	to call for a person	ເຮືອນຮ້າງ	abandoned house
ຮງກຮ້ອງ	to claim	ຮົວ	to leak
ຮງງ	to arrange order	ຮົ້ວ	fence

ຮໍ້ສອມ	garden fence	ໄຮ່	dry season rice field
ຮໍ້ຍາມ	house fence	ໄຮ່ສາລີ	cornfield
ຮວງ	ear of grain, beehive	ໄຮ່ນາ	ricefield (both dry and wet)
ຮວງເຂົ້າ	ear of rice	ໄຮ່ຝ້າຍ	cotton field
ຮວງລີບ	poor ear of grain	ໄຮ່ອາງຸ່ນ	vineyard
ຮວຍລູກ	fetus	ເຮົາ	we
ຮ່ວມ	to combine	ເຮົາທັງສອງ	both of us
ຮ່ວມກັນ	together	ເຮົາທັງໝົດ	all of us
ຮ່ວມງານ	to collaborate	ເຮົາເອງ	ourselves
ຮ່ວມໃຈ	to be unanimous	ຮໍາ	bran
ຮ່ວມຊາດ	throughout the country	ຮໍາເຂົ້າ	rice bran
ຮ່ວມທ້ອງດຽວກັນ	twins	ຮໍາໄຮ	to repeat, to reiterate
ຮ່ວມໄມ້ຮ່ວມມື	to cooperate		

TONE CODE TABLE

	Long or Nasal ending or ງ ມ ນ Semi-vowel ending ຍ ວ	Long + stop ກ ດ ບ	Short or Short + stop ກ ດ ບ	Tone Mark	
				່ ×́	້ ×̀
Kang ກ ຈ ດ ຕ ບ ປ ຢ ອ	1	6	3	2	5
Tam ຄ ງ ຍ ຊ ຫ ມ ນ ຝ ຣ ລ ວ ຮ	3	5	2	2	5
Sung ຂ ສ ຖ ຜ ຟ ຫ ຫງ ຫຍ ຫນ ຫມ ຫຼ ຫວ	4	6	3	2	6

Short: ×ະ ×̆x ×̆ ×̆ × ເ×ະ ເ×̆× ແ×ະ ແ×̆× ໂ×ະ ×̂x ເ×າະ ×̆9× ເ×̂

×̆ະ ×̆xະ ×̆x ເ×̂9 ×̂ວະ ×ວັ× ໃ× ໄ× ເ×̂າ ×÷ ×9ຍ

Long: ×າ ×̆ ×̆ × ເ× ແ× ໂ× ×́ ×9× ເ×̂

ເ×̂ວ ×ວ× ເ×̂9 ×̂ວ ×ວ×

CONSONANT ORDER

ก – g^1 – 264	ท – t^3 – 339	ล – l^3 – 390
ข – k^4 – 272	น – n^3 – 346	ว – w^3 – 396
ค – k^3 – 281	บ – b^1 – 353	ห – h^4 – 398
ง – ng^3 – 293	ป – bp^1 – 361	หง – ng^4 – 402
จ – ch^1 – 294	ผ – p^4 – 368	หย – ny^4 – 402
ส – s^4 – 299	ฝ – f^4 – 372	ฒ – n^4 – 402
ซ – s^3 – 309	พ – p^3 – 373	ฆ – m^4 – 404
ย – ny^3 – 315	ฟ – f^3 – 378	ฦ – l^4 – 407
ด – d^1 – 318	ม – m^3 – 379	หว – w^4 – 408
ต – dt^1 – 324	ย – y^1 – 386	อ – --^{1} – 409
ถ – t^4 – 336	ร – l^3 – 388	ฮ – h^3 – 411

VOWEL ORDER

×ะ	a:	แ××	aa:/ae:	เ×ี	ia
××	a:	แ×	aa/ae	×ี×	ia
×า	a	โ×ะ	o:	เ×ือ	eua:
×ี	i:	××	o:	เ×ือ	eua
×ิ	i	โ×	o	×ือ	ua:
×ื	eu:	เ×าะ	oh:/aw:	×ือ	ua:
×ึ	eu	×อ×	oh:/aw:	×อ	ua
×	u:	×	oh/aw	×อ×	ua
×ุ	u	×อ×	oh/aw	ใ×	ay:/ai:
เ×ะ	e:	เ×ื	er:	ไ×	ay:/ai:
เ××	e:	เ×	er	เ×า	ow:/ao:
เ×	e	เ×ือ	ia	×ำ	a:m
แ×ะ	aa:/ae:	×ื×	ia:	×อย	oy:/oi:

"Books to Span the East and West"

Tuttle Publishing was founded in 1832 in the small New England town of Rutland, Vermont [USA]. Our core values remain as strong today as they were then—to publish best-in-class books which bring people together one page at a time. In 1948, we established a publishing office in Japan—and Tuttle is now a leader in publishing English-language books about the arts, languages and cultures of Asia. The world has become a much smaller place today and Asia's economic and cultural influence has grown. Yet the need for meaningful dialogue and information about this diverse region has never been greater. Over the past seven decades, Tuttle has published thousands of books on subjects ranging from martial arts and paper crafts to language learning and literature—and our talented authors, illustrators, designers and photographers have won many prestigious awards. We welcome you to explore the wealth of information available on Asia at **www.tuttlepublishing.com**.